New Perspectives on Native North Amer

New Perspectives on Native North America

Cultures, Histories, and Representations

SERGEI A. KAN &
PAULINE TURNER STRONG

UNIVERSITY OF NEBRASKA PRESS
LINCOLN & LONDON

The generous support of the Claire
Garber Goodman Fund of the Department
of Anthropology, Dartmouth College,
and the University of Texas at Austin
is gratefully acknowledged.

⊗

Library of Congress Cataloging-
in-Publication Data
New perspectives on native North America :
cultures, histories, and representations /
edited and with an introduction by
Sergei A. Kan and Pauline Turner Strong.
p. cm.
Includes bibliographical references and index.
ISBN-13: 978-0-8032-2773-6 (hardcover : alk. paper)
ISBN-10: 0-8032-2773-6 (hardcover : alk. paper)
ISBN-13: 978-0-8032-7830-1 (pbk. : alk. paper)
ISBN-10: 0-8032-7830-6 (pbk. : alk. paper)
1. Indians of North America—History—
Sources.   2. Indians of North America—Social
life and customs.   3. Ethnohistory—North
America.   4. Ethnology—North America.
5. North America—History—Sources.
6. North America—Social life and customs.
7. Fogelson, Raymond.   I. Kan, Sergei.
II. Strong, Pauline Turner, 1953–
III. Fogelson, Raymond.
E77.N48 2006
970.004'97–dc22
2005025331

In honor of Raymond D. Fogelson

Contents

Raymond D. Fogelson, *Courtesy of Sergei A. Kan*

Introduction

SERGEI A. KAN & PAULINE TURNER STRONG

The essays in this volume were influenced and inspired by Raymond D. Fogelson, who has taught in the Department of Anthropology at the University of Chicago since 1965. The contributors, mainly Fogelson's students, include some of the leading anthropologists and ethnohistorians working on Native North America, and their essays exemplify the broad interests and interdisciplinary approach of their mentor. Grounded in historical, ethnographic, and linguistic research, the essays span four centuries and focus on the Subarctic, Northeast, Northwest Coast, California, Southwest, Great Basin, and Plains as well as the region at the core of Fogelson's research, the Southeast. The contributors explore many of the theoretical issues central to Fogelson's work and, more broadly, scholarship on Native North America at the turn of the twenty-first century: culture, history, and power; personhood and creativity; historical consciousness and ethnographic representation; identity, alterity, and hybridity; and the politics of culture.[1] Many of the essays also exhibit a penchant for reflexivity, collaboration, irony, and wordplay—all of which were characteristic of Fogelson's work long before they became hallmarks of postmodern and postcolonial anthropology.

The contributors represent several generations of Fogelson's students, from notable senior scholars to others in the early stages of their careers.[2] Two contributors, Regna Darnell and Peter Nabokov, are close colleagues of Fogelson rather than former students. Most of the essays gathered here were originally presented in two double sessions honoring Fogelson at the 1996 annual meeting of the American Anthropological Association. A handful of papers presented at the sessions could not be included in this volume—most tragically, a paper on representing indigenous peoples by the late Sharon K. Stephens. A student of Fogelson's as both an undergraduate and graduate student, Stephens's research on the Sami of Finland and Norway (e.g., Stephens 1995) advanced the tradition of scholarship on the circumpolar North pioneered by Fogelson's mentor, A. Irving Hallowell

(1926). Stephens's work also exemplifies the research that Fogelson and some of his students and colleagues have carried out on indigenous land claims and cultural rights.[3]

The volume is divided into four sections: Perspectives, Cultures, Histories, and Representations. Fogelson considered each of these themes extensively in his publications—although, as the essays attest, many of the contributors were influenced even more by Fogelson's informal teaching and mentoring. The remainder of this introduction presents the essays in each section in the context of Fogelson's research, teaching, and intellectual roots. It concludes with a sketch of Fogelson's life and scholarship, followed by a selected bibliography of his publications.[4]

Perspectives: On the Genealogy and Legacy of an Anthropological Tradition

From A. Irving Hallowell and Anthony F. C. Wallace, his mentors at the University of Pennsylvania, Ray Fogelson inherited an abiding interest in intellectual history—particularly the history of anthropology but also the history of religion, psychology, and sociology (see Fogelson 1976, 1982b, 1985b, 1987b, 1991a, 1999a). This interest, enhanced by his close association with the historian George W. Stocking Jr. at the University of Chicago, was passed on to many of Fogelson's students. For decades now Fogelson and Stocking have collaborated, commented on each other's works, and supported each other in training graduate students (including many of the contributors to this volume).

The essays in part 1 place the works of Fogelson and the contributors in the context of the history of anthropology. The first chapter, "Keeping the Faith: A Legacy of Native American Ethnography, Ethnohistory, and Psychology," is by Regna Darnell, who did her graduate work at Penn a few years after Fogelson. Using a characteristically Fogelsonian phrase—*gardez le foi*—as a metaphor for allegiance to what she calls the Americanist tradition, Darnell explores the intellectual genealogy of Fogelson's work, focusing on the distinctive manifestation of that tradition at Penn (see also Darnell 2001; Valentine and Darnell 1999). By emphasizing the importance of "the native point of view" in the Americanist tradition she traces from Boas through Frank Speck, Edward Sapir, Hallowell, and Wallace, Darnell sheds light on the ubiquity of the prefix *ethno-* in Fogelson's work—the significance of which is noted in many of the subsequent chapters.

Jennifer S. H. Brown's "Fields of Dreams: Revisiting A. I. Hallowell and the Berens River Ojibwe" explores Hallowell's rich legacy in several contexts, including the work of Brown's own mentors, Fogelson and Stocking; the subfield of psychological anthropology; and Brown's conversations with the descendants of Chief William Berens, Hallowell's foremost Ojibwe consultant. Brown's approach to the significance of dreams among the Ojibwe—which draws on extensive research in Hallowell's unpublished papers as well as fieldwork on the Berens River—exemplifies the melding of historical and ethnographic methodologies that Fogelson has advocated and practiced. Though she is critical of Hallowell's foray into Freudian interpretation, Brown praises his fieldwork and his (more typical) interpretations of dreams in terms of Ojibwe ontology and what Fogelson (1976) calls ethnopersonality theory (see also Straus 1977, 1982). Invoking Fogelson's (1989b) call for attention to "native theories of history," Brown interprets Ojibwe dreams as "ways of framing, telling, and remembering history."

As Darnell's chapter indicates, the Speck-Hallowell-Wallace-Fogelson line of inquiry has centered on the Algonquian and Iroquoian cultures of the Subarctic and eastern Woodlands. Nearly a dozen of Fogelson's students have worked in these areas.[5] Margaret Bender, however, has most directly followed in her mentor's footsteps, conducting fieldwork among the Eastern Cherokees of North Carolina three decades after Fogelson's first visit there as a young graduate student. Bender's essay, "Framing the Anomalous: Stoneclad, Sequoyah, and Cherokee Ethnoliteracy," considers the mysterious life of Sequoyah, the inventor of the Cherokee syllabary, in the context of Fogelson's writings and teachings about fieldwork, interpretation, and Cherokee culture and history. In comparing Sequoyah to the Cherokee culture hero Stoneclad (Fogelson 1980c), utilizing Fogelson's (1989b) concept of "epitomizing events" to interpret Cherokee views of Sequoyah, and employing the term *ethnoliteracy* to refer to the meanings of literacy within Cherokee culture, Bender builds upon and extends Fogelson's lifelong inquiry into Cherokee beliefs, practices, and historical processes.

Significantly, both Bender and Brown invoke the cultural and semiotic theories of a fellow contributor, Greg Urban, while Brown cites collaborative work she has conducted with still another contributor, Robert Brightman. Darnell notes earlier collaborations between Fogelson and one of his fellow students at the University of Pennsylvania, Paul Kutsche, as well as between Fogelson and one of his students at the University of Chicago, Amelia Bell (Fogelson and Bell 1983; Fogelson and Walker 1980). The bibliography to this chapter also includes collaborations between Fogelson and his mentor, A. F. C. Wallace; his colleagues Richard N. Adams,

Melford E. Spiro, and George Stocking; and several other students, including the editors (Fogelson 1981, 2001a; Fogelson and Brightman 2002). Such collaborations and cross-fertilizations have continued among Fogelson's students (and now include students of students), indicating the extent to which he is a central node in a vibrant social network and scholarly tradition.[6]

Cultures: On Persons and Power, Rituals and Creativity

Although currently a contested term, *culture* remains important both to Native American peoples and to those who write about them. The opening essays of parts 2, 3, and 4 offer theories of culture that respond to postmodern and postcolonial critiques while remaining true to what Bender calls Fogelson's "deep cultural relativism." Thomas Buckley (part 3) presents culture as a construction, inscription, possession, dispossession, and repossession, while Robert Brightman discusses Western concepts of culture as only one kind of "ethno-anthropology" (part 4). Greg Urban's essay, "Power as the Transmission of Culture," enters an arena, the anthropology of power, that has been central to Fogelson's research since he co-edited an important volume on that theme (Fogelson and Adams 1977; Fogelson 1977). Urban, however, turns from Fogelson's interest in the cultural construction of power to the complementary "relationship of power to the movement of culture." Analyzing a set of examples ranging from ethnographic documentations of Cherokee and Yanamamö culture to the feature film *Babe* and, finally, to one of his own interactions with Ray Fogelson, Urban considers how culture is both replicated and transformed through power relations.

The relationship between culture and power is considered in a more traditionally political sense in Larry Nesper's "Ironies of Articulating Continuity at Lac du Flambeau." Based on extensive ethnographic and ethnohistorical research among the Lac du Flambeau band of Lake Superior Chippewa Indians, Nesper's essay considers a recent conflict over the exercise of off-reservation hunting, fishing, and gathering rights. He places this conflict in the context of the growing articulation between local and global economies at Lac du Flambeau over the past century. Viewing cultural difference as dynamically related to political and economic relations, Nesper demonstrates how geographical knowledge, hunting and fishing skills, and indigenous crafts were revalued as Lac de Flambeau became a tourist destination. In demonstrating the process through which the spearfishing of walleyed pike became central to Chippewa (or Anishinabeg) identity, Nesper shows that, ironically, as the Anishinabeg of

Lac de Flambeau "grew more connected, they grew more distinct from the dominant society."

Power and powerlessness are central themes in the work of one of Fogelson's favorite authors, the ethnologist James Mooney. Arapaho texts recorded by Mooney are the subject of Jeffrey D. Anderson's "The Poetics of Tropes and Dreams in Arapaho Ghost Dance Songs." Anderson analyzes key tropes such as pity, exchange, and metamorphosis in order to demonstrate how Ghost Dance songs exemplify "creative ritual responses to external sources of power"—be they spiritual beings or colonial powers. Cultural creativity is a longstanding concern of psychological anthropology, but it is also central to linguistic anthropology, and Anderson's chapter is one of several showing the influence on Fogelson's students of Chicago linguistic anthropologists Paul Friedrich and Michael Silverstein.

Creativity often takes the form of humor, as Raymond A. Bucko, S.J., points out in an essay that evokes Fogelson's ready sense of humor in its title as well as in its content and style. "Night Thoughts and Night Sweats, Ethnohistory and Ethnohumor: The Quaker Shaker Meets the Lakota Sweat Lodge" utilizes one of Fogelson's favorite images—the reduplication and infinite regress evident on a cylindrical container of Diamond Crystal Shaker Salt.[7] Comparing dry ethnographic descriptions to his own experiences of the Lakota sweat lodge, in which humor is central, Bucko suggests that joking and wordplay are such an implicit and contextual aspect of the sweat lodge that they are rarely included in Lakota descriptions of the ritual. He also speculates that sweat lodge participants or observers may censor themselves in order not to give offense and, furthermore, that observers may simply be oblivious to the humor around them. It is clear from Bucko's analysis that although there are occasions when a more somber attitude is appropriate, humor is integral to the sweat lodge ceremony because it invokes conscious reflection, helps to produce harmony and equality, corrects unacceptable behavior, and serves to present the participants as weak and pitiful in order to invoke spiritual aid.

Like Anderson and Bucko, Robert E. Moore is among the many scholars inspired by Fogelson to focus on the meanings of religious symbols and rituals.[8] In his essay, "Self-consciousness, Ceremonialism, and the Problem of the Present in the Anthropology of Native North America," Moore discusses two rites of passage that each exhibit innovations from the perspective of the culture in which they originated. The first is a birthday party at which the honored guest is absent—a fairly common occurrence for rites of passage at the Wasco-Wishram community of Warm Springs, however uncommon it may be in the dominant society. The second rite of passage Moore considers is a naming ceremony in which a young woman chooses her own name—not the custom at Warm Springs and, in fact, a violation of a proscription against explicitly acknowledging a relationship with a guardian spirit. These innovations lead Moore to a renewed appreciation of an anthropology that, as Sapir puts it, "boldly essays to bring every cultural pattern back to the living context from which it has been abstracted in the first place, and, in parallel fashion, to bring every fact of personality formation back to its social matrix" (1934:410). Many of the contributors to this volume consider themselves part of this project, one that resonates strongly with the psychological anthropology of Hallowell, Wallace, and Fogelson (see Fogelson 1982b).

Histories: On Varieties of Temporal Experience and Historical Representation

Nowhere is Ray Fogelson's influence clearer than in the field of ethnohistory or historical anthropology (see Krech 1991). Critical of the ethnocentrism of much scholarship labeled "Indian history" or "ethnohistory," Fogelson has called for an "ethno-ethnohistory" that embodies native historical consciousness and theories of history, and even an "ethno-ethno-ethnohistory" written by indigenous scholars (Fogelson 1974a, 1989b; Turner 1988). As Thomas Buckley points out in the opening essay in part 3, Fogelson's reduplications of the prefix *ethno-* might best be understood as parody—aimed, it would seem, at getting the original *ethno-* in *ethnohistory* taken seriously. Viewed as a whole, Fogelson's work makes it clear that all histories are ethnohistories—that is, representative of a particular cultural perspective—just as all logics are ethnologics; all psychologies, ethnopsychologies; and all anthropologies, ethno-anthropologies.

Nearly every essay in this volume is concerned with the interplay of the cultural and the historical—a key tenet of Fogelson's research and teaching, reinforced at Chicago by scholars such as Jean Comaroff, John Comaroff, Marshall Sahlins, George Stocking, and the late Bernard Cohn. However, the essays in part 3 are most centrally concerned with the writing of ethnohistory. Buckley's "Native Authorship in Northwestern California," offers an expansive consideration of indigenous voices and perspectives, one that has relevance far beyond the region in which the analysis is centered. Buckley begins by complicating Fogelson's methodological statements about ethnohistory by placing them in the context of Vine Deloria's (1969) critique of non-Native scholarly authority and the subsequent deconstruction of the unified category of the "native anthropologist." Indigenous perspectives often appear in print these days—as Fogelson (1974a) recognized early on—and there are instructive parallels as well as significant differences in the way indigenous and nonindigenous perspectives are circulated and received. Focusing on histories and ethnographies written by five twentieth-century Native authors from California, Buckley considers how these texts respond to outsiders' accounts, establish authority and strategic alliances, pursue historically variable agendas and maintain historically variable silences, express distinctive theories of history and take advantage of distinctive publication venues—and, finally, receive dramatically different kinds of responses.

Raymond DeMallie, Mary Druke Becker, and Joseph C. Jastrzembski explore somewhat similar issues in their considerations of accounts of Native peoples dating to the seventeenth through nineteenth centuries. In "The Sioux at the Time of European Contact: An Ethnohistorical Problem" DeMallie corrects four common misconceptions about the Dakota and Lakota peoples—misconceptions he attributes to a tendency to view Siouan culture through Iroquoian lenses. Through a critical reading of original sources, DeMallie describes the Sioux in the early seventeenth century as buffalo hunters (not horticulturalists) organized in bands (not clans or a confederacy), and exhibiting relative consistency from east to west. Both the Eastern Siouan resemblance to Woodland groups and the famous political metaphor of the Seven Council Fires, DeMallie maintains, are postcontact developments.

Becker's "Proto-Ethnologists in North America" analyzes a number of non-Native accounts of North American Indians from the mid-eighteenth to the mid-nineteenth centuries, seeking not so much to reconstruct Native cultures as to delineate the forms of inquiry and interpretation the accounts reveal. In an essay that draws on extensive research in colonial archives, Becker argues against monolithic interpretations of colonial knowledge production. Following Fogelson (1979b) in characterizing colonial traders, missionaries, officials, and translators as "proto-ethnologists," Becker stresses their intellectual curiosity, openness to the unexpected, willingness to learn other languages and engage in extensive social interaction, and ability to generalize as well as to recognize cultural specificities.

In "Folklore, Personal Narratives, and Ethno-Ethnohistory," Jastrzembski considers Chiricahua Apache folklore and personal narratives as a reflection of Chiricahua historical consciousness. Synthesizing Ruth Benedict's theory of folklore with Fogelson's approach to ethnohistory, Jastrzembski focuses in particular on a Chiricahua version of the captivity narrative on the Southwestern frontier. Given the ubiquity and longevity of Anglo-American captivity narratives in the Southwest (see Brooks

2002; Strong 2002), Jastrzembski's essay addresses a clear need to consider Native experiences and expressions of captivity.

Like those of many other contributors, Sergei Kan's essay is inspired by Fogelson's "The Ethnohistory of Events and Nonevents" (1989b), which was originally delivered as a presidential address before the American Society for Ethnohistory. At an occasion traditionally used to define the nature of ethnohistory, Fogelson aligned himself with the *Annales* school's critique of positivist, event-centered history, urging ethnohistorians to attend to various kinds of "nonevents."[9] Fogelson's important and influential article offers an open-ended typology of nonevents, including nonrecognition or nonvalorization of what others consider eventful (as in political events), imagined events (as in prophecies), latent (unrecognized) events, erasures (as in a society's conscious adoption of a low profile, or the repression of a traumatic event), and mythic or "epitomizing events" (as in the Cherokee narrative of the demise of the Aní-kutáni priesthood that he analyzes elsewhere) (Fogelson 1984).

The contributors to this volume offer many additional examples of nonevents, including Sequoyah's life story (which Bender analyzes as an epitomizing event), Spunky's birthday party (a nonevent for Spunky, according to Moore), ritual humor in the Lakota sweat lodge (a "Cheshire cat" event in Bucko's eyes), and the extinction of New England Indians (analyzed by Jean O'Brien in part 4). A nineteenth-century conflict in southeastern Alaska, largely an altercation between two Tlingit clans, is the focus of Kan's "Events and Nonevents on the Tlingit/Russian/American Colonial Frontier, 1802–1879." In an essay that relies on U.S. and Russian Orthodox Church archives as well as Tlingit oral history, Kan considers how the conflict became an epitomizing event for Russian Creoles—a manifestation of Tlingit "savagery" and "treachery" that was expected to turn into a "massacre" of the local non-Indians—while it remained more or less a nonevent for the Tlingits and for the Americans who had recently claimed control of the area.

The final essay in part 3, David W. Dinwoodie's "Time and the Individual in Native North America," places Fogelson's concern with native historical consciousness in the context of the anthropology of time (incidentally, a central concern of Nancy Munn, with whom many of Fogelson's students have worked). Dinwoodie begins with a critical review of Ekkehart Malotki's refutation of Benjamin Lee Whorf's famous hypothesis about Hopi "timelessness." He maintains that Malotki's work actually appears to substantiate Whorf's claim that "the Hopi language is seen to contain no words, grammatical forms, constructions or expressions that refer directly to what we call 'time'" (Malotki 1983: vii).

Differentiating modern Western "time" from culturally variable "temporalities," Dinwoodie shifts our attention from linguistic structure to the individual experience of multiple temporalities, taking as his examples a well-known Hopi life history, *Sun Chief* (Taleyesva 1942). Dinwoodie's examination of the discursive movement from one time frame to another in *Sun Chief* is intended less to resolve the longstanding debate about the Whorf hypothesis than to underscore (as does Moore) the continuing relevance of Sapir's call for centering analysis on individual experience—a key concern of contemporary psychological anthropology.

Representations: On Selves and Others, Hybridities and Appropriations

Perhaps the most striking way in which Ray Fogelson's research and teaching have anticipated current developments in anthropology is his longstanding interest in what now falls under the rubric of the representation of identity and difference (see Strong 2004b). An outgrowth of his interest in the history of ideas, psychological anthropology, and what Hallowell (1965) called "the history of anthropology as an anthropological problem," Fogelson's articles on such diverse subjects as Cherokee monsters, booger masks, and little people (1980c, 1982a, 1985a; Fogelson and Walker 1980; Fogelson and Bell 1983), European, American, and Native American identities (1982b, 1985b, 1998b), and the representation of colonized peoples in world fairs (1991b) consider how selves are constructed in relations of identification with and opposition to various kinds of others.

Part 4 opens with a general essay on Native American "ethno-anthropologies," Robert Brightman's "Culture and Culture Theory in Native North America." Brightman, who has published related articles on Missinippi Cree primitivism and Maidu clown performances (Brightman 1990, 1999), is here interested in Cree and other Native "objectifications" of cultural identity, cultural difference, cultural transmission, cultural change, cultural hierarchy, and cultural purity or authenticity. Looking first at myths, cosmologies, and parodies that objectify culture, Brightman then turns to the historical processes through which tribal and pan-Indian identities have been constructed in opposition to the dominant culture. Although he views hybridity as the "default condition of culture" (see also Kapchan and Strong 1999), Brightman notes that many Native and Boasian anthropologies converge in viewing culture as essentialized, differential, socially contextualized, and subject to contamination and appropriation.

The five remaining essays in part 4 are case studies in the representation of cultural identity and difference. Barrik Van Winkle's "Cannibals in the Mountains: Washoe Teratology and the Donner Party" considers how the cannibalism of the Donner Party, which was marooned by a snowstorm near Lake Tahoe in 1846, became an epitomizing event for the Washoe Indians indigenous to the region. Though considered a tragic exception in white historical memory, for Washoes the incident became central to the typification of whites (including the ethnographer) as belonging to a dangerous set of voracious predators including mountain lions, grizzly bears, wolves, and monsters.

The tropes of cultural purity and contamination—which Brightman finds common to Native and Boasian anthropologies—are explored further in Jean M. O'Brien's " 'Vanishing' Indians in Nineteenth-Century New England: Local Historians' Erasure of Still-Present Indian Peoples." O'Brien's analysis of the trope of "the last of his tribe" considers how nineteenth-century local histories constructed a regional and national identity by narrating the extinction of local Indians—while also recognizing, at some level, their continuing presence. This ideological feat was accomplished, O'Brien suggests, by invoking concepts of racial and cultural purity that denied the Indianness of the remaining Algonquians and Iroquoians in New England.

Sharply contrasting with the "vanishing" Indians of nineteenth-century New England histories is the ubiquitous Pocahontas, the romanticized Powhatan "princess." In "Pocahontas: An Exercise in Mythmaking and Marketing," Frederick W. Gleach traces representations of Pocahontas from John Smith's histories through the Disney cartoon, attending in particular to the increasingly intense commodification of her image. Although the image of Pocahontas has never before been marketed as vigorously as by Disney, earlier contexts for commodification include commemorations of the English landing at Jamestown in 1907 and 1957 as well as the production of pottery for the tourist trade by the Powhatan Indians beginning in the 1930s. Instead of vanishing, Pocahontas has been subjected to endless reproduction and simulation, but the result is much the same as in New England: the Powhatan people are not recognized as living people.

The last two essays also consider romantic appropriations of Indian culture. In "I'm an Old Cowhand on the Banks of the Seine: Representations of *Le Far West* on the Left Bank," Michael E. Harkin analyzes the efflorescence of Parisian simulations of the West as a contemporary manifestation of a French tradition of exoticism reaching back to Montaigne. But Harkin also finds contemporary motivations for representing the West—and the Indian—as consummately natural, free, and egalitarian in a France that is suffering a crisis in economic freedom and national identity.

Pauline Turner Strong's essay, " 'To Light the Fire of Our Desire': Primitivism in the Camp Fire Girls," reflects on the use of Indian-inspired rituals and symbols in the Camp Fire Girls from the organization's founding in 1910 until the present. Drawing on her own experience as a Camp Fire Girl as well as historical sources, Strong traces links between the organization and what Stocking (1989) calls "romantic motives" in the history of anthropology, specifically those of Lewis Henry Morgan, Frank Hamilton Cushing, John Collier, Ella Deloria, Benedict, and Sapir. Like each of the essays in part 4, Strong's contribution is inspired by Fogelson's interest in the many manifestations of primitivism.

An afterword by Peter Nabokov brings the volume to a close. Nabokov, who dedicated a volume on "American Indian ways of history" to Ray (Nabokov 2002), served as the final discussant for the AAA sessions honoring Fogelson. The chapter is included not so much for its commentary on particular essays, for there is only a loose connection between the conference papers Nabokov mentions and the essays published in this volume.[10] Rather, the chapter stands as a tribute to the warmth, wit, and wisdom of the scholar, mentor, and friend honored in this collection of essays.

The Life and Scholarship of Raymond D. Fogelson

Born in Red Bank, New Jersey, on August 23, 1933, Raymond D. Fogelson describes himself as "an anti-intellectual child who did not read much and wanted to become a professional ping-pong or baseball player." As a young teenager Ray liked to read sports books. A biography of John McGraw of the New York Giants was one of his favorites.

Ray has had a lifelong interest in music. He had an aunt who was a concert pianist and taught at the Julliard School, while his older sister, who graduated from Julliard, was a soloist with the Robert Shaw Chorale. As a teenager Ray would make pilgrimages to New York City to hear Charlie Parker, Dizzy Gillespie, and other revolutionaries of American jazz.

Ray's father had high ambitions for his son: he wanted Ray to become a physician. After studying at a "mediocre local high school" for a while, Ray was sent for three years to a private school in eastern Pennsylvania, partially on a football scholarship. There he improved his grades, and in 1951 he was admitted as a premed student at Wesleyan University. Ray found chemistry and other required disciplines "boring," however, and finally decided that medical school was not for him. He did become interested in psychology, and ended up majoring in that discipline.

Wesleyan had an excellent psychology department at the time, with such prominent scholars on the faculty as Joseph Greenbaum (who later became a dean at the New School for Social Research), David McClelland (who later served as the head of the Department of Social Relations at Harvard), Michael Wertheimer, David Beardslee, and others. Ray began to work particularly closely with Beardslee, writing a bachelor's paper for him on sexual arousal in music. The paper compared differential sexual arousal in female and male college students, using projective essays written by students in response to music. A published essay based on this project (Beardslee and Fogelson 1958) was assigned as required reading for years at several universities to exemplify an interesting experimental design in psychology.

Despite this scholarly accomplishment, Ray began to question whether he wanted to become a psychologist. As he put it, "I had this image of psychology controlling and predicting human behavior, which I didn't want to do, since I was very idealistic. I thought psychology was going to take over the world." Gradually he became interested in anthropology (which only seemed to aim at describing and explaining human behavior), even though his grade in his first anthropology course was rather low. David McAllester, a well-known specialist in Navajo ethnology and ethnomusicology, taught this course. Despite his poor performance Fogelson and McAllester became good friends, with McAllester supporting Ray's experimental study of music and writing recommendations for his graduate school applications.

Even after his shift to anthropology, Ray retained a strong interest in psychology and psychoanalysis. The latter interest developed when he took a course in classical mythology from Wesleyan's prominent classicist, Norman O. Brown, for whom he wrote a number of Freudian interpretations of Homeric hymns. It was in Brown's course that Ray first read such anthropological classics as James Frazer's *The Golden Bough* and Bronislaw Malinowski's *Magic, Science, and Religion*.

In 1955 Ray arrived at the University of Pennsylvania to begin his graduate work in anthropology, which led to an MA in 1958 and a PhD in 1962. Penn's primary attraction for him was the University Museum and the presence of psychological anthropologist A. I. Hallowell. At the time the anthropology department at Penn was rather small, and although it included a number of leading anthropologists representing the discipline's four subfields, physical anthropology and archaeology were dominant. That situation began to change soon after Ray arrived, with the hiring of two young professors, Ruben Reina and Robbins Burling, who were later followed by Paul Friedrich. A. F. C. Wallace, who had completed his PhD under Hallowell in 1950, began teaching courses in the anthropology department in 1957. Among the department's older and more established members were Hallowell, Carleton Coon, Loren Eiseley, Ward Goodenough, Alfred Kidder II, Wilton Krogman, and Linton Satterthwaite. Ray did very well in his graduate anthropology courses, although he received a C– in Goodenough's introductory freshman course! A number of fellow graduate students at Penn—particularly Igor Kopytoff, Paul Kutsche, and Ben Saler—became Ray's lifelong friends.

Ray learned a great deal from most of his teachers in graduate school, but he attributes his abiding interest in psychological anthropology, religion, and ethnohistory to Pete Hallowell and Tony Wallace. Because Wallace was younger than Hallowell, Ray developed, as he put it, a "somewhat closer relationship with him than with Hallowell." During his second year at Penn, Ray enrolled in Wallace's course on the anthropology of religion, which focused on religious experience and revitalization movements. Ray recalls being "very impressed with both the course and the instructor," who at the time had an adjunct affiliation with the anthropology department. Inspired by Wallace's research on what are now known as "culture-bound syndromes," Ray conducted research on the Windigo disorder, which led to an article published in Hallowell's festschrift (Fogelson 1965; see also 1980c). At the same time, because Wallace had himself been Hallowell's student, Ray was indirectly absorbing many of the senior psychological anthropologist's ideas.[11]

Ray's decision to focus his doctoral research on a Native American culture was fortuitous. While taking a course on culture change, he, like all the other students, had to pick a geographic area of specialization. Initially he chose the Caribbean "because of the nice beaches there," but since another student had already done field research in Trinidad, Ray was assigned the American Indians instead. His interest the Eastern Cherokee developed due to a special field project run by John Gulick, an anthropologist at the University of North Carolina, Chapel Hill. Funded by the Ford Foundation, the Cross-Cultural Laboratory of the Institute for Research in Social Science initiated in 1956 a summer field project focusing on the Cherokee Indian Reservation in western North Carolina. For three summers a group of graduate students (mainly from the University of North Carolina) conducted field research on various aspects of contemporary Cherokee culture and society under the direction of a few professional anthropologists (see Gulick 1960). Ray's participation in the project began in the summer of 1957 and continued in December of that year and again during the summer of 1958. Two years later he returned to the area on his own to conduct additional research for his doctoral dissertation.

Although the stipend given to each graduate student participating in the project was minimal, it did cover some of Ray's basic living expenses. Most importantly, participation in the Cherokee project provided the young anthropologist with a group of colleagues with whom he could discuss his findings, try out various ideas and interpretations, and so forth. Ray names four older colleagues—John Witthoft, William C. Sturtevant, William N. Fenton, and the Cherokee scholar Robert K. Thomas—as his most important informal mentors.[12] Among the participating graduate students, Paul Kutsche was Ray's closest associate. The two of them worked together on traditional Cherokee work cooperatives (*gadugi*), eventually publishing an important paper on the subject (Fogelson and Kutsche 1961). Another graduate student taking part in the project, whom Ray credits with "teaching him more about field methods than anyone else," was Charles Holzinger, an older PhD candidate at Harvard who was already a professor at Franklin and Marshall College.

Ray recalls the Eastern Cherokee reservation of the late 1950s and early 1960s as being a rather isolated and poor community where "life was hard and the dogs were skinny." However, he found the people generally friendly toward anthropologists. Although Gulick and most of his associates focused on the contemporary sociocultural life of the Cherokee and issues of acculturation, Ray became much more interested in traditional Cherokee culture, aspects of which could still be found on the reservation, particularly among the members of the older generation. Although Ray's initial assignment was to administer Rorschach tests to the more acculturated Cherokees, neither he nor the Cherokees were comfortable with this. By this time he had clearly made the transition from experimental and clinical psychology to a more humanistic psychological anthropology and to cultural anthropology more generally.

A number of factors seem to have influenced Ray's turn from acculturation studies to more ethnohistorically inspired studies of those aspects of Cherokee culture that could still be traced directly to their eighteenth- and nineteenth-century antecedents. On the one hand, there was a lot of social disorganization in the Cherokee community at the time, including alcoholism and fighting. Ray felt that he "did not have to go to an isolated Indian village to study anomie." On the other hand, he felt inspired by the research of such prominent ethnologists and ethnohistorians of the past as James Mooney and Frank Speck as well as by that of one of his contemporaries, John Witthoft. Mooney's work (e.g., Mooney 1890, 1891, 1900; Mooney and Olbrechts 1932) was particularly influential on the young anthropologist. It was exciting for Ray to return to a society Mooney had studied fifty years earlier and to find aspects of the old Cherokee medicine and religion still alive. As Ray put it in his interview, "I used to read Mooney every day. I love to just kind of read the myths and think of new interpretations and so forth. [Mooney] is one of my bibles. So he was very important as an indirect kind of teacher."

Ray describes his approach to the study of the traditional Cherokee culture as "iceberging," contrasting it with William Fenton's (1955) "up-streaming." While Fenton would take a present-day institution and work his way backward to uncover its earlier version, Fogelson's method was to look for institutions that the Cherokees themselves considered to be traditional or old. In his words, by searching through those institutions "you kind of get to the deeper and deeper levels of the culture, which would expand, so that the tip of the iceberg would lead you down into the deeper cultural structure." One of the institutions that Ray's Cherokee consultants clearly identified as traditional was the free-labor association known as *gadugi*. Though the outer forms of the *gadugi* as well as some of the tasks it accomplished had changed since the eighteenth and the nineteenth centuries, it still remained "a kind of native social security," as Ray put it. Moreover, the members of the *gadugi* kept rosters of their officials and took minutes, so as Ray continued to study this institution he was able to uncover vestiges of the old Cherokee town system and gain a better understanding of its nature.

Ray also became interested in the Cherokee stickball game. By the late 1950s the game was played mainly as a tourist attraction, but the players still took it seriously, purifying themselves in the traditional manner by "going to the water" and performing other rituals. A number of Ray's Cherokee teachers were willing to talk to him about this. Fascinated by the game, Ray began working his way from its contemporary version back to its earlier manifestations, as documented by Mooney (1890) and others. This research led Ray to insights into patterns of political organization and warfare, and eventually the traditional Cherokee ball game became the subject of his PhD thesis (Fogelson 1962; see also Fogelson 1971).

Similarly, Ray's work on what he called the local "medico-magical beliefs"—the subject of his 1958 master's thesis (Fogelson 1958) and several subsequent articles (Fogelson 1961, 1975, 1980a)—led him to interesting discoveries about the relationship between past and present. The medicine man with whom Ray worked most closely was Lloyd Run-ningwolf Sequoyah, who was well regarded in North Carolina and served as the conjuror for the stickball team of the Big Cove community. One of Ray's favorite methods of working with Lloyd Sequoyah, which es-tablished a relationship of openness and reciprocity, was to bring him copies of the old magical formulas contained in Mooney's field notes at the Smithsonian Institution. Important moments in the relationship between the medicine man and the young anthropology student were trips the two of them took to Oklahoma in the summers of 1958 and 1960, when they attended several stomp dances and contacted the more traditional Cherokees affiliated with the Redbird Smith movement, including Redbird's youngest son, Stokes Smith. This political and religious revitalization movement, rooted in the older "Keetowah movement," was initiated by traditional ("full-blood") Cherokees in the Indian Territory in the late 1890s and early 1900s in response to the Allotment Act and the dissolution of the Cherokee Nation. It has continued to attract followers to this very day (Thomas 1961; Fogelson 1993a).

The trip to Oklahoma was important for Ray's growth as a student of the Cherokees, since it gave him a comparative view and allowed him to see firsthand the continuing exchange of ideas between the Eastern Cherokees and the Oklahoma Cherokees. He watched Lloyd Sequoyah reacquaint his Oklahoma relatives with social and ceremonial dances that the Eastern Cherokees had retained but that were no longer being performed in the west (see Jackson and Levine 2002). Sequoyah also shared with the Western Cherokees some medicinal plants from the original Cherokee homeland. As Ray put it, "this was the beginning of a kind of a cultural exchange."

When asked why Lloyd Sequoyah might have been willing to share his knowledge with an anthropologist, Ray pointed out that in the 1950s few local younger people "took the elders seriously." The medicine men might have been feared for their spiritual power, but the idea of "progress" was still strong among most of the people, and the traditionalists were seen as being "in its way." In Ray's words, "at that time, not too many community members or even other anthropologists were interested in what Lloyd and the other medicine men had to teach, except for this white guy from Philadelphia." Sequoyah even entrusted Ray with the books in which he recorded his sacred formulae in syllabary. By comparing these texts with the ones recorded earlier by Mooney, Ray was able to get a much better sense of continuities in the Cherokee magico-religious worldview. For his part, Sequoyah came to appreciate Mooney's work in preserving the ancient formulae, which led him to see the value of Ray's own ethnographic research. A kind of mentoring relationship developed between the two of them, somewhat similar to that between a medicine man and a younger Cherokee interested in his knowledge.[13]

In addition to working closely with a small group of medicine men and other traditionalists, Ray participated fairly regularly in various community social activities, such as "pie socials" and church meetings. One of the highlights of those activities was participating in the stickball game (which proved to be utterly exhausting) and going over the mountains through Smokey Mountain National Park to Cosby, Tennessee, for moonshine. On the whole, Ray enjoyed his doctoral fieldwork and, in his words, "learned a lot there about culture and society in operation."

While writing his dissertation Ray received some advice from Hallowell and Wallace, but he says that he was "on his own" for much of the time. During that period (1960–61) Ray was a research fellow at the Eastern Pennsylvania Psychiatric Institute, where Wallace was the director of clinical research. Ray's research at the institute—which involved an ethnography of an open ward of schizophrenic women with good prognoses—strengthened his interest in psychological anthropology. The research resulted in two joint publications with Wallace, including a major paper on identity struggles arising in family therapy sessions (Wallace and Fogelson 1961, 1965).

Ray's work at the Eastern Pennsylvania Psychiatric Institute was interesting but time consuming, and the dissertation progressed rather slowly. Luckily, a job offer from the University of Washington's anthropology department in 1962 made him work very hard to complete the PhD. It was then that Pete Hallowell was particularly helpful—even coming to his student's apartment to read sections of the dissertation as they were being written!

Ray found the prospect of teaching large undergraduate classes at the University of Washington a bit daunting, since he had not gained much teaching experience at Penn. Among the courses he taught at UW were "Introduction to Anthropology," "Anthropology of Religion," "Psychological Anthropology," "Theories of Race," and a course on "The History of Anthropology" with Simon Ottenberg. The course on race was a particularly memorable experience, since it was offered at 7:30 a.m. during the winter quarter, when it was still pitch dark. Only by the end of the lecture would the sun finally come up. Because courses at UW were more or less permanently assigned to particular faculty members, Ray never had the opportunity to teach Native American ethnology. This was the domain of senior colleagues such as Viola Garfield, Erna Gunther, Melville Jacobs, and Verne Ray. Nevertheless, Ray learned a great deal from them about Boasian anthropology as well as the indigenous cultures of the Plateau and the Northwest Coast. Mel Jacobs was a particularly important source of stories about Boas.

While in Seattle Ray initiated a new research site by conducting some preliminary psychological and ethno-ecological research among the Shuswap Indians of interior British Columbia. His teaching and research experience at UW contributed to a broad, comparative view of American Indian cultures, which served Ray well in his subsequent research and teaching. Ray has always insisted that his graduate students specializing in Native North America develop a similar comparative view, familiarizing themselves with ethnographic works (especially the classics) that deal with topics and geographic areas far beyond the immediate focus of their dissertation research.

The presence of colleagues such as Ottenberg, Edward Harper, Kenneth Read, Mel Spiro, and James Watson added to the attractiveness of the position at the University of Washington. Ottenberg and Spiro, both of whom shared Ray's interest in psychological anthropology, became his lifelong friends, as did Gananath Obeyesekere, who had just completed his PhD and was temporarily holding a postdoctoral teaching position. Spiro and Fogelson had another common bond, as both had been graduate students of Hallowell. The two of them coauthored the introduction to the Hallowell festschrift edited by Spiro (Fogelson and Spiro 1965). Eleven years later, when Fogelson edited a major posthumous edition of Hallowell's papers (Hallowell 1976), Spiro wrote the introduction to one of the book's sections (the others were authored by Wallace, Fred Eggan, George Stocking, and Wilcomb Washburn).

Being at the University of Washington was a good learning experience, but the position had its drawbacks. Ray began to dread the thought of having to teach the same courses year after year. (He had to teach the anthropology of religion course six times in three years!) In addition, the UW administration was not delivering on its earlier promise to help fund the department's expansion. So when the University of Chicago made him an offer in 1965, he reluctantly left the Northwest for the Midwest, where he joined his former associates Paul Friedrich, Mel Spiro, and Manning Nash (who had taught briefly at the University of Washington). Ray has remained at Chicago ever since, except for occasional visiting appointments at Princeton, the University of California at San Diego, the University of California at Santa Cruz, and the University of Texas at Austin.

Ray's appointment was the first of a new type of appointment at Chicago: he was an assistant professor in both the anthropology department and the social science division of the (undergraduate) college. Later he also accepted appointments in the Committee on Human Development and the Department of Psychology. After having been at Washington for three years he appreciated Chicago's approach to teaching, in which faculty could choose what they taught. Over the three and a half decades of his tenure at Chicago, Ray has taught an impressive variety of courses, from his standard psychological anthropology and North American Indian ethnology lecture courses to seminars on such topics as primitivism, shamanism, and "The Culture of Nature," which was developed in response to Marshall Sahlins's popular course "The Nature of Culture." In reminiscing about the teaching he has done at Chicago, especially in the late 1960s and 1970s, Ray uses such words as "fresh," "exciting," and "experimental." He also recalls fondly his experiences team-teaching with such colleagues as Bob Adams, Jim Fernandez, Les Freeman, Bill Hanks, Tanya Luhrman, Marshall Sahlins, George Stocking, and two former students, Sharon Stephens and Anne (Terry) Straus.

When the editors of this volume look back at the highlights of our own graduate education at Chicago in the late 1970s and early 1980s, Ray's North American Indian ethnology course stands out. The course not only inspired many of the contributors to this volume to specialize in this particular area but also introduced them to each other and encouraged them to collaborate and exchange ideas. Among Ray's effective pedagogical methods was his use of guest lectures by the department's more senior North Americanists (Sol Tax and Fred Eggan, who were professors emeritus at the time). A recent PhD, Terry Straus, was also a guest lecturer, and she gave the class a sense of the excitement and challenges of doing ethnographic research in contemporary Native American communities. Another way of helping his students find common intellectual ground was an assignment that required each student to write a research paper on a single aspect of American Indian culture. In 1977–78, when this book's editors took the class, the topic was Native American architecture, and several of the research papers were incorporated into theses and publications.[14]

Ray played an instrumental role in developing a popular undergraduate program in anthropology at the University of Chicago, both by teaching a variety of undergraduate courses and encouraging his departmental colleagues to do likewise. He points out that reading classical works in anthropology and the social sciences more generally with bright undergraduates has been a rewarding teaching experience and helped to broaden his own theoretical outlook. It is well known that at a research university such as Chicago not every faculty member takes undergraduate teaching seriously, but Ray always has. He attributes his attitude, at least in part, to his own undergraduate experience at Wesleyan, where "teaching was where it was at." He also notes that he was exposed to some fine teachers at Penn. Thanks to Ray's dedication to undergraduate teaching, an innovative undergraduate concentration in anthropology was established at Chicago, and many alumni of the undergraduate program have gone on to do successful graduate work in anthropology and other social sciences (Fogelson 1999).

At Chicago Ray developed a strong interest in Lévi-Straussian structuralism and symbolic anthropology, which he has retained to this day. In the 1960s and 1970s Chicago was a major center of symbolic anthropology, with such prominent scholars as Clifford Geertz, Nancy Munn, Marshall Sahlins, David Schneider, Terry Turner, and Victor Turner on its faculty (see Fogelson 2001b; Handler 1995; Stocking 1979). In the area of American Indian ethnology Ray benefited greatly from having two senior colleagues who worked in the area, Fred Eggan and Sol Tax (DeMallie 1994; Eggan 1974; Fogelson 1980b; Foley 1999; Hinshaw 1979; Stocking 2000). Ray found Eggan (who had been a close friend of Hallowell) particularly supportive as a colleague. Other Chicago colleagues with whom Ray has been particularly close over the years include Friedrich, Nash, Stocking, Jim Fernandez, Les Freeman, and Raymond Smith.

Although Chicago's anthropology department has had its share of fine lecturers and effective mentors, Ray Fogelson is well known as one of the most "student-friendly" professors. As Ray stated in the remarks he delivered at the close of the last of the AAA sessions held in his honor, he has always found himself learning as much from his graduate students as from reading or talking to colleagues. Ray's office door is always open, and his graduate students have benefited greatly from conversing with him in his cluttered office, borrowing books from his vast library, and interacting with him, his friends, and each other at the famous parties at his North Side home. Known to some of his students' children as "Uncle Ray," he has always shown an interest in his students' lives and families as well as their scholarship. Ray has successfully created a true community of scholars, and many of his students, including a significant number of the contributors to this volume, have become lifelong friends as well as colleagues.

Ray's commitment to mentoring graduate students is further illustrated by his longstanding support for the Central States Anthropological Association, which he served as president in 1983–84. He has faithfully participated in its annual meetings, and encourages his students to present their first scholarly papers at these small and supportive meetings. Ray has also been deeply involved in the American Society for Ethnohistory, whose presidency he assumed in 1987–88 and whose membership he helped increase (particularly by encouraging his graduate students and recent doctorates to join and attend meetings). Ray's talent for composing thought-provoking and humorous comments on his colleagues' papers at scholarly meetings is legendary. His talent in this area is particularly worthy of admiration because quite often this work is done the night before the session, if not at the session itself. Not all of these comments find their way onto the printed page, but when they do we are treated to wonderful ethnological essays in their own right (see Fogelson 1981, 2001a).

Ray has also been a strong supporter of the D'Arcy McNickle Center for the History of the American Indian at the Newberry Library. He served on the center's advisory board from 1971 to 1985 and again from 1989 to 1992, and contributed some of his most provocative papers to its curriculum series (Fogelson 1985c, 1986, 1989a). Ray's involvement with the American Society for Ethnohistory and the D'Arcy McNickle Center coincided with the further development of his interest in exploring Cherokee culture through a combination of ethnographic and ethnohistorical research. During the Chicago years Ray has continued publishing articles on the Cherokees, while also exploring other areas of interest such as psychological anthropology (Fogelson 1982b, 1994a), the anthropology of power (Fogelson 1977; Fogelson and Adams 1977), ethnohistory (Fogelson 1984, 1985c, 1989b), the anthropology of religion (Fogelson 1987b; Fogelson and Brightman 2002), the history of anthropology (Fogelson 1985b, 1987a, 1987b, 1997, 1999a), and the history of representations of American Indians in Europe and the United States (Fogelson 1991b).

Since the mid-1960s Ray has carried on ethnographic research among the Oklahoma Cherokees and Creeks (Muskogees), a natural development after his trips with Lloyd Sequoyah. One of his major contacts in Oklahoma was his old friend and colleague Bob Thomas (see Fogelson 1998a). An important new development in Ray's involvement with southeastern Indian people occurred in 1986 when he and a group of Newberry Library Fellows (Jay Miller, C. B. Clark, Robert McKinley, and Richard Sattler) participated in the stomp dances of the Oklahoma Creeks. Since being welcomed into the stomp dance community, he has been going there almost every summer (see Fogelson 2001a; Miller 2001). Ray has not published any works based on this experience and emphasizes that he does not view it as fieldwork in the strict sense of the term. But the experience of fasting and following other prohibitions, taking medicinal teas, getting initiated into the ritual system, and being given a Creek name has informed his teaching and helped him better understand many aspects of Southeastern Indian culture and history. He has also been invited to present papers at scholarly conferences organized by the Oklahoma Cherokees (e.g., Fogelson 1993a). When discussing his experience in Oklahoma, Ray talks about "a new kind of fieldwork" that he calls "observant participation."

Always keeping an eye on the most recent political and cultural developments in Indian Country, Ray continues to publish thoughtful and provocative essays on such topics as Native American identity, past and present (Fogelson 1998b). An important but relatively unknown dimension of Ray's involvement with Native American people and issues has been his congressional testimony on federal recognition criteria and on specific recognition cases, such as that of the Lumbees (Fogelson 1988b, 1989c). Congressional testimony has also given him a chance to do informal ethnographic research on the Branch of Acknowledgment and Recognition (a subdivision of the Bureau of Indian Affairs). At the 1993 Mashantucket Pequot History Conference and the 1998 meetings of the American Anthropological Association he gave papers exploring the cultural and political biases entailed in recognition criteria (Fogelson 1988a, 1993b). Ray also became involved in the Dickson Mound controversy in the state of Illinois—a controversy that eventually ended public visits to a large complex of exposed prehistoric graves (Fogelson 1991c). He has been an early and consistent supporter of the Native American Graves Protection and Repatriation Act (NAGPRA), which has caused some disagreements between him and some of his friends and colleagues at the Smithsonian. He has spoken out on the Indian mascot issue on a number of occasions, and maintains a keen interest in the vibrant cultural and artistic life of Chicago's diverse Native American community.[15]

Ray recently completed one of his most significant scholarly projects: editing the monumental *Southeast* volume of the Smithsonian Institution's *Handbook of North American Indians* (Fogelson 2004b). One of twenty projected *Handbook* volumes, the *Southeast* contains Fogelson's latest articles on the history of anthropology (Jackson, Fogelson, and Sturtevant 2004) and Eastern Cherokees (Fogelson 2004a), while the introduction (Jackson and Fogelson 2004) offers a valuable discussion of the principles that have organized scholarly knowledge about Native North America. The latest in a series of important general works he has published on the cultures of the Southeast (Fogelson 1974b, 1979a, 1994b), the *Handbook* volume is among the most impressive accomplishments of the great scholar, mentor, and friend this volume honors.

Acknowledgments

The editors gratefully acknowledge the support of their families and institutions during the years this volume was in preparation. We thank Gary Dunham and the staff at the University of Nebraska Press for their interest, and the contributors for their dedication and patience. The generous financial support of Dartmouth College and the University of Texas at

Austin is also gratefully acknowledged. Above all we are grateful to the faithful mentor and friend who inspired this project, Ray Fogelson.

Notes

1. The works of many of the contributors are included in a recent survey of innovative ethnographic research on the indigenous peoples of North America (Strong 2005).

2. A more recent generation of Fogelson's students is listed on the website of the anthropology department at the University of Chicago, http://anthropology.uchicago.edu. (See "World of Chicago" and "Graduate Program.") Accessed July 8, 2005.

3. On the work of Stephens, who died of cancer in 1998, see Malkki and Martin 2003. Other treatments of indigenous cultural rights and legal claims by Fogelson and his students include Art 1981; Brown and Morrow 2001; Brown and Rieger 2001; Buckley 1996; Fogelson 1981, 1988a, 1988b, 1989c, 1993b; Jacknis 2002; Nesper 2002, 2004; Sooktis and Strauss 1981; Strong 1981, 2001, 2004a; Strong and Van Winkle 1993, 1996; Van Winkle and Poor 1981. See also Nesper's essay in the present volume.

4. The biographical sketch is based on a 1998 interview with Sergei Kan as well as subsequent communications with Kan and Strong.

5. In addition to Brown and Bender, these include David Blanchard and Amelia R. Bell (see, for example, Blanchard 1982; Fogelson and Walker 1980; Fogelson and Bell 1983) as well as contributors Mary Druke Becker, Robert Brightman, Frederick Gleach, Larry Nesper, Jean O'Brien, and Pauline Turner Strong.

6. Collaborations among Fogelson's students include, in addition to the present volume, Bender 2002; Brown and Brightman 1988; Gleach 2003a; Harkin and Kan 1996; Kan 2001; Mauzé, Harkin, and Kan 2004; Nesper 2003; Strong 1981; Strong and Van Winkle 1993, 1996; Van Winkle and Poor 1981.

7. Fogelson discusses this image in "On the Varieties of Indian History" (1974:105). See also Bender's chapter in this volume.

8. In a review of the state of ethnohistory, Shepard Krech (1991:354) noted that "the privileging of cultural meaning in interpretation" is particularly characteristic of the work of Fogelson and his students. Many of Fogelson's own publications concern the cultural meaning of Cherokee rituals, including healing and conjuring ceremonies (Fogelson 1958, 1961, 1980a; Fogelson and Bell 1983), sorcery and witchcraft (1975), and the stickball game (Fogelson 1962, 1971).

9. Among the contributors, Brown (1991) and DeMallie (1993) have also published presidential addresses on the nature of ethnohistory.

10. In addition to early versions of the essays in this volume by Buckley, Urban, Van Winkle, and Brightman (see also Brightman 1999), Nabokov comments on conference papers on "reinventing the Veddas" by James Brow, neotraditional architecture in northwest California by Ira Jacknis, the Great Irish Exhibition of 1853 by Jamie Saris, and the politics of representing indigenous peoples by Sharon Stephens. (For related works, see Brow 1997; Jacknis 2002; Saris 2000; Stephens 1995). Many essays included in the volume remain unmentioned because they were not part of Nabokov's assignment as discussant. His comments on particular papers illustrate the range of work influenced by Fogelson, which extends far beyond this volume's focus on Native North America.

11. On Wallace's career and ideas, see Grumet 1998; Jennings 1990; and Wallace 1978.

12. See Fogelson 1998 (honoring Thomas); Fogelson and Brightman 2002 (honoring Sturtevant).

13. For a 1959 photograph of a young Ray Fogelson with Lloyd Sequoyah, see Jackson, Fogelson, and Sturtevant 2004:40.

14. See Art 1979; Kan 1978, 1989; Strong 1979. As Nabokov notes in the afterword and elsewhere (Nabokov and Easton 1989:413), these and other seminar papers were sources for his book *Native American Architecture*.

15. The Chicago Indian community is described in two volumes edited by Ray's student and colleague Terry Straus (1990; Straus and Arndt 1998).

Bibliography
Selected Works by Raymond D. Fogelson

Beardslee, David C., and Raymond D. Fogelson
1958 Sex Differences in Sexual Imagery Aroused by Musical Stimulation. *In* Motives in Fantasy, Action and Society: A Method of Assessment and Study. John William Atkinson, ed. Pp. 132–142. Princeton NJ: D. Van Nostrand.

Fogelson, Raymond D.
1958 A Study of the Conjuror in Eastern Cherokee Society. MA thesis, Department of Anthropology, University of Pennsylvania.

1961 Change, Persistence, and Accommodation in Cherokee Medico–Magical Beliefs. *In* Symposium on Cherokee and Iroquois Culture. William N. Fenton and John Gulick, eds. Pp. 213–225. Bureau of American Ethnology Bulletin 180. Washington: U.S. Government Printing Office.

1962 The Cherokee Ball Game: A Study in Southeastern Indian Ethnology. PhD dissertation, Department of Anthropology, University of Pennsylvania.

1965 Psychological Theories of Windigo "Psychosis" and a Preliminary Application of a Models Approach. *In* Context and Meaning in Cultural Anthropology: Essays in Honor of A. Irving Hallowell. Melford Spiro, ed. Pp. 74–99. New York: Free Press.

1971 The Cherokee Ballgame Cycle: An Ethnographer's View. Ethnomusicology 15(3): 327–338.

1974a On the Varieties of Indian History: Sequoyah and Traveller Bird. Journal of Ethnic Studies 2(1):105–112.

1974b Southeast American Indians. *In* Encyclopedia Britannica. 15th ed., 17:218–222.

1975 An Analysis of Cherokee Sorcery and Witchcraft. *In* Four Centuries of Southern Indians. Charles Hudson, ed. Pp. 113–131. Athens: University of Georgia Press.

1976 General Introduction. *In* Contributions to Anthropology: Selected Papers of A. Irving Hallowell. Raymond D. Fogelson, ed. Introductions by Fred Eggan, Raymond D. Fogelson, Melford E. Spiro, George W. Stocking Jr., A. F. C. Wallace, and Wilcomb E. Washburn. Pp. ix–xvii. Chicago: University of Chicago Press.

1977 Cherokee Notions of Power. *In* The Anthropology of Power: Ethnographic Studies from Asia, Oceania, and the New World. Raymond D. Fogelson and Richard N. Adams, eds. Pp. 185–194. New York: Academic Press.

1979a The Cherokees: A Critical Bibliography. Bloomington: Indiana University Press.

1979b Major John Norton as Ethno-ethnologist. Journal of Cherokee Studies 3(4):250–255.

1980a The Conjuror in Eastern Cherokee Society. Journal of Cherokee Studies 5(2):60–87.

1980b Fred Eggan. *In* Encyclopedia of the Social Sciences 19 (Supplement):163–166. New York: Macmillan and Free Press.

1980c Windigo Goes South: Stoneclad Among the Cherokees. *In* Manlike Monsters on Trial: Early Records and Modern Evidence. Marjorie M. Halpin and Michael M. Ames, eds. Pp. 132–151. Vancouver: University of British Columbia Press.

1981 Commentary. Special issue, "Native American Land." Pauline Turner Strong, ed. Chicago Anthropology Exchange 14:130–145. Chicago: Department of Anthropology, University of Chicago.

1982a Cherokee Little People Reconsidered. Journal of Cherokee Studies 7(2):92–98.

1982b Person, Self, and Identity: Some Anthropological Retrospects, Circumspects, and Prospects. *In* Psychological Theories of the Self. Benjamin Lee, ed., with the collaboration of Kathleen Smith. Pp. 67–109. New York: Plenum Press.

1984 Who Were the Ani-Kutani? An Excursion into Cherokee Historical Thought. Ethnohistory 31(4):255–263.

1985a Cherokee Teratology and the Unity of Opposites. Paper presented at the American Society for Ethnohistory, Chicago.

1985b Interpretations of the American Indian Psyche: Some Historical Notes. *In* Social Contexts of American Ethnology, 1840–1984. June Helm, ed. Pp. 4–27. 1984 Proceedings of the American Ethnological Society. Washington DC: American Anthropological Association.

1985c Night Thoughts on Native American Social History. Occasional Papers on Curriculum 3:67–89. Chicago: D'Arcy McNickle Center for the History of the American Indian, The Newberry Library.

1986 A Final Look and Glance at the Bearing of the Bering Straits on Native American History. Occasional Papers on Curriculum 5:233–261. Chicago: D'Arcy McNickle Center for the History of the American Indian, The Newberry Library.

1987a Robert H. Lowie. *In* Encyclopedia of Religion 9:40–41. New York: Macmillan and Free Press.

1987b North American Indian Religions: History of Study. *In* Encyclopedia of Religion 10:545–550. Mircea Eliade, ed. New York: Macmillan and Free Press.

1988a Federal Indian Recognition. Paper presented at Plenary Session, Annual Meeting of the American Anthropological Association, Phoenix.

1988b Testimony to the U.S. Senate Select Committee on Indian Affairs and H.R. Committee on Interior and Insular Affairs on Recognition of the Lumbee Indians. Congressional Record, S2672, 19–21, 77–84.

1989a The Context of American Indian Political History: An Overview and Critique. Occasional Papers on Curriculum 11:8–21, 171–177. Chicago: D'Arcy McNickle Center for the History of the American Indian, The Newberry Library.

1989b The Ethnohistory of Events and Nonevents. Ethnohistory 36(2):133–147.

1989c Testimony to the U.S. Senate Select Committee on Indian Affairs on Recognition of Indian Tribes. Congressional Record, S611, part 2, 80–82, 176–182.

1990 On the "Petticoat Government" of the Eighteenth-Century Cherokee. *In* Personality and the Cultural Construction of Society: Papers in Honor of Melvin E. Spiro. David K. Jordan and Marc J. Swartz, eds. Pp. 161–181. Tuscaloosa: University of Alabama Press.

1991a A. Irving Hallowell and the Study of Cultural Dynamics. *In* The Psychoanalytic Study of Society. L. Bryce and R. M. Boyer, ed. Pp. 16:9–16. Hillsdale NJ: Analytic Press.

1991b The Red Man in the White City. *In* Columbian Consequences, vol. 3. The Spanish Borderlands in Pan-American Perspective. David Hurst Thomas, ed. Pp. 73–90. Washington DC: Smithsonian Institution.

1991c Testimony to the Illinois House of Representatives on Dixon Mound, Springfield, Illinois.

1993a The Keetowah Movement in Indian Territory. Paper presented at the Cherokee History Conference, Tahlequah, Oklahoma.

1993b On Recognition Criteria: Myth-making and History-making at the Branch of Acknowledgement and Research of the Bureau of Indian Affairs. Paper presented at the Mashantucket Pequot History Conference, Mystic, Connecticut.

1994a (principal consultant) Cycles of Life. Alexandria VA: Time-Life Books.

1994b (principal consultant) Tribes of the Southern Woodlands. Alexandria VA: Time-Life Books.

1997 Mary R. Haas and Southeastern Ethnography. Anthropological Linguistics 39(1): 585–589.

1998a Bringing Home the Fire: Bob Thomas and Cherokee Studies. In A Good Cherokee, A Good Anthropologist: Papers in Honor of Robert K. Thomas. Foreword by Thomas J. Hoffman. Steve Pavlik, ed. Pp. 105–118. Contemporary American Indian Series, 8. Los Angeles: American Indian Studies Center, University of California.

1998b Perspectives on Native American Identity. In Studying Native America: Problems and Prospects. Russell Thornton, ed. Pp. 40–59. Madison: University of Wisconsin Press.

1999a Nationalism and the Americanist Tradition. In Theorizing the Americanist Tradition. Lisa Philips Valentine and Regna Darnell, eds. Pp. 75–83. Toronto: University of Toronto Press.

1999b On the Uses and Abuses of Undergraduate Programs in Anthropology. Journal of Undergraduate Honors. Manuscript in Raymond D. Fogelson's possession.

2001a Commentary. In Strangers to Relatives: The Adoption and Naming of Anthropologists in Native North America. Sergei Kan, ed. Pp. 243–255. Lincoln: University of Nebraska Press.

2001b David Schneider Confronts Componential Analysis. In The Cultural Analysis of Kinship: The Legacy of David M. Schneider. Richard Feinberg and Martin Ottenheimer, ed. Pp. 33–45. Urbana: University of Illinois Press.

2004a Cherokee in the East. In Vol. 14: Southeast. Raymond D. Fogelson, ed. Pp. 337–353. Handbook of North American Indians. William C. Sturtevant, gen. ed. Washington DC: Smithsonian Institution.

2004b (editor) Vol. 14: Southeast. Handbook of North American Indians. William C. Sturtevant, gen. ed. Washington DC: Smithsonian Institution.

Fogelson, Raymond D., and Richard N. Adams, eds.

1977 The Anthropology of Power: Ethnographic Studies from Asia, Oceania, and the New World. New York: Academic Press.

Fogelson, Raymond D., and Amelia R. Bell

1983 Cherokee Booger Mask Tradition. In The Power of Symbols: Mask and Masquerade in the Americas. N. Ross Crumrine and Marjorie Halpin, eds. Pp. 48–69. Vancouver: University of British Columbia Press.

Fogelson, Raymond D., and Robert A. Brightman

2002 Totemism Reconsidered. In Anthropology, History, and American Indians: Essays in Honor of William Curtis Sturtevant. William L. Merrill and Ives Goddard, eds. Pp.

305–313. Smithsonian Contributions to Anthropology, 44. Washington DC: Smithsonian Institution.

Fogelson, Raymond D., and Paul Kutsche

1961 Cherokee Economic Cooperatives: The Gadugi. *In* Symposium on Cherokee and Iroquois Culture. William N. Fenton and John Gulick, eds. Pp. 83–123. Bureau of American Ethnology Bulletin 180. Washington DC: Government Printing Office.

Fogelson, Raymond D., and Melford E. Spiro

1965 Introduction. *In* Context and Meaning in Cultural Anthropology: Essays in Honor of A. Irving Hallowell. Melford E. Spiro, ed. Pp. xv–xxii. Glencoe: Free Press.

Fogelson, Raymond D., and Amelia B. Walker

1980 Self and Other in Cherokee Booger Masks. Journal of Cherokee Studies 5(2):88–102.

Jackson, Jason Baird, and Raymond D. Fogelson

2004 Introduction. *In* Vol. 14: Southeast. Raymond D. Fogelson, ed. Pp. 1–13. Handbook of North American Indians. William C. Sturtevant, gen. ed. Washington DC: Smithsonian Institution.

Jackson, Jason Baird, Raymond D. Fogelson, and William C. Sturtevant

2004 History of Ethnological and Linguistic Research. *In* Vol. 14: Southeast. Raymond D. Fogelson, ed. Pp. 31–47. Handbook of North American Indians. William C. Sturtevant, gen. ed. Washington DC: Smithsonian Institution.

Wallace, Anthony F. C., and Raymond D. Fogelson

1961 Culture and Personality. *In* Biennial Review of Anthropology. Bernard J. Siegel, ed. Pp. 42–78. Stanford CA: Stanford University Press.

1965 The Identity Struggle. *In* Intensive Family Therapy: Theoretical and Practical Aspects. Ivan Boszormenyi-Nagy and James L. Framo, eds. Pp. 365–406. New York: Hoeber Medical Division, Harper and Row.

Other Works Cited

Art, Karen Majcher

1979 The Hogan: Microcosm of the Navajo Universe. Chicago Anthropology Exchange 12(2):36–43.

1981 Natural and Supernatural Resources: Mining on Navajo Land and the American Indian Religious Freedom Act. Special issue, "Native American Land." Pauline Turner Strong, ed. Chicago Anthropology Exchange 14:4–26. Chicago: Department of Anthropology, University of Chicago.

Bender, Margaret

2002 Langue, Parole, and Gender: Literacy in Cherokee. *In* Southern Indians and Anthropologists: Culture, Politics, and Identity. Lisa J. Lefler and Frederic W. Gleach, eds. Pp. 77–88. Athens GA: University of Georgia Press.

Blanchard, David Scott

1982 Patterns of Tradition and Change: the Recreation of Iroquois Culture at Kahnawake. PhD dissertation, Department of Anthropology, University of Chicago.

Brightman, Robert A.

1981 Cree Land Tenure in Northwestern Manitoba. Special issue, "Native American Land." Pauline Turner Strong, ed. Chicago Anthropology Exchange 14:70–98. Chicago: Department of Anthropology, University of Chicago.

1990 Primitivism in Missinnippi Cree Historical Consciousness. Man 25:399–418.

1999 Traditions of Subversion and the Subversion of Tradition: Maidu Clown Performances. American Anthropologist 101(2):272–287.

Brooks, James

2002 Captives and Cousins: Slavery, Kinship, and Community in the Southwest Borderlands. Chapel Hill: University of North Carolina Press.

Brow, James

1997 Demons and Development: The Struggle for Community in a Sri Lankan Village. Tucson: University of Arizona Press.

Brown, Caroline L., and Phyllis Morrow

2001 A Resource Most Vital: Legal Interventions in Native Child Welfare. The Northern Review 23.

Brown, Caroline L., and Lisa Rieger

2001 Culture and Compliance: Locating the Indian Child Welfare Act in Practice. Political and Legal Anthropology Review 24(2):58–75.

Brown, Jennifer S. H.

1991 Ethnohistorians: Strange Bedfellows, Kindred Spirits. Ethnohistory 38:113–123.

Brown, Jennifer S. H., and Robert Brightman

1988 "The Orders of the Dreamed": George Nelson on Cree and Northern Ojibwa Religion and Myth, 1823. Winnipeg: University of Manitoba Press.

Buckley, Thomas

1996 The Pitiful History of Little Events: The Epistemological and Moral Contexts of Kroeber's California Ethnology. In Volksgeist as Method and Ethic: Essays on Boasian Ethnography and the German Anthropological Tradition. George W. Stocking Jr., ed. Pp. 257–297. Madison: University of Wisconsin Press.

Darnell, Regna

2001 Invisible Genealogies: A History of Americanist Anthropology. Lincoln: University of Nebraska Press.

Deloria, Vine, Jr.

1969 Custer Died for Your Sins: An Indian Manifesto. New York: Macmillan.

DeMallie, Raymond J.

1993 "These Have No Ears": Narrative and the Ethnohistorical Method. Ethnohistory 40:515–538.

1994 Introduction: Fred Eggan and American Indian Anthropology. In North American Indian Anthropology: Essays in Society and Culture. Raymond J. DeMallie and Alfonso Ortiz, ed. Pp. 3–22. Norman: University of Oklahoma Press.

Eggan, Fred

1974 Among the Anthropologists. Annual Review of Anthropology 3:1–20.

Fenton, William N.

1955 Cultural Stability and Change in American Indian Societies. Journal of the Royal Anthropological Institute 83:169–174.

Foley, Douglas E.

1999 The Fox Project: A Reappraisal. Current Anthropology 40(2):171–191.

Gleach, Frederic W.

2003a Controlled Speculation and Constructed Myths: The Saga of Pocahontas and Captain John Smith. In Reading Beyond Words: Contexts for Native History. Jennifer S. H. Brown and Elizabeth Vibert, eds. Pp. 39–74. Petersborough ON: Broadview Press.

Grumet, Robert S.

1998 An Interview with Anthony F. C. Wallace. Ethnohistory 45(1):103–127.

Gulick, John

1960 Cherokees at the Crossroads. Chapel Hill: Institute for Research in Social Science, University of North Carolina.

Hallowell, A. Irving

1926 Bear Ceremonialism in the Northern Hemisphere. American Anthropologist 36: 389–404.

1965 The History of Anthropology as an Anthropological Problem. In Contributions to Anthropology: Selected Papers of A. Irving Hallowell. Raymond D. Fogelson, ed. Pp. 21–35. Chicago: University of Chicago Press, 1976.

1976 Contributions to Anthropology: Selected Papers of A. Irving Hallowell. Raymond D. Fogelson, ed. Chicago: University of Chicago Press.

Handler, Richard, ed.

1995 Schneider on Schneider. Durham NC: Duke University Press.

Harkin, Michael E., and Sergei Kan, eds.

1996 Special Issue, "Native American Women's Responses to Christianity." Ethnohistory 43(4).

Hinshaw, Robert

1979 Currents in Anthropology: Essays in Honor of Sol Tax. The Hague: Mouton.

Jacknis, Ira

2002 Storage Box of Tradition: Kwakiutl Art, Anthropologists, and Museums, 1881–1981. Washington DC: Smithsonian Institution.

Jackson, Jason Baird, and Victoria Lindsay Levine

2002 Singing for Garfish: Music and Woodland Communities in Eastern Oklahoma. Ethnomusicology 46(2):284–306.

Jennings, Francis

1990 Anthony F. C. Wallace: An Ethnohistorical Pioneer. Ethnohistory 37 (1990):438–444.

Kan, Sergei

1978 The Winter House in the Tlingit Universe. MA thesis. Department of Anthropology. University of Chicago.

1989 Symbolic Immortality: The Tlingit Potlatch of the Nineteenth Century. Washington DC: Smithsonian Institution.

2001 (editor) Strangers to Relatives: The Adoption and Naming of Anthropologists in Native North America. Lincoln: University of Nebraska Press.

Kapchan, Deborah A., and Pauline Turner Strong

1999 Introduction: Theorizing the Hybrid. Journal of American Folklore 112(445):239–253.

Krech, Shepard, III

1991 The State of Ethnohistory. Annual Review of Anthropology 20:345–375.

Malkki, Lisa, and Emily Martin

2003 Children and the Gendered Politics of Globalization: In Remembrance of Sharon Stephens. American Ethnologist 30:216–224.

Malotki, Ekkehart

1983 Hopi Time: A Linguistic Analysis of the Temporal Concepts in the Hopi Language. New York: Mouton.

Mauzé, Marie, Michael E. Harkin, and Sergei Kan, eds.

2004 Coming to Shore: Northwest Coast Ethnology, Traditions and Visions. Lincoln: University of Nebraska Press.

Miller, Jay

2001 Naming as Humanizing. *In* Strangers to Relatives: The Adoption and Naming of Anthropologists in Native North America. Sergei Kan, ed. Pp. 141–158. Lincoln: University of Nebraska Press.

Mooney, James

1890 The Cherokee Ball Play. American Anthropologist, o.s., 3:105–132.

1891 The Sacred Formulas of the Cherokees. The Seventh Annual Report of the Bureau of American Ethnology for 1885–1886, 301–397. Washington DC: U.S. Government Printing Office.

1900 Myths of the Cherokee. The Nineteenth Annual Report of the Bureau of American Ethnology for 1897–1898, part 1, 3–576. Washington DC: U.S. Government Printing Office.

Mooney, James, and Frans M. Olbrechts

1932 The Swimmer Manuscript: Cherokee Sacred Formulas and Medicinal Prescriptions. Revised, completed, and edited by Frans M. Olbrechts. Bureau of American Ethnology Bulletin 99. Washington DC: U.S. Government Printing Office.

Nabokov, Peter

2002 A Forest of Time: American Indian Ways of History. Cambridge: Cambridge University Press.

Nabokov, Peter, and Robert Easton

1989 Native American Architecture. Oxford: Oxford University Press.

Nesper, Larry

2002 The Walleye War: The Struggle for Ojibwe Spearfishing and Treaty Rights. Lincoln: University of Nebraska Press.

2003 (editor) Special issue, "Native Peoples and Tourism," Ethnohistory 50(3).

2004 Treaty Rights. *In* A Companion to the Anthropology of North American Indians. Thomas Biolsi, ed. Pp. 304–320. Malden MA: Blackwell Publishers.

Sapir, Edward

1934 The Emergence of the Concept of Personality in a Study of Cultures. *In* Selected Writings of Edward Sapir in Language, Culture, and Personality. Pp. 590–597. Berkeley: University of California Press, 1949.

Saris, A. Jamie

2000 Imagining Ireland in the Great Exhibition of 1853. *In* Ireland in the Nineteenth Century: Regional Identity. Glen Hooper and Leon Litvack, eds. Pp. 66–86. Dublin: Four Courts Press.

Sooktis, Rubie, and Anne Terry Strauss

1981 A Rock and a Hard Place: Mineral Resources on the Northern Cheyenne Reservation. Special issue, "Native American Land." Pauline Turner Strong, ed. Chicago Anthropology Exchange 14 (1–2):27–35. Chicago: Department of Anthropology, University of Chicago.

Stephens, Sharon

1995 The Cultural Fallout of Chernobyl Radiation in Norwegian Sami Regions: Implications for Children. *In* Children and the Politics of Culture. Sharon Stephens, ed. Pp. 292–318. Princeton NJ: Princeton University Press.

Stocking, George W., Jr.

1979 Anthropology at Chicago: Tradition, Discipline, Department. Chicago: Joseph Regenstein Library, University of Chicago.

1989 (editor) Romantic Motives: Essays on Anthropological Sensibility. Vol. 6, History of Anthropology. Madison: University of Wisconsin Press.

2000 "Do Good, Young Man": Sol Tax and World Mission of Liberal Democratic Anthropology. *In* Excluded Ancestors: Inventible Traditions: Essays Toward a More Inclusive History of Anthropology. Richard Handler, ed. Pp. 171–264. Madison: The University of Wisconsin Press.

Straus, Anne S. [Terry]

1977 Northern Cheyenne Ethnopsychology. Ethos 5:326–57.

1982 The Structure of the Self in Northern Cheyenne Culture. *In* Psychosocial Theories of the Self. Benjamin Lee, ed., with the collaboration of Kathleen Smith. Pp. 111–128. New York: Plenum Press.

Straus, Terry, ed.

1990 Indians of the Chicago Area. Chicago: NAES College Press.

Straus, Terry, and Grant P. Arndt, eds.

1998 Native Chicago. Chicago: McNaughton & Gunn; distributed by the Master of Arts Program in the Social Sciences, University of Chicago.

Strong, Pauline Turner

1979 The Delaware as Dwellers. Chicago Anthropology Exchange 12:24–35. Chicago: Department of Anthropology, University of Chicago.

1981 (editor) Special issue, "Native American Land." Chicago Anthropology Exchange 14. Chicago: Department of Anthropology, University of Chicago.

2001 "To Forget Their Tongue, Their Name, and Their Whole Relation": Captivity, Extra-Tribal Adoption, and the American Indian Child Welfare Act. *In* Relative Values: Reconfiguring Kinship Studies. Sarah Franklin and Susan McKinnon, eds. Pp. 468–93. Durham NC: Duke University Press.

2002 Transforming Outsiders: Captivity, Adoption, and Slavery Reconsidered." *In* A Companion to American Indian History. Philip J. Deloria and Neal Salisbury, eds. Pp. 339–356. Malden MA: Blackwell Publishers.

2004a The Mascot Slot: Cultural Citizenship, Political Correctness, and Pseudo-Indian Sports Symbols. Journal of Sport and Social Issues 28(1):79–87.

2004b Representational Practices. *In* A Companion to the Anthropology of North American Indians. Thomas Biolsi, ed. Pp. 341–359. Malden MA: Blackwell Publishers.

2005 Recent Ethnographic Research on North American Indigenous Peoples. Annual Review of Anthropology 34:253–268.

Strong, Pauline Turner, and Barrik Van Winkle

1993 Tribe and Nation: American Indians and American Nationalism. Social Analysis: Journal of Cultural and Social Practice 33:9–26.

1996 "Indian Blood": Reflections on the Reckoning and Refiguring of Native North American Identity. Cultural Anthropology 11:547–576.

Talayesva, Don

1942 Sun Chief. Leo Simmons, ed. New Haven: Yale University Press.

Thomas, Robert K.

1961 The Redbird Smith Movement. Symposium on Cherokee and Iroquois Culture. William N. Fenton and John Gulick, eds. Pp. 161–166. Bureau of American Ethnology Bulletin, 180. Washington DC: Government Printing Office.

Turner, Terence

1988 Ethno-Ethnohistory: Myth and History in Native South Americans' Representations of Contact with Western Society. *In* Rethinking History and Myth. Jonathan Hill, ed. Pp. 235–281. Urbana: University of Illinois Press.

Valentine, Lisa, and Regna Darnell, eds.
1999 Theorizing the Americanist Tradition. Toronto: University of Toronto Press.

Van Winkle, Barrik, and Robert Poor
1981 The Opposition of Nevada Indians to the MX System. Special issue, "Native American Land." Pauline Turner Strong, ed. Chicago Anthropology Exchange 14 (1–2):36–49. Chicago: Department of Anthropology, University of Chicago.

Wallace, Anthony F. C.
1978 Basic Studies, Applied Projects, and Eventual Implementation: a Case History of Biological and Cultural Research in Mental Health. *In* The Making of Psychological Anthropology. George D. Spindler, ed. Pp. 203–216. Berkeley: University of California Press.

New Perspectives on Native North America

Part One

Perspectives

On the Genealogy and Legacy
of an Anthropological Tradition

1. *Keeping the Faith*

A Legacy of Native American Ethnography, Ethnohistory, and Psychology

REGNA DARNELL

Like the Native American elders with whom many contributors to this volume work, Ray Fogelson's nuggets of wisdom are often delivered cryptically—embedded in the discourse of the moment, often in the context of a very late party at the annual meetings of the American Anthropological Association (AAA). When I was invited by a contingent of Ray's former students to contextualize *his* intellectual genealogy as a context for their own, I sought a metaphor that would draw us all into a single extended lineage. Unsurprisingly, I found that metaphor in Ray's own practice. When I tried it out on some of his former students, it became clear that I was not alone in treasuring accumulated hand-scrawled notes breezily signed "Gardez le Foi—Ray."

I found myself musing, not for the first time, "What are the tenets of this faith we are keeping together?" and "Who are the 'we' who are keeping them?" To guard an unspecified faith presumably involves standing alongside various equally unspecified others. Any attempt to over specify the tenets of the faith would, I think, foreclose the open-ended possibilities for overlap and cross-fertilization that might bind us together in webs of mutual significance. The network of the potentially faithful is in principle almost infinitely expandable. Ray employs a remarkably inclusive and undyadic image for the ritualized closing of personal letters to many known persons. But it is thoroughly consistent with his tenacious sociability, which has brought together and sustained many of us in this faith over the years. We have something in common: membership in a vital and ongoing tradition of research and scholarly civility—of which knowing Ray is more symptom than cause.

I want to reflect on this Americanist heritage that Ray and I share. The two of us were, in somewhat different senses, the last students of A. Irving

"Pete" Hallowell—Ray at the University of Pennsylvania and me at Bryn Mawr, where Pete taught a seminar in the history of anthropology the year after he retired from Penn at the age of seventy. He wasn't old and he didn't want to retire. I remember when we all persuaded him that classes always meet on the lawn in nice weather. Reassured that no one would harass him if we were caught, he spearheaded our migration to the library cloister. We brought him a chair, thinking it a courtesy. But he was crushed at his exclusion and sat with us on the grass, cross-legged, bolt upright, for two hours without squirming. Meanwhile, the ten young women in the seminar sprawled, squirmed, and fidgeted. That was when I began to understand that Pete was a fieldworker and that the Ojibwe had taught him well. He could sit and listen respectfully, even to students.

Ray received his PhD from Penn in 1962, three years before I began my graduate program there. I received my PhD seven years after his, having followed in his firm, decisively planted footsteps. Although we never overlapped directly, many of our experiences of professional socialization did. Now and again, I heard the name Fogelson mentioned with the approval the elders show for a young man whom it is already clear will carry on the tradition, "keep the faith."

Pete mentioned casually that I had to talk to this Fogelson character, that he knew a lot about several of the things I was interested in: history of anthropology, psychology and culture, and Indians, for example. None of the interests were so bizarre in themselves, but the combination was sufficiently rare to forge friendships rapidly. Although Pete did not then make it explicit, Ray was a young, dynamic example of his own dictum (Hallowell 1965) that anthropologists studying their own history should apply the methods of their own discipline. That is, they should do ethnographies within their own professional tribe. It wasn't a grand leap to use archival documents in addition to or even instead of field notes. After all, the ethnohistorians in our midst had been doing so for a long time. And the combination of methods, for me, remains the link between my own work in the history of anthropology and my praxis as an Americanist linguist, ethnohistorian, and symbolic anthropologist.

Although, of course, the larger faith is that of Americanist anthropology, with Franz Boas as its prophet, the University of Pennsylvania, like all major institutions that have trained substantial segments of the national profession, had its own unique, local, particularistic version of that tradition. Hallowell (1967: 152) was both explicit and prescient about the significance of such local intellectual genealogies:

> Anthropology at large has not yet developed an acute historical consciousness. As I see it, the history of anthropology in Philadelphia is

only a small segment of a larger whole. I hope that I have said enough, however, to indicate that anthropological activities here, when viewed in historical perspective, have been an integral part of a wider flow of events elsewhere and have influenced them as well. Awareness of past events should lead to a more rational appraisal of contemporary aims and achievements, as well as a sounder evaluation of our future goals and the best means to achieve them.

In spite of two decades of intervening scholarship, we still know too little about the institutional particularities of our major departments (Darnell 2002). Hallowell did his part, writing about his own career in Philadelphia anthropology as well as about the intellectual roots of what we now call anthropology. The latter articles were replete with footnotes and exhaustive in detail. His full-year seminar did not emerge from the Middle Ages in Europe until after Christmas; and Malinowski was about to burst upon the scene near the conclusion of his final lecture.

When we do explore our own genealogies, both professional and individual, the emphasis is all too often on origins and founders, dates and "epitomizing events" (Fogelson 1989) that condense actual historical context and process into easily grasped but highly simplified symbolic forms. Of stopping at this point, I too have been guilty. As historians of anthropology, however, we ought to be prepared to extend our genealogies to situate ourselves. Our innovations do not arise full blown from a vacuum. Let us begin, then, by rendering visible the shared genealogy that grounds Ray Fogelson's work in Philadelphia Americanist continuities.

In the good rabbinical fashion from which much of our Americanist-Boasian standard for scholarship derives, let us review some relevant begettings. Franz Boas begat Frank Speck who begat Hallowell. Together, Hallowell and Speck produced Anthony Wallace. Speck's death in 1950, the year of Wallace's PhD, left Hallowell and Wallace to beget Fogelson. In the latter two cases, the Americanist psychology and culture tradition was transmitted at the University of Pennsylvania through professional socialization by two generations of mentors working together to train their successors and future colleagues. This dual-generation pattern was an unintended consequence of hiring practices rather than a conscious ideology; mid-career scholars have the stature and local authority to insist on hiring someone they can talk to. The expansion of American anthropology in the years following World War II encouraged this kind of generational collaboration and local specialization. In the Penn case, Hallowell began as the younger partner to such a pedagogical line of transmission and became its senior in due course. Ray was the last student at Penn in that mold and the natural successor to his teachers. But his career led him away from Philadelphia to pursue the faith transmitted to him through Speck, Hallowell, and Wallace.

At Pennsylvania, the result was a partial discontinuity. Hallowell's position was filled by Dell Hymes, a linguist whose work overlapped with that of Wallace (and Ward Goodenough), not in culture and psychology but in ethnosemantics. Although he shared Hallowell's commitment to history of anthropology, Hymes came to it through a very different genealogy, grounded in overlaps with linguistics rather than psychology.

By the time I arrived at Penn, Pete was already emeritus, although for me he remained both mentor and friend to the end of his life. I thought of him as my grandfather, not my uncle as Ray suggests the kinship read for him. But I eventually learned to call him Pete because he was quite explicit that anything else made him feel old.

Meanwhile, away from the home ranch, Ray returned from the University of Washington to the University of Chicago at the behest of Melford Spiro (who, not incidentally, was a student of Hallowell as well as of Melville Herskovits, another Boasian, at Northwestern). Spiro received his PhD in the same year as Wallace, re-creating with Ray at Chicago the earlier Pennsylvania pattern of dual-generation mentors in psychology and culture. So the tendrils of the Penn tradition were extended by way of a highly productive Chicago grafting. Or, to employ a more ethnographically grounded metaphor, the Penn tradition migrated to Chicago.

Another Penn transplant was James VanStone, who also worked with Speck and Hallowell. Based at the Field Museum in Chicago, VanStone shared Ray's interests in ethnohistory and world's fairs. He was just older enough than Ray to provide a link to Speck in the Penn version of the Boasian tradition.

Although it's something of a tangent, that's about the time that I went job hunting at the AAA meetings in Seattle (where Ray introduced me to a lot of his friends) and just after George Stocking moved from Berkeley to Chicago by way of a semester at Penn—perfect timing to reinforce and legitimate my own work in history of anthropology—which had proceeded in a discontinuous genealogical line from Hallowell to Hymes. Hymes and Stocking were contemporaries, and both had been at Berkeley until about then.

There is, I suppose, no necessary connection between an interest in psychology and culture, ethnohistory, history of anthropology, and ethnosemantics. Nevertheless, my experience of them within University of Pennsylvania anthropology, and Philadelphia anthropology more generally, has certainly been closely linked. Similar theoretical positions were developed at Yale and at Berkeley in the same period, but they did not develop the intensely Americanist emphasis characteristic of the Philadelphia version of ethnosemantics. The American Indian commitments and resources of the American Philosophical Society, beginning with Thomas Jefferson and Benjamin Franklin, may well have influenced the university and its museum to maintain such a clustering of ethnographic specialization in a period when elsewhere the discipline was increasingly characterized by overseas ethnography.

Turning to the Chicago transplant, there is no question that when George Stocking arrived, Ray Fogelson, as part of his heritage from Hallowell, was willing and able to reinforce Stocking's work in the history of anthropology. Ray and George already had a lot in common: George was a historian, whose formal training in anthropology consisted of two courses in anthropology from Hallowell while he was a Penn graduate student in American civilization. Again, psychology and culture and history of anthropology—the subjects of Hallowell's two graduate seminars—were poles in the line of genealogical transmission, this time across disciplinary boundaries.

Since I was a student of Hallowell and Wallace but never of Fogelson, I have a certain hesitation in adding my own name to this genealogy. So I emphasize the direct continuity to Ray's students and former students at Chicago. (Nonetheless, my own adventures in Canada constitute an interrelated grafting. When I went to Edmonton in 1969, Pete told me that he had learned to ride a horse there in 1925. And after a long pause, he observed that "it's cold up there." This was the sum total of my instruction prior to undertaking my first fieldwork. Although the fieldwork was reasonably successful, the grafting was reinforced within my own scholarship but not in the direction taken by the anthropology program at the University of Alberta.)

I won't attempt to trace the ultimate origins of the genealogy. All post-Boasian Americanists know that origins are ultimately unrecoverable. In this case, they recede into a disciplinary prehistory of German idealism that Boas brought to North America (see Stocking 1996). Rather, let us begin with the legitimacy of the link to Boas. When Frank Speck came to Penn in 1907, George Byron Gordon, the new director of the museum, was scrambling to revive the abortive academic anthropology nominally associated with the honorary professorship of Daniel Garrison Brinton, who died in 1898 and was not replaced. Speck completed his MA with Boas at Columbia and came to Penn to take up a prestigious Harrison fellowship. Although he received his PhD from Penn, he continued to maintain close ties to New York anthropology. Speck vacated the Harrison fellowship just in time for it to be taken up by Edward Sapir in 1908 (Darnell 1970, 1988, 1990).

Speck and Sapir formed the two poles of the anthropology Hallowell acquired at Penn. They were peers in a founding generation that divided up the wide-ranging interests of Franz Boas. Hallowell (1972: 5) recalled: "Boas had said the last word. What one strove for was to follow Boas in his ubiquitous interests." None of the students fully succeeded in attaining the scope of their teacher. But between them, Speck and Sapir encompassed the ethnographic approaches of Boasian anthropology. Speck was immersed in the point of view of the northeastern Algonquian and Iroquoian hunters and gatherers and was particularly intrigued by their theories and practices regarding what his own society classified as ecology and natural history. Sapir was more interested in symbolic culture, with an emphasis on language and the verbal articulation of culture in texts from native speakers of Native languages (Darnell 2001).

Speck and Sapir were also mirror images in personality, completing and balancing one another. Sapir's review of Carl Jung's *Psychological Types* in 1923 lyrically articulated his lifelong sense of alienation from North American mainstream culture; Speck anchored him in that normalcy. Although Sapir left Penn in 1910 to organize Canadian anthropological work along Boasian lines, his two years at the University of Pennsylvania were formative for Hallowell's anthropology, particularly insofar as both men later turned to culture and personality. The movement from Sapir's locus of culture in the individual to Wallace's mazeway within an organization-of-diversity model of cultural transmission is fundamentally continuous, despite its mediation through Speck and its consequent loss of Sapir's focus on language as the methodological entree to the point of view of the individual.

Tony Wallace was Speck's last student and absorbed his commitment to northeastern ethnography. Wallace, like Speck, specialized in both Iroquoian and Algonquian cultures (in addition to many other areas of research, particularly in the Southeast). He also inherited a Boasian commitment to exploring the native point of view. Speck wasn't around by the time Ray arrived at Penn, but his influence persisted indirectly, mediated by the continued reliance of both Hallowell and Wallace on this genealogy. Fogelson became a specialist in Iroquoian but focused primarily on the Southeast, writing his MA thesis on the role of the conjurer among the Eastern Cherokee and his PhD thesis on the Cherokee ball game. This work reflected his fieldwork with both the Eastern Cherokee and the Oklahoma Cherokee and his extensive archival work on both Cherokee communities. His ethnohistory and his multisite ethnology formed a continuum.

The emphasis on ethnohistory alongside culture and psychology in the Pennsylvania instantiation follows the same genealogical line. Wallace adds to this the influence of his father, historian Paul Wallace, whose biography of Conrad Weiser remains a classic for anthropologists working in the Northeast. The position of both Wallaces is consistent with Boas's insistence that anthropology ought to move between the explanatory poles of history and psychology, with the former a necessary prelude to the latter (Darnell 2001). Wallace's 1950 dissertation on modal personality and the persistence of aboriginal worldview among the contemporary Tuscarora built on this foundation. It demonstrated that history and psychology are inseparably linked in particular cases and, in the process, operationalized Sapir's notions of intracultural variability. Wallace's biography of Teedyscung applied an equally Sapirian life-history method.

Fogelson developed the ethnohistoric tradition, in combination with contemporary fieldwork, along a range of theoretical dimensions. History was not to be understood as linear, static, or relevant only on antiquarian grounds. The past could not be understood apart from its ongoing resonances in the present; "the sunny chunks of memory culture" refused to stay in separate temporal compartments (Fogelson and Kutsche 1961: 109). Fogelson's early interest in magic, medicine, sorcery, and witchcraft (1961, 1975) led to consideration of how traditional materials were incorporated into contemporary religious practices. The Keetowah Society, which originated to protest long-defunct land allotment policies, persists today as "traditional religion," reworked by the Cherokee in line with their pragmatic worldview (Fogelson 1977:189). It is a revitalization movement without the rhetoric of revolution (as Wallace's typology of revitalization movements would predict). Links between gender and politics emerge from Fogelson's discussion of eighteenth-century Cherokee women and their "petticoat government" (1990).

Fogelson's early efforts to locate the Cherokee in relation to Northern Iroquoians remain as standards for theoretically sophisticated ethnohistory. For example, he documented that the Cherokee booger mask tradition (Fogelson and Bell 1983:54) involved features of form, function, and meaning similar to those among the five nations of the Iroquois Confederacy, for example, begging, disease connection, speaking in whispers or exotic languages, the carrying of weapons, facial expressions, and, among old people, walking with bent gait or using canes. A genetic relationship between the masking complexes thus seems clear in spite of major surface differences.

This symbolic-interpretive work has been highly significant for Iroquoian studies in general. For example, William Fenton's monumental synthesis on Iroquois masks frequently cites Fogelson's proposed interpretations (1987:180, 463, 488, 507). "Fogelson reminds us," Fenton writes, of patterns that "no Iroquois has ever suggested . . . as an explanation, to the author's knowledge." Some of these connections involve "a speculative leap" although they are grounded in ethnohistorically attested practices. This is "a deep level of analysis" of the meaning of symbols that brings "startling results." Fogelson's work creates a symbolic anthropology grounded in ethnohistoric and ethnological detail, giving it a verisimilitude that neither theory nor descriptive data alone can begin to match. Fenton was a mentor in his ethnographic work and encouraged theoretical open-endedness even when his own inclinations remained closer than Ray's to the analytic perspective of his Iroquois consultants.

The native point of view is also crucial, however, to Fogelson's version of the Americanist tradition. He is particularly eager to explore the implications of the prefix *ethno-* when applied to any semantic domain insofar as it is understood in terms intelligible in its originating culture. An ethnohistory meeting this standard, then, would have to be called "ethno-ethnohistory." Cherokee disease beliefs involve an "ethnospecificity" that cannot be generalized easily across cultures (1961:221). Fogelson called for an "ethnopersonality theory" (1975:127) and for an "ethnopsychology which involves working through native languages to gain insights into world view and knowledge of the localized behavioral environment" (1985:5), language directly reminiscent of Hallowell. Fogelson suggests that "the American Indian psyche" can be understood through Western eyes but must also be approached in terms of the psychological ideas of various American Indian groups (1985:4).

Not only is the native point of view significant, but it is privileged alongside that of anthropological science. Fogelson speculates that prophecy is the appropriate genre for indigenous history and that its continuous adaptation permits contemporary survival (1985:23). Indeed, such survival is based in the stabilities of Native American cultures (1989:139), in

> the internal strengths of Indian societies as expressed through the idiom
> of kinship, in the abiding sense of community, in the adaptive significance
> of what we derogatively view as factionalism, and in the political and
> legal effectiveness of native advocates.

A "highly developed level of historical consciousness" (1989:139) is also a survival mechanism. Moreover, having attempted to understand the Native point of view, the ethnohistorian must also acknowledge that he or she works in "bi- or multicultural frames of reference," in which points of view must be juxtaposed and balanced (1989:141). The American Indian tribes studied by ethnohistorians do not exist in isolation from contact and adaptation; their cultures cannot be studied without acknowledging the complex borrowings and mergings of a shared history of groups in contact.

I would now like to turn to what some of the members of this Philadelphia-based anthropological extended family have said about their own understandings of these genealogies. My evidence is who cites whom and how ideas and problems are related in terms specific to the Penn tradition. When I reread Tony Wallace's *Culture and Personality* (1962) in preparing this paper, I was struck by how often he cites (albeit sometimes only implicitly) people who were part of my own professional socialization. Ward Goodenough, Loren Eiseley, Carleton Coon (albeit before my time), John Alden Mason (whom I met through Hallowell), John Witthoft, and Dell Hymes were all Wallace's colleagues at Penn on whom he tried out his own ideas and whom he cited as authorities for substantiating his own arguments.

The Penn version of culture and psychology (the term preferred by Wallace) was always clearly distinguishable from what Ruth Benedict and Margaret Mead called culture and personality. The latter tradition focused on how socialization produced differences in national character (Mead) and holistic cultural pattern (Benedict). Both Mead and Benedict grounded their work in the discipline of anthropology, assuming that culture rather than biology would explain variations in human personality. Their contacts with psychologists were primarily with Neo-Freudians, particularly John Dollard, Karen Horney, and Erik Erikson, who modified Freudian psychoanalysis in terms of cultural context (cf. Darnell 1990). With a somewhat different twist, this is the crux of the challenge posed to Mead's work by the late Australian sociobiologist Derek Freeman, who charges that all of the Boasians ignored the biological basis of cultural diversity and similarity.

Hallowell was more interested in the psychoanalytic basis of psychology and culture, which he asserted in retrospect "had nothing to do . . . with personality studies as they later developed" (1967:4). Both Hallowell and Wallace explored the relationship of mind and body in the context of human and primate evolution. That is, they applied physical anthropological expertise not available to Sigmund Freud and his colleagues. Hallowell acknowledged Sapir as the model for his early involvement with psychoanalysis (1972:8). The decline in popularity of culture and personality "in the narrow sense" did not bother him because his own view of "psychological anthropology" had always been broader (1967:8).

For both Hallowell and Wallace, a broadly defined psychology and culture involved the relationship of mind and body in the context of human evolution. Fogelson (1976:xii) contextualizes Hallowell's concern with "the behavioural environment of the self" as a way of reconciling Charles Darwin and Freud. The link between social evolution and ecology came by way of Speck. Interestingly, it was Wallace who coined the term *ethnoecology* (1976:xiii) to refer to a combination of evolutionary process and the cultural particularism of detailed Boasian ethnography.

The native point of view was a piece of the Boasian program that was particularly emphasized at Penn. Hallowell (1967:5) believed that

> Speck's self-involvement with the study [of] a people and their problems was perhaps greater than that of other anthropologists of the period. . . . And I imitated my mentor for a long while. I too identified myself with the Indians, and tried to avoid serving on university committees.

(Others will have to report whether the latter also characterized Wallace or Fogelson). This identification was not entirely positive. In retrospect, Hallowell believed that it had prevented him from recognizing the complexity of Indian-white relations and the continuing multicultural character of present-day cross-cultural interactions.

But the native point of view did not entirely replace that of the analyst. Indeed, Hallowell's early work with the St. Francis Abenaki documented changes in the kinship system "unknown to the Indians themselves" (1967:6). Hallowell saw no contradiction between this analytic standpoint and his efforts to seek out and report the theorizing of social life that was formulated by his consultants. For example, when he asked hesitantly if people ever married their cross-cousins, Chief William Berens replied: "Who the hell else would they marry?" (1967:8). Both the absurdity of the anthropologist's question in local terms and the conviction of the consultant that he understands his own culture are clear.

Over and over in Hallowell's ethnography the perception of the individual actor emerges, as Wallace noted (Fogelson 1976:159). Spiro (Fogelson 1976:353) described this as the phenomenology of the self as understood by the actor. Spiro also emphasized (Fogelson 1976:355) that ethnography was not studied solely for its own sake but for the light it could shed on social behavior. Certainly this fits the sense I had of what ethnoscience was about in the late 1960s at Penn. It is also consistent with Hallowell's introduction to Wallace's *Culture and Personality*, where he emphasized the need for anthropology to be a science. Culture cannot be explained in terms of itself. Only the move to another level of structure, in this case the psychological, has the potential to lead from description to explanation.

Hallowell's fascination with Ojibwe ontology, that is, with things that are believed by the Ojibwe to exist in the world, also reflects his interest in folk science and Western science. In line with the relativistic turn that began in the mid-1980s, however, I prefer to speak of his ethnography as setting a standard for cross-cultural epistemology. I wonder now if Pete would have been willing to talk about epistemology and situated knowledge or if the ontological claim made by the Ojibwe would have seemed to him quite a different matter. Certainly there is no reason to expect that the Ojibwe would accept alternative epistemologies as equally valid.

Hallowell's later work (brought together in Fogelson 1976) evinces a similar intertextuality. Section introductions by various specialists in areas of Hallowell's expertise both document the scope of his interests and add evaluative reflexivity that reinforces the unity of the continuous and continuing genealogy traced in this chapter. These essays include Wallace on cognition and culture, Washburn on transculturation, Spiro on phenomenology, and Fred Eggan on social structure and what Hallowell called "the behavioral environment of the self."

This exploration of Ray Fogelson's professional roots in the Penn tradition raises as many questions as it answers. To date, the history of anthropology has produced very few examinations of the intellectual, institutional, and social interactional networks of individual scholars. Conference sessions and thematic volumes honoring particular scholars come closest to facilitating such historicist reflexivity. I would argue that the identification of our own genealogies, individually and collectively, is an important part of what we do both as practicing anthropologists and in our histories of anthropology. I take some pride in acknowledging ancestors and relatives among my contemporaries and descendants, treasuring the continuities and situatednesses that come from our overlapping experiences. Although the Americanist tradition has not produced a "school" in any rigid sense, there is an inclusive open-ended group of scholars who talk productively to one another, to the considerable enhancement of our discipline (Valentine and Darnell 1999). Among the scholars standing at multiple cross points in such genealogies, and thus in a position of considerable influence, is Ray Fogelson.

I think Ray might be the last of the latter-day Boasians who seems to know everything. A few of us still aspire to talk intelligently across the subdisciplines, but even fewer read the detailed literature with any enthusiasm or consistency. Ray has always prided himself on being the last book review editor of the *American Anthropologist* who dealt with all four subdisciplines. It's hard to find a topic Ray doesn't know a lot about. Usually he has read something about whatever it is very recently. And then there are the piles of books on his coffee table, and every other surface in sight. It's even more fun than a good bookstore because every item is selected by Ray's wonderful quirky intelligence. I can entertain myself browsing in those stacks indefinitely. Anthropology isn't supposed to be narrow. Ray reminds us that it is not.

Ray is a teacher who doesn't need hierarchy or formality to maintain his authority. He's so approachable and unpretentious that some people, more fools they, have been known to underestimate him. I have known many of Ray's students over the years—for the simple reason that he has always introduced me to them and made sure they were at meetings to meet people like me. None of his students has ever failed to acknowledge his breadth of intellect, wealth of knowledge, and conscientious attention to students and colleagues as whole people whose professional socialization goes way beyond library, classroom, and keyboard or foolscap (in respect for Ray's conscientious resistance to technological interference in the life of the mind).

Pete's students, and Ray's, and some of mine, pass on that legacy, keeping the faith in a continuously emergent and revitalized set of interpretive practices and ethnographic engagements. Our collaborations have led us to redefine, during Ray's career and my own, the kinds of values toward scholarship and colleagues (including students and consultants) that we must take with us when we do fieldwork. Otherwise the Indians will tell us to go back where we came from. In Ray's own words (Valentine and Darnell 1999:82–83):

> As Indian sovereignty has been re-affirmed, as movements for self-determination have gained momentum, and as formerly mute Indian voices become more strident, native confrontations with anthropology and anthropologists become inevitable. For many, these developments herald the death of the Americanist tradition. . . . If there is to be a resurrection of Americanist studies, and I think there will be, anthropologists will have to become wards to the people they study. They will have to pledge allegiances to new nationalisms. They will have to face the challenges of transmitting and translating the past and continuing results of Americanist research to new audiences in new contexts.

This, I believe, is a powerful contemporary statement of the legacy we share, of the faith we all continue to keep with Ray Fogelson.

References

Darnell, Regna

    1970 The Emergence of Academic Anthropology at the University of Pennsylvania. Journal of the History of the Behavioral Sciences 6:80–92.

    1988 Daniel Garrison Brinton: The 'Fearless Critic' of Philadelphia. Philadelphia: University of Pennsylvania Department of Anthropology Monograph Series 3.

    1990 Edward Sapir: Linguist, Anthropologist, Humanist. Berkeley: University of California Press.

    2001 Invisible Genealogies: A History of Americanist Anthropology. Lincoln: University of Nebraska Press.

    2002 Departmental Networks and the Cohesion of American Anthropology. Centennial Address, American Anthropological Association, Washington DC.

Fenton, William

    1987 The False Faces of the Iroquois. Norman: University of Oklahoma Press.

Fogelson, Raymond D.

    1961 Change, Persistence and Accommodation in Cherokee Medico-Magical Beliefs. In Symposium on Cherokee and Iroquois Culture. William Fenton and John Gulick, eds. Pp. 213–225. Bureau of American Ethnology Bulletin 180. Washington DC: U.S. Government Printing Office.

    1975 Analysis of Cherokee Sorcery and Witchcraft. In Four Centuries of Southern Indians. Charles Hudson, ed. Pp. 113–131. Athens: University of Georgia Press.

    1976 (editor) Contributions to Anthropology: Selected Papers of A. Irving Hallowell. Introductions by Fred Eggan, Raymond D. Fogelson, Melford E. Spiro, George W. Stocking Jr., A. F. C. Wallace, and Wilcomb E. Washburn. Chicago: University of Chicago Press.

    1977 Cherokee Notions of Power. In The Anthropology of Power. Raymond D. Fogelson and Richard N. Adams, eds. Pp. 185–194. New York: Academic Press.

    1985 Interpretations of the American Indian Psyche. In Social Contexts of American Ethnology, 1840–1984. June Helm, ed. Pp. 4–27. 1984 Proceedings of the American Ethnological Society. Washington DC: American Anthropological Association.

    1989 The Ethnohistory of Events and Nonevents. Ethnohistory 36: 133–147.

    1990 "On the 'Petticoat Government' of the Eighteenth Century Cherokee." In Personality and the Cultural Construction of Society. K. Jordan and M. J. Swartz, eds. Pp. 161–181. Tuscaloosa: University of Alabama Press.

    1999 Nationalism and the Americanist Tradition. In Theorizing the Americanist Tradition. Lisa Valentine and Regna Darnell, eds. Pp. 75–83. Toronto: University of Toronto Press.

Fogelson, Raymond D., and Amelia Bell

    1983 Cherokee Booger Mask Tradition. In The Power of Symbols. N. R. Crumrine and Marjorie Halpin, eds. Pp. 48–69. Vancouver: University of British Columbia Press.

Fogelson, Raymond D., and R. P. Kutsche

    1961 Cherokee Economic Cooperatives: The Gadugi. In Symposium of Cherokee and Iroquois Culture. William Fenton and John Gulick, eds. Bureau of American Ethnology Bulletin 180:83–123.

Hallowell, A. Irving

    1964 Anthropology at the University of Pennsylvania. Proceedings of the Philadelphia Anthropological Society.

1967 Anthropology in Philadelphia. *In* Philadelphia Anthropological Society. Jacob W. Gruber, ed. Pp. 1–31. New York: Columbia University Press.

1965 The History of Anthropology as an Anthropological Problem. Journal of the History of the Behavioral Sciences 1:24–38.

Jung, Carl Gustav

1923 Psychological Types. New York: Harcourt, Brace.

Stocking, George W., Jr., ed.

1996 Volksgeist as Method and Ethic. Madison: University of Wisconsin Press.

Valentine, Lisa, and Regna Darnell, ed.

1999 Theorizing the Americanist Tradition. Toronto: University of Toronto Press.

Wallace, Anthony F. C.

1962 Culture and Personality. New York: Random House.

2. Fields of Dreams

Revisiting A. I. Hallowell and the Berens River Ojibwe

JENNIFER S. H. BROWN

The boreal forests of Canada have been the setting for diverse dreams and visions—those of Northern Algonquians who have resided there for centuries and those of a long series of questing newcomers who, experiencing their personal "first contacts" with the inhabitants, have recurrently framed those experiences in tropes that foster exotic illusion. In July 1998 the *Winnipeg Free Press* featured an article headlined, "Heart of Magic: Up the Berens River, Time Has Stood Still." The journalist author, Bill Redekop, and a friend had flown to the Ojibwe reserve community of Little Grand Rapids, Manitoba, from Winnipeg, and then spent a week canoeing downriver to the Berens River reserve on the east shore of Lake Winnipeg. Redekop vividly described how, leaving behind such things as TVs, computers, and cell phones, they "entered a region where Ojibway stories and superstitions of hundreds of years ago were still told . . . total wilderness, as if travelling back in time" (Redekop 1998).[1]

These outsider dreams reaffirm the relevance of Johannes Fabian's critique of Western travelers' habits of constructing and distancing exotic Others, including those living today, as belonging to some other time or as situated in "a system of coordinates (emanating . . . from a real center—the Western metropolis) in which given societies of all times and places may be plotted in terms of relative distance from the present." The habit of locating "remote" spaces and peoples in some other temporal universe is symptomatic of an underlying "cosmological myth of frightening magnitude and persistency" (1983:26, 35). Fabian's analysis awakes us from the dreaming in "Heart of Magic." Of course, the Ojibwe along the Berens River live in the same calendar year as everyone else and are just as subject (or more so) to pressures and problems of "our" times. They are not as remote as city types make them out to be; scheduled air flights reach

[margin handwritten note: outside the mainstream]

them every day, and for three months a year winter roads across frozen lakes and muskeg allow transport on a large scale. Their community band offices and schools have telecommunications and computers and people who know how to use them. And their time has never stood still; to say so is to overlook a complex past, full of changes, and in essence to deny them a history.

Ironically, however, Redekop drew upon a source that I had provided to him when he expressed geographic remoteness in terms of temporal distance. His canoe trip came about partly because of his interest in the people whom anthropologist A. Irving Hallowell met on the Berens River in the 1930s. Some years ago, I drew his attention to one of Hallowell's books, *The Ojibwa of Berens River, Manitoba: Ethnography into History*; written in the 1960s, it was finally published in 1992, eighteen years after his death. Hallowell entitled its first chapter "The Living Past in the Canadian Wilderness," and a journalist caught by that image could easily miss my gentle caveat about such phrasings in my afterword to the book (Brown 1992:112).

Similarly, the *Winnipeg Free Press* article's title, "Heart of Magic," nicely evokes the exotic distancing of Joseph Conrad's *Heart of Darkness* (1902), published almost a century earlier. As Robert Brightman points out in his chapter in this volume, Hallowell's portrayals of Ojibwe bands as "growing increasingly 'traditional' [and remote from 'civilization'] as one ascended the Berens River into the boreal forest interior" readily call forth such imagery. Given that these journalistic and ethnographic tropes dovetail so well with the mythic questing language that has long typified wilderness canoeists' discourse (James 1985), Redekop's abstinence from such images would have been more surprising than his use of them. Of course, a vast disparity exists between his brief *Free Press* article and the profound understanding of Berens River people that is reflected in Hallowell's writings. Their shared reference to the upriver people in terms of some other time dimension, however, highlights what might be called a powerful waking dream common among parvenus in Indian country. The difference is that Hallowell's repeated research trips to the Berens River through the 1930s kept his dreaming in check and ultimately led him to far deeper cultural and historical perspectives (e.g., 1992:3, 11).

The main Ojibwe personage appearing, somewhat exoticized, in Redekop's narrative was Percy Berens, an individual he had heard about from me and my colleague, documentary radio journalist Maureen Matthews. Percy Berens's father was William Berens, the chief of the Berens River band at the mouth of the river, who made Hallowell's work possible. Our talks with Percy in the 1990s gave us a living link to the two men who for a decade, 1930–40, collaborated to share and attain deeper understandings of Berens River Ojibwe history, culture, and worldviews. Hallowell led us (and Redekop) to him, and he in turn, through memories, helped to lead us back to Hallowell, to the chief who befriended him, and to the fieldwork that engaged them both. Percy Berens became a nexus for tales of the field, past and present, journalistic and other, and for genealogies both familial and culture-historical.

In their intellectual lives, as in families, scholars too have genealogies. Raymond D. Fogelson and George W. Stocking Jr., who had formative roles in my graduate education at the University of Chicago, have vivid recollections of Hallowell from a period and place very different from those in Percy Berens's memory. As a senior professor at the University of Pennsylvania in the 1950s and 1960s, Hallowell had a great influence on both—"my anthropological godfather," as Stocking has described him (1968:x). This paper is grounded in an appreciation of the ideas, insights, and stories that Hallowell brought from Berens River and wove into his writings and teachings, particularly on the subject of dreams. More immediately, it credits Ray Fogelson for his generative role both in building on the rich legacies of Hallowell in North American Indian studies and in freely sharing his knowledge and insights with all those fortunate enough to work with him. Fogelson led me to Hallowell, and thereby to two locales that could hardly offer a greater contrast: first, the venerable precincts of the American Philosophical Society in Philadelphia where Hallowell's papers and photographs reside; and second, the living communities on the Berens River where his pictures and his small, posthumously published book about them (1992) and his photographs from the 1930s stirred vivid memories of Hallowell and of the ancestors whom he met.

In 1986 when I ventured into the Hallowell papers, they had just become accessible, and I had no idea what doors they would open. Ever since then they have given momentum and new directions to my research. Beyond the richness of their own content, they led to renewals of conversations that Hallowell was not able to pursue once his Berens River visits ended in 1940. Hallowell learned a tremendous amount from the Ojibwe, particularly through his partnership with Chief William Berens. It was Chief Berens who, in 1930, planted in his mind the idea of focusing his studies along the Berens River, diverting him from an initial focus on the more northerly Cree, who had proved to be less isolated than he had hoped. They met at the right moment. Hallowell, aged thirty-seven, was still very much a Boasian comparative ethnologist; his major publications (on bear ceremonialism and on historical changes in Abenaki kinship) were strongly based on library sources (Hallowell 1926, 1928).

His limited fieldwork among the more easterly Abenaki and Nipissing had followed in the empirically oriented ethnographic footsteps of his mentor, Frank Speck. He had not yet defined a satisfactory field space of his own beyond where other anthropologists had ventured. William Berens gave him that gift, inviting him into his community and those of his relatives, up the river—Little Grand Rapids, Pauingassi, Poplar Hill, Pikangikum, and others (Hallowell 1992:6, 8). Here Hallowell could find, as James Clifford puts it, "a cleared place of work" that allowed the "specific practices of displacement and focused, disciplined attention" and the resultant travel discourse that have been hallmarks of field anthropology (Clifford 1997:186, 196). Although time did not "stand still" for Hallowell on his trip upriver with Chief Berens, he later recalled his sense of how that first journey led into "a more primitive world of temporal orientation. The days of the week melted away. . . . The hours of the day soon disappeared since I was the only one who carried a watch and it stopped" (1992:8).

As for William Berens, he was about sixty-five in 1930. For twenty-three years he had been chief of the Ojibwe band at the mouth of the Berens River. When he was a boy, his father, Jacob Berens, the first treaty chief in the region after Treaty 5 was signed in 1875, had said to him, "Don't think you know everything. You will see lots of new things and you will find a place in your mind for them all" (Brown 1989:210). Berens lived by that advice. Like his father, he and his family belonged to the Methodist Church (part of the United Church of Canada after 1925), which had established a mission at Berens River in 1873. But like his father he spoke two languages and combined in his own way two bodies of knowledge and experience. He gathered freely from the knowledge and opportunities that outsiders brought, and Hallowell was one of his most productive harvests.

More profoundly, Berens also had unusual breadth from his upbringing by an Ojibwe father and grandfather on one side and a mother of Scots-Cree descent (Mary McKay) on the other. When Hallowell appeared he was prepared to talk to him at length and to travel with him up the river on several occasions, introducing him to venerable elders and into communities whose ways had been little touched by missionaries and Indian agents. His openness may have reflected a retrospection related to aging, a sense of cultural losses and pressures that had intensified during his life, and the agreeable prospect of revisiting upriver relatives he had not seen in a long time. More immediately he had lately experienced some conflict with the local mission day school over a son's schooling, and although he did not sever his church connection he may have been ready to reorient himself toward the Aboriginal culture and ways that he had learned from a succession of powerful ancestors as well as to transmit what he knew to an eager student opportunely arrived (Brown 1989:218–219).

Amid his researches on many other topics, Hallowell quickly learned how central dreams and dreaming were to Ojibwe experience and worldview. Eventually he was to link his understandings of Ojibwe dreaming to an analysis of dreaming as a universal human characteristic. In his article "The Role of Dreams in Ojibwa Culture" (1976 [1966]), for example, he speculated on when dreaming had first appeared in human evolutionary history. Noting that dreaming appeared to be a distinctly human phenomenon, he suggested that its advent was one marker of human beings' attainment of "a new behavioral plateau," one that was "vitally linked with man's psychobiological functioning and his distinctive level, perhaps, of behavioral adaptation" (1976:451, 450).

Hallowell also learned how, for the Ojibwe themselves, dreams had a central place in their worldview, quite aside from their interest for students of psychobiology. "At the level of group adaptation," he argued, "the Ojibwa interpretation of dreams may be seen as a positive and necessary factor in the maintenance of the sociocultural system that gives meaning to their lives" (1976:453). He took the point further in some of his unpublished notes, and in an undated handwritten diagram that shows how closely dreams intersect with myths and waking experience. On this chart three sectors of a circle representing the individual are divided by dotted rather than solid lines and connected by arrows to represent their mutual influences. These relationships are not easily fathomed by Western observers: as Hallowell noted, the Western habit of creating conceptual divisions between myths, dreams, and waking experience leads outsiders to see them as more distinct from each other than they actually are in Saulteaux culture. In a more elaborate chart, published when his long-lost book manuscript, *The Ojibwa of Berens River*, appeared in 1992, Hallowell placed Ojibwe dreaming in a still more ramified and complex setting. In that volume, figure 17, "The role of dreams in the Ojibwa sociocultural system," maps the integral links between dreaming, the socialization of the child, concrete individual experience, worldview, and central institutions of traditional Ojibwe society such as the puberty fast and the shaking tent (1992:86).

Within what scholarly frame and by what means did Hallowell arrive at these formulations? The answers reside in two domains: intellectual genealogy and methodology. Regna Darnell, in her chapter in this volume, succinctly traces the intellectual line: "Franz Boas begat Frank Speck who begat Hallowell." At the University of Pennsylvania, Hallowell's professional home, "the Americanist psychology and culture tradition was transmitted . . . through professional socialization by two generations of mentors working together to train their successors and future colleagues [including, of course, Ray Fogelson]." Hallowell's dynamic relating of individual psychology to social system and worldview combined, in his analysis of dreams, with a strong concern, shared by his close colleagues, to grasp Native perspectives, logic, and understandings and map them as accurately as possible.

As for method Hallowell listened carefully; he cared about understanding the significance of dreams and their integration in Ojibwe culture and thought; he gained people's confidence so they talked to him about such things; and he had William Berens as mentor, intermediary, and translator. I can say with confidence that when Hallowell came up the river the elders he met found that the level of conversation they could achieve with him through Chief Berens was beyond that possible with any other white man they had known. The name by which he is still remembered, sixty years later, echoes that relationship; people at Little Grand Rapids and Pauingassi refer to him as *Midewigimaa* or *Mide* master because he understood these things so well and took such interest in them (Matthews and Roulette 1996:333).[2]

As Hallowell explored dream experiences and their ramifications, he learned, as had a stream of outsiders before him, that the vision quest was central (for males in particular) to the process of growing up Ojibwe and receiving necessary powers and instruction (for a fuller discussion, see Brown and Brightman 1988:138–146). Many younger men of the 1930s had not undertaken dream quests, but their older relatives had, and the process by which a boy left home, fasted alone in a "nest" in a tree, and awaited the blessings of dream visitors (*bawaaganak*, literally, "the dreamed [ones]") was often and amply described. Usually not talked about were the nature and content of the actual visions and the other-than-human persons who conferred them. Dreamers were restricted from revealing these matters unless they were prepared to lose the gifts given (Hallowell 1955:360), or under certain other conditions.

The prohibition against a dreamer telling his vision-quest dreams might be inferred to signify that Ojibwe people had a more general rule against the telling of dreams. But Hallowell's materials, along with the writings of others and the ongoing praxis of Ojibwe themselves, indicate that this conclusion is simplistic. If one had dreamed but had failed to receive blessings, were near death and unable to use these gifts any more, or belonged to a Christian church and had no plans to use the spirits' offerings (as was the case with William Berens) one might talk more freely of them. A dream that predicted the future might be told once the event had happened; and dreams that validated the gift of and rights to a ceremony and to telling the ceremony's origin might be recited as part of that ceremony. Dreams, with the usual exception of the specifics of a person's empowering vision, were communicated on proper occasions and to appropriate audiences, and necessarily so if they were to become part of a shared culture. As Greg Urban has observed about another society where dreaming is central, the Ibirama of Brazil, "Each dream must be put into words, if it is to have the possibility of becoming a cultural object" (Urban 1997:7).

Dreams were not simply interesting to talk about. They were ways of learning from and about the other-than-human dreamed ones, the mythic personages (*aadizookaanag*) also known as "our grandfathers," who appeared also in legend (Hallowell 1992:84–85). They taught about how to interact properly with these beings and, more deeply, about the importance of remembering and attending to dreams, which is a skill one needs to learn and practice. Vision dreams, in particular, had much to teach, even if they were never explicitly revealed. Sometimes they became subjects of conjecture and discussion by others, although the recipient himself never told them. Observers of a powerful medicine man's behavior could pick up clues about the identity and powers of his *bawaaganak*, the dream visitors from which his blessings had come, and how to interact with them properly. Hallowell was told that at Pauingassi, Manitoba, Fair Wind (Naamiwan), a venerable religious leader, was seen to speak with and understand Thunderbirds (*binesiwag*) and offer them a smoke during thunderstorms. Other people assumed that they were his *bawaaganak*, and watching him they learned about that relationship and about how Thunderbirds should be treated. The carved wooden bird symbol (*obineshishikaniwan*) placed on a post at the entrance to his Wabano pavilion, and silently recorded in Hallowell's photographs, also confirmed the association. No one needed to talk about this; its significance needed explaining only to outsiders (Matthews and Roulette 1996:332, 357; Matthews 1995:7).

Fair Wind's circumspection about his vision-fast dream contrasted with his public recitation, at his Drum Dance of the 1930s, which Hallowell attended, of the charter dream that had consoled him and guided his founding of the ceremony two decades earlier following the death of a favorite grandson (Hallowell 1955:166). In this instance, the giver of the dream evidently mandated its telling as part of the ceremonial performance. But vision-fast dreams are not distinguished terminologically from other sorts of dreams. The general term for "dream" in the region is *bawaajigewin*, related to *bawaaganak*, the dream visitors who are implicated in all dream experiences.[3]

Though the content of a successful vision-fast dream was typically kept private, such dreams might be revealed if they had gone badly wrong. On the upper Berens River, a man named Birch Tree told Hallowell of a dream that his father had heard from a young man just before he died; he wanted it known "as a lesson to the people." When he went on his vision quest, he had wished to dream of all the leaves on every tree in the world:

> Sure enough, he began to dream about all sorts of different leaves. Finally he heard a voice speaking to him. "Grandchild," it said, "that is enough. I'm a little scared for your sake. You have dreamed of half the leaves in the world now. If you dream of every leaf in the whole world you will gain nothing by it." So the young man went home. He was very proud of his power. Very little was hid from him [i.e., the leaves told him everything that went on—AIH]. Yet he was not satisfied. He wanted to know more and more. So he went back to his nest in the tree and slept again. He heard a voice. It said, "What do you want?" "I'm not satisfied with half," the boy said, I want to dream of every tree that bears a leaf." "It will not be a good thing for you to do that," the voice said. "But I want to," the boy replied. So the voice said, "Alright, then." And so the young man dreamed of all the remaining leaves in the world. After this he heard the voice again. "Grandson," it said, "you've been dreaming of every tree in the world that bears a leaf but as soon as the leaves start to fall, you will get sick. Then, when all the leaves drop to the ground, your life will end. You can't blame me. It is your own fault. I told you it was not good to know everything."
>
> "That is what the Indians taught their children," [Birch Tree] commented. "It is better to dream of many things than too much of one thing."

Hallowell added that the reason for dreaming of many things rather than one was that "a man needs many different kind of pawaganak [*bawaaganak*] in order to help him in a variety of circumstances. The more he has, then, the better. Some men, I was told, have hundreds of guardian spirits" (Hallowell 1892–1981, Series I, file 1, "Dreaming." pp. 22–24).[4]

As Hallowell pointed out, this story parallels two Ojibwe tales recorded by William Jones, with the difference that, in these, it was a father who pushed his son too fast until he knew everything. Both quests ended in the loss of the faster; one became a robin and flew away, and as for the other the father later found only his son's bones lying where the boy had been fasting. Over-fasting and efforts (or claims) to know everything in the world both carried penalties (Hallowell 1976:418 and n. 24). The stories evoke Jacob Berens's admonition to his son, William: "Don't think you know everything." Arrogance and greed carried a price, just as hubris or overweening pride did for the ancient Greeks.

Another Berens River story about vision fasting emphasized the need for proper preparation and purity. Boys were not to engage in sexual relations until after their fast and were to avoid any association with females immediately before and after the quest (Hallowell 1992:88). One boy who wanted to fast admitted to his father that he had gotten involved with a girl. The father warned him his quest would probably fail, but the boy went anyway. He lay down and slept. Someone came and said, "What do you want?"

> I've come here to try to receive a blessing.
>
> Nothing will bless you because you are not clean—go back.
>
> The boy went home but wanted to try again. He made a sweat lodge and sweated four times, washing himself in water each time. Again he tried and was told he was not clean. He returned home, sweated and bathed seven times, and had all his clothes washed. Then he went out again and slept and dreamed. Someone asked what he wanted. He answered, a blessing.
>
> Nothing will come to you.
>
> So he gave up the quest. [Hallowell 1892–1981, series V, Research, misc. notes, file 3].

Interpretations of rules against a vision-faster's contact with females have varied. Hallowell's informants explained them by saying that women, because of menstruation, were relative to men *wiinizi*, in a state of impurity, which put at risk the cleanness or religious purity (*bekize*) required when interacting with *bawaaganak*. Recently, Margaret Simmons (granddaughter of William Berens) and Roger Roulette (Ojibwe linguist) elaborated as follows: the problem is not "dirt" as in a dirty house, but rather the risk of a spiritual disorder or chaos. A woman after menarche and before menopause, and especially during her monthly periods, "can put everything into disorder because of the strength of her powers" (Roulette, in Brown and Matthews 1995:9). Berens River Ojibwe women did not engage in an institutionalized vision fast because they were said not to require the spiritual powers that men needed; some, however, did receive unsolicited dream visitors and blessings (Hallowell 1992:88).

Another anecdote about a failed quest emphasized the self-discipline needed to fast. Sometimes two boys went out fasting together. One time, two parallel cousins ("brothers" in Ojibwe terminology) went to a "nest" to fast. When they were alone the older boy said,

> Do you want something to eat?" He had secreted a roasted rabbit under his clothes. At first the younger boy refused. But after his companion had eaten some of the rabbit, he, too, ate a portion. They stayed in the 'nest' that night and the next day they finished up the rabbit. Later the same day they went back to camp in time for the evening meal. They knew that it was no use to expect a dream revelation. [Hallowell 1892–1981, "Dreams," 12–13]

 Dream experiences might also be revealed if the teller had no intent or plan to use the powers offered in them. Chief William Berens, as a church-going Methodist, never mentioned trying a vision quest. But sometimes he had dreams in which spiritual beings presented powers and gifts that he could have accepted if he had chosen. Since he declined their offers, he recounted the dreams to Hallowell. In the most elaborate of these dreams, he encountered the *memegwesiwag*, small beings who lived in rock cliffs above water and were known for their medicines, while he was hunting:

> I climbed a high rock to have a look across the lake. I thought I might sight a moose or some ducks. When I glanced down towards the water's edge again, I saw a man standing by the rock. He was leaning on his paddle. A canoe was drawn up to the shore and in the stern sat a woman. In front of her rested a cradleboard with a baby in it. Over the baby's face was a piece of green mosquito netting. . . . The man was a stranger to me but I went up to him. I noticed that he hung his head in a strange way. He said, "You are the first human being ever to see me. I want you to come and visit me." So I jumped into his canoe. When I looked down I noticed that it was all of one piece. There were no ribs or anything of the sort, and there was no bark covering. I do not know what it was made of.
>
> On the northwest side of the lake there was a very high steep rock. The man headed directly for this rock. With one stroke of the paddle we were across the lake. The man threw his paddle down as we landed on a flat shelf of rock almost level with the water. Behind this the rest of the rock rose steeply before us. But when his paddle touched the rock this part opened up. He pulled the canoe in and we entered a room in the rock. It was not dark there, although I could see no holes to let in any light. Before I sat down, the man said, "See, there is my father and my mother." The hair of those old people was as white as a rabbitskin. I could not see a single black hair on their heads. After I had seated myself

I had a chance to look around. I was amazed at all the articles I saw in the room—guns, knives, pans, and other trade goods. Even the clothing these people wore must have come from a store. Yet I never remembered having seen this man at a trading post. I thought I would ask him, so I said, "You told me that I was the first human being you had seen. Where, then, did you buy all of these articles I see?" To this he replied, "Have you never heard people talking about *pagiticigan* [offerings; cf. *bagijigan*]? These articles were given to us. That is how we got them." Then he took me into another room and told me to look around. I saw the meat of all kinds of animals—moose, caribou, deer, ducks. I thought to myself, this man must be a wonderful hunter if he has been able to store up all this meat. I thought it very strange that this man had never met any other Indians in all his travels. Of course, I did not know that I was dreaming. Everything was the same as I had seen it with my eyes open. When I was ready to go I got up and shook hands with the man. He said, "Anytime that you wish to see me, this is the place where you will find me." He did not offer to open the door for me so I knew that I had to try and do this myself. I threw all the power of my mind into opening it and the rock lifted up. Then I woke up and knew that it was a dream. [Hallowell 1992:90]

A second dream, about a boy in a red tuque (the Canadian spelling of *toque*], drew William Berens into a contest of powers and rewarded him with a gift of protection from bullets if he should ever go to war. Since he never did so, even though he was offered a chance during World War I, he concluded that he did not need the blessing and again felt that he could tell about it:

I was walking along and came to a house [not a wigwam]. I went in. There was no furniture in the room I entered. All that I saw was a small boy in a red tuque. He said to me, "Oh, ho, so you're here." "Yes," I replied, "I'm here." This boy had a bow in his hand and two arrows. One was red and the other black. "Now that you've found me," he said, "I'm going to find out how strong you are." I knew that if he ever hit me that would be the end of me. But I went to the middle of the room, as he told me, and stood there. I filled my mind with the thought that he would not be able to kill me. I watched him closely and, as soon as the arrow left the bow, I dodged. I saw the arrow sticking in the floor. He had missed me. Then he fitted the other arrow to his bow. "I'll hit you this time," he said. But I set my mind just as strongly against it. I watched every move he made and he missed me again.

"It's your turn now," he said and handed me the bow. I picked up the two arrows and he went to the middle of the room. Then I noticed a strange thing. He seemed to be constantly moving yet staying in the same place. He was not standing on the floor either, but was about a foot above it. I knew that it was going to be hard to hit him. I let the black arrow go first and missed him. I made up my mind that I was going to hit him with the red arrow and I did. But it did not kill him. He took the bow from me, tied the arrows to it and laid it aside. "You have beaten me," he said. I was very anxious to know who it was but I did not wish to ask. He knew what I was thinking, because he asked, "Do you know who you have shot? I am a fly [i.e., smaller than a bulldog fly but constantly moving]. [Hallowell 1892–1981, Research, Saulteaux Indians, Dreams; see also the briefer account in Hallowell 1976:467]

The boy then went on to say that Berens would never be shot and killed by a bullet unless the marksman could hit a spot as small as a fly. The two dreams speak to other themes besides powers offered but then not used by the dreamer. In telling them Chief Berens vividly and perhaps strategically affirmed to the visiting anthropologist not only his immersion in Ojibwe ways of thought and experience but also the fact that other-than-human beings selected him more than once to receive gifts in dreams and allowed him to choose among options. (The theme of a dreamer making choices about accepting blessings or accepting the advice offered by dream visitors also appears in the story of the boy dreaming about the leaves.) Berens's dreams also highlighted the power of mind and will. Confined inside the rock cliff of the *memigwesiwag*, Berens escaped by throwing all the power of his mind into opening the rock. Similarly, when attacked by the boy with the red tuque, Berens recalled, "I filled my mind with the thought that he would not be able to kill me"—and indeed, the boy failed to hit him.

Dreams (or the *bawaaganak* through dreams) also offered gifts of foresight about what was to happen. At Pauingassi Fair Wind told Hallowell that he had dreamed four years earlier that Hallowell was coming; and Fair Wind's son had dreamed the previous year (1932) "that I was coming (a stranger)." Similarly, some other old men told Hallowell "that they knew what I was going to ask—*a very marked pattern*. Foresight is the basis of power" (Hallowell 1892–1981, Research). In these instances the telling of a past dream served to establish that the teller had predictive powers and to validate and perhaps affirm control, to an extent, over what was happening in the present. Within this framework Hallowell's visit and questions were not surprises. (One is reminded of the predictive dreams about first contacts with white men reported in oral traditions from the coasts of North America [e.g., Prins 1996:44].)

A dream could also validate a waking experience that someone had already reported. When Peter Berens was a boy of eleven or twelve, he saw a Thunderbird [*binesi*] lying with wings outspread on the rocks at Flathead Point near Berens River. It was bluish gray with striped feathers and a red tail. It was just after a storm had passed; the rain had ended, but there was still thunder. Peter ran back to his family's camp to tell them, but when they came no bird was there. He was not believed at first "because it is so unusual to have seen pinesi with naked eye." Later, however, an old man who had dreamed of Thunderbirds confirmed Peter's description and said that Peter too would live to be an old man because he had seen a Thunderbird (Hallowell 1892–1981, Research, ser. V, Religion). In this instance, the old man was perhaps impelled to reveal a clue about his own vision-fast dream so Peter would understand the blessing he had received and so others would accept the boy's account as truthful. Ojibwe perspectives on the world gave weight to empirical observation and verification, as Hallowell recognized by 1934 in his article, "Some Empirical Aspects of Northern Saulteaux Religion" (Hallowell 1934). In Fogelsonian terms one might speak of Ojibwe ethno-empiricism—an outlook also found among Plains groups for whom dreams serve as "a reality base for the lived world" (Irwin 1994:64).

Sometimes dreams retrospectively provided ominous foreshadowings or warnings about the future or about happenings in a certain place. William Berens told Hallowell,

> When I was a young man I dreamed that I fell through the ice of the river at a spot . . . where the current is very swift. I found 2 otters in the water there. I turned into an otter, and swam along with them to a hole in the ice. There was my father ready to help me out.
>
> Ten years later I fell through the ice at the same place I had dreamed about. At first I lost my senses. The swift water swept me along to a place lower down where the river was open. My father called out, "Hold up your hand." I heard him, did so, and he saw me coming. He pulled me out by my parkey [parka], just in time. [Hallowell 1892–1981, ser. V, Dreams, W.B. 1.4]

In another dreamlike experience one night, half awake, Berens saw a winged angel with golden hair who made him tremble all over. "I wondered," he said, "what was going to happen." He was at Poplar River at the time, some distance north of Berens River, his home. The next day,

Berens's fur trader boss unexpectedly and urgently asked that he help him out on a trip to Berens River, so he went. There he found his sister was very ill, and the family had been wanting to send for him. As his sister died a few days later, he was glad that he had come (Hallowell 1892–1981, Dreams, "An Apparition.").

Still another dream with Christian elements foreshadowed to Berens the Methodist-Roman Catholic religious conflicts that came to Berens River in his later life, as well as the role he would play in them as chief and as member of a family that had had Methodist ties since the 1860s. It took place near the Hudson's Bay Company's woodpile at Berens River:

> Two Catholic priests were holding me, one on each side. Another Indian was there too (named). One of the priests took his head off. There he stood without any head. I was fighting them but they dragged me off towards where the Catholic mission now stands. We came to a big furnace and these priests tried to push me into it. At the same time there was an old man who stuck his head out of the flames and tried to pull me in. But they were not able to get me in. I kept on fighting them and they dragged me to another place where there was another furnace. There the same thing happened. . . . I got pretty close to the flames that time: then I woke up.

Berens told Hallowell that the dream provided foreknowledge of his later struggle with the Catholic Oblate missionaries at Berens River (see Gray 1996, chapters 6–7, and 2000). The image of the Indian losing his head signified "that the priests can do what they want with Indians who do not think for themselves. They can put any ideas in your head they want to" (Hallowell 1892–1981, ser. V, W.B., Dreams 1.8).

As noted before, tellings of dreams sometimes served to explain what a ceremony was about and to declare and validate its leader's role and spiritual powers. At Pauingassi in 1933, Hallowell and Chief Berens attended Fair Wind's Drum Dance, a ceremony whose cultural and musical connections reached far south of the American border (Matthews 1993; Vennum 1982). Fair Wind, blind and in his eighties, began the proceedings with a speech recounting how the ceremony had come to him in a dream some years before, after the death of a favorite grandson whom he had been unable to cure (Hallowell 1955:166–167). Grieving deeply, he was away by himself in the bush one day.

> I made up my mind to die. I lay down on the point of a rock, where I could be found. When I closed my eyes, towards the sky I saw something like a nest. When I looked towards the east, I heard something saying:

"This is something that will stop you from crying. You'll not die. For this is one of the finest things to play with."

Later in the ceremony, Fair Wind's son, Angus, told of his own mourning for his brother's son, Fair Wind's grandchild, and the blessing that he had received—a dream in which a voice told him, "I'll give you something to ease your mind and that of others. But you must take care and carry things through as you are told" (Hallowell 1955:167). Hallowell observed that dreams, in the absence of rules about inheritance, could be subtle markers of succession. Angus was the head drummer in Fair Wind's ceremony, and was "also the active leader of the *wabanowiwin* [Waabano ceremony] at Pauingassi, of which his father is the ostensible head." His dream experience, Hallowell wrote, "is undoubtedly the reason why Angus takes a leading role in the ceremony mentioned and after his father dies will undoubtedly succeed him as the 'owner' of this ceremony as well as the wabanowiwin" (Hallowell 1892–1981, Series I, file 1, typescript, pp. 20–21). Angus indeed did succeed his father but had no children of his own. He brought up, instead, another of his brother's sons, Charlie George Owen (d. 2001), who in turn had the appropriate dreams and received gifts and powers. The ways in which dreams gave (and still give) structure to family history and to the transmission of cultural and spiritual knowledge, privileges, and responsibilities are demonstrated by conversations from both the 1930s and the 1990s.

When Maureen Matthews and I talked with Charlie George Owen about his memories of Fair Wind (and Hallowell) in 1992, the first thing he wanted to tell us about was a dreamlike healing experience in which his grandfather's powers brought him back from the dead. He also retold several times Fair Wind's vision, the one that founded the Drum Dance, as it was his legacy. His details complement and go beyond those recorded by Berens and Hallowell in 1933 (Brown and Matthews 1994; Matthews and Roulette 1996). Charlie George Owen was a practicing Mennonite for over thirty years, and the big drum he once owned was burned in a house fire in 1972. But he was also heir to Fair Wind's knowledge and to strong traditions and blessings passed down in part through the experiencing and telling of dreams. The two streams of belief, firmly dammed apart in conventional missionary doctrine, flow together or at least side by side in many Ojibwe minds, as they evidently did in Fair Wind's (Brown and Matthews 1994). Both Christian and Ojibwe spirit beings can empirically prove to be sources of power and spiritual support.

At Pauingassi, Fair Wind's grandnephew, Jacob Owen, also exemplified this pattern. As a young ceremonial helper, he stood wearing a feather in his cap in one of Hallowell's photographs of the 1930s. Others told us that this was a sign of his connection with Thunderbirds. Visiting him one time with Margaret Simmons (Chief Berens's granddaughter) to interpret, we left the initial conversation to him, and he offered a long discourse on the Bible (like his cousin he had become a Mennonite during the sojourn of a Mennonite missionary in Pauingassi in the 1960s). Then Margaret asked whether he had ever seen Thunderbirds. "No, never," he replied; "I have never seen them with my own eyes. But I knew them and they spoke to me. And today, I use it [the power] some days." He went on to tell us of his encounter with them, a story he said he had never told before, and to recount an instance of his use of their power (Matthews 1995:5–6).

Why did he speak of these things at that moment? Several reasons may have converged. Perhaps the fact that Chief William Berens's granddaughter asked the question made a difference. Also, he appreciated the connection Maureen Matthews and I had with *Midewigimaa* (Hallowell's name at Pauingassi, see note 2), and may have been among the elders there who had decided to call us *Midewigimaawikwewag*, the Hallowell women. (In fact, there was some surprise that we weren't related to Hallowell in some way, and one person asked why his children never came back to visit.)[5] Two other possible reasons arise. First, Jacob Owen had just, in essence, preached a Christian sermon, and the giving (away) of his Thunderbird dream may have signaled a tip in the balance toward the Mennonite side of his life, just as William Berens's Methodism offered him license for the telling of otherwise privileged experiences. Second, he was then the oldest man in Pauingassi, almost blind, and in failing health (he died in 1996). Maybe he felt that few chances were left to use his powers and that this was the moment to pass on something of what he knew, which he knew we cared about and which would otherwise be lost.

When Hallowell came to interpreting the meanings of the dreams he was told, he was, on the whole, an excellent listener, and worked to understand the ways in which dreams were integrated into Ojibwe life and world-views. But as a professional anthropologist, he was also deeply involved in the social science of his times. Especially from 1938 into the 1940s, he became absorbed by possibilities of applying psychological methods such as the Rorschach inkblot tests to his subjects, as well as by the potentialities of looking at their myths and dreams in psychological terms (Spindler and Spindler 1991). One short report concerning a dream of William Berens, in the journal *Man*, in 1938, marked perhaps the peak of his engagement with Freudian psychology, the use of which was then on the rise among American anthropologists.[6] Berens and Hallowell were traveling upriver to Little Grand Rapids, a 100-mile trip with 50 portages.

One morning, Hallowell asked Berens if he'd had any dreams, and Berens described one he had just had. He was walking on snowshoes, evidently in spring because not much snow was on the ground:

> I was travelling with a boy. I sighted a camp but there was no one in sight. Then I heard the sound of chopping in the bush. As we came closer a man appeared. This man handed me some money, over one hundred dollars in bills. I could see an X on some of them. But the bills were the colour of that (pointing to my sleeping bag, which was yellow-brown in hue). This man also gave me some silver and I gave some of it to the boy. I asked whether this was all right and the man said "yes."

Hallowell asked Berens what he thought the dream signified. Berens replied that it might mean "that he would catch a fox the next winter. He inferred this from the colour of the bills, which he thought so inexplicable." He could not identify either the man or the boy, and said he was also puzzled by the color of the bills.

Hallowell went on to state his own analysis of the dream in remarkably assured terms: "The Freudian symbolism in this dream is so transparent that it needs no further comment. On account of the colour of my sleeping bag it could hardly have been more forcibly emphasized." The money motif, he wrote, "unconsciously associated with faeces." The reason that Berens had this dream was that the chief, having been his "interpreter and mentor during several summers of field work," was getting rather tired of it, and here he was starting off on yet another trip. Further, the dream was probably an expression of repressed aggression:

> I was the man he failed to recognize. . . . I gave him the money, which approximated the amount he would earn, but this money was also faeces, metaphorically speaking. . . . since we have been close friends, he could not turn me down, and he needed the money as well. But he was not anticipating a pleasurable trip, because internally he very much resisted going.

To Hallowell, this Freudian interpretation served to "make the dream intelligible in terms of the circumstances in which it occurred." Interestingly, Hallowell added, "When I explained the Freudian symbolism [to Berens], he seemed in no way resistant to the idea" (Hallowell 1938:47–48).

We must wonder what actually happened when in the middle of their conversation Hallowell supplanted Berens's analysis with his Freudian theory. Was Berens convinced, or polite, or struck dumb by his friend's interpretation? We can't tell. In any case, such a determinedly etic analysis was not typical of Hallowell's writings. Cast as a brief letter to a journal rather than a full article, it was also less measured, perhaps representing the apex of his enthusiasm for Freudian analysis. The main interest of the note probably lies more in what it tells us about Hallowell than about Berens. By 1938 Hallowell was evidently concerned about his relationship with the aging chief and worried that he had made too many demands upon him. Psychologically, his own sense of guilt, and perhaps his projections of his feelings about the chief and about the money involved, are the things that most shine through.

I would like to conclude with one further dream that Hallowell recorded. The interpretation and context in which Hallowell placed this dream appear more typical of his best work, and are more revealing and interesting. They also take us back to the dream charts mentioned earlier. One of the men whom Hallowell met up the Berens River had been told this dream by an old man who evidently felt he had no further use for the powers of the dream visitor involved, and the hearer in turn passed it on.

A father left his son on an island to fast. Several times, the boy dreamed of an *ogimaa* (a chief or leader) who finally said to him, "Grandson, I think you are strong enough (in magic power) to go with me." The visitor began dancing around him and turned into a golden eagle, and the boy noticed that now his body too was covered with feathers. They flew south together, a long distance, to the land of the summer birds where there were many people living. (For Berens River Ojibwe, this land was also the abode of the dead.) The boy shot lots of ducks, geese, and other birds while he was there. Then, in springtime, the two flew north again to the island:

> "Your relatives must wonder where you are," said the Eagle to him. "But you stay here and in a day or two your father will come for you and you can go back home with him. Any time you want me, just mention my name and I will always help you." The next day the boy's father came for his son. He was glad in his heart to see him but he asked no questions. [Hallowell 1892–1981, "Dreams," p. 15]

This dream, as Hallowell observed, echoed patterns often found in dreams. But Hallowell also drew attention to how its motifs and structure paralleled another story that he was told, by a Cree several hundred miles to the north. This story, about events said to have happened long ago, was represented as a boy's real waking experience, not as a vision or myth. A boy canoed out to an island in God's Lake (northern Manitoba) to gather birds' eggs. His canoe drifted away, and he was marooned and became very hungry. Finally as he sat on the shore, he heard someone say from the water, "Nojis [grandson], come down here." When the boy did so, he saw the Great Trout:

"Get in under my fin," the fish said. So the boy did as he was told. It was as comfortable there as if he were in a wigwam. There was plenty of food too.

The fish dived and travelled to many different lakes during a whole season, teaching the boy "everything there was to know about the different kinds of fish." Then he returned the boy to the island in God's Lake. One day, when the boy's father was out paddling, he saw four otters swimming. He followed them to the island and "saw his son sitting on the shore. He was very glad to see him. He brought him home but he asked him no questions." [Hallowell, 1892–1981, "Dreams," pp. 2–3]

Hallowell pointed out how stories told from long ago could resemble dreams in both outline and content. According to what he called the Ojibwe "psychology of belief" (Hallowell 1892–1981, "Dreams," p. 3), both were accepted as plausible and true, being consistent with the larger framework of the Ojibwe worldview. As Hallowell made clear elsewhere (1939:32), this was not the prelogical or childlike confusion of fantasy and reality that Lucien Levy-Bruhl (1922) postulated when writing about "the primitive mind." Rather, there was consistency, feedback, and parallelism, as shown in Hallowell's charts. The pattern appears to resemble what Greg Urban found in Brazil among the Ibirama: old dream narratives "may ultimately transmogrify into myths," conforming as they do to durable patterns common to both myths and dreams (1997:7).

As Hallowell learned, the myths told on long winter nights in fact echoed the motifs of stories and dreams and served as "a kind of invocation" to the other-than-human "grandfathers" to come and listen (Hallowell 1976:460). Children falling asleep with the stories and myths in their heads dreamed of the personages that the stories featured; as well, they knew their voices because they heard them speak in their diverse distinctive manner whenever shaking tent ceremonies were held. Through life, one's waking, sleeping, and ceremonial experiences served to reinforce one another in a coherent, meaningful, and long-established system that guided both thought and action, values and belief. Dreams, the (re)telling or discussion of dreams in appropriate settings, and the overt interaction of a medicine man with his *bawaaganak* (as with Fair Wind and the Thunderbirds) on the basis of an untold dream were means of teaching and learning, and were deeply integrated into what Hallowell called the Ojibwe "culturally constituted behavioral environment" (1955:86, 1992:80).

In recent times, changed ways of living and learning in reserve communities and schools have damaged the fragile personal and familial contexts in which communication of and learning from dreams could occur. Along the Berens River the language, culture, and stories of dreams and of legendary "grandfathers" can be found, but the knowledge often seems imprisoned in the older people's heads as they sit alone in their small frame houses on the reserves, or in corners of the crowded homes of offspring, surrounded by the tumult of younger generations. Intergenerational rifts and misunderstandings have created islands of solitude with too few means for crossing the gulfs between them. Quiet chances for telling stories and dreams and for mutually respectful conversation and communication are casualties of the conditions of life in many reserve communities today; and off the reserve things are often even worse.

There is a role for insider/outsider communication and dialogue here. The patient study and conversation carried on by Hallowell with Chief Berens in the 1930s fostered learning and teaching not only for the two collaborators, but for a young man named Percy Berens as he watched and listened to his father hard at work with the visitor, and for others. Up the river, at Pauingassi, Hallowell attended Fair Wind's ceremonies and photographed both the old man and his descendants. These apprentice ceremonial attendants (*oshkaabewisag*), Charlie George Owen, Jacob Owen, and others, could still recall rich details from the 1930s when they looked at Hallowell's photographs, over sixty years later. In 1992, still farther upstream at Poplar Hill, a young translator, rather mystified about what Maureen Matthews and I were doing, took us around to visit old people who might remember Fair Wind (or Hallowell—*aadizookwewinini*, story man, as they call him up there). As the young man gradually located those who could be most helpful, he was clearly hearing about such things as Fair Wind's dream, his Drum Dance, and the Midewiwin for the very first time. Finally, one elderly woman, recognizing that we already knew rather more than he did, said firmly to him, "Your grandmother danced in that dance; you should know about this!" It was like dropping pebbles in a pond and watching the ripples spread, or perhaps relighting candles of memory and wondering how far their light would travel.

Dreams are ways of framing, telling, and remembering history. Raymond Fogelson has asked us to make "a determined effort to try to comprehend alien forms of historical consciousness and discourse . . . taking seriously native theories of history as embedded in cosmology, in narratives, in rituals and ceremonies, and more generally in native philosophies and worldviews" (1989:134–135). We may add dreams, broadly defined, to the list. This essay began with outsiders' waking dreams in Ojibwe country—reveries of travel that are grounded in cosmic assumptions about time and history (or its lack) along the Berens River. These reveries themselves make and reinforce history in that they structure so many outsiders' initial perceptions and representations of their "first contacts." The test for the newcomers is whether they manage, as Hallowell did, to move beyond the reveries and write beyond the tropes.

Within Ojibwe country, selective and strategic tellings and retellings of dreams, verbally and through overt ceremonial demonstrations of powers, have long helped to structure historical and cultural knowledge and memory. They persist but they do not stand still; they move onward through time and through changing contexts with lengthening pasts—what Fogelson has called "a series of contiguous past presentisms." As Fogelson emphasizes, "The awareness of the interface between the past and present has theoretical and practical significance for ethnohistorians" (1989:136). Practically speaking, as illustrated here, enriched insights can arise from juxtaposing oral and written sources with contemporary observation.

On a theoretical level, however, a look at the Ojibwe field of dreams must lead us to ask whether the drawing of dichotomies between past and present is one more instance of outsider imposition. In Ojibwe terms, it seems more useful to speak of what Clifford Geertz, in a different context, described as "experience-near" and "experience-distant" (1983:57–58). From the people's insider perspective, powerful other-than-human beings such as Thunderbirds and other dream visitors are very much alive and available despite missions, schools, and efforts to explain thunder and other "natural phenomena" through science. (In fact, they are embedded in language; one cannot name thunder without referring to these giant birds.) Some Ojibwe, such as Fair Wind or Jacob Owen, carried the blessings, and weights, of "experience-near" relationships with Thunderbirds. Charlie George Owen could speak at first hand of Fair Wind; his oral texts are sprinkled with *mii iwe*, a particle indicating veracity and certainty. When speaking of topics he was less certain of, or more distant from, he used other markers indicating "a subtle declension . . . from personal experience to hearsay" (Matthews and Roulette 1996:358 n.). Others, ranging from Peter or Percy Berens to Margaret Simmons or Roger Roulette, speak from experiences or observations that are more distant, while the great majority of outsiders may only look and listen from outside. But the beings are there, to be sought in the proper ways. As Maureen Matthews was told by Roger Roulette, "everyone has a guardian, even me. It doesn't matter that I might be ignorant of it and not know how to show my respect" (Matthews 1995:5). In this context images of spreading concentric circles seem more useful than Hallowell's acculturational gradients (see Brightman, chapter 15 of this volume) or linear histories that oppose past to present. Owing to language loss and all sorts of other pressures, the dwellers of the inner circles are fewer at present than in the 1930s. Nevertheless, renewals of spiritual contacts and powers are always possible, and indeed they are rising in numbers all the time, even if their terms of reference change and vary from the old ways (see, for example, Williams 1992).

To conclude, even though we may emend a few of the conclusions and conceptual frames that Hallowell developed, his papers and writings have offered special opportunities to follow his student Fogelson's advice about doing ethnohistory. Without Hallowell, none of the work discussed here would have gone forward. His writings are not the whole story, however. He also, unlike many visitors, left warm memories among the people he met. He respected them, listened well, and treated them well (elders at Pauingassi, for example, told us how he had given Fair Wind the shirt he wore in Hallowell's photograph of the 1930s). His attitude shines forth in his short essay "On Being an Anthropologist," written in 1972: "I deeply identified myself with the Berens River Ojibwe. To the small number of white people in the area I paid practically no attention. . . . I was completely oriented toward Indians and their culture rather than the total community [of Hudson's Bay Company traders, clergy, and others]" (1976:10). Of course, as he went on to admit, this meant that, at the time, he overlooked studying Ojibwe relations with others (Indian-white relations), the prejudices they experienced, the constant outside pressures. We can forgive him that, however, given his lasting contributions; and in any case, those topics have not been at risk of neglect in more recent years (for diverse examples, see, for example, Dunning 1959; Gray 1996, 2000). As fieldworker and as scholar, Hallowell left a legacy that allowed the reopening of conversations that he and the Berens River Ojibwe never finished, helping us learn how to ask better questions, how to listen better and what to listen for, and how to teach a little when our turn comes.

Notes

1. This paper began life as the annual Edward S. Rogers Lecture in Anthropology at the Royal Ontario Museum, Toronto, in February 1997. My thanks to Maureen Matthews; to the people we have consulted along the Berens River; to Margaret Simmons, Percy Berens, and Roger Roulette; to Cory Willmott (McMaster University) who contributed valuable ideas, information, and suggestions; to the staff at the American Philosophical Society Library in Philadelphia; and to Sergei Kan and Pauline Turner Strong for the invitation to participate in this volume and for their helpful editorial comments, patience, and labors.

2. *Mideg* (plural) are persons with spiritual powers and gifts received from dream visitors, *bawaaganak*. The term has been variously translated as priest, conjuror, or shaman; Manitoba Ojibwe people now commonly use "medicine man" in English. Hallowell's Ojibwe nickname evoked not only his interest in the *Midewiwin* (Grand Medicine Society) of the

Ojibwe (see Angel 2002 for a recent overview), but his broader interest in dreams and spiritual beliefs and practices.

The orthography of Ojibwe words in this chapter, except for those quoted from Hallowell's writings, follows that provided in Nichols and Nyholm (1995), with supplementary advice gratefully received from linguist Roger Roulette for Berens River vocabulary. A number of linguists prefer the spelling *Ojibwe* to the more common *Ojibwa* or *Ojibway* because it more closely elicits the correct pronunciation of the word in the language itself. *Saulteaux*, a term often used by Hallowell, is a synonym still common in Manitoba and refers back to Sault Ste. Marie where the French first met Ojibwe people. The Ojibwe term of preference is now often *Anishinaabe*, which means "human being" or often "Ojibwe" or "Indian" in contradistinction to white folk.

3. As Neil McLeod (Cree) put it to Maureen Matthews, for Ojibwa/Cree people there is no such thing as a "secular" or nonspiritual dream; definitionally, all dreams are, on some level, encounters with these spirit beings (McLeod to Matthews, December 8, 1998).

4. Hallowell Papers, Ms. Coll. 26, APS, Series I, MSS, file 1, typescript entitled "Dreaming," pp. 22–24. Hallowell Papers hereafter cited as Hallowell 1892–1981.

5. Hallowell had one adoptive son whose life took some tragic turns. Surprised by the question, we were not quick enough to try to explain the sense in which we, intellectually, were Hallowell's grandchildren. But the Pauingassi elders must have gotten the idea anyway, when they named us.

6. Lee Irwin, commenting on the application of Freudian theory to Native American dreaming generally, comments on how its use "creates a climate of suspicion with regard to the value or significance of the manifest dream" and gives priority to its latent "hidden and disguised" content. It certainly led for a time to analyses very different from those offered by the dreamers themselves (Irwin 1994:11, 246 n. 3).

References

Angel, Michael
    2002 Preserving the Sacred: Historical Perspectives on the Ojibwa Midewiwin. Winnipeg: University of Manitoba Press.
Brown, Jennifer S. H.
    1989 "A Place in Your Mind for Them All": Chief William Berens. *In* Being and Becoming Indian: Biographical Studies of North American Frontiers. James A. Clifton, ed. Pp. 204–225. Chicago: Dorsey Press.
Brown, Jennifer S. H., and Robert Brightman
    1988 "The Orders of the Dreamed": George Nelson on Cree and Northern Ojibwa Religion and Myth, 1823. Winnipeg: University of Manitoba Press.
Brown, Jennifer S. H., with Maureen Matthews
    1994 Fair Wind: Medicine and Consolation along the Berens River. Journal of the Canadian Historical Association 4:55–74.
Brown, Jennifer S. H., and Maureen Matthews
    1995 "Tackling the Women": A. I. Hallowell and Unfinished Conversations along the Berens River. Paper presented at annual meetings of the American Society for Ethnohistory, Kalamazoo, Michigan.
Clifford, James
    1997 Spatial Practices, Fieldwork, Travel, and the Disciplining of Anthropology. *In* An-

thropological Locations: Boundaries and Grounds of a Field Science. Akhil Gupta and James Ferguson, eds. Pp. 185–222. Berkeley: University of California Press.

Dunning, R. W.
   1959 Social and Economic Change among the Northern Ojibwa. Toronto: University of Toronto Press.

Fabian, Johannes
   1983 Time and the Other: How Anthropology Makes Its Object. New York: Columbia University Press.

Fogelson, Raymond D.
   1989 The Ethnohistory of Events and Nonevents. Ethnohistory 36(2):133–147.

Geertz, Clifford
   1983 Local Knowledge: Further Essays in Interpretive Anthropology. New York: Basic Books.

Gray, Susan Elaine
   1996 The Ojibwa World View and Encounters with Christianity along the Berens River, 1875–1940. PhD dissertation, Department of History, University of Manitoba, Winnipeg.
   2000 "They Didn't Get Along So Good Them Two!": Tales of an Oblate and a Methodist Missionary at Berens River, Manitoba, 1920–1940. Western Oblate Studies 5 / Etudes oblates de l'Ouest 5, Raymond Huel and Gilles Lesage, eds., 37–58. Winnipeg: Presses universitaires de Saint-Boniface.

Hallowell, A. Irving
   1892–1981 Papers. Ms. Coll. 26, American Philosophical Society Library. Philadelphia.
   1926 Bear Ceremonialism in the Northern Hemisphere. American Anthropologist 28: 1–175.
   1928 Recent Historical Changes in the Kinship Terminology of the St. Francis Abenaki. Proceedings of the 22nd International Congress of Americanists, 97–145.
   1934 Some Empirical Aspects of Northern Saulteaux Religion. American Anthropologist 36:389–404.
   1938 Freudian Symbolism in the Dream of a Saulteaux Indian. Man 38:47–48.
   1939 Growing Up—Savage and Civilized. National Parent-Teacher 34(4):32–34.
   1955 Culture and Experience. Philadelphia: University of Pennsylvania Press.
   1976 Contributions to Anthropology. Raymond D. Fogelson, ed. Chicago: University of Chicago Press.
   1992 The Ojibwa of Berens River, Manitoba: Ethnography into History. Edited with a preface and afterword by Jennifer S. H. Brown. Fort Worth: Harcourt Brace College Publishers.

Irwin, Lee
   1994 The Dream Seekers: Native American Visionary Traditions of the Great Plains. Norman: University of Oklahoma Press.

James, William C.
   1985 The Quest Pattern and the Canoe Trip. In Nastawgan: The Canadian North by Canoe and Snowshoe. Bruce W. Hodgins and Margaret Hobbs, eds. Pp. 9–23. Toronto: Betelgeuse Books.

Kan, Sergei, ed.
   2001 Strangers to Relatives: The Adoption and Naming of Anthropologists in Native North America. Lincoln: University of Nebraska Press.

Levy-Bruhl, Lucien

1922 La mentalité primitive. Paris: Felix Alcan.

Matthews, Maureen

1993 Fair Wind's Drum Transcript of Ideas program. Toronto: CBC Radio Works.

1995 Thunderbirds. Transcript of Ideas program. Toronto: CBC Radio Works.

Matthews, Maureen, and Roger Roulette

1996 Fair Wind's Dream: Naamiwan Obawaajigewin. In Reading Beyond Words: Contexts for Native History. Jennifer S. H. Brown and Elizabeth Vibert, eds. Pp. 330–360. Peterborough ON: Broadview Press.

Nichols, John D., and Earl Nyholm

1995 A Concise Dictionary of Minnesota Ojibwe. Minneapolis: University of Minnesota Press.

Peers, Laura, and Jennifer S. H. Brown

2000 "There Is No End to Relationship among the Indians": Ojibwa Families and Kinship in Historical Perspective. The History of the Family: An International Quarterly 4(4):529–555.

Prins, Harald E. L.

1996 The Mi'kmaq: Resistance, Accommodation, and Cultural Survival. Fort Worth: Harcourt Brace College Publishers.

Redekop, Bill

1998 Heart of Magic: Up the Berens River, Time Has Stood Still. Winnipeg Free Press, July 12, Sunday magazine, p. C1.

Spindler, George, and Louise Spindler

1991 Rorschaching in North America in the Shadow of Hallowell. Special issue honoring A. I. Hallowell, The Psychoanalytic Study of Society 16. Bryce Boyer and Ruth Boyer, eds.

Stocking, George W., Jr.

1968 Race, Culture, and Evolution: Essays in the History of Anthropology. New York: Free Press.

Urban, Greg

1997 Culture: In and about the World. Anthropology Newsletter 38(2):1, 7.

Vennum, Thomas, Jr.

1982 The Ojibwa Dance Drum: Its History and Construction. Smithsonian Folklife Studies, no. 2. Washington DC: Smithsonian Institution Press.

Williams, Shirley

1992 Women's Role in Ojibway Spirituality. Journal of Canadian Studies 27(3):100–104.

3. *Framing the Anomalous*

Stoneclad, Sequoyah, and Cherokee Ethnoliteracy

MARGARET BENDER

Raymond D. Fogelson, Mentor and Scholar

It was in 1989, as a new graduate student in the University of Chicago's anthropology department, that I first began talking with Ray Fogelson about the possibility of doing fieldwork with the Eastern Band of Cherokee Indians.[1] He gave me a sly look and said, "well, you know . . . that's a subject I happen to know something about!" Nevertheless, I fearlessly, some might say foolishly, plunged ahead into one of my teacher's most precious domains. As I prepared to go to the field to study contemporary Cherokee literacy, Fogelson steered me toward the classic histories, primary texts, and ethnographic materials. But much more importantly, he shared with me some of his own experiences of being in the field in that rural North Carolina community and offered well-grounded advice. "Don't over-cue," was one such piece of advice, which I took to mean that I should try to suppress my dense and clumsy *yo:nek* nature and learn to give and receive subtle social cues.[2] Fogelson always encouraged me to be low key and was quick to point out once when, in the field, I was on the verge of becoming "a pain in the [neck]" to my consultants. He wisely advised me that if I arrived during tourist season, people would wait to see if I was still around in the wintertime. If I was, he suggested, then they would take me seriously. He urged me from the beginning to find a way to give something back to the community while I was there. In my case, that meant establishing an ongoing working relationship with a local Cherokee language education and preservation project.

Fogelson's advice was practical as well as anthropological, however. He asked me before I left if I knew how to pack a wood stove so that the fire wouldn't go out during the night. Before going to North Carolina, I had never to my knowledge been in the same room with a wood stove. So the initial answer was no, but I proudly told him later that I had pretty much gotten the hang of it.

But when Fogelson shared his advice and memories of the community with me, in the back of my mind there was always a lingering concern that the world he described and the one I would encounter would be very different. In particular, I was afraid that I would not be able to explore further Fogelson's interests in medicinal beliefs and practices and traditional ceremonialism. But though it was true that I did not explicitly study Cherokee medicine and ceremonialism, thinking about the significance of what I had observed in the field nearly always brought me back to the context of the invention and subsequent history of usage of the syllabary, a history necessarily linked with all aspects of Cherokee life, including the spiritual. This history of usage connects the time of my fieldwork with that of Fogelson, as well as the many facets of Cherokee spiritual belief and practice, like pages in the same book.

On my return visits to Chicago, Fogelson loved to talk about the community and the place we both knew, its dynamic politics, prominent families, the breathtaking natural beauty of the mountains, and the food! Bean bread, fatback, fried potatoes, and ramps. One time I tried to come back to Chicago smelling like ramps, a favorite vegetable of Cherokees and white mountaineers alike, which is something like a cross between garlic and onion. If I had little knowledge of spiritual or medicinal power to share, I thought I could at least offer olfactory potency. However, like the form of power that Fogelson has associated with Cherokee conjuring (1977), the smell of ramps must be actively maintained, and, alas, my trip had taken too long. Despite my best efforts, my potency waned by the time I arrived in Fogelson's office. Occasionally I brought back gifts of sourwood honey or darts for Fogelson's blowgun. I obtained these darts in an empty parking lot in downtown Cherokee, from a knowledgeable and respected elder. This community leader was wearing a baseball cap and was so slumped down in his car seat that the innocent exchange took on the air of a clandestine, forbidden revelation of sacred knowledge—at least, in my imagination.

My most enduring memory of Fogelson's presence in my fieldwork, however, is not of our sharing the same dissertation field site but of the compassion and concern that Fogelson shows his students as whole people. When my mother died while I was in the field, Fogelson sent me what was probably the kindest, warmest, most empathetic letter I have ever received from anyone.

There were definite traces of my teacher in the field. One consultant said, yes, he remembered "those anthropologists living in Big Cove" but didn't say much else. Another said that she had marveled as a young girl at the white man recording—in syllabary!—the proceedings of the Big Cove community meetings. Knowing that my advisor and I had been in some of the same buildings, along the same rivers, on the same roads, and in the presence of the same people, gave me a sense of connectedness and continuity that few graduate students are fortunate enough to experience.

At many levels, then, Fogelson was there for me in the field. But before and after my fieldwork his scholarly interests and work have always, inevitably, informed and enriched my own. One important area of influence involves Fogelson's focus on individuals as subjects of scholarly attention.[3] This emphasis on the individual can be seen at many levels—from his faith in the value of getting to know small numbers of consultants very, very well, to his critical interpretations of the perspectives and potential biases of chroniclers of Cherokee history and culture, be they Major John Norton (1978), James Adair (1990), or Traveller Bird (1974). Fogelson's respect for the importance of the individual is so deep that he is prepared to observe in Cherokee historical consciousness a personalized model of the course of human events, one in which human motivation and agency are the most powerful causes of change (1984).

Much of Fogelson's work illustrates the possibility of making insightful and illuminating connections if only the subject is seen from the proper perspective. This is another area in which I deeply feel his influence. Those familiar with Fogelson's famous Diamond Crystal Shaker Salt analogy will probably agree that a similarly strenuous refocusing of the analytic apparatus is necessary when trying to grasp the numerous analogies that appear in his work, as when grasping the principle of infinite regress.[4] Certainly the reader is shaken into a new perspective and awareness when following Fogelson along as he *almost* proposes the usefulness of the term ethno-ethno-ethno-ethnohistory (1974:110), and as he points out the urgent, and suddenly—to the reader—obvious, importance of studying *non*events (1989). Fogelson's shifting lenses allow him to see the psychologically similar in the apparently diverse, as when he points out parallels between the Algonquian Windigo and the Cherokee Stoneclad (1980b). These lenses also reveal to him, and to his readers, the fallacy of externally imposed cultural categories, as when he observes that eighteenth-century Cherokee society may have been more deeply triadic than it was dyadic. Despite the common ethnohistorical analysis of Southeastern societies as containing two structurally opposed "red" (warlike young men) and "white" (diplomatic old men) divisions, Fogelson suggests that women serve as a mediating third category. This triad of young men—women—old men may be more fundamental, he suggests, than the red-white division or one drawn strictly along gender lines (1977).

Fogelson's work also suggests a cultural relativism of a very deep kind, and it is this quality that has probably made the most indelible impression on me. He has contributed to that stream of voices in anthropology that suggests that what are often seen as basic, uniform, universal essences— power, gender, history, and time, for example—may in fact take culturally specific forms. In an article whose very title suggests the nonuniformity of history, "On the Varieties of Indian History: Sequoyah and Traveller Bird" (1974), Fogelson gently suggests some of the ways in which ethnohistory might free itself from the grasp of ethnocentrism. Rather than providing an alternative to standard "history" merely by focusing on non-Western sub-jects, he argues, ethnohistorians should engage in ethno-ethnohistory— that is, "ethnohistory written from a native point of view" (106). This entails "a kind of anthropological ethnohistory in which a central role would be given to intensive fieldwork, control of the native language, use of a native time perspective, and work with native documents" (106). Fo-gelson also echoes Sturtevant's (1966) call for a broadened conceptualiza-tion of the "document" to include "not only maps and pictorial evidence, but also cultural artifacts and fresh field notes" (Fogelson 1974:106). It is the quest to understand what "native documents" constitute and *how they mean* that to me is at the heart of at least one aspect of both eth-nohistory and anthropological fieldwork. Indeed, if we take this practice seriously, we find that this disciplinary distinction between history and anthropology, with its related presupposition that the past and the present are distinct objects of study, falls apart in the actual practice of studying culture. Finding and interpreting such nonconventional "documents" is an exercise in the deep cultural relativism about which Fogelson has so much to teach us.

Fogelson pushes his argument further by arguing that the event-centric-ity of historical accounts may itself be culture bound. In "The Ethno-history of Events and Nonevents" (1989), he revisits his exploration of the ethno-ethnohistorical domain, arguing that ethno-ethnohistory re-quires "taking seriously native theories of history as embedded in cos-mology, in narratives, in rituals and ceremonies, and more generally in native philosophies and worldviews. Implicit here," he goes on to say, "is the assumption that events may be recognized, defined, evaluated, and endowed with meaning differentially in different cultural traditions" (1989:134–135). He proceeds to illustrate several types of "nonevents" that might be significant in a culture's view of its own history. These are "nonevents" in that they are not occurrences documentable in the conventional sense as having "occurred at a given time and place" (133). Hence they would not be recognized as events by positivist historians. Nonevents include, for Fogelson, failure to participate in documentable events like censuses; nonrecognition of something, considered eventful by others, as an event; events that are differentially interpreted or valued by the participants; events "that never happened but could have . . . or . . . should have" (142); general social, environmental, or psychological conditions, which he calls "latent events" (143); and events that "can be documented, but are so traumatic they are denied" (143). Seeking out and learning from nonevents forces one to look beyond history as it might be narrowly conceived and to embrace the human sciences and condition more generally.

One of the most intriguing types of nonevents (also discussed in Fogelson 1984) is the epitomizing event:

> Epitomizing events are narratives that condense, encapsulate, and dramatize longer-term historical processes. Such events are inventions but have such compelling qualities and explanatory power that they spread rapidly through the group and soon take on an ethnohistorical reality of their own. [1989:143]

These nonevents reflect historical reality from the local point of view, but they do so at a highly elevated, one might say poetic, level. Of the many tools Fogelson offers us for grasping cultural difference I have found this to be one of the most powerful. His recognition of the significance of the epitomizing event in structuring historical consciousness certainly explains why he urged me, upon leaving to do fieldwork among the Eastern Cherokees, to read the myths collected by James Mooney in the late nineteenth century (Mooney 1982) over and over again.[5] He was trying to prepare me to understand some of the categories and structures through which the past and present might be interpreted in that community.

Exploration of the epitomizing events central to a culture's view of its own history is a key source of information in and of itself, and it may also provide evidence of the narrative structures that make locally intelligible accounts of events and nonevents alike.[6] When such an "epitomizing" narrative structure occurs in more than one context in a particular culture's narrative repertoire, we may be seeing evidence of the kind of linguistic meaning-through-resemblance, or iconic meaning, that Greg Urban has shown us (1991) is so essential to grasp in a deep, and yet grounded, understanding of culture.

Fogelson's work clearly suggests the ethnocentrism of presuming that the Western distinction between myth and history works the same way, or is even relevant, universally. Studying the parallelism between narratives of epitomizing events (be they "mythic" or "historical" from a Western perspective) is a technique that allows us to perceive the way the past is understood and related to the present in the cultures we study.

Sequoyah and Stoneclad

I began thinking concretely about this parallelism about ten years ago. Terry Straus, one of my committee members at Chicago, asked me whether Sequoyah, the nineteenth-century inventor of the Cherokee syllabary, wasn't a kind of Cherokee culture hero. I thought this to be a reasonable conjecture: he was a creator whose work in the world made new things possible and contributed to the characterization of Cherokee society by both insiders and outsiders as "civilized." Sequoyah's original invention of a writing system for the Cherokee language, accomplished without the benefit of familiarity with any other orthography, is unparalleled in modern times. The invention, seen as miraculous by many of its beneficiaries, made possible a cultural legacy that includes social and political documents and religious and medicinal texts. The Cherokee Nation's written constitution, its newspapers, the Cherokee New Testament that serves today not just as the Bible but as an authoritative source of information about the Cherokee language itself, written versions of Cherokee myths and formulas—all these were made possible, in form at least, by Sequoyah's gift.

Sequoyah's life and death have been much mythologized. Nearly everything about him has been contested at one time or another, including his paternity, his racial identity, the authenticity of his invention, and his place of death and burial. Many of the contemporaneous accounts of Sequoyah refer to an anonymous sketch of the man that appeared in the *Cherokee Phoenix* as their source, lending mystery to his biography.[7] As Fogelson has written (1974:108), "the scarcity of reliable documentary evidence makes the task of piecing together the facts of Sequoyah's life reminiscent of the quest for the historical Jesus." Indeed, the lack of concrete information about Sequoyah's life story may have allowed it to become something of an epitomizing event. Although I am not challenging the historical reality of Sequoyah's life, I think it fair to say that his life story has become "a narrative that condenses, encapsulates, and dramatizes longer-term historical processes" (Fogelson 1989:143) for those who tell, receive, and know it. Certain aspects of his life are generally agreed upon: he was a silversmith who fought during the Creek War, advocated Cherokee relocation to the Arkansas Territory, held positions of political leadership, and traveled in search of Cherokee speakers with whom to share the syllabary.[8] But beyond this, the syllabary, its invention, and its inventor have come to represent to those who use it, talk about it, and write about it many significant and contradictory trends in historic Cherokee life: Cherokee autonomy, Cherokee nationalism, Cherokee progress, Cherokee "civilization," Cherokee resiliency, Cherokee "renascence," the conversion of Cherokees to Christianity, and the preservation of traditional Cherokee medicine and spirituality.[9]

Not only, then, can Sequoyah be interpreted as a culture hero, but his received life story can be seen to transcend short-term historical accounts as epitomizing events do.

Thinking about the mysterious Sequoyah as a kind of culture hero led me to a comparison of the great inventor with another, more monstrous, culture hero that had captured the imagination of my mentor some years earlier (1980b). Stonecoat, or Stoneclad, is the figure in Cherokee mythology responsible for bestowing on the Cherokees specific medicinal formulas and knowledge, hunting songs, the crystals used for divining, and the red clay used for face and body painting (Mooney 1982). In the version of the myth collected by James Mooney around the Turn of the Century, Stoneclad is a "wicked cannibal monster [whose] whole body is covered with a skin of solid rock" (Mooney 1982:319) and who has a particular taste (and olfactory predilection) for hunters. Using his cane as a nasal extension, Stoneclad sniffs out a particular group of hunters who are under the protection of a medicine man. This medicine man advises them that Stoneclad has only one weakness—he cannot be exposed to menstruating women. The hunters promptly recruit seven menstruating women to greet the monster along the trail into the camp. As he encounters each one, Stoneclad becomes sicker and sicker, finally vomiting blood and collapsing. The medicine man then pins him to the ground with seven sourwood stakes, and the community piles logs all around him and begins a great fire. As he slowly burns to death, Stoneclad, known to possess considerable sacred powers and knowledge, tells the Cherokees of all the medicines he knows and sings them his hunting songs. At daybreak all that remains amongst the ashes are the magic crystal, the *ulv:hsati*, which the medicine man keeps for his own purposes, and the lump of red clay, or *wo:ti*. According to the myth, whatever "each person prayed for while [being painted with the clay]—whether for hunting success, for working skill, or for a long life—that gift was his" (Mooney 1982:320). A division is thus made between that part of Stoneclad's gift that is sacred and upper worldly—the crystal, for use by the medicine man—and that part which is secular, of this earth, and for general distribution: the clay.

This reduction of Stoneclad to two substances, one white or clear and one red, reverberates in a complex way with traditional Cherokee beliefs about human souls and bodily substances. According to Witthoft, Cherokee traditional belief asserts the existence of four souls (1983). First, there is a soul of conscious life. This soul left

> the body immediately at death and continued its personal life, sometimes remaining nearby for a time, often seen as a ghost, harmless and powerless. This soul is located in the head, immediately under the front fontanelle. The magic of scalping and the ritual treatment of scalps is directed against this soul. This soul is conscious, self-conscious, has personality, memory, continuity after death, and is unitary, not quantitative in its essence. It creates or secretes the watery fluids of the body: saliva, phlegm, cerebro-spinal fluid, lymph, and sexual fluids. Magical attack upon this soul by the conjurer is called "spoiling his saliva." [Witthoft 1983:68–69]

In addition, there are held to be three other "body" souls:

> The second soul, that of physiological life, is located in the liver, and is of primary importance in doctoring and in conjuring. This soul is a substance, is not anthropomorphic in any [way], has no individuality, and is quantitative, there is more or less of it. Its secretions are yellow bile, black bile, gastric juice, etc.
>
> The third soul, that of the circulation, is located in the heart, and blood is its secretion. This soul is non-individual and quantitative; it takes a month to die, its substance gradually diffusing back into nature as a life force.
>
> The fourth soul is located in the bones. . . . It takes a year to die, its essence gradually returning to nature, contributing its material to the growth of crystals in the ground, especially to the quartz crystals used in divination and conjuring. [Witthoft 1983:69–70]

Although Stoneclad is not a human being, the substances left behind in the wake of his death seem at least to overlap with these human souls and their associated substances. The *ulv:hsati* seems analogous to the crystals associated with the human bone soul, though this part of Stoneclad's legacy also seems to represent the soul of his "conscious life," since it includes his knowledge and, perhaps, memory. The *wo:ti* or red clay seems more like the other body souls—a substance, positive in this case, but without consciousness. Fogelson (personal communication, May 1990) has suggested that together the human bone and blood souls may represent the red and white aspects of Cherokee social organization, that is, the young warriors and the elder statesmen whose complementary leadership together represents a healthy Cherokee social life. Once Stoneclad has been absorbed and transformed by the united seven Cherokee clans, one might argue, what emerges is a strengthened and enriched Cherokee infrastructure with its red and white components.[10]

In a version of the myth recorded by Fogelson in 1960,

> what remained in the morning ashes was [Stoneclad's] crystal heart. This was broken up and distributed to different medicine men to serve as powerful divining instruments. By scrying and interpreting revealed signs in the crystal, the future could be foretold and answers to critical questions obtained. [Fogelson 1980b:137][11]

Parallels with the generally accepted life story of Sequoyah are illuminating. On the surface both Stoneclad and Sequoyah are characterized as loners distinguished by their use of a cane. As Stoneclad uses his cane to divine for hunters, Sequoyah uses a stick to scratch the earth in the quest for his dream. In portraits Sequoyah is often shown using a stick to point to characters on a syllabary chart. But the iconicity runs deeper. Fogelson has argued that Stoneclad, like other monsters, served the role of delimiting the normally human (Fogelson 1980b). Although certainly not considered to be a monster, Sequoyah was in his day seen to exceed the bounds of normalcy. He reportedly holed up in a shed or a hut while working on his writing system, muttering to himself, and neglecting his duties as a husband and community member. His muttering and isolation led to accusations of witchcraft, and the hut containing his work, like Stoneclad's body, was burned to the ground.

Both Sequoyah and Stoneclad endure a trial by fire that leads to the adoption of their symbolic representatives, their gifts, by the community as a whole. These events reverberate with a more general Cherokee process in which important and sacred gifts come from fire. For example, Cherokees still described the use of ashes for divining in the mid-1990s, and sacred fires figure largely both in the traditional consecration of mounds and in stompground ceremonialism. Fire is more specifically seen as a cleansing source of renewal in the pan-Southeastern Green Corn Ceremony. In the cases of Sequoyah and Stoneclad, through the action of fire the anomalous is not only reincorporated into the mainstream of Cherokee life, but each gift becomes one of the culture's most important tools and symbols.

Stoneclad's behavior in the throes of his fiery death is strikingly similar to that expected of Cherokee war captives: "in defiance of [the] pain" of being burned alive, "they were to sing war songs about their heroic deeds" (Perdue 1979:5). Some such captives were spared by the women of the community and adopted.

While Stoneclad plays the role of a captive, Sequoyah plays the role of an in-law. Sequoyah's story epitomizes the experience of the in-marrying Cherokee male, who at the time of marriage must relocate to his wife's village and subordinate himself to the authority of her matrilineal kin group. Young men often congregated in men's houses that provided relief from this stressful environment. Sequoyah's hut, a men's house for one, is simultaneously anomalous and typical. While Stoneclad confronts the "blood" of seven women (representatives of the seven Cherokee matrilineal clans), Sequoyah confronts the "blood" of one woman (his wife's matrilineal kin). It was Sequoyah's wife and her family, resentful of his neglect and irresponsibility, who were the supposed instigators of the fire.

That vomiting blood is the final manifestation of the sickness brought on by Stoneclad's exposure to menstruating women suggests a kind of metamorphosis, and more specifically an absorption of the patient into the fold of the agents of illness. Stoneclad comes to resemble that which has made him sick, and through a deathbed metathesis he trades divine knowledge for this symbolic incorporation of human qualities. A parallel is suggested by Fogelson's discussion of the symbolic transformation of bloody Cherokee warriors. In the process of preparing for war, being transformed in status from "white" to "red," being ritually scratched, and ultimately shedding the blood of others and themselves, they became "the symbolic equivalent of menstruating women" (1990:175). Fogelson argues that this transformation can be understood as a "male effort to expropriate the presumed destructive power of menstruating women" (175). In the case of Stoneclad the "destructive power of menstruating women," while fatal to the being himself, is put to extremely positive use for humanity, releasing from a source of danger, fear, and death essential tools and knowledge for life. Though Sequoyah's trial by fire was not facilitated by menstruating women, women's metaphorical blood (his wife's matrilineal kin) is the force that reincorporates him.

Sequoyah redeems himself through his daughter, his first student, when she demonstrates the efficacy of the syllabary. In one version of the myth, Stoneclad calls the menstruating virgins his "granddaughters" (Herndon 1980:177). Stoneclad thus redeems himself by succumbing to and transforming himself into the symbolic equivalent of these granddaughters.

According to some versions of the Sequoyah story, the burning of his work was ultimately productive, like Stoneclad's burning. Sequoyah was said to be at a dead end in the invention process, having tried to invent a pictographic, ideographic, and/or logographic system that, once burned, he could not reconstruct.[12] This burning could be said to have "crystallized" the creative process, so Sequoyah's work took a new and much more concentrated form, resulting ultimately in the syllabary of only 85 characters.[13] It should also be noted that the bilingual newspaper made possible by Sequoyah's invention was called the *Phoenix*—named after the bird that, according to Egyptian mythology, rose from the ashes like the syllabary that formed the newspaper's words.[14]

The crystals left among the ashes at Stoneclad's burning were an indirect source of knowledge. "By scrying and interpreting revealed signs in the crystal, the future could be foretold and answers to critical questions obtained." The syllabary, after its invention and acceptance, was similarly treated as though its relationship with language and knowledge were not entirely transparent. Fogelson has noted that it was often treated as a mnemonic device that held encapsulated information, and that letters written in these early years were often telegraphically brief. I have argued elsewhere (2002a) that even today the syllabary is treated in Cherokee language education and elsewhere as a kind of code rather than as a neutral and productive system for phonetic transcription. Briefly, what I mean by this is that its phonemic efficacy is deemphasized while its cultural, linguistic, and even situational specificity are emphasized; it is treated as alternately obfuscating and revelatory; its order is considered meaningful; and it is frequently used with the aid of a standard syllabary chart that functions as a kind of "key" and in combination with other Cherokee orthographies seen as more "transparent." Furthermore, like the "signs in the crystal," much of what is written in the syllabary, particularly medicinal formulas, must be decoded or interpreted before it is of any use. Some medicine men have deliberately cultivated idiosyncratic handwriting so the revelatory potential of their formulas remains theirs alone.

Both the crystal and the syllabary are treated in Cherokee mythology and history as precious gifts, specifically for Cherokees, that must be cared for. A version of the Stoneclad myth offered by Marcia Herndon indicates that the heart must be "properly cared for" in order to maintain its efficacy (1980:177). I heard very similar sentiments expressed about the syllabary in the early 1990s. The syllabary was a gift from God, I was told by more than one consultant, and its use must therefore be maintained.

Two additional Cherokee myths further the parallelism between the life stories of Stoneclad and Sequoyah. Mooney treats these, the myth of the book and the bow and the myth of the crystal and the silver, as parallel myths of the same "class" (1982:351). Both narratives seek to explain how the white man and the Indian have wound up with their respective gifts. In the first case, the Indian originally possessed the capacity of "the book" and the white man the bow, but due to white treachery or theft, or Indian misuse (depending on the version), possession of these gifts was reversed. Mooney presents three versions of this myth from different sources. The one from an 1844 issue of the *Cherokee Advocate* goes as follows:

> When Sequoya, the inventor of the Cherokee alphabet, was trying to introduce it among his people, about 1822, some of them opposed it upon the ground that Indians had no business with reading. They said that when the Indian and the whiteman were created, the Indian, being the elder, was given a book, while the white man received a bow and arrows. Each was instructed to take good care of his gift and make the best use of it, but the Indian was so neglectful of his book that the white man soon stole it from him, leaving the bow in its place, so that books and reading now belong of right to the white man, while the Indian ought to be satisfied to hunt for a living. [1982:351]

This narrative helps us to understand the life story of Sequoyah in and of itself because it places Sequoyah in position to achieve a historic reversal of mythic proportions: that which was lost in mythic times is regained through the effort of the culture hero. But the parallelism between this and the myth of the crystal and the silver shed even more light on the significance of Sequoyah's gift.

In this next myth, crystal—in fact, the very same *ulv:hsati* that forms the core of Stoneclad's heart—occupies the structurally opposite position from the book: originating with the white man but ending up in the possession of the Indian. Mooney recounts:

> At the creation an *ulv:hsati* was given to the white man, and a piece of silver to the Indian. But the white man despised the stone and threw it away, while the Indian did the same with the silver. In going about the white man afterward found the silver piece and put it into his pocket and has prized it ever since. The Indian, in like manner, found the *ulv:hsati* where the white man had thrown it. He picked it up and has kept it since as his talisman, as money is the talismanic power of the white man. [1982:350-351]

This myth speaks to the respective gifts and priorities of the two peoples: Cherokees have access through the crystal to the world of spiritual and medicinal knowledge, while whites control the capital. The myth astutely suggests, though perhaps with some irony, that money is more than a pragmatic resource to the white man. However, in the larger context of

Cherokee culture and worldview, we know that money, for Cherokees, is antithetical to spirituality. Working with Cherokees in North Carolina in the early 1990s, I was told that medicine men could not accept money as a direct payment for treatment. To do so, I was told, would ruin their medicine. One consultant told me that money was "too heavy" to be exchanged directly for medicine. Thus this myth, like that of Stoneclad, structurally opposes the *ulv:hsati*, associated with the spiritual realm, to the more profane things of this earth.

The life story of Sequoyah asserts a new structural equivalence between these two exchange stories as well as between the crystal and the syllabary because it constitutes a reappropriation of the alienated gift of literacy. As Stoneclad bequeathed crystal and its accompanying knowledge to the Cherokees, so Sequoyah bequeathed them his invention and its priceless preservational and generative potential. What the myths of the crystal and silver and the bow and the book suggest to us is that both of these gifts, though temporarily in the hands of others, have ultimately returned to their rightful owners. As culture hero Sequoyah simultaneously creates and restores traditional culture. The parallelism also suggests that literacy (now in syllabary) stands in a similar relationship to hunting as the crystal does to money, namely, it constitutes a gift of knowledge as opposed to a gift of physical subsistence, it is more sacred than profane, and it is more otherworldly than clay, bow-and-arrow, or coin.

The emerging parallel between the syllabary and the *ulv:hsati* is reinforced between a linguistic relationship between the Cherokee words for reading and (medically) examining. "He is reading" and "He is (medically) examining (someone or something)" take the same form: *ako:liyeʔa* (Feeling 1975). Cherokee syllabary characters, one might suggest, undergo a similar sort of analytic scrutiny and interpretation as a medical patient that is also analogous to the "scrying and interpreting" applied to crystals.

Stoneclad was consumed by fire so the portion of his essence that was good and useful could be appropriated by man. Sequoyah, in a parallel way, disappeared as a tangible historical figure once his gift had emerged from the fire to be appropriated by the Cherokee people, leaving only his valuable code behind. An important point of indexical connection lies in the fact that the medicinal knowledge made available through Stoneclad's death is now, and has been since the last century, largely available via Sequoyah's invention. Medicinal formulas are written in the syllabary, with which they are very strongly associated.

The story of Stoneclad is only one of the traditional Cherokee myths that illuminates the narrative shape and symbolism of the commonly circulated biography of Sequoyah. Yet in the absence of this story, this received life history would be at some level opaque. It would be opaque because while its most straightforward referential content might still be grasped, an important iconic dimension of its meaning—its resemblance to another, very similar narrative—would not be accessible to the would-be outside interpreter. A cultural insider, however, would not need to superimpose the two narratives and note their structural similarity, nor would he or she likely be inclined to articulate this similarity. To the cultural insider, this similarity is likely experienced as familiarity, intelligibility, and depth of meaning.

The similarity of Sequoyah's received life story to the Stoneclad narrative implies, among other things, the continuity of past events, despite the heterogeneity that an outsider might attribute to the *kinds* of past these events represent. Everyday artistic and linguistic practices in Cherokee, and the tangible artifacts that result from them, also suggest that the *present* is in continuity with the past. Each mobilization of the image or name of Sequoyah or of the syllabary draws for part of its meaning on a string of resemblances to similar past utterances or events. Thus the parallelism in these epitomizing events in turn allows us to understand the culturally specific nature of Cherokee literacy.

Cherokee Ethnoliteracy

Seeing Stoneclad and Sequoyah as parallel helps us to understand many aspects of the syllabary's use. The comparison lends depth and meaning to the association of the syllabary with medicine and with religion more generally. It helps us to understand why the syllabary is treated as a special gift, for Cherokees alone (and not even for all Cherokees). It may also shed light on why the syllabary is seen as having special aesthetic properties. These understandings open up a window into what Fogelson might call Cherokee *ethno*literacy.

Because the syllabary is associated with the sacred in general, it has been able to survive the general conversion of the Eastern Cherokees to Christianity over the course of the 180 years since its invention. One of the fascinating things that has happened during this time has been a fragmentation of syllabary usage into separate components along the lines of functional specialization. This fragmentation is particularly significant between the reading and writing of syllabary. There seems to have been a major shift in this regard between the time of Fogelson's fieldwork and my own, a shift in which writing (producing what is seen as new text) in syllabary has become a rarer and more suspect activity, while reading remains more widespread and accepted. This shift is associated with a shift in beliefs about appropriate religious practices, as I will seek to explain next.[15]

Several times, when I shared with Fogelson my impressions of Eastern Cherokee Christian disapproval of traditional medicinal practice and "conjuring," he responded by saying that when he was in the field consultants had suggested that the two realms of belief and practice were to a degree complementary. As he has written, "the conjuror, by omitting mention of black magic including certain types of love magic and witchcraft, sees no great discrepancy between his goals and methods and those of Christianity" (1980a:83). Some members of the Eastern Cherokee community still distinguished between medicine and conjuring in the mid-1990s, although some used the combination designation "conjure-doctor" to refer to medicine men. Though some do not see either as compatible with Christianity, some Cherokees who make this distinction today see medicine, but not conjuring, as a potentially appropriate practice for a Christian. One consultant told me how her father, a medicine man, had specifically broken down his medicinal notebooks into "good" and "bad" categories. This woman wanted access to the notebooks, but her father first required her to pass a simultaneous test of morality and literacy by studying the New Testament.

Although reading, and especially reading print, is associated with Christianity, writing (and reading handwriting) are associated with medicine. One young Cherokee man I knew encountered considerable resistance in his efforts to read and write the syllabary because of its association with medicinal writing. Because other members of his family were known to be specialists in traditional medicine, he raised suspicions that he was involved in "witchcraft," as he called it. One of the community's main concerns, he thought, was that there was no legitimate reason to learn to read and write the syllabary at a young age. The belief was that someone was "training him."

Some Cherokees who read and write today try to solve this problem and avoid the suspicion that goes hand in hand with such skill by modeling their handwriting after the printing in the Cherokee New Testament. They thus index their devotion to Christianity in their handwriting style itself.

In understanding the divergence among Cherokee literacy practices like reading, writing, copying, and possessing text, the parallels between Stoneclad and Sequoyah, crystal and syllabary, and medicine and literacy offer some insight. Cherokee medicine, which descends from Stoneclad, requires the performance of medicinal texts or chants. The delivery of these takes place in one of four registers: thought, whispered, spoken, and sung, in ascending order of potency (Herndon 1980:178). Each register is appropriate for specific medicinal contexts. Similarly, there is a functional and associational specialization among the possible uses of the syllabary, which may be read silently, read aloud, sung, written, copied, or possessed.

I do not have much information on the significance of silent reading, but I believe that it is a less significant category of usage than reading aloud. Reading aloud, particularly of the New Testament, is for most readers a performative demonstration of faith. It is thus an inherently social act.

Singing is somewhat marginal as a literacy practice because, as one might expect, many Cherokees who are not literate (and also many who are not fluent speakers) can sing the most popular hymns. Though the hymns are printed syllabary texts, then, their performance does not require literacy. Nevertheless many Cherokees possess the hymnal, and many will "read along" as they sing the hymns regardless of their reading proficiency. In terms of its potency, then, and as a source of local respect and authority, singing is less powerful than reading aloud. Though there may be many hymn singers in a congregation, someone who is truly proficient at reading aloud from the New Testament is likely to be seen as an expert and may be a Sunday school teacher.

Copying is important in many ways. Copying hymns or Bible verses, usually enlarging them at the same time so they can be shared with a group or displayed, was a fairly common activity among literate Cherokees in the mid-1990s. This copying was usually fairly exact, of both the language and the print itself. Similarly, medicine men traditionally transcribed formulas carefully so as to avoid alteration. Copying is a fairly neutral mobilization of the syllabary, and perhaps for this reason it is the mode of use most commonly seen in the production of tourist commodities like pottery and in formal, public language education.

Writing in the syllabary is a rare and specialized activity, except in the context of formal language classroom exercises, and it is significant that there is no parallel to writing if we return to our analogy with medicinal registers. At an abstract level this is because the texts or chants are the legacy of Stoneclad and do not come from human beings. In practice, new medicinal texts must have developed over time, but this fairly rare occurrence is greatly overshadowed by the processes of reproduction and inheritance of existing texts. Writing in the syllabary thus does not have a legitimate mythic parallel that would make it justifiable or perhaps even comprehensible. For Eastern Cherokee Christians in the mid-1990s (in North Carolina, this meant nearly all Cherokees), the texts of relevance had already been written and the necessary knowledge already bequeathed. New texts were at best superfluous and at worst suspect. The possibility of the production of new medicinal texts was greeted with alarm; there was already enough work to do in sorting out the more from the less dangerous existing texts.[16]

Though Fogelson stated that a reading knowledge of the Cherokee syllabary was traditionally necessary in order for an individual to train to become a conjuror, this was clearly a very specialized reading knowledge. "Although several members of the Band are competent enough to read the Bible, hymnals, and secular documents in the syllabary," he wrote, "a native practitioner is required to work with the formulas, since these documents are written in a highly stylized ceremonial language unintelligible to the Cherokee non-specialist" (1962:75). A medicine man, then, would have to master a special style of writing in order to produce his own unique texts and to interpret those he inherited or bought from others. Today just knowing how to read printed syllabary well enough to read aloud from the Bible is a highly specialized form of knowledge that is generally prerequisite to the positions of Sunday school teacher or cultural specialist. Though the acceptable texts and contexts have shifted, then, the specialized nature of syllabary use remains.

The narrative iconicity we have been tracing also helps us to understand why and how the syllabary is so importantly linked with power. In "Cherokee Notions of Power" (1977) Fogelson argued that the type of power associated with conjuring—and by association and analogy, I would argue, with writing—is not inherited but can be acquired, via regular practices and observances, over a lifetime. Power is not a permanent attribute of objects and individuals, but rather it requires periodic renewal. It is thus the individual, and his actions, that are responsible for generating and maintaining power. Certainly, the accumulation of written texts, through their original production and/or exchange, could be seen as a buildup of individual power of this sort. Many Cherokee Christians today, however, would view this model of power as being in direct conflict with the genuine source of power available via the written word. The Bible reader serves mainly as a point of *access*, for himself and others, to Truth and Power. Learning to read may be seen as a one-time, relatively permanent transformation, parallel to "getting saved." Reading syllabary, as a more passive or receptive engagement with the power of language, may thus be more highly compatible with Christian practice and belief than is writing. If, as Fogelson argues, Cherokee power is also strongly associated with knowledge, then the kind of knowledge accessible through syllabic literacy may be powerful enough; the kind of power generated by the production of new knowledge through text may seem dangerous.

In addition to the questions that would surround the content of new, original writing, there is the question of readership. There are few enough readers of conventional, printed syllabary; very few Eastern Cherokees would be able to read an original handwritten text. The individual writer therefore isolates himself or a very small reading community, whereas the goal of most syllabary Bible readers is to come together with others in the Word.

Reading Biblical syllabary thus indexes a different model of community than does generating new text via handwriting. Individual *writers* may be seen as divisive or antisocial, whereas Bible *readers* serve as spiritual leaders for small subcommunities on the Eastern Cherokee reservation that were once unified and structured in other ways—for example, by the cooperative labor organizations and ball teams about which we have learned so much from Fogelson (1961, 1962). Like the anomalous Stoneclad and Sequoyah the syllabary and its use must be properly framed, incorporated, and made a regular, acceptable, and comprehensible part of the Cherokee cultural world. Christian life provides this incorporation in a way that medicine perhaps no longer can.

The question of how Sequoyah's syllabary functions, of how it has meaning in the culturally and historically specific contexts of its use, turns out to be a highly complex one. Implicated are narrative patterns of Cherokee biography and myth, variable interpretations of Sequoyah's life and work, and a long and rich history of practical usage, evaluation, and association of this unique set of 85 characters. Studying the relationship of *literacy* to the Cherokee linguistic and cultural life of the past 175 years or so would be fruitless; if we take seriously the lessons in the work of Raymond D. Fogelson, we can see that a search for *ethno*literacy is truly our only meaningful starting point.

Notes

1. My 1993–95 fieldwork among the Eastern Cherokees was made possible in part by a grant from the Phillips Fund of the American Philosophical Society and a fellowship from the Spencer Foundation, both of which are gratefully acknowledged. I would also like to thank an anonymous reviewer for the University of Nebraska Press for his or her very helpful suggestions. Most thanks of all go to the Eastern Cherokee community for teaching me about Cherokee's rich language and culture.

2. *Yo:nek* is Cherokee for "white person." Spellings of Cherokee words in this chapter will follow Cook 1979, regardless of the source.

3. Raymond DeMallie has recently noted that Fogelson shared this sense of the importance of the individual with him as well (1996).

4. In "On the Varieties of Indian History: Sequoyah and Traveller Bird" (1974), Fogelson leads his readers toward an appropriate perspective from which to consider the meanings and implications of the term *ethno-ethno-ethnohistory* by way of the following anecdote:

> When I was a young boy growing up on the sandy outer fringes of the New Jersey Coastal Plain, I remember exploring the kitchen cupboard one day and making an astounding discovery. I seized a cylinder of Diamond Crystal Shaker Salt on which was printed a portrait of a friendly-looking Shaker lady holding an identical cylinder of salt. Turning the container from side to side, I successively discovered— as deeply as my vision could penetrate—additional Shaker ladies bearing cylinders of salt. In my own naive and independent fashion, I had stumbled upon the principle of infinite regress. [1974:105]

5. A few years ago I was criticized, understandably, by a student in one of my classes for using the word *myth* to refer to a Native American creation account. I believe that the student felt that the word *myth* implied falsehood. What Fogelson reminds us of is that those narratives most often called "myths" are epitomizing events *par excellence*. Myths, "sacred narratives explaining how the world and man come to be in their present form" (Dundes 1984:1), are in the most meaningful sense *truer* than history.

6. In the course of this exploration, it is important to realize that not everyone in a community may agree on what the central epitomizing events are, nor on how they should be interpreted.

7. The text of this sketch, and several of the other accounts that appeared thereafter, may be found in Kilpatrick's *Sequoyah of Earth and Intellect* (1965).

8. Agreement is not universal about even these very general biographical characteristics. Cherokee historian Traveller Bird (1971) has challenged the identity of Sequoyah as the man called "George Guess" in English and argues that the syllabary was a longstanding tool of Indian warrior-scribes that predated Sequoyah by hundreds of years.

9. In *Cherokee Renascence in the New Republic* (1986), McLoughlin argues that Sequoyah's invention was one of the factors that enabled the Cherokees to persevere and even thrive as a nation in the late eighteenth and early nineteenth centuries.

10. Herndon writes that "a Stoneman's heart must be wrapped in a moccasin or a piece of thin leather, and in the old days it was kept in a rock cliff. The spirit of the heart must be fed blood once a week, either from oneself or from a bird or animal" (Herndon 1980:177). The obligatory incorporation of blood into the crystal (essence of bone) further suggests the importance of the duality of Stoneclad's legacy. Herndon also states that the crystal in question "is a rutile quartz crystal, red on one end." If that is so, then red and white are both integral parts of the legacy.

11. *Scrying* means gazing with interpretive intent, as into a crystal.

12. In a pictographic system, pictures represent spoken words or ideas. In an ideographic system, individual characters represent ideas. In a logographic system, individual characters represent spoken words. Alphabets and syllabaries, by contrast, use individual characters to represent isolated consonants or vowels of the spoken language (alphabets) or consonant-vowel combinations (syllabaries). An alphabet or syllabary will generally require only a small number of characters, in comparison with the other types of writing systems, and these are therefore often considered to be more "efficient" systems.

13. The syllabary, like the crystals produced by Stoneclad's death, has proved to be indestructible to this day. Neither the attempts by missionaries and progressives often characterized as "mixed-bloods" to introduce a different orthography for Cherokee in the 1820s,

nor the violent destruction of the Cherokee Nation's syllabary printing press, have deterred the Cherokee preference for, and continued usage of, this writing system.

14. According to Mooney (1982:539) the paper's name was devised by Samuel Worcester, a white missionary to the Cherokees, and Elias Boudinot, the Cherokee editor of the *Phoenix*. In Cherokee, it is *tsule:hisanv:hi*, meaning "the one who was down and has risen."

15. For a more detailed treatment of Cherokee ideologies of literacy and the functional specialization of syllabary use, see Bender 2002a.

16. In the mid-1990s, women were more likely to mobilize the syllabary in copying mode, while men were more likely to be both readers and writers, both more potent forms of syllabary use. For a more extensive discussion of the division of linguistic labor by gender in Cherokee, see Bender 2002b.

References

Bender, Margaret
  2002a Signs of Cherokee Culture: Sequoyah's Syllabary in Eastern Cherokee Life. Chapel Hill: University of North Carolina Press.
  2002b Langue, Parole and Gender: Literacy in Cherokee. *In* Southern Indians and Anthropologists: Culture, Politics, and Identity. Lisa J. Lefler and Frederic W. Gleach, eds. Pp. 77–88. Athens GA: University of Georgia Press.
Cook, William Hinton
  1979 A Grammar of North Carolina Cherokee. Ph.D. dissertation, Department of Linguistics, Yale University.
DeMallie, Raymond
  1996 Remarks preceding the presentation of " 'To Make the Dakota Understandable, as human beings': Ella Deloria and the Sioux," delivered at the Annual Meeting of the American Society for Ethnohistory. Portland, Oregon.
Dundes, Alan
  1984 Introduction. *In* Sacred Narrative: Readings in the Theory of Myth. A. Dundes, ed. Pp. 1–3. Berkeley: University of California Press.
Feeling, Durbin
  1975 Cherokee-English Dictionary. William Pulte, ed. Tahlequah OK: Cherokee Nation of Oklahoma.
Fogelson, Raymond D.
  1961 Cherokee Economic Cooperatives: The Gadugi. *In* Symposium on Cherokee and Iroquois Culture. Bureau of American Ethnology, Bulletin 180. William N. Fenton and John Gulick, eds. Pp. 88–98. Washington DC: Smithsonian Institution.
  1962 The Cherokee Ball Game: A Study in Southeastern Ethnology. PhD dissertation, Department of Anthropology, University of Pennsylvania.
  1974 On the Varieties of Indian History: Sequoyah and Traveller Bird. Journal of Ethnic Studies 2:105–112.
  1977 Cherokee Notions of Power. *In* The Anthropology of Power: Ethnographic Studies from Asia, Oceania and the New World. Raymond D. Fogelson and Richard N. Adams, eds. Pp. 185–194. New York: Academic Press.
  1978 Major John Norton as Ethno-ethnologist. Journal of Cherokee Studies 3(4):250–255.
  1980a The Conjuror in Eastern Society. Journal of Cherokee Studies 5(2):60–87.
  1980b Windigo Goes South: Stoneclad among the Cherokees. *In* Manlike Monsters on

Trial: Early Records and Modern Evidence. Marjorie M. Halpin and Michael M. Ames, eds. Pp. 132–151. Vancouver: University of British Columbia Press.

1984 Who Were the Ani-Kutani? An Excursion into Cherokee Historical Thought. Ethnohistory 31(4):255–263.

1989 The Ethnohistory of Events and Nonevents. Ethnohistory 36(2):133–147.

1990 On the 'Petticoat Government' of the Eighteenth-Century Cherokee. *In* Personality and the Cultural Construction of Society. David K. Jordan and Marc J. Swartz, eds. Pp. 161–181. Tuscaloosa AL: University of Alabama Press.

Herndon, Marcia
1980 Fox, Owl and Raven. Selected Reports in Ethnomusicology: The Traditional Music of North American Indians 3(2):175–192.

Hufford, Mary
1998 Tending the Commons: Ramp Suppers, Biodiversity, and the integrity of "The Mountains". Folklife Center News 20(4):3–11.

Kilpatrick, Jack Frederick
1965 Sequoyah of Earth and Intellect. Austin TX: The Encino Press.

McLoughlin, William G.
1986 Cherokee Renascence in the New Republic. Princeton NJ: Princeton University Press.

Mooney, James
1982 Myths of the Cherokee and Sacred Formulas of the Cherokees (reproduced from U.S. Bureau of American Ethnology Bulletins 7 and 19). Cherokee NC: Cherokee Heritage Books.

Perdue, Theda
1979 Slavery and the Evolution of Cherokee Society, 1540–1866. Knoxville: University of Tennessee Press.

Sturtevant, William
1966 Anthropology, History, and Ethnohistory. Ethnohistory 13:2–51.

Urban, Greg
1991 A Discourse-Centered Approach to Culture. Austin: University of Texas Press.

Witthoft, John
1983 Cherokee Beliefs Concerning Death. Journal of Cherokee Studies 8(2):68–72.

Part Two

Cultures

On Persons and Power,
Rituals and Creativity

4. *Power as the Transmission of Culture*

GREG URBAN

An anthropological cliché: language is a mechanism for the transmission of culture. Around the crackling campfire at night (to continue the cliché), shadows flickering against the loblolly pines, someone tells a story. Others listen to it, and later themselves retell it. The "it" here, the myth, is not intrinsic to the language; one can speak the language without knowing the myth. However, two individuals, let's say A and B, must share a language in order for the myth to pass between them. Language facilitates the passage of myth between people. It is the medium through which myth moves on its journey across space and over time. And in the course of that journey, the myth maintains its integrity as a thing or cultural object. Myth, in this way, is quintessential culture; it is passed on or transmitted via social learning.

From this point of view, imperatives, as part of language, pose a problem.[1] They seem not to facilitate the transmission of culture in the way that language more generally facilitates the transmission of myths. If A tells B to do something, A is not transmitting (or not necessarily transmitting) a piece of socially learned, socially circulating culture. A may be ordering B to do something that A has never done before and, indeed, that B has never done before. There is a factor of novelty here.

In addition, in the case of the myth, B copies or tries to copy what A has done or, in this case, said. B has heard A tell the myth, and, in his or her own turn, B tells the myth to someone else. B replicates the actions of A. However, in the case of the imperative, A socially transmits something to B, but B does not simply parrot A's words—pace the scenario in which A says "repeat after me," and B echoes "repeat after me." Instead, the transmission that takes place involves a magical conversion. The meaning of the words uttered by A becomes the reality of the actions performed by B—the words transubstantiate; they, in effect, become flesh.

I want to argue in this paper that, despite the foregoing comparison, imperatives are, indeed, closely bound up with the transmission of culture. The problem is not with imperatives, which seem to lie outside of "culture." Rather, it is with the concept of culture itself, which makes those imperatives seem alien, something other than culture. We need a new way of thinking about the motion of culture through space and time. A study of imperatives as facilitators of the flow of culture forces us to rethink the nature of that flow, of what culture is and how it moves. I will argue, in this chapter, that when culture flows through imperatives that culture itself is modified or reshaped; its movement is altered. Culture, in short, undergoes acceleration.

Within classical culture theory, power is problematic. Scholars have looked at folk conceptualizations of power (see the papers in Fogelson and Adams 1977, especially those by Bean, Black, DeMallie and Lavenda, Fogelson, Issacs, Lane, Mackenzie, Pandey, and Stross)—at the way power is construed by culture but not at the relationship of power to the movement of culture itself.[2] This is in part because, within classical culture theory, culture is unproblematically inertial; once set in motion it tends to continue in motion. What has been in the past will be in the future. From this point of view, culture appears to be only backward looking. In thinking about it, one traces everything back to antecedents. The antecedents are the source of culture's strength and vitality—the force behind its movement. Power is only culture if it replicates what has been. Since power is linked to newness or change, it always in some measure eludes culture as understood inertially.

The problem in this formulation is with the construal of culture itself. We need to focus attention not just on the inertial—where what has been will be—but also on those situations in which the flow of cultural elements is deflected from its course or in which the element is reshaped—where what has been is becoming something else. In these cases culture is accelerating, in the sense of changing its course of motion or changing its own shape. Such accelerating culture is forward looking. In thinking about it, the past appears as prelude to the future. What rivets attention is not custom or tradition but newness, innovation, originality. This is the side of culture, or so I want to contend, with which power is intimately bound up.

Part of my argument in this paper will be that, for this reason, imperatives create a problem for thought and, hence, tend to become the focus of narrative reflections. They are problematic within a metacultural understanding of culture as traditional—as old things handed down from the past—because they are aligned with the new. However, even within a metacultural understanding of culture as modern—as new, rational, cut off from the past—they pose a problem because they are identified with the passage of something between people, and hence with connection over time. The interesting question for me, therefore, will be: How are imperatives narrativized? Where do they figure into stories about the movement of culture over time and space?

Imperatives Can Be Placed in the Service of Tradition

Before I get to the question of narrativization, I want to sharpen my earlier claim about imperatives and newness. In that characterization, or caricaturization, I suggested, first, that when A tells something to B using imperatives, A is not simply transmitting a piece of extant culture but rather getting B to do something that may be wholly new—action that neither has done before and even that A will not do. There is a factor of novelty here. Second, B is not simply imitating A's behavior—"do as I do"—but rather acting out the meaning of A's words—"do as I say." This is the factor of transubstantiation. Taken together these two factors would make the relationship of imperatives to culture distinct from that of language to myth, where a traditional object (myth), fashioned out of language, passes through language on its journey between people across time and space. The imperative would be linked to the construction of new objects in the world (new actions), and the process of construction would involve the conversion of words into deeds.

So the first question is whether imperatives in the real world conform to this characterization, and the answer is: "No!" or, at least, "Not exactly." Examples can be found and, indeed, abound in many Amerindian communities in Brazil and adjacent countries in which both characterizations seem doubtful. In these cases imperatives appear to be so much a part of inertial culture that it is difficult to see what newness their issuance produces, or even to be sure that transubstantiation has taken place. I would like to think of this as one pole—the traditional pole—of a continuum between tradition and modernity.

In a brief segment of a film by Timothy Asch and Napoleon Chagnon (1970) called *The Feast*, shot in the Yanomamö village of Patanowä-teri on March 3, 1968, at 2:30 p.m., we see a Yanomamö man squatting on his haunches, wielding a machete in his right hand, scraping and cleaning the ground around him. We see him gesticulate and hear him call out in a language we infer to be Yanomamö. The line is repeated, the English translation on the screen appearing as: "—All of you there. Come help clean the plaza." In an earlier explication of this segment, the narrator tells us that, although the man we see on the screen is a headman and "sponsor of the feast," he "cannot order people to work. He leads by example both in cleaning the village and in providing the largest share of the food."

What is going on in this scene? By our inference the headman's imploring is successful, and we imagine others coming to clean the plaza. From the point of view of the flow of culture over time, the actual act of plaza cleaning is a traditional behavior—socially learned and socially passed on. Presumably all adults in the village are familiar with it, and adult men have probably engaged in it on numerous occasions. If the headman is A and another villager who heeds the command is B, it is apparent that A, through his behavior, is transmitting a piece of extant culture, pace my original formulation in which the use of the imperatives in effecting behavior is distinguished from the use of language in transmitting myth. The acts being performed by A and B alike are traditional acts, not new ones.

Moreover, we can question the factor of transubstantiation. According to that factor, what B imitates is not the words that A utters. In the Yanomamö example, B would not simply go around saying: "All of you there. Come help clean the plaza." Instead, or in addition, B would actually engage in the activity described by A's words. B would clean the plaza, conforming to the semantic description in the imperative: "Come help clean the plaza." A conversion would take place. The semantically understandable utterance would get enacted as a behavior that could be characterized by that semantic information—for example, by the sentence "he is cleaning the plaza." In the ideal imperative I have sketched, therefore, something that is abstract (a meaning) gets converted into something concrete (a behavior). The word takes shape in the world as the thing described by it.

The Yanomamö example differs from my ideal case in that B's production of behavior in the world is not exclusively a response to the semantic content of A's utterance. Instead B may be in part copying A's behavior, in addition to or instead of heeding A's words. Moreover, B's behavior may be—indeed, probably in most cases is—not just a copy of A's behavior or an enactment of A's words, but also the reproduction of behaviors B himself has already learned. In other words, A's words and/or actions may only call up in B cultural patterns of behavior that B had acquired previously. The same cultural pattern is already present in A and B, and the pattern is summoned by A—whether by A's behavior or A's words or both. This is, therefore, an example of imperatives that are maximally in the service of tradition, fostering the movement of what would otherwise be inertial culture through time.

But this does not mean that no acceleration takes place, that the imperatives, even here, are merely inertial. For without the imperative it would be possible for B to construe A's cleaning of the plaza as an idiosyncratic act. B could rationalize A's behavior, or even imagine that it was A's job alone to clean the plaza. However, the imperative makes it absolutely clear that A expects or wants B to engage in similar behavior—to help out. The imperative brings to consciousness A's expectation that B will activate the cultural patterns he has already acquired. The imperative summons B's behavior by drawing B's consciousness to A's desire—"Come help clean the plaza." Therefore, A's words—the imperatives A utters—have some accelerative effect. They help to kindle the flow of culture through B at a precise moment. They therefore impart an incremental force to the culture that is already there but that may not otherwise take shape in the world at that exact time. A's words act as a catalyst to precipitate those actions in the world.

Of course, the efficacy of A's utterance is aided by his status as "headman." That status itself appears from Chagnon's (1992[1968]) descriptions to be, in considerable measure, a result of past evidence of leadership. Take the following example:

> a group of men from Patanowä-teri arrived [in Upper Bisaasi-teri] to explore with Kãobawä [the Upper Bisaasi-teri headman] the possibility of peace between their two villages. They were brothers-in-law to him and were fairly certain that he would protect them from the village hotheads. One of the ambitious men in Kãobawä's group saw in this an opportunity to enhance his prestige and made plans to murder the three visitors. This man, Hontonawä, was a very cunning, treacherous fellow and quite jealous of Kãobawä's position as headman. He wanted to be their village leader and privately told me to address him as the headman.
> [Chagnon 1992[1968]:134]

According to Chagnon, Hontonawä issued a bootstrapping imperative to him—"[he] told me to address him as the headman"—hoping, apparently, to achieve the status by having people call him by the title. However, and critically, he also attempted, as the story unfolds, to organize a murder that would have undermined Kãobawä's current leadership. His issuance of imperatives in the latter case would precipitate actions designed to demonstrate his own leadership as well as the incompetence of Kãobawä. So past evidence of having imperatives obeyed is one basis for expecting that future imperatives will be obeyed. There is a key element of traditionality here. The position of headman is part of an inertial culture but one that can and must be incrementally accelerated by each successful instance of leadership itself.

Maintenance of Tradition Requires Accelerative Force

What is the main idea here? I started by arguing that imperatives, in the Yanomamö example and more generally, can be placed in the service of tradition. Now I am arguing that tradition itself requires that service; it needs accelerative force. Inertia alone is not sufficient to carry cultural elements indefinitely into the future. Forces of various sorts—forgetting, competition from other cultural elements, physical quirks of persons or the environment, and more—are at work to dissipate tradition. This is especially true in oral transmission—the basis for the movement of myths through space and time. The forces of dissipation must be counteracted if culture is to continue on its journey. In the Yanomamö example it is apparent that the imperative issued by the headman is part of an attempt to carry on a tradition where that tradition—plaza-cleaning in preparation for the feast—might otherwise dissipate. The imperative supplies an incremental force that counteracts the dissipative forces at work on traditional culture.

If my argument is correct—if imperatives even when placed in the service of tradition supply an accelerative force however incremental that force may be—the question becomes: what is the source of that force? An answer that I hope to begin to give in this chapter is that the force derives in part from narratives. In particular it originates in the expectations surrounding imperatives—within a given discourse community—that stem from the dominant ways in which imperatives are used in narratives, such as myths. Those narratives encode an understanding of what imperatives are and of how they function socially. Understanding in turn shapes expectations and behaviors.

Paradoxically such understanding can be stabilized within a community only if the narrative construction of the imperatives can be stabilized. In the case of myths the problem of stabilization is synonymous with the problem of ensuring the replication of the myth itself. There is an important difference when it comes to mass-mediated forms, such as films or novels, as I will argue in the next section. But in the case of myths stabilizing the understanding of imperatives, fixing the narrative expectations surrounding them, means ensuring that the myth will be told again and again in the same way, at least insofar as the role of the imperatives is concerned. The "insurance" is the aesthetic design that makes the role of the imperatives so central and so salient, so interesting, that the role will be reprised in subsequent tellings.

One design feature of so many myths that makes them intriguing in this regard is their very topic: change. As has been long observed, myths tend to be about the epic transformation of the world, how it came to be as it is today. Transformation often involves creating new culture or moving old culture into new territory. We are dealing here with monumental, life-altering change that, once effected, leaves the world in a new equilibrium. The myths therefore deal explicitly with what I have been calling the problem of acceleration. Correspondingly, or so I want to argue, the accelerative function of imperatives is construed, in these myths, as stabilizing or restorative. The imperatives help to harness a world in flux, to produce a new equilibrium that in some important respects resembles the older equilibrium that the changes disrupted. The imperatives are therefore at the service of the maintenance of tradition. This is acceleration but acceleration designed to overcome the dissipative forces at work on inertial culture.

A corollary of this is that imperatives are to be obeyed—with obeyance being evidence of understanding and, hence, of the passage of meaning and culture between the individuals involved. I say "corollary" because were the imperatives to be represented as self-consciously disobeyed then their accelerative force in effecting the transmission of traditional culture would be compromised. If one can't expect imperatives to be obeyed one can't expect culture to move. Hence to facilitate the oral transmission of traditional culture it is crucial that imperatives be represented as something to be complied with and that noncompliance be represented as the result of misunderstanding and also the source of negative rather than positive consequence. I will try to show that the opposite is true in the case of the dissemination of culture through mass media. There, movement through space and time is rendered easier, but the replication of culture is harder since replication requires the production of new cultural forms—new films or videos or books or CDS—not simply watching or reading or listening to older cultural forms. In that case the questioning of imperatives becomes of paramount importance. Such questioning becomes evidence of a different kind of understanding.

In many of the Amerindian examples at which I have looked obeying (and hence understanding) is simply taken as a matter of course. There is no question of compliance or noncompliance. This can be seen in the case of the first of the imperatives in the myth fragment I quote later in this section. But where the question of compliance is raised within the narratives, the noncompliance is represented as negligence rather than disobedience, failure to fully understand the imperative in all of its details, or failure to grasp the significance of those details. The person commanded endeavors to do as he or she is told, but—for whatever reason—fails. The result of this failure is change. Because the imperatives are restorative, when they are not faithfully followed irreversible change takes place.

Let's look now at a fragment of a Cherokee Indian myth. This fragment —a self-contained episode in its own right—is one part of the longer myth "Kana'ti and Selu: The Origin of Game and Corn," as rendered in James Mooney's (1900:242–249) *Myths of the Cherokee*:

> Every day when Selu got ready to cook the dinner she would go out to the storehouse with a basket and bring it back full of corn and beans. The boys [her two sons—the Wild Boy and his younger brother] had never been inside the storehouse, so wondered where all the corn and beans could come from, as the house was not a very large one; so as soon as Selu went out of the door the Wild Boy said to his brother, "Let's go and see what she does." They ran around and climbed up at the back of the storehouse and pulled out a piece of clay from between the logs, so that they could look in. There they saw Selu standing in the middle of the room with the basket in front of her on the floor. Leaning over the basket, she rubbed her stomach—*so*—and the basket was half full of corn. Then she rubbed under her armpits—*so*—and the basket was full to the top with beans. The boys looked at each other and said, "This will never do; our mother is a witch. If we eat any of that it will poison us. We must kill her."
>
> When the boys came back into the house, she knew their thoughts before they spoke. "So you are going to kill me?" said Selu. "Yes," said the boys, "you are a witch." "Well," said their mother, "when you have killed me, clear a large piece of ground in front of the house and drag my body seven times around the circle. Then drag me seven times over the ground inside the circle, and stay up all night and watch, and in the morning you will have plenty of corn." The boys killed her with their clubs, and cut off her head and put it up on the roof of the house with her face turned to the west, and told her to look for her husband. Then they set to work to clear the ground in front of the house, but instead of clearing the whole piece they cleared only seven little spots. This is why corn now grows only in a few places instead of over the whole world. They dragged the body of Selu around the circle, and wherever her blood fell on the ground the corn sprang up. But instead of dragging her body seven times across the ground they dragged it over only twice, which is

the reason the Indians still work their crop but twice. The two brothers sat up and watched their corn all night, and in the morning it was full grown and ripe.

A first point to note about this episode is that the imperatives, in which the mother tells her sons what to do, follow the ideal type pattern I laid out earlier: A (the mother) orders B (the children) to do something that she will not herself do. The situation thus differs from that in the Yanomamö example, where the headman "orders" others to do what he himself is already doing. In this narrative B's behavior is characterizable (more or less) by the semantic description contained in A's words. A conversion thus takes place—at least as it is represented in the narrative. The meanings of A's words take shape as the behavior performed by B.

Since this is a narrative I should note that the "behaviors" of B, in this case, are actually, and obviously, descriptions of the behaviors encoded in words. The "conversion" in this case is thus between quoted speech and framing speech. In an earlier book, *Metaphysical Community*, I developed an understanding of the importance of this relationship with regard to the ethnographic endeavor. If we compare the Cherokee myth fragment above with the Yanomamö case discussed earlier, the narrative takes the place of the ethnographer-observer's description of the nonlinguistic event in which the imperative is embedded. Here is an excerpt of that description again:

> we see a Yanomamö man squatting on his haunches, wielding a machete in his right hand, scraping and cleaning the ground around him. We see him gesticulate and hear him call out in a language we infer to be Yanomamö. The line is repeated, the English translation on the screen appearing as:

> —All of you there. Come help clean the plaza.

In this case, I—an external observer of the film—have quoted the translated imperative, have described the behaviors on screen, and made some inferences from these observations. In the myth, the narrator plays the same role.

The interconversion process between meaning and behavior is thus analogous to the relationship between quoted speech and quoting speech. And, indeed, one hypothesis about the cultural organization of behavior I have advanced, and advance again here, is that people act so their behavior is narrativized or narrativizable (by themselves or others) in a certain way. That certain way corresponds to the available circulating narratives in the community of which the individual is part.

A second point to be observed about the preceding example is that the behavior expected of B by A is *new*. It is presumably not part of a culturally acquired pattern already available to B. Hence the imperatives issued by A affect the inertial flow of culture. They are "accelerative" in this sense. The kind of culture produced by them that flows from A to B is a new culture. Its shape is different from that of the inertial culture out of which they grew. The imperatives participate in a process of change.

At the same time what is intriguing is that the "newness"—the planting of corn in this case—is an attempt to carry on an older pattern. The narrator is at pains to tell us that the boys had always had corn when growing up: "[they] wondered where all the corn and beans could come from." The mother's act, when the boys decide to kill her, is far from a retributive one. She wants the boys to continue to have corn as they always have. And so she instructs them how to make it from her dead body.

From the point of view of the inertial flow of culture over time, therefore, the imperative, while effecting something new, is also and simultaneously endeavoring to restore something old. It is working at the behest of tradition, attempting to preserve it as it moves over time in the face of tumultuous and irreversible changes.

Another point: according to the narrative the boys do not willfully resist their mother. Instead they attempt to carry out her commands. This is shown in the linguistic parallelism. Parts of the imperative are matched by parts of the behavior that is subsequently described. However, they fail to carry out what is really a complex set of commands in all of their detail. From the point of view of the transmission of culture, therefore, the conversion of A's initial command into B's behavior is described as improperly executed. B fails to precisely reproduce the behavior that A is transmitting to B through the semantic meaning of her words. Cultural transmission is only partially successful here. Moreover, the failed part of transmission leads to a consequence, and that consequence is negative for B. B has to work harder or gets less corn. There is an admonition here: had B replicated A's semantic meaning in his/their behavior, life would be better for B. Alas, transmission is difficult. Reproduction of the semantically coded material in actual behavior involves inaccuracies of transmission. In the following schematization (Figure 1) of the relevant portions of this narrative you will observe the elegant structure, which, I submit, is part of what makes this myth aesthetically interesting and hence keeps it circulating. Imperatives 1 and 3 involve mistakes, from which negative consequences follow; imperatives 2 and 4 involve simple compliance, from which positive consequences follow:

Imperative 1:	"when you have killed me, clear a large piece of ground in front of the house.
Behavior:	The boys killed her with their clubs . . . Then they set to work to clear the ground in front of the house.
Mistake:	but instead of clearing the whole piece they cleared only seven little spots.
Bad Consequence:	This is why corn now grows only in a few places instead of over the whole world.

Imperative 2:	"drag my body seven times around the circle."
Behavior:	They dragged the body of Selu around the circle.
Good Consequence:	wherever her blood fell on the ground the corn sprang up.

Imperative 3:	"Then drag me seven times over the ground inside the circle."
Behavior:	they dragged it over
Mistake:	only twice
Bad Consequence:	which is the reason the Indians still work their crop but twice.

Imperative 4:	"stay up all night and watch"
Behavior:	The two brothers sat up and watched their corn all night.
Good Consequence:	in the morning it was full grown and ripe.

Figure 1.

Transubstantiation Appears as Replication When It Is Narrativized

If we ratchet up our microscope one notch further and zoom in on these fragments of discourse an interesting pattern emerges. The transubstantiation referred to earlier—that is, the conversion of the meaning of an imperative into a behavior in the world—reappears here as the replication of micro-strings of discourses. Figure 2 highlights this for imperative 1.

In this figure the upper line contains the actual words from the imperative. The bottom line consists of the words from the description of the behavior that followed from the imperative. I have drawn boxes around the words that are physically replicated between the command utterance

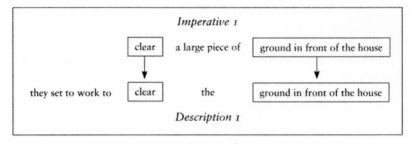

Figure 2. One example of transubstantiation as replication

and the description of the resultant behavior and drawn arrows to trace the replication process.

What is interesting is that the description of the behavior, as a collection of words, appears as a partial (at least) replication of the imperative, as a collection of words. The mystery of transubstantiation, wherein meanings transmitted through language take shape as objects in the world—behaviors or sequences of behaviors—is thus resolved at the level of narrative where transubstantiation appears as discourse replication. This discourse replication involves the simultaneous reproduction of meaning and material form. Moreover, the reproduction is itself an actual instance of the movement of culture over time, however microscopic that movement may be. Because the narrative unfolds in time, whether reading time or spoken time, the subsequent stretch of discourse occurs after the initial imperative. At the micro levels of discourse, therefore, the problem of commands and power in relation to the movement of culture is resolved as the micro-replication of discourse fragments.

Lest this one example appear anomalous, I have also diagrammed two others, which I give below in Figures 3 and 4.

These examples make it clear that imperatives, in the case of the Amerindian myths I have been studying, are more akin in their efficacy to the retelling of myths than my initial contrast at the beginning of this essay seemed to suggest.

At the same time, I want to now train our sights on a different fact: the replication here is only partial. We see evidence of change as well. The wording of the imperative is distinct from the wording of the description. Part of the difference is a matter of linguistic design. In the case of imperatives, replication crosses the line between metadiscourse and discourse (or reporting speech and reported speech). This kind of crossing introduces regular changes (see Lee 1997, and also the papers in Lucy 1993). For example, "my body," a phrase in the first person, be-

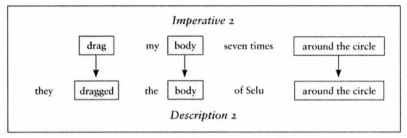

Figure 3. Another example of transubstantiation as replication

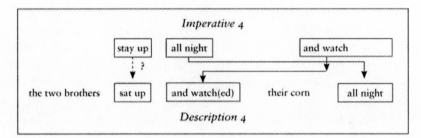

Figure 4. Complexities in transubstantiation as replication

comes "the body of Selu," a third person phrase; "watch," a verb in the
present tense, becomes "watched," a verb in the past; and so forth. Systematic projections transform the reported imperative into the described
action.

But there is more to change than systematic projection. There is also,
firstly, random alteration, part of the entropic forces of the universe at
work on culture as it moves through the world. A possible example is in
Figure 4—the transformation of "stay up" into "sit up." In a more perfect
replication we would expect either "stay up" or "sit up" to occur in both
the imperative and the description. Instead, we find one in the former,
the other in the latter. Someone who did not know the significance of the
internal replication—such as an anthropologist recording or translating
the myth, or even a Cherokee youth learning it—might easily introduce
a random change of this sort.[3] Such random alterations constitute errors
in the replication process across tellings, and they reshape the myth over
time. But they are simultaneously errors within a single telling, affecting
the relationship between imperatives and descriptions. Copying errors of
this sort—assuming this is indeed a copying error—must be counteracted
by accelerative force if the cultural element is to conserve its shape over
time.

In addition to random alteration there is also change that holds significance for the plot. Aesthetic tension and interest build around such change, where the fulfillment of the original command is shown to be incomplete. Such a change occurs, in Figure 2, where "a large piece of" is dropped from the description of the behavior. We learn that this change has profound significance. The boys made a mistake. Instead of clearing a "single large piece of" ground, they cleared "only seven little spots." The change is of aesthetic interest because the audience, like the character, could not have readily foreseen its significance. The audience overlooks it just as the character does. How could the boys have known that clearing "only seven little spots" would produce the consequence that "corn now grows only in a few places instead of over the whole world"? The lesson to be learned here is that one must pay careful attention to the command, carrying it out in all of its details and as precisely as possible even if one does not know its significance. The slightest deviation could have monumental consequences.

What, finally, is this pattern of inept or inexact compliance all about? My contention is that, as a piece of traditional Cherokee culture, the pattern focuses attention on the need to carefully listen to and follow commands. The myth, in effect, argues for imperatives as a force that can be used to counteract the dissipation of inertial culture.

Intriguingly, in the case of the "Origin of Game and Corn" myth, the pattern may have accomplished its goal. The evidence suggests that, for a considerable portion of the nineteenth century at least, the myth was successfully transmitted across the generations. Witness Mooney's (1900:431) claim that the "story was obtained in nearly the same form from Swimmer and John Ax (east) and from Wafford (west)," the Eastern and Western Cherokee having been separated since the removal in 1838, and Mooney's field research having taken place between 1887 and 1890.[4]

The myth, though dealing with cosmological problems of change and continuity in its overt plot line and though focusing on the difficulties of replication within its microaesthetic detail, of course had its own problems of historical reproduction. The forces of random change that gnaw away at culture more generally gnaw away at this myth as well. The myth's success in propagating itself may have been due in part to its microdesign features, which reinforce its overt topic. The micro features focus conscious attention on the need for precise copying. In doing so, they supply an accelerative force to the copying of the whole myth itself over time and, hence, impel its physical circulation in the world. They act like a lens, concentrating different spectral lines on a single point—the need for precise replication. In doing so, they help to bring about that replication, and they help to propel the myth through time.

Resisting Commands Can Lead to Newness

Thus far I have focused on the role of imperatives in accelerating culture as a means of maintaining tradition. The pattern in this Cherokee (and also many other Amerindian myths) is one of inexact or inept compliance with imperatives. But there is another pattern in the use of imperatives, this one involving narrative evidence of conscious resistance to them. If, as I have now argued, faithful compliance is necessary to achieve the continuity of traditional culture, what are we to make of the pattern of overt resistance? One clue is that this pattern is especially prominent in contemporary novels, films, and songs. Could the pattern be linked to the nature of movement of these kinds of mass-mediated elements?

As in the case of the "Origin of Game and Corn" myth, my interest is in instances in which the resistance pattern becomes the aesthetic focus of the narrative. There are numerous examples of this, of which I'll pick one: the children's movie *Babe*. The story line centers around a pig named Babe who early in life is orphaned and sold to a farmer named Arthur Hoggett—his human master. Babe is befriended by Fly, a female sheepdog whose children are being taken away from her to be sold. Fly becomes a mother figure for Babe, who refers to her as "Mom." Hoggett, the farmer, gets the idea that the pig can play the role of sheepdog and so in the following excerpt orders Babe to round up the sheep to see whether the pig can handle the task. The pig does and is eventually entered in the sheepdog competition, which it not only wins but achieves the highest marks ever recorded. Babe becomes a historic or world-transforming figure. Here is the transcript of the excerpt:

1. Farmer Hoggett: *Get 'em up pig!*
2. Fly (the sheepdog mother): He wants you to drive them out of the yard.
3. Farmer Hoggett: *Away to me, pig!*
4. Mother/Sheepdog: Remember, you have to dominate them. Do that, and they'll do anything you want. *Go! Go!*
   [The pig runs out to the sheep.]
5. Young pig: Woof, ruff, ruff, ruff (with baaas in the background) . . . Woof, ruff . . . ruff, ruff, ruff, woof (laughter in background, continuous) ruff, ruff, ruff, woof (laughter),
   [The pig returns to the sheepdog.]

6. Young pig: This is ridiculous, mom.

7. Mother/Sheepdog: Nonsense. It's only your first try. But you're treating them like equals. They're sheep. They're inferior.

8. Young pig: Oh no they're not.

9. Mother/Sheepdog: Of course they are. We are their masters, Babe. Let them doubt it for a second and they'll walk all over you.

10. Rex (the sheepdog father): Fly! *Get that pig out of there.*

11. Mother/Sheepdog: *Make them feel inferior!*

12. *Abuse them.*

13. *Insult them.*

14. Father/Sheepdog: Fly!

15. Young pig: They'll laugh at me.

16. Mother/Sheepdog: *Then bite them!*

17. *Be ruthless!*

18. *Whatever it takes, bend them to your will!*

19. Father/Sheepdog: Enough!

20. Mother/Sheepdog: *Go on! Go!*

[The pig goes back out to the sheep.]

21. Young pig: *Move along there ya, ya uh big buttheads!*

22. Sheep: laughter

[The pig bites one of the sheep on the leg.]

23. Female Sheep: *Young one, stop this nonsense!* What's got into you all of a sudden? I just got finished tellin what a nice young pig you been.

24. Young pig: Ma, I was just trying to be a sheepdog.

25. Female sheep: Huh! Enough wolves in the world already, without a nice lad like you turnin nasty. Ya haven't got it in ya, young 'un.

26. _____

27. Father/Sheepdog: You and I are descended from the great sheepdogs. We carry the bloodline of an ancient bahu. We stand for something. And today I watched in shame as all that was betrayed.

28. Mother/Sheepdog: Rex, dear. He's just a little pig.

29. Father/Sheepdog: All the greater the insult!

30. _____

31. Young pig: I'm sorry I bit you. Are you alright?

32. Female sheep: Well, I wouldn't call that a bite, myself. You got teeth in that floppy mouth of yours, or just gums?

33. Young pig and sheep: (laughter)

34. Female sheep: Ya see ladies, a heart of gold.

35. Chorus of sheep: A heart of gold.

36. Female sheep: No need for all this wolf nonsense, young 'un. All a nice little pig like you need do is ask.

37. Young pig: Thanks very much. It was very kind of you.

38. Sheep: A pleasure.

39. Another sheep: What a nice little pig!

40. _____

41. Mother/Sheepdog: Alright, how did you do it?

42. Young pig: I asked them and they did it. I just asked them nicely.

43. Mother/Sheepdog: Now we don't ask sheep, dear; we tell them what to do.

44. Young pig: But I did, mom. They were really friendly. Maybe Rex might, ya know, be a little more friendly if I had a talk with him.

45. Mother/Sheepdog: No, no, no. I think you better leave that to me.

This excerpt is complicated in terms of commands. We have the human master issuing commands to the pig (lines 1 and 3), the mother sheepdog commanding the pig (lines 4, 11–13, 16–18, 20), the father sheepdog commanding the mother sheepdog (line 10), the pig commanding the sheep (line 21), and the sheep issuing a command back to the pig (line 23).

There are interesting parallels between the scene and the "Origin of Corn and Game" myth. Both focus on an adopted child—the Wild Boy, in the Cherokee myth and the orphaned pig in the case of "Babe." In each the mother-child relation figures centrally. Moreover, in each there are key transformations in the nature of the social relationships.

However, there is a salient difference with respect to the problem of replication. Whereas the boys in the Cherokee myth follow their mother's commands without any explicitly narrativized evidence of resistance, the pig exhibits conflict over the imperatives issued by the mother. It is not that the pig does not attempt to fulfill the commands. He does. In this episode's turning point, the mother tells the pig: "abuse them, insult them." And the pig later says to the sheep: "Move along there ya, ya uh big buttheads!" The mother tells the pig: "bite them!" And we later see the pig biting the sheep on the leg.

Yet there is something importantly different here vis-à-vis the myth. The pig's obeying is reluctant and conflicted, and that reluctance is narrativized. After his initial attempt to comply with his mother's command, he tells her, "This is ridiculous, mom," calling her authority into question. She reasserts the correctness of her position, saying: "Nonsense. It's only your first try. But you're treating them like equals. They're sheep. They're inferior." The pig argues back, in dialogic fashion: "Oh no they're not."

This kind of back-and-forth argument is completely absent from the myth, where commands are executed matter of factly, even if the execution is bungled.

A good example of this difference—which gives an entirely distinct feel to the narrative—can be found in two different tellings of the story of Abraham from the Old Testament (Genesis 22). The first is from the King James Version:

> 1 And it came to pass after these things, that God did tempt Abraham, and said unto him, Abraham: and he said, Behold, [here] I [am].
>
> 2 And he said, Take now thy son, thine only [son] Isaac, whom thou lovest, and get thee into the land of Moriah; and offer him there for a burnt offering upon one of the mountains which I will tell thee of.
>
> 3 And Abraham rose up early in the morning, and saddled his ass, and took two of his young men with him, and Isaac his son, and clave the wood for the burnt offering, and rose up, and went unto the place of which God had told him.

Here Abraham complies unhesitatingly with God's command. Compare this with Bob Dylan's sung version in "Highway 61 Revisited":

> Oh God said to Abraham, "Kill me a son"
> Abe says, "Man, you must be puttin' me on"
> God say, "No." Abe say, "What?"
> God say, "You can do what you want Abe, but
> The next time you see me comin' you better run"
> Well Abe says, "Where do you want this killin' done?"
> God says, "Out on Highway 61."

What to make of this difference? I want to argue that the resistance, apparent in *Babe*, in "Highway 61 Revisited," and in numerous other contemporary cultural expressions in which imperatives become the aesthetic focus of narration, has to do with the transmission of culture. However, it has to do with a distinctive version of the transmission of culture—one associated with modernity and with the mass mediation of culture through print, magnetic recordings, television, and similar vectors of culture. The resistance exhibited here is really a manifestation of the way cultural replication works in the contemporary United States and, perhaps increasingly, elsewhere.

This may seem paradoxical. On the surface, resistance to commands would seem to be resistance to the transmission of culture if my earlier observations about the Cherokee myth are correct. In that case I argued that the myth contained an implicit moral—you should follow the semantic content of commands as precisely as possible. If you do, good consequences follow; if you do not, the result will be negative. If there were an analogous moral in the case of *Babe* it would be: if you do what you know inside of you to be right, rather than just listen to others, then good consequences will follow. Finding the right inside of oneself is a hallmark of the "modern" individual. Correspondingly, blindly obeying the commands of others is anathema. Hence, Dylan's Abe strikes a contemporary listener as more real than the biblical Abraham. He acts the way a modern individual would and should—with horror at the thought of sacrificing his own son. He, initially at least, resists God's command.

The problem is: how can this finding of right inside of oneself be cultural transmission? It seems the opposite of transmission. The idea of an internal moral compass is opposed to the idea of commands that come from without. You cannot blindly obey the commands of others, but rather must carefully weigh them and decide what is right. Your conduct is determined by your decision, not by the imperatives issuing from another. Babe resists his "mother" Fly. Fly resists her husband Rex. The sheep resist Babe. Where is the cultural transmission in this?

A first observation is that Babe, while resisting the details of Fly's command, in fact endeavors to do what Fly and Hoggett, the human master, want: he gets the sheep to file in orderly fashion out of the yard. Moreover, in the long run, Babe effectively exerts more control over the sheep than Fly or Rex had. Indeed, as the story approaches its climax, we learn that Hoggett has entered Babe in the sheepdog competition, and we later see how, through cooperation, Babe not only wins the sheepdog contest but receives the only perfect score in the history of the competition. Babe—a little pig—becomes, in effect, the best "sheepdog" that ever lived.

On the one hand, Babe resists the culture that Fly endeavors to transmit to him. On the other hand, he grasps the purpose or objective of that culture and comes up with a better way of achieving the end. Babe is thus a reshaper or accelerator of culture. It is not that Babe, as an individual, does something that falls outside the orbit of culture in some kind of naturalistic realm. What he does is take an existing piece of culture and refashion it into something new, something better. Culture flows through him, but it is shaped by him in the course of that flow.

Babe not only works with the culture that was transmitted to him by his "mother" Fly. He also works with the culture that has been passed down among the sheep and that he has acquired by virtue of his friendship with one of the sheep, Ma. This is the one who, in line 23, tells him: "stop this nonsense! What's got into you all of a sudden? I just got finished tellin what a nice young pig you been." Babe explains (line 24) that he was trying to acquire the culture of the sheepdogs: "Ma, I was just trying to be a sheepdog." Ma—apparently a second mother figure for Babe—then attempts to summon the culture of the sheep that Babe has gotten, presumably, from her: "Huh! Enough wolves in the world already, without a nice lad like you turnin nasty. Ya haven't got it in ya, young 'un."

Babe's achievement, therefore, depends upon the synthesis of two different lines of culture, two different ways of doing things in the world: the culture of the sheepdog and the culture of the sheep themselves. As if to drive home this point, we later see that Babe's success at the sheepdog competition depends on something he acquires from the sheep—a secret password. The sheep at the competition are not the same ones that Babe has been dealing with on the farm. Consequently, they act indifferently to him, despite his attempts to be friendly. Initially, at least, they only pay attention to Fly. Realizing the problem, Fly sends Rex back to the farm to learn the password from the sheep there. He then tells it to Babe, who uses it to get the sheep to comply with his commands—which are stated as requests rather than overt imperatives. Hence, Babe acquires a tangible piece of sheep culture that makes his sheepdoggish control possible. The secret of his success is his fusion of distinct strands of culture. The fusion results in the acceleration or change of the culture itself. The result is a new and improved culture—a better system of control.

Of course, it is the case also that the sheepdog culture and the sheep culture are both deflected from their normal course when they are transmitted to Babe, who synthesizes them. And it is not Babe who is solely responsible for this deflection. The farmer Hoggett, Babe's human master, is the one who originally gets the idea that Babe might be able to perform the work of a sheepdog. He says to Babe (line 1): "Get 'em up Pig!" But the deflection would not be possible either without Fly's encouragement. She translates the initial command to Babe and encourages him to carry it out. This deflection is one of the key precipitating factors behind the synthesis. Nor would the synthesis be possible without the firm assertion of sheep culture that Ma issues. Though Babe is a conduit for these two strands of culture, both deflected from their normal course, and though the synthesis takes place through him, one can hardly say that his distinctive "achievement" is the result of characteristics that he uniquely possesses as an individual. The power that Babe ultimately wields is a power that results from the flow of different strands of culture through him; indeed, it is the power *of* those strands as they came into conflict in specific social situations. The power, in this sense, emanates from the movement of culture and, indeed, is nothing other than the movement of that culture—the movement of distinct strands that come into conflict and then, as a result of that conflict, fuse into a new kind of culture. Modernity—to make this claim baldly—is the celebration of such fusions.

Resistance Can Occur in Oral Narrative

In the previous section I suggested that the resistance pattern may be linked to a "modern" idea of cultural transmission, in which the ideal is not precise replication of a prior element (such as a myth) taken as a unit of culture, but rather the synthesis of distinct strands that result from the challenging of prior elements, or the attempt to produce elements that are "better." I have linked this to the phenomenon of mass mediation, where durable physical materials—books, videos, CDs—make it possible for discourse to be disseminated without necessarily being replicated. This is fundamentally unlike oral transmission, where dissemination—getting the message out—depends upon replication. In order for other people to get exposure to a myth, the myth must be retold, re-created, in short, replicated. In order for other people to get exposure to a video, however, it is not necessary for one to redo the entire video. On the other hand, for the social learning that went into the making of that video to be passed on, that is, replicated, dissemination is not sufficient. The test of replication of a video is the production of a "new" video. This pattern of cultural movement—based on the production of something putatively "new"—is analogous to the pattern of resistance in narrative, where the straightforward replication of the imperative is called into question in the description.

This raises one question: Is the resistance pattern a direct function of the channel of transmission, oral versus electronic, for example? As evidence that it is not, I present the narrativization of an actual incident that involved the author of this chapter and the honoree of this volume, my esteemed mentor Ray Fogelson. I began sharing this narrative with others almost immediately after the event it describes occurred, somewhere back in the late 1970s. I have told the story orally to generations of graduate students, who now carry on—in what measure I am uncertain—the culture passed down to me from Ray Fogelson. The narrative was finally written up in 1996, in preparation for an American Anthropological Association presentation that formed part of a session honoring Ray. It is not unsullied by mass media, since I did commit it to writing, but this version was meant to be heard and is as close to the previous oral versions as I could make it. Here is the narrative:

> I was a graduate student at the University of Chicago, just back from the field, looking for a job, and giving my first talk at a professional meeting. I had the good fortune to have Ray Fogelson as my adviser, and he actually let me stay in his hotel room, so that I wouldn't have to pay for the hotel bill.
>
> Well, Ray was at that time a party animal—I'm not sure, of course, that there was ever a time when he was not a party animal. In any case, he was out until about 4:00 or 4:30 a.m., and I had to deliver my paper at an 8:00 a.m. session. So I got up at 6:30 a.m., showered, and was about to walk out the door when I heard this voice say: "*read me your paper!*"
>
> I said, "*shhh, Ray, go back to sleep.*" But he insisted: "*read me your paper!*" I thought, "this is ridiculous." But he was my professor, after all. So I got my paper out of my briefcase, turned on the light, and started to read. Then I heard this voice from the bed say: "that's terrible."
>
> Ray switched on the light by his bed, put on his glasses, picked up a newspaper, and started to read the first thing he saw. "This is what you sound like," and he read in a boring monotone: "apples are fifty cents, but oranges are forty cents. Now here's what it should sound like: APPles are FIFTY cents, BUT, ORANGes are FORTY cents."
>
> Well, I started in on my paper again, and Ray said, "that's a little better." Before you know it, he was snoring, but when I tried to sneak out, he said: "*finish it!*" And I did. And my paper went infinitely better as a result.

I don't know how many times I've told this story. However, it was a "new story"; I narrated it for the first time back in the late 1970s. As such, it was not the retelling of an ancient tradition.

The pattern of resistance is patent: "I heard this voice say: 'read me your paper!' " This could be Dylan: "Oh God said to Abraham, 'Kill me a son.' " Indeed, my response: "shhh, Ray, go back to sleep!" parallels Abe's: "Man, you must be puttin' me on." Ray persists—as, note, did Fly after Babe's initial resistance. He reiterates his command, in response to which I think but don't say: "This is ridiculous." These are the same words actually spoken by Babe, who, however, appended a kinship address term: "This is ridiculous, mom."

My point is not that this narrative instantiates the film *Babe*, or even the vignette from "Highway 61 Revisited." It is that the pattern of resistance found in these mass-mediated narratives also occurs in what was an oral narrative. Of course, it is an oral narrative spun out in a community saturated with mass-mediated narratives, and such narratives may have been the originals from which my specific production was copied—that is, from which the resistance pattern was copied. But the point is that the relationship between medium and rhetorical pattern is not direct and simple. We are dealing with a cultural pattern, or metacultural pattern— resistance to commands—that is compatible with mass-mediated cultural replication and its attendant idea of "modernity," but not a simple reflex of those media themselves.

Resistance to Commands May Be "Rational"

In his paradigm-fixing account of legitimate domination or authority, Max Weber (1978[1925]:215) distinguished three bases on which persons might be granted authority by others: the charisma of the commander, tradition, and rationality. The pattern of inept compliance discussed earlier obviously correlates, in some measure, with Weber's traditional grounds: "an established belief in the sanctity of immemorial traditions and the legitimacy of those exercising authority under them." But the connection between the resistance pattern and Weber's rational grounds ("a belief in the legality of enacted rules and the right of those elevated to authority under such rules to issue commands") is not obvious. Indeed, a microdiscursive account of resistance suggests a different way of thinking about the relationship between rationality and command.

An important point to note in regard to the aesthetically foregrounded resistance pattern is that resistance does not equal rejection of the command. Indeed, in each of the examples discussed in this chapter, the addressee of the imperative attempts to carry out the command. This is obviously true of the boys in the Cherokee myth, but it is also true of Babe, who indeed succeeds in complying with farmer Hoggett's initial command beyond Hoggett's wildest dreams. It is even true of Dylan's rendition of the story of Abraham, and also of the Fogelson story. These are stories about *complying* with commands. Resistance may involve rejecting a command, but this is not its essence, only a possible consequence of its nature.

From a microdiscursive point of view, resistance is manifested first and foremost by a questioning of the initial command. The questioning can be overtly stated in the narrative by the person commanded, or it can be revealed to the audience by the narrator. When Fly, the mother sheepdog, says to Babe: "Remember, you have to dominate them. Do that, and they'll do anything you want. Go! Go!", Babe, after his initial failed effort, says:

"This is ridiculous, mom." When Dylan's God says to Abraham: "Kill me a son," Abraham responds: "Man, you must be puttin' me on." When Ray Fogelson says to me: "Read me your paper!", I respond: "Shhh, Ray, go back to sleep!" and I think (thereby revealing to my audience): "This is ridiculous."

What is happening here is that the imperative, rather than being simply replicated in the description of the subsequent action, is *responded* to. The response pattern makes compliance something other than knee-jerk. It makes it the negotiated outcome of a dialogical interaction. It is this dialogical negotiation of the initial command—where the response could be internal (to the audience) rather than external—that is the hallmark, or so I want to claim, of a rational grounding of authority. Dialogical response to imperatives is as or more important than a belief in the legality of enacted rules, although legality is no doubt, as Habermas argues (1989[1962]:57–88), a consequence of the negotiation of imperatives.

At the same time, I believe that the microdiscursive pattern does reflect what Weber had in mind when dubbing this form of authority "rational."[5] From a microdiscursive perspective, the response to the imperative is narratively problematized. The initial command is subjected to doubt but *not rejection*. The person commanded appreciates the authority of the command-giver but cannot, for various reasons, simply carry out the command. The doubt places the initial command in a discursive relationship to other factors, including other imperatives. The persons commanded may, after scrutiny of the command, simply comply with it. Or their behavior may constitute partial compliance. Or, again, it may signal their rejection of the command. What is important to the phenomenon, understood as a pattern within narratives, is that the discursive pathway to the behavior is complicated and that the initial imperative is, along the way, subjected to scrutiny. Compliance is rational because discursive ratiocination intervenes between the imperative and the description of the subsequent behavior.

From the point of view of a theory of cultural motion under modernity the accordioning out of the relationship between imperative and description makes sense. If the inept compliance pattern brings into crisp focus the need for careful replication, the resistance pattern zooms in on the need to contextualize and scrutinize the initial cultural element, with the behavior then produced being something new—the output of that scrutiny or weighing. Even where the ensuing behavior is, apparently, straightforward compliance with the initial command, the description of the compliance is only distantly related, and via complex transformations, to the initial imperative. In the case of Dylan's Abraham, the only trace of "Kill me a son" is the recurrence of "*kill*" in the second to last line: "Well Abe says, 'Where do you want this *killin'* done?' " Note that "kill" here appears not as a description of behavior but as part of reported speech: these are Abe's words. Furthermore, the reported speech is in the form of a question back to God, and hence is part of a continuing negotiation of the original imperative. It is not a description of the actual behavior.

The biblical story of Abraham is intriguing in this regard. It does not show the pattern of inept compliance found in the Cherokee case. But, at the same time, we do see there evidence of a similar almost word-for-word replication of the imperative in its description, as shown in Figure 5.

A new factor that is prominent here, however, is paraphrase. Parts of the initial command are fulfilled, in the narrative, not by a simple replication of the words taken from the imperative but instead by an elaborate paraphrase. Thus, the command "get thee into the land of Moriah" is followed by the description "went unto the place of which God had told him." "Moriah" becomes "the place of which God had told him," and, indeed, the name Moriah is never repeated in this entire story. In such paraphrase we do not find the simultaneous copying of meaning and linguistic material that is characteristic of replication in the Cherokee case. A chasm opens here between meaning and behavior that is not resolved at the level of narrative by word-for-word replication. Hence, the narrative does not allow us to see imperatives as part of the replication of culture. Perhaps paraphrase, in this regard, is closer to response and represents an incipient form of analysis of the initial imperative, along the lines that Voloshinov (1986[1929]:115–123; see also Bakhtin 1984) has suggested for discourse more generally. Imperatives in this case appear to partake of that mysterious transubstantiation process with which this chapter began. Even at the level of narrative the words of the imperative become something else: the words of the paraphrase.

In any case, the response pattern more generally problematizes the relationship between imperatives and the motion of culture, suggesting that cultural replication may be an inadequate way to think of cultural movement in this case. Instead, we are forced to construe cultural elements as decomposable into parts or strands. Confronted with a cultural element, modern recipients of culture do not (or do not in this ideal world of narratives) simply replicate the element. Instead, they place it in relation to others, take strands from one and intertwine them with strands from others, thus weaving something that, although a continuation of what has come before, is also arguably something new and different, as in the case of Babe's transformation of the form of leadership of sheep. The sheep are still being led, but they are being led now in a new way.

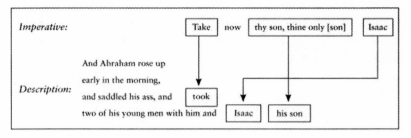

Figure 5. Replication in the Biblical story of Abraham

Power Is the Acceleration of Culture

By now it is obvious that, from the point of view of a theory of cultural movement, tradition is far from simply inertial. It requires the infusion of accelerative force to propel it forward in time, overcoming dissipative forces at work on it. Perhaps it is not as obvious that the kind of movement I have just described—movement under modernity, connected with a pattern of resistance to imperatives within narrative, and an emphasis on the production of new cultural elements—generates its own problems of movement that require accelerative force.

What kinds of problems? To answer that question, we need to look at what is peculiar about the motion of culture in modernity. What is peculiar is that the processes of dissemination and replication have become, relatively speaking, disentangled. In the case of oral transmission, the dissemination of culture depends upon its replication. For a cultural element such as a myth to get from one individual (or group) A to B and from B to C, A must tell the myth to B (dissemination), but then B must retell it to C (replication). The movement from A to C depends upon replication in a direct way.

In the case of modern mass-mediated culture, however, A could get a book or video or CD to C without the intermediation of B as replicator. Mass media offer the possibility of broader dissemination and of greater temporal durability of the element. But, at the same time—and this is one problem created by the nature of modern cultural movement—the production, and hence also reproduction, of social learning has become more difficult. If someone has already written a book there is no need for another individual to write that same identical book—pace the Borges story ("Pierre Menard, Author of *Quixote*") in which an author wishes to write the already-written book *Don Quixote*. Hence, there is no need for precise word-for-word replication. The fact that the book has already been written and is publicly accessible obviates this need.

Correspondingly, the replication of the social learning that went into writing that book becomes difficult. True, great effort must be expended to learn something in word-for-word fashion. But one does not have to invent a new combination of words that has the grabbing power of the old one. The benefit of the word-for-word replication is that small changes can be made over years and even centuries, so that there is gradual accretion of artistic input. In writing a new book, one must create a new and different combination that is equally as compelling as the old one and that contains within it all the artifice of generations without precisely duplicating that artifice. How can culture stimulate its own reproduction under these circumstances?

Culture's answer to this challenge is a metacultural emphasis on modernity, on the new. Such an emphasis counteracts the tendency of social learning to fade out because of the ease of dissemination. In some sense, this is the opposite of the case of myth. There, dissemination depends upon replication; hence, to ensure dissemination of culture one must ensure its precise replication. In the case of modern mass mediation, dissemination is easy—at least, it is easy to ensure that the cultural element as a physical thing has such durability in the world that it can be inspected by others after its producer is gone. But the reproduction of the social learning deposited in mass-mediated cultural elements is difficult. Since that reproduction depends on the production of a putatively "new" element—a new book or new video or new CD—to ensure the transmission of the old social learning one must place a premium on newness. The metacultural ideology of newness thus itself imparts an accelerative force to culture, ensuring replication where that replication might not otherwise take place.

The pattern of resistance to imperatives embodies this metacultural privileging of newness. The imperatives, like the whole cultural elements of which they form part, are not simply reproduced in the ensuing behavior. Instead, they are scrutinized, weighed against other factors, dialogically engaged. The outcome may be—indeed, typically is—compatible with the initial imperative, but that outcome does not appear as the simple reflex of the initial imperative. In just this way does the "new" cultural element, under modernity, fail to appear as the simple copy of any one earlier element. Rather, various elements, various factors have gone into it.

Increased difficulty of replication is not the only problem engendered by the nature of modern cultural movement. There is also a problem of competition among elements, which makes dissemination itself, at least in one sense, problematic. Because the elements are durable and because they are constantly being produced, it becomes difficult for any one element to gain the attention of individuals who would view it or listen to it or touch it. The element is out there in the perceptible world as a thing that could be paid attention to. But if the attention of individuals is otherwise occupied, how can the element surface?

Two answers to this question suggest themselves. One view gives priority to the social pathways of dissemination. The ability of an element to surface into the attention of individuals is a product of its social positioning. An established film producer makes an uninteresting film that nevertheless gets out there. It circulates. This happens because of the producer's access to the pathways and networks of circulation. Correspondingly, an unestablished filmmaker produces what would be an interesting film but cannot get it disseminated.

This view tends to construe the social networks as independent of the elements that circulate within them. But the problem of attention cannot be purely a mechanical one, since individuals could, presumably, opt out of a given network and into another. Even if they were presented with a cultural element by virtue of their participation in a network, that element would not necessarily grab or hold their attention. And if only elements of that nature were disseminated the network itself would break down. Some uninteresting elements can pass by, living off the reputation of the others, but uninteresting elements cannot be the only ones in circulation.

This would suggest that one look for the motive or attractive force within the elements themselves. Roman Jakobson (1960), following on the work of members of the Prague School, has argued that parallelism in discourse—the formal basis of the poetic function—serves to make the discourse of which it is part salient. Parallelism calls attention to itself and hence also to the broader discourse of which it is part. It says, in effect: "Look at me." Might not this aspect of the cultural element be responsible for effecting its own dissemination? Indeed, the replication I have demonstrated in the inept compliance pattern conforms to this expectation. The description of the compliance behavior looks like the imperative from which it stems.

However, and in contrast, the resistance pattern is not grounded so much in this kind of direct, highly salient reprising. There is a key difference here with respect to inept compliance, where the characters unthinkingly and unhesitatingly try to carry out the command but bungle the task. In the resistance pattern, the imperatives—like the whole cultural elements themselves—must be scrutinized, weighed against other factors, dialogically engaged. The description of the outcome bears traces of the initial imperative, in greater or lesser measure, and hence the description does contain parallelism, but the parallelism is not nearly as salient as in the other case.

Given the considerable differences between the two patterns, can it be the pattern alone—apart from the social network in which the pattern circulates—that supplies the motive force, effecting dissemination by a kind of bootstrapping? The empirical question might be posed this way: could the resistance pattern be plucked from its social context, plopped down in a new social context in which the pattern has not before appeared—say, an Amerindian village in Brazil—and immediately attract attention?

What is critical about this pattern, or so it seems to me, is that it models the processes of cultural movement within the very context of which it is part. There is a recognition of aptness to the immediate social situation of which the element forms part. The Dylan version of the story of Abraham sounds contemporary. Dylan's Abe fits into the social networks in which the song circulates. In this sense, self-reflexive modeling of the social processes of circulation in which the cultural element itself moves is one key to the success of the pattern.

If I am correct, the two patterns of imperative usage I have described are really instructions: they tell those who behold them what to do with the discourse of which they are part. In the case of inept compliance, the pattern instructs a listener to precisely replicate the myth of which it is part. In the case of resistance the admonition is: produce a new piece of discourse that takes account, in some fashion, of the existing one.

But granted that such instructions are embedded in discourse, why should people follow them? The analogous question arises (and arose earlier in this chapter) in connection with imperatives themselves: why do people respond to imperatives the way the do? Imperatives work the way they do, or so I have argued, because of the models for how to respond to them that are contained in prior discourse. The resistance pattern cannot work immediately if it is plopped into a social context where that pattern has not previously existed. The cultural element may be interesting to the people who behold it, but the instruction does not take hold as efficacious—reshaping the expectations about proper responses to imperatives—until a sufficient history of occurrences of the pattern has developed. That history, of course, is a strand of culture. The efficacy of the instruction depends upon its position within such a strand, its relation to prior instances of the pattern.

Do we have here a chicken-and-egg problem? For an implicit or explicit instruction about cultural replication to be efficacious in one instance the instruction must resonate with prior instances. But then how can such instructions, or imperatives for that matter, really accomplish anything genuinely new? And is not newness, after all, the hallmark of imperatives?

My answer is that the instruction, as well as the imperative, is never wholly new; it is not something created ex nihilo. The accelerative forces I have been describing are changing or modifying or deflecting forces. They reshape an existing cultural element or course of movement, but they do not create something that bears no traces of what has come before it. This is obvious in the case of the Cherokee pattern, where the instruction is at the service of maintaining a tradition in the face of dissipation—newness here means overcoming the decay of something old and, hence, preserving that old thing. However, and less obviously, it is also true in the case of the resistance pattern, where the instruction is to produce something new but something that simultaneously reprises the old. The pattern is compatible with mass-mediated cultural circulation, where cultural elements have temporal longevity but are difficult to replicate. The instruction gives a boost to the replication process and, hence, actually preserves old cultural learning.

What light does all this shed finally on the nature of power? If, following the resistance pattern, I dialogically engage the view of power as first and foremost about social relations, my retort—recall Babe's "This is ridiculous, mom"—is that power is first and foremost about the mysteries of the motion of culture. Indeed, power is nothing other than that which accounts for extra-inertial cultural movement: the acceleration, reshaping, and deflecting of culture as it passes through individuals, making its way across space and over time. Such a view allows the study of culture to takes its proper place alongside the study of motion more generally, from the awe-inspiring spectacle of heavenly bodies in cosmic motion to the microscopic reduplication of DNA molecules, whose accumulated information thereby makes its way through the universe.

Notes

A portion of this chapter appeared as chapter 4, entitled "This Is Ridiculous," in Urban (2001a), *Metaculture: How Culture Moves Through the World*, although the general argument is framed differently there. A related article but using different empirical material and focusing on the aesthetics of imperative usage is Urban (2001b), "The Proto-Aesthetics of Imperatives."

1. I use the term *imperative* here to highlight linguistic form. Imperatives are grammatically describable linguistic expressions that signal themselves as devices for telling someone to do something, rather than, for example, as devices for communicating information. The term *command*, in contrast, draws attention to function, to what it is that A is trying to get B to do. Of course, imperatives may serve functions other than commanding, and commands may be expressed through linguistic forms other than imperatives (see Ervin-Tripp 1972, 1976). However, I am especially concerned in this paper with situations in which there is a confluence between the two, with imperatives that are used functionally in grammatical

terms to express commands. Hence, my particular choice of the term *imperative* versus *command* at any given moment in this chapter is a matter of relative emphasis.

2. Fogelson (1977b), for example, following on J. N. B. Hewitt's (1902:32–46) influential explication of the Iroquois concept of *orenda*, examines a Cherokee term related to power, *ulanigugu*, which, however, he finds "somewhat amorphous" (186). Nevertheless, he is able to cull an implicit understanding of "power" from traditional (i.e., inertial) Cherokee magical practices.

3. This particular story was obtained by Mooney "in nearly the same form from Swimmer and John Ax (east) and from Wafford (west)" (Mooney 1900:431), which suggests that Mooney may have compiled this version from several others. He could have been the source of the change, or the change could have been introduced by the translator(s) (Chief N. J. Smith or someone in his family—see Mooney 1900:13), or, again, by an editor.

4. The energy concentrated on replicating the myth was harnessed in part also by ritual; the myth was "held so sacred that in the old days one who wished to hear it from the priest of the tradition must first purify himself by 'going to water,' i.e., bathing in the running stream before daylight when still fasting, while the priest performed his mystic ceremonies upon the bank" (Mooney 1900:431).

5. Although this kind of rationality is perhaps more akin to what Habermas (1984, 1987) calls "communicative rationality."

References

Asch, Timothy, and Napoleon Chagnon, dirs.
    1970 The Feast. 29 min. documentary. Available through Penn State Audio-Visual Services, Pennsylvania State University, University Park PA.
Bakhtin, Mikhail
    1984 Problems of Dostoevsky's Poetics. C. Emerson, trans. Minneapolis: University of Minnesota Press.
Bean, Lowell John
    1977 Power and Its Application in Native California. In The Anthropology of Power. Raymond D. Fogelson and Richard N. Adams, eds. Pp. 117–129. New York: Academic Press.
Black, Mary B.
    1977 Ojibwa Power Belief System. In The Anthropology of Power. Raymond D. Fogelson and Richard N. Adams, eds. Pp. 141–151. New York: Academic Press.
Chagnon, Napoleon A.
    1992[1968] Yanomamö. New York: Harcourt Brace College Publishers.
DeMallie, Raymond J., and Lavenda, Robert H.
    1977 Wakan: Plains Siouan Concepts of Power. In The Anthropology of Power. Raymond D. Fogelson and Richard N. Adams, eds. Pp. 153–165. New York: Academic Press.
Ervin-Tripp, Susan
    1972 On Sociolinguistic Rules: Alternation and Co-occurrence. In Directions in Sociolinguistics: The Ethnography of Communication. J. J. Gumperz and D. Hymes, eds. Pp. 213–250. New York: Henry Holt.
    1976 Is Sybil There? The Structure of American English Directives. Language in Society 5:25–66.

Fogelson, Raymond D.

    1977 Cherokee Notions of Power. *In* The Anthropology of Power. Raymond D. Fogelson and Richard N. Adams, eds. Pp. 185–194. New York: Academic Press.

Fogelson, Raymond D., and Richard N. Adams, eds.

    1977 The Anthropology of Power: Ethnographic Studies from Asia, Oceania, and the New World. New York: Academic Press.

Habermas, Jürgen

    1984 The Theory of Communicative Action, vol. 1: Reason and the Rationalization of Society. T. McCarthy, trans. Boston: Beacon Press.

    1987 The Theory of Communicative Action, vol. 2: Lifeworld and System: A Critique of Functionalist Reasoning. T. McCarthy, trans. Boston: Beacon Press.

    1989[1962] The Structural Transformation of the Public Sphere: An Inquiry into a Category of Bourgeois Society. T. Burger, trans. Cambridge MA: MIT Press.

Hewitt, J. N. B.

    1902 Orenda and a Definition of Religion. American Anthropologist 4:33–46.

Issacs, Hope

    1977 Orenda and the Concept of Power among the Tonawanda Seneca. *In* The Anthropology of Power. Raymond D. Fogelson and Richard N. Adams, eds. Pp. 167–184. New York: Academic Press.

Jakobson, Roman

    1960 Linguistics and Poetics. *In* Style in Language. T. Sebeok, ed. Pp. 350–377. Cambridge MA: MIT Press.

Lane, Robert B.

    1977 "Power Concepts in Melanesia and Northwestern North America." *In* The Anthropology of Power. Raymond D. Fogelson and Richard N. Adams, eds. Pp. 365–374. New York: Academic Press.

Lee, Benjamin

    1997 Talking Heads: Languages, Metalanguage, and the Semiotics of Subjectivity. Durham NC: Duke University Press.

Lucy, John A., ed.

    1993 Reflexive Language. Cambridge: Cambridge University Press.

Mackenzie, Margaret

    1977 Mana in Maori Medicine—Rarotonga, Oceania. *In* The Anthropology of Power. Raymond D. Fogelson and Richard N. Adams, eds. Pp. 45–56. New York: Academic Press.

Mooney, James

    1900 Myths of the Cherokee. *In* Nineteenth Annual Report of the Bureau of American Ethnology, Part I. pp. 1–576. Washington DC: Government Printing Office.

Pandey, Triloki Nath

    1977 "Images of Power in a Southwestern Pueblo." *In* The Anthropology of Power. Raymond D. Fogelson and Richard N. Adams, eds. Pp. 195–215. New York: Academic Press.

Stross, Brian

    1977 Tzeltal Conceptions of Power. *In* The Anthropology of Power. Raymond D. Fogelson and Richard N. Adams, eds. Pp. 271–285. New York: Academic Press.

Urban, Greg

    1996 Metaphysical Community: The Interplay of the Senses and the Intellect. Austin: University of Texas Press.

2001a Metaculture: How Culture Moves through the World. Minneapolis: University of Minnesota Press.

2001b The Proto-Aesthetics of Imperatives. *In* Verbal Art across Cultures: The Aesthetics and Proto-Aesthetics of Communication. Hubert Knoblauch and Helga Kotthoff, eds. Pp. 223–236. Tübingen: Gunter Narr Verlag.

Voloshinov, V. N.

1986[1929] Marxism and the Philosophy of Language. L. Matejka and I. R. Titunik, trans. Cambridge MA: Harvard University Press.

Weber, Max

1978[1925] Economy and Society: An Outline of Interpretive Sociology. G. Roth and C. Wittich, eds. Berkeley: University of California Press.

5. Ironies of Articulating Continuity at Lac du Flambeau

LARRY NESPER

Introduction

To account for the "Walleye War" between the Lac du Flambeau band of Lake Superior Chippewa Indians and organized groups of non-Indians opposed to treaties in northern Wisconsin in the 1980s we must undertake a certain kind of archaeology of cultural dispositions. I will argue here that although the reservation moved rapidly from obscurity to the front pages of the nation's newspapers during that decade there are far more sociocultural and historical continuities than discontinuities.

In 1983 the Seventh Circuit Court of Appeal in Chicago surprised everyone when it reversed a district court decision and found all of the Chippewa bands' off-reservation hunting, fishing, and gathering rights (originally reserved in the mid-1900s in treaties ceding lands to the federal government) to be good law. Those lands had become northern Wisconsin, the upper peninsula of Michigan, and northeastern Minnesota. The three states had been infringing on the Indians' rights for more than a century by undertaking projects of self-definition that marginalized the Indian communities legally, politically, economically, and socially. By the last quarter of the twentieth century, off-reservation usufruct rights did not exist de jure, though they were surreptitiously exercised, often nocturnally, and were justified by ongoing Indian legal resistance projects that had significant consequences.

Spearfishing, Culture, and Conflict

The Lac du Flambeau people have deeply identified with night hunting and fishing for about two and a half centuries. François Mahliot traded at "Lac au Flambeau" in 1805–6, as he recorded it in the journal required by his employers, the Northwest Company. His is the first published reference to what would subsequently be translated "Torch Lake" (Mahliot 1910). In William Whipple Warren's history, written in the winter of 1852–53 based on conversations he had in the late 1840s, the bilingual, mixed-blood historian offers 1745 as the approximate date for the establishment of permanent villages in the region of Wisconsin that had formerly been Dakota and Fox territory. Furthermore, he adds:

> The French early designated that portion of the tribe who occupied the head-waters of the Wisconsin, as the Lac du Flambeau band, from the circumstance of their locating their central village or summer residence, at the lake known by this name. The Ojibways term it Waus-wag-im-ing (Lake of Torches), from the custom of spearing fish by torch-light, early practiced by the hunters of their tribe who first took possession of it. [1985(1885):190]

Though the practice of spearing fish was widespread (the only areas of the continent where fish were not speared were the Great Plains and the Great Basin [Rostlund 1952:293]), the practice of spearing at night may have been coterminus with the Algonquians' residence in the area. The first description of this practice in the published North American literature is by Paul Le Jeune (1897:311) in his "Relation of What Occurred in New France in the Year 1634." He writes about Algonquian people in the area of Quebec. David Thompson's *Narrative of His Exploration in Western America, 1784–1812* gives an account of spearing at Red Lake in mid-April in what would become Minnesota (1916:267–268). Johann Georg Kohl (1860:328), the German ethnographer, geographer, and travel writer, visited the Lake Superior country in the mid-1850s and described both spearing fish and hunting at night by torchlight. In the early twentieth century Frances Densmore notes that "the larger fish were speared and were best secured at night" (1929: [1979]:125) and went on to describe five different kinds of torches, distinguishing torches used for fishing from all the others. In her survey of the Wisconsin Chippewa bands in the 1940s, Sister Clarissa Levi (1956:357) recorded people's memories of how torches had been made from cedar bark, hazel brush, and basswood; dipped in pitch; and stored. By the early twentieth century, some Lac du Flambeau people were using Coleman lanterns and rowboats. This method was widely replaced with automobile headlights powered by 12-volt batteries duct-taped to construction helmets, which spearers wore while standing in motorized aluminum boats. Today, people "shine" the county trunks and old logging roads at night from their cars using a hand-held apparatus also made of auto headlights.

Though technologically evolving, the scale of the Lac du Flambeau community's commitment to a hunting mode of life did not prevent them from being designated by observers as rather acculturated in the middle of the twentieth century (Gillan 1942:546; Caudill 1949:409; Boggs 1956:192). Nonetheless, in the late twentieth century the Lac du Flambeau band came to lead the other Ojibwe bands in exercising off-reservation hunting, fishing, and gathering rights in the face of violent opposition, in the process revitalizing and reorganizing itself.

The conflict between the bands and both the state and the local non-Indian residents came to focus on the meaning of Indian people spearfishing spawning walleyed pike at night in the weeks between the ice breakup and the opening of the sports-fishing season in early May on the hundreds of lakes in the region. This was a social conflict whose magnitude residents of the state had not seen since the late 1960s when Madison burned and exploded with the antiwar movement. Non-Indians feared the impact on the tourist economy of Indians harvesting game fish by the tens of thousands. They attacked the practice of spearfishing by drawing upon the wide and intuitive appeal of a liberal political philosophy that would extend "equal rights" to all U.S. citizens, all the while assuming inevitable Indian assimilation.[1] Much of this protest was orchestrated by Protect America's Rights and Resources (PARR), a local anti-Indian organization ambitious to assume leadership of the national anti-Indian movement (Ruyser 1995).

Tribal members and their supporters defended the practice by drawing upon the value of a historically distinct cultural tradition and the legal history of the relationship between autonomous indigenous peoples and the federal government. They symbolized this difference by an appeal to "treaty rights." As the conflict unwound during the late 1980s and early 1990s, the Indian people would represent the difference between non-Indian and Indian exploitation of resources as the difference between a sporting ethic and a harvesting ethic (Schlender 1991). This opposition subsumes the history of the relationship between Indians and non-Indians as well as the differences in political philosophy. But it entailed even more. The conflict was a debate of cosmological significance about the proper relationship between human and non-human life and therefore the possibility of a future for both. Indeed, a number of the spearfishing men and women had been in the habit of making tobacco offerings before they fished in a tacit recognition of the relationship of reciprocity that obtains between human and non-human "persons" in the Ojibwa cosmos (Hallowell 1955). Indian people often spoke of the relations between Anishinabeg and the other beings who lived on "Mother Earth" as the moral basis of the harvesting ethic. They thought of it as a responsibility.

Drawing upon Robert Brightman's work (1993) I would suggest that, in practice, spearfishing in the spring is an aspect of human beings' obligation to use the bodies of animals as a mode for their own reproduction. The Indians, by honoring the animals' spirits in generously distributing their corporeal form throughout the community, placed those spirits in debt, a debt that would be paid through more fish the following year, hence the morality of harvesting. Hunting and fishing, then, made the indigenously imagined good life possible.

The motivational value of these relations of reciprocity for Indian people was inadvertently intuited when non-Indian individuals within the antitreaty movement adopted the slogan "Spear an Indian, Save a Walleye." It was a version of the slogan that had emerged the decade before in the lower peninsula of Michigan in the conflict over Indian commercial fishing, and it was intended to degrade Indian human life. However, insofar as the slogan effectively expressed what was at stake in sarcastically equating human and nonhuman life, they showed that conditions for a serious conflict had been met (Simmel 1955). Non-Indians in the area imagined that their lives were made possible by walleye as well as by a tourist industry.

In 1989 the state of Wisconsin offered the Lac du Flambeau band $50 million in per capita payments, social programs, employment opportunities, and money for a much-needed elementary school in exchange for foregoing the exercise its spearfishing rights for ten years. The band turned the offer down. The decision shocked and dismayed non-Indian local and state leaders, who had persuaded both their constituents and the tribal council to support and endorse the deal. Reflecting on the meaning of the vote, Indian opponents saw their refusal to lease their treaty rights as a condition for the continued possibility of their cultural distinctness. Hunting and fishing, especially at night, lay at the core of the very identity of this community.

Indigenous ethnonationalism developed in a number of places in North America over the last third of the twentieth century, but at Flambeau it only emerges in the late 1980s with this conflict. In the words of Gail Guthrie Valaskakis, who grew up in both Indian and white worlds on the reservation, "Flambeau receded into the 1970s behind the boarded windows of empty shops. . . . The raised fists of the American Indian Movement were never welcome here" (1988:281). This is true enough, as the community had temporarily loaned or exported its radical element to the Chicago Indian community. Flambeau tribal member Mike Chosa led the first Indian occupation east of Alcatraz with the establishment of the Chicago Indian Village near Wrigley Field in 1971 and then the occupation of Belmont Harbor in the same city the following year. Chosa aside, though, no one in the 1970s would have predicted that in the late 1980s the Flambeau band would lead a regional Indian nationalistic revitalization that came close to turning into a civil war.

Ray Fogelson's Influence on the Project

The history of these events takes a long time to relate (see Nesper 2002). It would not have been told at all, at least not by the present author, had it not been for Ray Fogelson's seminar entitled "Religious Movements in Native North America" in the spring of 1989. It was in that forum that Ray taught the elements of doing ethnohistory through his extended exploration of the Cherokee movement led by Redbird Smith. It was his interpretation of the relationship between factionalism, religious ideology, and culture that permitted me to begin to see the significance of what was transpiring on the boat landings of northern Wisconsin that spring. His "Factionalism Revisited" (1987) helped me to appreciate some of the more counterintuitive combinations that came together in the emergence of the Wa-Swa-Gon Treaty Association, a neotraditionalist faction at Lac du Flambeau that was redefining both the significance of the federal treaties signed in the mid-nineteenth century and their historical subsistence practices. And later his analysis of the representation of American Indian ethnicity at the World's Columbian Exposition, in "The Red Man in the White City" (1991), caused me to attend to the scale of the stage on which movements and ethnic reorganizational projects are undertaken.

Herein lies the basis for the argument that follows: the controversy over off-reservation hunting, fishing, and gathering rights in the 1980s in northern Wisconsin was a culturally specific social process of remembering and reorganizing a distinct history and identity set in a much larger context. Ray's discussion of "forms of historical consciousness and discourse" and "native theories of history" (Fogelson 1989:134) disposed me to attend not only to the ways in which Anishinabeg people talked about what they were doing, but also the significance of the fact that they were still spearfishing at all.

Hunting, Fishing, "Violating," and Local Identity

In this chapter I want to examine a single incident—an arrest—that occurred near the end of the nineteenth century. Minimally, I hope it sheds some light on the fervor with which Flambeau speared fish in the lakes off their reservations in the late twentieth century. But the event also reveals some of the economic and political circumstances that would shape a set of dispositions as well as a regional ethnic identity. As such this chapter is an effort to show how historical and cultural processes are related to each other. Ideally, the incident reveals some of the ways in which this little society has reproduced itself by transforming itself over the past one hundred years. Its people would simultaneously resist and accommodate domination, all in an effort to improvise a collective life with the outcome of producing and retaining a distinct sense of themselves.

By the 1890s Lac du Flambeau had a population of about 800 people, who were organized into about 150 nuclear families and a far smaller number of extended families. Collectively they were barely making a living by gardening and doing seasonal wage work in the lumber industry. They were also hunting, fishing, making wild rice and maple sugar, and gathering berries, some of which they sold. Ten years of the General Allotment Act of 1887, in addition to the implementation of the allotment provisions in the Treaty of 1854, had concentrated much of the band's population on a 144-square-mile reservation in the north-central area of the state. By 1897, 306 tribal members had been allotted land parcels and so shared in the nearly $40,000 the local lumber mill paid out for the 20 million board feet of pine, hemlock, and birch that was cut each winter, though the money was controlled by the government agent.

In July 1897 two old men were arrested. The incident is reported in a letter written by Fred Vine, the government farmer at Lac du Flambeau, to the acting Indian agent at Ashland, one Lieutenant Scott, Sixth Cavalry (it can be found in the Letters Received File of the La Pointe Agency at the National Archives, Great Lakes Branch):

Lac du Flambeau Reserve
July 30, 1897
Acting U. S. Indian Agent, Ashland Wisconsin

Sir: The Game Wardens of Iron County have in jail at Hurley 2 of my old indians [sic] under sentence of 4 months imprisonment and $50 fine. They are Wa bish ki bi nesi who is blind and 88 years old and Na wa kwa gi jig who is 72 years old.

The facts are that these two old men and the wife of Wabiskibinesi went down the river after birch bark to make canoes and when on their return were given some venison by some other indians and when near the reservation line were arrested by John Sealy, Wm Henderson and Alex Gauthier who were all drunk. The two old men were hand cuffed together and made to walk to the station, taken to Hurley and their case rail roaded through without any chance for their friends to assist them in any way. They were not even given an interpreter. The indians say that the men had plenty of whiskey and gave them all they would drink. The old woman, the wife of Wabishkibinesi was turned adrift without any thing to eat to get home the best should could. What Venison they had was in the canoe of Wabishkibinesi and I fail to see by what authority they arrested the other old man.

I believe in enforcing the game law on white men as well as indians. But to be so harsh on these old men who were told when the treatys were made with them that the game belonged to them and they should have the privilege of hunting any where they pleased the punishment seem to me to be out of proportion to the offence. If it was some of the young men I would not feel so hard but the drunken ruffians do not interfere with them but jump on such inofensive old people as these who are very poor neither having any money to their credit who under my orders were trying to do such work as they could in making canoes to sell to make a living. Can not something be done to get these old men out of jail. it is hard for them to be locked up so long and I do not beleive either of them would do an intentional wrong. I have made complaint to U.S. Attorney at Madison of these men giving the old indians whiskey. If these game wardens want to enforce the law let them do it right.

Respectfully,
Fred J. Vine Govt Farmer

P.S. Write to District attorney of Iron County at Hurley and have him send the old fellows home do not think they will [?hinder?] the deer.

Interestingly, the antagonism between the federal and state agents is palpable here. As such, the letter indexes the ascendancy of state power, with the federal agents attempting to moderate a *fait accompli*. Beyond that it also shows federal acquiescence in the state's usurpation of the federal-Indian relationship.

Clearly both federal and state officials knew that Indians believed that "the game belonged to them," in Fred Vine's words, because of "treatys," though this belief was regarded lightly by non-Indians. Vine's letter was addressed to Captain J. C. L. Scott, Sixth Cavalry, who was about to retire from the position of acting agent at La Pointe, 65 miles by train northwest of Flambeau. Seven months on the job and a year after the incident, the good captain's successor, one S. W. Campbell, in his own report to the Commissioner of Indian Affairs, would reveal his tacit and apparently widely shared ignorance of the supremacy clause of the United States Constitution ("all Treaties made . . . shall be the supreme Law of the Land") by including the following:

> The recent enforcement of the stringent fish and game laws in Wisconsin and Minnesota are felt by the Indians to be a great hardship, although they have learned by severe experience that the same must be obliged. [Campbell 1898:320]

The Wisconsin Supreme Court had ruled in 1879 that criminal laws applied to Indian on the reservations (Satz 1991:83–85) so we should understand Campbell's appraisal as generous for the time. Nonetheless, here is a locus of the reproduction of paternal relations between the federal government and Indians, with the former intervening on behalf of Indian people, against the state, on a case-by-case basis. It is a moment that also speaks to and assists in producing the ascendancy of state power over Indian people.

On the Anishinabeg side of the matter we might note that when the 1837 treaty, ceding the southern parts of Lake Superior Ojibwe land, was signed, it explicitly retained the rights to hunt fish and gather on the ceded lands in Article V. At the time of that first treaty the arrested men would have been 28 and 12 years old. In 1842 the northern part of the Southwestern Ojibwe bands' lands was ceded. The right to hunt, fish, and gather on those ceded lands was stipulated in Article II. The men would have been 33 and 17. There is every likelihood that Wabishkibinesi attended the proceedings as the head of a household and his companion Nawakwagijig as a youth loosely attached to his natal family. After all, Secretary Verplanck Van Antwerp wrote that "upwards of a thousand individuals, men, women and children" (Satz 1992:131) were present at Fort Snelling for the first treaty. Whether they were at the proceedings or not, however, they would have made the yearly trip to LaPointe, where they were paid for the cession. The Reverend Alfred Brunson (1872:182–183) attended the payment in 1843:

> And now runners had to be sent out to all the bands of this agency to call in the Indians to the payment. Some of these bands were two hundred or more miles from Lapointe, and ten days were allowed for the return of the runners and the coming in of the Indians, and it was a matter of surprise to me that they could be gathered in so short a time. Not only the bands that were parties to the treaty, but the Leech Lake and Pigeon River bands, still more distant were present.

No matter exactly where Wabishkibinisi and Nawakwagijig were living when the Anishininabeg of this region were referred to in the plural as the Lac du Flambeau *bands*, they would have either been well aware of the terms of the treaties or have lived their daily hunting lives as they always had.

The old men were going off the reservation to harvest birch bark to build canoes to sell to the first generation of fishing tourists, when the two met some younger men who had been hunting off the reservation. Since the reservation had only been surveyed in the 1807s and it was allotment that concentrated people there, the valence of "on" and "off" the reservation was only just developing however. Besides, these men apparently only spoke Ojibwemowin.

Flambeau in the World System

Hunting was a longtime subsistence and commercial activity at Lac du Flambeau. François Mahliot, agent of the Northwest Company, for example, made several references to his purchases of rice and venison (Mahliot 1910). The old men were clearly involved in commerce. The young men might or might not have been, though commercial hunting was common at the time. In both cases we see an implicit effort to retain control over the social relations of production—that is, to sell the product of collective labor and not the labor itself (Sider 1986:29–33). This was part of an improvised overall strategy to remain socially distinct in the face of a complex of federal and state policies, economic practices, and demographic shifts.

An increase in Indian commercial hunting, allotment, and the concentration of the Lac du Flambeau bands into two population centers within the confines of reservation were all aspects of the same articulatory process. Logging drove these practices. The effect was the creation of a new social formation at Lac du Flambeau. With the emergence of the state of Wisconsin, which facilitated the logging industry, the articulation of this community in the world system developed a second aspect in the form of wage labor. People both sold their labor and continued to sell the product of their labor, and these modes of production had implications for each other.

Logging on the reservation began in 1886, eleven years before the arrest, when 10 million feet of Flambeau timber was cut from allotted lands. This was an aspect of a far larger transformation of the landscape. As Robert Gough notes, "In the quarter-century following 1873 sixty billion board feet were cut by Wisconsin sawmills" (Gough 1997:18) in the northern third of the state, and Lac du Flambeau is near the geographic center of this region referred to as "The Cutover." Logging would continue on the reservation until 1912 when the lumber mill built in 1894 was shut down. The entire logging project was facilitated by the completion of a shorter railroad link between the Iron Range and the city of Milwaukee (Anonymous 1889:5–6) that traversed Flambeau in 1889 (Anonymous 1937:9), incorporating the reservation and its transforming resources into the hinterland of Milwaukee and Chicago. Ironically, this incorporation into and by the "metropolitan corridor" (Stilgoe 1983) made possible Flambeau's greater differentiation from the putatively homogenizing metropolitan juggernaut.

By the time the old men were arrested the fragmented post—fur trade economy had both diversified to include wage labor in the logging camps and hypertrophied, with Flambeau people producing and selling wild or "country foods," as it was sometimes called. Fewer than 800 tribal members produced 8,000 pounds of maple sugar in 1894—and this was regarded as low—as well as tons of frog legs, for example, and great quantities of straw and blue and black berries, in addition to their contribution to the $1.5 million-a-year venison market in Chicago, which started in the 1870s (Oberly 1991). This elaboration would not have been possible without the railroad.

It is also perhaps ironic that this economic improvisation—led by commercial hunting and all of its attendant social forms—was somewhat enhanced by the coming of the lumber interests. Elders today will tell you that their ancestors had to go south to hunt deer in the middle of the nineteenth century and before because the pinelands did not support much of a deer population. Leveling the pine forest made for great deer habitat, as the deer fed on the emerging second growth. This had the effect of increasing the numbers of deer close by Lac du Flambeau (Habeck and Curtis 1960:49). People didn't have to travel south to hunt anymore as they had for generations. So just at the historical moment when greater incorporation into the wage economy loomed, Flambeau people were able not only to fish, gather wild rice, and hunt in the area of their eighteenth-century village settlement; they could also sell the surplus more extensively. As they grew more connected, they grew more distinct from the dominant society that was their market. And it was an expanding market at that.

The Emerging State of Wisconsin

But the state was expanding too and defining itself, at least in part, by facilitating the commoditization of the wildlife and lands within its borders. This would have implications for Anishinabeg identity, society, and culture. Within three years of entering the Union, the state had imposed a season on deer hunting (in 1851) and proscribed gill netting (in 1853). In 1868 the state hunting seasons for deer, game birds, and fur-bearing animals were applied to what were called at the time "uncivilized Indians," treaties made between the Lake Superior bands and the federal government notwithstanding. The law reduced the land base of the Flambeau's traditional and changing economy from 16 million acres to 450,000 (Oberly 1991:81), a loss of 97 percent. The laws and the policies that followed from them criminalized Indian subsistence. The game wardens brought Indian people before judges who, in turn, confiscated meat and rifles and fined a people who largely had no cash or sent them to jail, severely damaging families' ability to sustain themselves. This exercise of state power would have the long-term effect of creating an opposition between Indian and non-Indian identities and sensibilities, as the full meaning of the criminalization of an Indian way of life was realized.

Transformation of Local Indian Identity and Culture

Stimulated by a transformation of their natural resources, constrained by a new legal context for exploiting those resources, and motivated by a desire and expectation to remain a distinct people, the Flambeau people revalued and refined indigenous geographical knowledge and hunting skills. Importantly, their knowledge and skills were also conjoined with those of warfare as the cultural category of "violating" emerged with all of its oppositionary connotations and implications. "Violating," of course, refers to violating the game laws, and everyone has stories of doing this. In the early 1990s I never heard the term *violating* uttered without it being accompanied by a knowing, mischievous smile because the term referred to an entire history of relations in which white representatives of state power had come to reveal themselves to Indians as moral inverts. By the late nineteenth century many Indian people had several different kinds of relationships with non-Indians. Some of the most consequential of these were with game wardens who arrested them and the county magistrates who fined and imprisoned hunters for the crime of providing for their families, for being generous, and for using the land and its resources in a traditional manner.

Indian Fishing Guides

Even as an oppositionary identity developed for those selling the products of their labor, Flambeau was also developing at the other pole of local articulation—selling specialized labor directly. The 1870s brought the first publications of guidebooks for fishing in northern Wisconsin. The development of an economic infrastructure that would accommodate sports fishing in the form of hotels, guides, cooks, and oarsmen (Les 1988:2) was soon to follow. Even the industrial curriculum at the boarding school that arrived in Flambeau in 1896 sought to accommodate the needs of this new industry by teaching the girls domestic skills and the boys construction trades.

On the lakes, in 1878 the state prohibited the use of spears, nets, seine, baskets, grapnels, traps, or devices other than hooks and lines for taking fish. This was an effort to deter harvesting by both Indians and whites as fish were exoticized and anthropomorphized in the state-sanctioned and corporately managed commoditization process. In 1884 the Milwaukee Lake Shore and Western Railroad sponsored the publication of a pamphlet, *Forests, Streams, Lakes and Resources of Northern Michigan*, that reprinted five columns from *American Field* magazine entitled "A Bohemian Adrift in a Wonderland of Lakes." The author, "a prominent sportsmen, over the nom de plume of 'Carey,' " according to the editor, waxes eloquent over the North. He describes the first bass he takes:

> How very black the handsome fellows are, these piscatorial Ethiopians, and they are so nearly of one weight—three or four pounds! Always gamy, these boreal heroes fight with the pluck, spirit and endurance of Old Norsemen. [Anonymous 1884:10]

Similarly in an 1895 fishing and hunting guidebook sponsored by the Chicago and North-Western Railroad and published by Rand McNally, the game fish are "the finny tribe" (Leffingwell 1895:5). These invitations simultaneously anthropomorphize nature and naturalize at least a segment of humanity in the project of producing both a kind of metropolitan person and a kind of regenerative landscape. All the while, of course, Flambeau people continued to hunt, gather rice, and spear fish on and even off their reservations in the hundreds of lakes throughout the area.

In 1879 the Wisconsin Supreme Court ruled that Indians were subject to state laws on their reservations, making only passing reference to the treaties. In 1881 the first closed seasons on game fish were established. This was followed by a flurry of species-specific bag and size limits in the first years of the twentieth century. The year 1883 brought the state's prohibition of the export of venison. The hunting season was shortened from November 1 to December 15, and hunting at night with lights was interdicted (Schorger 1953:213), the very practice that distinguished Indian people at Lac du Flambeau. In 1887 Wisconsin again shortened the deer season, now to twenty days and appointed the first fish and game wardens (Oberly 1991:84). Hunting licenses were required for all deer hunters for the first time in 1897. Two years later no game at all could be taken without a license (Anonymous n.d.:1). All of this was to facilitate a particular economic relationship with Great Lakes cities.

Members of the urban elite and the rising white metropolitan middle class, now connected with northern Wisconsin by rail—and soon to be connected by highway—began to venture north. They would enhance and validate their regenerative and recreative (if ephemeral) fishing experiences in the north woods by bringing back more enduring tokens of their interaction with the indigenous inhabitants, like birch-bark canoes and other Indian-manufactured goods. For these tourist-adventurers, possession and display of Indian material goods were signs of their own prowess at home, or "authenticity" in Handler's terms (1986:4). Railroad-sponsored travel literature touted the recreative and regenerative value of contact with Indians, clearly opposing the value of their presumed aboriginality to the fishing tourists' sophistication:

> It follows as a matter of course that here must be a very Eden of piscatorial delight—a whole district in which the fisherman can ply his craft without stint, in which the sportsman may linger for days amidst primeval scenery and indulge in mighty sport, and where the student of Indian life and manners may gather great store of aboriginal folk lore from the red men, or those familiar with their traditions, or perhaps co-actors with them in more modern incidents of stirring forest adventure. [Anonymous 1891:6]

Anishinabeg people did not stand idly by as these processes of objectification proceeded. The recognition of the value of their own domestic goods outside local Indian society as commodities sold to urban whites transformed those goods into signs of ethnic difference and bicultural competence for Ojibwes in the Great Lakes sector of the world system. The Lac du Flambeau Cultural Center and Museum possesses no more than five items older than about 1890, according to Gregg Guthrie, the museum's first president. The tracks crossed Flambeau only the year before. This dearth of material culture is a measure of Indians' participation in shaping the cultural dimension of this articulation process. After 1890 it proliferates. Published and private photographs from the first decade of the twentieth century commonly show miniature canoes along with other craft items (Goc 1995:81, 104, 112). In one of the photos used in a recently published community history, the canoes are rather ostentatiously displayed (Goc 1995:112). This suggests local appropriation of this means of objectification, which clearly advertises the availability of such goods at Lac du Flambeau.

The Symbolic Value of Birch-bark Canoes

It is not surprising that among the first generation of icons of indigenous authenticity in the region are watercraft, or models of the real thing. "Carey" recommends that the fishing tourist procure either "a light wherry . . . or an Indian birch bark canoe" (Anonymous 1884:16). Just a few years before Fred Vine had directed these old men to make "canoes to sell to make a living," the World's Columbian Exposition in Chicago had featured "means of transportation as object lessons of human progress." Fair designer Frederick Law Olmstead had written to the fair's chief of construction, Daniel Burnham, and called for birch-bark canoes, "managed by Indians suitably trained, equipped and costumed for the purpose" (de Wit 1993:63). Watercraft made relationships between peoples possible and were also emblems of their differences, a lesson Flambeau people had learned and were teaching, actively and for profit, at the train station between the two settlements on the reservation.

Technologies and Culture Change

It would not be until the 1920s that the state of Wisconsin's intellectuals working in and around Richard Ely's Institute for Research in Land Economics (first in Madison, then at Northwestern University) abandoned the project of transforming the lands cut over by the lumber companies into farms. Instead they recommended the redevelopment of the forests for industrial and recreational use (Gough 1991, 1997). Indeed, the forest had been regenerating, and the tourists had been coming north for decades by this time. In 1927 the state passed the Forest Crop Law, which exempted reforesting lands from taxation (Gough 1997:168). In 1933 Oneida County, the county adjacent to Flambeau, adopted the nation's first rural zoning ordinance, "establishing forestry and recreation districts closed to new settlement" (Wilson 1957:105), on the advice given by the state's first forester two decades earlier. Early in the same year President Herbert Hoover established the Nicolet National Forest in four counties (Gough 1997:170), one of which bordered Lac du Flambeau. This shift in land-use policy in a thinly settled region facilitated what had been going on for decades. Large sections of the cutover's reforesting lands had been evolving as a de facto (if often illicit) common-property, open-access resource for deer hunting since the 1880s. This physical process and this reorientation in land-use policy would have the effect of stimulating both poles of Flambeau's articulation. As more tourists came north to consume the regenerative signs and experiences of authentic indigenous life, and more "country food" was harvested, Indian people had the opportunity to sell their labor, though on terms they did not control. But they also sold the products of their labor, on terms they largely did.

Part of the state's project had been to transform the lakes' fish populations, filling them with the kinds of game fish that metropolitan sports fishermen would travel far and spend money to catch: mostly walleye but some muskie and bass as well. So, for example, already in 1902 the first fish hatchery was established by the state's conservation department in Woodruff, twelve miles east of Lac du Flambeau. The next year Chicago and Northwestern Railroad published a detailed tourist map showing all of the transportation routes and hunting and fishing resorts in Vilas and Oneida counties, with the Flambeau reservation rather near the center of that map. A tourist booklet published in 1919 by the United States Railroad Administration lists seven such resorts reachable by train from the Flambeau station (Anonymous 1919:72).

The railroad stimulated processes of autoexoticization, realized mostly as a local craft industry, that permitted some continued Indian control over the social relations of production. At the same time the railroad also created Indian guiding, which was a valorization of traditional geographical knowledge at the cost of retaining control over those relations. Hotels and resorts in the area hired Indian men to guide non-Indian sports fishermen to the walleye, muskie, and bass for the day. "It is the land of the Ojibway and many of the tribe still linger," Albert Britt, the editor of *Outing* would write in *The Wilderness Next Door: An Appreciation of the Northern Lake Region*. "If you can have an Ojibway paddler in the stern of your canoe, you will be a fortunate man" (Anonymous 1919:3). This was not the only opportunity tribal members had to sell their labor, however. As indicated earlier, a sawmill opened in 1894 in the town, and "75% of the Indians were employed by the logging company"—though "every time the drums sounds the 900 Indians in the company's employ immediately drop their work and start for the place where the dance is held" (Scrobell 1988:75–76). In the case of guiding, however, Indian people were selling access to knowledge and skills that had a higher place in the traditional order of value than did the work undertaken by the employees of the mill.

The succeeding technology and mode of relationship—articulation with the metropole vis-à-vis motor highway—supplanted the crafts industry but accelerated the motivation to transform the lakes themselves. That change stimulated both subsistence and commercial harvesting, including the practice of spearfishing.

The "Big Fish Auto Road" made it to Eagle River, which is 40 miles east of Flambeau, in 1917. It would be a few more years before a usable road followed the tracks across the reservation from the towns of Woodruff-Minocqua. When it did, however, it devastated the crafts industry. Where the railroad centralized the Indian/non-Indian nexus, the automobile decentralized it. The railroad was worth $10,000 a year to Indian people in handicrafts sold to tourists, much of it from the platform at the station. The highway reduced that figure by 90 percent (Goc 1995:38), and the crafts industry was struggling to fill the income void created when the mill shut down in 1912. But the auto itself would play a very important role in simultaneously connecting Flambeau to and differentiating Flambeau from the metropole because of the different things that autos meant in this metamorphosing local system of the world.

There is a difference between the *presence* of automobiles in Lac du Flambeau and the fact of Lac du Flambeau being connected with the cities of the south by motor highway. Owning a car was a sign of an ability to access cash—mostly through guiding and craft sales as well as wage labor at Cushway's mill. And though it was a sign of emerging class differences within Flambeau society, it was not a sign of acculturation. Lac du Flambeau people assimilated the automobile as a terrestrial canoe, as it was ideally suited for hunting the old logging roads at night in somewhat the same way that their parents and grandparents had hunted the lakes at night in canoes.

There is a photograph, from the second or third decade of the twentieth century, in the archives of the Lac du Flambeau Cultural Center and Museum showing fishing guide Frank Wild Cat standing in front of a side view of his car. He has strung a stringer of fish one-half the car's length, in a dramatic statement in a non-Indian register of the value of traditional Indian knowledge. But far more importantly for this argument, there is also a photograph dating from the same period of a middle-aged Indian woman standing in a stylish knee-length black woolen coat, pointing her rifle in the direction of the dead buck at her feet in the snow. She is also standing in front of an automobile. The curator of the museum's collections, Marcus Guthrie, reports that the photo was recently taken to the Elder's Center and shown to tribal members Reva Chapman and Celia DeFoe, both of whom are in their early eighties. They said that the woman in the picture was either Josephine (Burgess) Peterson or Agnes Kobe, who, in addition to Mary King, Celia Boniash, Susan Menominee Catfish, Josephine Kobe, and Josephine Poupart, "would go off hunting, usually because their men were in jail for violating [the game laws] or something. So they had to go." The women reported that "Mary King purchased a Model T when they first came out and the women would hook a travois to the back and go off" (Guthrie, personal communication, 1997)—go off hunting, that is. Mary's car would have had to come up on the train and was more than likely purchased from the proceeds of beadwork and other craft items sold to tourists, supplemented perhaps by money her husband contributed.

As a result of the availability of cars, hunting and the attendant social relations were stimulated. At the same time, with Indian guides making five to seven dollars a day and increasing numbers of white people coming "up North" for the fighting game fish, the Indian Agency in Lac du Flambeau built a hatchery in the 1913, the year after the mill closed. The hatchery was capable of producing 9.6 million walleye fry per year for the chain of lakes on the reservation. This influx of walleye transformed the structure of the fish population in the chain of lakes that had been created by the logging company's dam 30 years earlier. A bigger hatchery capable of producing 50 million walleye fry per year was built in 1936 (Guthrie 1997). By this time, there were 40 to 50 Flambeau men working as guides, according to Nelson Sheppo who began guiding in 1934 and continued into the mid-1980s.

Local non-Indian businessmen facilitated this aspect of Flambeau's articulation. According to Joyce Laabs, "In 1912, a forward looking group of men formed the Fish and Game Protective Association of Northern Wisconsin and published a booklet aimed at attracting tourists." They saw their purpose as "protecting and fostering the fish and game of Northern Wisconsin . . . touted the scenery, the crystal lakes, the tumbling trout streams and the bracing and reviving air," and aimed the message at "the office worker or city dweller who can spare only a week or 10 days for an outing" (Laabs 1980:95).

Internal Differentiation in the Division of Labor

The gift of meat from the young men, who escaped the drunken wardens in Fred Vine's letter, to the older men, who did not, is a significant moment that represents a division of both economic and symbolic labor in this complex of evolving indigenism. As noted earlier, the lumber mill was built where three lakes came together about two miles from what had been the main settlement since the late eighteenth century. It was closed in 1912, the same year a windstorm destroyed most of the houses in the main settlement as well as three Indian-owned and -operated stores (Valaskakis

1988:274). Some of the refugees took over the abandoned company-built housing that same year, but the presence and disappearance of the mill had an important impact on local society. By the first decade of the twentieth century, Flambeau Indian society had two cultural and geographic poles defined in opposition to each other that were largely co-extensive with its two modes of production. There was the "town" where people were even thought to speak slightly differently and now the "Old Village," a self-consciously nativistic settlement that had both historic roots in that location and had been marketing its indigenous material culture for three decades or more. This intraethnic opposition was energized, in turn, by its opposition to a third term: the non-Indian society in all of its complexity and manifestations.

There is an interesting homology here. The young men mentioned in Fred Vine's letter, who were more than likely commercially hunting off the reservation in the last decade of the nineteenth century, fed and provisioned old men who were also involved in intersocietal trade of relatively more durable goods: birch-bark canoes. In the same way the "town" and "The Old Village" developed and transformed different indigenous resources, both cooperating and competing with each other.

The evidence for this symbiosis is drawn from the industrial survey that was undertaken at Lac du Flambeau. On two days in 1922, 132 households were surveyed. The name of the head of the household, allotment number, age, degree of blood, legal status, location and condition of the house, years of birth for all household residents, and details about their occupations were all recorded. Considered in aggregate, the data presents a clear image of the importance of both selling labor and selling the products of labor. For example, of the men ten had no listed occupation, typically due to age or illness. Twenty-one were involved in wage labor exclusively, in jobs such as guiding or farming or labor or carpentry. Seventy-four men identified themselves as both having a job (such as teamster, laborer, guide, proprietor or railroad worker) and hunting and fishing. A few added trapping, and/or "works with birchbark" to the rest of these activities. The data clearly indicate that 70 percent of Indian men who listed occupations in the census also were involved in traditional economic practices.

Of the women, twenty-five had no occupation listed, three were exclusively involved in wage labor, and eighty-five did at least one (and typically three or four) of the following: "beadwork"; "makes baskets, moccasins, reed mats"; "tans hides"; "makes maple sugar or syrup." Two women were identified as "traps, hunts and fishes." Like the men, a full 75 percent of the women were involved in occupations that required their use of traditional resources (Anonymous 1922). Much of this produce was sold.

The similarity of these percentages and the individual household portraits indicate that families were either more inclined toward wage labor or more inclined toward more traditional forms of making a living. All of this has a spatial dimension. Overall and in general, traditional skills and knowledge were deployed on a geographic axis wherein Old Villagers became craftspeople and townsmen became fishing guides. In a dense exchange of value, prized game fish—icons of knowledge of the lakes on and off the reservation for Indian people—were availed to affluent non-Indian fishing tourists by culturally "mixed-blood" Indians living in the town of Flambeau. In the same exchange, and in another register, signs of the regenerative power and authenticity of those icons were transmitted in the form of craft items. These included twine and reed mats, woven bags, moccasins, beadwork, tanned hides, and miniature birch-bark canoes in addition to processed country foods like wild rice, berries, maple syrup, and sugar packed in *mukoks* (birch-bark baskets)—typically made by so-called full-bloods in the Old Village.

Conclusion

Here is the locus of a key indigenization: the process by which the relationships with larger forces and relations are given local meaning. The Flambeau people undertook greater articulation with the regional economy and society while producing greater ethnic difference through an ongoing internal debate on practices. They appropriated the changes the railroad and automobile made in the landscape and the state made in the structure of the fish populations of the northern lakes. They became fishing guides, and they marketed craft items to the guide's clientele. They increased both their subsistence and commercial hunting and fishing. They changed the distribution of species in their own lakes' fish populations, favoring walleye, muskie, and bass, fish that brought tourists north. At the same time they were seen and saw themselves as party to a multidimensional oppositional relationship with the larger society. All of these changes represent traditional processes of ethnic reorganization (Snipp and Nagel 1993) that were informed by a local order of value. They reveal the ways in which articulation can operate: Flambeau became more culturally distinct form "the surrounding" or "dominant" society, as people refer to it, even as the community became more socially and economically connected.

The people I spent time with and interviewed in 1991 who had spear-fished off the reservation since 1985 when the tribes and the state agreed on the season's length and the number of lakes to be speared, were in their twenties, thirties, forties, and fifties. In their youth all of them had speared on the reservation those very walleye that had been tacitly produced to attract non-Indian metropolitan sports-fisher folk. Most had "violated"—hunted and fished off the reservation—and could tell stories of deceiving game wardens, a privileged activity in the reproduction of this oppositionary identity. Some remembered pulling oars for their fathers, brothers, and uncles in the days before motors and using Coleman lanterns before the 12-volt battery-driven car headlamps were duct-taped to construction helmets to illuminate the shallows and rock bars where the walleye spawned. It was so common at Flambeau to spear walleye that one young spearer said, "We are all spearers," and an older spearer, when asked if he would talk about the history of spearing, said, "You don't keep track of everyday life." Tom Maulson, the leader of the group that aggressively speared the lakes off the reservation in the 1980s at the peak of the conflict, said "It's in their blood. That's our way."

The practice was not common throughout the ceded territory, however. Flambeau, after all, was the only reservation where there were so many lakes—two thousand in Vilas and Oneida counties alone, "about one sixth of the surface area " (Gough 1997:10). Lac du Flambeau spearers may never let Bad River people forget that the latter showed up on the boat landings with the nearly useless short ice-fishing spears when they first came down from the southern shore of Lake Superior to the inland lake region. Flambeau spearers took, and continue to take, the lion's share of the collective tribal quotas. In 1986 and 1987, for example, they took more than 70 percent of all the walleyes taken by the five bands (Kmiecik 1987, 1988). In 1988, 1989, and 1990 they accounted for half the "spearer-nights" and one-third to one-half of the total boat hours while harvesting more efficiently than all the bands that speared (Kmiecik 1991). Nearly the same proportions hold for the early twenty-first century.

It should not be surprising, then, that by the middle of the twentieth century, and certainly toward its end, those who did spearfish speared walleyed pike exclusively because there are so many of them and because their eyes are so big and easy to see at night in the water illuminated by a light fixed to spearfishermen's construction helmets. "Their eyes look like the headlights of a car seen from an airplane," a middle-class tribal member told me matter of factly. It should not be surprising that they would represent this practice to themselves and others as traditional and as being at the very center of their sense of themselves as a distinct people. And it should not be surprising that contesting this practice's legitimacy would evoke the deep sense of outrage, mobilize the broad spectrum of

Flambeau society, and motivate the nativistic ethnic reorganization and cultural renaissance that it did.

Note

1. On March 25, 1950, the recently formed Wisconsin Commission on Human Rights sent a letter to all 6,500 resort operators in the state that addressed the issue of widespread discrimination against Jews and Negroes by the resort industry. The commission referred to the relevant Wisconsin statute as "Wisconsin's 'equal rights' law" (Recknagel 1950:8). The use of quotation marks in the letter suggests that the term had standing at the time, forty years before it became such a powerful symbol for the non-Indians resisting the exercise of the off-reservation rights. The righteousness with which the phrase was used during this conflict may reflect the hostility northern whites have historically expressed toward the state's expectation and desire to democratize access to public accommodations.

References

Anonymous
   n.d. License Chronological History. Department of Natural Resources. Madison, Wisconsin. Typescript.
   1884 A Bohemian Adrift in a Wonderland of Lakes. *In* Forests, Streams, Lakes, and Resources of Northern Michigan. Marquette MI: Messrs. J. M. Longyear and J. M. Case.
   1890 Fifteenth Annual Report of the Milwaukee, Lake Shore and Western Railroad Company for the Year 1889. Milwaukee WI: The Company.
   1891 The Northern Wisconsin Lakes. Published by the Chicago, Milwaukee and St. Paul Railway. Chicago: Knight and Leonard.
   1919 The Northern Lakes: Minnesota, Wisconsin, Upper Michigan, Iowa, Illinois. United States Railroad Administration.
   1922 "Lac du Flambeau Industrial Survey" National Archives and Record Service, Correspondence of the Office of Indian Affairs and Related Records. Lac du Flambeau Agency. Record Group 75: Bureau of Indian Affairs. Great Lakes Branch, National Archives. Chicago.
   1937 The Railroads of Wisconsin 1827–1937. The Railway and Locomotive Historical Society, Inc. Baker Library, Harvard Business School, Boston.
Boggs, Stephen
   1956 An Interaction Study of Ojibwa Socialization. The American Sociological Review 21:191–198.
Brightman, Robert
   1993 Grateful Prey: Rock Cree Human-Animal Relationships. Berkeley: University of California Press.
Brunson, Alfred
   1872 A Western Pioneer: or, Incidents of the Life and Times of Rev, Alfred Brunson, A.M., D.D., Embracing a Period of Over Seventy Years. Written By Himself. Vol. 2. Cincinnati: Hitchcock and Walden.
Campbell, S. W.
   1898 Report of La Pointe Agency. *In* Reports to the Commissioner of Indian Affairs. Washington DC: Government Printing Office.

Caudill, William

    1949 Psychological Characteristics of Acculturated Wisconsin Ojibwa Children. American Anthropologist 51:409–427.

de Wit, Wim

    1993 Grand Illusions: The Chicago World's Fair of 1893. Neil Harris, Wim de Wit, James Gilbert, and Robert W. Rydell, eds. Chicago: Chicago Historical Society.

Densmore, Frances

    1979 [1929] Chippewa Customs. Minnesota Historical Society. First published in 1929 by the Smithsonian Institution Bureau of American Ethnology Bulletin #86.

Fogelson, Raymond

    1987 Factionalism Revisited. Paper presented at the American Anthropological Association Meetings, Chicago.

    1989 The Ethnohistory of Events and Nonevents. Ethnohistory 36:2.

    1991 "The Red Man in the White City." In Columbian Consequences, Volume 3: The Spanish Borderlands in Pan-American Perspective. David Hurst Thomas, ed. Washington DC: Smithsonian Institution.

Gillan, John

    1942 "Acquired Drives in Culture Contact." American Anthropologist 44:545–554.

Goc, Michael

    1995 Reflections of Lac du Flambeau: An Illustrated History of Lac du Flambeau, Wisconsin, 1745–1995. Compiled by Ben Guthrie. Friendship WI: New Past Press.

Gough, Robert

    1991 Richard T. Ely and the Development of the Wisconsin Cutover. Wisconsin Magazine of History, autumn 1991.

    1997 Farming the Cutover: A Social History of Northern Wisconsin, 1900–1940. Lawrence KS: University Press of Kansas.

Guthrie, Marcus

    1997 M. Guthrie to L. Nesper, February 27.

Habeck, J. R., and Curtis, J. T.

    1960 Forest Cover and Deer Population Densities in Early Northern Wisconsin. Wisconsin Academy of Science Arts and Letters 48:49–56.

Hallowell, A. Irving

    1955 Culture and Experience. Philadelphia: University of Pennsylvania Press.

Handler, Richard

    1986 Authenticity. Anthropology Today 2(1) (February):2–4.

Kmiecik, Neil

    1987 Results of Spearing During Spring 1986 Data Summaries. Administrative Report 87–3. Biological Services Division. Odanah WI: Great Lakes Indian Fish and Wildlife Commission.

    1988 Spearfishing of the Lake Superior Tribes of Chippewa Indians Spring 1987 Summary Report. Administrative Report 88-2. Biological Services Division. Odanah WI: Great Lakes Indian Fish and Wildlife Commission.

    1991 Spear Fishery of the Lake Superior Tribes of Chippewa Indians Spring 1990 Summary Report. Biological Services Division. Odanah WI: Great Lakes Indian Fish and Wildlife Commission.

Kohl, Johann Georg

    1985 [1860] Kitchi-Gumi: Life Among the Lake Superior Ojibway. St. Paul: Minnesota Historical Society Press.

Laabs, Joyce

    1980 A Collection of Northwoods Nostalgia from the Pages of the Lakeland Times. Vol. 2. Sun Prairie WI: Royale Publishing.

Lefingwell, Bruce William

    1895 Hunting and Fishing Along the North-Western Line. Chicago: Rand McNally.

LeJeune, Paul

    1897 "Relation of What Occurred in New France in the Year 1634." *In* The Jesuit Relations and Allied Documents. Vol. 6. R. G. Thwaite, ed. Cleveland: Burrows.

Les, Betty

    1988 Summary: History of Fishing in Wisconsin. Bureau of Research Wisconsin Department of Natural Resources. Madison WI. Typescript.

Levi, Sister Clarissa M.

    1965 Chippewa Indians of Yesterday and Today. New York: Pageant Press.

Mahliot, François

    1910 A Wisconsin Fur Trader's Journal, 1804–05. Collections of the State Historical Society of Wisconsin 19:163–233.

Nesper, Larry

    2002 The Walleye War: The Struggle for Ojibwe Spearfishing and Treaty Rights. Lincoln: University of Nebraska Press.

Oberly, James W.

    1991 The Lake Superior Chippewas and Treaty Rights in the Ceded Territory of Wisconsin: Population, Prices, Land, Natural Resources, and Regulation, 1837–1983. Report written for the Great Lakes Indian Fish and Wildlife Commission. Odanah WI.

Racknagel, Kenneth

    1950 The Uninvited: A Study of the Resort Discrimination Problem in Wisconsin. Governor's Commission on Human Rights. Madison WI.

Rostlund, Erhard

    1952 Fresh Water Fish and Fishing in Native North America. University of California Publications in Geography. Vol. 9. Berkeley: University of California Press.

Ryser, Rudolf C.

    1995 Anti-Indian Movement on the Tribal Frontier. Occasional Paper #16–3. Center for World Indigenous Studies. Olympia WA.

Satz, Ronald

    1991 Chippewa Treaty Rights: The Reserved Rights of Wisconsin's Chippewa Indians in Historical Perspective. Transactions of the Wisconsin Academy of Sciences, Arts and Letters 79(1).

Schlender, James

    1991 "Treaty Rights in Wisconsin: A Review." Northeast Indian Quarterly, (spring):4–16.

Schorger, A. W.

    1953 The White-tailed Deer in Early Wisconsin. Transactions of the Wisconsin Academy of Sciences, Arts and Letters 42:197–247.

Scrobell, Daniel D.

    1988 Early Times. Minocqua WI: Heritage House.

Sider, Gerald

    1986 Culture and Class in Anthropology and History. Cambridge Studies in Social Anthropology. Cambridge: Cambridge University Press.

Simmel, Georg

    1964 Conflict and the Web of Group Identity. New York: Free Press, Macmillan.

Snipp, Matthew, and Joann Nagel

1993 Ethnic Reorganization: American Indian Social, Economic, Political and Cultural Strategies for Survival. Ethnic and Racial Studies 16(2) (April):203–235.

Stilgoe, John R.

1983 Metropolitan Corridor: Railroads and the American Scene. New Haven: Yale University Press.

Thompson, David

1916 David Thompson's Narrative of His Expeditions in Western America, 1784–1842. J. B Tyrell, ed. Toronto: Champlain Society.

Valaskakis, Gail Guthrie

1988 The Chippewa and the Other: Living the Heritage of Lac du Flambeau. Cultural Studies 2(3) (October):267–293.

Warren, William Whipple

1984 [1885] History of the Ojibway People. Minnesota Historical Society Press. First published in 1885 by the Minnesota Historical Society as volume 5 of the Collections of the Minnesota Historical Society. St. Paul MN.

Wilson, R. G.

1957 Zoning for Forestry and Recreation: Wisconsin's Pioneer Role. Wisconsin Magazine of History 41 (winter):102–106.

6. The Poetics of Tropes and Dreams
in Arapaho Ghost Dance Songs

JEFFREY D. ANDERSON

In June 1892 ethnologist James Mooney heard from the Indian agent
and from Arapahos themselves at the Shoshone (now Wind River) Reservation agency that Northern Arapahos no longer practiced the Ghost
Dance. But later at a log-cutting camp in the Wind River Mountains,
Mooney reported that when he went to a nearby *tipi* to visit the old men
he "heard from a neighboring hill the familiar measured cadence of the
ghost songs" (1896:809). After the massacre at Wounded Knee, after the
date of the predicted world renewal had passed, and after the Southern
Arapaho apostle Sitting Bull had been shunned by the Northern Arapaho
(Fowler 1982:123), the ghost songs were still sung at Wind River. The
songs, along with the dance forms they inspired, were more durable than
the message of the Northern Paiute prophet, Wovoka, and took a detour
off the beaten path of history. Indeed, the Arapaho variation of the Ghost
Dance movement would have been nearly a complete nonevent (Fogelson 1989) to anthropologists and historians if not for Mooney's classic
ethnographic account.

Through the songs and his own interpretations, Mooney's account conveys a sense of "being there," a closeness to the Ghost Dance phenomenon
gained by his relationship to the Arapaho, which was stronger than to any
other group. The study was unusual for its time in paying close attention to
cultural creativity as it emerged in history, rather than ignoring it in order
to salvage pre-reservation culture. In contrast, subsequent perspectives on
the Ghost Dance have treated the phenomenon as a single movement and
formulated causal models or chronologically ordered narratives that rely
primarily on Mooney's first section, entitled "The Narrative." Moving
against that strong current, this chapter steps into the second section of

Mooney's work to flesh out the details and connectivities that shaped the distinctive Arapaho experience of the Ghost Dance.

In Arapaho the Ghost Dance is referred to either as *3iikonohwoo*, "ghost or skeleton dance," or *koo'einohwoot*, "round dance."[1] The former derives from the word *3iik* or *3iikonehii*, referring to a ghost-skeleton of a deceased person who wanders about in this world. As Hilger's informant notes (1952:79–80), *3iikonehii* was among the worst things one could say about another person in Arapaho ways of speaking. It is likely, as Fowler (1982:326 n.) suggests and Curtis (1934:200) renders it, that the second term, *koo'einohwoot*, was preferred. By early spring of 1889 some Northern Arapahos had begun performing the Ghost Dance after a visit by Sherman Sage and five Shoshones to Wovoka earlier that year (Mooney 1896:894). Near the end of 1889 a larger delegation followed, including Sitting Bull and Friday. In April 1890, Black Coyote initiated the first dance in Oklahoma among the Southern Arapaho. Though Mooney observes that the Arapaho kept dancing until 1892, some songs, elements, and forms persisted even longer.

Mooney collected the songs in his extensive fieldwork among both the Northern and Southern Arapaho between 1890 and 1893 (1896:653–654). Several other songs are distributed elsewhere in the literature (see Densmore 1936 and Curtis 1934). It appears that most of the 73 songs were recorded on cylinders at traditional Southern Arapaho song rehearsals (Mooney 1896:918). During a practice session, Mooney asked the group led by Black Coyote to perform specific songs or repeat others. In presentation Mooney then arranged the songs by common theme or function into groups that contained similar elements such as whirlwind, crow, the sweat lodge, games, and age grade societies. Performative sequence is only retained for the opening song at the beginning and the closing songs at the end of the Arapaho section. Musical transcriptions for eight songs are provided (numbers 1, 9, 28, 44, 45, 52, 67 and 73; Mooney 1896:958, 965, 977, 990, 991, 996, 1006–1007, 1011–1012).

Remarkable in the collection is the discrepancy between the detailed and exact transcriptions and translations on one hand and Mooney's general exegesis on the other. The former reflects an extensive engagement in the Arapaho language that does not seem possible for Mooney given the brief duration of his field visits. There is direct evidence that the transcriptions and translations were completed by the Mennonite missionary Reverend H. R. Voth with the assistance of Southern Arapaho informants (Voth n.d.). Voth's manuscripts in the Bethel College archives retain many of the original translation notes and a list of informants' initials, all in Voth's handwriting. The orthography and glosses are also consistent with notes and manuscripts throughout his papers. Though Mooney acknowledges Voth in the introduction (1896:655), he makes no reference to this specific contribution for the song texts. Mooney apparently employed Voth and his informants to transcribe the song texts from the cylinders he provided. From the transcriptions Voth in turn produced the English translations. Based on those translations, Mooney's interpretations do trace relevant cultural connections for song elements but also provide many that are detached from the salient linguistic and cultural features in the texts themselves.

Because of this gap the songs and the context of their creation and performance contain much more linguistic and cultural evidence than Mooney provided. Retranslation and closer attention to the linguistic features and cultural associations of the songs will make possible interpretation beyond Mooney's original comments, which were apparently based on the translations Voth completed.[2] In most cases I have been able to transpose the songs into modern Arapaho orthography and refine some translations, though some forms elude clarification.

The gist of Mooney's presentation of the Ghost Dance songs follows the emerging American anthropological tradition for elaborating connectivity. Cultural particulars are identified, then related unsystematically to the rather limited linguistic, historical, and ethnographic data available at the time. Though Mooney offers a wealth of descriptive material for the songs, his interpretation and translation tend at times to reify elements of the millenarian doctrine of the Ghost Dance. The present discussion carries the interpretation further to ethnosemantic and poetic elements discernible from the wealth of Arapaho evidence accumulated since 1896.

There are thus a number of reasons to now pay even closer attention to the songs of the Arapaho Ghost Dance. As in other groups songs are at the center of Arapaho religion and practice as the source of movement for performance and participation. Though all languages are musical and suited to music, Arapaho carries its own modality, rhythm, and resonance that have struck not only other American Indian peoples but non-Indian observers as well, including Mooney himself: "Their religious nature has led them to take a more active interest in the Ghost dance, which, together with the rhythmic nature of their language, has made their songs the favorite among the tribes of Oklahoma" (1896:958). Second, various forms of Arapaho music have been borrowed and adapted by other Plains groups throughout the unwritten history of Plains cultural development. Mooney in turn verifies this by noting that the Arapaho Ghost Dance songs were often the first songs learned by other Plains tribes. Though not within this chapter's scope here, it would be possible to trace Arapaho cultural elements in songs identified for other groups. Third and to reemphasize, Arapaho Ghost Dance songs are poetry that contain much more than can be encompassed by attending to the doctrine of the movement as a whole or even cultural variations of it. As Mooney notes quite explicitly, the songs were the center of the Ghost Dance. Moreover, he adds, "First in importance, for number, richness of reference, beauty of sentiment, and rhythm of language are the Arapaho songs" (1896:953). As Mooney estimates each performance caused 20 to 30 persons to fall into trance, who then created many new songs. Rather than a new religion bounded by doctrine, the Ghost Dance was an explosion in and of ritual practices of poetic and musical creativity without parallel before or since in Arapaho culture.

Another broader reason for looking at the songs is that the Arapaho Ghost Dance has been more or less left out of the accepted, written history. Occasionally, a drawing by Mary Irvin Wright, an Arapaho song text, or a full-page color photograph of an Arapaho Ghost Dance shirt decorates works of larger scope focusing on or merely citing the "religious movement." Despite Voth's rich translations and Mooney's intensive ethnography of the ceremony among both the Southern and Northern Arapaho tribes, there has been little subsequent, systematic study of the songs as ethnohistorical texts that reflect Arapaho experiences of the time. Similarly, few of the acknowledged studies of the causes of the Ghost Dance have been conclusive, as Kehoe notes (1989:103–111), and none have explained the involvement of relatively broader groups of Arapaho, including predominately women. Also, much has been written about the beginnings and ending of the Ghost Dance "movement," yet the middle of the historical trajectory, where Mooney placed the Arapaho, has subsequently been ignored. The Northern Arapaho in Wyoming provided the link between the Great Basin and the Northern Plains (i.e., Lakota and Cheyenne) while the Southern Arapaho, who learned it from the northern tribe, spread the ritual among various groups in Indian Territory (see Miller 1959:31ff.).

Arapaho peoples have eluded the historical gaze both because they practiced what Fogelson calls "low-profile invisibility as a defensive strategy" (1989:142) and because historians have been preoccupied with more visible tribes and events. Ironically, though, Arapahos have long been at the center of indigenous Plains cultural developments. There is thus a contradiction between the written history that is pervasively vague and thin about Arapaho participation in "events" and the local perspective that places Arapahos as the "mother tribe" in the center of Plains cultural history, including what Mooney recognized as their central role as messengers, apostles, and song composers for the Ghost Dance (1896:955). For over a century, then, the rich material Mooney provided on the Arapaho Ghost Dance has been left out of ethnohistorical study.

The Arapaho Ghost Dance is treated here as a "nonevent" along paths suggested by Fogelson (1989). As such, our concern is not to place it within an historical plot of events, a model of causality, or a stage synopsis of the movement, but with understanding how the Arapaho people experienced the Ghost Dance and created it within their own sociocultural space and lived history. For one thing, it is hard to situate the Ghost Dance in a time slot with a beginning and end for the Arapaho peoples. On one side, much of the content of the Ghost Dance is carried over from mythical and ritual contexts preceding the dance itself, thus placing it in the long duration of Arapaho history. On the other, though Mooney notes that the last performance among the Arapaho was in 1892, the songs persisted long after 1900. Exactly when the Arapaho tribes stopped practicing the ceremony is not altogether clear. In 1924 several Arapahos working in northern California on a silent motion picture, *The Thundering Herd*, were able to meet Wovoka through Tim McCoy, their friend and technical director for the film. At that meeting they performed the dance and accompanying songs (McCoy 1977:221). Consistent with McCoy's description, Arapaho participants at that time still regarded Wovoka as a powerful medicine man. Contemporary oral history also suggests that the Ghost Dance songs were remembered at least by the generation of Arapaho singers that passed away by the 1980s. For the Arapaho case, little has been done to follow the elements backward or forward in time from Mooney's frame of reference itself. An intensive analysis of the songs is one place to begin.[3]

One principal reason for the elision of Arapahos is the weak presence of what Fogelson calls an "ethnoethnohistorical approach": "the vast majority of ethnohistorical works produced by historians and anthropologists either neglect or consciously eschew the native point of view" (1972:105). The problem is not so much that evidence for indigenous perspectives is thin, as Mooney's material on the Arapaho Ghost Dance illustrates. The lack of attention to indigenous perspectives, as Fogelson realizes, has been a symptom of a misplaced concreteness that identifies objectivity with a plot-generated narration of events bounded by a thin, restricted reading of documents (1989:135–137). His deconstruction of this equivocation of linearity with objectivity evolves from two converging strands in social scientific thought. One is the French Annales critique of positivist history that opened a closed historical consciousness to multiple levels of time outside the narrow chronology of events or reduction to monocausal explanation. The other critical current flows from Hallowell's insight that culturally constituted realities can be studied objectively only by eschewing "categorical abstractions derived from Western thought" (1960:359). Simply stated, positivist or narrative history *is less objective* for ignoring the residuum of "nonevents" and details of concepts that are contained in indigenous texts (Fogelson 1989:141).

A third trajectory to be woven into this is the need to study cultural creativity in ethnohistory by attending to the linguistic and ethnopoetic dimensions of Native texts. Extending the approach set forth in Judith Vander's work (1997) on Shoshone Naraya songs, I will explore some of the dominant tropes, mythico-ritual core concepts, and sociocultural contexts of a few Arapaho Ghost Dance songs. As Fernandez and others have noted, "what is done in human affairs is not to be taken literally at face value," and the assumption of an "immaculate perception" or interpretation is betrayed by the intercession of figurative devices that are not merely expressive but constitutive of culture" (1991:1).

One task for ethnohistorical translators of texts is to identify figurative devices and their functions relative to indigenous contexts rather than impose a Euro-American reading. To cite an obvious example, metaphor is not the dominant trope in Arapaho narrative or poetics. A Euro-American standard definition of trope assumes distortion or shift from a primary or basic meaning, that is, as a figure that changes the meaning of a word from its ordinary meaning (Lanham 1991:154–155). This concern with metaphor derives from the Western preoccupation with the referential function of language, thus distinguishing poetic language as deviating from literal, or "standard language." Across cultures it is not so easy to define boundaries between standard and poetic language, or between the work of words and the play of tropes. The opposition should be phrased, following Friedrich (1986), as a continuum instead of a dichotomy.

An alternative definition of tropes is offered by Bohuslav Havránek of the Prague School who identifies poetics in the process of foregrounding "the use of the devices of the language in such a way that this use attracts attention and is perceived as uncommon, as deprived of automatization, as deautomatized" (1964:10). This broadens the definition beyond a semantic function to include images, dreams, musicality, myth, and other figures. When applied to other cultural contexts, the challenge is to elaborate an understanding of the contexts of *both* automatization and improvisation. In the Ghost Dance songs it is necessary to distinguish what is "ordinary" for the cultural context from what is "foregrounded" as novel. In particular, the poetic function of forms in Arapaho contexts is to foreground and generate movement from stasis and closeness from distance in social relations.

Dell Hymes's (1981:7) recognition of the lack of linguistic and ethnopoetic attention to Native American original texts certainly applies to much ethnohistory and to the Arapaho Ghost Dance songs in particular. There has been no intensive study of the Arapaho songs for over a century. It is thus necessary to retranslate and reinterpret the songs by utilizing ethnographic, linguistic, and historical evidence accumulated since Mooney's time. It is equally essential to consider the multiple levels upon which the songs function, for the Arapaho Ghost Dance was an expression of poetic imagination, interweaving myth, dream, ritual, individuality, referentiality, style, and social relations.

Permeating formulations about revitalization movements is a Western psychology of aesthetics that assigns creativity to individual psychopathology or collective disequilibrium. In this sense Anthony Wallace's original model of revitalization (1956) has often been applied to the Ghost Dance without consideration for the Arapaho's unique contribution. Mooney's observation that Arapahos embraced the Ghost Dance more profoundly than other Plains groups is a test for all theories that attribute cultural creativity to psychological, economic, or political causes. For the former to hold Arapahos must have experienced the greatest stress and deprivation among Plains groups, but there is no evidence or even possibility for supporting that hypothesis.

Mooney's answer to the difference of receptivity is the Arapaho "character" as "devotees and prophets" in comparison to other groups, such as the Cheyenne, that he defines as "more skeptical" (1896:775). Such a caricature has informed subsequent characterizations of the Arapaho, though it deserves qualification. There is indeed an Arapaho cultural schema for practice that anticipates mystery or things unknown behind the appearances of the world, though such things when known could be accepted or rejected. Some Arapaho people were in fact skeptical about Wovoka's message, while others accepted it. Among Northern Arapahos, those in Black Coal's Forks People band, for example, did not as readily give up their commitment to Catholicism for the Ghost Dance.

Nor is it clear that all Arapahos saw the messiah as an extraordinary visionary or historical figure. Recounting his first encounter with Wovoka, Sherman Sage did not speak of the messiah's death and resurrection as uncanny or miraculous:

> "Yes he died. It is harder for me to believe than it is for Yellow Calf. So I kicked him in the ribs."

"When I kicked him in the ribs," he continued, "he did not move, so he was dead. Then, pretty soon, his eyes opened, he sat up, stood before us and gave us a message from the Great Mystery." [McCoy 1977:214]

The sense that the supernatural or sacred inspires great mystery or awe among the Arapaho—or other indigenous peoples—must be reconsidered and properly contextualized. One Arapaho view I heard in the contemporary context is that such things and experiences are dangerous, and proper precautions must be followed, but they are not necessarily exceptional or extraordinary. Such behavior does not necessarily reflect intense devotion to doctrine. In particular, Arapaho medicine men (*beetee3i'*) were known to have powers similar in form and effect to those Wovoka exhibited.

The difference in Arapaho involvement must also be situated in the strategies that Arapaho people used toward non-Arapaho cultures. During the first decades of the reservation period, both Arapaho tribes attempted to sustain continuity by appropriating and placing cultural innovations and Euro-American introduced forms within channels of Arapaho practice and cultural creativity. For example, Christianity and the mission schools were not perceived as threats to be resisted but as sources of knowledge and power to be appropriated for Arapaho practice (see Anderson 2001b). As Carl Starkloff (1974) has argued, Arapaho Catholics appropriated sacraments and other practices in Arapaho terms. The Ghost Dance was thus part of a local cultural movement and strategy to indigenize imposed, adopted, and newly created forms not through assimilation or syncretism, but through compartmentalization within Arapaho practice.[4]

Over a longer duration the Ghost Dance was brought into an Arapaho theory of creative practice to appropriate life-giving power or displace the negative power of what is "crazy," chaotic, or unknowable. Arapaho ritual practice and language preserves, produces, and appropriates ambiguity and mystery, or *cee'inoo'*—to use the Arapaho term that Alfred Kroeber curiously glosses with the German term *unergründlich*, or "unfathomable" (Kroeber 1916–20). Zdenek Salzmann offers a gloss of the same stem as "confused" (1983:69). The fringes on the sides of a rawhide bag that Kroeber describes are called *niitcäantetanani*, which contains the *c(e)e'in-* stem and means "what we do not know; that is, objects out of our possession, or various things too numerous to mention" (1902:125). In Arapaho practice the power of this mystery can be channeled into human life through appropriate ritual practices, though it is always to some extent beyond human grasp. Out of this, movement follows from stasis, and closeness from distance.

Most of the songs that Mooney recorded are short entitlements of larger dream or trance narratives that aim to appropriate such power. The trances that Ghost Dance hypnosis created were regarded as "crazy" forms of behavior in the Cheyenne, Lakota, and Arapaho cultures alike (see George Sword's narrative in Mooney 1896:797–798). The Western dream theory that maintains that alternative states of consciousness contribute to personality organization must be qualified here, as much as the revitalization-from-disequilibrium thesis must be qualified at a collective level. In the Arapaho context dreams and visions are not as much about reorganizing the "self" as about channeling acquired power for life through social relations with both human and other-than-human persons, to borrow Hallowell's distinction (1960).

For besides Wovoka himself, trance was not part of the original Paiute ceremony, though it became central and even "epidemic," according to Mooney (1896:772), in Arapaho performance, especially among women participants. Arapaho practice seems to have copied and then generalized Wovoka's trance practices and less so his "message." The life-death metamorphosis and travel to the above were not without precedent in mythico-ritual experience, though the general accessibility of trance to both genders of all ages was unique to Arapaho practices. On the one hand, the practice parallels the mythical acquisition of knowledge through death and rebirth as in the Arapaho story of Lime-Crazy, who died and came back to the camp to share the knowledge of the men's Crazy Lodge (Dorsey and Kroeber 1903:23–31). On the other, such experiences outside of the traditional age-ranked system were part of unprecedented collectivized ritual participation that proliferated in cultural inventiveness from the 1890s on.

In Arapaho interpretations a trance or dream does not necessarily affect equilibrium or a better life, for it may indeed bring obligations and "roads" to follow that are more difficult than those before the vision (see Anderson 2001a:255–256). Mooney mentions one Ghost Dance leader whose power was negative and dangerous, though the man himself was pitied and not held responsible for his actions (1896:924–925). Thus, it is necessary to overcome the assumption that dreams or visions are always curative and that alternative religious movements "move" crisis toward equilibrium. An Arapaho dream or vision always poses some open-endedness or new "mystery" about meaning and associated obligations, the risks or benefits of which only become known as subsequent actions unfold.

Another Euro-American preoccupation framing the Ghost Dance is the construction of religion as an a priori, ordered belief system or "doctrine."

As DeMallie argues, there was no unified "creed" for the message from the prophet Wovoka (1982:387). Vander reiterates that "there was not a single Ghost Dance religion" but a bifurcation into Great Basin and Plains branches and, within each, considerable variation (1997:30). For this break, Arapahos were instrumental. On the smaller scale, each individual visitor to the prophet or participant back home had his or her own interpretation. At the level of indigenous perspectives, the content of songs themselves can thus be related to unique individuals. At another level, no Arapaho song literally mentions the coming of an apocalyptic destruction and renewal, though many express a coming reunion with the spirits of the dead through trance, a road between earth and sky via the messenger Crow, or the revivification of the buffalo (Mooney 1896:983). Foregrounding millenarian imagery in particular are songs attributed to Sitting Bull, who was the link in bringing the ceremony from Wyoming to his own southern tribe and others in Indian Territory. His own allegiance to Wovoka's message would eventually alienate him from the North Arapaho tribe (Fowler 1982:123).

At a very general level the Ghost Dance doctrine does fit, as Mooney suggests, with Arapaho cosmogony involving succession of four worlds to this the final one:

> And Nih'āⁿçaⁿ gave the Arapaho the middle of the earth to live in, and all other were to live around them. Since then there have been three lives [generations]; this the fourth. At the end of the fourth, if the Arapaho have all died, there will be another flood. But if any of them live, it will be well with the world. Everything depends on them. [Dorsey and Kroeber 1903:16]

Mooney relates that the Arapaho recognized this world as the sixth cycle and the coming end as the seventh (1896:701). All Arapaho views of time and space were shaped by the same homologous order, a pattern with its own variant among many Northern American Indian peoples (Anderson 2001a:91–114). There have been four worlds, each associated with a different direction and color. According to most this world is the last one or the black or blue world. Similarly, there are four hills of life (*yeneini3i' 3030utei'i*), four seasons, four directions, and four buttes at the periphery of the world upon which the Four Old Men sit, protecting the world at the periphery from the outside. Seven cycles are included when the intervening transitions or valleys are added to the four hills.

Rather than a cosmic renewal and return of all the dead, though, it seems that the Ghost Dance trances functioned for some practitioners as a way to meet particular deceased relatives or return to specific cherished practices relevant to individual life experiences. In Song 23 (Mooney 1896:973) the composer meets his own father and in 19 (1896:971) a brother. In Song 68 (1896:1007) a mother sees her children playing. As Mooney suggests a dominant theme is a journey to reunite with the dead. As in other Arapaho ritual contexts, practice is defined by the social relations in one's family or among peers rather than inspired by visions of cosmological change.

Mooney was less interested in, and leaves to "common sense," the function of the Ghost Dance to bring about ends specific to this world and to individuals. In surveying Ghost Dance variations he says that "The idea of obtaining temporal blessings as a reward of a faithful performance of religious duties is too natural and universal to require comment" (1896:786–87). On the contrary, these motives are cultural and particular. Arapaho songs were tied less to cosmological reflection and more to individuals' immediate, short-run concerns, to generate life, maintain social relations, and establish paths for action. The Ghost Dance was brought into an Arapaho theory of ritual practice through which life-generating elements could be appropriated and life-negating ones discarded (see Anderson 2001a:240–273). It is in the terms of this Arapaho sense of practice that the Ghost Dance songs begin to make sense.

Pity and Release

Attending to the ways in which core concepts and tropes work is indispensable if ethnohistory is to overcome ethnocentric psychological and theological assumptions. This is most evident in Mooney's exegesis of and others authors' recurring references to Song 28:

> *Neixoo nehcih'owouunoni,*
> *Neixoo nehcih'owouunoni*
> *Woow, biixonokooyeinoo*
> *Woow, biixonokooyeinoo*
> *Hoowuuni biiȝitii*
> *Hoowuuni biiȝitii*

> Father, have pity on me!
> Father, have pity on me!
> Now, I am wailing-fasting-thirsting.
> Now, I am wailing-fasting-thirsting.
> There is no food.
> There is no food.
> [Mooney 1896:977][5]

Most of the attention drawn to this song derives from Mooney's comment: "This is the most pathetic of the Ghost-dance songs. It is sung to the plaintive tune, sometimes with tears rolling down the cheeks of the dancers as the words bring up thoughts of their present miserable and dependent condition" (1896:977). As will be discussed in detail, the song itself does not necessarily foreground historical events or socioeconomic conditions precipitating the Ghost Dance. Though pity is common to other American Indian cultural systems, among the groups for which Mooney supplies Ghost Dance songs it is most conspicuous and pervasive in the Arapaho collection. Where pity appears in songs from other Plains groups, such as a few Kiowa songs (1896:1084–1088), the Arapaho influence is clear.

Appeals to pity and ritualized crying are continuous with other Arapaho relations of ritualized exchange. Ceremonial "weeping for pity," which Arapaho distinguishes from other ways of crying, is part of all the most sacred rituals (see Dorsey 1903:49; Kroeber 1902:74). In fact, referring to pity is typical for a prayer or song of petition in many contexts of Arapaho ritual practice, from individual fasting to the Offerings-Lodge (i.e., Sun dance). To give one example, a song that Curtis recorded was performed during the preparation of the buffalo hide prior to the actual performance of the Offerings-Lodge:

> *Heetih'owouuneeneino'*
> *Hiisiis neisonoo*
>
> May he pity us
> Sun, my father
> [Curtis 1934:198]

In Arapaho ways of speaking, pity is the medium for any human request directed to other-than-human persons. Such petitions must be made not only with sacrifice and offerings but also with channeled creativity through song, painting, and production of ritual objects. Pitiful situations are expressed in a modality that draws attention, through condensation of emotion, to a center. All thinking, seeing, hearing, and speech are focused on a central object or being in order to attract blessings to mobilize life. In this way the earth was created, all life motion in ritual occurs, and the Ghost Dance itself sought to call forth buffalo, the deceased in the above, and powerful other-than-human persons. It is also in this condensed modality that alternative states of consciousness attract new knowledge. In short, pity is a core modality but not historically specific to an "event" or time period.

Song 28 parallels many Arapaho prayers and songs. One specific correspondence is Yellow Calf's ritual prayer for calling buffalo, recorded by the cowboy-actor Tim McCoy: "Then the people outside the circle of stones around the buffalo skull moved inside the circle and shouted: '*Nechawunania!* Have pity on us! *Niibithi!* We have nothing to eat! *Nechawunania! Niibithi!*'" (McCoy 1977:112). According to McCoy, Yellow Calf described this prayer, conspicuously similar to the song recorded by Mooney, as part of a ceremony to recall buffalo: "When the *etheninon* [*hii3einoon*], buffalo herd, would disappear, it was I who asked the people of the village to come to a hill. There, on the highest point, I placed a painted buffalo skull inside a circle of stones. I would ask the people to think of the buffalo and thank them for giving us food for life, shelter for protection and clothing for warmth" (1977:112). Two of the terms used by Yellow Calf are clearly identical to those of Song 28. Two other Ghost Dance songs (34 and 35) refer to the *3i'eyoo*, a stone monument placed on hills or mountains at places of fasting or prayer as a symbol for the center of pity and sacrifice (Mooney 1896:981). The term also refers to the same monument in the path toward the sun outside a sweat lodge. On one level the song is a call for the return of buffalo that is consistent with a practice that predates and postdates the Ghost Dance itself. As in myth (see Dorsey and Kroeber 1903:48) buffalo come out of pity, like any distant being, when they hear Arapaho cries.

Although original Arapaho texts for all translations are not available, enough are accessible from notes of Kroeber, Mooney, and Cleaver Warden (Dorsey's interpreter) to verify that the form *hoowouuno-* (or *-owouuno-* when prefixed) is consistently translated as "pity," "sympathy," or "mercy," connoting action as well as sentiment in the sense of "easily moving" or "moving another." Pity as a state blocks or slows movement, while the reaction generates movement. Pity as an action is thus to make it easy for another person to move. Pity is thus only comprehensible in relation to Arapaho ways of spatializing time and temporalizing space in myth, ritual, language, and art. To explore some of this here, the stem *hoowouuno-* can be reduced further to *hoow-*, suggesting "downward" or "downhill" motion, and —*ouu*—, which is derived from -*[h]onouu-* or "climbing." Consistent with the four hills temporality, pitying connotes making it easy for someone through downward motion as in descending or coasting down a hill. This is especially clear when the opposite term for "difficulty" is considered. The term *honouneenoo'* ("it is difficult"), connotes by virtue of the *honouu-* form a climb or ascent upward, as in the verb phrase *honouuhunoo* ("I am climbing uphill"). In all, to pity someone is to "make it easy" for them, as in a downhill motion, to make one's burden light or to empower one to "push on hard" (Mooney 1896:966).

Pity is the modal device (see Friedrich 1991:34) linked to a root chrono-type, or schema for shaping space-time, for affecting a shift or break-through from immobility to mobility, from inattentiveness to listening, from diffuseness to focus, from isolation to engagement, and from dis-tance to closeness in social relationships. As a modal trope pity carries more than a literal sense of pathos, for it requires action, generates social relations, and initiates subsequent exchange. It is way of moving an or-dinarily unmoved being to engage in exchange and a means for closing the distance between two persons of different rank. Those senior in age or highest in the above are the least moved by circumstances. Similarly, the highest being, Our Father, moves less than the sun, moon, or other sacred beings. As both a narrative device and a pragmatic process in social relations, pity "moves" the unmoved.

A narrow interpretation based on the assumption that the Ghost Dance was solely a response to the harsh conditions of reservation life cannot be supported by referring to the songs in total. This is not to deny that physical and demographic conditions were harsh for the 1880s and 1890s, which were among the most difficult periods the Arapaho tribes faced. It is only to assert that the mood of this song and its accompanying affect do not just reflect the "stress" of reservation life but rather borrow formalized figures and pragmatic schema from mythico-ritual forms of much longer duration.

One of the advantages of ethno-ethnohistory viewed through ethnopo-etics, then, is that imposed and assumed universal psychological concepts can be discarded or refined to fit the local ethnopsychological context. The Arapaho concept of "pity" raises many difficulties for attempts to translate it into Euro-American psychological concepts. It is neither a universal mood nor demeanor, but an action taken and an exchange re-lation between persons for ritual practice and life movement in time. The historical conditions of "pity" thus should not be overgeneralized either by a Euro-American association of indigenous peoples as "Other," as thus saturated with pathos, tragedy, or even apocalypse.

Within the collection of the Arapaho songs, not all expressions fore-ground a so inwardly "pathetic" tone and condensed gist. In contrast to songs of pity, various other songs affect lighter and dissipated mood and imagery. Flight in particular is almost as pervasive as pity in the songs taken as a whole. Suggesting motion around the earth or to the above, flight is foregrounded in Song 29, which is especially complex linguisti-cally and rich in imagery:

Neniihoonih'ohunoo
Neniihoonih'ohunoo
Yeneisitii'inookuunih'ohunoo
Yeneisitii'inookuunih'ohunoo
Hihcebe'—He'e'e'!
Hihcebe'—He'e'e'!
Hei'ei'ei!
Hei'ei'ei!

Yellow I am flying.
Yellow I am flying.
Wild roses I wear on my head, I fly.
Wild roses I wear on my head, I fly.
Above—
Above—
[Mooney 1896:977]

This song is especially interesting because of the imagery created by compounding verb forms, a unique Arapaho contiguity trope, paralleled in many other American Indian languages. Much of Arapaho poetics involves combining verb forms in creative ways in order to foreground a striking visual image, as clever, beautiful, humorous, or uncanny. The first line combines *-niihoon-* and *-nih'ohu* ("yellow" and "flying"), two forms not normally together. The second line compounds three forms: *yeneis* ("wild rose"), *-nookuu-* ("worn in hair"), and *-nih'ohu* ("flying"). Both the first and second constructions end in the *-noo*, a first-person singular, intransitive verb suffix. Also there is an antistrophic repetition of the *nih'ohunoo* verb form at the close of each of the first two lines.

Mooney concedes that "The meaning of this song is not clear" (1896: 978). He follows this with an association to the uses of rose berries, though other connotations are worth considering. The juxtaposition of red and yellow is part of the duality of Ghost Dance painting and art, as Kroeber recognizes (1907:417). Red here could mean earth as well as rose, and yellow the sky or above (*hihcebe'*). The song also follows a gist from attending to the flyer's color to a hair ornament, to the *hihcebe'* ("above") and a sense of spatial dissipation. Song 29 contrasts free movement, then, with the immobility, fasting, and pity of the oft-quoted Song 28 directly preceding it. The former moves upward into dissipation, the latter downward into a condensed immobility. These two types of songs recapitulate two moments in Arapaho mythopoetic space-time that are carried into the Ghost Dance, a transition from immobility to mobility and from earth to the above.

Revolving around pity and released motion, there are specific cultural continuities and creative figures that advance Mooney's interpretation of the Ghost Dance songs and movement as functioning to reconfigure relations between Arapaho people and the non-Indian world. The Arapaho term for a Euro-American person is *nih'oo3oo* (*nih'oo3ou'u*, plural form), which refers to the spider and the mythical trickster figure of stories who became *hihcebe' nih'oo3oo* ("Spider-Above") and *heisonooonin* ("Our Father"), which we will discuss later in this chapter. Early and contemporary Arapaho informants are careful to make the separation, however, between these two extensions of the term by stressing that the creator-trickster of myth is not a "white man" (Hilger 1952:146). For *nih'oo3oo* Mooney offers the meaning "expert, skillful, and wise" (1896:962). This does not mean that whites were perceived as godlike, only that they had powers unfixed and mysterious, with the potential to give life if appropriated correctly or negate it if not. Anything confusing or mysterious (*cee'inoo'*) can be bad or good, depending on the movement of exchanges, relations, and practices in and through time.

Song 3 places the relation to whites in the context of exchange and pity:

> *Hee, teebe tih'owouunonou'u, neniisono'*
> *Hee, teebe tih'owouunonou'u, neniisono'*
> *Nih'oo3ou'u*
> *Nih'oo3ou'u*
> *Niibinou'u koh'owootino*
> *Niibinou'u koh'owootino*
>
> Yes, at first when I pitied them, my children.
> Yes, at first when I pitied them, my children.
> The whites.
> The whites.
> I gave to them, fruits.
> I gave to them, fruits.
> [1896:961]

As part of the vision that accompanies Left Hand's experience of this song "the father showed him extensive orchards, telling him that in the beginning all those things had been given to whites, but that hereafter they would be given to his children, the Indians" (1896:962). In the beginning the creator pitied the whites and gave them fruits but from this time on will pity Arapahos instead.[6]

Drawing on mythical elements, this song thus presents an epitomizing event that synecdochically represents the historical and continuing relationship between Arapahos and *nih'oo3ou'u*. Its function of connecting part to whole in time operates on a number of levels. In mythical time whites received different technology that excluded Arapahos (Dorsey and Kroeber 1903:6). In Left Hand's vision, Arapahos will receive it in the next age, thus returning to the proper balance. In broader perspective the Ghost Dance directs that "power" given to whites—with the implication that they have no rights to it—will be given to Arapahos.

Connected to the song's focus on gift giving, another song (30) about *nih'oo3ou'u* recognizes that whites are "without pity" and will therefore receive no pity from other-than-human persons or Arapahos in return:

> *He'yoho'ho! He'yoho'ho!*
> The yellow-hide, the white skin [man].
> I have now put him aside—
> I have now put him aside—
> I have no more sympathy [pity] with him.
> I have no more sympathy [pity] with him.
> *He'yoho'ho! He'yoho'ho!*
> [Mooney 1896:978, brackets added]

Much Arapaho and other North American Indian discourse directed to Euro-Americans requested that the latter show pity and thus engage in genuinely human relationships. For Euro-Americans, though, such requests were often perceived as "begging," with negative connotations of dependency, lack of initiative, or the nagging talk of poverty. What Arapahos and perhaps other tribes in their own ways were trying to do, however, was to engage Euro-Americans in a "human" exchange in their own terms of pity, conceived as a positive motive for giving when others have an obvious need, without concern for moral or material "cost."

As another phase in the relationship, the song relates that whites are to be "put aside," which parallels a moment of Arapaho ritual practice in which life-threatening things and persons must be discarded to a distance from human lived space. All Arapaho ritual practice sought to place life-threatening elements at a distance or discard them, either on the periphery of the camp circle or world, or in the above somewhere. Wovoka's message that whites would be placed somewhere else, then, is continuous with Arapaho strategies for placing distance between themselves and Euro-American society in the history of contact. In general, the Ghost Dance songs revolve around the theme of "putting things in their proper places."

A third song (21) relates that whites will be rendered "desolate," although "poor" or "pitiful" is probably a better translation of the phrase *hootowouuhono'* (Mooney 1896:972). The final verse states *nih'oo3ou'u hohookee niʒi'*—that is, "whites they are crazy." Craziness (*hohookee*) connotes "having no sense," "not caring about what you do," "not seeing the consequences of one's actions," being "not in one's right mind," or "always jumping into a situations without thinking."[7] Another connotation of craziness is "overdoing things," or "going to extremes," that is, violating the limits of respect and caution for ritual and some nonritual practices. In these senses, though, craziness is not morally bad but rather a source of power for life movement when it is channeled properly through ritual.

This song follows the gist of Left Hand's vision more than it does a millenarian belief in the coming of a new world, as Mooney emphasizes (1896:973). There is no direct mention of a new earth for Indians or of whites being destroyed. Rather, Song 21 relates the mytho-logic of Song 3, that is, that the whites will become poor because they are "crazy" and will be put aside, discarded, or collectively shunned. In many respects this ambiguity seizes on irony. Whites are crazy and without pity yet they multiply and have much food and technology. Such a contradiction has generated a multiplicity of Arapaho views and strategies throughout history, all of which question whether Euro-Americans participate in Arapaho definitions of personhood or in a separate reality.

As a group the songs that pertain to *nih'oo3oo* employ various tropes to place boundaries on the relationship between Arapaho and non-Indian people. All these devices revolve around the asymmetry of intercultural exchange and juxtapose an explicit or implicit "then" to a "now" in the shift in the relationship to whites. "At first," Arapahos approached them on the human ground of pity and did not know them; now they have no pity for them and know they are crazy but powerful. Such songs are allegorical and synecdochic in generalizing from part to whole the real contradictions of cultural contact retained in collective memory. One conspicuous aspect of trance narratives and songs is, then, to shape the space and time of the relationship between Arapaho and non-Indian worlds by foregrounding traditional images and shapes.

Our Father

The focal addressee and apparent speaker of many songs is *heisonoonin* (translated "Our Father"), *neisonoo* ("my father"), or *neixoo* ("father!," vocative form). One of these variants appears in 24 (32 percent) of the 73 songs.[8] As Mooney notes for the Arapaho context, "father or grandfather are terms of reverence and affection, applied to anything held sacred or awful" (1896:970). In their ritual uses, these terms are extensions of the "generational principle" of Arapaho kinship terminology as Eggan defined it (1937). The term *father* extends to father's brothers, and the term *grandfather* ultimately extends to all men of two generations above or higher.

Sherman Sage refers to *heisonoonin* as "Everybody's Father" since it is a third-person plural inclusive possessive (Hilger 1952:65). Some other forms used in ritual contexts also employ the *hei-* or *hii-* prefix with the *-n* inclusive suffix used for sacred forms to mark collective possession, such as when the afterlife is referred to as *hiiyein* ("our home") and the Four Old Men as *hii(t)een(i)* (literally denoting "our hearts").

Elsewhere, Mooney states that for the "Opening Song" (1), which originated with the Northern Arapaho and was adopted by southern followers, *heisonoonin* refers to the messiah who speaks to his followers as "my children" (*neneisono'*) (1896:959). Mooney's confusion over the usage reflects his selection of only part of the range of the term's meaning from the polysemy and metonymic function that surrounds this and many similar terms in indigenous North American religious practice and ethnopoetics. The *Our Father* term is unique to prayers and petitions directed to the creator. However, any contiguity with the creator by mythical kinship, message, or exchange can extend the term to the person or thing involved.

The term *Our Father* mediates distance and closeness in relations with other-than-human persons. In most songs there is a spatial configuration shaped by the position of the voice of the speaker and addressee. Songs that address Our Father speak from the point of view of the dreamer or the human realm itself to the above. Those songs addressing "my children" speak from above or, according to Mooney, from Wovoka or a messenger (e.g., Crow) to an audience below. By way of contrast, a few other songs evoke equal relations, such as those that refer to a male (*beenii'*) (1896, 4:962) or female (*hiseihihi'*) "partner," as among best friends or chums of the same gender (1896, 64:1002). Songs pertaining to gambling and game playing, for instance, generate a sense of equality. Whereas hierarchical relations require respect and indirect appeals, equality implies open relations and play.

Other beings addressed in prayer can be referred to as "father," though according to much evidence Our Father is specific to the highest being or creator who sits unmoved "above" all others. In mythical time Father-Above and Mother-Above are the parents of the brothers, Sun and Moon, who marry earthly wives, one of whom brings culture to the people below. *Hihcebe' Nih'oo3oo*, translated as "Man-Above or Spider-Above," is thus really the father of all other beings, both human and sacred (Dorsey and Kroeber 1903:6). Consistent with a nearly pan-Algonquian archetype, *heisonoonin* is an "owner of earth water, and everything," which again parallels the age hierarchy in which senior men and women own the most sacred bundles and knowledge, subsuming all others. Each being prayed to is an owner, such as the water-monster *hiincebiit*, who is "owner of waters" and turtle, who is "owner of rain." Beneath Our Father are the other owners, who are also referred to as "fathers," except for the earth, which is called "mother" (*neinoo*).

In mythical time, the trickster *nih'oo300* (spider) created the world and humans. Then, from this, the earthly level he was placed above, or *hihcebe'*, where he know "sits." Though Dorsey and Kroeber refer to the creator as "white-man above" it seems that the sense of "spider" preceded the reference to white man and that the term relevant to the present mythical period is *heisonoonin*. Jessie Rowlodge, one of Hilger's informants (1952:144), further states that Spider-Above should not be addressed directly but rather spoken of as Our Father or *beeteet* ("medicine" or "mystery") and that only the most senior old men of the last degree of lodges should pray to him. As in many cultures, to address by name a senior person or relative deserving respect is inappropriate. Elders I spoke to at Wind River also agreed that *heisonoonin* is more appropriate for prayers than *hihcebe' nih'oo300*.

The mythical evolution of other-than-human persons recapitulates the life trajectory for humans, which moves from mobility in youth to immobility in old age. Beings once itinerant or "crazy" (e.g., *nih'oo300*) become placed in the cosmos as *honouuneiht* ("he/she is difficult"), meaning, according to Kroeber's notes (1916–20), "not easily moved or persuaded, can't hurt it, hard to satisfy, or grant benefits." To be powerful (*beetee*) is thus also to be difficult to move to pity. To approach such a being requires sacrifice or dream states. All high-ranking human or other-than-human persons must be referred to carefully and indirectly and approached through the mediation of others, such as messengers, elders, or medicine men. Thus the call for poetry or nonliteral ways of speaking in Arapaho prayers and songs fits with ritual action.

To be reconsidered, then, is Mooney's suggestion that Wovoka and the Arapaho leader Sitting Bull were referred to as "Our Father."[9] If this is correct it is clear that the Arapaho Ghost Dance songs employed the term for prophet and apostle in a new way that broke significantly with prior usage, which was confined to the creator only. It is clear from existing narratives and oral history that Arapaho people regarded Wovoka as a powerful medicine man, although Mooney overstates the connection between prophet and Our Father. The material he provides on trance and the songs themselves suggests that Arapaho followers did not place Wovoka in the center of imagery and "doctrine." They sought to appropriate the practice of his vision rather than totalize their belief in his message or raise his charismatic authority to sacred status above humans. As discussed below, *houu* ("crow") became a new term for God with the Ghost Dance, and in turn *houusoo* came to refer to both Wovoka and Jesus, as offspring or son of Crow/God.

One curious shift for the Arapaho is the tendency of the Ghost Dance, Christianity, and Peyote religion to allow more immediate petitions to *heisonoonin* without elders' intercession. The dreams, visions, and appropriated religious forms of this era allowed more open access to the above through prayer and song. The Ghost Dance was unprecedented in its direct visionary experiences, musical improvisation, and openness to so many participants.

Exchange

As relevant to our preceding discussion of dreams and pity, many of the Arapaho songs contain or imply exchange as a trope for establishing connectivity. To my knowledge there has been no treatment of the symbolic dimensions of exchange in the Ghost Dance, yet much of the movement was about the exchange of "goods," whether knowledge or material forms. At one level the Arapaho relationship to Wovoka was defined by the exchange of medicine and knowledge between a medicine man (*beeteet*) and his clients. Well into the early 1900s, Arapaho people continued to write and send money to Wovoka to order the red paint from Mount Grant (Mooney 1896:778–79), which the prophet sent for a price in used tin cans (Dangberg 1957). As Mooney observed, objects he brought from Wovoka to the Arapaho were regarded as medicine deserving respect. Within the ceremony itself, those "given feathers" became leaders of the dance. Much of the ritualized transfer of the dance between tribes revolved around intertribal gift giving, for which there are only scattered references in the ethnographic literature. Throughout history Plains peoples have "given" ceremonies to each other in order to form enduring bonds of friendship and alliance. Kroeber mentions, for example, that the Crow Dance was given to the Arapaho by the Lakota, as a *ce'eek3oo*, that is, a bundle given to form friendship between tribes (1907:368). The "giving of the Ghost Dance" to other tribes, then, was a way of forming or reaffirming bonds of exchange between tribes. More immediately the Ghost Dance songs are about relations of exchange between humans and other-than-human persons moving toward, though never achieving, balanced reciprocity once and for all (Hallowell 1960:384).

Though extensive in literature and poetry outside North America (see Mauss 1990:1–2), exchange as a "trope" is especially pervasive in Arapaho and other American Indian narrative forms. Gifts as tropes "mean" more than their face value. They extend the time and space of relations beyond the self, immediate social situation, narrative frame of reference, or discursive event (see Munn 1986:3–20). Performing these functions, gifts are focal in a number of Arapaho Ghost Dance songs. In Song 18 (Mooney 1896:971), a man of the extinct Arapaho "Rock" band (*hoho'nookowunnen*) gives paint to the dreamer. Many of the songs give access to goods no longer available, such as buffalo meat, new bed coverings, and, in this case, paint. A gift thus bridges past and present. As mentioned earlier, an other-than-human person more distant in space and time must be compelled by sacrifice, singing, crying, praying, and ceremony to "listen" and then pity human beings with gifts for life, knowledge, and motion. Song 26 refers to turtle's gift of the earth to humans in myth, as well as the knowledge of it from "my father":

> *Hee, teebe tihne'etiitoonehehk*
> *Hee, teebe tihne'etiitoonehehk*
> *Niiteehehk be'enoo neeceeheiht*
> *Biito'owu'*
> *Biito'owu'*
> *Tihtowuuneinoo neisonoo*
> *Tihtowuuneinoo neisonoo*

> Well, just when there was life.
> Well, just when there was life.
> It was turtle who gave this gift.
> It was turtle who gave this gift.
> The earth.
> The earth.
> When he told me this, my father.
> When he told me this, my father.
> [1896:975]

In the Arapaho earth-diver myth, only turtle is able to bring up earth from beneath the water that covers the world. He gives it to the Flat Pipe who spreads it out, then turtle himself becomes the earth-island. In the opening song (1896:958), discussed next in this chapter, earthquakes and other tectonic events are caused by his movements. Also, as Mooney recognizes, the turtle is a common image on Arapaho Ghost Dance shirts.

Kroeber records a fasting vision that a Southern Arapaho man experienced around the time of the Ghost Dance in which, after seven days of fasting, turtle visits him:

> I am not the father nor the messenger, but I whom you have heard of and talked of,—the turtle. I own the rain. When you want rain, pray to me, for I am the fog. . . . When you are at a feast, let the people take a little food and give it to me. Let them do this whenever they can, and I will remember them and protect them. [Kroeber 1907:428]

In Arapaho, the word for "fog" and "turtle" are the same. As for other spirit helpers, the individual who receives such aid must offer a piece of food to him at each meal. The dance sticks, and paraphernalia made by the man and described by Kroeber connote connections to the Ghost Dance as well. As the preceding quotation suggests, there is an ongoing exchange between humans and other-than-human beings that involve daily food offerings and other sacrifices. Many of the Ghost Dance songs are continuous with the form of vision experiences in which people receive gifts for protection, life, and well-being from other-than-human beings. As a result, a lifelong exchange is set in motion.

Exchange is one of the dominant tropes of the Ghost Dance songs since it is the basis for shifts in relations, changes of form, and even movements in nature. Pity is the initial mover of exchange between those distant in space or rank. As a trope, exchange extends the frame of reference of the text itself to an ongoing temporality of social relations among persons. Much of the Arapaho sense of "doing things in a good or right way" involves ongoing proper exchange between humans and other-than-human beings. When violated the exchange becomes potentially life threatening. One of the functions of the Ghost Dance was to create new exchanges, balance some, and recognize the imbalance of others. As discussed earlier the imbalance in exchange between Arapahos and Euro-Americans in the history of contact is the generative source of distance as a strategy expressed in the Ghost Dance songs. In short, exchange defines history.

The Ghost Dance "doctrine" apparent in the songs and surrounding performance is about the polytropic interrelationship of exchange, pity, and movement on both small and large scales of space and time. The opening song begins, for instance, with Our Father addressing his children:

> *Eyehe'! neneisono'*
> *Eyehe'! neneisono'*
> *Hinee ceese' hetiicooninoo Hei'eiyei'!*
> *Hinee ceese' hetiicooninoo Hei'eiyei'!*

Nohooni ne'niʒeetouhunoo Hei'eiyei'!
Nohooni ne'niʒeetouhunoo Hei'eiyei'!
Biito'owu' tohno'oobenowoo Hei'eiyei'!
Biito'owu' tohno'oobenowoo Hei'eiyei'!

Eiyeihei! My children.
Eiyeihei! My children.
That is another of your pipes.
That is another of your pipes.
Look! Thus I shouted.
Look! Thus I shouted.
The earth, where I moved it.
The earth, where I moved it.
[Mooney 1896:958]

Mooney seeks to clarify the ambiguity surrounding this song by making connections to the "messiah" and the regeneration of the earth. The last line, according to Mooney, refers to the "new earth" prophesied by Wovoka. He identifies "another pipe" with the newer revelation and thus an extension of the sacredness that Arapaho religion places on the sacred Flat Pipe. However, no historical evidence exists that Wovoka actually gave a pipe to the Arapaho. The pipe symbolism characterizes some Arapaho artistic representations on Ghost Dance paraphernalia, especially from Oklahoma. A man holding a pipe appears on Southern Arapaho Ghost Dance shirts and women's dresses. Kroeber describes a "model of the sacred pipe" that was made by an elderly Southern Arapaho man in compliance with his Ghost Dance dream (1907:359–360). The pipe itself deviates in form from the sacred prototype, though the symbolism synthesizes elements from the Arapaho earth-diver story (e.g., turtle and duck) with distinctly Ghost Dance elements. Interestingly, most of the pipe symbolism seems to have been confined to Southern Arapahos.

One Arapaho practice in the Ghost Dance, suggested by symbolism and the song above (1), involved imitating traditional ritual forms in ways that would be considered unacceptable in former times. Some Southern Arapahos in Oklahoma, at a considerable distance from the most sacred pipe in Wyoming, perhaps imagined the possibility of "another pipe," to be given through the Ghost Dance. Whatever the case it is logical in Arapaho mythopoetics that the Flat Pipe should precede everything else at different levels of time: in the ceremony itself, at the beginning of the earth, and in any prophesied renewal. Through the pipe Arapaho people initiated and sustain the most durable relationship to Our Father, the creator. In the context of exchange it embodies and maintains the most sacred and crucial of all exchanges for the Arapaho, for the pipe must be cared for and receive offerings in order for the life of the tribe to continue. It is the center of all the most sacred vows and sacrifices made by humans for the well-being of others. This ongoing exchange is the most real and powerful "time," one that transcends life history, eventful history, and the material world it preceded. The pipe precedes all exchanges between people and ensures that talk, knowledge, and goods transferred will all be practiced in a good or right way. Overall, the songs seek to create or regain the paths of exchange among human groups and between humans and other-than-human persons in order to generate life and empowerment.

Play and Movement

As Mooney recognizes many songs express youthful images of games and play. Here there is some continuity with Wovoka's vision of people in the spirit world "engaged in their old-time sports and occupations, all happy and forever young" (1896:771). There are Arapaho songs about various toys and games: the hummer, or bull-roarer (25); top (65); snow snakes (68); the *beexotii*, or large-wheel stick target game (44, 49, 50), which Mooney cites as being revived through the Ghost Dance (1896:994); the awl game (64); and the hand game or "hunt the button game," which Mooney called *ga'utut* (1896:1008ff.) and Salzmann referred to as *koxouhtiit* (1983:109; Mooney 1896:974, 1005–1006, 1007, 990, 994, 995, 1002).

All Arapaho ritual contexts and social gatherings involved some form of game or sport. Bounded competition, especially between two groups or individuals, was central to traditional Arapaho lower age grade lodges, which involved races and other contests between two sides of the lodge, namely, the short and stout men (Kroeber 1904:166). As in many other American Indian rituals, games, play, and gambling channeled the motion of "craziness" into life and power. Following this pattern, the hand game lent to the Ghost Dance a medium for generating motion through competition among equals. Games and gambling were part of the social relations that complemented joking or play among equals. Toward those deserving respect in adult social relationships—or what is generally referred to as "avoidance" (see Eggan 1937) such as one's ceremonial grandfather, opposite sex sibling, or opposite sex parent-in-law—one could not gamble, joke, or play games. Toward equals as age peers or kin one can "play." In brief, play and equality go together.

Related to play, one recurrent theme in the songs is the capacity for expression that is also traditionally encouraged in youth, including telling

(2, 7), singing itself (8, 11, 13), humming (25), and weeping (42, 43, 44), all of which can be placed within an Arapaho understanding of expression (Mooney 1896:959, 964–967, 974, 985–986, 990). In childhood the ability to speak or sing was cultivated, stressed, and rewarded (see Hilger 1952:41). According to Kroeber, expression defined one's disposition and place in the afterlife: "When quiet or timid people die, their spirits are noisy and troublesome; but the ghosts of people who in life are loud and active are harmless after death" (1907:317). Therefore, loud expression was important to some life transitions, such as ear piercing, (Kroeber 1902:18; Hilger 1952:27) as a preemption of future pain or unrest. Toward those above, crying, singing, and other loud expressions are part of the normal Arapaho ritual process for discarding life-threatening things and attracting life-giving forces. Through sacred exchanges other-than-human persons can speak to humans and thus offer knowledge. In Song 2 (Mooney 1896:959), the *se'eicoo*, Flat Pipe, tells the dreamer that "all shall be put together again." Sacred beings or ritual objects, as in other Arapaho ceremonies, can make people speak or sing, as in Song 8 (1896:965) in which the "wind makes the head-feathers sing." Along two axes and in reciprocal fashion, the Ghost Dance attempted to open up lines of communication with other-than-human beings and through games and music so as to rejuvenate play and relations among equals.

The association of flying motion with loudness and power is further reflected in Song 27:

> *Neneisono', neneisono' neneeninoo (nii)touhnoo ne'nih'ohunoo*
> *Neneisono', neneisono' neneeninoo (nii)touheteihnih'ohunoo*
>
> My children, my children. It is I. I yell-thunder; as I fly.
> My children, my children. It is I. I yell-thunder-roar-flying.
> [1896:976]

Flight is thus combined with sound, music, and life.

The connection of games to expression and motion through music is conspicuous in the hand game. Though Mooney offers a description of the hand game and Kroeber provides material on the game and its paraphernalia, there is unfortunately no intensive treatment of its role or position in the Arapaho Ghost Dance performance. Lesser's detailed treatment of the Pawnee hand game identifies the revitalizing synergy between the game and the dance and recognizes that it was introduced by the Southern Arapaho (1978:332). Though the Pawnee adapted the hand game to their former sacred bundle practices for defining inter-kin group relations, the

Arapaho adaptation of the game is less evident, though its significant role in Ghost Dance gatherings would be difficult to dispute.

One of the more striking connections is supplied by Frances Densmore's observation that the obvious "paired phrasing" of lines in Arapaho Ghost Dance songs also characterizes hand game music, though the tempo of the former is somewhat slower (1936:65ff.). In Arapaho music history it is not certain whether such a form originated with Ghost Dance and hand game songs. As Herzog contends (1935:403) the "paired progression" may be a result of the fact that both the hand game and the Ghost Dance developed in the Great Basin and diffused to the Plains. Vander extends this by situating the original musical and dance form in Great Basin traditions predating the Ghost Dance (1997). Ake Hultkrantz (1981:276) also documented among the Wind River Shoshone a pre—Ghost Dance "Father Dance," a form of round dance held in the fall to petition for blessings of food, good weather, and continued life. In fact, many images in Arapaho Ghost Dance songs are suggestive of calling forth buffalo and bounty, as in Yellow Calf's song version earlier. Similarly, the musical form of the Ghost Dance survived readily up to the present in the modern Round Dance and Forty-Nine styles. In its history the form has proved to be multifunctional and more open to improvisation in performances.

Densmore extends Mooney's point by attributing the pairing of each line to the hypnotic effect shared by both types of songs. In the Ghost Dance, the repetition of lines and of the song itself combined with the hypnotic effect of the leader's waving feather and whirling cloth (1896:924) before the participants' eyes. Similarly, in the hand game, the guessing side tries to distract and lull the team hiding the buttons so they will reveal cues or hints as to which hands hold the marked button. There is among the Arapaho a strong relation between song, medicine power, "seeing" into others' minds, and the power of guessing.

The shape and sequence of lines became formal tropes for the Arapaho Ghost Dance songs. Each of from two to four lines was repeated in a pattern of aa/bb/cc/dd. There seem to be relatively more lines for both the opening and closing songs. Without accompaniment by a drum or other percussion, each song generated a round dance side-step cadence in which the left foot moved sideways followed by the right (1896:921). The dance step thus localizes in the bodies of dancers a trochaic cadence of the left foot stepping more sharply than the right in order to cover a greater distance as the group moves clockwise holding hands. As with much Arapaho and other Plains music, the synaesthetic effect of the songs is to juxtapose cadence and melodic verse. The songs, then, have shapes at different levels: the cadence, the prosody of poetic language, and the melodic movement of musical voice.[10]

Bruno Nettl identifies a tendency in Arapaho song phrases to move upward in pitch and tone with the prosody from low to high vowels, and conversely downward in musicality with high to low vowel transitions (1954). In a sample of songs, the former correlation held in 75 percent and the latter in 72 percent of relevant categories. There is a general, though not universal pattern for the Ghost Dance songs to move downward in each phrase, as in Songs 1 and 9 (Mooney 1896:958, 965). Coincident with the musical structure is the tendency for phrases to end on the back vowels -o(o) or -u(u), a pattern produced by the predominance of verbal suffixes with these phonemes. This relationship of music and prosody lends a unique musicality to the overall aesthetic quality of Arapaho songs:

> When all is ready, the leaders walk out to the dance place, and facing inward, join hands so as to form a circle. Then, without moving from their places they sing the opening song, according to previous agreement, in a soft undertone. Having sung it through once, they raise their voices to their full strength and repeat it, this time slowly circling around in the dance. The step is different from that of most other Indian dances, but very simple, the dancers moving right to left, following the course of the sun, advancing the left foot and following it with the right, hardly lifting the left foot and following it with the right, hardly lifting the feet from the ground. For this reason it is called by the Shoshone the "dragging dance." All the songs are adapted to the simple measure of the dance step. As the song rises and swells the people come singly and in groups from the several tipis, and one after another joins the circle until any number from fifty to five hundred men, women, and children are in the dance. When the circle is small, each song is repeated through a number of circuits. If large, it is repeated only through one circuit, measured by the return of the leaders to the starting point. [Mooney 1896:920]

There are a number of remarkable insights on the relationship between form and affect in the music as part of a ritual dance. The pairing of a loud with a following soft beat is coincident with the shuffling round dance step, as well as hand game songs. Each song also begins softly while dancers are stationary, then crescendos in the second repeat as the music "moves" the dancers. At multiple levels the Ghost Dance was about generating motion from stasis and expression from quietness.

Specifically, repetition and circularity co-occur. Just as each of from two to five lines is repeated, the whole song is repeated for the duration of the circuit(s) of the round dance. This raises the question of the relation between form and practice, that is, between the shape of a song and the dance itself, both of which have interwoven circles that return to the same place. The temporal phasing and songs became standardized according to the directions of Wovoka, though it seems that Arapahos themselves formalized the dance process in their own way. Each ceremony had to begin with the opening song (1896:958) and end with the morning star song (72) to greet the sunrise (1896:1010–1011), followed then by the appropriate closing song (73; 1896:1011–1012). Song 72 asks that the morning star take pity on the dancers for dancing until daylight. Again, one way of gaining the pity of other-than-human persons is to show strength through endurance—a pattern apparent in the Arapaho ceremonial lodges. The final song is interesting, for it involves and refers to five circuits in order to end the ceremony. In Arapaho ritual logic five circuits or stops completes any circular movement.

Mooney remarks that the tempo and mood of songs are interrelated. He noticed that the hypnotic practice and its trance effects occurred as the music and songs became louder and faster in tempo (1896:925). In Arapaho ritual logic rapid motion is closely associated with durability as well as states of "craziness," as in the men's Crazy Lodge, in which men danced through fire (see Kroeber 1904:190). Crazy types of behavior can thus be appropriated within the boundaries of ritual for life and knowledge. Within repetitions and circles the dance itself sought to generate these effects, what others would call "renewal," though they are much more specific to the poetic-kinesic practice of Arapaho games, dance, and music than to "doctrine."

Metamorphosis

Explicit in several of the songs and implicit in others is another related trope—metamorphosis, a device that is present in much American Indian verbal art, including myths and dream narratives. As for other Arapaho tropes, metamorphosis is a device that is more about motion than analogy, the dominant cognitive function assumed for Euro-American devices (see Lakoff and Johnson 1980). It is also related to the power of medicine men (*beetee3i'*) who in many cultures can transform themselves into animals or other human forms, as well as die and return to life. Transformation from one form into another by humans, animals, and other-than-human beings effects a breakthrough in the syntagmatic sequence of songs and narratives. In the Ghost Dance it also provides the medium for the transition between living and death. In the vision cited earlier, the dreamer saw a "stout man" who spoke to him, announcing that he was the "turtle."

When the man turned to walk away he appeared as a turtle, thus revealing his power and knowledge to the dancer. As elsewhere, in Arapaho myth and ritual practice the shift of "turning around" reveals the real identity behind appearance.

Songs 5 and 23 (Mooney 1896: 962, 973) relate dream images of metamorphosis. In the former the dreamer goes to a camp where he is taken around by his dead father to meet other deceased friends. As Mooney relates, "While they were thus going about, a change came o'er the spirit of the dream, as so often happens in this fevered mental condition, and instead of his father he found a moose standing by his side. Such transformations are frequently noted in Ghost-dance songs" (1896:962–63). In Song 23 a similar experience unfolds, though the shift to a bird reveals Our Father (*heisonoonin*) rather than "my father," a difference Mooney fails to mention. Other songs imply a transformation of the dreamer. One of the songs (20) from the Arapaho apostle Sitting Bull relates: "My father did not recognize me [at first]. / When again he saw me, / He said, "You are the offspring of a crow." As Mooney interprets it the song expresses Sitting Bull's transition to the role of messenger or "Crow's offspring" (*houusoo*), a term that also means "son of God" and was applied to Jesus and Wovoka (1896:972).

As Hallowell contends for Ojibwe ontology, metamorphosis is an attribute of persons of the other-than-human category (1960:372ff.). Humans, both dead and living, animals, and other-than-human persons share an animacy that allows for metamorphosis. In Arapaho myth the most sacred beings possess the greatest power for readily shifting shape into human or animal form themselves or for changing the shape of other beings or dimensions of the natural world. This includes the transition between life and death, as in Wovoka's vision experience itself. In the Arapaho play of categories, as in Ojibwe and other American Indian ethnopoetics, the boundaries between domains are not solidified a priori but are ever open and fluid. It is upon this fluid movement among permeable categories that the trope of metamorphosis activates movement in time and thus life. The tendency in a Western, modern "semantic language," to borrow Kenneth Burke's term (1973), is to prefer clear and distinct boundaries among categories and then to examine how tropes move the frame of reference through analogy or specifically metaphor from a source to a target domain. In Arapaho categories, analogy is less operative than syntagmatic contiguity as a shift through movement, transformation, or turns of perception. Among these metamorphosis is an expression of the mysterious, chaotic, and confusing possibilities of the world always available to careful appropriation through ritual, visions, or ritual exchange.

Crow

One innovation of the Ghost Dance that broke from prior mythico-ritual traditions is the figure of Crow, central in the dance and various Arapaho songs. In Arapaho mythology Crow is a minor figure, though a "trickster" of sorts when he does appear. The story "White Crow Marries Blood-Clot Girl" begins with a famine in the camp. The young man, White Crow, gathers the men for a hunt, but when they approach the man/bird helps the buffalo get away. Again he tries the same trick to "starve the people," but the people capture him before he can mislead them again. White Crow then delivers himself for his punishment to the chief, who uses smoke to turn the bird black (Dorsey and Kroeber 1903:319–321). As a result of this change, he will remain black and only eat the chips, eyes, and skulls of animals. In a similar story Crow steals a kit fox kill from the culture hero Found-In-Grass in order to receive the reward of a chief's daughter as wife (Dorsey and Kroeber 1903:341–348). The chief then marries his elder daughter to Crow, while Found-In-Grass marries the younger sister. Found-In-Grass becomes a handsome provider and attracts the attention of his sister-in-law. In both stories Crow is a messenger/stealer of game, a "false provider," carrion-eater, and trickster.

This image is expressed in Ghost Dance Song 58 (Mooney 1896:999), in which seven crows that Mooney identifies as the seven leaders of the Ghost Dance among the Arapaho fly about a carcass. As messenger, guide, and mediator of exchange Crow is associated with the transition between life and death and the revivification of buffalo. In the prereservation Arapaho ecology crows followed the buffalo herds to scavenge for food. Thus they were guides to herds. As trickster, like the mythical *Nih'oo3oo*, he mediates between humans and the above, humans and animals, and center and the west, the periphery of the world. Though introduced through the message of Wovoka, Crow is appropriated in Arapaho contexts of meaning and imagination. In the closing song (73; 1896:1011–1012) he is referred to as Our Father and thus identified with the creator, based on his part-whole relation with Our Father as messenger and mediator. Such a role was at that time unprecedented in Arapaho myth and ritual and was neither preceded in Great Basin versions of the dance nor foregrounded in subsequent variations extended to other tribes.

As a bird he is able to "see" from above. Song 48 speaks from Crow's point of view:

> *Beih'ineniitootee' niitobeenoo*
> *Beih'ineniinootee' niitobeenoo*
> *Neneeninoo houu*
> *Neneeninoo houu*

Everything, I hear. I hear well.
Everything, I hear. I hear well.
I am crow.
I am crow.
[1896:993–94]

Shared with other-than-human persons above is Crow's ability "to per-ceive all" in the human world, while the difference is his capacity to move about along the vertical and horizontal axes, movement denied the highest being of all, Our Father.

At another level birds are associated with human expression, as in singing and speaking. In one song (8) the head-feather, as part of Crow, sings to the dancer (1896:965). The Crow, like the meadowlark, sings in a way that speaks the Arapaho language and is thus among various animals that talk to human beings (Michelson 1910). Mooney mentions that followers in Left Hand's camp in Oklahoma kept a live crow that eventually died but "which was claimed had the power of speech and prophetic utterance, and its hoarse inarticulate cries were interpreted as inspired messages from the spirit world" (1896:982). The first line of Song 38 relates that Crow "calls" the dreamer, though the verb form suggests "yelling," at least in modern usage: *nihneniitoubeinoo houu,* or "he yelled [called] for me, crow" (-*neniitou-* = "yell or holler") (1896:983–984).

Crow is therefore a likely messenger from *hihcebe'* ("above") or *hi-iyein* ("our home," the place of the afterlife), not only because he can both speak and fly but also because he is black, the color associated with west, the route to the above. Crows also hover and circle like birds of prey, such as eagles and hawks, which also figure prominently as messen-gers and sources of feathers. They also eat meat like these birds, as well as carrion, like magpie, another bird of the Ghost Dance (1896:999). Crow feathers and the stuffed body figure prominently in Ghost Dance headdresses and paraphernalia, as well as in the belts of the Crow Dance (*houunohwoot*), which once accompanied the Ghost Dance and is still performed in Wyoming. As Mooney notices, "crow" refers in some songs not only to the messenger, but, through part-whole association, to the feathers used by Ghost Dance leaders to induce trances during the per-formance itself. Song 52 (1896:996) suggests this connection by referring to crow's role in the timing and rhythm of the dance, that is, in making people move or stop, as in the closing song (73; 1896:1011–1012). The feathers are a part-to-whole representation of the crow, as well as being associated with trance states, the world above, black to the west, and Our Father.

One of the "structural" mythic functions operating throughout the Ghost Dance songs is the union of near and far and, specifically, a mediation of earth and sky. As Mooney narrates it Crow gathered the people on the border of the earth and the people of the other world at the border of their land to the west. With a piece of earth from his beak he creates first a mountain, then a land bridge between the two worlds. With a piece of grass he then makes the land green, and with a twig generates trees (1896:983). In this manner Crow parallels the role of turtle in the earth-diver tradition. From a part he can generate the totality. The Crow thus gives people a "road" (*bóoó*) and a new earth, as several songs (36, 37, 38, 40) suggest (1896:982–984). Song 40 speaks from Crow's point of view:

> *Hee, neniisono' Ei'e'yei!*
> *Hee, neniisono' Ei'eiyei!*
> *Hiiyou hee3eibenowoo*
> *Hiiyou hee3eibenowoo*
> *Biito'owu', Ei'eiyei!*
> *Biito'owu', Ei'eiyei!*
>
> My children—Ei'eiyei!
> My children—Ei'eiyei!
> Here it is, I hand it to you.
> Here it is, I hand it to you.
> The earth— Ei'eiyei!
> The earth— Ei'eiyei!
> [1896:984]

As a result he joins earth and sky, just as turtle once brought up land from below the water.

The mediation of sky and earth is further supported by Mooney's description of Ghost Dance paintings and Kroeber's material (1907:328ff. and 417) on the dresses, headdresses, and other objects inspired by trances and made for the dance. Prior to dancing, participants were painted with a red or yellow line along the hair part dividing the head; accompanying the "road" were suns, moon crescents, stars, crosses (i.e., morning stars), and bird designs, all of which enriched Arapaho songs and their symbolism (Mooney 1896:920). In Kroeber's study of decorative art, many of the Ghost Dance objects are half one color and half another, though the duality departs from the traditional red and black of Arapaho sacred ceremonies, such as the Offerings-Lodge (see Dorsey 1903:60–61). Depending on the pairing, Kroeber notes that the common Ghost Dance color dualities are blue and red, green and yellow, or red and green, respectively connoting earth and sky (1907:417). The two- or three-dimensional art of the Ghost Dance is thus homologous in many respects to the poetics of the songs in forming symmetry, duality, and mediation. The distinct color duality and presence of Crow in Ghost Dance songs thus replicates mythic forms with new emphases and content.

Along with "roads" and color duality, circular motion also mediates different levels of reality. Several songs (numbers 17, 27, 39, 45) refer to the former:

> Nonoo'onih'ohunoo
> Nonoo'onih'ohunoo
> Biito'owu' heneiisei'i
> Biito'owu' heneiisei'i
> Heeneih3i' ne'nih'ohunoo
> Heeneih3i' ne'nih'ohunoo
>
> I am flying in circles.
> I am flying in circles.
> The earth's boundaries.
> The earth's boundaries.
> They are long [feathers], as I fly.
> They are long [feathers], as I fly.
> [Mooney 1896:970; see also 976, 984, 990–991]

In this song the dreamer flies around the boundary of the earth where the land meets the water. Circling the boundaries is conventional motion in Arapaho ritual and myth at multiple levels, such as the tipi, camp, ceremonial lodge, and world. It is thus isomorphic to the motion of the Ghost Dance itself, the flight of Crow, and the swirling hypnotic movement of the leader's trance-inducing whirling feather, handkerchief, or hand (1896:925). Complementarily, within this song is a suggestion of linearity or "length," of the feathers. Long flowing fringes, feathers, hair, grass, and other materials are associated with the beauty of dancing and in this case flying. They can mean long life, a road, or other linear modes of motion. Thus, the song brings together circularity and linearity, as so much Arapaho motion does.

The connection of circular movement to "crazy" states is found in Song 39:

> Nonoononoo'ooteinoo houu
> Nonoononoo'ooteinoo houu
> Tohce'no3einoo houu
> Tohce'no3einoo houu

The crow is circling and circling me.

The crow is circling and circling me.

Because he crow is coming after me again.

Because he crow is coming after me again.

[1896:984]

Song 45 (1896:991) has the same first line, but in the second Crow tells the dreamer he will receive a hawk feather as a gift. As Mooney relates Song 39 is sung with a rapid tempo and at the point in the dance when trance is most suggested. Here rapid movement and circularity combine. As a reduplicated construction of the verb stem *nonoonoo'ootei-* ("to go in circles"), *nonoononoo'ootei-* thus refers to repeated action, that is, "going in circles over and over again." The dreamer of this song relates that the crow came to "conduct him to his friends who had gone before" (1896:984). Circular helix-shaped motion is strongly associated with the sacred and above, as in the whirlwind of several songs; the flight of birds, including crows and eagles; and the motion of smoke carrying prayers to the above.

Conclusion

By activating traditional forms of longer duration and breaking through into new elements the Ghost Dance—as improvised poetics in practice— was a medium for generating social relations, life motion, expression, and mediation of near and far. The Ghost Dance, too, was part of a much larger process of Arapaho creative ritual response to external sources of power, including Euro-American society. Clearly, then, it is not enough to understand the Arapaho Ghost Dance and the songs, in particular, as events in a sequence of others, at a generic level of American Indian history. Songs, prayers, myths, and other creative forms offer as much insight into what Fogelson (1974, 1989) calls ethno-ethnohistory as do oral history and other narrative forms that are ostensibly more related to events. It has been shown here that, first, it is productive to use available ethnographic and linguistic evidence to retranslate and retranscribe indigenous texts. Second, ethnohistorical approaches to texts must critically examine concepts that import Euro-American assumptions about motives, religion, or tropes. Third, it is essential to consider how traditional and invented poetic forms and devices function or "play" in the narratives and practices that are the subject matter of ethnohistory. Finally, ethnohistorical research must consider dimensions of temporality and historical trajectories that are outside the constructed mainstream of American Indian history. One way to do this is through detailed and comprehensive study of indigenous texts.

The ghost songs reveal that Arapaho people were dreaming, dancing, and singing within mythical and ritual boundaries of longer duration, while infusing new colors, rhythms, transformations, figures, and shapes into their experiences. The generativity of poetic language is its ability to enliven conventional tropes and forms while foregrounding new materials. Indigenous texts do not just refer literally to assumed objective historical conditions, universal motives and emotions, or collective reactions to contact with Euro-Americans. Only by appreciating indigenous creativity as bridging continuity and change is it possible to understand not only the structure, schema, and orders of symbols and meanings but also their openings, fluidity, and dynamics in history.

Notes

1. Contemporary Arapaho orthography is as follows: *b* is pronounced as in English, except like a "p" sound at the end of words; *c* is like a "ch" in English (e.g., "church"), but voiced like a "j" sound at the beginning of words; *e* sounds like the "a" in the English word *cat* and just held longer when written double /*ee*/; *h* is like the English "h" but always also pronounced at the end of a syllable or word; *i* is similar to the short "i" in English *bit* but in the long double-form that is written as /*ii*/ it sounds like the long "e" sound in English (e.g., "meet"); *k* is usually produced like the "k" in English but voiced as a "g" sound at the beginning of words; *n* is the same more or less as in English; *o* is almost the same as in English "got" and in the long form rendered as /*oo*/ it sounds like the vowel sound held longer in the pronunciation of *caught*; *s* is the same as in English though never voiced as a "z"; *t* is a voiceless alveolar stop much like English "t" but voiced as a "d" sound at the beginning of words; *u* is like the "u" in English *put*, and in the long form written as /*uu*/ it is held longer like the long "u" sound in English *cute*; *w* is the same as in the English word *water* but also pronounced as voiceless at the end of words; *x* is uncommon in English and is most like the rough "ch" as in German *ich*; *y* similar to the English form but also pronounced as voiceless at the end the end of words; *3* is a voiceless dental fricative as in English *thin* or *three* (thus the symbol) but never voiced as in English *than*; ' is a glottal stop in which the glottis at the base of the throat is closed. The vowel combination *ou* sounds like the long "o" sound as in *boat*. The *oe* diphthong sounds like the long "i" sound in English *bike*. The *ei* combination is just as in English *reins*. Triple vowel forms are pronounced longer yet than their double-vowel counterparts but with a double stress, as in /*éeél*/ or /*óuúl*/.

2. The songs are generally phrased in first-person singular or occasionally plural forms. They are all articulated in the nonnarrative present or past tense, marking firsthand knowledge actually perceived, in this case, by dreamers. Traditional narratives, for example, are constructed throughout by a prefix *he(e)'ih-*, which marks second-hand information or a narrative past tense that places the events in another mythical "time." Unlike myths, dream narratives and the songs are not constructed in the past tense, marked for distance between observed and observer.

3. For the Kiowa, as Kracht describes (1992), the dance itself persisted much longer than previously realized. Likewise, Lesser (1978) has shown the enduring power of the

hand game, which evolved out of the Ghost Dance, for Pawnee cultural revitalization. As central to Vander's extensive research (1997) the Naraya songs (Round Dance/Ghost Dance) predated the Ghost Dance of 1890 and survived into the 1980s among Eastern Shoshone, neighbor tribe of the Northern Arapaho.

4. As I have shown elsewhere (2002), the *Our Father* in Arapaho replaces all alien concepts of sin and salvation with Arapaho concepts of pity and life movement (Anderson 2001b). Loretta Fowler (1982) has also documented the degree to which the Northern Arapaho have appropriated political and economic forms within Arapaho age-structured authority in order to sustain tribal solidarity and continuity in intermediation with Euro-American society.

5. All song transcriptions and translations are the author's, unless otherwise indicated.

6. The term *koh'owootino* is a generic word for round fruits and is now used to refer to canned goods in general.

7. A moth, for instance, is *hohookehe'* ("little crazy") because of the way it flies into fire. *Hohookee-* is also associated with "not listening to what others tell you" or "having blocked up senses."

8. There is also continuity of "Our Father," as Mooney suggests, with Shoshonean groups (the Eastern Shoshone also refer to the creator as Our Father). Concurring with Vander's bifurcation, though, the Arapaho "Our Father" for the creator is more directly connected with Plains usage and, even more strongly, with extensions among Algonquian-speaking groups (see Cooper 1934:19, 31).

9. There is also a connection, reaffirmed in the Arapaho case, between Jesus and Wovoka as father, which in turn overlaps with the new term Crow, for "God" (*houu*). In Arapaho Christian liturgy, the Crow also figures, since Jesus is *houusoo*, that is, son of God or Crow. Overall, ties to the Shoshonean or Christian usage are much weaker, though not without some relevance, than those to the enduring Arapaho and even Algonquian usage.

10. With respect to the last dimension, as Herzog adds (1935:405–406) all Ghost Dance songs are limited in range, usually to a fifth and at most an octave. Almost all phrases and virtually all songs end on the tonic, usually ascending from higher tones. In short, range is "limited," and all phrases return to a central tonic.

References

Anderson, Jeffrey D.

    2001a The Four Hills of Life: Northern Arapaho Knowledge and Life Movement. Anthropology of North American Indians Series. Raymond J. DeMallie and Douglas R. Parks, eds. Lincoln: University of Nebraska Press.

    2001b Northern Arapaho Conversion of a Christian Text: The Our Father. Ethnohistory 48(4):689–712.

J. Beden, and D. Wellbery, eds.

    1991 Chronotypes: The Construction of Time. Stanford: Stanford University Press.

Burke, Kenneth

    1973 Semantic and Poetic Meaning. *In* The Philosophy of Literary Form. Berkeley: University of California Press.

Cooper, John M.

    1934 The Northern Algonquian Supreme Being. Washington: Catholic University Press.

Curtis, Natalie

    1934 The Indians' Book. New York: Dover.

Dangberg, Grace M.

1957 Letters to Jack Wilson, the Paiute Prophet, Written Between 1908 and 1911. Smithsonian Institution, Bureau of American Ethnology, Bulletin 164 (Anthropological Papers, no. 55). Pp. 279–96. Washington DC: Smithsonian Institution.

DeMallie, Raymond J.

1982 The Lakota Ghost Dance: An Ethnohistorical Account. Pacific Historical Review 51(4):385–405.

Densmore, Francis

1936 Cheyenne and Arapaho Music. Southwest Museum Papers 10:1–112.

Dorsey, George A.

1903 The Arapaho Sun Dance; the Ceremony of the Offerings-Lodge. Field Columbian Museum, Publication 75, Anthropological Series, vol. 4. Chicago: Field Museum.

Dorsey, George A., and Alfred L. Kroeber

1903 Traditions of the Arapaho. Field Columbian Museum, Publication 81, Anthropological Series, vol. 5. Chicago: Field Museum.

Eggan, Fred

1937 The Cheyenne and Arapaho Kinship System. *In* Social Anthropology of North American Tribes: Essays in Social Organization, Law, and Religion. Fred Eggan, ed. Pp. 35–95. Chicago: University of Chicago Press.

Fernandez, James

1991 Introduction: Confluents of Inquiry. *In* Beyond Metaphor: The Theories of Tropes in Anthropology. J. Fernandez, ed. Stanford: Stanford University Press.

Fogelson, Raymond

1974 On the Varieties of Indian History: Sequoyah and Traveller Bird. Journal of Ethnic Studies 2(1):105–112.

1989 Ethnohistory of Events and Nonevents. Ethnohistory 36(2):133–147.

Fowler, Loretta

1982 Arapahoe Politics, 1851–1878: Symbols in Crises of Authority. Lincoln University of Nebraska Press.

Friedrich, Paul

1986 The Language Parallax: Linguistic Relativism and Poetic Indeterminacy. Austin: University of Texas Press.

1991 Polytropy. *In* Beyond Metaphor: The Theory of Tropes in Anthropology. James Fernandez, ed. Pp. 17–55. Stanford: Stanford University Press.

Hallowell, A. Irving

1960 Ontology, Behavior, and World View. *In* Contributions to Anthropology: Selected Papers of A. Irving Hallowell. Raymond Fogelson, ed. Pp. 357–390. Chicago: University of Chicago Press.

Havránek, Bohuslav

1964 The Functional Differentiation of the Standard Language. *In* A Prague Reader on Esthetics, Literary Structure, and Style. Pp. 3–16. Washington DC: Georgetown University Press.

Herzog, George

1935 Plains Ghost Dance and Great Basin Music. American Anthropologist 37:403–419.

Hilger, Sister M. Inez

1952 Arapaho Child Life and Its Cultural Background. Smithsonian Institution, Bureau of American Ethnology, Bulletin 148. Washington DC: Government Printing Office.

Hultkrantz, Ake

  1981 The Changing Meaning of the Ghost Dance as Evidenced by the Wind River Shoshoni. *In* Belief and Worship in Native North America. Christopher Vecsey, ed. Pp. 264–281. Syracuse NY: Syracuse University Press.

Hymes, Dell

  1981 In Vain I Have Tried to Tell You. Philadelphia: University of Pennsylvania Press.

Kehoe, Alice B.

  1989 The Ghost Dance: Ethnohistory and Revitalization. New York: Holt, Rinehart, & Winston.

Kracht, Benjamin R.

  1992 The Kiowa Ghost Dance, 1894–1914: An Unheralded Revitalization Movement. Ethnohistory 39(4):452–477.

Kroeber, Alfred L.

  1902, 1904, 1907 [Reprint 1983] The Arapaho. Foreword by Fred Eggan. Lincoln: University of Nebraska Press.

  1916–20 Smithsonian Institution National Anthropological Archives. Manuscript 2560, Notebook 6. Washington DC.

Lakoff, George, and Mark Johnson

  1980 Metaphors We Live By. Chicago: University of Chicago Press.

Lanham, Richard A.

  1991 A Handlist of Rhetorical Terms. Berkeley: University of California Press.

Lesser, Alexander

  1978 The Pawnee Ghost Dance Hand Game: Ghost Dance Revival and Ethnic Identity. Madison: University of Wisconsin Press.

Lévi-Strauss, Claude

  1968 The Origin of Table Manners: Introduction to the Science of Mythology. Vol. 3. J. Weightman and D. Weightman, trans. New York: Harper & Row.

Mauss, Marcel

  1990 The Gift: The Form and Reason for Exchange in Archaic Societies. New York: W. W. Norton.

McCoy Tim, with Ronald McCoy

  1977 Tim McCoy Remembers the West: An Autobiography. Garden City NY: Doubleday.

Michelson, Truman

  1910 Field Notes. Smithsonian Institution National Anthropological Archives. Washington DC.

Miller, David Humphreys

  1959 Ghost Dance. Lincoln: University of Nebraska Press.

Mooney, James

  1896 The Ghost-Dance Religion and Sioux Outbreak of 1890. Fourteenth Annual Report of the Bureau of Ethnology, 1892–93. Part 2. Pp. 641–1110. Washington DC: Government Printing Office.

Munn, Nancy

  1986 The Fame of Gawa: A Symbolic Study of Value Transformation in a Massim (Papua New Guinea) Society. Cambridge: Cambridge University Press.

Nettl, Bruno

  1954 Text-Music Relationships in Arapaho Songs. Southwestern Journal of Anthropology 10:192–199.

Salzmann, Zdenek

1983 Dictionary of Contemporary Arapaho Usage. Arapaho Language and Culture Instructional Materials Series, No. 4. Northern Arapaho Tribe, Wind River Reservation.

Sapir, Edward

1949 The Grammarian and His Language. *In* Selected Writings of Edward Sapir: Language, Culture, and Personality. David G. Mandelbaum, ed. Pp. 150–159. Berkeley: University of California Press.

Starkloff, Carl F.

1974 The People of the Center: American Indian Religion and Christianity. New York: Seabury Press.

Vander, Judith

1997 Shoshone Ghost Dance Religion: Poetry Songs and Great Basin Context. Urbana: University of Illinois Press.

Voth, H. R.

n.d. H. R. Voth Collection. Bethel College, Mennonite Library and Archives. Newton, Kansas.

Wallace, Anthony F. C.

1956 Revitalization Movements: Some Theoretical Considerations for their Comparative Study. American Anthropologist 58:264–281.

7. Night Thoughts and Night Sweats, Ethnohistory and Ethnohumor

The Quaker Shaker Meets the Lakota Sweat Lodge

RAYMOND A. BUCKO, S.J.

There are many things I deeply appreciate about my mentor, Ray Fogelson, though they are the kinds of things that, like one's parents, sometimes go unappreciated until one has really grown up. To my frustration as someone who wanted to finish his dissertation in a single weekend, Ray calmly counseled me to put up my feet and think about things for a while. Indeed, his own works are open ended, suggesting avenues of fertile exploration rather than trying to corner the epistemological market. In this chapter, a tribute (I hope) to Ray and the many things he has taught me, I propose to look in a reflexive way at humor in the context of ritual among the Lakota. In doing so, I seek to understand why humor has been generally omitted or bracketed in ethnohistorical literature, anthropological analysis, and at times in contemporary Lakota practice. Like Ray, however, I do not propose to sew up the situation but to recommend possible avenues of investigation and reflection for a deeper understanding of these phenomena.

It was Ray who introduced me to the Diamond Crystal Quaker Shaker lady, that paradigm of reflexivity (also known as "ethno ethno" [1974]) who once graced the Diamond Crystal salt container. As Ray himself describes both her and his metaphoric intentions: "The image in the salt trope is that of a Quaker woman on the label of a cylindrical Diamond Crystal salt shaker (note Quaker/Shaker) holding an ideational salt shaker in her lap, leading to the illusion of infinite regress."[1] From my own youth I recall a different blue, round salt container, made by the Morton salt company, on which appears a young girl holding an umbrella and a round, blue container on which she appears holding an umbrella and a round, blue container on which she appears holding an umbrella and a round, blue container as far as the eye and imagination can see. I suggest that an examination of Lakota humor will reveal something about influences and reflections: Lakota reflections on other Lakota or Lakota at other times, Euro-American reflections on Lakota culture, and Lakota reflections on Euro-American culture and on the intricate interrelationships the Lakota had and continue to have both among themselves and with these outsiders who insist on writing down everything.

The day when that Ray introduced this Ray to the Diamond Crystal Quaker Shaker lady I was reminded of my own childhood introduction to reflexivity. My parents were both hairdressers and ran their own shop. The shop had mirrors on opposite sides of the room so there were hundreds of people in the room and multiple Ray Buckos. I loved to sit on the barber chair and spin around and around. I could see my selves, my many sets of parents, and a multiplicity of their customers. The faster I spun myself in the chair the bigger all their eyes grew. I've been going around in circles ever since, reflecting and becoming part of the reflection itself.

Ritual humor, I propose, is an event that became a nonevent and then later an event and nonevent through the interactions and reflections of both Lakota and Euro-American participants and observers. Insiders and outsiders continue to debate its significance and place in ritual practice. It is for the ethnohistorian to reflect on these reflections and reflectors, both past and present, in order to interpret this and other phenomena properly.

Ray, a man of opulent humor, also introduced me to the delights of paper titles. In one of his own moments of self-reflexivity he states: "I chronically suffer from a pathological form of premature entitlement. When asked or required to present a paper, I usually invent a clever title and then expend much worrisome effort trying to justify it" (1989). Taking off from Milton Singer's *Man's Glassy Essence* (1984), Ray presented a paper entitled "Man's Gassy Essence: The Social History of Balloons" (1987b). By a twist of fate and with a twist of words he wrote "A Final Look and Glance and the Bearing of the Bering Straits on Native American History" (1987a). My own title, a tribute to his work as well as his skills of entitlement, takes its cue from "Night Thoughts on Native American Social History" (1985). However, the inspiration for the analysis contained in this work comes from another of Ray's writings, "The Ethnohistory of Events and Nonevents" (Fogelson 1989). In this article Ray challenges his readers to examine why events become nonevents and nonevents become events. This is the task I set for myself in looking at the seeming "disappearance" and "appearance" of humor in Lakota ritual in general and specifically in the sweat lodge.

The humor of Native people was extensively remarked upon in the earliest European recordings of Native life. My own "apical ancestor" and brother Jesuit, Father Paul Le Jeune, superior of the Residence of Kebec (Quebec), writes in his relation of 1634:

> I do not believe that there is a nation under heaven more given to sneering and bantering than that of the Montagnais. Their life is passed in eating, laughing, and making sport of each other, and of all the people they know. There is nothing serious about them, except occasionally, when they make a pretense among us of being grave and dignified; but among themselves they are real buffoons and genuine children, who ask only to laugh. [Thwaites 1897:243]

On the other side of the continent, another priest, this one the Russian Orthodox Hiermonk, Father Gedeon, who arrived in Alaska in 1804, said this of the inhabitants of Kodiak Island:

> The Kadiaks are for the most part not loquacious, though they are quick to answer, witty and amusing. One answered my query as to where he had sought a cure of his illness by saying: "In me, in my wife, in the water and on the shore." Seeing on a high cliff a great number of seabirds I asked another Kadiak whether he could count them all. He answered, "I could if only they did not lay eggs each year." [Pierce 1978:136]

Lakota themselves have commented on their particular sense of humor. Vine Deloria Jr., a contemporary Lakota scholar and social critic states:

> The Indian people are exactly opposite of the popular stereotype. I sometimes wonder how anything is accomplished by Indians because of the apparent overemphasis on humor within the Indian world. Indians have found a humorous side of nearly every problem and the experiences of life have generally been so well defined through jokes and stories that they have become a thing in themselves. [Deloria 1988:146–147]

Another astute contemporary observer of his own culture, traditional singer and cultural expert Severt Young Bear, says this about the centrality of humor in Lakota life:

> Among the Lakota, no matter what the hardship there is, whether it's a death in the family or a serious ceremony or a discussion of a problem we might be concerned about, there's always humor connected with it. I think that humor brings us back to reality and reminds us that we are not really that important, or that the issue on the floor is not really that bad, or that somebody who is a good speaker or a mature leader

knows when to lighten things up by telling a funny story or making fun of himself or somebody in the audience. We all get a smile on our faces and nod agreement and feel better. When somebody can't laugh or enjoy a joke in the middle of something else, we take it as a sign that they're not comfortable with themselves, aren't too sure of themselves and can't laugh at times. No matter how serious the situation, there's always humor which is told in such a way that it doesn't hurt people's feelings. [Young Bear and Theisz 1994:169]

So, too, individuals who have dealt with the Lakota have frequently noted their sense of humor. Historian Stanley Vestal comments on one of his interviews with the octogenarian Joseph White Bull, noted Lakota warrior:

Four times he tried to have 2 wives at once—always with unhappy results due to jealousy. . . . One pair was so jealous that when he went to bed one woman clung to his arm and leg on one side, the other on the other, so that he couldn't sleep and was all cramped and stiff in the morning. He acted it all out for me. It was a scream! [Tassin 1973:167]

Still, one of the most persistent images of Indian people remains their stoicism and lack of humor despite abundant evidence to the contrary. Robert Easton addresses the stereotype:

"All Indians are stoic, stolid and devoid of humor." This is a popular misconception shared by most white people, particularly those who have never known any Indians. Nothing could be further from the truth, for despite what many white people think, American Indians enjoy a rich legacy of laughter. This marked disparity between common belief and fact was explained as early as 1882 by Colonel Richard Irving Dodge in his *Our Wild Indians—Thirty-three Year's Personal Experience Among the Red Man of the Great West.* "In the presence of strangers he is reserved and silent . . . the general impression seems to be that the Indian, wrapped in his blanket and impenetrable mystery, and with a face of gloom stalks through life unmindful of pleasure and pain. Nothing can be further from the truth. The dignity, the reserve, the silence, are put on just as a New York swell puts on his swallow tail coat and white choker for a dinner party, because it is his custom. In his own camp, away from strangers, the Indian is a noisy, jolly, rollicking, mischief-loving braggadocio, brimful of practical jokes and rough fun of any kind making the welkin ring with his laughter." [Easton 1970:38–39][2]

One of my most salient and enjoyable experiences in the field has been encountering the humor of the Lakota people. Most remarkable for some-one raised in the Catholic tradition of solemn ritual events is the sheer infusion of humor in about every ritual I have attended on the Pine Ridge Reservation. This is particularly true for the sweat lodge.

Humor has reached a high level of conscious reflection among individuals who participate in the sweat. My own field experiences provided rich material on humor, generally volunteered by my teachers and experienced by myself during actual sweats as well as afterward.[3] Humor is employed in a very self-conscious manner in the sweat. Participants are quite articulate about the use of humor, taking time to include humorous occurrences to illustrate their point. As some of my teachers explained to me:

> We believe in laughter. Humor is a good medicine. When a person is on the verge, laughter takes that away. A warrior is one who can laugh at death. Folks also say we are stoic and serious. They are stereotyping. We are humans. There is lots of joking and teasing, even in the sweat, especially with brothers-in-law. Once my uncle was trying to be serious. He wanted to say "hand me the deer antlers." He said instead "Hand me the antlers dear." The reply from his wife was, "Honey, you haven't said that in years, we should sweat more often." We learned that there is a time to be serious and a time to let it out. There's a time when it is not proper to laugh and a time when it is not proper to be serious.
>
> Humor is important. It makes you stick to reality. Don't get too serious. You tease someone who is really serious or down and out. You can nearly feel it. *Hé niyé nitháwa* ['That one belongs to you']; they say that when a big hot rock rolls into the sweat. Humor brought me to my senses. I went in the first time with fear, anxiety, uncertainty. We use it so you don't get too mysterious and holy. Somehow out of this comes humility—we go in serious and afflicted—come out *hécheglalaška*, 'not so bad after all.' The first humor I came across: A mouse crawled all over us in the sweat. Some women even screamed. The leader said in a mixture of Lakota and English that itself was comical: "*Tókhašni* ['It doesn't matter'], that's our sacred mouse. *Ki yelo* ['that sure is']!" I thought, that's absurd, you don't say that here! "*Ó niyé cha, Ó* ['It was you'],"[I said] thinking a spirit was moving around [when it was just a mouse]. [Bucko 1998:138–139]

Another of my teachers stated as a sweat began: "Laughter is the best medicine and it helps you feel comfortable. Jokes are to help you get used to the heat but also to relax and ease you" (Bucko 1998:139). Besides peace and comfort for the individual, humor has social ramifications, providing a way to create or reconstruct group harmony. This is clear again from another participant's testimony:

> *Kichígnapi*, 'respect each other.' That's humor; the good part of you comes out. The spirits do that. You might hate each other but the spirits make sure you have one mind. They don't intimidate you but they joke. If someone is sick then everyone is serious. Otherwise just crack up any joke. Go in with shoes on or your glasses on. It happens, they forget. That will make them laugh. [Bucko 1998:139]

Ray Fogelson defines an event as "that which occurs at a given time and place" (1989:133). Thus humor, which is always keyed to context, can be classified as an event. Despite the rich array of contemporary humor in the sweat, early ethnographic descriptions treat humor in the sweat as a nonevent: there is simply no mention of humor in a considerable number of texts. From the late 1950s onward, however, the nonevent becomes an event, at least in the ethnohistorical record.

The question becomes not only the reality of humor in the sweat but the generation of the very nature of "eventfulness." Humor in the sweat constitutes an event. So, too, the recording (in text or memory) of the occurrence of humor is also an event. Finally the recovery of that event through reference to text or memory is also an event. Forgetfulness (or loss of textual reference), inability to recognize an event, the suppression of the event before curious outsiders or insiders, or simple nonoccurrence all constitute nonevents. Is the early lack of humor in the sweat due to the observers (missionaries and explorers who did not generally associate ritual with humor), the record (a failure to remember or find the documentation of ritual humor), the observed (a few contemporary Lakota will say that ritual in the past was indeed thoroughly solemn), or the very act of observation (suspension of humor lest the ritual be misinterpreted by outsiders)? As Fogelson astutely points out: "Implicit here is the assumption that events may be recognized, defined, evaluated, and endowed with meaning differentially in different cultural traditions" (Fogelson 1989:135). Equally important is the same dynamics applied *across* cultures. Finally Lakota ritual practice is highly heterogeneous. Thus the presence or absence of humor, just like the quality and quantity of humor, is variable across time and space, situation and assembly.

In order to more deeply appreciate humor as an event and/or nonevent in the Lakota sweat lodge, it is important to have a general understanding of Lakota ritual humor. Ritual humor is not restricted to the sweat lodge. One can find it today in almost every contemporary Lakota ritual. The Heyoka ceremony was consistently seen as one based in humorous performance: ceremonial obligation carried out through the reverse behavior of the participants.[4] The ethnohistorical record presents the humor of the ceremony but always and properly in the context of the dire necessity for members of this society to fulfill their ceremonial obligations through contrary behaviors.

Remarkably, though recognized in the nineteenth century, ceremonial humor has not been extensively noted or analyzed except for the *heyoka*. Concerning the *heyoka* ceremony, Black Elk states that "the people should be in a happy, jolly frame of mind before the great truth is presented" (De-Mallie 1984:232) and, once his *heyoka* ceremony was over, "Everybody was glad and they regarded this as a medicine to make them happier all around" (DeMallie 1984:235). Thus ceremonial humor is a consistent "event" in this particular ritual.

The Sun Dance also has significant elements of ritual humor although this event becomes a nonevent in the ethnohistorical literature. Walker has the most extensive observations on humor in the course of this ritual. He states that during the preparation for the Sun Dance "the people jest and have sports that all may be merry" (Walker 1917:95). On the day of the feast that prepares for the actual Sun Dance he says, "men and women should treat others on terms of equality and with friendly hilarity" (Walker 1917:105). Concerning the raising of the Sun Dance pole he states:

> Immediately, men and women commingle and then follows a period of license when they banter each other and jest of sexual things. At that time a man or a woman may be familiar with one of the opposite sex in a manner that would be an indignity at other times, and the ribald merriment may become boisterous. [Walker 1917:110]

It is clear from Walker's description that there are marked periods for both humor and solemnity in the course of this sacred ritual. Walker fails to pursue the implications of his findings, however. James Dorsey, in *A Study of Siouan Cults* (1894), says nothing of the humor connected with the Sun Dance or other rituals. The same is true for Frances Densmore (1918), who does state, however, that the Sun Dance is held at the full moon of midsummer " 'when all nature and even men were rejoicing' " (1918:98). Joseph Brown's recording of Black Elk's description of the Sun Dance similarly states that people "were rejoicing" when the pole was raised (Brown 1987:79), but no mention of ritual humor is made except that at the conclusion of the ritual "The people all rejoiced, and the little children were allowed to play tricks on the old people, at this time, but nobody cared; and they were not punished, for everybody was very happy" (Brown 1987:99). Contemporary descriptions of the Sun Dance, specifically Amiotte (1987), Powers (1975), Lewis (1968), Mails (1978), and Holler (1995) say little about humor in the ritual.

In the case of the sweat lodge ethnohistorical literature makes no mention of ritual humor until the 1950s. Until then, at least in the context of the sweat, humor is a nonevent that is only later presented (or perhaps recognized) as event. Steven Feraca makes the first specific reference to humor in the Lakota sweat lodge in 1956. During a sweat that he attended he observes that "constant joking was indulged in by all present and included many humorous references to the salutary nature of the bath" (Feraca 1961:157). What is interesting is that the "event" is presented not as an innovation but as though it were (and perhaps it was) a normal part of the ceremony itself. William Powers provides some of the content of the humor in describing a ceremony in which he participated:

> Some of the jokes allude to this cramped situation, and one participant will chide another, saying, "You always want to sit next to the door so you can get out in a hurry." Others are jokingly accused of lifting the lodge covering a few inches so that fresh air can blow in. [Powers 1975:135][5]

Powers actually provides two descriptions of the sweat lodge in *Oglala Religion*, one with and one without humor. When he describes the "classical" sweat (1975:89–91), based on ethnohistorical sources as well as his own experience, he completely omits any reference to humor (he also does this in his Sun Dance description). His second more experiential and less structural description of the sweat lodge includes humor (1975:134–136). Clearly Powers's earlier description is more influenced by "classical" texts, which omit humor, than by his own observation as he omits humor from his structural analysis of ritual in *Oglala Religion*. As in the nineteenth century, there is a tendency to omit humor or treat it as epiphenomenal. To find a "place" for ritual humor in the sweat we need to look at its nature and context.

Though there is a general consensus that humor has a place in this ceremony opinion varies greatly as to where, when, and how to use humor. Rather than creating disharmony and bad feelings within the sweat, a dangerous thing to do, there are various regulating devices that can be enlisted. None of these actions involve direct interpersonal confrontation, which is quite rare. The sweat leader can disrupt banter by beginning another round of sweating (rarely is joking behavior engaged in during a round of sweating when the door is shut), he can start a song or prayer, or any participant can "change the subject." Just as individuals were able to start their own band if they disagreed with the policies of the leaders of the band to which they belonged (and provided they had enough supporters to become a viable unit), so too individuals will "hive off" to create a new sweat group:

> I respect that [someone who wants the sweat entirely serious], but this is our sweat and Church and it is how we do it. We don't do it out of disrespect. When you get your own sweat you can do it that way. Now respect our ways. Somehow you can tell if laughter is disrespectful. Some sweats are really rigid. I couldn't handle it. [Bucko 1998:137–138]

Consistently, humor is deprecating—either self-deprecating (telling stories or jokes "on oneself") or other-deprecating, "teasing," as a Lakota speaking English would put it.[6] It is important to note that humor, like everything else in the sweat, is part of normal daily life, only more so. Though generally classified as a rite of purification and passage, the sweat is also a rite of intensification. Every element in the sweat is from the ordinary world, only compressed into the time and space of the lodge and amplified through intensification—both ritual (the foregrounding of symbolic objects and activities) and environmental (the regulated physical extremes in the lodge). These elements are at the service of producing a heightened, controlled, and transformative experience of the ordinary world of physical, spiritual, and social interaction. Thus humor is intensified from ordinary life rather than shifted into a specific pattern, such as the reversals apparent in *heyoka* activity.

Self-deprecation, particularly on the part of the leader, is essential to produce harmony and *communitas* in the sweat.[7] This harmonious interrelationship is generally expressed in Lakota through the extension of kinship terms.[8] This helps a generally egalitarian society balance positions of superordination and subordination with the individual freedom inherent in joking and teasing behavior. A sweat leader told the following story as part of this process of leveling his role to that of the participants. A sweat leader will give his or her spiritual credentials for running a sweat before beginning and will then deprecate his or her position:

> Once an older man asked me to conduct a sweat lodge ceremony. His duty was to inform the people. It was late spring, the thunder storm season. I started the fire. This older man said he told everyone but no one was around. I said, "Let's us two do it." The wind was blowing. It was the feeling like just before a storm. The rocks were hot enough to have a good sweat but not that hot. He sang, we both prayed, sang again. The flap was opened and someone came in. It was a good sized person.

I told my partner to make the person welcome. He spoke in Lakota to the person, asked how he was and all the social amenities. That guy who came in just sat there and licked his chops, didn't pay attention to us or say anything. My partner got closer and started talking again, giving him a welcome, this time in English. He moved closer and I heard my partner say: "Hey, cut that out." I said I'm going to start the sweat again. My partner closed the door, the first dipper was poured, and then we heard a howling. The door opened and a big black dog ran out. My partner only recalls the black dog but not the words. [Bucko 1998:164]

Besides the leader, other participants in the sweat also engage in humor. One participant spoofed the leader's ability to eat dog quickly: meat in one side of the mouth and then bones out the other. Another related how in one sweat a then present participant brought in what he thought was a rock but turned out to be a smoldering stump, which nearly suffocated the participants when it was placed in the pit. At one sweat the leader's sister came to a sweat in between rounds while the door was open. Her brother-in-law, who was also in the sweat, called out from the darkness of the lodge: "Take all your clothes off and come on in." This is also in keeping with the Lakota custom, observed by many, of maintaining joking relationships between brothers- and sisters-in-law (Bucko 1998 141, 142).

Not only are the participants apt to be teased, but also there is teasing about the ceremony itself. One doorkeeper casually remarked that he was going up to the house to watch television as he closed the flap. Upon entering one lodge another doorkeeper would say in a deep, serious voice as participants passed him: "Tickets, tickets please!" People also joke about the discomforts of the sweat, stressing their own inability to endure the ceremony. Commonly jokes are made about the cramped conditions in the lodge, the intensity of the heat, the darkness, and the weakness they feel afterward. People joke too about modernizing their sweats with ceiling fans, air conditioners, sprinkler systems, picture windows, rail cars to transport the hot rocks, and après sweat showers (Bucko 1998:139, 141).

Much self- and other-deprecating humor revolves around mistakes made in the sweat. The most common theme of humor involves linguistic errors. One subject concerns variations on the prayer *mitákuye oyás'į*, or "all my relatives" in English. This is the most frequently utilized prayer in a sweat ceremony. Confusion over the basic prayer in English, "all my relatives," include such misappropriations as "all my rattlesnakes" and "all in the family." Humorous variations on mispronunciations of the Lakota *mitákuye oyás'i* include "My tacos are done" or "*mitawicu oyás'i*" (all of my wives). I was told that when someone once said in a sweat "*mitákuye oyás'i*," someone else replied, "Would you shut up, I'm trying to pray" (Bucko 1998:140). Joking about the sweat allows participants to allay their fears and discomforts and to encourage each other. Strong bonds are forged in the interplay of shared suffering and shared delight. A Lakota friend who knows of my interest in the sweat lodge told me this story:

> Two Lakotas from Rosebud [one can also substitute Pine Ridge] were walking down the road really hungry. They saw a turtle walking across the road so they picked it up and carried it home. When they got there they decided to put it in the microwave. Just as one of them was closing the door the other said to wait while he put in a little dish of water so the turtle would not dry out. He put in the water, closed the door and set the timer for twenty minutes. Here, when that bell rang the door swung open and that turtle sticks his head out and says: "Mitakuye Oyas'in."

In addition to interpersonal joking, humorous stories about the sweat are very important in defining the purpose of the sweat as well as the proper behavior of participants. These stories are sometimes told outside of the context of the sweat ceremony itself. Again the leveling process is essential in these tales. Each story told about the sweat involves people known to, and named by, the narrator.[9] Generally the same story is told, naming different individuals, either people there present or well known to the audience. Like interpersonal humor these stories can level participants' status by presenting them as foolish. At the same time they act as behavioral guides by highlighting the consequences of pride and foolish behavior. One of the most popular motifs involves individuals and groups who are convinced that they have great spiritual powers. One of the stories of this type involves a bull and a group of sweaters. This is but one of many variations on this story:

> Once all these guys were sweating and this mean big black bull comes along. As it comes the woman outside hollers "*Tablóka wą él ú ye!*" ['There's a bull coming!'] She heads out but they don't hear her in there. The bull stops at the sweat and starts sniffing under the covers. The leader says "*Thųkášila hí s'elél—anáǧoptą po! Thukášila ahí yelo!*" ['Grandfather is here—listen! Grandfather has arrived!'] Then that bull hooks his horns under the sweat and pulls it up. Those men inside were *itunkala cinca sala s'elel* ['pink just like baby mice']. [Bucko 1998:158–159]

The contents of the lodge—men pink, naked, blinded by the bright light, and shriveled, who look all the world like baby mice in a disturbed nest, an image of helplessness and pitifulness—is considered highly amusing. This image of weakness or pitifulness is in contrast to individuals focusing on their spiritual dignity, strength, and proximity to the divine. A similar story is told involving the exposure of the contents of the lodge:

> There was once an old guy who late one afternoon was going to sweat with two cousins and two brothers. They all were invited to his place for a sweat. When everything was ready they all went in and he began with the *hablóglaka* ['recitation of visionary experiences'], talking about himself first, his visions and things like that. He was sitting on the west side in the place of honor. It was a social sort of thing. He's talking and everyone is listening.
>
> Outside a relative was going to break a team of horses, one was wild and the other was tame. He caught them both and roped them together with the same rope when a whirlwind came up and scared the horses. The rope got out of his hands and they got away, heading for the lodge with the rope between them. The rope took off the lodge cover. The four in the lodge were bowed over listening so when the lodge cover headed away they were sitting there all pink like newborn mice when you disturb the nest. The old man was sitting upright so the rope took him along with the lodge over the hill. Pretty soon here comes the old man all muddy with the canvas cover over him, mad as hell. The women saw this and they all died laughing. He shook his fists at his son-in-law and said that I'm gonna get you for this. [Bucko 1998:158]

These stories of weakness are also extended to spiritual leaders, showing that they are just as human as everyone else is. Though there are many such stories, this one specifically refers to the sweat lodge:

> This story happened around here, as my Grandfather tells it. Long time ago, the medicine men didn't get along with one another. When they have a ceremonial, they would put down each other. They said the others don't have powers. When they do meet up in a sweat they try to chase each other out. *Íya yútapi* ['they eat rocks']; they could stand a lot of heat. There's an old medicine man. They said no one could chase him out of the sweat. No matter how hot it is in there he'll sing. Some roughnecks decided to fix this man. Long time ago they had this *yamnúmnuǧapi zi* ['yellow pepper,' perhaps powdered mustard]. I don't know what it is— pepper now is less powerful. They got hold of some of that. They put it in a bag. The old man poured lots of water—they all shouted *mitákuye oyás'į*. They can't stand the heat. The roughnecks went in and sat right

beside the old man. The man with the *yamnúmnuǧapi zi* took it out and put some on the old man's back under his neck. His sweat made it run down his back and it ran into his crack and burned his backside. He jumped up and out of there. The door flew open—he ran towards the creek. The water made it worse when he jumped in. It was just like fire down there. He was jumping up and down hollering. His mother and grandmother were there. He was old but they were still living. His mother said, *Cįkš, tókha he?* ['Son, what's the matter?'] He said, "Get out of here you crazy old ladies, I'm dying." Pretty soon he's *ųzé ša so?* ['his butt is red, hey?'], sliding his rear end in the mud trying to cool it off, but even that made it worse. That's the story he told. This happened. [Bucko 1998:160–161]

A similar story is told where the antagonists use iron filings. A third story involves some kids throwing hot pepper into a sweat while everyone is in there. The occupants all shot out of there buck naked (Bucko 1998:161).

Stories making spiritual leaders look foolish are also extended to Christian clergy. One frequently told tale is of the priest who is shaking hands at Mass (sometimes a powwow is used as the locus) and saying "Peace be with you!" One old man who is a Lakota speaker (and thus speaks English using Lakota vowels) replies, "Peees on you too, Father!" Another story has a priest telling an old man through a translator that if he does not go to Mass he will be sent to hell. Since there is no Lakota word for hell the translator tells the old man that he will go where it's hot all the time. The old man tells the translator in Lakota to tell the priest that that would be fine with him as he is cold all the time anyway. At Church one day the minister warns his congregation of the evils of peyote. "*Lila pa*" ['it's really sour'], he states. An old lady in the congregation looks up at him and replies: "How do you know, did you ever taste any?"

Other stories highlight the activities of unscrupulous medicine men whose names are often inserted into these rather standard narratives. These stories are employed as warnings to anyone who would exploit the position of medicine man rather than used against spiritual leaders as a class of people. This story chides both unscrupulous leaders and naive participants:

Once a medicine man invites nuns [sometimes "women"] to go to his sweat. He asked some singers to sing at 4:00. When he sees all the nuns, he told them to take off all their clothes. The nuns did this. When the singers saw this, they wouldn't go in the lodge. So they sat outside and sang for him. Well, the medicine man's wife comes over the hill and the leader sends his wife away before she sees anything. The sisters just sit in there quietly. The medicine man told them that the spirits might touch you. After the sweat they commented on how the spirits were doing that. The nuns were saying that the spirits had big hands and one nun said, "That one spirit sure had big lips too." [Bucko 1998:161]

It is clear that humor is both present and important to the Lakota sweat lodge as well as to Lakota life in general. Thus humor has the status of an "event" both by its widely observable and recognizable occurrence and by its intimate relationship to a multiplicity of social interactions. In the tradition of Ray Fogelson, let me now suggest some avenues for interpreting ritual humor.

Deprecating humor is utilized both to ease the tensions of individuals about the sweat and to create harmony within the sweat among the participants. It does so by foregrounding individuals' shortcomings in order to emphasize equality. Everyone and, at times, everything is teased. This harmony is essential in creating and stabilizing social relationships. At the same time humor itself can be employed as a corrective to unacceptable behavior without directly confronting the offending individual or causing him or her public embarrassment. The sweat lodge often serves as a locus for an individual's introduction to Lakota social relationships and culture as well as for the reintegration of individuals into these relationships.

The sweat represents a culturally Lakota place of transformation. Weakness is exchanged for strength, fragmentation for wholeness, disease for health, discord for harmony, and sorrow for joy. It is also a place of intensification where vivid physical and spiritual experiences revitalize individuals and groups. When Lakota pray in a sweat, they present themselves as poor and pitiful in order to invoke spiritual aid. Humor in the sweat is social discourse in which one presents himself or herself (or others) similarly as weak and needful in order to petition for and subsequently establish spiritual and communal aid and support.

The sweat is a break from routine, a movement into another world, just as it is an intensified but controlled experience of this world. At the same time it is a controlled intensification of present reality, for it is the condensation of the entirety of the Lakota social, natural, and spiritual world. The sweat lodge ritual is infused with humor to enable participants to move more facilely between these worlds and to apprehend the intensified presentation of the cosmos. The universe created by the sweat is a world that reflects the ordinary world, a place of harmony and joy yet pain and suffering, power and wisdom yet weakness and foolishness. The symbolic and literal mastery of suffering in this ritual context renews the determination of individuals and groups who experience an outer world replete with alienation, pain, and sorrow.

In a structuralist vein ritual humor is a binary banana peel that propels people swiftly from one set of oppositions to another, creating oppositions, reversing them, and thereby quickly dissolving them, establishing structure and proposing antistructure. Mary Douglas observes that jokes are "expressive of the total situations in which they occur" (Douglas 1991:98). The sweat lodge intensifies normal experience—and humor is one of many vehicles of intensification. Indeed, to understand the joke one must understand both the culture of a people as well as the ritual expressions that it produces.

Yet humor can also be a delicate matter. In my two years of fieldwork and many years of sweating I was reprimanded only once for behavior in a sweat lodge. This was for making jokes about modernizing the sweat during a break. Though others were making similar jokes, a non-Lakota Native participant took offence at what I said. Although nothing was said to me in the lodge, later in the day the person, who knew I am a Jesuit, called me aside and commented that he would never make fun of things in church such as during Communion or suggest ways to change the Catholic ritual.[10] When I explained that in my experience many people joked in the lodge (in fact, in that lodge I was joining in the general joking), the individual cited experience in stating that jokes were never told in the sacred sweat lodge. Event became nonevent right before my eyes.

To understand how humor appears and disappears, one must understand how cultures, and individuals within those cultures, interact, interpret, and are interpreted by one another. This is crucial for interpreting the nature of the specific event under discussion—ritual humor in the sweat—as well as for understanding why humor in the sweat is variously interpreted as an event or nonevent over time. I propose a variety of reasons for the nonevent status of humor in early sweat lodge descriptions. First, with the exception of Father Hennepin, none of the early observers of the sweat lodge actually participated in the ritual.[11] Their informants, generally converts to Christianity, which then focused on a vehement rejection of traditional religion, were their only source for what went on inside the lodge. Though Father Hennepin was literally an insider, he probably did not speak Dakota well enough to pick up any humor (and Dakota and Lakota humor is highly verbal). We must also consider the possibility that due to an outside presence humor was simply not employed. This is consistent with the awareness the Lakota had of the seriousness demeanor of Christian ritual.

Clearly, the Lakota were careful in presenting themselves to outsiders whose prejudices and expectations they fairly accurately anticipated. Thus the omission of ritual humor in oral narrative delivered to outsiders as well as rituals performed under the observation of outsiders (the stuff of ethnohistorical records) may well have been deliberate and reflective of the Lakota perception of Christian ritual rather than their own practice. Reciprocally, outside observers, in their attempts to both ennoble and/or vilify the Lakota, remove humor as a source of common humanity, placing these people either above or below such emotion. Joseph Epes Brown is far more Mircea Eliadian than Milton Berlesque.

My own fieldwork made me quite aware of the predominance of humor in the sweat lodge. However, whenever I asked one of my teachers how he or she would structure and conduct a sweat, the response, though highly detailed, normally lacked any reference to humor. When I asked deliberately about the use of humor in the sweat, people were quite forthcoming with both stories of humorous occurrences and their own analysis of the importance of humor. It seemed that humor is so spontaneous and contextual in this ritual that it is difficult to view it as part of the structure of the ritual itself. It is a taken-for-granted, if not simply unreflected, element of the ritual assemblage.

Humor has been and continues to be essential to Lakota ritual. First, Walker notes that humor is integral to the focal Lakota ritual, the Sun Dance. Second, Black Elk makes clear that humor is essential to ritual practice and the welfare of the people. During my own field observations between 1988 and 1990, there was no contestation by Lakotas themselves over the presence of humor in a sweat in my experience, as there was over other elements in the sweat such as the use of particular songs, the participation of non-Lakota or non-Natives, or the utilization in the sweat of what was considered New Age paraphernalia such as crystals. Finally, individual Lakota with whom I worked consistently cited humorous stories as well as joking behavior from the past and considered humor to be always present in some way in the sweat.

Although jokes and stories are frequently reused in different sweats, humor remains part of oral performance. Oral performance is keyed not only to text but also to context. Thus humor is more appropriate at some times than at others. Sweats I have been to after a family member has experienced some tragedy have been quite solemn. So, too, sweats for people who are experiencing social tension can be quite humorous as participants work to relativize the crisis. Joking is an intimate act and is not engaged in casually. Like the sweat ceremony itself, joking can act to increase social intimacy and equality and, at the same time, demarcate social boundaries, roles, and statuses.

Some individuals are funnier than others, more appreciative of humor, and more willing to engage in verbal banter and storytelling. I found in my own work that the more funny stories I heard about the sweat, the more Lakota folks would ask me to tell the ones I knew just as I was asking them to tell me the ones they knew! In this exchange it was sometimes confusing as to who was interviewing whom about humor. Stories, like any other object of value and beauty, are to be exchanged and generously shared. Finally, humor is central to the enjoyment of life, and the sweat is preeminently about life.

Clearly, humor has in some cases been removed, censored, or ignored by some observers because of a variety of preconceptions, both by Lakota and non-Lakota, just as participants shielded certain behaviors based on the presumed sensibilities of their observers.[12] Anthropologist Alice Fletcher was given a Sun Dance figurine "sans penis" to protect what the Lakota perceived to be her sensibilities (Mark 1988:80). They thereby invented the Ken doll with this deft act of chivalry. So, too, James Walker's informants altered the story of "The Wizard and His Wife" (Walker 1983:118–130) by substituting a rattle for an air-filled bladder that emulated the sound of defecating (thus laying the invention of the whoopie cushion at the feet of the Lakota). One of Ella Deloria's informants explained the substitution: "The interpreter must have changed it so as not to offend Dr. Walker. Of course, it was right to do so" (Jahner 1983:20). Lakota ritual participants were and are quite aware of their "observers," as a result either omitting references in discourse or actually changing their ritual forms at times.

Let me return to the nature of events and nonevents. Today, as in the nineteenth century, humor continues to appear and disappear, thus becoming event and then becoming nonevent. Sometimes, depending on the humor and circumstances, this becoming and unbecoming may itself become an unbecoming event. I have been to sweats that were more solemn than a Pontifical Mass and have laughed away entire evenings and nights at others. Lakota have quit other lodges and built their own sweats because their former sweat groups were getting too solemn or too frivolous. Lakota and other Native people who are integrating themselves into traditional culture sometimes move with a convert's zeal and seriousness. Non-Lakotas sometimes approach Lakota ritual with solemnity and a desire to do things "by the book," usually referring to Walker (1980), Brown (1953), Neihardt (1971), Stolzman (1986), or McGaa (1990, 1992, 1995, 1998). At a talk I gave in 1998, a tribal leader complained to me about outsiders coming in and telling them how to do sweats based on their reading of ethnographic materials. I confessed to him that my one fear about the book I had just published (Bucko 1998) was that if a flash-light suddenly popped on in one of his future sweats a participant might solemnly say "Wait a minute, it says on page 233 of Bucko's book that you should . . . ."

Humor is essential to a sweat, and just as a good sweat leader regulates the heat and duration of each round, so too he or she will regulate the mood and intensity of the prayers and interactions. I was once asked by a spiritual leader to start making jokes because things were getting too serious in the sweat. I also became material for sweat lodge stories that are still told (mostly when I'm around!). Once I was asked by a sweat lodge leader to ask the fire keeper to bring in seven rocks. I put my head out the door and said: "Seven rocks, please." When I sat back down in the lodge the leader explained to me that he had told the other participants about how I had learned some Lakota and that he was hoping that I would have said it in Lakota! I was known after that as "Seven Rocks Please" (Bucko 1998:141).

It was with Ray Fogelson that I began to understand the importance of reflection to ethnography and ethnohistory. He reminds us that "historians are never free from history. There is a continual interaction between past and present" (1989). In looking at the appearance and disappearance of humor in the sweat lodge and other ceremonies as well as in the representations of these events, we need to reflect on both the observer (the ethnohistorian) and the observed (the Lakota in a specific ritual event). We must also take into consideration the fact that the observed are also the observers and that the observers are also the observed. In addition to this interethnic reflexivity, as Ray points out, past and present create yet another set of influences as observer and observed generate and modulate their own understandings of the past as well as their relationships to the present. Thus the need, as Fogelson points out in his work, for an ethno-ethnohistorical approach (1974; 1989). At the same time we are looking at two events—the actual production of humor in a ritual and the recording and/or remembrance of such an event. Thus if ritual humor is not recorded or remembered, it does not necessarily mean it was not present. Then again, its absence does not necessarily guarantee its presence. If I relied only on my teachers' formal descriptions of sweats rather than also participating in them I could have concluded that humor was absent from the sweat. On the other hand, I have attended sweats, albeit very few, which were entirely serious. So, too, the observer has to recognize when humor is present—he or she has to "get it" for the event to be recognized as an event. In this blur of perspectives and reflections of how others see one another lies the important issue of whose history this is (Fogelson 1989:142). The ethnohistorian writes the history and indeed becomes part of the history, but the constructed history does not belong to him or her. At a time when groups focus on the implications of the concept of cultural property not only are lines drawn (becoming themselves "events") but "No Trespassing" signs are appearing all over town. Thus restriction and omission can be as much an act of defiance as they were acts of deference to another's sensibilities in the past. So, too, denial of the accuracy and/or validity of ethnographic description and ethnohistorical analyses can itself be a declaration of independence.

Thus I propose to add another "type" of event to Fogelson's Fogelso-nian typology of events and nonevents: the oscillating or, to use a literary metaphor, the Cheshire Cat event—one that is an event that becomes a nonevent and again becomes an event. Humor in the Lakota sweat lodge provides an instance of this phenomenon. In the ethnographic record and indeed in contemporary practice now you see it, now you don't. And now you see it again. It depends on how you look at it, when you look at it, who's looking, and from what perspective. This multi-perspective and multi-reflective approach is part of Ray's legacy to ethnohistory and is essential for understanding the dynamics both of contemporary Lakota ritual humor and the way in which it has been and continues to be ana-lyzed.

"My speculations here are intended only to suggest the explanatory possibilities of considering nonevents in the writing of ethnohistory" (Fo-gelson 1989:145). As one of Ray's students I have attempted a brief walk here in his famous saddle shoes, hopefully to add a few more suggestions and reflections to the discussion. Description and practice, interpreter and interpreted, past and present, variation and pattern, event and non-events, like the Diamond Crystal salt lady, reflect to a considerable depth. Ethnohistory is about understanding the process as well as the results. Ethnohistory, itself about time, takes a lot of time and requires a lot of putting up of one's feet and thinking . . . good advice from a cherished mentor, as I am learning in my anthropological almost-maturity.

Notes

This article began as a chapter in my dissertation and the book *The Lakota Ritual of the Sweat Lodge* (Lincoln: University of Nebraska Press, 1998). It is used here with the permission of the University of Nebraska Press.

    1. Personal e-mail correspondence, Pauline T. Strong, June 27, 2005, who was quoting from a letter from Fogelson to Kan and Strong, dated April 27, 2005. See also Fogelson (1974).

    2. For similar statements on the stereotype of Indian humorlessness (and subsequent data

to dispel the myth) see Dorson 1946:113; Edmunds 1974:141–142; Emmons 2000:ix; Hill 1943:7; Hymes 1979:ix–xi; Lincoln 1993:4; Opler 1938:3; Price 1998:255; Sayer 1985:68–72; Steward 1931:187; and Wallace 1953:135.

3. The field material and some of the analyses in this present work can also be found in my dissertation (Bucko 1992) as well as my book on the sweat lodge (Bucko 1998), which is based largely on my dissertation. Ray Fogelson directed my dissertation.

4. For analysis of the *Heyoka* see Densmore 1918; Eastman 1849; Erdoes and Lame Deer 1972; Hassrick 1964; Howard 1954; Lewis 1974; Lewis 1990; Lowie 1913; Powers 1975; Sandoz 1961; and Walker 1980.

5. Powers provides an earlier description of a Lakota sweat lodge he participated in that is full of humorous interaction (Powers 1969:126–131).

6. Vine Deloria also points out that teasing is used to correct individuals without shaming them and as an act of self-deprecation (Deloria 1988:147). Interestingly, his chapter in *Custer Died for Your Sins* on humor deals primarily with politics and intertribal and interpersonal relations and makes no mention of ritual humor.

7. For a description of communitas in the context of ritual see Turner 1969.

8. One of the individuals with whom I sweat refers to the group at the sweat as her "sweat clan."

9. To protect the privacy of individuals I omit or change names in each of the stories I reproduce. Lakota jokes and stories are normally told mentioning specific people, usually a relative or someone present whom the narrator wants to tease.

10. W. Hill notes that Kluckhohn makes the same observation concerning the Navajo: "According to Kluckhohn conservative Navajo resent and object to joking during the performance of a chant way. They think of it as in the same category as joking in church" (Hill 1943:8 n. 8).

11. Father Hennepin entered a Santee sweat lodge in 1680. Subsequent accounts of Dakota lodges do not appear until the middle 1800s. Lakota lodge descriptions are even later.

12. Hieb (1972:163–164), drawing on the ethnography of Pueblo ritual clowns, gives examples of how early observers disdained and censored what they encountered.

References

Amiotte, Arthur
   1987 The Lakota Sun Dance: Historical and Contemporary Perspectives. *In* Sioux Indian Religion: Tradition and Innovation. R. DeMallie and D. Parks, eds. Norman: University of Oklahoma Press.
Brown, Joseph E.
   1953 The Sacred Pipe: Black Elk's Account of the Seven Rites of the Oglala Sioux. Norman: University of Oklahoma Press.
Brown, Joseph Epes
   1987 The Sacred Pipe. New York: Penguin Books.
Bucko, Raymond A.
   1992 Inipi: Historical Transformation and Contemporary Significance of the Sweat Lodge in Lakota Religious Practice. PhD dissertation, Department of Anthropology, University of Chicago.
   1998 The Lakota Ritual of the Sweat Lodge: History and Contemporary Practice. Lincoln: University of Nebraska Press.

Deloria, Vine, Jr.

1988 Custer Died for Your Sins: An Indian Manifesto. Norman: University of Oklahoma Press.

DeMallie, Raymond J., Jr.

1984 The Sixth Grandfather: Black Elk's Teachings Given to John G. Neihardt. Lincoln: University of Nebraska Press.

Densmore, Frances

1918 Teton Sioux Music. Bulletin 61. Smithsonian Institution, Bureau of American Ethnology. Washington DC: Government Printing Office.

Dorsey, James Owen

1894 A Study of Siouan Cults. In Eleventh Annual Report of the Bureau of American Ethnology. Pp. 351–544. Washington DC: Government Printing Office.

Dorson, Richard M.

1946 Comic Indian Anecdotes. Southern Folklore Quarterly 10(2):113–128.

Douglas, Mary

1991 Jokes. In Implicit Meanings: Essays in Anthropology. M. Douglas, ed. Pp. 90–114. London: Routledge & Kegan Paul.

Eastman, Mary H.

1849 Dahcotah; or Life and Legends of the Sioux around Fort Snelling. New York: John Wiley.

Easton, Robert

1970 Humor of the American Indian. Mankind 2(9):37–41, 72–73.

Edmunds, R. David

1974 Red Men and Hat Wearers. In Red Men and Hat-Wearers: Viewpoints in Indian History: Papers from the Colorado State University Conference on Indian History, August 1974. D. Tyler, ed. Pp. 141–53. Boulder CO: Pruett.

Emmons, Sally L. A.

2000 A Disarming Laughter: The Role of Humor in Tribal Cultures, An Examination of Humor in Contemporary Native American Literature and Art. PhD dissertation, Department of English, University of Oklahoma.

Erdoes, Richard, and John Lame Deer

1972 Lame Deer—Seeker of Visions. New York: Simon and Schuster.

Feraca, Stephen

1961 The Yuwipi Cult of the Oglala and Sicangu Teton Sioux. Plains Anthropologist 6(13):155–163.

Fogelson, Raymond D.

1974 On the Varieties of Indian History: Sequoyah and Traveller Bird. Journal of Ethnic Studies 2:105–112.

1985 Night Thoughts on Native American Social History. Occasional Papers in Curriculum No. 3. Pp. 67–89. Chicago: D'Arcy McNickle Center for the History of the History of the American Indian, The Newberry Library.

1987a A Final Look and Glance at the Bearing of the Bering Straits on Native American History. In Occasional Papers in Curriculum No. 5. Pp. 233–261. Chicago: D'Arcy McNickle Center for the History of the American Indian, The Newberry Library.

1987b Man's Gassy Essence: The Social History of Balloons. Central States Anthropological Society, Columbus OH.

1989 The Ethnohistory of Events and Nonevents. Ethnohistory 36(2):133–147.

Hassrick, Royal
1964 The Sioux: Life and Customs of a Warrior Society. Norman: University of Oklahoma Press.

Hieb, Louis A.
1972 Meaning and Mismeaning: Toward an Understanding of the Ritual Clown. *In* New Perspectives on the Pueblos. A. Ortiz, ed. Pp. 163–195. Albuquerque: University of New Mexico Press.

Hill, W. W.
1943 Navajo Humor. General Series in Anthropology 9:5–28.

Holler, Clyde
1995 Black Elk's Religion: The Sun Dance and Lakota Catholicism. Syracuse NY: Syracuse University Press.

Howard, James H.
1954 The Dakota Heyoka Cult. Scientific Monthly 78(4):254–258.

Hymes, Dell
1979 Foreword. *In* Portraits of "The Whiteman": Linguistic Play and Cultural Symbols among the Western Apache. K. H. Basso, ed. Pp. ix–xviii. Cambridge: Cambridge University Press.

Jahner, Elaine
1983 Introduction. *In* Lakota Myth. E. Jahner, ed. Pp. 1–40. Lincoln: University of Nebraska Press.

Lewis, Thomas
1968 The Oglala Sun Dance. Pine Ridge Research Bulletin 5:52–64.
1974 The Heyoka Cult in Historical and Contemporary Oglala Sioux Society. Anthropos 69:17–32.
1990 The Medicine Men: Oglala Sioux Ceremony and Healing. Lincoln: University of Nebraska Press.

Lincoln, Kenneth
1993 Indi'n Humor: Bicultural Play in Native America. Oxford: Oxford University Press.

Lowie, Robert H.
1913 Dance Associations of the Eastern Dakota. Anthropological Papers of the American Museum of Natural History 11(2):101–142.

Mails, Thomas E.
1978 Sundancing at Rosebud and Pine Ridge. Sioux Falls SD: The Center for Western Studies.

Mark, Joan T.
1988 A Stranger in Her Native Land: Alice Fletcher and the American Indians. Lincoln: University of Nebraska Press.

McGaa, Ed (Eagle Man)
1990 Mother Earth Spirituality. San Francisco: Harper and Row.
1992 Rainbow Tribe. New York: Harper San Francisco.
1995 Native Wisdom: Perceptions of the Natural Way. Minneapolis: Four Directions.
1998 Eagle Vision: Return of the Hoop. Minneapolis: Four Directions.

Neihardt, John G
1971 Black Elk Speaks: Being the Life Story of a Holy Man of the Oglala Sioux. Lincoln: University of Nebraska Press.

Opler, Morris E.

1938 Humor and Wisdom of Some American Indian Tribes. New Mexico Anthropologist 3:3–11.

Pierce, Richard A.

1978 The Russian Orthodox Religious Mission in America, 1794–1837: with Materials Concerning the Life and Works of the Monk German, and Ethnographic Notes by the Hieromonk Gedeon. Kingston ON: Limestone Press.

Powers, William K

1969 Indians of the Northern Plains. New York: G. P. Putnam's Sons.

1975 Oglala Religion. Lincoln: University of Nebraska Press.

Price, Darby Li Po

1998 Laughing without Reservation: Indian Standup Comedians. American Indian Culture & Research Journal 22(4):255–271.

Sandoz, Mari

1961 These Were the Sioux. New York: Hastings House Publishers.

Sayer, Robert F.

1985 Trickster. North Dakota Quarterly 53:68–81.

Singer, Milton B.

1984 Man's Glassy Essence: Explorations in Semiotic Anthropology. Bloomington: Indiana University Press.

Steward, Julian H.

1931 The Ceremonial Buffoon of the American Indian. Papers of the Michigan Academy of Science, Arts, and Letters 14:187–207.

Stolzman, William, S.J.

1986 How to Take Part in Lakota Ceremonies. Pine Ridge SD: Red Cloud Indian School.

Tassin, Ray

1973 Stanley Vestal, Champion of the Old West. Glendale CA: Arthur H. Clark Company.

Thwaites, Reuben Gold, ed.

1897 The Jesuit Relations and Allied Documents. Vol. 6. Cleveland: The Burrows Brothers Company.

Turner, Victor W.

1969 The Ritual Process: Structure and Anti-Structure. Ithaca NY: Cornell University Press.

Walker, James

1917 The Sun Dance and Other Ceremonies of the Oglala Division of the Teton Sioux. Anthropological Papers of the American Museum of Natural History 16(2):51–221.

1980 Lakota Belief and Ritual. Lincoln: University of Nebraska Press.

1983 Lakota Myth. Lincoln: University of Nebraska Press.

Wallace, William J.

1953 The Role of Humor in the Hupa Indian Tribe. Journal of American Folk-lore 66:135–141.

Young Bear, Severt, and Ron D. Theisz

1994 Standing in the Light: A Lakota Way of Seeing. Lincoln: University of Nebraska Press.

8. Self-consciousness, Ceremonialism, and the Problem of the Present in the Anthropology of Native North America

ROBERT E. MOORE

Introduction

Students of Raymond D. Fogelson have often shown a propensity for two seemingly different kinds of anthropological work: the use of documentary archives to understand *the past*(s) of American Indian communities—the now vital field of ethnohistory—and the use of ethnography to understand *the present* in these same communities. Often enough, one body of documentation (e.g., field notes) can be made to illuminate the other (e.g., the archive).[1]

And vice versa. In this respect, of course, Fogelson's students follow his example, even if there are few, if any, who can do it as gracefully as he can (see, e.g., Fogelson 1984).

Now, this attempt to conjoin the past with the present would hardly deserve mention at all except for the fact that several decades of "memory ethnography," followed by acculturation studies, followed by the era of repatriation and federal recognition, have made the problem of the present in American Indian studies an acute one.

The absence of the present in earlier decades of American anthropology is quite noticeable, especially when one searches the literature of the 1920s and 1930s for descriptions of (then) contemporary reservation life. Two exceptions that come to mind are Margaret Mead's *The Changing Culture of an American Indian Tribe* (1932) and Clark Wissler's *Red Man Reservations* (1938; previously titled *Indian Cavalcade*). Mead's account, of course, is "ethically challenged"—the research, as she admits, was carried out under false pretenses—while Wissler's account was travel literature aimed at a general readership (as its two titles suggest).

The situation today is dramatically different. Anthropologists, together with linguists, archaeologists, and sometimes physical anthropologists, now routinely serve tribal groups and reservation communities in a range of advisory and consultative capacities. Moreover, they are often called as expert witnesses in land claims cases, federal recognition cases, and other court proceedings (cf. Clifford 1986; notice the shadow life, outside the academy, of the Boasian "four fields").

Most if not all of these activities involve mapping (often quite literally) from populations in the past to existing social groups in the present through a framework of legal rights of possession and/or usufruct of lands and other such "cultural resources"—a term that sometimes includes surviving elders with traditional knowledge (e.g., of language). The focus may be on the past, but these discussions are taking place in the present and are constitutive of it.

Like other ethnographers and linguists whose focus, if not their training, is "Americanist" (Darnell and Valentine 1999), many of the contributors to this volume have been struggling to develop an analytic vocabulary for talking about these and other aspects of contemporary life in Native American communities in a way that contributes to wider discussions (in anthropology and related fields) of globalization, modernity, and indigeneity (see, e.g., Cattelino 2005, Carneiro da Cunha 2005).

In this chapter I will be attempting something far more modest. The ethnographic material will be more or less contemporary (mid-1980s to the present), and my focus will be on the variety of roles that individuals play, or don't play, in observances whose manifest function is to mark and effectuate their transition from one status or stage of life to another. By using different modes of participation in life-cycle ceremonials as a set of lenses through which to view the changing significance of personhood, I hope to describe the emergence of a kind of "identity politics" in the community I know best, Warm Springs Indian Reservation in central Oregon.[2]

I will discuss two examples, both of which are marginal in one or more respects. One is an observance of obviously Euro-American origin—a birthday party—while the other, a Wasco naming ceremony, is clearly traditional. The former example comes from my own field notes, the latter from field notes and conversations shared with me by Kathrine S. French and her late husband and colleague David H. French (1918–1995).

I will describe the first example briefly, the second in more detail. I will then move from an interpretation of the second example into a brief discussion of the fundamental questions that it seems to raise about the possible future(s) of American Indian studies in anthropology.

The point of this chapter is precisely to call the whole issue of authenticity—how is it ritually invoked and what forms of authority are called upon in creating it?—to our ethnographic attention. For it is clear that authenticity, which can function both as a symbol of the (essentialized) historical continuity ("tradition") of populations and communities and as a primordial modality of selfhood and identity for individuals, has become a Foucauldian "discourse of truth" in the present. It is just as clear that anthropologists and anthropology, thanks in part to decades of painstaking "salvage ethnography" in Indian communities across the United States and Canada, are deeply implicated in it.

At Warm Springs today, social ceremonials marking "life-crisis" events like birth, death, marriage, a boy's first successful hunt, or a girl's first huckleberry picking or root digging continue to be a focus of much interest and activity. The logistics, planning, and expenditures involved in the sponsorship of these events—which usually involve some distribution of gifts to the assembled public, and always, always involve "putting up a dinner" for a large group of people (with ample leftovers to take home)—continue to govern the activities of whole families for weeks and months leading up to one of these events (see K. French 1955).

Control over the format—and thereby over the meaning—of ceremonial events like these is currently passing into the hands of a new generation, some of whom seem to be operating in part with a new set of notions about the very nature and purpose of such public enactments. At issue are matters such as the relationship between the historical contingency of individual lives and more enduring social categories, for example, that of "person" (Mauss 1985[1938]), and the relationship between the stereotypically "primitive" existence of a locally bounded cultural universe—located in a past—and the contemporary experience of communities that are open to and embedded in wider cultural and institutional formations.

Spunky's Birthday Party

In July 1986 at Warm Springs a family gathering was held in the household of Mrs. M., where at the time I was living and "helping around."

Mrs. M., the matriarch of a large family, had recently been widowed, and so the management of the household and surrounding rangeland (including a dozen or so head of cattle) fell to her. Mrs. M. was (and is) in vigorous good health. I'll not soon forget the sight of her, with her bright kerchief tight over her long gray braids, driving rapidly around and through the sagebrush near the house—herding cattle behind the wheel of a small Ford Pinto she kept for that very purpose. She was about 65 years old at the time, and her daughter's husband, who ran a cattle ranch over the ridge to the north, rendered help with veterinary and other ranch-related matters.

By ancestry both Chinookan (Wasco) and Sahaptin, Mrs. M. speaks both of those languages but has always identified herself as a Wasco, partly because she was raised by her Kiksht-speaking maternal grandmother. Her late husband (and the father of her five children) came from a large Paiute family from the south end of the reservation (where we now were). In addition to Wasco (Kiksht) and Sahaptin, Mrs. M. can speak some Paiute (and understand more), but when it came to Kiksht she always disclaimed full fluency and urged me to "double check" her responses to my linguistic queries with other speakers whose Kiksht she held in higher esteem than her own. She is known as a skilled maker of baskets using Wasco, Sahaptin, and Paiute techniques and designs, and participates in basket-making demonstrations at the new Museum at Warm Springs and elsewhere in the region.

The gathering over the July Fourth weekend, celebrating the birthday of Spunky, as the youngest of Mrs. M.'s grown children is known, had become an annual event in the family. Over time it became almost like a small family reunion, "a chance to get everybody together," as Mrs. M. put it. Naturally, when the day came, I agreed to help her with the preparations.

We'd cook salmon and eels on thick planks of cedar leaning over the fire, and hamburgers and hot dogs on the barbecue grill for the kids. Chips, celery, potato salad, cole slaw, and soft drinks rounded out the feast. It was too hot to eat inside, and so we set up the table, the grill, and the rest of it in the shade of an "arbor" adjoining the long house she'd built on her property several years before (it was now used mostly for storage, and that summer for my lodging).

The grocery list composed, I was sent off to the Erickson's IGA supermarket in the nearby town of Madras, Oregon. Among my instructions was to go to the bakery counter to pick up a cake that Mrs. M. had ordered several days before. I was told to make sure the bakery people had remembered to inscribe the cake, in icing, with "HAPPY BIRTHDAY SPUNKY."

I arrived back with the cake and other supplies, and we cleaned off the table and got things ready. Soon everyone had arrived, and we had a pleasant, relaxed meal in the quickly cooling evening air outdoors, where the kids could run and play in the sagebrush with the several dogs that lived around the place. And then I was instructed to go to the house and bring forth the cake. I set the cake down in the middle of the table, we gathered the kids, and we all sang "Happy Birthday, Dear Spunky."

But Spunky was not there. Indeed, he was lodged at the Warm Springs Tribal Jail and, as everyone knew, had been there for a couple of days (too much celebrating). There was absolutely no middle-class shame or embarrassment attached to this, nor had it prevented us from going ahead with the annual family gathering in his name (in this as in many other communities, the police and community jail perform a broad range of social service functions).

As one of Mrs. M's grown daughters cut the cake and distributed the slices, she asked if anyone had talked to Spunky that day. Apparently, Mrs. M. had called over to the jail earlier. As we began dessert she replayed the phone call in the locally characteristic narrative style that omits all the "he-said, she-said" material and depends instead on direct quotation, with distinctive voice qualities to signal conversational turn-taking: " 'Is Spunks there?'—'He's asleep'—'Oh, well don't wake him up'—'Can I take a message?'—'Just tell him his mom called to wish him a happy birthday'—'Okay.' "

Now, the observance of people's birthdays is obviously not ancient in these societies. But the practice of going ahead with a life-cycle ceremonial and recognizing and marking an important transition in the life of an individual, even when that individual can't be present at the event, is far from unheard of. The ethnographic archive of ceremonialism at Warm Springs is replete with reports as well as observed instances of life-cycle ceremonies, including namings and even (until the 1950s) "wedding trades," in which, for one reason or another, the individual(s) whose change of status was being marked could not be present (see K. French 1955 and ms.). Often, someone else (a sibling, perhaps, or a cousin) functions in the event as a substitute and receives payment.

The traditional approach, then, provides for such contingencies: if the actual individual is unavailable you simply hire someone, "stand them up" (in the local nonstandard variety of "Reservation English"), and go ahead. Just as our courts of law convict people of crimes in absentia, so individuals at Warm Springs can advance into adulthood or receive an Indian name in absentia. That is what happened in this case, right down to the singing of "Happy Birthday," and no one remarked about it.

The point is that Spunky's birthday party was *not* ideologically marked as an "Indian" activity, and yet it was conducted in a way that fits very well with everything we know about "traditional" ceremonialism in relation to "traditional" forms of social organization in this community. The small difficulty of the honoree's being detained elsewhere was handled with aplomb and in keeping with standards according to which such observances are defined as relevant *not* primarily to the honoree as an individual but to *the family*. The family is the major participant, the "principal" (Goffman 1981), and the sponsor of all such life-cycle ceremonies; its oldest living members officiate and make the arrangements (see K. French 1955 for a full discussion of social ceremonialism at Warm Springs).

In the present case, Spunky accedes to a new status within the family upon his birthday (a Euro-American "culture trait," whatever that means), and that change of status needs to be marked by a gathering, a dinner, and an observance of some sort. Spunky's actual presence is desirable, of course, but not critical.

It is no wonder, then, that the familiar Euro-American linkage of marriage with romantic love is, if not unknown at Warm Springs, patently insignificant. Everyone knows that marriages constitute alliances between families. Accordingly, "weddings" and related ceremonials do not function significantly as occasions for self-expression on the part of the bride and groom as individuals.

And all of this is in keeping with principles that are associated with the social organization of traditional times, which centered on the family as a kin-based corporate group. Kinship in Wasco (and Sahaptin) is reckoned bilaterally, with "Hawaiian"-style cousin terminology. The enduring units of social organization among Chinookans and their descendants at Warm Springs are bilateral descent-groupings that hold title, as corporations, to bodies of inherited wealth—sets of titles (personal names), along with other valuables and privileges (see Silverstein 1984 and Hymes 1966 for full details on this central aspect of Chinookan traditional culture; see Ackerman 1994, where the broader area context is sketched).

With respect to inherited names and valuables, at Warm Springs as elsewhere in the Northwest Coast, the oldest family members function as officiants on ritual occasions, and otherwise as custodians and caretakers (compare the "keeper" of an archive). The valuables remain corporate property. Names are "invested" in younger family members and can just as easily be divested from them, at the (dis)pleasure of an elder (see Silverstein 1984).

Hence the image arises of such a kin group as a set of structural slots, consigning the actual individuals to the realm of historical contingency: what's needed on a ceremonial occasion marking a change of status is the actual individual whose status is being changed—or, failing that, a reasonable facsimile, a hired stand-in who will act appropriately in the event. As Hymes points out, in traditional society the name itself had a title-like character, and a certain socio-cultural content (or set of connotations). . . . More importantly, a name was necessarily obtained by transmission along kinship lines. It was a social property, maintained in the group, and this continuity was explicitly stressed in the ceremony of conferral. In Wishram social theory, the set of names endured, and particular lives passed through them. [Hymes 1966:145]

Chinookan names, as Silverstein has observed, are "explicitly like what we call antiques." A name is an object, one that can be "displayed, brought out like an object of value from the trunk where it has been stored, and index the ordinal position of the bearer in an economy of total worth" (Silverstein 1984:1–2).

Though the term *family* is in wide use at Warm Springs for these groupings, one also hears other terms, including *outfit*—as in, "So-and-so's outfit." I have more recently heard the term *entourage* being used in this way.

As Lévi-Strauss (1982) suggests, the historical background is clear enough: demographic collapse due to disease epidemics and other causes at (or even prior to) European contact brought about a situation in which a large number of valuable titles and other inherited privileges fell into the hands of the relatively few who survived—hence the Kwakiutl situation, which led to marriages with ever "closer" kin (or even one's own arm or leg) in the struggle to maintain proprietary control over the wealth.

Such, in any case, was the fate of many such "societies of the House" up and down the Northwest Coast during the early historical period. Concurrent with demographic resurgence over the last several decades has come rapid obsolescence of linguistic and other forms of traditional cultural knowledge and practice and a general opening up of once relatively isolated reservation communities to the wider world (U.S. Highway 26 connecting Warm Springs to Portland and Bend, Oregon, opened in 1949; TV followed). Today, as the population at Warm Springs skews ever younger, the number of elders who know the names and know how to dispose of them (in a ceremonial sense) decreases every year. Mrs. M. is now one of a handful of remaining speakers of any Chinookan language.

It is perhaps noteworthy that "identity politics" of a familiar sort has managed to make any inroads at all in a community like Warm Springs, where descendants of three culturally and linguistically distinct groups (Wascos, Sahaptins, and Paiutes—the three Confederated Tribes) have intermarried for generations (in the case of Sahaptins and Wascos, probably centuries). In this regard, the family of Mrs. M., a woman of Wasco and

Sahaptin descent who married into a family of Paiute (and, more distantly, Hawaiian) descent, is typical.

The key, of course, is that "the concept of culture"—with differences of language (and, less significantly, material and ceremonial culture) as its most salient diacritics—has arrived in the local community as a working category of people's understanding, a development in which anthropology is obviously implicated, especially in a place like Warm Springs, where anthropologists have been a more or less constant presence (mostly welcomed) for more than fifty years.

A "space" has been opened up, one might say, between *the social* in the sense of kinship, marriage, residence, and descent, and *the cultural* in the sense of (differences of) language, material culture, and the dynamics of contact history, especially as these have been swept up into a politics of recognition (Silverstein 2003). And in this space there is room to maneuver, in answer to varying interests and desires. This space has been open for maneuvering for a long time at Warm Springs—but recent institutional and other developments have provided new points of reference, and new ways of inhabiting it (see now Carneiro da Cunha 2005, whose distinction between culture and "culture" is similar in spirit). To show how this works is the point of the next ethnographic example.

In 1993 the tribally owned Museum at Warm Springs opened in an architecturally striking building whose design and displays are organized in a strictly tripartite fashion that gives roughly equal exhibition space to the distinct cultural backgrounds and historical experiences of the reservation's three "tribes" (Wasco, Sahaptin, Paiute). The effects of the Native American Graves Protection and Repatriation Act (NAGPRA, Public Law 101–601, 25 U.S. Code §3001 et seq.) continue to be felt at Warm Springs, as in other Native communities across the United States.

Meanwhile, important cultural heritage activities—including classroom teaching of the three ancestral languages—can hardly help but build upon, and support, whatever sense people may have of the distinctness of these three "tribal" heritages. Since the 1990s the teaching of the three ancestral languages has been handed off to a new generation of heritage workers who teach the languages in elementary schools. Many of them are computer literate and fully "plugged in" to emerging regional, national, and global networks of language maintenance and indigenous rights, even as they remain in closer-than-ever contact with "the grandmas."

To recapitulate: Spunky's birthday party was not ideologically captioned as "Indian" at all, and yet it was conducted in a way that fits very well into what we know of an older social organization centered on the "House" (or family "Outfit"). This fact, of course, in no way consigns the event to some neatly definable realm of "tradition," perhaps as opposed to "modernity" in some metaphysical sense. By celebrating Spunky's birthday at all (with hot dogs, hamburgers, and cole slaw, note, alongside eels and salmon), we were of course performing one version of modernity.

In the next example we encounter another version of modernity. This time the life-cycle observance is ideologically captioned, both as "Indian" (and specifically "Wasco") and as "traditional." However, in this case the honoree is anything but in absentia, and in fact she conducts herself in a way that fits very well within what we know about identity politics in the wider society, a pattern associated with the professional or "white-collar" class of what used to be called Yuppies (Silverstein 1998, 2003).

In this milieu, "self-actualization" (Maslow 1968)—like "modernity" itself!—is an unfinishable project, and at life-cyclically appropriate junctures people (often those who have some experience of the "wider world," e.g., college) may seek to reconnect with their ethnic, cultural, religious, or other heritage. Experientially vivid encounters with "heritage" are highly prized, and self-expression as a positive value in itself licenses a whole range of discourse genres with themes of self-discovery and self-revelation.

Hummingbird

The second example comes from the field notes of Kathrine French and her late husband and colleague, David French (1918–95), which they graciously shared with me in the form of numerous conversations and finally a typed document, dated November 29, 1993, that bore the heading "Cynthia Johnson [pseudonym], 11/29/93. (Phone conversation with DHF)."[3]

It is important to know as context for this document that both Frenches, whose fieldwork engagement with Wasco and Sahaptin people at Warm Springs began in 1948 and continues (in the work of Kathrine French) to this day, have had many longstanding friendships with families and individuals at Warm Springs. Increasingly they are seen by many in the community as cultural experts and "keepers" of an archive of linguistic and cultural heritage—indeed, by the 1980s, as "elders" themselves. Residing in Portland, they have remained in close touch with the reservation and are often consulted—and often are "consultants"—about details of traditional culture and language. I had been an undergraduate anthropology student of David French's at Reed College in the late 1970s. By the time of the events to be described here I had become, thanks in large part to the Frenches' guidance and support, a colleague, someone with whom they frequently discussed ethnographic and other reservation-related matters.

The notes the Frenches shared with me describe an unexpected phone call from "Cynthia Johnson," a woman in her mid-thirties who was in the process of moving back to Warm Springs after several years living off the reservation (square brackets enclose my editorial additions and clarifications):

> [Cynthia] phoned in the afternoon to ask how one says hummingbird in Wasco. She had asked [names of various Wasco-speaking elders resident at Warm Springs], and perhaps others [. . .]. None of them knew the word; [Mrs. A]—and perhaps others—suggested that DF might know. She got our phone number from a man unknown to DF. On Thanksgiving Day, someone, perhaps [Mrs. X], held a naming ceremony for about 4 people. Cynthia wanted to take the name Hummingbird, but since no one knew the Wasco name for it, it was given to her in English. Cynthia had wanted the name because of two experiences she had had:

> (1) Her cat had caught a hummingbird. Cynthia offered the cat some cat food, and it let the hummingbird go and proceeded to eat the cat food. The bird lay there for a moment, then realized that it was free and flew away. (2) Cynthia dreamed about a hummingbird (presumably after the event involving the cat).

> [French and French ms.]

It was, David French told me, the second time in recent years that he'd been asked "how to do a new name." He noted that "This is a Plains or Southwest naming pattern—she had experiences with hummingbirds and that's the name she wanted." (For an exhaustive treatment of Native North American personal names and naming practices, see French and French 1996.)

Ms. Johnson's slightly unusual request to receive the name 'Hummingbird' could be accommodated by the elders planning the naming ceremony, it seems, but the lack of a Wasco rendition of the name posed a real problem. French's wording of the situation (according to my own notes on a phone conversation I had with him the next day) seems to reflect someone's sense—probably Ms. Johnson's—that the name-bestowal was not considered to be complete without it: "She was recently given the name 'Hummingbird,' in English, *pending retrieval of the Kiksht word*" was how he explained it to me.

As she made the rounds of surviving fluent speakers of Wasco on the reservation seeking the Kiksht word for 'hummingbird,' Cynthia Johnson had other adventures, as when she approached Mrs. Z., a relatively young (ca. 60) but strongly opinionated Kiksht speaker:

> When Cynthia asked [Mrs. Z] for the word for hummingbird, [Mrs. Z] responded, "That's *my* name." Cynthia asked her whether it was wrong for two people to have the same name. [Mrs. Z] responded that that was true but that she could be called "Big Hummingbird" and Cynthia could be called "Little Hummingbird." [French and French ms.]

I know Mrs. Z well, and never heard from her or anyone else that she had a Wasco name meaning 'hummingbird.' In any case, she offered a helpful compromise but, notice, still no Kiksht translation. The notes continue:

> DF did not recognize CJ's [Euro-American] name (nor did KF, later). DF asked CJ about her relatives, in order to place her in terms of his knowledge of Warm Springs. She said that she was a granddaughter of . . . [etc.]. She and DF did discuss various people that he had known. [French and French ms.]

After discussing Warm Springs people they knew (or knew of) in common, in the course of which various aspects of CS's biography and genealogical connections emerged, David French requested "time out" to consult his linguistic files. He turned first to a Wasco word list compiled in the 1970s by his fellow Chinookanist and former student Dell Hymes, which was divided into "vocabulary domains":

> The above conversation had two parts with a half hour between the parts. DF requested the interruption in order to search for a word for 'hummingbird.' He found nothing in the DF/KF 3 x 5 slips, but DH's Domain List included
>
> (1) łiap'útskn ['hummingbird'] [= $(i)ł_3$-ia_4-p'úckn][4]
>
> which DF transmitted to CJ [in the second half of the phone call]. Because DH's typist had included only ł of the ił- ['neuter-collective'] prefix, and because DF tried in a flawed manner to diminutivize 'hummingbird,' CS received an imperfect version of "little hummingbird." DF plans to talk with her again and to suggest
>
> (2) iłgap'útskn [probably intended for $ił_3$-ga_4-p'úckn 'her$_4$ hummingbird' (?)] [French and French ms.]

Somewhat oddly, all these attested terms for 'hummingbird' have the form of a possessed noun: item (1) above could be structurally glossed as 'it(Neut.)$_3$-his$_4$-p'úckn [?]' and item (2) as 'it(Neut.)$_3$-her$_4$-.' . . . I will return to this matter later in this chapter.

The difficulty David French had in "diminutivizing" the form from the Hymes Domain List in accordance with pervasive Kiksht processes of "sound symbolism" is understandable. Such processes involve shifting the place and manner of (especially consonant) articulation to index speaker attitudes of endearment or revulsion toward the referent (evaluating the referent speaker-centrically as "little" or "dear" versus "big" and "gross" using so-called diminutive and augmentative sound symbolisms, respectively). The 'hummingbird' form as given in all known attestations shows every sign of being "diminutivized" already: the glottalized *p* [p'] and the appearance of *-ts-* [c] instead of the "ch-" sound [č] are both signs that this form, as a lexeme for 'hummingbird,' is already "frozen" in a diminutivized phonetic shape (not at all uncommon in bird and animal terms; see Silverstein 1994 for an explication of this whole system of indexical "sound symbolism" in Kiksht).

That is to say, the ordinary term for 'hummingbird' already conveys, in the quality of its consonants, the notion of "littleness." This being the case, the new and divergent form would be the one that Mrs. Z. proposed for herself, the form for "Big Hummingbird."

French had phoned Hymes in Virginia and asked for his help, and in a few days a letter arrived dated November 30, 1993, in which Hymes reported that he had checked his files and found a 'hummingbird' form with [b] instead of glottalized [p'], "from the first time I recorded Wasco, summer 1951, from Hiram [Smith]."

(3) ɬabuckn ['hummingbird'][=ɬ-ia-buckn]

After working through some of the issues of "consonant symbolism" discussed here, Hymes closed his letter with a brilliant *bon mot* suggesting another possible trade-off with Mrs. Z., this one at the level of "the phoneme" itself:

> Anyway, [Cynthia Johnson] probably has a good form by now. Don't know if she would appreciate having the glottal[ized] stop and giving the b to [Mrs. Z]?
> [Hymes ms.]

Surprisingly enough, it turns out that if we augmentativize the term for 'hummingbird', altering it so that it now might mean "Big Hummingbird," what we get is a kin term, one that can be glossed roughly as 'sibling-in-law.' Consider the items in (4), which are taken from the list of "Wishram kin terms" in Spier and Sapir's *Wishram Ethnography*:

(4)(a) a$_3$-ia$_4$-púčxan 'she$_3$-his$_4$-sister.in.law'

(b) i₃-ča₄-púčxan 'he₃-her₄-brother.in.law'
   [Spier and Sapir 1930:264]

This also explains the other oddity of the attested forms for 'humming-bird,' namely, that they are all possessed nouns. This is typical, if not obligatory, for kin terms in this language (and for many others). But it is very odd for zoological terms. Whether one takes the form from the Hymes Domain List or the forms from Hiram Smith (of which Hymes and I obtained from Mr. Smith minutely different examples 33 years apart), one has a form glossed as 'hummingbird' that appears to be nothing more than 'someone-his-sibling.in.law' with diminutive "sound symbolism." Compare the items in (5) and (6), which comprise a "minimal pair":

(5) iłiapúčxan [ił₃-ia₄-pučxan] 'someone₃-his₄-brother/sister in law'
   (cf. Spier and Sapir 1930)
(6) (i)łiap'úckan [(i)ł₃-ia₄-p'uckan] 'hummingbird'
   (Hiram Smith 07/51, to DH)[5]

In a society that practiced the levirate, an institution already clearly reflected in its kinship terminology, as Sapir (1916) long ago showed, "sibling-in-law" is a salient social category in a number of ways. With respect to this category the kin term would be a kind of emblem, especially for those who remember the social usages and customs of former times. There is no doubt that 'wives' sisters' count as 'potential spouses' from a man's point of view. It is interesting, then, to recall that Mrs. Z.—who perhaps disingenuously claimed, when approached by Cynthia Johnson, that 'hummingbird' was her name, and who suggested the compromise of "big hummingbird" and "little hummingbird"—was perhaps the last woman of the Wasco group to uphold this custom.

This much, at any rate, can be gleaned from the ethnographic and linguistic archive of Kiksht, supplemented by knowledge gained on the fly and in situ. But before we can begin to put all this into the context of Cynthia Johnson's larger project, we should ask about how that project was received on the Reservation.

Name and Identity under Erasure

To understand Cynthia Johnson's intervention into the naming system—including the pointed nonresponses of reservation elders to her queries—it is useful to ask about how her queries, and the "project" behind them, might have been interpreted. This opens up themes that connect Wasco naming practices with practices involving guardian spirits, subjects I can only sketch here (for full discussion of both, see Hymes 1966).

For the societies in which Wascos, Wishrams, and (in this respect culturally quite similar) Sahaptins lived and to some extent continue to live, the system of spirit-powers operates as a total theory of personality, embracing the whole range of diagnostic, interpretive, and "clinical" phenomena that are addressed by our own discourses of psychiatric and psychodynamic theory. The system of spirit-power beliefs and practices allows people—and to a fuller and more consequential degree shamans—to isolate and explain pathological processes, to define a behavioral horizon that constitutes the functioning of a "normal" personality, and to give a coherent (if conventionally "veiled" in practice) account of the relationship between individuals' outward behavior and their inner states, motivations, and the like.

Just as one might acquire several names over the course of a lifetime—including one given at a ceremony of bestowal during adolescence and others acquired more informally—so also one might acquire several guardian spirits over a lifetime, perhaps the first during a carefully planned "guardian-spirit quest" during youth.

But according to traditional Wasco and Sahaptin thinking about such matters, there are, in addition to the formalized "vision quest," other less formalized ways of initiating a relationship with a guardian spirit. This is especially relevant to adults, who may or may not have been successful in acquiring such a tutelary by more formal means in childhood. The fact is that any unusual encounter with an animal—especially when least expected and quite outside the context of any purposeful "questing"— can represent an attempt by the spirit to "reach out" and make contact with a potential human protégé.

Whether or not a full-blown relationship is initiated here between the spirit-power and the one who is "visited" in this manner depends entirely upon how the person responds to such an overture. The person may recognize it for the communicative act that it is and yet refuse "uptake," in which case the spirit withdraws, perhaps discouraged, perhaps "bothering" (in local English) the one who jilted him or her for a few days afterward. Alternatively, the person may not understand or notice, in which case he or she was, of course, not meant to respond. The obvious implication is that such things are more likely to happen to people who already have one or more guardian spirits, and/or that such people are more likely to interpret such happenings as possibly leading to something more.

It has been a very long time since any young person on the reservation has been 'sharpened' (to translate the Kiksht idiom into English) and sent out on a formal spirit quest—but odd encounters with animals still happen all the time.

In characterizing these happenstance encounters with spirit-powers at inauspicious or random times in daily life, people speak (in local English) in terms of "adoption": the spirit, in contacting the person, is seeking to be "adopted" by, or to "adopt," the human being (the English usage is apparently reciprocal).

The practice of sending adolescents (of both sexes) out on "power quests" may be long obsolete, but certain rules remain. The person who acquires a guardian spirit by whatever means is absolutely forbidden to disclose the identity of the spirit—that is, to identify it by name. Disclosure of this sort immediately ends the relationship. The fact of such a relationship, and the identity of the spirit involved, must be left for others to deduce. The commonest explanation for the prohibition on uttering the name is that the spirit will hear you, and it does not like to hear the sound of its own name being "called." Instead, one performs the "identity," which is to say, the relationship, in winter ceremonials where participants take turns performing the songs and dances they learned from their tutelary spirits (Hymes 1966). Such "Winter Power-Singing" continues at both Warm Springs and Yakama.

The point is that this interpretive framework is available to most everybody at Warm Springs (notwithstanding the discontinuation of formal spirit quests) and is almost perfectly suited to interpreting the significance of Cynthia Johnson's reports of her encounters with hummingbirds.

In any case, her decision to take "Hummingbird" as her Wasco name introduces complications. It would seem that Cynthia Johnson understood her naming ceremony as an opportunity for her publicly to acknowledge her hummingbird experiences, as if those experiences legitimated her claim to the name (which she herself suggested in the first place). But the relationship of all this to local standards is extremely problematic, in part because of the prohibitions on identifying one's guardian spirit by name (Hymes 1966; cf. Spier and Sapir 1930).[6]

It is interesting to note that "adoption" is what a hummingbird spirit-power may have been suggesting to Cynthia Johnson (whether she realized it or not), and "adoption" into the reservation community at Warm Springs—and specifically into the Wasco group—is exactly what she was right then trying to orchestrate for herself and for her young child. The naming ceremony held on Thanksgiving Day 1993 was an important step in this process.

But the particular form taken by Cynthia Johnson's project creates a perfect contradiction. Disclosure of the name of one's guardian spirit is absolutely forbidden, but public disclosure of a personal name and its "provenance" is the very raison d'etre of the naming ceremony (in local parlance, one "brings out" the name at the ceremony; reciting the provenance can take hours).

Mrs. X and the other elders who organized the naming ceremony (where four other local people also received names) solved the problem in a way that simultaneously accommodated both Cynthia Johnson's somewhat unusual wishes and the traditional prohibition on narrating and naming one's experiences with (actual or potential) sources of power (Hymes 1966). The solution is ingenious: Cynthia Johnson received her Wasco name "under erasure" as the deconstructionists say: "in English, pending retrieval of the Kiksht word."

There is an unmistakable irony in the involvement of anthropologists. By supplying Cynthia Johnson with a (less than perfect) Kiksht rendition of 'hummingbird' they may in effect have circumvented the wishes of the elders whose knowledge and memories of traditional culture they had so meticulously documented over many years.

In fact, several projects and several mediations are involved in this complicated story, and each one is associated with, and definitional of, the distinct social positioning of the various actors. We see this when we begin to use Cynthia Johnson's activities around her naming ceremony as a lens through which to view the local community's connections to broader social and institutional formations. Cynthia Johnson's quest to find the Wasco word for 'hummingbird' leads her from her own experiences of dreams and the uncanny first to Wasco elders who seem to have withheld the Kiksht translation of the name, and then to anthropologists whose files and documents do not offer "closure" but instead reconstrue 'hummingbird' as an open-ended linguistic problem—and who are involved with memories of their own ("from the first time I recorded Wasco, summer 1951, from Hiram [Smith]" [Hymes])—into now-unrecoverable mythological references and wordplay lurking in the kinship terminology.

It should come as no surprise that Indian reservations in the United States provide rich opportunities to study what Marshall Sahlins has called "one of the more remarkable phenomena of world history in the later twentieth century," namely, "the cultural self-consciousness developing among imperialism's erstwhile victims" (Sahlins 1993:3). Noting that "reified notions of cultural differences, as indexed by distinctive customs and traditions, can and have existed apart from any European presence," Sahlins argues that "what distinguishes the current 'culturalism' . . . is the claim to one's own mode of existence as a superior value and a political right, precisely in opposition to a foreign-imperial presence" (1993:4).

Note the prominence here of self-consciousness, a consciousness that sees "culture" as something that individuals can possess (or be dispossessed of), that sees culture as precipitated in concrete material things and practices (e.g., participation in ceremonialism, speaking the ancestral language), all of which can then be swept up into the contemporary "culturalist" inflection of what Wallace and Fogelson (1965) presciently called "the identity struggle."

This is what seems to make these recent developments different in kind from anything that had come before. This is also what instantly invalidates these contemporary manifestations of "culturalism" from some points of view. Sahlins, in fact, positions his own piece as "offer[ing] some theoretical justification for a return to certain world areas such as North America and Polynesia, areas which have been too long slighted by ethnographers, ever since it was discovered in the 1930s and 1940s that they were 'acculturated.'" (1993:1–2; cf. D. French 1961).

We could, then, define the "culture" that Cynthia Johnson is after as being "not historically authentic because it is a reified and interested value, a self-conscious ideology rather than a way of life" (Sahlins 1993:4; cf. Povinelli 2002). Cynthia Johnson, recall, put this whole process into motion when, recently divorced from the father of her young child, she decided to move from Portland, Oregon, back to Warm Springs, where she was born and spent most of her childhood. Her genealogical connections to the community—and thereby to a plausibly "Wasco" cultural heritage—were clear to everyone. She had spent virtually all her adult life off the reservation, had attended college, worked, and married and divorced a non-Indian, but now she wanted to return to Warm Springs, to reconnect with her heritage and begin the process of enrolling her young son as a tribal member—a "reified and [self-]interested value" perhaps, but one that she made no secret of, and that no one, so far as I know, questioned as such. Acquiring a Wasco name was an important first step in this process, and people were willing to accommodate her, even to the point of allowing her to select her own Indian name on the basis of personal experiences she had had. This, perhaps, was a small sticking point, but she did receive the name, "in English, pending retrieval" of the Wasco form. For purposes of "retrieving" the Wasco version of her name she consulted anthropologists in Portland, the Frenches—just as the elders had instructed her to do.

And so we can see how she maneuvered in the space between the social and the cultural, as anthropologists have sometimes been accustomed to differentiate them: Her stated purpose was to move back to the reservation (residence), to reenter the community as a single mother with a young child (domestic cycle), to re-embed herself in a network of kin. Her method, in part—for I have described only one facet of her larger project, neglecting all the administrative and bureaucratic details—was cultural: to identify herself as a "Wasco," partly by participating in a distinctively "Wasco" naming ceremony.

Needless to say I am not suggesting that anthropologists should essentialize any such distinction between "social" and "cultural" phenomena; indeed, my usage of "cultural" here merely adapts that of many people at Warm Springs, who use the term to denote precisely those things (language, material culture, ceremonialism, and activities involving them) that differentiate the three "tribal" traditions.

Moreover, Cynthia Johnson's situation may be less unusual than I have made it sound. "One feature of the non-unilinear descent group in the Plateau," notes Ackerman in a perceptive article based on fieldwork on and around the Colville Reservation in Washington State, "is its permeability" (Ackerman 1994: 294). Ackerman's account is worth quoting at length (the named groups here are all Interior Salishan):

> My consultant's son, though having grown [up] among the Moses-Columbia people, felt closer to his Chelan relatives and got along particularly well with his mother's sister. In pre-reservation times, he might have moved to Chelan territory when grown and become a member of the descent group there. Since residence is no longer so diagnostic of descent-group membership today, a person simply changes his or her emotional allegiance to another group and takes on new responsibilities. Nevertheless, this example shows that it is still possible in contemporary times for full siblings not only to become members of different descent groups or bands within the same tribe, but also to become members of different tribes. Thus, the personal identity of the Plateau individual is not set at birth: his or her ethnicity and residence can both change, and, as we will see, the person's name itself changes. A similar case of change of tribal affiliation today is that of a young woman who changed her tribal identity to that of her mother's close friend. The friend taught the young woman many of the customs and rituals of her descent group and finally gave her a new Indian name associated with the new descent group. Now the young woman considers herself and is considered as belonging to the same descent group as the friend, which is in a tribe or ethnic group different from the one she was born into. . . . Since both tribes live on the Colville Reservation today, she does not need to move physically, but she does participate in the ceremonies of her chosen descent group affiliation. Incidentally, her mother and siblings

are perfectly comfortable with her new affiliation. [Ackerman 1994: 294–295]

Ackerman's terminology and use of analytic categories is different in several respects from that of this chapter (she is concerned, e.g., with elucidating the social structure of "the Plateau culture area," whose existence she presupposes along with categories like 'band' and 'tribe')—but the resonances are striking nonetheless. In her conclusion, Ackerman notes that the presence of what she calls non-unilinear descent groups in the Plateau "is so subtle that it has been detected more by *process* than by *structure* in this research" (Ackerman 1994:305; emphasis added).

Conclusion

What could be more "Indian" than receiving an Indian name? What could be more "American" than being born on the Fourth of July and celebrating your birthday as part of a family reunion held over the long holiday weekend?

I am not able to bring closure to the philological puzzle of 'hummingbird.' The value of these two examples—Cynthia Johnson's naming ceremony and Spunky's birthday party—is that together they enable us to ask an interesting set of questions relevant both to anthropological "theory" and to the future development of American Indian studies.

First, both examples contain subtleties that "can be detected more by process than by structure," to borrow Ackerman's phrase (1994:305). More to the point, both examples show how matters of "structure" manifest themselves in and through "process," because they are in fact immanent in it—but how? Rituals, if they are anything, are "structured processes." The two examples discussed here are both "life-cycle" ceremonials, ritual events in and through which individuals mark, acknowledge, and achieve changes in their, and others' statuses and identities.

Second, this material also points to subtleties in the relationship between *individuals* as historically contingent beings with birth (and death) dates, and *persons* as socially constructed actors whose passages through definable life stages can be marked and observed whether they are physically present at the observance or not—or who can, in fact, receive an Indian name whether the name itself is available or not.

Finally, this same ethnographic material can also be used to raise questions about the changing status of American Indian studies in anthropology. Both examples look at first like marginal cases, perhaps even "non-events" (Fogelson 1989)—and indeed both would probably have been dismissed by earlier generations of anthropologists as inauthentic, if they were noticed at all. To be sure, many of the elements of both stories involve cultural forms and institutions—hot dogs, birthdays, anthropology—that originated outside the local traditions we associate with the distinct but overlapping "cultures" of the three Confederated Tribes. So why do they fall within our purview as students of "Native American" cultural traditions? The answer, of course, is that they do fall within our purview precisely to the extent that we, as ethnographers and as historians, hold ourselves responsible to *the present* in these communities.

We can, out of careful studies of events and projects like the two described here, develop an enlarged sense of anthropology's value, once we understand these as sites where exceedingly complicated mediations are playing themselves out. The second example especially makes clear the need to understand "the ethnographic encounter" as a cultural episode in its own right: recall that it was the Wasco elders themselves who, faced with Cynthia Johnson's queries about the word for 'hummingbird,' told her to ask the anthropologists.

If the project really is "to bring every cultural pattern back to the living context from which it has been abstracted in the first place, and, in parallel fashion, to bring every fact of personality formation back to its social matrix" (Sapir 1949[1934]:410), then it seems to me that American Indian studies is poised right now to reclaim the central place it once enjoyed in the discipline of anthropology—not in spite of the fact that new projects like Cynthia Johnson's are underway on reservations across the United States but because they are underway.

Acknowledgments

Fieldwork at Warm Springs Reservation and elsewhere in the region, 1983 to the present, has been supported at various times by research grants from the Melville and Elizabeth Jacobs Research Funds (Whatcom Museum Foundation), the Phillips Fund of the Library of the American Philosophical Society, and the Center for Psychosocial Studies (now the Center for Transcultural Studies) in Chicago.

The ethnographic material in this chapter has been presented in a number of settings over a number of years: first at the annual meetings of the American Anthropological Association in San Francisco in November 1996, in an invited session organized by Sergei Kan and Pauline Turner Strong, entitled "Selves, Power, and History in Native North America: Contemporary Papers in the Americanist Tradition in Honor of Raymond D. Fogelson." For comments and questions in San Francisco, I am grateful to Margaret Bender, David W. Dinwoodie, Sergei Kan, Suzanne Oakdale, and Pauline Turner Strong.

Some of the material formed the basis for a very different presentation to the Anthropology Colloquium Series at New York University on October 15, 1998. I am grateful to the audience on that occasion—notably Faye Ginsburg, Fred R. Myers, and Anupama Rao—for helpful questions and comments. I am further indebted to a number of NYU colleagues for valuable comments, questions, and criticisms: T. O. Beidelman provided a sweeping and exhaustive written critique of that manuscript, and the written comments of Karen I. Blu, Steven Feld, and Susan Carol Rogers led to the sharpening of many points.

A further development of the NYU manuscript was presented at Indiana University–Bloomington on February 5, 1999, in a lecture sponsored jointly by the Departments of Anthropology, Linguistics, and Folklore and the Horizons of Knowledge Program. I am grateful to my hosts, Ray DeMallie and Douglas R. Parks, for the opportunity (and for their gracious hospitality) and likewise to Della Cook, Paul D. Kroeber, Philip LeSourd, and others for their questions and comments.

As always I am grateful to Kathrine S. French, who graciously shared her field notes with me. Finally, conversations with Ray Fogelson, Michael Silverstein, Courtney Handman, James Slotta, Jessica Cattelino, Manuela Carneiro da Cunfia, and others at the University of Chicago since 2002 have been a great help as the current manuscript was being prepared. With so much good advice, I have no one but myself to blame for the infelicities that remain.

Notes

1. One obvious example is Brown and Brightman (1988). A complete list would include the work of most of the contributors to this volume, including that of the editors, and many others.

2. The language is known natively as Kiksht, in the linguistic and anthropological literature as the Wasco-Wishram dialect cluster of Upper Chinookan. A few of the standard sources on the language, the people, and/or the cultural tradition are Sapir 1909 (texts), Spier and Sapir 1930 ("memory ethnography"), D. French 1961 (acculturation study), Hymes 1966 (a reconstructed "ethnography of speaking" in the precontact period), Silverstein 1985 (language) and 1996 (textual analysis). The reservation community at Warm Springs is treated in K. S. French 1955 and 1960 and in French and French 1955; aspects of my own work are presented in Moore 1988 (language obsolescence) and 1993 (myth narration).

3. In the D. and K. French field notes (and generally in their own archives), persons are identified by initials. In the present case, DF or DHF refers to David French; KSF to Kathrine

French; CJ to "Cynthia Johnson" (a pseudonym); DH or DHH to Dell Hymes; and RM to Robert Moore.

4. Here and below, cross-referencing "pronominal" prefixes are labeled with subscript numbers in keeping with practices established in Chinookan linguistic studies since the 1970s (see, e.g., Silverstein 1985 for fuller explanation). In possessed nouns like those discussed here, the second pronominal, in order-class 4, gives the number and gender of the possessor; and the first element, in order-class 3, gives the number and gender of the thing possessed (denoted also by the noun "stem" that follows the set of prefixed "pronominal" elements; order-class positions 1 and 2 are reserved for verb forms).

5. Re-elicited from Mr. Smith by author on September 6, 1984.

6. Verbal disclosure of the identity of one's own spirit-power(s) is permitted only on one's deathbed, and such disclosures constitute the Wasco stereotype of what "last words" are all about. See Hymes 1966 for fuller discussion of all these matters on the basis of a reconstituted view of "precontact" Wasco-Wishram culture. See Sapir 1909:220–222 for an actual (reported) example—last words, describing a guardian spirit encounter, spoken by a Wasco infantryman mortally wounded while fighting on the side of the U.S. government against recalcitrant Paiutes in southeastern Oregon in 1866–67.

References

Ackerman, Lillian A.
    1994 Non-unilinear Descent Groups in the Plateau Culture Area. American Ethnologist 21(2):286–309.
Biolsi, Thomas
    2005 Imagined Geographies: Sovereignty, Indigenous Space, and American Indian Struggle. American Ethnologist 32(2):239–259.
Brown, Jennifer S. H., and Robert Brightman
    1988 "The Orders of the Dreamed": George Nelson on Cree and Northern Ojibwa Religion and Myth, 1823. St. Paul: Minnesota Historical Society Press.
Buckley, Thomas
    2002 Standing Ground. Yurok Indian Spirituality 1850–1990. Berkeley: University of California Press.
Carneiro da Cunha, Manuela
    2005 "Culture" and Culture: Traditional Knowledge and Intellectual Rights. Marc Bloch Lecture, Ecole des Hautes Etudes, delivered at the Sorbonne June 10, 2004. Ms.
Cattelino, Jessica R.
    2005 Florida Seminole Casinos and Sovereign Interdependency. Paper presented at Workshop on Comparative Colonialisms, University of Chicago. Ms.
Clifford, James
    1986. Identity in Mashpee. In J. Clifford, The Predicament of Culture: Twentieth-century Ethnography, Literature, and Art. Pp. 277–346. Cambridge MA: Harvard University Press.
Darnell, Regna
    1990 Edward Sapir: Linguist, Anthropologist, Humanist. Berkeley: University of California Press.
Darnell, Regna, and Lisa Valentine (eds.)
    1999 Theorizing the Americanist Tradition. Toronto: University of Toronto Press.

Fogelson, Raymond D.

1984 Who Were the Ani-Kutani? Ethnohistory 31:255–263.

1989 The Ethnohistory of Events and Nonevents. Ethnohistory 36(2):133–147.

French, David

1961 Wasco-Wishram. *In* Perspectives in American Indian Culture Change. E. Spicer, ed. Pp. 337–430. Chicago: University of Chicago Press.

French, David H., and Kathrine S. French

1996 Personal Names. *In* Vol. 17: Languages. Ives Goddard, ed. Pp. 200–221. Handbook of North American Indians. William C. Sturtevant, gen. ed. Washington DC: Smithsonian Institution.

French, Kathrine S.

1955 Culture Segments and Variation in Contemporary Social Ceremonialism on the Warm Springs Reservation, Oregon. PhD dissertation, Department of Anthropology, Columbia University.

1960 Ceremonial Segmentation. Actes du VIᵉ Congrès International des Sciences Anthropologiques et Ethnologiques. 2 vols. Vol. 1:101–104.

French, Kathrine S., and David French

1955 The Warm Springs Indian community. The American Indian 7(2):3–17.

1993 "Cynthia Johnson [a pseudonym], 11/29/93. (Phone conversation with DHF)." Unpublished manuscript in possession of K. S. French.

Hymes, Dell

1966 Two Types of Linguistic Relativity (with Examples from Amerindian Ethnography). *In* Sociolinguistics. W. Bright, ed. Pp. 114–167. The Hague: Mouton.

Lévi-Strauss, Claude

1982 The Social Organization of the Kwakiutl. *In* C. Lévi-Strauss, The Way of the Masks. Pp. 163–187. Seattle: University of Washington Press.

Maslow, Abraham H.

1968 Toward a Psychology of Being. Princeton NJ: Van Nostrand.

Mauss, M.

1985 [1938] A Category of the Human Mind: The Notion of Person; the Notion of Self. *In* The Category of the Person. M. Carrithers, S. Collins, and S. Lukes, eds. Pp. 1–25. Cambridge: Cambridge University Press.

Mead, Margaret

1932 The Changing Culture of an Indian Tribe. New York: Columbia University Press.

Moore, Robert E.

1993. Unpublished notes on telephone conversation by author with D. French, November 30, 1993.

Povinelli, Elizabeth

2002 The Cunning of Recognition. Durham NC: Duke University Press.

Sahlins, Marshall

1993 Goodbye to Tristes Tropes: Ethnography in the Context of Modern World History. Journal of Modern History 65(1):1–25.

Sapir, Edward

1909 Wishram Texts. Publications of the American Ethnological Society, vol. 2. Leyden: late E. J. Brill.

1916 Terms of Relationship and the Levirate. American Anthropologist (n.s.) 18: 327–337.

1949[1934] The Emergence of the Concept of Personality in a Study of Cultures. *In*

Selected Writings of Edward Sapir in Language, Culture, and Personality. D. Mandelbaum, ed. Pp. 590–597. Berkeley: University of California Press.

Silverstein, Michael

1984 The 'Value' of Objectual Language. Ms.

1985a Wasco-Wishram Lexical-Derivational Processes vs. Word-Internal Syntax. *In* Lexical Semantics. D. Testen, Veenz Mishra, and Joseph Drogo, eds. Pp. 270–288. Chicago:
Chicago Linguistic Society.

1994 Denotational Iconism vs. Relative Motivation in Wasco-Wishram "Sound Symbolism." *In* Sound Symbolism. John J. Ohala and Johanna Nichols, eds. Pp. 40–60.
Cambridge: Cambridge University Press.

1996 The Secret Life of Texts. *In* Natural Histories of Discourse. M. Silverstein and G.
Urban, eds. Pp. 81–105. Chicago: University of Chicago Press.

1998 Contemporary Transformations of Local Linguistic Communities. Annual Review
of Anthropology 27:401–426.

2003 The Whens and Wheres—as Well as Hows—of Ethnolinguistic Recognition. Public
Culture 15(3): 531–557.

Spier, Leslie, and Edward Sapir

1930 Wishram Ethnography. University of Washington Publications in Anthropology
3(3):151–300.

Wallace, A. F. C., and Raymond D. Fogelson

1965 The Identity Struggle. *In* Intensive Family Therapy: Theoretical and Practical Aspects. Ivan Boszormenyi-Nagy and James L. Framo, eds. Pp. 365–406. New York:
Hoeber Medical Division, Harper & Row, Publishers.

Wissler, Clark

1938 Indian Cavalcade; or, Life on the Old-Time Indian Reservations. New York: Sheridan House.

Part Three

Histories

On Varieties of Temporal Experience
and Historical Representation

9. Native Authorship in Northwestern California

THOMAS BUCKLEY

In 1976 I returned to northwestern California, where I had already spent some time with Native people, to undertake my first formal field work as a graduate student of anthropology. Since I was now there as a professional in training I thought it best to announce myself formally. The Yurok Indians, who were my first interest, had no tribal council in the 1970s (they were not fully, federally acknowledged as an Indian tribe until 1993, despite having been a federally recognized tribe since 1851). I went instead to the Tri-county Development Agency in McKinleyville, a government-funded Indian service organization, where I spoke with Christopher Peters (Yurok), who was then on the agency's staff. I told him about my plans to do anthropological research in the area.

"I won't try to stop you," he said, "but I won't help you, either. You're on your own. Maybe you'll find people who'll talk with you. We'll see." Peters paused, then continued: "We want to do our own anthropology now. We may not do it as well as white people from the universities, but we'll do it as well as we can."

Chris Peters's position—neither friendly nor unfriendly that day—reflected locally a growing sentiment and an incipient movement in Native North America. Vine Deloria Jr. had long since condemned "anthros" as necromancers and parasites, asking that they do something for living American Indians or get off the reservations (1969). Delmos Jones, an African American, had called for a new, "native anthropology"—anthropological research to be carried out by marginalized peoples within their own societies (1970).[1] Although Jones acknowledged that such practice contradicted then common assumptions about the inability of insiders to achieve social scientific objectivity, he argued that there were important new perspectives to be offered by "native anthropologists" and that anthropological objectivity was not all it was cracked up to be anyway. My own anthropological mentor, Raymond D. Fogelson, had noted, by 1976, the increasing numbers of published Native American–authored accounts of their authors' own culture histories that questioned the right of non-Indian historians and ethnographers to "possess" the native past (Fogelson 1974).

Fogelson is well known for his "exasperated" formulations of "ethno-ethnohistory" and of "ethno-ethno-ethnohistory" (1974, 1989:134). The writing in his cumulative historiography, beginning in about 1966 (Fogelson 1971), gives us a glimpse of Fogelson's characteristic whimsy, humane warmth, and astonishing erudition (from kitchen packaging here to particle physics there), which he has delighted, instructed, and inspired his many colleagues, students and friends with for years. Yet his formulations were and remain serious contributions, for all the tongue-in-cheek quality with which he has couched these concepts. And while these parodic formulations themselves are now familiar to many Americanists, it is worthwhile to outline the historiographic concepts that gave rise to them.

Fogelson's intention has been to formulate an alternative to a Eurocentric historiography that remains oblivious to native points of view as it pursues its own ends, even under the guise of "ethnohistory" that, in its most common version, is little distinguished ideologically from the received "history" it seeks to augment (1989). To fulfill its promise, Fogelson argues, ethnohistory needs to attend to native historical consciousness and native theories of history, as "embedded in cosmology, in narratives, in rituals and ceremonies, and more generally in native philosophies and world views" as well as in less obvious matrices like kinship systems and architecture (1989:134–135). Such "ethno-ethnohistorical" sources both complement and improve Western historical understanding, he argues, by contributing to new and long-promised sorts of accounts, and they also inform historical and anthropological theory—all points that he demonstrates brilliantly in an article on a seemingly mythic Cherokee elite, the *aní kutáni* (Fogelson 1984).[2]

Ten years earlier, in a review of Cherokee author Traveller Bird's mythic biography of Sequoyah (Fogelson 1974), Fogelson had also focused on recent Native American reworkings of received, more traditional native histories, terming such works "ethno-ethno-ethnohistories." Although Traveller Bird's remythologization of Sequoyah's already mythically constructed life was factually erroneous by the standards of academic historiography, Fogelson took it seriously. He asked, what was the historical and cultural significance of Traveller Bird's contemporary reenvisioning of older Cherokee mythologized biography?

Fogelson's approach, and his respect—at once critical and hermeneutical—for native authorship stimulated my cohort of his students, those who worked with him at the University of Chicago during the 1970s. In part because of the skeptical neutrality of Native people like Chris Peters toward my presence among them, I began paying closer attention to published American Indian accounts of their own cultures and histories in the lower Klamath River drainage of northwestern California.

I had, of course, my own degree of skepticism. Academic research disciplines are, after all is said and done (as indeed it was in the "culture wars" of the 1980s and 1990s), of perhaps indeterminate but, withal, certain value. The shared rules of argument and evidence, traditions of erudition and critical histories of theoretical development, the quests (however unconsummated) for objectivity—the entire, satisfying choreography of the professional scholar's dance—all indeed serve an endless interpretive spiral toward, if not truth, at least validity. This is my conviction: that academic scholarship has rendered the world a better understood (if not a better) place. Yet we professional academics are initiated into and enjoy the privileges of an elite, and like most elites are far from immune to hubris.

Rules of argument and use of evidence, dedication to historical grounding in our own traditions, and the rest are by no means exclusive to us, nor are consensual tests for validity—any more than all metropolitan scholars are good scholars or an Indian's name on a book's cover assures that book's virtue. Still, protecting our elite privileges, we academics perhaps tend—unconsciously, implicitly, unwillingly, or however—to equate the texts that fall within the broad area covered by Jones's "native anthropology" and Fogelson's multiple-ethno histories with "folk" histories and their ethnographic equivalents. We do this out of respect for our own disciplines but also, I think, in order to both celebrate and preserve our rank as "trained" and "objective" historians and ethnographers. We tend on the one hand to be involuntarily (speaking charitably) patronizing toward nonacademic Native historians and on the other to be blind to the similarities of our often quite distinct enterprises.

It seems to me that however distinct the two bodies of work may be, Native-authored history and ethnography gets constructed in much the same way as metropolitan anthropology and ethnohistory. That is, it gets constructed through processes of negotiation that are shaped both by cumulative traditions and by the transient historical and political-economic contexts within which they emerge. In both cases, work is produced by authors and is evaluated by its most pertinent audiences in relation to collective but historically variable standards of appropriateness, which are grounded in a consensual historical and/or cultural consciousness that has its own historicity. What separates the two sorts of works most demonstrably is not, then, a profound difference in the processes that shape them but the historically emergent, culturally and class-relative styles, metaphors, and other tropes through which these processes manifest at the surfaces of texts—that, and the degree of power writers have to impose their particular representations on a broader, multicultural society.

In the following readings of five books by Native authors, published between 1916 and 1994, I explore this area of similarity rather than focus on genre dissimilarities or the differential power relations of American Indian and non-Indian authors.

My renowned anthropological predecessor in northwestern California, A. L. Kroeber, was not oblivious to a "native anthropology" already emergent there during the period in which he was most directly involved in studying Native California. In 1921 he reviewed, for the *American Anthropologist*, the first book published by a Yurok author, *To The American Indian* by Lucy Thompson (Kroeber 1921; Thompson 1991[1916]). And in 1942 Kroeber published a collection of Yurok mythic and historical narratives (clearly discriminating between the two) together with commentaries upon them by his "co-author," Robert Spott, a Yurok Indian (Spott and Kroeber 1942). (I discuss both works later in this chapter.) Kroeber, however, had been well aware of both a particular Yurok historical consciousness and of Yurok Indians' reflexive insights into their own cultural traditions long before either of these works saw publication.

Beginning his Yurok fieldwork in 1900, Kroeber had found, for example, that despite strictures against naming the dead, Yuroks born before massive contact, in 1850, were quite capable of tracing genealogies five and more generations deep, largely for purposes of contracting prestigious marriages (Waterman and Kroeber 1934).[3] He also collected deep historical data on dance regalia ownership, house site occupation, and the transmission of subsistence usufruct rights through the testimony of his Yurok consultants (e.g., Spott and Kroeber 1942).

Again, Yurok self-consciousness about their precontact culture (including the Yurok language) as a "system of signification," as A. I. Hallowell put it, is well documented in Kroeber's field notes from 1900–1907—if not in his published work—as well as in surviving Yurok language use. A Yurok doctor, elderly when Kroeber first met her in 1905, gave him a prayer that spoke of gathering angelica root incense "from the middle of the sky." "That's not where I get it," she went on—"that's just the way I talk so that all kinds of money will come into my house." Kroeber printed the "formula" in his 1925 *Handbook of California Indians* but not the doctor's commentary on it (Kroeber 1905, 1925:66). In the same vein, the late Ella Norris (Yurok-Tolowa) gave me, in 1978, a wonderful invocation of "God," a Yurok phrase, *woɬkeloh `ela ci`n wegenoy`o:mom* (literally, " 'morning always early' you-are-being-called"), a reflexive, metalinguistic putting-in-quotes that, she said, is "just what I call it—'Early Morning [sun]Rise.' " Other examples of such reflexivity abound (see Buckley 1984).

Kroeber was well aware at the beginning of the twentieth century, then, of Yurok historical consciousness and of Yurok self-consciousness of their culture as a culture. The "co-authored" 1942 monograph "Yurok Narratives" is nonetheless somewhat frustrating to read today because Kroeber virtually ignores Spott's (often very subtle and always very Yurok) commentaries on the traditional narratives that he performed. Kroeber overrides them and caps each chapter with his own, ethnological commentaries that, finally, spin Spott's meanings to Kroeber's very un-Yurok ends.

By the same token in his review of Thompson's 1916 book, *To the American Indian* (Kroeber 1921), Kroeber praised this early work of Yurok authorship for the many new "items" of ethnographic information to be found in it, items that might add to his own trait-based account of "the world renewal cult" (cf. Kroeber and Gifford 1949:88–89). What he did not so much care for, however, was Thompson's far too postcontact glossing of ethnographic and mythological materials in terms of Masonic imagery (courtesy of her husband, Milton "Jim" Thompson, a white timber cruiser) and of biblical imagery (courtesy of, I believe, the Presbyterian ministry [see Buckley 1998]). All of these were, for Kroeber, "extraneous" and "irrelevant" and Thompson's prose "prolix" (Kroeber 1921; Kroeber and Gifford 1949), of little use in reconstructing the "native primitive culture before it went all to pieces" (Kroeber 1948:427)—the primary objective of his salvage ethnography. Since then-contemporary Yurok culture was of virtually no professional interest to him—was not, in fact, "Yurok" in his eyes—Kroeber had little use for these "extraneous" materials (cf. Buckley 1996).

But Lucy Thompson, born in 1853, was in no way un-Yurok, as Yurok culture had come to be during her lifetime. Though no Yurok student graduated from a public high school until the 1920s, Thompson was literate, and her English prose—at its best richly evocative—was but one instance of a Yurok respect for English literacy that must have emerged soon after contact, in 1850. By the 1880s Yuroks in the town of Requa were filing legal suits against the white school board, seeking admission to elementary school for their children—expressly in pursuit of literacy.

Clearly, by 1900, it was a matter of expedience and cultural survival to become literate as the only way to defend the remaining Yurok lands against continuing white encroachment through the Dawes Act and other written instruments. There were other motives at play as well among these people whose aristocracy had always valued multilinguality and taken pride in Yurok's abilities to speak Karuk, Wiyot, Tolowa, Hupa, and the other very diverse languages of their principal neighbors. Upriver on the Klamath, for example, Karuk Indians were apparently delighted to have missionary-sponsored English teachers sent to them. In 1908, young and old reportedly jammed Mary Ellicott Arnold and Mabel Reed's classroom with lively enthusiasm as reading and writing English became a virtual fad around Happy Camp and Orleans, California (Arnold and Reed 1957). Arnold and Reed's account strikes a lively, adaptive counterpoint to accounts of linguistic abuse by federal boarding schools at the same time.

Though Lucy Thompson's literacy was neither anomalous nor, necessarily, a sign of destructive acculturation that heralded the loss of real Yurok culture, neither were her historical consciousness or her reflexivity, her awareness of her culture as a culture and her creative commentary upon it in any way un-Yurok, or even un-precontact Yurok. Although Kroeber rejected these commentaries—Thompson's Masonic-Christian "ethno-ethno-ethnohistory," to apply Fogelson's concepts—as irrelevant to his own anthropological work, these aspects of the 1916 book are decidedly interesting today. They tell us much about Yurok efforts at the beginning of the twentieth century both to understand what had happened to them in the half-century since "the end of the world"—the cataclysm of the California Gold Rush (during which they had suffered a 75 percent population decline)—and to gain the understanding of the people who had done this to them.

Lucy Thompson was no "native primitive" Yurok everywoman. She was trying hard to figure out how her Yurok culture might survive the cataclysm that had overtaken it, at one moment co-opting white language for purposes of resistance, like her Sioux contemporary Zitkala-Ša (1921), at another chiding despairing and dissolute Yurok survivors angrily, much as Zora Neale Hurston was to do somewhat later when writing of her own, African-American people (Hurston 1984[1942]:213–237). On the next page still, Thompson transforms the ancient Yuroks and their mythic culture heroes into "Wandering Tribes," "Our Christ," "The Samson of the Klamath Indians," prophets, and mermaids. The men's ceremonial sweat house at the village of Pecwan, where she was born, becomes a "Lodge," its occupants a secret, mystic brotherhood led by "High Priests" who share the "secret name of the Deity." Despite these apologetic transformations, or reenvisionings, Thompson's writing is always proud and at once lovingly nostalgic and angry as well as, I think, fearful of being misunderstood by a powerful and dangerous white audience.[4]

Thompson wrote her book partially in response to then-available published accounts of her people—most especially, I believe, the journalist Stephen Powers's *Tribes of California* (1976[1877])—and argued for the legitimacy of her own, Indian voice as a Yurok aristocrat and trained cultural expert:

> As there has been so much said and written about the American Indians, with my tribe, the Klamath Indians [Yuroks], included, by the white people, which is guessed at and not facts, I deem it necessary to first tell you who I am, for which please do not criticize me as egotistical. [Thompson 1991[1916]:xxix]

Yet Thompson is not antiwhite, and *To the American Indian* is not a racist polemic. The book is dedicated to "My beloved husband, with whom all of my married life has been so pleasantly spent" (xxx). Indeed, Thompson had many other white friends besides her husband, such as the photographer Emma B. Freeman, an early, romantic bohemian sojourner in northwest California (Palmquist 1977). Such friends most likely alerted Thompson to the growing concern for Indian welfare spreading among liberal white thinkers of the era, with the—already apparent—failure of the federal allotment policy. People like Ruth Kellett Roberts, present on the lower Klamath at the time when Thompson was writing her book, were to be influential in the formation of the Indian Welfare committee of the California Women's Federation, one of the many precursors of John Collier's Indian Defense Association (Graves 1929:101). It was the same social and political climate that nurtured Zitkala-Ša and supported her early publications in the *Atlantic Monthly* beginning in 1900.

However supportive this plural social context was, it incorporated only a minority of white northern Californians, most of whom—in 1916— were still rabidly anti-Indian (e.g., Heizer and Almquist 1971). Thompson was all too aware that the fate of the neighboring Wiyot Indians, "almost exterminated by the white man" in 1867 (Thompson 1991[1916]:217), could as easily have been the Yuroks'. Yet her handling of the era of greatest conflict and Yurok population decline (1860–70) is restrained. Her Yurok people, here, are not hapless victims, like the Wiyots, but killers of whites (and each other) as well, agents in a world unbalanced—for Indians and whites alike—by greed, the desire for revenge, and whiskey. Her most sustained treatment of the perilous world that she and her devoted white husband lived in, through mortal violence, pandemic disease, unspeakable abuse, and humiliation is, finally, an argument for temperance rather than an indictment of the whites (1–24). Only briefly and toward the end of her book does Lucy Thompson's grief and bitterness flash through: "Sometimes it seems hard to think of man's inhumanity, but sure as the sun goes down, the white man will suffer for his wicked treatment of the . . . Indians" (220).

Harry Roberts, Robert Spott's protégé, told me more than once, in the eleven years I spent with him, to always "rehearse the good—let the bad go." In his view, which I came to believe manifested ancient tenets of "high" Yurok culture, "light is the normal course of events; darkness is only a temporary interruption." The essential nature of "creation" is "beauty," and it is ungrateful—even rude—to talk about dirty things, to cause pain with words. The dead should be mentioned only with the greatest discretion, and the world should be made beautiful with talk, not sullied by voiced recollection.

It is my feeling that this was Lucy Thompson's (aristocratic) sensibility as well. Remembering the great world-renewal dances of her girlhood she writes that the singing "is most perfect in time and tune and makes one feel the love of the great Creator of all things." People called each other "sister" and "brother," and Thompson lovingly remembered the

> flints, white deer skins, fisher skins, otter skins, silver grey fox skins and fine dresses made of dressed deerskins, with fringes of shells knotted and worked in the most beautiful styles, that clink and jingle as they walk and make one have a feeling of respect and admiration for them. The eyes will strain to look on this most pleasant sight, which can never leave one's memory that has seen it in its flowery days.

The dances, she concludes, make people "feel that there is some good to live for" (Thompson 1991[1916]:112–119).

Thompson takes refuge from her present in richly detailed accounts of the great dances of her girlhood and the ancient stories that were her education. But she protects these behind screens of biblical and Masonic comparison through which she proclaims herself human to her people's enemies, at the same time trying to appreciate those enemies' own humanity—and to explain to them in familiar terms something of what the old Indian ways meant. Overall, in this careful balancing act, it is the sacred itself and the Yuroks' religious practices that predominate.

Lucy Thompson was the first northwestern California Indian to publish a book, and the last to do so for another 62 years.[5] During these same years, more than 70 original anthropological and historical works were published by non-Indian authors on the Yuroks and their immediate neighbors—the Karuks, Tolowas, Hupas, and Wiyots. These 70-plus scholarly works do not include a sizable "grey literature," three unpublished doctoral dissertations on the Yuroks alone, any number of reprints and textbook syntheses, and so on. Little of this writing was readily accessible to the Native audience in northwestern California before the late 1970s and the establishment of the Indian Action Library in Eureka. Such was the elite, white effort to "possess" the Native past (Fogelson 1974).

Spott and Kroeber's important "Yurok Narratives" did, as I've mentioned, appear in 1942, yet it is hard to accept it as a Native-authored work. Aside from his already mentioned overriding of Spott's own interpretations, Kroeber's transcriptions of Spott's oral narratives (Spott's written English was quite limited) are so heavily edited—or written from memory by Kroeber—that it is nearly impossible today to reclaim Robert Spott's voice through them. In reality, in the 1942 volume Spott is Kroeber's informant, not his coauthor, and Kroeber was at once gracious and ingenuous in designating him first author.[6]

We come forward in time, then, to 1978–79 in tracing Native authorship of books in northwestern California. Two books, both by Hupa Indian writers, were published in these years—*Our Home Forever: A Hupa Tribal History* by Byron Nelson Jr. (1978) and *Genocide in Northwestern California: When Our Worlds Cried* by Jack Norton (1979). Though the two books came out in successive years, both were being composed at the same time and reflect, I think, the same moment in Hupa and broader, regional culture history—although, as we will see, they sprang from quite different contexts within that moment.

It was a time in which Thompson's emphases and silences had been reversed. Both Norton and Nelson decline discussion of indigenous spirituality and religious practice in any detail, and both place considerable emphasis on past genocide and present oppression by—among others— anthropologists.

Like Thompson, Norton begins his book in near repudiation of received, non-Indian authored ethnology and ethnohistory, but at far greater length and with considerably greater acrimony. For Norton, the ethnologization of Native cultures in the region after 1900 by Pliny E. Goddard, Edward Gifford, T. T. Waterman, and especially A. L. Kroeber must be understood as a continuation of the catastrophe that had befallen his people, beginning in 1849. Expressing a modicum of gratitude for the written records of the old ways that these ethnographers compiled, Norton also rejects this record as being "ethnocentric" and as serving the interests of the invaders, particularly in its blindness to Native spirituality:

It should be stated here that the Kroeber *Handbook* should most em-
phatically be re-worked, and a complete history of the tribes of the region
be produced. Those now reading this work are shocked and dismayed
by the evidence of ethnocentrism and prejudice shown by Kroeber, the
distinguished scholar. These need to be pointed out at some time soon,
for they have been picked up and made a part of the educational process, and contribute greatly to the misconceptions about native peoples
of California. [1979:18]

Though, like Thompson, Norton would address Native spirituality as
being central to communal life, he is committed to a prior focus on that
which Thompson underplayed as a prerequisite to further discussion of
spirituality. The facts of nineteenth-century genocide need, in Norton's
view, to be entered into the educational process before, ultimately, turning to the sacred. This is so that the received ethnographic record, and
especially its omission of spirituality (as well as genocide), might be understood in context and thus be accurately reworked. To omit this terrible
history is, in effect, to collude in ongoing ethnocide.[7]

Ultimately, Norton's objective is not so much to berate Kroeber, or even
the white perpetrators of genocide, but to reestablish the Native peoples
of northwestern California in the human race, as Lucy Thompson had
done with her use of non-Indian, comparative mythology and symbolism.
Thompson used biblical and Masonic themes in her efforts to humanize
the Yuroks for those who had dehumanized them, and to gain the understanding of the whites. In the secularized, legalistic, and global (and safer)
contexts within which he wrote, Norton used comparable texts and the
symbols of comparable power brokers—those of international law and of
the United Nations. The final third of *Genocide in Northwestern California* is taken up with appendices that begin with the 1948 United Nations
Convention on the Prevention and Punishment of Genocide. They go on
to include rosters of federal, state, and local officials and military units
that were actively engaged in the subjugation of northwestern California
between 1850 and 1880, naming the hitherto unmentionable and also
restoring *their* humanity, recovering these individual actors from a general
and amnesiac "them."

Norton's approach compares Native Californians and biblical peoples
in a new and terrible way and amounts to an indictment that reaches much
closer to most contemporary homes in the region than did the Nuremberg
trials. There are many familiar North Coast family names on the more local rosters. Second, Norton portrays American Indians as innocent victims
of genocide—quite differently, that is, than had Thompson, whose Yuroks

No longer do Native ppl. look first to specific signifiers of their culture when reflecting on a cultural identity;

There is a trend now to when contemplating one's Indianness, to see the commonly shared genocide of all Indian people first.

(Sherman Alexie's realization)
↳ double consciousness)

are agents and only the white man's rum is truly a demon. This victimized portrayal was to be characteristic of a good deal of Native and non-Indian writing about genocide in North America that led up to and extended beyond the national Columbian quincentennial in 1992. Norton's use of the 1948 United Nations Convention on Genocide and his portrayal of northwest California Indians as pure victims of white aggression begin to suggest the wider contexts of his particular early contribution.

Genocide in Northwestern California was written because "a great deal is now known about the injustices committed against Indians of the Plains, the Eastern seaboard, and the Southwest [but] . . . [l]ittle is known, and less is understood . . . of the genocide committed against the native people of California, particularly those of Northwestern California . . . this most inhumane of all American tragedies" (Norton 1979:vii). Its local context rests within wider, then-contemporary, national and international contexts.

Norton was both representing and responding to a growing impatience among many Native thinkers with the habitual denials by dominant society of genocide and ethnocide in the colonization of North America and with the historical oblivion those denials had promoted. Second, he and other Native and non-Indian writers understood (though not in *Genocide in Northwestern California* itself) this denial and oblivion as continuing in part because of an attempted co-optation of the experience of genocide itself—along with the term *holocaust*—that they attributed to Israeli nationalists and their American allies. Both parties, they charged, were seeking moral justification of controversial Israeli government policies. Norton was to make explicit an argument for broadening the reference of the term *holocaust* at international conferences in the 1980s.

Both resistance to denial and historical oblivion in North America and the political contest for language were also evident in a number of publications by other Native and non-Indian authors during the same period: for example, Russell Thornton's *American Indian Holocaust and Survival: A Population History Since 1492* (1987), Ward Churchill's *A Little Matter of Genocide: Holocaust and Denial in the Americas* (a collection of earlier essays published as a book in 1998), as well as David E. Stannard's *American Holocaust: Columbus and the Conquest of the New World* (1992). Among these writers, Churchill (Keetoowah Cherokee) was the most analytical as well as the most outspoken in his condemnation of both denial and oblivion at home and of the co-optation of the experience of genocide for political purposes that he and others perceived (1998).[8]

There are many and complex reasons for the full emergence of the discourse on North American genocide in the later twentieth century. At least one anthropologist has argued cogently that this discourse emerged among Native Americans through a shared narrative dialogue with anthropologists (Bruner 1986). In Native northwestern California, one might surmise, this discourse was taken up both because traditional strictures against "rehearsing the bad" were weakening (and because the shame of violation had turned to less internalized anger), and also because it had become safer to speak the once unspeakable. As Lucy Thompson undoubtedly knew, it is not safe to remind the powerful of their crimes. It was not, in 1916, in Del Norte and Humboldt counties, nor was it all that safe in 1979, though safe enough by then to make it a reasonable risk—even for a historian seeking tenure at a state university, as Jack Norton was. (One really needs to understand what a short time ago the 1860s were in local consciousness, both Indian and white, and the enormous investment that the State of California has made in its sanitized history of intrepid pioneers, saintly Franciscans, and a single dead Indian—Ishi.)

But if the silence surrounding nineteenth-century genocide in northwestern California was ready for breaking, a new reticence was emerging at the same time, in the late 1970s, regarding that about which Lucy Thompson had been most forthcoming—Native spirituality and local religious practice. This new reticence is equally in evidence in Byron Nelson's *Our Home Forever* as in Jack Norton's book contemporaneous with it.

Norton was breaking what amounted to a local and national silence on genocide at a time when the region's Indian people were regrouping powerfully, both socially and culturally. Nowhere was this truer than at Hoopa, where the Hupa Indian tribe, federally acknowledged, was positioning itself economically and politically for a new period of consolidation and growth.[9] It was as determined to break a logjam of withheld federal timber payments as it was to reinvigorate its traditional culture with reconstructed villages, a tribal museum, language programs, and continued sustenance of public spirituality—particularly through curative brush dances and the more momentous, biennial white deerskin dance. *Our Home Forever: A Hupa Tribal History* by Byron Nelson Jr. (1978) emerged from this context: a tribally authorized history by an author who has served several terms on the Hupa tribal council. It is both complementary to Norton's work and unlike it in many ways.

The tone of Nelson's history is unemotional and rooted in the canons of academic historiography. Though mildly critical of received ethnographies and histories, his introductory ethnographic chapters are unabashedly based in Pliny Goddard's work, published at the turn of the century (Goddard 1903–4). Like Norton, Nelson acknowledges the central importance of spirituality in both precontact and contemporary Hupa culture. Yet he too declines to discuss it in any detail—not because there is a prior historical experience to be understood before spirituality might be properly considered, however. In accord with the Hupa elders who have contributed to the work, Nelson holds that Native spirituality should not be discussed publicly. He dismisses the topic briefly: simply, he "does not try to describe those parts of the culture which are most closely interwoven with the people's religious beliefs" (Nelson 1979:3). While Thompson sought to communicate the meanings of Yurok spirituality through analogy with Western traditions and Norton postponed discussion of these meanings until an historical, moral debt had been acknowledged, Nelson essentially says that they are no one's business outside of the Hoopa Valley. He would seem to be invoking a tribal secrecy regarding the sacred that is often invoked in Native North America as elsewhere, and is just as often attributed to Native peoples by outsiders who would describe them. Yet stereotypes are simplistic by definition, and Nelson's reticence regarding the sacred (in strong contrast to, say, Lucy Thompson), seems to me more complex in origin than a comparatively simple observing of putatively traditional taboos.

Certainly, Nelson (and the book's contributing elders) are as concerned with maintaining cultural boundaries as with territorial sovereignty. But it seems likely that their defensiveness was as much in response to the rising tide of New Age wannabes threatening the Hoopa Valley from nearby Arcata, California, as an invocation of traditional secrecy. I also think that it reveals something of Hupa and neighboring Native peoples' insecurity regarding their own spiritual heritage. Elders at the time—a generation removed from Lucy Thompson—were generally dubious that the old "Indian Way" could survive, and Nelson's own, still more recent generation of spiritual students had yet to achieve the confidence in their own abilities to carry on that was to be clearly in evidence by the late 1980s. In the interim, spirituality and religion remained, sensibly enough, local knowledge closely guarded by politically acute thinkers such as Byron Nelson (though some Native cynics have alleged that "people say things are 'secret' because they don't know anything about them themselves!").

Foregoing cynicism, it seems more appropriate to assume that Nelson was writing in a professional manner, supported by the Hupa tribe, and taking care of business. What he deemed to be *everybody*'s business (and here Nelson's book resembles Norton's appendices) was the chronological and factual administrative and territorial history of the Hoopa Valley Indian Reservation.

In this context genocide becomes more complex than in Norton's victimized account, and more like Thompson's: there are good Indian agents as well as bad, collaborating warriors as well as resisters and victims. Again, while Norton's crying "worlds" are cultural, spiritual, and above all moral territories, Nelson's "home" is more simply territory. His book is most useful and compelling as a finely researched and documented bureaucratic and economic reservation history, a valid (by external legal and political standards) and valuable record that, taking care not to issue a blanket indictment, might earn the respect of non-Indian federal bureaucrats, legislators, and judiciary. (Norton's appended rosters, in contrast, include lists of U.S. presidents, senators, and representatives as well as more local officials.) Nelson's *Our Home Forever* was a foundational text upon which the Hupa tribe might move ahead—toward, as it was to turn out, the congressional Yurok-Hupa Settlement Act of 1988, which was enormously beneficial to the Hupas in terms of land-base and economic stability, though at some cost to their northern neighbors, the Yuroks. In this regard, *Our Home Forever* came into being, most pertinently, within the context of the high-stakes federal tribal acknowledgement proceedings and land-claims cases of the late 1970s, particularly in the eastern United States, with all of their technicalities and legal stringencies (e.g., Brodeur 1985; Campisi 1991).[10]

Fogelson's focus on indigenous reenvisioning of indigenous histories and revoicings of Native historical theory takes on new complexities in this boundary-setting, competitive, fully modern discourse. It becomes clear, for instance, that reticence may be as much a vehicle for expressing Native perspectives on their own histories as voiced emphases. Precontact renderings of the region's history were cast in part in terms of the sacred in a mythologized history of villages and houses, of the great dances and of the regalia that dances in them (and stands at the heart of the local ceremonial economy)—all projected back into a "before time," when the creators and First People chartered the world that human beings were to inherit and steward (e.g., Kroeber 1976). This is the aspect of local historical consciousness and narration that Lucy Thompson centered her own narrative upon. She reenvisioned and translated it here and there in terms of nonindigenous mythologies, spirituality, and hierarchies, but she stated it nonetheless, while she treated with far more reticence both the more recent and obscene, entirely human history and the grief-stricken and angry historical consciousness to which it gave rise.

Consciousness of this modern history is voiced by both Norton and Nelson who choose, however, to communicate its spiritual concomitants through a new order of understatement, declining discussion of indigenous spirituality in the region while voicing loudly what Thompson had uttered sotto voce. These were not, I think, individual choices so much as communal ones, just as, for example, A. L. Kroeber's virtual neglect of both contact history and of Native women's points of view reflected collective decisions and styles in Boasian salvage ethnography (Buckley 1988, 1996).

The 1916 edition of Thompson's book is to be found, well cared for, in many Yurok houses, whose inhabitants speak of her with respect. The new edition, published in 1991 by Malcolm Margolin's Heyday Books—arguably, the contemporary publisher most responsible to Native Californian sensibilities—has a glowing introduction by the modern Karuk Indian artist-scholar Julian Lang.[11] Nelson's reservation history is, again, a tribally authorized one, originally published by the Hupa Tribe. Its author's work was assisted by an acknowledged board of 21 "Contributing Elders." Norton's book was published by Rupert Costo (Cahuilla) and the activist, Native-focused Indian Historian Press and continues to be widely read by American Indian audiences in the region. The emphases and understatements that I have discussed were not simply individual then but communal and, as such, highly communicative of the northwestern California Indian community's changing historical consciousness and theories of history as well as the changing, external contexts within which history is recorded.

Norton and Nelson's reserved approaches to the specifics of local spirituality were countermanded in 1982, however, by another Native writer—although, significantly, an outsider. Robert G. Lake Jr. is a Cherokee–Seneca scholar who came to work in the ethnic studies program at Humboldt State University in Arcata in the 1970s. Marrying a local Yurok woman, he took a serious interest in the region's own Native peoples. Out of this conjunction came *Chilula: People of the Ancient Redwoods* (Lake 1982), an effort to reconstruct the culture of the Hupa's Athabascan neighbors and kindred to the south and west, who were decimated and dispossessed in the genocide that Norton detailed.

Lake sets out to write from what he calls an "endogenous perspective" (e.g., as one of Jones's "native anthropologists"), hoping to set right perceived errors and omissions in the outsider ethnographies of Kroeber, Goddard (1914), and others. To ensure validity, he enlists the aid of eleven named elders and of his wife, Tela Donahue Lake (now Star Hawk), a clairvoyant and apprentice Indian doctor. He also takes another step, augmenting and interpreting local historical consciousness with his own new "endogenous" perspective. As Thompson remythologized Yurok Indians through the images of Western spirituality and Norton reenvisioned moral history through post—World War II international law, so Lake applied the metaphors and conceptual tools of alternative Western psychology, citing C. G. Jung, Bruno Bettleheim, the holistic therapists Kenneth Pelletier and Patricia Garfield, and other New Age thinkers, including John Lilly.

Lake is reticent neither about genocide nor Chilula spirituality. Indeed, spiritual meanings are at the center of his interpretation and exegesis of traditional Chilula culture and history. Where data are lacking, he seeks his wife's clairvoyant assistance to retrieve it, revealing through her the significance of a number of disused sacred sites. This focus was in part in response to conflict with the U.S. Forest Service over Yurok and Karuk sacred sites in the Siskiyou Mountains and elsewhere. The conflict, well underway by 1978, involved both Native and non-Indian activists in a struggle for protection of Native American religious freedom under both environmental legislation and the First Amendment to the United States Constitution (Buckley 2002:170–201).

While Thompson speaks lovingly but in passing of the "mystic shadows of dreamland mountains" (1991[1916]:226) and Norton touches briefly on the "clues to possible solutions to today's environmental crises" offered by traditional Native cultures (1978:6), the environment and environmentalism are central to Lake's book, which is dedicated to many people, including the "Save the Redwoods League . . . and the ancient Redwood Trees that have an aboriginal right to live and to flourish" (Lake 1982:iii).

Lake's book, and his particular "endogenous perspective" were then in part products of particular local political situations and shared goals that, like Nelson's tribal history, it supported. And too it reflected broader contexts—in this case, the New Age movement that Nelson partly sought to discourage but that provided a good many of Lake's (and Norton's) students at Humboldt State as well as the then florescent national environmentalist movement. However, rather than going into publication through what amounts to an indigenous peer-review system (the Hupa Tribal Council, the Indian Historical Press, Heyday Books, etc.), Lake published *Chilula* through the University Press of America, a general academic publisher with a very large, author-subsidized catalog. And unlike Thompson's, Norton's, and Nelson's books, it was repudiated by local people, including the elders that Lake had consulted.

These elders, embarrassed by having their names in the book, charged that Lake broadcast (secret) sacred knowledge they had given him as a student and a seeker, never intending it for publication. There seem to me to be other problems inherent in the book as well, including the detailed intimacy of family histories; the linking of specific informants with specific, privileged information; and the verbatim transcription of other, nonesoteric testimony that the elders themselves could not have intended for publication:

> Last summer I had to fast and walk up the mountains all by myself in the hot weather to get the Deerskin and Jump Dance medicine. Soon I won't be able to do this anymore. And I ask, who is willing to learn the old ways for our tribe and for the Creator? . . . Most of the young people won't dance in the Sacred Dances, but they sure like to get drunk and dance the Whiteman's dances. [Lake 1982:164]

On the face of it, Lake reports nothing new here and reports it not much differently than Lucy Thompson had in 1916, inveighing against drink and lamenting the dissoluteness of the young. There are significant underlying differences, however. First, Lake edits and represents the voices of respected, named elders in such passages, while Lucy Thompson spoke for herself, as such an elder. (Alternatively, Nelson, while working with 21 contributing elders, linked none of them directly with potentially controversial information in his text.) Second, one cannot avoid the impression, from Lake's prose, that he uses his transcribed interviews to validate himself. In the just-quoted passage, the elder, after all, confides in Lake, a younger man who has gone to the elder as an earnest student of the sacred, one who is not drunk and dancing "the Whiteman dances." All of this is in contrast to Thompson's wariness of "egocentrism" and is in breach of still-regnant local manners. Finally, Lake, although a Native anthropologist in Jones's terms, was also an outsider to the environment he described and interpreted: his view was not *pertinently* endogenous from a local point of view.

The book was rejected locally in the local way, largely by being met with silence. This was harsh treatment, for *Chilula* has its virtues. Lake's scholarship is detailed and careful, drawing together in a comprehensive way much of the scattered, published information on the Chilula Indians and arriving at some provocative and valid interpretations of both received texts and new oral testimony. He collates a variety of useful environmental information and indeed sheds light on regional spirituality, new to the published literature. In most of this *Chilula* resembles both Norton's and Nelson's locally popular works. Perhaps it will be consulted more graciously by Native readers once the critical dust has settled.

The local reaction to his book took Lake by surprise: somewhere, communications had broken down without his knowing it. However the misunderstandings occurred, archetypal energies, creative dreaming, holistic approaches to preventing stress disorders, clairvoyance, environmentalism, and the rest were not at issue—any more than Thompson's Masonic lodge and biblical imagery, Norton's United Nations, or Nelson's federal bureaucracy, to my knowledge, have been foci of the critiques of Native readers. What was offensive was Lake's breaching of the community's reserve regarding specific sacred knowledge and its respect for individual privacy, and his seeming self-aggrandizement.

Lake left the region some time after *Chilula: People of the Ancient Redwoods* was published. The language of depth psychology that he explored in it has found its way into ongoing discourse on the sacred among younger spiritual people in the region, but the book itself is not often mentioned. Lake now writes on healing for a New Age audience under the name of Medicine Grizzly Bear (Lake 1991).

A certain balance between boldness and careful recognition of regnant discursive strictures finally may be what characterizes the three locally *successful* books that I have discussed so far. Adding further "ethnos" to ethnohistory and to ethnography is not a risk-free undertaking, as Medicine Grizzly Bear discovered. From another perspective, while Fogelson's infinitely regressing Shaker Salt Ladies on the kitchen package pose a pleasing, whimsical trope, I don't think that we need entertain multiple "ethnos" more seriously than the "exasperated" Fogelson first did. Beyond Native reenvisioning of indigenous histories and reconfigurations of received Native historical consciousness, we would seem rapidly to leave behind the collective and communally constituted and acceptable—that is to say, all "ethnos." Departing from both culture as shared knowledge and practice and history as shared experience, we would enter the domain of fiction or something else: sometimes "self-help," the bookstore section where we find Medicine Grizzly Bear Lake's *Native Healer* today, published by Quest Books of the Theosophical Publishing House (1991).

Recognizing this distinction between the ethnic and the individual leaves unaddressed the question of how an ethnic group's shared historical consciousness and theory of history change. Largely by responding to extrinsic political-economic changes, as is so often the case in academic anthropology (e.g., Stocking 1992)? Or do varying theories indeed make progress through innovation, as is also widely if implicitly assumed in academe? However so, a final example of such change remains to be mentioned: Julian Lang's *Ararapíkva, Creation Stories of the People: Traditional Karuk Indian Literature from Northwestern California*, published by Heyday Books in 1994—more than a decade after Norton, Nelson, and Lake's contributions.

Julian Lang, the Karuk scholar, artist, and cultural activist introduced earlier in this chapter, leaves aside, finally, what had by 1994 become *de rigueur* anthro-bashing and condemnation by faint praise. More, it would seem, has been unnecessary. Rather, Lang acknowledges (in the book and elsewhere) his profound debt to the anthropological linguists who have made ongoing study of Karuk language and texts possible—J. P. Harrington, Helen Roberts, and especially William Bright (Lang 1989, 1990, 1994:6). He does this gracefully, leaving his own Karuk language teachers and older storytellers at center stage.

It seems to me that this reorientation toward received academic texts is historically illuminating as well as revealing of Lang's individual graciousness. (Anthro-bashing is "like swearing," he once said to me—referring to the old use of the names of enemies' dead relatives as a [litigable] form of insult-curse.)

During the 1980s Lang's generation of ceremonial leaders and participants had successfully reinvigorated, under the guidance of elders, many of the great "world renewal" dances of the Karuks, Yuroks, Hupas, and Tolowas, gaining considerable confidence through doing so. The contribution of such habitually castigated salvage-ethnographic texts as Kroeber and Gifford's "World Renewal" (1949) to this successful renaissance was undeniable. Both a new appreciation for some of the efforts of the early ethnographers and increasing local cultural confidence (the two are not unrelated) have nurtured a general improvement in relationships between Native people and contemporary, non-Indian researchers.[12] Though DeLoria's 1969 polemic, *Custer Died for Your Sins*, still rings true for many, many other Native cultural and spiritual experts and activists—including Julian Lang—have arrived at more complex and nuanced views of the century-long collaboration between academics and their own peoples. Lang's *Ararapíkva* manifests this new confidence and complexity alike.

The book is organized around six retranscribed Karuk texts with interlinear English translations. These are filled out with portraits of the original storytellers, sections on Karuk culture and language, a glossary, photographs, and very careful suggestions as to what each story or prayer might be about: "Knowledge, which is what the story is, gives power" (Lang 1994:45); "We live in a world created by yearning and sexuality, and every time we look at the moon and see Frog Woman there, we are reminded of this wonderful fact" (p. 49); "wonder is at the heart of creation" (p. 55). To an extent, Lang returns to Thompson's approach, which he admires (Lang, in Thompson 1991[1916]:xv–xxvi).

Lang positions himself, as author and editor, firmly within Karuk culture and culture history—reviewing, for instance, his own family's experience of the "wanton destruction" that Norton chronicles (Lang 1994:11 ff.). However, he also shifts the received discourse by delving into meanings of the sacred—as Lake did, though far more discretely. His presence as reinterpreter and innovator is felt in a single noun, *love*, which occurs four times in the slim (112 pages) volume: in the dedication "To Indian Love," in the introduction ("The power of love has been instrumental in keeping indigenous peoples together"), and twice more in the main text. "The affirmation of love as the greatest force on earth is balanced by the knowledge that even love has its limits: life must be lived according to the rules that have been laid down for us" (Lang 1994:5, 13–14, 63). *Love* is not a word to be found in the ethnographies and histories of Kroeber or Goddard, nor one used so pervasively in any of the works of the other Native authors I have discussed (though Thompson, as we have seen, indeed invokes it). Yet, like spirituality and genocide, Lang implies, it is at the heart of Native northwestern Californian cultures, past and present, and it is at the very center of his book.

Lang's work, reaching back into the past for its stories and its many subtle reflections of Lucy Thompson's pioneering work (much as non-Indian scholars continue to reach back toward Kroeber's oeuvre [e.g., Keeling 1992]), equally reflects the new period of cultural confidence that dawned in Native California in the 1980s. Lang is close to the center of this renaissance, grounded in a federally acknowledged tribe still holding a portion of its aboriginal territory, in command of his tribal language, participating in the traditional ceremonialism resurgent in northwestern California today, and knowing that there is far more to this practice than the individual "power" that Lake emphasized. He can, in effect, fully afford to be generous, wealthy in his knowledge that "there is no love like Indian love" (personal communication, 1992). Though his use of the English *love* has a Christian resonance, that resonance is rather different from Thompson's apologetic use of Christian comparisons. Lang subtly suggests that the Christian whites are not so much to be feared, as Thompson implies, or hated, as Norton needed to convey, but pitied for their loneliness in their secularized and alienated world.

Books are and are not like precontact "cosmologies, narratives, rituals and ceremonies" (Fogelson 1989). They exist in a different world that books themselves have had no little part in creating. It is in part for this reason that "ethno-ethnohistory" and a parallel ethno-ethnography has developed, throughout this century in Native northwestern California, in much the same way as elite, academic anthropology and history do. Theoretical and methodological paradigms rise and fall, subject to external contextualization and to communal validation, old themes are woven into new patterns, disappear and reemerge, and certainly the Native authors I have reviewed are as respectful of their "data" as any metropolitan scholar. If

Norton, Nelson, Lake, and Lang did not invoke Lucy Thompson's biblical and Masonic "ethno-ethno-ethnohistory," it was not because they held it to have been inappropriate to her time but to their own, when analogies with Holocaust victims, the criteria of federal courts, the insights of depth psychology, and the power of enduring love simply made more sense. If local readers rejected Lake's earnest but ill-advised breaching of local etiquette it was because it fell outside of the disciplinary canons of their own anthropology and historiography. Such indigenous processes seem no more unusual or exotic than those of elite academic disciplines viewed historically.

The elements entered into these processes, however, are not necessarily the elements entered into elite academic developments over time. Kroeber, for example, pretty much ignored genocide and spirituality alike (not to mention love) as well as the dialectical roles of white society in shaping present Indian societies. On the other hand, Native writers have not been much concerned with trait inventories or with kinship and culture itself as general systems, for example. Their theories and methods, broadly speaking, have different sources and different objectives than those of most non-Indian academics.

In our time, academic and Native concerns have come to overlap in some areas—in questioning elite ethnographic authority, for instance (Clifford 1983), and in understanding that narratives of Indian-white relations have never been truly monological but always dialogical (Bruner 1986). These overlappings are, I believe, results of that very dialogue. In general, however, differing theoretical paradigms have prevailed. There was, for example, a virtual cottage industry in psychoanalyses of Yurok culture between 1943 and 1970 in academe. Native writers in northwestern California have never taken up this approach, although they have proposed parallel theories: depth psychology and a general theory of a love that is not exclusively erotic, for instance. Many non-Indian academics and Native writers would like to think that these are differences that make a difference, but I am not so sure.

Lucy Thompson's comparative use of biblical imagery in the interpretation of indigenous spirituality is, arguably, no more nor less appropriate than Erik Erikson's (1943) appropriation of Freud's Viennese mythology in the interpretation of that same spirituality, or so it would now appear with the widely accepted downgrading of Freud's psychology from positive science to humanistic, even poetic intellectual improvisation. One could even argue that Thompson's analogies are more appropriate in comparing spiritual tradition to spiritual tradition rather than reducing all such traditions through profoundly secular analysis: an apples-and-oranges affair if there ever was one. One could go on in this way, though such comparisons—as opposed to either Thompson's or Freud's—indeed tend toward the odious.

More certainly, it is clear that psychoanalysis, trait inventories, formalized studies of social structure, and the rest have prevailed for cultural reasons that have had to do with power and with dispossession. It is clear, that is, that the study of successive efforts in elite, metropolitan descriptions and analyses of Native northwestern California is a study as much of Euro-American culture history and politics as of Yurok, Karuk, Hupa, or Chilula Indians. We cannot easily dismiss Native models for studying themselves, and the analogies and metaphors embedded in these, as merely "subjective," as nonscientific, or as though the history of European models for studying those people had been anything else in any truly defining way. Chris Peters in 1976 need not have been so diffident about his colleagues' abilities to do their own anthropology. Rather than worrying that these colleagues would "not do it as well" as non-Indian outsiders, he might have said "we will do it differently." Studying these differences takes us a ways into understanding real differences between non-Indian elites and Native northwestern California—into understanding *both* sides of the cross-cultural equation better.

All cultural and historical interpretation is reflective of its authors, if not always reflexively so. (In this, the Yurok doctor whom Kroeber interviewed in 1905 was well ahead of the academic anthropologists of her time.) Perhaps it is time to come up with some new terms for the operations and processes involved in this creative effort. Since we remain in dialogue, Native abilities to confidently repossess their own histories and cultural accounts depend in part on non-Indians' abilities to stop segregating these accounts as hyphenated forms, with their implications of "folk"—that is, non-"objective"—status. These matters seem, finally, to underlie Fogelson's "exasperation" in the 1970s and the seemingly parodic nature of his reduplicative "ethnos."

Notes

1. Delmos Jones's notion of "native anthropologists" has since been problematized by later theorists. See, for example, Les Field (1998) for an overview of recent discussions of the intricate intertwinings among and contradictions within the analytic categories of "metropolitan" and "native" anthropologists. These considerations are entirely pertinent to my discussions of works by Jack Norton and Robert Lake later in this chapter, although I do not delve far into them here.

2. Fogelson's insights have had a profound impact on Americanist ethnohistory. See,

for example, Peter Nabokov's recent, detailed examination of modes of American Indian historical consciousness and its communication, particularly through narrative (2002).

3. The late Arnold R. Pilling claimed to have collected a Yurok genealogy in the 1970s that reached back into the fifteenth century (personal communication 1982).

4. Thompson's use of Christian analogies, as well as her motives, might be compared to those of her contemporary "Red Progressive," Dr. Charles A. Eastman (1911).

5. During these years there were indeed some shorter works published by Native authors from the region—pamphlets like the Karuk Indian *Peek-wa Stories*, by Chief and Mrs. Eaglewing, published in 1938, and another good—if brief—account of Yurok life coauthored by Timm Williams (Seiter and Williams 1959). There were also various columns in local newspapers by Native authors, some important speeches that were transcribed and published, and so on. These all deserve close attention, but my present focus is on published, Native-authored books.

6. For example, a thorough search of Lowie Museum and Bancroft Library archives by Richard Keeling, who worked cataloging Kroeber's notes and recordings at Berkeley during the 1980s, failed to turn up any preliminary notes on or transcriptions—in English or in Yurok—of Spott's "The Inland Whale," perhaps the best known of the narratives in the published volume.

7. Norton indeed went on to write about Native spirituality, in continuing commitment to education, in *Natasha Goes to the Brush Dance* (Norton 2000), a children's book with an accompanying teacher's guide (Norton and Norton 2000), both written in collaboration with his wife, Jana Norton. These works are not discussed in the present chapter, which covers only the period 1916–94.

8. I have reported Norton's and others views in order to put Norton's 1979 book in its full, relevant context, as I have done with the other four works by Native authors discussed in this chapter. I do not see it as part of my proper scholarly role to either support Norton's (or the others') views or to argue against them. My responsibility in all five cases, as I define it, is only to assure that I have represented all such views accurately.

In January 2003, making final revisions, I resubmitted this essay to Jack Norton, asking him to attend especially closely to drafts of the foregoing paragraphs and inviting his critique of them. Mr. Norton had no objection to my representation of his views. In his response he wrote,

> At the 1988 International Conference on the 50th Anniversary of Kristallnacht, Oxford, England—I ran into intransigence and overt anger from some Jewish scholars when I used the term "genocide" in relationship to white/Indian contact. There was almost complete rejection for using the term "holocaust" in regards to the Indian experience even in the most limited sense such as the Yontoket [Tolowa] massacre. But after Stannard's work "American Holocaust" in 1992, the firestorm of death, disease, and carnage is undeniable.
>
> To claim exclusivity in human suffering has the potential of limiting universal empathy, but I also recognize the need for group identity and therefore the term "Shoah" may define the Jewish tragedy and should not be co-opted. Sam Oliner and I used to teach [in a class on genocide at Humboldt State University] that every genocide is different and for healing to take place requires empathetic regard for that suffering. [e-mail to author, January 10, 2003]

Norton goes on to quote Elie Wiesel on the need for storytelling to create empathy and promote healing, concluding that "In the telling and listening humanity meets" (e-mail, January 10, 2003).

None of the writers of conscience that I have mentioned should be facilely accused of anti-Semitism, certainly not Jack Norton, a lifelong activist in antiracism. (Churchill dedicates his book to Raphaël Lemkin, the late Polish Jewish exile credited with coining the term *genocide*.) It is worth noting that during the years relevant to my discussion of Norton's book, parts of the Israeli left were also condemning "Shoah Business," as they themselves called alleged use of the Holocaust to justify Israeli governmental policy (Beth Goldring, personal communication, 1985).

I note that some Holocaust scholars and curators have been sensitive to some of the issues raised by Norton and others, including Israeli dissenters. In January 2003, for example, the U.S. Holocaust Memorial Museum in Washington DC announced that it was mounting a show on "Nazi Persecution of Homosexuals 1933–1945" and that it had plans for further exhibits on "the Holocaust's other victims," including "the handicapped, Gypsies, Poles, Soviet prisoners of war and Jehovah's Witnesses" (*New York Times*, January 4, 2003).

Personally, I feel that any questions of "ownership" of the experience of genocide were mooted by well-publicized (if inadequately responded to) events in Iraqi Kurdistan, in Rwanda, and in the Balkans in the 1990s. I also recognize and accept that the term *holocaust* has long since entered into general English-language discourse on genocide and related tragedies and that languages have irrepressible lives of their own. That I have been called upon to provide this lengthy note, however, suggests that the issues raised by Norton and others have yet to be resolved and that, in 2003, they are perhaps more sensitive than ever.

9. Through the cumulative vagaries of transcription, the territory that the "Hupa Indians" occupy has customarily been represented in written English as "the Hoopa Valley." Aboriginally, these people did not call themselves "Hupa" (or "Hoopa")—words derived from the Yurok language—but "Natinook-wa" and their valley "Natinook" (Nelson 1978:3).

10. Critics of Nelson's *Our Home Forever* have pointed out that a team of non-Indian historical researchers, working for the Hupa tribe, played an important role in its composition. Yet I do not see this as reason to refute its authenticity as a Native-authored text. All published writers receive support and help, from editors if no one else, and researchers often receive considerable assistance from other researchers. The present chapter, for example, has directly benefited from and been substantially changed by the comments of this volume's editors, an anonymous reviewer, participants and audience members at the two academic meetings where I presented shorter versions of it, and one of the authors whom I discuss in it. Lucy Thompson's *To the American Indian* was vetted by her husband, Jim Thompson, whose florid Victorian prose occasionally overwhelms her more straightforward (if poetic) writing. Jack Norton received support from his mentor and publisher, Rupert Costo (Cahuilla), in writing *Genocide in Northwestern California*; the anthropologist Arnold R. Pilling contributed importantly to Robert G. Lake Jr.'s *Chilula* (discussed later in this chapter); and the linguist William Bright assisted Julian Lang while Lang was writing *Ararapíkva* (also discussed later). Such collaborations, however, have often seemed to raise more—and different sorts of—questions in the cases of American Indian authors than in those of others, as though "Indians" aren't *supposed* to be literate, scholarly, or analytic. Full exploration of this situation would demand an entire essay and would fall outside of my objectives in the present chapter.

For my purposes, it suffices to deal with the named authors of the books under consideration in this chapter as simple indicators of the people who wrote them. However complex the actual circumstances of their composition might have been, what directly concerns me about the books under discussion is not what help their authors received but the changing contexts within which the books were written and the degree to which they have been received by the communities that they represent as authentic and desired reflections of those communities' self-understandings.

11. Margolin inaugurated Heyday Books in 1978, going on to publish the currently definitive print vehicle for California Indian voices, the bimonthly *News from Native California*, beginning in 1987. Until the founding of Heyday Books, the Naturegraph Press was probably the most widely accepted Indian-advocacy publisher in the state, having published Jack D. Forbes's (Powhatan) highly regarded *Native Americans of California and Nevada* in 1969, for example.

12. Many other factors contributed to the easing of relationships between Native and non-Indian researchers in northwestern California during the 1980s. Non-Indian advocacy anthropologists, like the late Arnold R. Pilling, were useful and supportive in the effort to stop federal construction of "the GO-road"—a protracted legal battle that, though ultimately lost, was of considerable importance in building awareness and solidarity among the new spiritual traditionalists (Buckley 2002:170–201). Others, like Lee Davis and Richard Keeling, did much to secure Native access to the University of California's vast collection of northwestern Californian ethnographic materials. The annual California Indian Conference, which began bringing Native and non-Indian experts together in the mid-1980s, has also been effective in bettering relationships between "anthros," "histos," and Indians. Yet other factors and events have contributed importantly to the process as well.

References

Arnold, Mary Ellicott, and Mabel Reed
    1957 In the Land of the Grasshopper Song. New York: Vantage Press.
Brodeur, Paul
    1985 Restitution: The Land Claims of the Mashpee, Passamaquoddy, and Penobscot Indians of New England. Boston: Northeastern University Press.
Bruner, Edward M.
    1986 Ethnography as Narrative. *In* The Anthropology of Experience. Victor Turner and Edward M. Bruner, eds. Pp. 139–155. Urbana: University of Illinois Press.
Buckley, Thomas
    1984 Yurok Speech Registers and Ontology. Language in Society 13(4):467–488.
    1988 Menstruation and the Power of Yurok Women. *In* Blood Magic: The Anthropology of Menstruation. Thomas Buckley and Alma Gottlieb, eds. Berkeley: The University of California Press.
    1996 The Pitiful History of Little Events: The Epistemological and Moral Contexts of Kroeber's Californian Ethnology. *In* History of Anthropology, vol. 8: Volksgeist as Method and Ethic: Essays on Boasian Ethnography and the German Anthropological Tradition. George W. Stocking, Jr., ed. Pp. 257–297. Madison: University of Wisconsin Press.
    1998 The Shaker Church and the Indian Way in Native Northwestern California. American Indian Quarterly 21(1):1–14.
    2002 Standing Ground: Yurok Indian Spirituality, 1850–1990. Berkeley: University of California Press.
Campisi, Jack
    1991 The Mashpee Indians: Tribe on Trial. Syracuse NY: Syracuse University Press.

Churchill, Ward

1998 A Little Matter of Genocide: Holocaust and Denial in the Americas, 1492 to the Present. San Francisco: City Lights Books.

Clifford, James

1983 On Ethnographic Authority. Representations 1(2):118–146.

Deloria, Vine, Jr.

1969 Custer Died for Your Sins. New York: MacMillan.

Eaglewing, Chief, and Mrs. Eaglewing

1938 Peek-wa Stories: Indian Legends of California. Los Angeles: B. N. Robinson Publishing.

Eastman, Charles Alexander

1911 The Soul of an Indian: An Interpretation. Boston: Houghton Mifflin.

Erikson, Erik H.

1943 Observations on the Yurok: Childhood and World Image. University of California Publications in American Archaeology and Ethnology 35(10):257–302.

Field, Les

1999 Complicities and Collaborations: Anthropologists and the "Unacknowledged Tribes" of California. Current Anthropology 40(2):193–201.

Fogelson, Raymond D.

1971 The Cherokee Ballgame Cycle: An Ethnographer's View. Ethnomusicology 15(3): 327–338.

1974 On the Varieties of Indian History: Sequoyah and Traveller Bird. Journal of Ethnic Studies 2:10–12.

1984 Who Were the Ani-Kutani? An Excursion into Cherokee Historical Thought. Ethnohistory 31:255–263.

1989 The Ethnohistory of Events and Nonevents. Ethnohistory 36(2):133–147.

Goddard, Pliny E.

1903–4 Life and Culture of the Hupa. University of California Publications in American Archaeology and Ethnology 1(1):1–88.

1914 Notes on the Chilula Indians of Northwestern California. University of California Publications in American Archaeology and Ethnology 10(6):265–288.

Graves, Charles

1929 Lore and Legends of the Klamath River Indians. Yreka CA: Press of the Times.

Heizer, Robert F., and Alan J. Almquist

1971 The Other Californians: Prejudice and Discrimination under Spain, Mexico, and the United States. Berkeley: University of California Press.

Hurston, Zora Neale

1984(1942) Dust Tracks on a Road: An Autobiography. Urbana: University of Illinois Press.

Jones, Delmos J.

1970 Towards a Native Anthropology. Human Organization 29 (4):251–259.

Keeling, Richard

1992 Cry for Luck: Sacred Song and Speech among the Yurok, Hupa and Karok Indians of Northwestern California. Berkeley: University of California Press.

Kroeber, A. L.

1905 Field Notes—Yurok Indians. Kroeber Papers. Bancroft Library, University of California, Berkeley.

1921 Review: Mrs. Lucy Thompson, To the American Indian. American Anthropologist 23(2):220–221.

1925 Handbook of the Indians of California. Bulletin 78, Bureau of American Ethnology of the Smithsonian Institution. Pp. xviii, 1–995.

1948 Anthropology: Race, Language, Culture, Psychology, Prehistory. 4th ed. New York: Harcourt, Brace & World.

1959 Ethnographic Interpretations, 7–11: Yurok National Character. University of California Publications in American Archaeology and Ethnology 47(3):236–240.

1976 Yurok Myths. Berkeley: University of California Press.

Kroeber, A. L., and E. W. Gifford

1949 World Renewal: A Cult System of Native Northwest California. Anthropological Records 13(1):1–155.

Lake, Medicine Grizzly Bear

1991 Native Healer: Initiation into an Ancient Art. Wheaton IL: Quest Books/Theosophical Publishing House.

Lake, Robert G., Jr.

1982 Chilula: People from the Ancient Redwoods. Washington DC: University Press of America.

Lang, Julian

1989 Pat pananúararáhih: Our Indian Language. News from Native California 3(3):3–4.

1990 How They Almost Killed Our songs. News from Native California 4(2):22–25.

1994 Ararapíkva, Creation Stories of the People: Traditional Karuk Indian Literature from Northwestern California. Berkeley CA: Heyday Books.

Nabokov, Peter

2002 A Forest of Time: American Indian Ways of History. Cambridge: Cambridge University Press.

Nelson, Byron, Jr.

1978 Our Home Forever: A Hupa Tribal History. Hoopa CA: The Hupa Tribe.

Norton, Jack

1979 Genocide in Northwestern California: When Our Worlds Cried. San Francisco: Indian Historian Press.

2000 Natasha Goes to the Brush Dance. Hemet CA: c/o Center for the Affirmation of Responsible Education.

Norton, Jack, and Jana Norton

2000 A Teacher's Guide to Natasha Goes to the Brush Dance. Hemet CA: c/o Center for the Affirmation of Responsible Education.

Palmquist, Peter E.

1977 With Nature's Children: Emma B. Freeman (1880–1928)—Camera and Brush. Eureka CA: Interface California Corporation.

Powers, Stephen

1976[1877] Tribes of California. Berkeley: University of California Press.

Seiter, Herbert D., and Harry D. (Timm) Williams

1959 Prince Lightfoot: Indian from the California Redwoods. Palo Alto CA: Trubador Press.

Spott, Robert, and A. L. Kroeber

1942 Yurok Narratives. University of California Publications in American Archaeology and Ethnology 35(9):i–viii, 143–256.

Stannard, David E.

    1992 American Holocaust: Columbus and the Conquest of the New World. New York: Oxford University Press.

Stocking, George W., Jr.

    1992 The Ethnographer's Magic and Other Essays in the History Anthropology. Madison: University of Wisconsin Press.

Thompson, Lucy

    1991[1916] To the American Indian. Introduction by Julian Lang. Berkeley CA: Heyday Books. (Orig. pub. Eureka CA: Cummins Print Shop.)

Thornton, Russell

    1987 American Indian Holocaust and Survival: A Population History Since 1492. Norman: University of Oklahoma Press.

Waterman, T. T., and A. L. Kroeber

    1934 Yurok Marriages. University of California Publications in American Archaeology and Ethnology 20(30):1–14.

    1938 The Kepel Fish Dam. University of California Publications in American Archaeology and Ethnology 35(6):49–80.

Zitkala-Ša.

    1921 American Indian Stories. Washington DC: Hayworth.

10. *The Sioux at the Time of European Contact*

An Ethnohistorical Problem

RAYMOND J. DEMALLIE

The earliest period of European contact with the Sioux Indians (the Dakotas and Lakotas) dates approximately from 1660 to 1720, when they lived in the area of present-day Minnesota and eastern South Dakota. Many misconceptions concerning the Sioux of that time have been perpetuated in the anthropological and historical literature by simply repeating as fact what earlier writers presented as surmise. In anthropology such misconceptions have frequently been fostered by a predisposition to use the Sioux case to prove some more general theoretical point about American Indian society. In this chapter I will examine four persistent misconceptions concerning the Sioux, each of which has been repeated in the literature over the past century. All four misconceptions are articulated in the influential comparative study of the Sioux by the late James H. Howard (published in article form in 1960 and in expanded monograph form in 1966 and 1980). That a scholar as meticulous as Howard accepted these misconceptions attests to the extent to which they have permeated the literature:

1. The Sioux at the time of European contact were a typical Woodland people whose economy "was based upon hunting, fishing, and the gathering of lake and forest products supplemented by slash and burn horticulture" (Howard 1980[1966]:2).

2. Sioux society at the time of European contact was organized in clans, or clanlike villages, paralleling the social organization of other Woodland and Prairie groups (Howard 1980[1966]:5, 13, 22).

3. The Sioux at the time of European contact were united in a political alliance known as the Seven Council Fires (or Seven Fireplaces), whose seat was at the Mdewakantonwan village on Spirit Lake, generally assumed to be Mille Lacs Lake (Howard 1980[1966]:3).

4. The Santees (Eastern Dakotas, living in Minnesota) represented an older, original form of Sioux culture, from which the Yankton-Yanktonai and Teton groups subsequently diverged as they moved westward and adapted to new ecological zones and interacted with other tribes. [Howard 1960:250, 1980[1966]:10]

The roots of these misconceptions lie deep in the published literature and can be traced at least to the writings of William H. Keating, the "historiographer" of Stephen H. Long's exploring expedition up the Minnesota River in 1823:

> Like all the Indian nations with whom the white man has come in contact, the Dacota presents to us at this day but a noble ruin. No longer united for purposes of common defence, they have long since ceased to meet at the same council fire; their alliances with other nations are now mere mockeries; their wars have dwindled into petty conflicts. Instead of marching, as they formerly did, by hundreds, they now issue forth in small detachments, presenting rather the character of a band of marauders than of an expedition of warriors. When they lighted the common calumet at the General Council Fire, it was always among the Mende Wahkantoan, who then resided near Spirit Lake, and who were considered as the oldest band of the nation, their chiefs being of longer standing than those of the other tribes; among themselves they used the appellation of brothers. [Keating 1959[1825], 1: 442–443]

Keating indicated that Joseph Renville, a fur trader married to a Dakota woman, was the primary source of the information on the Dakotas included in his book, but there is no way of ascertaining whether these historical conclusions came directly from Renville. Earlier in his narrative, Keating mentioned the prehistoric mounds found near Lake Pepin, concluding that they attested to "the former existence of a very dense population. . . . It must have been a stationary one, for these works could not have been executed in a short space of time" (Keating 1959[1825], 1:258–259). At the same time—especially since he liberally cites the *Jesuit Relations* and other published sources—it may be hypothesized that Keating had in mind the model of the Iroquois confederacy, which, in his day, was indeed "a noble ruin." The Five Nations of Iroquois (later the Six Nations), an alliance whose central council fire was at Onondaga, served early Euro-American explorers and government representatives as the model of American Indian political organization, so shaping their perceptions of other tribes with which they came into contact farther west. Indeed, in the *Jesuit Relations*, Jacques Marquette (JR 54:190) characterized the Sioux ("Nadoüessi") as "the Iroquois of the country beyond La Pointe," that is, west of Lake Superior. For Keating, the Seven Council Fires readily suggested the League of the Iroquois, who used the image of a single longhouse with five fireplaces as the symbol and metaphor of their alliance.

Keating's publication became the main source from which later writers drew to characterize the organization of the Sioux groups. In his official report for 1849, Alexander Ramsey, superintendent of Indian affairs for the new Minnesota Superintendency of the Office of Indian Affairs, presented an account of the "Seven Grand Council-Fires" of the Sioux that is apparently derived entirely from Keating (Ramsey 1849:1014–1024). The missionary Stephen Return Riggs, introducing the grammar and dictionary of Dakota that was published by the Smithsonian Institution, commented only that the seven bands of the Dakota "sometimes speak of themselves" as the "Seven council fires" (Riggs 1851:vii). In his synthetic outline of Siouan social organization, J. Owen Dorsey (1891:257) transformed Riggs's qualified statement into a general assertion: "The Dakota call themselves 'Otcheti cakowiⁿ' [ochéthi šakówį], *The Seven Fire-places*, or *Council-fires*, referring to their original gentes, now tribes."

The analogy between the Sioux and the Iroquois was sharpened and given scientific standing in anthropology in the writings of Lewis Henry Morgan. In *Systems of Consanguinity and Affinity of the Human Family* (1871), Morgan interpreted the "Dakotan Confederacy" of the Seven Council Fires as an attempt—like that of the Iroquois—to prevent the practically independent subdivisions of the Sioux from breaking entirely from one another. He wrote: "The important uses of the federal principle to arrest the constant tendency to denationalization was understood by the Dakotas, although it never ripened into a permanent and effective organization" (Morgan 1871:172). Morgan seems to have blamed this failure on the adoption of the horse and the subsequent development of a nomadic lifestyle based on buffalo hunting. In terms of kinship, he found the Sioux system to be structurally identical to that of the Senecas, which, in his judgment, indicated a social system that necessarily reflected the same organizational principles and ideas, as well as suggesting a genetic relationship between the Sioux and the Iroquois. Expanding his argument further in *Ancient Society* (1963[1877]:158), Morgan hypothesized that the Sioux had formerly been organized in patrilineal clans but as they became nomadic bands they "allowed the gentile organization to fall into decadence."

This, the first picture of the Sioux at the time of contact presented by an anthropologist, was drawn without systematic recourse to historical documents to corroborate or revise the conjectured reconstruction. Since Morgan's time, vastly more historical sources in better editions have become available, making an ethnohistorical reconstruction possible. Anthropological studies that use these historical sources include Holder (1970), Hickerson (1970), Wedel (1974), Birk and Johnson (1992), and Gibbon (2003). Yet to date no extensive account of the Sioux that makes full use of available historical sources has been published, and the misconceptions fostered over more than a century of anthropological study continue to be perpetuated. The Sioux case offers a good opportunity to demonstrate the value of an ethnohistorical approach, combining anthropological perspectives with historical methodology. This chapter is a step in that direction, focusing on the data from the earliest period of European contact with the Sioux.

Major Sources

The writings of missionaries, traders, and explorers from French Canada and Louisiana provide the earliest sources for reconstructing Sioux culture. Using these documents presents a multitude of problems stemming from the additions and deletions made by copyists and editors through the years. In her ethnohistorical studies, Mildred Wedel (1974, 1988) demonstrated the importance of using such documents in their most original forms, comparing variants, and not relying on translations.

The earliest information on the Sioux appears in the *Jesuit Relations,* where they are first mentioned in 1640 by Father Paul Le Jeune, who reported information learned from the coureur de bois, Jean Nicollet (JR 18:231). However, Pierre Esprit Radisson and Médard Chouart, Sieur des Groseilliers, were the first Europeans known to contact the Sioux. They visited them in 1659–60, and Radisson's account provides the first description of the Eastern Sioux. Radisson, who shifted his allegiance from France to England, wrote the account of his travels in idiosyncratic English that lacks the clarity that might be expected had he composed his narrative in French. His manuscripts were not published until 1885. A modernized edition appeared in 1961 but is not considered reliable (see Warkentin 1996).

The manuscript writings of Nicholas Perrot, a fur trader who lived among the Indians of the Midwest from 1665 until 1699, provide the second major source on the Sioux. In 1686 he built the first trading post in Sioux country, known as "the post of the Nadouessioux," at Lake Pepin. Some of Perrot's writings (the originals of which are now lost) were incorporated in Bacqueville la Potherie's *Histoire* (1722); his memoir on

Indian life was published in 1864 (Perrot 1968[1864]). An English translation of both was published by Blair (1911–12).

The expeditions from 1679–81 surrounding the enterprise of Robert Cavelier, sieur de la Salle, and that of Daniel Greysolon Dulhut, both representing the government of New France, provide the first specific information on the locations of Sioux tribal groups. Most of these documents were collected in Pierre Margry's *Découvertes et Établissements des Français* (1876–86). Margry was free with his editorial changes, however, and the documents he published cannot be relied on without systematically checking his original sources.

In the spring of 1680 La Salle sent a party of three men, led by Michel Accault and including Antoine Augelle and the Recollect priest Louis Hennepin, to explore the upper Mississippi. Hennepin published accounts of these explorations in two self-glorifying books that, although they must be evaluated carefully, nonetheless present valuable ethnographic detail. English translations are available of both the *Description of Louisiana* (1693), edited by Grace Lee Nute (Hennepin 1938) and *A New Discovery of a Vast Country in America* (1698), edited by Rueben Gold Thwaites (Hennepin 1903). They should be used in conjunction with the careful assessment of Hennepin's writings by Jean Delanglez (1941).

In the late 1680s Pierre-Charles Le Sueur continued to trade with the Sioux at Lake Pepin. In 1695 he built a new trading post at Isle Pelée (now Prairie Island), and in 1700 he constructed Fort L'Huillier, on the Blue Earth River, in order to mine what he mistakenly thought was copper ore. Le Sueur was the first to describe the Sioux who lived west of the Mississippi River. Some of his accounts are collected in Margry (1876–86, 6:55–92), and the ethnographic material on the Sioux, extracted from copies of his original manuscripts (Le Sueur 1700), is summarized in Wedel (1974). A map of North America drawn by Jean-Baptiste Louis Franquelin in 1697, with additions in 1699 and 1702 by Claude and Guillaume Delisle, records the names and locations of Sioux villages as reported by Le Sueur (Wedel 1974:167; DeMallie 2001, 2:722–724). The writings of Pénicault, edited by Richebourg Gaillard McWilliams (1953), provide a supplementary account by a member of Le Sueur's expedition to the Blue Earth River.

A problematical source closes this initial period of French contact: an anonymous, undated memoir on the Sioux, written after 1719. An English translation was published by Edward D. Neill (1890); the original manuscript, said to be in the Archives de la Marine, Paris, has not been located.

Divisions of the Sioux

The familiar three-part division of the Sioux into Santees, Yanktons, and Tetons, based on dialect and geographical location, was not noted in any of these early accounts. Nor was any mention made of a division into seven groups. Instead, the French distinguished only between the Sioux of the East and the Sioux of the West, reflecting their location in relation to the Mississippi River. The Sioux of the East told Le Sueur (1700), attempting to persuade him to build his post on the Mississippi River, that the region to the west, up the Minnesota River, belonged to the Sioux of the West and to the Iowas and Otoes; and that the Sioux of the East and the Sioux of the West did not hunt on one another's lands without permission. Judging from the village names given by Le Sueur, the Sioux of the East all belonged to what was later termed the Santee division, while the villages comprising the Sioux of the West included all three divisions: Santee, Yankton, and Teton (see DeMallie 2001, 2:723–724).

In 1695 LeSueur brought to Montreal a Sioux chief named Tioscaté, who laid at the governor's feet 22 arrows, each representing a Sioux village, and asked for an alliance and trade with the French. The Franquelin-Delisle map locates 22 Sioux villages, and lists a twenty-third without showing its location. Eleven of these villages are indicated as Sioux of the East, 12 as Sioux of the West. In his journal, Le Sueur (1700) named 20 Sioux villages, of which 7 were Sioux of the East and 13 were Sioux of the West. Among the western groups are four names given on the Franquelin-Delisle map as Sioux of the East, apparently reflecting a western movement of these four groups.

Because most of the early French contacts were with the Sioux of the East, they are more fully described in the literature. Le Sueur gave their population as about 300 dwellings (600–900 families). He estimated the Sioux of the West at over 1,000 dwellings (more than 2,000–3,000 families), although he admitted that he had seen only a small portion of them and that most of his information about them came from their eastern relatives (Wedel 1974:163–166).

The Sioux of the East

On the Franquelin-Deslisle map the villages of the Sioux of the East are shown around Mille Lacs and on the eastern tributaries of the Mississippi, from the Platte River to below the mouth of the Crow Wing River. Their yearly cycle was a nomadic one. Toward spring, the winter camps began to break up as the men set off in small groups to hunt, taking their families with them. The first important social event of the year was a spring gathering. Such was undoubtedly the nature of the multitribal gathering mentioned by Le Jeune in 1640:

> We have been told this year that an Algonquin, journeying [westward] beyond these peoples [the Central Algonquians], encountered nations extremely populous. "I saw them assembled," said he, "as if at a fair, buying and selling in numbers so great that they could not be counted"; it conveyed an idea of the cities of Europe. I do not know what there is in this. [JR 18:233]

This account suggests that large numbers of people gathered annually for social and religious purposes as well as for trade. They came from all over the Midwest and thus included groups hostile toward one another at other times of the year. The Feast of the Dead, held in the early spring of 1660, described by Radisson (1885:210–219) was such a gathering. It was clearly held during a period of suspended hostilities between warring groups. When Radisson and Groseilliers arrived they found a camp of over 1,500 people from "eighteen several nations," including both Siouans and Algonquians. Later, another 1,000 people arrived. Radisson exhorted the Sioux to cease their war with the Crees and convinced them, instead, "to lead them [the Crees] to ye dance of Union, which was to be celebrated at ye death's feast and banquet of kindred." Unfortunately, Radisson gave few details concerning the 14 days of festivities. He mentioned "playes, mirths, and battails for sport," games and physical contests, dances, and a feast made "to eat all up. To honnor the feast many men and women did burst [vomit]." Further, he added, "The renewing of alliances, the marriages according to their countrey coustoms, are made; also the visit of the boans of their deceased friends, ffor they keepe them and bestow them uppon one another." Doubtless the interband and intertribal alliances formed through these marriages were central to the feast and were solemnized by the "dance of Union" (Radisson 1885:219). According to Radisson, the celebration of the Feast of the Dead occurred every seven years.

Later that spring, the Sioux returned to their summer villages in the Mille Lacs area. Perrot provided a graphic description of their location:

> The country where the latter [Sioux] dwell is nothing but lakes and marshes, full of wild oats [rice]; these are separated from one another by narrow tongues of land, which extend from one lake to another not more than thirty of forty paces at most, and sometimes five or six, or a little more. These lakes and marshes form a tract more than fifty leagues square, and are traversed by no river save that of Louisiana [the Missis-

sippi]; its course lies through the midst of them, and part of their waters discharge into it. Other waters fall into the Ste. Croix River, which is situated northeast of them, at no great distance. Still other marshes and lakes are situated to the west of the St. Pierre River [the Minnesota], into which their waters flow. Consequently, the Sioux are inaccessible in so swampy a country, and cannot be destroyed by enemies who have not canoes, as they have, with which to pursue them. Moreover, in those quarters only five or six families live together as one body, forming a small village; and all the others do the same, removed from one another at certain distances, in order to be near enough to lend a helping hand at the first alarm. If any one of these little villages be attacked, the enemy can inflict very little damage upon it, for all its neighbors immediately assemble, and give prompt aid wherever it is needed. Their method of navigation in lakes of this kind is to push through the wild oats with their canoes, and, carrying these from lake to lake, compel the fleeing enemy to turn about; they, meanwhile, pass from one lake to another until they clear them all and reach firm ground. [Blair 1911–12, 1:166–167]

Le Sueur noted that the canoes used by the Sioux were small and covered with birch bark; they were more easily maneuvered in the marshes and small lakes than were the larger canoes of their enemies (Wedel 1974:170). The summer villages of the Eastern Sioux, described by Perrot, were apparently very small, although perhaps a number of these small communities, adjacent to one another, might have been considered a single village. Issac Jogues reported in 1641 that he was told (apparently by the Hurons) that the Sioux villages were "larger, and in better state of defense" than those of the Hurons (JR 23:225). Radisson, visiting in 1660, described one of these Sioux villages as follows:

> We being arrived among yt nation of the beefe [the Sioux] we wondered to find ourselves in a towne where weare great cabbans most covered with skins and other[s with] close matts. They tould us that there weare 7,000 men. This we believed . . . They have no wood, and make provision of mosse for their firing. This their place is environed with pearches wch are a good distance one from an other, that they gett in the valleys where the Buffe [is] use to repaire, upon wch they do live. [Raddison 1885:220]

Although the population estimate can only be an exaggeration or a scriptographic error, we may assume this was a large village. Radisson did not describe the "cabbans," a word used for any kind of Indian dwelling, but he had earlier described the Sioux lodges when they arrived at the

Feast of the Dead. We may be justified in assuming that if those of the village had been any different, he would have mentioned the fact. At the Feast of the Dead he described the Sioux lodges as round, constructed "wth long poles wth skins over them . . . the cottages weare all in good order; in each 10, twelve companies or families" (Radisson 1885:210). I interpret this to mean that the lodges were conical tipis, each housing ten to twelve persons, that is, a family group. Radisson indicated that the tent poles were not carried from place to place but were gathered anew at each camping site by parties of young men. The tent coverings were carried by women: "Then [came] ye women laden unto so many mules, their burdens made a greater shew than they themselves; but I suppose the weight was not equipolent to its bignesse. They were conducted to the appointed place, where the women unfolded their bundles, and flang their skins whereof their tents are made, so that they had howses [in] lesse than half an houre" (Raddison 1885:212–213).

Le Sueur also described the Sioux *cabanes* as made from "several buffalo hides, dressed and sewn together and they take them wherever they go[;] in each dwelling there are usually two or three men with their families" (Wedel 1974:165). On the occasion of a feast held at Le Sueur's fort on December 1, 1700, the Sioux joined together four individual lodges to make one large structure that accommodated the 100 men who participated. He noted the use of buffalo robes as carpets inside the lodges.

The anonymous French memoir (Neill 1890) also described the lodges of the Eastern Sioux, stating that they were made "in sugar loaf shape [conoidal], covered with various designs such as sun, calumets, arrows, etc." These lodges were 12 to 15 feet high and 60 to 80 feet in circumference; each housed 12 to 15 persons. The fire was built in the middle. There was only one door, covered by a bearskin.

Taken together, the evidence from this early period suggests that the Eastern Sioux were living in tipis, usually constructed with buffalo hide covers, that sound much like those of the nineteenth century. The most significant difference appears to be that since transporting them was difficult, each woman carried only a portion of a tent cover, and several women joined their pieces together to form multifamily dwellings.

The Sioux village that Hennepin visited in 1680 was apparently small, and was situated on an island. Unfortunately, he did not provide a good description of it. From the lack of agreement in the sources concerning the size of Eastern Sioux villages, we may conclude that village size probably varied considerably, as it did during the nineteenth century.

When the Sioux returned to their village sites in the spring, they would open cache pits in which surplus wild rice from the last harvest was stored. Le Sueur wrote that it provided them with nourishment throughout the year (Wedel 1974:170).

According to Le Sueur (Wedel 1974:170) and the anonymous French memoir (Neil 1890:235), the Sioux of the East did not cultivate the ground, and Hennepin made no mention of horticulture. To the contrary, Radisson (1995:220) wrote: "They sow corns, but their harvest is small. The soyle is good, but the cold hinders it, and ye grains [are] very small." Evidence from the *Jesuit Relations* is likewise conflicting. In 1642, mention is made that the Sioux "harvest Indian corn," but in 1670–72 the opposite is stated, that the Sioux "know not what it is to till the soil for the purpose of sowing seed" (JR 23:225, 55:169). On the basis of this limited and conflicting information, it seems likely that only some of the Eastern Sioux practiced horticulture, and only on a limited scale. Tobacco, grown for ritual purposes, may have been the most important crop.

During the summer, when the buffalo congregated in large herds, the Sioux also gathered together for communal hunts. These hunts were extremely important because they provided the meat to be dried for winter use, as well as the hides for their lodge coverings. The hunts were directed by chiefs who cooperated to ensure that the various hunting parties would not interfere with one another. When scouts returned after locating a herd, the hunters and their families traveled as quickly as possible by canoe to get near the buffalo, then marched overland on foot, leaving some old men behind to guard the canoes and watch for enemies. One such hunting party seen by Hennepin in July 1681 numbered 250 men (80 families). He reported that sometimes 100 to 120 buffalo were killed in a single hunt. The hunters circled the herd and kept the animals milling while they killed as many as possible with arrows. Apparently, fire was sometimes used to encircle the herd. After the kill the buffalo were skinned and butchered, the meat preserved by drying in the sun, the hides cared for, and everything cached. Then the group was ready to search for another herd (Hennepin 1903, 1:271–272, 279, 290).

Because of the large size of the buffalo herds during the summer, and the long distances between them, it would disastrous if careless hunting by a single individual or a small group frightened the herd away before the communal hunt. The hunts were therefore controlled by the chiefs for the common good, and anyone hunting before the communal hunt took place was liable for punishment. These sanctions were strictly enforced. Hennepin and his party were invited to join a small group of Sioux who had violated the rules of the hunt. He described the event as follows:

As we were falling down the River *Meschasipi* [Mississippi] . . . we found some of the Savages of our Band, in the Islands of the River, where they had set up their Cabins, and were well provided with Bulls Flesh. They offer'd us very freely of what they had. But about two Hours after our landing, we thought we should have been all murder'd: Fifteen or sixteen Savages came into the middle of the Place where we were, with their great Clubs in their Hands. The first thing that they did was to over-set the Cabin of those that had invited us. Then they took away all their Victuals, and what Bears-Oil they could find in their Bladders, or elsewhere, with which they rubb'd themselves all over from Head to Foot.

We took them at first for Enemies . . . but it appear'd they were some of those that we had left above at the Fall of St. *Anthony.* One of them, who call'd himself my Uncle, told me, that those who had given us Victuals, had done basely to go and forestal the others in the Chase; and that according to the Laws and Customs of their Country, 'twas lawful for them to plunder them, since they had been the cause that the Bulls were all run away, before the Nation could get together, which was a great Injury to the Publick; For when they are all met, they make a great Slaughter amongst the Bulls; for they surround them so on every side, that 'tis impossible for them to escape. [Hennepin 1903, 1:279–280]

Evidently the clubs carried by these men were symbols of their office as police appointed by the chiefs to supervise the hunt.

The Eastern Sioux seem to have done much of their traveling during this period by canoe. Both birch-bark and dugout canoes were made; the former were light and easier to handle, while the latter were capable of carrying large loads. Hennepin (1903, 1:234) reported that the Sioux could sometimes row 30 leagues (75 miles) in a single day. The Sioux had domesticated dogs, according to Radisson (1885:206), but no mention is made during this period of the use of dogs as beasts of burden. In the early nineteenth century the Mdewakantonwans did not use dog travois, although their use is reported among other Eastern Sioux groups (Pond 1908:359–361).

After the communal hunts, the Eastern Sioux returned to their village sites in the lake country for the harvest season. Wild rice stalks were tied in bundles before ripening for protection against waterfowl; when ripe, the bundles were untied, and the grain was collected by being beaten with clubs into birch-bark canoes. The wild rice was then dried, threshed, and winnowed, and part of it was stored in underground caches for later use (Radisson 1885:215; Hennepin 1903, 1:224). Most of the corn was doubtless eaten as soon as it ripened. Various roots, fruits, and berries were gathered and eaten fresh or preserved by drying (Hennepin 1903:256; Bacqueville de la Potherie in Blair 1911–12, 2:73; LeSueur in Wedel 1974:170).

As winter approached, the Eastern Sioux moved their camps northward into forested areas where they trapped beaver, hunted deer, and fished (Radisson 1885:220; Hennepin 1903:230, 256).

The Sioux of the West

The Sioux of the West were first mentioned by Hennepin in 1680. From the Eastern Sioux he learned "that about twenty or thirty Leagues above the Fall of *St. Anthony*, there is another Fall; near which a Nation of Savages inhabit at certain Seasons of the Year. They call those Nations *Tintonha*, that is, *The Inhabitants of the Meadows*" (Hennepin 1903, 1:223). At the eastern end of Lake Erie, Hennepin met an Iroquois war party returning from an expedition against the Western Sioux, whom they reported lived 400 leagues from there (Hennepin 1903, 1:107). During his stay with the Eastern Sioux, Hennepin met some of the *Tintonha*. One day four men arrived from "a people in alliance with them [the Sioux of the East], with whom they had danced the calumet" (Hennepin 1903, 1:266–268). He reported that these men had marched four moons in order to reach the Eastern Sioux—surely an exaggeration—and he calculated, therefore, that their country was 400 to 500 leagues to the west (1,000 to 1,250 miles). They told him that in the western country there were few forests, and that sometimes they made fires out of dry buffalo dung over which they cooked their food in earthern pots, since they had no metal ones. "Tinton," translated as "nation of the prairies," was also recorded by Le Sueur as one of the groups comprising the Sioux of the West. However, in the nineteenth century "Prairie Village" was the name of a prominent Mdewakantonwan band among the Santees (DeMallie 2001, 2:723, 736).

Le Sueur provided more detail on the Sioux of the West. He wrote that they lived "only by the hunt" and roamed on the prairies and plains between the upper Mississippi and the Missouri, where canoes were not needed. They practiced no horticulture and did not gather wild rice. They had no fixed villages. All their travel was by foot. They carried their buffalo-skin lodges with them—probably using dog travois, although he does not mention them. Apparently their lodges were identical to those of the Sioux of the East, each housing two to three men and their families (Wedel 1974:165–166).

Sioux Social Organization

The picture of Sioux social organization that emerges from the literature of this period is of a large number of small village groups held together by common language and customs. An account in the *Jesuit Relations* for 1660 places the number of Sioux villages at 40 (JR 46:69); Le Sueur gives between 20 and 23 (Wedel 1974:163); and the anonymous memoir gives 20 to 26 (Neill 1890). Le Sueur noted that the Eastern Sioux were the "masters of all the other Sioux and the Ioways and Otos because they are the first with whom we traded and to whom we gave arms so that they are rather well armed" (Wedel 1974:166).

Sioux villages appear to have been independent social groups. The small communities described by Perrot (Blair 1911–12, 1:166), consisting of only five or six families, may be taken as a lower limit. Each village may have been a separate band, or, more likely, several villages may have comprised a single band. Their dispersion probably reflected the necessity of delegating to each extended family a large enough area of the wild rice marshes to make the harvest profitable. At other times of the year, particularly during the summer buffalo hunts, several villages came together. The Yanktons who wintered with Le Sueur at his fort on the Blue Earth River in 1700–1701 numbered 150 lodges, the Wahpekutes 60 lodges. By May 1701 Le Sueur noted that 200 lodges were camped near the fort (Wedel 1974:170). Similarly, as noted earlier, Hennepin observed a buffalo-hunting party numbering 80 families (250 men).

The total Sioux population is given as 7,000 men by Radisson (1885: 220); 8,000–9,000 men (5,000 families) by Hennepin (1903, 1:226); and 4,000 families by Le Sueur (Wedel 1974:163). These figures doubtless reflect better information over time, not decreasing population.

There are no indications of any type of unilineal organization. The anonymous memoir states that boys were named after elders of the father's family, while girls were named after the mother's family (Neill 1890:237). Each lodge seems to have housed an extended family comprising 12 to 15 persons (Neill 1890:236), representing two or three men with their families (Wedel 1974:165)

Radisson's account of the Feast of the Dead (1885:210–219), describing the arrival of the Sioux men, suggests distinct social statuses for youths, adults, and elders. Some of the young men are represented as scouts wearing body paint that was probably distinctive to their office. Some of the men wore crow skins at their belts, clearly the prototype of the "crow belt" bustles worn in the nineteenth century by officers in certain men's societies.

Two types of chiefs were described. Council chiefs were the village leaders, while war chiefs were both leaders in war as well as conjurors, seers who were called "those who seek after truth in the dark," according to the anonymous memoir (Neill 1890:230, 238). (It is likely, judging from Jonathan Carver's account in the 1760s, that these conjurors were what he called the "chief of the warriours," who directed war parties but did not participate in them [Parker 1976:99].) The offices of both council chief and war chief, according to the anonymous memoir, were said to be hereditary, passing to the deceased chief's brother's son (presumably in the case where a chief had no son of his own). The same writer says that the chief's name was hereditary. The anonymous author also describes totemic "signs" that he seems to have understood as being analogous to Huron and Iroquois clan names and were said to designate the various Sioux villages. He listed five of them. For example, the "sign" of the "River Sious" was said to be "a bear wounded in the neck" (Neill 1890:235). If these signs have any basis in ethnographic reality, they may have represented hereditary personal names of the council chiefs of the various villages.

The families of chiefs apparently had higher status than others. Sometimes the daughter of a chief would retain her virginity long beyond the usual age of marriage. This, according to the anonymous memoir, was a mark of her status (Neill 1890:229). Hennepin (1903, 1:214) reported that hunters took the best part of the game that they killed and presented it to the chief as an offering to the sun. Chiefs, however, did not exercise any real authority. For example, when Hennepin asked a chief to bring his band and travel with him to meet Dulhut, the chief "heard my Proposal, and was willing to embrace it; but those of his Band wou'd not let him" (Hennepin 1903, 1:271–272). This was at the beginning of July, and the people were anxious to be off on a buffalo hunt.

In addition to the war conjuror mentioned earlier, the anonymous author mentioned two other types of medicine men. "Those who strive against death" were said to be old men who were conjurors (apparently in matters not involving war) and curers, doubtlessly religious curers. "Those who dress wounds" seem to have been more strictly herbalists and healers (Neill 1890:230).

An additional social category was the berdache, described by Hennepin as follows (1903, 2:653):

> I don't know by what Superstition some of the Illinois and *Nadouessians* [Sioux] wear Womens Apparel. When they have taken the same, which they do in their Youth, they never leave it off; and certainly there must

be some Mystery in this Matter, for they never Marry, and work in the Cabins with Women, which other men think below them to do. They may go however to their Wars, but they must use only a Club, and not Bows and Arrows, which are fit, as they say, for Men alone. They assist at all the Superstitions of their *Juglers*, and their solemn Dances in honour of the *Calumet*, in which they may sing, but it is not lawful for them to dance. They are call'd to their Councils, and nothing is determin'd without their Advice; for, because of their extraordinary way of Living, they are look'd upon as *Manitous*, or at least for great and incomparable Genius's.

Kinship, Marriage, and the Life Cycle

The sources from this period provide few details concerning the Sioux kinship system. The anonymous memoir notes that the father and father's brother were classed together, as were the mother and mother's sister. Father's sister and mother's brother were called by aunt and uncle terms (Neill 1890:229). This classification agrees with the bilateral kinship system as recorded among the Sioux during the nineteenth century, but, of course, it does not differentiate it from a unilineal system.

Radisson (1885:220), Le Sueur (Wedel 1974:165), and the anonymous memoir (Neill 1890:229) all report that the Sioux commonly practiced polygyny. According to Le Sueur, a Sioux man was not considered worthy of marriage until he had killed an enemy. The anonymous memoir records that marriage was preceded by a period of courtship lasting perhaps three months. During this time the man visited the girl nightly, making presents to her parents. Sexual relations were not permitted during courtship. If the union was approved, one night the man would arrive at the girl's lodge, fire his gun at the doorway, then hand it to one of her near relatives (evidently as gift). Then he led his bride away (Neill 1890:229). Radisson (1885:220) reported that women were respected according to the number of children they had borne. He stated that "the maidens have all manner of freedome, but are forced to marry when they come to the age."

According to the anonymous memoir, a man might offer the sexual services of his wife to another man, in proof of his friendship. A refusal of this offer was taken as an insult. Sometimes a marriage would not last long, and the man would send his wife back to her parents' lodge. In the case of adultery, the husband might cut off his wife's nose, ears, or hair. Sometimes the wronged husband would give a feast "in honor of the lover. They do this so as to kill him" (Neill 1890:229). Radisson

(1885:220) also mentions cutting off the nose, presumably of the woman, or "crown of the head" of the man as punishment for adultery.

In the case of murder, the anonymous memoir states that the victim's nearest relatives were obliged to avenge the death. Sometimes this resulted in a brawl during which several men might be killed. Such a quarrel was not allowed to develop into a blood feud, however, for the elders of the two families would agree to stop it. The last murderer would undergo a ritual of forgiveness, and doubtless of adoption into the family of his victim (Neill 1890:234).

The dead were either placed on scaffolds or buried in the ground; the anonymous memoir does not indicate the reason for the differentiation. If a person died while on a journey, the body was burned and the ashes preserved. The dead were greatly respected and probably feared. After a man's death a "Crow Feast" was held at which the participants emulated the call of that bird as well as its habits, eating without using their hands. The purpose was to send the soul of the deceased to the country of souls (Neill 1890:233). Both Radisson (1885:219) and Hennepin (1903, 1:241, 255) recorded that the bones of the dead were sometimes preserved, honored, and carried on war expeditions. According to Le Sueur, each individual was believed to possess three souls. After death the good soul went to the warm country, the bad soul to the cold country, while the third remained with the body (Wedel 1974:165). The anonymous memoir reports that the souls of the dead go to the country of souls, "where is game in profusion, and where they dance day and night, and taste all manner of delights without trouble or toil" (Neil 1890:233).

Peace Making and Adoption

Adoption ceremonies involving the red pipestone calumet or feathered pipe stems played an important part in intertribal relations during this period. According to Perrot (Blair 1911–12, 1:184–186), when the pipe was "sung" for a person of another tribe, "they render him who has had that honor a son of the tribe, and naturalize him as such." The calumet ceremony was a sacred ritual that compelled the suspension of hostilities between the groups involved, since the individual adopted served as a representative of his tribe. Regarding the calumet itself, Perrot wrote, "The savages believe that the sun gave it to the Panys [Pawnees], and that since then it has been communicated from village to village as far as the Outaouas [Ottawas]." The calumet was thus a symbol of peace; it was presented to travelers to give them safe passage among the various Midwestern tribes. Hennepin (1903, 1:228, 236–237) noted that a calumet was also symbolic of war; men who wished to fight the enemy danced the calumet of war.

In order for the Sioux to be at peace and friendship with any individual or group, the outsiders had to be symbolically incorporated into the group. For this reason, all of the early explorers had the calumet danced for them, and pipes were presented to them as symbols of the relationship so established. Many accounts note that visitors were ritually fed, like children, to symbolize their adoptive status.

There was apparently another, perhaps more specifically personal, adoption ritual that incorporated an individual into the Sioux people. According to Hennepin (1903, 2:476–477), it was referred to as "bring[ing] them forth." Antoine Augelle (called Picard du Gay), one of Hennepin's companions, was so adopted by the Sioux. They placed a gourd rattle in his hand and made him sing, and attached feathers to his hair. Persons adopted in this manner, Hennepin wrote, were "cherished as if they were natural relatives" and were called by kin terms. Captives were adopted to take the place of deceased relatives. Thus Hennepin and his two companions were adopted by two of the chiefs in place of sons who had been killed in battle. Hennepin reports that he was called "brother" by the chief of one village, "uncle" by another man, and so on. Once adopted, he was fitted into the entire kinship network.

Social Integration

From these seventeenth- and early-eighteenth-century sources it is clear that the basic mechanism for social integration was voluntary cooperation, undoubtedly based on kin relationships, with their associated obligations and behavioral expectations. No individuals in society commanded real authority, not even chiefs, and no punishments were effected at a tribal level with the single exception of the policing that accompanied the all-important summer buffalo hunts. Village life was directed by council chiefs, while warfare was in the hands of separate war leaders and seems to have been embedded in a religious context. Village councils were undoubtedly informal groups of elders who directed the yearly cycle through consensus. Crimes, even murder, were handled by the families directly concerned, not at the village or tribal level. Bands were small and autonomous, traveling over large areas in the course of their regularly established annual rounds. The bands seem not to have been territorial units, except inasmuch as the permanent village sites claimed adjacent wild rice marshes or possibly horticultural areas for the exclusive use of the inhabitants of the village. There is no evidence that these bands were unilineal groups; rather, they were organized bilaterally. There is the suggestion of patrilocal residence and patrilineal succession of chiefs. Household groups were extended families. There is no evidence of any overarching tribal organization. The largest gatherings were the spring trading fairs and the summer buffalo hunts. On all levels, the cooperation between individuals and groups that kept society together was voluntary and not rigidly structured.

Conclusions

The sources at the time of contact are too sketchy to provide a detailed reconstruction of Sioux society and culture. Nor do they give us a picture of the Sioux lifestyle before it was influenced by Europeans. By 1660 they were already involved in the fur trade. They told Radisson (1885:213) that their doors were always open to him because it was the European traders who "kept them alive" by their merchandise. Guns were already essential to maintaining the balance of power among the tribes, and the Sioux were quickly coming to depend on manufactured items—particularly metal goods—for many everyday needs.

Nonetheless, the early sources do provide sufficient documentary evidence to review and correct the four misconceptions with which this discussion began:

1. It is inaccurate to characterize the Sioux at the time of contact as typical Woodland people with an economy based on hunting, wild rice gathering, and corn horticulture (e.g., Howard 1980[1966]:2; see discussion in Birk and Johnson 1992:212–213, 218). There is no evidence that the Sioux groups practiced horticulture to any extent, and the limits of distribution of wild rice precluded many of the Western Sioux groups from gathering it. The food staple for the Sioux was buffalo meat, and even the Sioux of the East were so dependent upon it that in 1660 Radisson (1885:207), the first European to describe them, called them "the Nation of the beefe." Radisson (1885:220) noted that the Sioux used forest resources during the winter for trapping and hunting, and all sources noted their use of the lakes in the fall for wild rice gathering, but the focus of subsistence was the hunting of buffalo on the prairies.

2. There is no historical evidence to give any support for the existence of clans among the Sioux at the time of contact (a point convincingly made in Stipe 1971 and accepted by Howard 1980:iii–iv). Howard (1979:138–139) suggested that the animal taboo names used to des-

ignate some Sioux bands, which are similar to or identical with clan names among such tribes as the Omahas and Poncas, suggest that Sioux band organization was in a structural sense equivalent to that of the unilineal clans among other tribes. Though the argument itself is not a strong one, it might be noted that none of the 23 village names recorded by Le Sueur at the end of the seventeenth century are animal taboo names. It is therefore more plausible to suggest that animal taboo names were a later introduction to the Sioux, probably directly from such groups as the Omahas and Poncas.

3. There is no historical evidence to substantiate the existence of the Seven Council Fires as a political alliance. Nor is there any evidence to suggest that the number seven had any social significance in terms of group organization. The often-repeated assertion (e.g., Powers 1977:16) that the Sioux at the time of contact identified themselves as the Seven Fireplaces, an alliance—albeit temporary, with shifting leadership—of seven named groups, lacks any foundation in the documentary record. The attempt to provide scientific support for the existence of the Seven Council Fires by pushing the alliance back to a time before European contact and linking it with archeological remains (e.g., Gibbon 2003:43) is mere speculation, following in the tradition established by Keating (1959[1825]:442) that assumes American Indian political organization degenerated after contact with Euro-Americans. Nor does it explain why there is no mention of the Seven Council Fires in seventeenth- and early eighteenth-century accounts. All historical evidence suggests that the Seven Council Fires was a metaphorical expression of the relatedness of the many scattered Sioux groups that developed during the late eighteenth or early nineteenth centuries. The Seven Council Fires has cultural validity as a symbol of ethnic identity, but not historical validity as an actual political alliance.

4. Though the record is sparse, there is no indication that at the time of contact the culture or society of the Eastern Sioux was substantially different from that of the Western Sioux. Rather than argue that the Santees retained many original Woodland traits and were the most conservative of all the Sioux (e.g., Howard 1960:250), it would be more plausible to argue that the Woodland characteristics of Santee culture, particularly of the Mdewakantonwans, represent a subsequent development during the late eighteenth and early nineteenth centuries. This obviates the need to portray the Santees as more culturally conservative than the other Sioux groups, and also under-

scores the importance of differentiating among the Mdewakantonwans, Wahpetonwans, Sissetonwans, and Wahpekutes, rather than
obscuring the differences among them by using the general designation "Santee."

Each of these misconceptions has considerable tenacity in the thinking and writing of anthropologists and historians, yet each is clarified
by even cursory examination of the documentary sources. This example
from the Sioux exemplifies the importance of reading original sources
critically to provide the basis for an ethnohistorical perspective that combines the methods of anthropology and history to reach more insightful
understandings of the American Indian past.

Acknowledgments

This article originated in the introductory section of my PhD dissertation
(DeMallie 1971), which was written under the supervision of Raymond
D. Fogelson, whose suggestions for structuring the material are reflected
here. I am grateful to him for three decades of intellectual support and
encouragement and for setting an exemplary standard in his own work for
his students to emulate. For assistance with this chapter, special thanks are
due to Douglas R. Parks, Francis Flavin, and Carolyn R. Anderson. The
ethnohistorical material discussed here is presented in a different context
in DeMallie (2001).

References

Bacqueville de la Potherie, Claude C. Le Roy
  1722 Histoire de l'Amérique septentrionale. 4 vols. Paris: J. L. Nion and F. Didot.
Birk, Douglas A., and Elden Johnson
  1992 The Mdewakanton Dakota and Initial French Contact. In Calumet and Fleur-de-
    Lys: Archaeology of Indian and French Contact in the Midcontinent. John A. Walthall
    and Thomas E. Emerson, eds. Pp. 203–240. Washington DC: Smithsonian Institution.
Blair, Emma H., ed.
  1911–1912 The Indian Tribes of the Upper Mississippi Valley and Region of the Great
    Lakes, as Described by Nicolas Perrot, French Commandant in the Northwest; Bac-
    queville de la Potherie, French Royal Commissioner to Canada; Morrell Marston,
    American Army Officer; and Thomas Forsyth, United States Agent at Fort Armstrong.
    2 vols. Cleveland: Arthur H. Clark.
Delanglez, Jean
  1941 Hennepin's Description of Louisiana: A Critical Essay. Chicago: Institute of Jesuit
    Study.
DeMallie, Raymond J.
  1971 Teton Dakota Kinship and Social Organization. Unpublished PhD dissertation, De-
    partment of Anthropology, University of Chicago.
  2001 Sioux until 1850. In Vol. 13: Plains. Raymond J. DeMallie, ed. Pt. 2, pp. 718–760.

Handbook of North American Indians. William C. Sturtevant, gen. ed. Washington DC: Smithsonian Institution.

Dorsey, James Owen

1891 The Social Organization of the Siouan Tribes. Journal of American Folk-Lore 4(14): 257–266, 4(15):331–342.

Gibbon, Guy

2003 The Sioux: The Dakota and Lakota Nations. Malden MA: Blackwell.

Hassrick, Royal B.

1964 The Sioux: Life and Customs of a Warrior Society. Norman: University of Oklahoma Press.

Hennepin, Father Louis

1903 A New Discovery of a Vast Country in America, Reprinted from the Second London Issues of 1698. Reuben Gold Thwaites, ed. 2 vols. Chicago: A. C. McClurg.

1938 Father Louis Hennepin's Description of Louisiana; Newly Discovered to the Southwest of New France by Order of the King. Marion E. Cross, trans. Minneapolis: Minnesota Society of the Colonial Dames of America, University of Minnesota Press.

Hickerson, Harold

1970 The Chippewa and Their Neighbors: A Study in Ethnohistory. New York: Holt, Rinehart and Winston.

Holder, Preston

1970 The Hoe and the Horse on the Plains: A Study of Cultural Development among North American Indians. Lincoln: University of Nebraska Press.

Howard, James H.

1960 The Cultural Position of the Dakota: A Reassessment. In Essays in the Science of Culture in Honor of Leslie A. White. Gertrude E. Dole and Robert L. Carneiro, eds. Pp. 249–268. New York: Thomas Y. Crowell.

1979 Some Further Thoughts on Eastern Dakota "Clans." Ethnohistory 26(2):133–140.

1980[1966] The Dakota or Sioux Indians: A Study in Human Ecology. Anthropological Papers 2, Dakota Museum, University of South Dakota, Vermillion. Reprints in Anthropology 20. Lincoln NE: J & L Reprint Co.

Jesuit Relations [JR]

1896–1901 The Jesuit Relations and Allied Documents: Travel and Explorations of the Jesuit Missionaries in New France, 1610–1791; the Original French, Latin, and Italian Texts, with English Translations and Notes. Reuben Gold Thwaites, ed. 73 vols. Cleveland: Burrows Brothers.

Keating, William H.

1959[1825] Narrative of an Expedition to the Source of St. Peter's River, Lake Winnepeek, Lake of the Woods, &c. Performed in the Year 1823, by Order of the Hon. J. C. Calhoun, Secretary of War, Under the Command of Stephen H. Long, U.S.T.E. 2 vols. London. Minneapolis MN: Ross & Haines.

Le Sueur, Pierre-Charles

1700 [Journal en forme de lettre de M. Le Sueur sur le Mississipi et l'intérieur des terres en 1700.] Paris, Archives Nationales, Archives de la Marine, 4JJ14, no. 4.

Margry, Pierre, ed.

1876–86 Découvertes et établissements des Français dans l'ouest et dans le sud de l'Amérique septenrionale, 1614–1754. Mémoires et documents originaux. 6 vols. Paris: D. Jouaust.

McWilliams, Richebourg Gaillard, trans. and ed.

1953 Fleur de Lys and Calumet: Being the Pénicault Narrative of French Adventure in Louisiana. Baton Rouge: Louisiana State University Press.

Morgan, Lewis Henry

    1871 Systems of Consanguinity and Affinity of the Human Family. Smithsonian Contributions to Knowledge 17. Washington DC: Smithsonian Institution.

    1963[1877] Ancient Society: Or, Researches in the Lines of Human Progress from Savagery through Barbarism to Civilization. New York: Henry Holt. Cleveland: World Publishing.

Neill, Edward D.

    1890 Memoir of the Sioux. Macalester College Contributions 1:223–240.

Parker, John, ed.

    1976 The Journals of Jonathan Carver and Related Documents 1766–1770. [St. Paul]: Minnesota Historical Society Press.

Perrot, Nicolas

    1968[1864] Mémoire sur les moeurs, coustumes et religion des sauvages de l'Amérique septentrionale. With an introduction by R. P. J. Tailhan. Leipzig and Paris: A. Franck. Reprint, New York: Johnson Reprint Corporation.

Pond, Samuel W.

    1908 The Dakotas or Sioux in Minnesota as They Were in 1834. Minnesota Historical Society Collections 12:319–501.

Powers, William K.

    1977 Oglala Religion. Lincoln: University of Nebraska Press.

Radisson, Peter Esprit

    1885 Voyages of Peter Esprit Radisson, Being an Account of His Travels and Experiences among the North American Indians, from 1652 to 1684. Gideon D. Scull, ed. Boston: Prince Society.

    1961 The Explorations of Pierre Esprit Radisson from the Original Manuscript in the Bodleian Library and the British Museum. Arthur T. Adams, ed.; modernized by Loren Kallsen. Minneapolis MN: Ross & Haines.

Ramsey, Alexander

    1849 [Annual report, Ex-officio Superintendent of Indian Affairs, Minnesota Superintendency, Oct. 13–17.] In Annual Report of the Commissioner of Indian Affairs. 31st Cong., 1st sess., serial 550. Pp. 1004–1036. Washington DC: Government Printing Office.

Riggs, Stephen Return

    1851 Grammar and Dictionary of the Dakota Language. Smithsonian Contributions to Knowledge, vol. 4. Washington DC: Smithsonian Institution.

Stipe, Claude E.

    1971 Eastern Dakota Clans: The Solution of a Problem. American Anthropologist 73(5): 1031–1035.

Warkentin, Germaine

    1996 Discovering Radisson: A Renaissance Adventurer between Two Worlds. In Reading Beyond Words: Contexts for Native History. Jennifer S. H. Brown and Elizabeth Vibert, eds. Orchard Park NY: Broadview Press.

Wedel, Mildred Mott

    1974 Le Sueur and the Dakota Sioux. In Aspects of Great Lakes Anthropology: Papers in Honor of Lloyd A. Wilford. Elden Johnson, ed. Pp. 157–171. St. Paul: Minnesota Historical Society.

    1988 The Wichita Indians 1541–1750: Ethnohistorical Essays. Reprints in Anthropology 38. Lincoln NE: J & L Reprint Co.

11. *Proto-Ethnologists in North America*

In 1974 Raymond Fogelson published an article entitled "On the Varieties of Indian History: Sequoyah and Traveller Bird." In it Fogelson explores, against an image of infinite regress, three types of American Indian history: (1) "the historical study of non-Western peoples, sometimes also including distinctive ethnic or religious groups within Western society; for such studies a native perspective may be deemed desirable but is not considered essential;" (2) "ethnohistory written from a native point of view;" and (3) "Indian writing of Indian history." His analysis of the diversity of these interpretations and the value of each to intellectual discourse demonstrates the reflectivity, as well as reflexivity, that characterizes his work.

Here I will explore some examples of what Fogelson has elsewhere referred to as a "proto-ethnologist": an individual who predates professional anthropologists yet was a "keen observer of the particular" and possessed the "capacity to generalize . . . observations for purposes of comparison and reconstruction" (1979: 254). I will investigate the nature of some writings by people who interacted with cultural others in eastern North America before the mid-nineteenth century in ways that were far from stereotypical. This investigation will enable me to demonstrate that these writings can help us to reflect not only on these proto-ethnologist' roles in cross-cultural interaction or their place in the development of ethnographic thought but also on the nature of ethnography, and in doing so can provide a mirror for ethnologists today. This is particularly appropriate as anthropologists enter the twenty-first century increasingly evaluating and critiquing ethnography, the hallmark of anthropology. The writings of proto-ethnologists may be, and in many cases have been, employed in each of the three Fogelsonian types of American Indian history. This chapter suggests that analyses of the data they have left would benefit from more of the reflexivity and reflectivity so characteristic of Raymond Fogelson's work.[1]

While doing research at the British Library in London in the spring of 1977, I was struck by a letter written by an unidentified person sometime during the mid-eighteenth century to a Mr. Lellycrow or Pellycrow (the handwriting is unclear), a South Carolina trader residing at the village of Coosa. The letter gives instructions that include questions to be asked of Indians with whom he or she trades.[2] I shall quote at length from the section on government to give a sense of the nature of the inquiries:

> When any Person is injur'd by his Neighbour, or has any Dispute or Controversy with him, how are their differences determined & adjusted, does Might overcome Right, and must the weakest sit down with the wrong & is every one Judge for himself, & also Executioner of what he thinks right, or do they apply to any other Person or Power for Redress of Wrongs. . . . In whom is the Supreme Power of making, explaining & executing their Laws lodged—in One, in a few, or in Many, or partly in all of these. What is the Title of the Person that has the chief Power in their Language, & what is the true Meaning of that Word in English, is it head or chief or First or Eldest, or Ruler, Governor, Judge or General, Is it annex'd to this or that particular Family, & do they inherit it from Father or Mother, or is it given by the consent & Election of the People, to the most prudent & Brave . . . and what Ceremonies are used at the making or crowning a King or Headman, and Whither he has any particular Badge of Authority. Is the Obedience of the Rest blind & absolute Obedience to these headmen, or is their Duty bounded & Limited by Laws & Customs . . . Who has the Power of declaring War or making Peace. Do they punish such as resist or disobey lawfull Authority And what Authority have Parents over their Children. [Anonymous n.d.]

This passage is full of interesting questions. The writer expresses an awareness of the possibility of matrilineal as well as patrilineal descent. The association of the authority of parents over their children with governmental authority is noteworthy. It suggests a much more holistic approach to cultural phenomenon than was characteristic of that time period or of thinkers for many generations to come.

It is clear that the author of this letter wished to gather information about Indians with whom South Carolina traders were dealing. There is nothing particularly remarkable about this. What should be noted, however, is the systematization of the questioning and the writer's openness to different cultural forms, to different meanings.[3] Under the section of the manuscript on history, instructions are given to inquire into

> What Notion they have of the World, whither it for ever Existed as we now see it, or if it had a Beginning. Whither they have any Vestige among them of the Account of the Deluge, or whither they have ever heard of Men's making a very high Tower; What Notion they have of so many Indians speaking so many different Languages. Whither they look upon all Men white, red & Black as the same Original & to have Sprung from the same man, or that they are perfectly different, & what accounts they give of the Creation or beginning of each-where their Nation came from, the Sun rising, or Sun Setting, the South & North or whether they came out of the Earth, where they at present Live. [Anonymous n.d.][4]

The author also advises how to take field notes. In one section of the letter it is suggested that the trader, when delivering presents from the governor of South Carolina to the Choctaws, "Should make short Notes by way of Memorandum without any Connection or studying to make it read well; You will find when you have time to think of these things more fully afterwards, that such Notes or Jottings will wonderfully help your Memory." In suggesting subjects of inquiry, the writer instructs: "As to all of these in their Order, You may have a Separate Page or Sheet for each of them, and when you hear any Thing upon any of these Subjects, Set it down under its proper head, & leave it 'till you gather Something else" [Anonymous n.d.]. In this letter, therefore, the writer not only presents the questions of concern but also provides insight into how the desired information should be gathered. The 20-page document is a testament to a searching mind.

This manuscript from the mid-eighteenth century does not stand alone as an example of individuals attempting to understand others different from themselves. Data about American Indians left by missionaries such as the Jesuit Joseph François Lafitau and John Heckewelder (a Moravian), traders like James Adair, naturalists like John Bartram, and colonial administrators such as Sir William Johnson have long been used in analyses of American Indian history. They have also come to the attention of scholars doing intellectual history (Adair 1775; Bardram 1995; Lafitau 1974–77[1724]; Heckewelder 1819, 1820, 1876; Heckewelder, Manuscripts; Sullivan 1921–65). A. Irving Hallowell's "The Beginning of Anthropology in America" describes such individuals as being on the threshold of developing anthropological thought in America. That thought, he noted, had been "stimulated by the rise of rationalism, the development of scientific aims and methods in the study of natural phenomena and, in particular, by rapidly increasing information about the aborigines of remote parts of the world during the Age of Discovery" (1976:36). I will suggest here that their value to modern anthropologists resides not in the extent to which they embraced "rationalism" or "scientific aims and methods" but rather in their inquisitiveness, their openness in cross-cultural interaction, and in most cases, their participation in that interaction.

participant observer

Anthropologist William N. Fenton characterized Joseph-François Lafitau as an early "precursor" of anthropological thought (1969a; see also Hodgen 1971[1964]:346–349, 446, 490–491). Charles Hudson identified James Adair as a nascent anthropologist (1977); and Raymond Fogelson called John Norton—a late eighteenth- and early nineteenth-century gentlemen born in Scotland who claimed to have been of Cherokee descent and who spent a great deal of his adulthood among American Indians—a "proto-ethnologist" (1979:254). In "North American Religions: History of Study," Fogelson, while pointing out the stereotypical nature of early data from North America pertaining to American Indian religions, notes:

> Lack of sustained observation tended to diminish the reliability of . . . reports, but this deficiency was overcome by exceptional traders and administrators who resided for long periods in Indian communities, learned Indian languages, and often married Indian women. (1987:546).

The British ethnologist James Cowles Pritchard relied, in his own writings, on data from the missionary to the Delawares John Heckewelder. The extent to which Heckewelder may or may not have influenced the direction of Pritchard's thought is unknown, however (Stocking 1973:lxiv). Many, if not most, of the individuals writing before the mid-nineteenth century in North America who are named in studies of the history of anthropology may have had little immediate influence on the development of intellectual thought. However, it is well accepted that they anticipated that development in certain ways.[5] I do not intend here to retread ground already well covered. I will explore instead the nature of their ethnology, or rather their proto-ethnology, and suggest that they can have a place in contemporary anthropological thought.

Perhaps the most characteristic feature of early proto-ethnologists was their curiosity, their openness, their probing minds. They asked questions. They sought to learn. They entertained the possibility of a different frame of reference.[6]

Questionnaires were commonly used by proto-ethnologists. They provided a well-established technique for gathering information by the mid-eighteenth century, when the manuscript we quoted extensively earlier was written. They had been used to guide European travelers in searching for "empirical knowledge" about unfamiliar peoples and places from as early as the sixteenth century, and perhaps much earlier by persons interested in unfamiliar people and places (Stagl 1995:64; Fowler 1975:17–18). According to Justin Stagl, author of *A History of Curiosity: The Theory of Travel 1550–1800*, one early participant observer of Aztec culture in America, "the Franciscan Bernadino de Sahagún (1499–1590) based his comprehensive survey of Aztec language, culture and religion on oral and written interviews following standardized lists of questions" (Stagl 1995:126).[7] Don D. Fowler, in his "Notes on Inquiries in Anthropology," suggests that Sahagún conducted "perhaps the first true anthropological inquiry . . ." (1975:17). However, Tzvetan Todorov maintains that because "Sahagún expects the Aztec gods to resemble the Roman gods" his questions "impose[d] a European organization on American knowledge." He made inquiries that fit into his conceptual framework (Todorov 1984:233–234). Not to be ignored, however, is the fact that he also provided data generated by his inquiries that did not fit into that framework (Todorov 1984:233).

Hodgen notes that William Petty, a seventeenth-century English gentleman-scholar, "drew up in 1686 a series of questions concerning 'The Nature of the Indians of Pensylvania.' Part of this was concerned with demography, the remainder with straight ethnology" (Hodgen 1971[1964]: 190). Typical questions were as follows:

What is the proportion between their males & Females. . . .
   Suppose there bee 1000 of them, within a certain scope of ground. Q How many of them are under 5 years old? How many between 5 & 10, 10 & 15 . . . how many above 75? . . . What is the nature & weight at a medium of men & women distinctly, which are over 20 years old?
   . . . What is the true meaning of 'King' amongst them? hath hee power over Life and Death? and over the Plantations and Goods of his subjects? . . . By what Title doth hee clayme his Power, as oldest, strongest, &c.? as the eldest of his race &c.? [Petty 1927, 2:115, 116][8]

Petty's inquiries were not as sophisticated and as open ended as those posed by the anonymous mid-eighteenth-century author quoted earlier. They too, however, indicate a quest for knowledge.

An eighteenth-century illustration of a spontaneous search for answers is provided by George Croghan, a frontiersman appointed Deputy Superintendent of Indian Affairs in the Northern Department by William Johnson. In June 1763, Croghan reported an interview with a Cayuga Indian named John Hudson about an Indian attack on English settlers near Fort Bedford (now Bedford, Pennsylvania). Croghan, in attempting to discover who was responsible for the attack, asked careful questions about individuals. One can witness an exchange of information in the following, as reported by Croghan: "Q: Is not the Wolf, son to Kickiuskum? and therefore a Delaware A: The Wolf is Son to Kickiuskum but born of a Wiandot [Wyandot] Woman. and consequently according to the Customs of the Indians a Wiandot" (Croghan 1763).

Croghan was not the most perceptive or broad-minded of the people interacting with American Indians. Yet, as can be seen, even he engaged in some open-ended questioning. Although matrilineal kinship was not part of his heritage, he provided clear evidence of it among the Wyandot. One can almost see his mind stretch.

Questionnaires fostered a systematization of knowledge and have been a basic tool of anthropological research (see Fowler 1975). The well-known *Notes and Queries in Anthropology for the Use of Travellers and Residents in Uncivilized Land* was published as late as 1951 (Stagl 1995:295). As is well known, systematization can have its limits, however. Many very early questionnaires, developed before the advent of professional anthropology in the late nineteenth century, were designed to gather statistical information. Many were so extensive and detailed that they either were never used in the field or data from them was filed away without being processed (Stagl 1995:123–124, 226–277, 275–276). Moreover, the extent to which questionnaires shape data calls for scrutiny to be paid to the evidence derived from them, scrutiny that may be based in part upon analysis of extant questionnaires. Such analyses can provide valuable information. They can be a guide to the conceptions of individuals using or composing the questionnaires (Fowler 1975:16). As an anthropologist, what is significant to me both in the questionnaire embedded in the anonymous mid-eighteenth-century letter quoted extensively earlier and in George Croghan's spontaneous questions is the degree to which they allow for new, unexpected responses. There were people in the eighteenth and early nineteenth century who were open to the possibility of something different from that with which they were already familiar. In this, they strongly resemble modern ethnologists.

For William Petty, the author of questions about Indians in Pennsylvania and for the writer of the mid-eighteenth-century manuscript cited earlier (at least at the time he wrote the questions), the search for information was initiated from afar, from an armchair, rather than from the field.[9] On the other hand, Sahagún was on location, asking his questions. Roger Williams was a seventeenth-century Englishman whom Margaret Hodgen asserts must have followed a "program of investigation" that was "very similar" to Petty's "forty years earlier among the American

Indians" judging by the categories into which he grouped the information he presents in his *A Key Into the Language of America*: "Of Eating and Entertainment"; "Concerning Sleepe [sic] and Lodging"; "Of their Numbers"; "Of their relations of consanguinitie [sic] and affinitie [sic], or, Blood and Marriage," and so on. Williams also gathered his data in person (Teunissen and Hintz 1973).

Sahagún and Roger Williams both knew the language of the people they wrote about. George Croghan, too, was in the field and was "thoroughly familiar with the natives' customs, language, and traditions" (Kawashima 1988:247). A characteristic of many of the most notable early reporters on American Indian culture was that they were "fieldworkers," that is, they had extended, face-to-face interaction with people of another culture. They often stayed among them for long periods of time and, in some cases, lived among them or adjacent to their villages. I will explore what constitutes fieldwork as I proceed with my analysis.

Charles Hudson, in "James Adair as Anthropologist," states:

> Adair, not surprisingly, was a man of his time. What made his *History* [*History of the American Indians*, first published in 1775] unusual, so that he at times sounds almost like a modern anthropologist, was that he was well-educated, was blessed with an enquiring intellect, possessed super social insight, and was by nature of his situation, a long-term participant-observer. He understood best what he *had* to understand in order not only to function successfully as a trader and as a British colonial agent but, in fact, to survive. [Hudson 1977:325]

Almost without exception, the individuals such as Adair whose writings have been used and reused in studies of American Indian history were interacting directly with the people about whom, and in the situations about which, they reported. In cases in which they were not, they relied heavily on input from people in the field.[10] For example, the author of the mid-eighteenth-century unanimous letter quoted at the beginning of this chapter was addressing a particular trader because "The Governor [of South Carolina?] . . . has a great Opinion of your Veracity, and also of your Ability . . ." (Anonymous n.d.). This concern with obtaining information on the ground was characteristic as well of early anthropologists who did much of their analyses using data derived from others. An example is John Cowles Pritchard who considered missionaries to be "more reliable" sources of information because of their "long residence" than " 'naturalists' making 'short visits' " (Stocking 1973:lxxxiii–iv). The fluidity of cultural boundaries provides an environment for learning that cannot be underestimated. Proto-ethnologists often are significant testimony to it. The notes and observations of these individuals—their "ethnography"—provide snapshots of cultural interfaces.

Often the tendency is to analyze the data left by proto-ethnologists to determine its accuracy, its reliability. They have more to offer, however. The observations and reflections that proto-ethnologists recorded as the result of their experiences among people different from themselves provide perspectives on cross-cultural interaction as well as personal insights into preparations that were made for, and experiences that resulted from, contact with persons of other cultures. The evidence left by these individuals indicates that some, if not many, of them were actively searching for questions and answers to aid them in interactions with others in their social environment. They were thinkers, analyzers, people looking to understand. Reanalysis of their work can lead modern anthropologists to reflect on their own roles in cross-cultural encounters, including fieldwork, and at the same time encourage anthropologists to consider the reflexive nature of the representations provided by these individuals and the uses made of them in scholarly study (St. George 2000).[11]

John Heckewelder has left notes about his attempts to learn an Indian language while serving as a missionary among the Delawares in Pennsylvania. He relates that when he first began learning he would constantly ask "How, or What, is this called?" and would write down and memorize the answers. Occasionally he would read some back to his Delaware friends, who informed him that the answers were incorrect. One day, an Indian who knew German (Heckewelder's native language), Delaware, and English came to the village. Heckewelder showed the man the notebook into which he had been writing down words for "some months." The man advised him to throw the book into the fire. He suggested to Heckewelder that the way to learn the language was to listen, to come to hear the sounds correctly. He asserted that only then would it be of any use to write the words down. This Heckewelder did, and "thro listening to them so repeatedly for a Month or two, I learnt to *hear distinctly*. I wrote, & they understood every word perfectly well—I could *hear* and distinguish sounds—" (Heckewelder, Letters, June 20, 1816). Heckewelder has left a rich record of his residence among the Delaware Indians (Heckewelder 1819, 1820, 1876; Heckewelder, Manuscripts).

Proto-ethnologists such as James Adair, William Johnson, Bernadino de Sahagún, Roger Williams, and Samuel Kirkland (a missionary for the Society in Scotland for Propagating Christian Knowledge among the Iroquois) resided for decades in close proximity with, if not directly among, American Indians. Samuel Kirkland provides an example of a proto-ethnologist who specifically went to live in an Indian village, in a Seneca household, to learn about Iroquois culture (Pilkington 1980:3–39). In his journal of his initial contact with the Senecas of Kanadesege, Kirkland reported that he had been advised by the Superintendent of Indian Affairs, William Johnson, "by no means to ridicule any of the traditions of the fathers—till I was master of their language and then I might take them up gently & on rational grounds" (Kirkland, Journal, November 1764–June 1765). This passage both reveals Kirkland's disposition to learn and hints at his motivations for doing so. He was a missionary who wished to convert the Senecas to Christianity. He spent most of the remainder of his life in Iroquois country.

The motivations of many early fieldworkers for learning about Indian culture were often quite clear. Many were missionaries hoping to convert American Indians to their religion. Others were traders intending to profit from economic relationships with Native people. Still others were colonial administrators concerned with exerting control over what was to them new territory. It is common for scholarly studies to have focused on the limitations of orientations such as these, to point out the imposition of Western cultural norms during the process of the colonialization and conquest of North America that these orientations entailed (Todorov 1984; Cheyfitz 1997[1991]). Although these motivations influenced the records that the individuals left, they do not necessarily abrogate the ethnographic value of their data (Washburn 1976, 1:355–356). For one thing, information that the proto-ethnologists present is often evidence of the roles these individuals themselves played in the cultural interaction in which they were involved. One is granted a glimpse of John Heckewelder and Samuel Kirkland in the field from the observations just quoted, for example. Much more may be gathered from the extensive records that they and others have left (See Guzzardo 1976; Ibbotson 1938; Wallace 1971[1958]).

It is common knowledge that although anthropologists may not have motivations, like missionaries and traders, that actively promote change in people of other cultures, they have nevertheless personal, theoretical, and cultural perspectives that undoubtedly influence what they observe and record and may have a lasting impact on the people they do fieldwork among. The records left by proto-ethnologists and the lives they led provide data that anthropologists might profitably use to reflect upon themselves and their work.

Another characteristic of some of the most remarkable observers of the past is that they foreshadowed anthropologists in systematizing data. Lafitau is renowned for this (Fenton 1969a; Fogelson 1987:346; Hallowell 1976:46–47; Tax 1955). He was not alone, however. As discussed earlier, questionnaires fostered systematization. There were other means of systematizing as well. Sometimes, as in the cases of the southern trader James Adair and a number of Catholic missionaries of New France, new and different cultural phenomena were interpreted in terms of the familiar. For Adair, it was Hebrew culture; for Lafitau, Greek and Roman civilization; and for Jesuit and Recollect missionaries attempting to learn North American Indian languages, it was the grammars of the Romance languages (see Hudson 1977; Hanzeli 1969). Others, like the author of the questions presented at the beginning of this article, were more open to alternative interpretations. Even those like Lafitau and Sahagún who were very committed to particular paradigms, however, were willing to admit new data. They did so, not in the realm of fantasy, as was common in the Middle Ages when reports of monsters filled records (Hodgen 1971[1964]:49, 66), but on the basis of their participation, observation, and interviews in the field (Lafitau 1974–77[1724], 2:112; Todorov 1984:234–235). How do the differences in perspectives, and how do the motivations of the proto-ethnologists to learn about people of another culture, affect the value of these sources' contributions to the writing of American Indian history?

It is sometimes easier to evaluate the data left by individuals who used familiar frameworks than those left by persons who interpreted more freely. The frames of references and biases inherent in the former are clearer than those of the latter. However, it is important in understanding the nature of the cross-cultural interaction involved to realize that among those using familiar paradigms and those less committed to a particular theory or motivation there were individuals who were trying to interpret and find meaning. These latter were willing, like Sahagún, Lafitau, and most probably the anonymous mid-eighteenth-century author seeking information about Native peoples in the southeastern United States, to report what did not always easily fit their models (Lafitau 1974–77[1724], 2:112; Todorov 1984:234–235, 237). Their success is evidenced to some degree by their ability to function in the cultures in which they found themselves (see Hudson 1977:325; Fogelson 1979:252). Their success, or lack thereof, provides substantial evidence of their roles in cross-cultural interaction. It has been suggested that using a familiar framework to categorize data may have helped some individuals to understand what was unfamiliar to them. Charles Hudson argues that Adair's theory of Hebrew origins "helped him [Adair] to understand the culture and society of the Indians more than it hindered him" (1977:312; see also Fenton 1988).

What also distinguished a number of these proto-ethnologists was their ability to identify unfamiliar relationships and to recognize cultural specificity in relationships while at the same time relating them to the history of man. They could recognize both differences and similarities between their own culture and that of another (Lafitau's description of matrilineal kinship is a case in point [Lafitau 1974–77[1724], 1:333–336]).[12]

One need only compare the work of Lafitau with the journal of Warren Johnson, an Irishman visiting his brother William Johnson in the colony of New York 1760–61 to see that there is more to systematization than simply categorizing (Lafitau 1974–77[1724]; Sullivan 1921–65, 13:180–214). In his journal Warren Johnson recorded his impressions and observations in a haphazard fashion, as follows:

> the Indian women have very great Influence over the Indians, soe that if the young Warriours are going to War they can almost hinder them. but when going all Sing the War song, & get a Charge from the Old Women, particularly to behave well, & not to be a Discredit to themselves, or their forefathers. The Dutch make great Use of Stoves, which keep the Room next to them, very warm, which is intirely disagreable to all Strangers & gives them a Head-ach. [Sullivan 1921–65, 13:192][13]

Lafitau, in contrast, writes that if Iroquois "Elders" wish to stop a war party from going out

> the surest way they have at hand to break up the enterprise is to reach the matrons of the lodges, where those who are engaged with the leader have their *Athonni* (paternity) for these have only to interpose their authority to turn aside all the best devised plans. This is a sign that they have a prestige somewhat more important than the Council of the Old Men itself. This means is rarely employed, however, because the Indians treat each other with great respect and are not eager to set in motion these means of prestige and authority to constrain others against their will. [Lafitau 1974–77[1724], 2:101–102][14]

Warren Johnson's journal, although containing much information about Iroquois Indians, resembles a curio cabinet rather than a careful analysis (Hodgen 1971[1964]:114–115). The data are useful to modern ethnohistorians but are not as rich or as deep as when put into a paradigm by a thoughtful, inquisitive individuals such as Lafitau.[15]

There is, of course, an attractiveness about data of the type that Warren Johnson presents. They appear to be somewhat more pure, untainted by analysis. Yet it is widely accepted that "The facts do not speak for themselves; they are emplotted rather than collected, produced in worldly relationships rather than observed in controlled environments" (Clifford 1997:67).[16] This characterizes the data provided by ethnologists as well as by proto-ethnologists, no matter how "pure" or how objective they may appear. If data cannot be judged against a standard of objectivity, then how is it to be evaluated if one is trying to learn about the "other"?[17] Should anthropologists be striving for "a native point of view" if that point of view is forever out of grasp? I would suggest, as have others, that the goal in attributing meanings to phenomena is to approximate as much as possible those attributed by the "other"—to translate, to make understandable (Cheyfitz 1997[1991]:xxv; Geertz 1973:15–16; Wallace 1970). The extent to which proto-ethnologists were able to do this varied. They undoubtedly struggled, in most cases unconsciously, to explain the new and unfamiliar in ways that they and those for whom they recorded their observations could understand.[18] This involved, of course, interpretation, that is, translating from one language or culture to another.[19]

Learning the other's language seems to have been an objective linked to the openness of participants in cross-cultural interaction. The predilection to become verbally conversant with the other was certainly more common in people trying to communicate meaningfully. Most of the European and Euro-American observers who have left perceptive accounts were persons who attempted to learn Indian languages. William Johnson, in written observations about missionary work going on around him in the 1760s and 1770s, often lamented the fact that missionaries of the Society for the Propagation of the Gospel (S.P.G.) did not reside among the Indians to learn their "Way of Living" and language (Sullivan 1921–65, 5:389, 5:598, 11:741; see also Klingberg 1939:134–138). The missionaries worked through interpreters and moaned that their efforts among the Indians were meeting with little success. This reinforced their image of Native Americans as being in a debilitated state. One S.P.G. missionary wrote that the Indians " 'are but a few and are moreover prejudiced by covetous persons who traffic with them for their skin and furs" (Klingberg 1939:134). Such interpretations were made and are characteristic of frustrations of cross-cultural interaction. There were numerous other individuals, however, who learned, some of whom became fluent in languages other than their own.

In his study, *The Poetics of Imperialism: Translation and Colonization from The Tempest to Tarzan*, Eric Cheyfitz (1997[1991]) dwells upon problems of translation, in terms of both language and the interpretation of cultural phenomenon. They should not be underestimated, of course. In learning a new language or familiarizing themselves with a new culture, the proto-ethnologists on whom I have focused attributed meaning to new vocabulary, new grammatical and semantic structures, new behavior, and new material culture. Moreover, they then translated what they learned back into their own native languages. It goes without saying that much undoubtedly was lost, added, and/or misinterpreted in the process. Cheyfitz focuses on disjunctures, misunderstandings, and failures to communicate in analyzing early encounters between Westerners and Natives in North America (Cheyfitz 1997[1991]).[20] Westerners appear in his work, therefore, as personifications of a colossal monolith, speaking and living the "metaphors" of colonization. There were, however, numerous people before the mid-nineteenth century who were searching to understand others who lived very differently from themselves. Some did a better job of it than others, that is, came a little closer to "touch[ing]" (Cheyfitz 1997[1991]:xxv) the lives, meanings, and experiences of people of another culture.

An example of this is that in March 1755 the English superintendent of Indian affairs for the Northern Department, William Johnson, wrote the following in a letter to the Pennsylvania statesman Richard Peters:

> The Old Man [an Oneida Indian, named Scaroyady] pressed me much to let You know his desire, which is, that Mr Weiser, or Montour, may be there [at Philadelphia], to interpret what he has to Say to Your Government. He allows Davison to Understand ye. language as well as any Man, (and I realy think he does) but says he is foolish, and unguarded in his Cups. which is a pitty, as otherwise he might be a verry usefull Man at this time. [Sullivan 1921–65, 9:164–165]

It is clear from this letter that Scaroyady had an opinion about who was capable of making acceptable linguistic translations.

Another Iroquois, the Mohawk Hendrick, speaker for the Six Nations of Iroquois, protested Johnson's forced resignation (the result of controversy between Johnson and the Commissioners of Indian Affairs) as administrator of Indian Affairs for the colony of New York at a meeting with Governor George Clinton in 1751. Hendrick stated,

> We were very much shocked when Coll. Johnson sent a Belt of Wampum through the Six Nations, to Inform us that he declined acting any more with us, and it was the more Terrible, because he was well acquainted with our publick Affairs. We had in War time when he was Like a Tree, that grew for our use, which now seem to be falling down, tho it has many roots; his knowledge of our affairs made us think him one of us (an Indian) and we are greatly afraid as he has declined, your Excellency will appoint some person, a stranger both to us and our Affairs; and we give your Excellency this Belt of Wampum to raise up the falling Tree. [Sullivan 1921–65, 1:340][21]

Johnson was installed as superintendent of Indian affairs in 1755. He remained in that position until his death in the middle of a conference with the Six Nations in 1774, having first settled along the Mohawk River Valley on land acquired from the Indians in 1738.

We should analyze successes, honest attempts to communicate, and failures to gain a broader understanding of the nature of the processes of cross-cultural interaction. There were individuals, such as the proto-ethnologists discussed here, who respected and sought to understand others different from themselves (Hallowell 1976:46–47). They were able to grasp "social nuances" (see Hudson 1977:317). Granted, in their attempts to do so they interpreted through layers of their own cultural and personal perspectives. The fact remains, however, that they tried and in more than a few cases succeeded. Their efforts are as illustrative of processes of cross-cultural interaction as are more common stereotypical responses.

To some extent, those living in North America, or staying for a long period of time, were forced to make translations, sometimes in order "to survive" (Hudson 1977:325), but perhaps more commonly in order to become an accepted part of the cross-cultural networks in which they found themselves. Perhaps they share something with modern ethnographers in this respect. Today fieldwork in North America is conducted less and less in isolated communities where the ethnographer is a temporary resident—Malinowski in his tent—and more and more in cooperative, ongoing, extended relationships, where the lives of non-Native anthropologists are increasingly linked with Native Americans, and vice versa (Clifford 1997:52–91, 299–334). Indeed, in many instances the distinction between Native and non-Native no longer applies. Ethnographers and collaborators participate in overlapping worlds, united by technological advances in communication and transportation (Gleach 2002:501–502; Marcus 1998c:241).

In the processes of cross-cultural interaction, the interpretations or translations—the meanings attributed to phenomena—by individuals seeking to understand the "other" were, of course, never exactly parallel to the interpretations or translations by the "other." However, roughly equivalent interpretations were frequently made that facilitated interaction (see Wallace 1970). When a translation is made, it does not necessarily capture the original meaning. In most cases, it probably does not. People accommodate themselves to differences by tolerating them or by changing. Without a doubt, change is often a by-product of cross-cultural interaction, as individuals fit into one another's lives.

Proto-ethnologists did not plunge self-consciously into the field, and they seldom reflected upon their role in interaction, as do modern ethnologists. Note that Charles Hudson writes, "Adair was not a participant-observer in the modern sense. It is clear that in comparison with other traders, he neither participated in Indian life as fully as they, nor gave as much credence as they to Indian beliefs" (1977:318). Yet he was able to grasp subtle "social nuances," participated for 30 or more years in social networks with Indian people, observed, analyzed, and recorded his observations and analyses. The clearest distinction between proto-ethnologists and modern ethnologists lies less in the extent and nature of their participant observation than in this: proto-ethnologists rarely, if ever, engaged in self-conscious reflection. Perhaps it is this self-conscious reflection—an awareness of one's role in a cross-cultural "dialogue"—that characterizes ethnology, albeit in a more muted form before 1950 than at present. It is this perhaps that distinguishes ethnology from proto-ethnology.

Attempts to understand the other were not only made by Europeans and Euro-Americans, of course. Evidence of the openness of American Indians to outsiders is abundant. However, it has largely been analyzed within the context of Western expansion, particularly within traditional histories that often suggest, if not explicitly assert, that somehow Indian openness resulted in the adoption of Western cultural practices and beliefs with a concomitant loss of Native cultures. However, more and more analyses of Indian history within the past 20 to 30 years have concentrated both on Native Americans' active role in the processes of cross-cultural interaction and on the cross-flow of symbols, ideas, habits, and practices as individuals interacting together have interpreted and reinterpreted these phenomena in their own ways (Axtell 1981; Blu 1980; Fowler 1994; Griffiths and Cervantes 1999; Rollings 1988; White 1991; Richter 1992, to name but a few). The tendency of writers of Indian history to focus on Indian-white relations as a process of acculturation has been lamented and criticized (Ortiz 1988). As a result, Native Americans, as well as other people involved in colonial encounters, have increasingly been seen as equal, active participants in the historical processes in which they were or are involved.

One example from the eighteenth century of an American Indian "proto-ethnologist" involves the handling of the Euro-American conception of rank. In July 1754, Tanacharison (Half King), a Mingo, was in the English Fort Necessity (in present southwestern Pennsylvania, near the West Virginia border) when it was besieged by the French. The acting commander of the fort, Ensign Edward Ward, was a young, inexperienced officer who could not decide what to do when the French demanded that he surrender. (He was only in control of the fort temporarily, his commanding officer having left a few days earlier for a brief trip up the

Ohio). Ward sought advice from Tanacharison, who recommended that he explain that he did not have the rank to capitulate but that his superior would return shortly and could negotiate with the French commander.[22] Ward took Tanacharison's advice. The French would not buy the logic; Ward was forced to surrender (see Ward 1754). This case, however, indicates not only Tanacharison's awareness of rank as an important Euro-American military concept but also his efforts to manipulate his understanding of it.[23]

Many of the proto-ethnologists mentioned in this paper were not part of anthropological tradition. Their value to anthropologists and ethno-historians extends beyond determining the degree to which they resemble modern ethnologists or directly influenced anthropological thought. It can be enhanced by studying their roles as individuals in the processes of cross-cultural interaction—processes not exclusive of colonial periods but ongoing—in which twentieth-century ethnologists are as much engaged as were the proto-ethnologists. In studying change in situations of cultural contact that concentrate on processes as well as results, it can be profitable to focus on the disposition of individuals involved in such interaction. One can then go on to see what this disposition tells us about the interaction in which they were involved—about the extent of communication and understanding achieved. Within this perspective, focusing on proto-ethnologists "in the field" can help us view ethnology as an ongoing, continually evolving study of cultural interactions rather than as a rigid, defined discipline characterized by specific methods and procedures. Contemporary controversy between humanistic and scientific perspectives in anthropology calls for more analysis of the nature of ethnology.

There were certainly some individuals before the mid-nineteenth century who made earnest efforts to understand others different from themselves. Some, such as the anonymous author of the questions presented at the beginning of this article, were disposed to be open, truly inquisitive, in ways similar to modern ethnologists. They were all, however, individual cultural beings and had varying degrees of success in reaching their goals of understanding. Studying their writings can remind us to be aware constantly that equivalencies are always only approximations, that, with the layering of interpretations entailed by the writing of ethnography or of Indian history, one must treat with caution not only one's sources but also one's work with them.

The length and intensity of the face-to-face interaction of these proto-ethnologists with the people they described varied, as did the degree to which they systematized data. What distinguishes them most from their compatriots are their inquiring minds and openness to others different from themselves. More extensive study of them is justified.

These proto-ethnologists also indicate that there is hope in searching for equivalencies, as long as we realize that they may never be completely found. Some people come closer to understanding, communicating, and functioning with people of different cultures than others. Trying to discern how close one, and/or one's sources, can come can increase our knowledge of the nature of the sources we use to study American Indian history and the cross-cultural interaction they evidence. But it can also help us understand the nature of the writing of that history, for ethnohistory is, in a sense, doing fieldwork among documents. We must not despair at discrepancies. They will always be there. They are, in fact, the stuff of which history and anthropology are made. A historical study, an ethnohistory, and an ethno-ethnohistory (Fogelson's three types of Indian history) all provide different views, different pictures. So, too, do the variety of sources available to writers of American Indian history. All can be valuable additions to intellectual dialogue and an understanding of the nature of that dialogue.

Notes

1. An early version of this chapter, "Eighteenth-Century Fieldworkers," was presented on November 30, 1979, at the American Anthropological Association meetings in a session entitled "Pioneers in Anthropology." I am indebted to Pauline Turner Strong for the valuable comments she provided to me while I reworked this chapter.

2. Although I am far from certain about the identity of the addressee, one possibility is John Legrove, an English trader who was killed "in the Chickasaw Nation" by Choctaw in July 1750 (McDowell 1958:6). The letter gives instructions to gather information about

> the several Tribes you trade with, particularly the Savanoes, or Schawanaes [sic], the Chickewsaws [sic], and the Creeks; And as I have above all things sent you upon his Majestys Service with a present to the Chactaw [sic], you are above all things to be careful in making remarks there . . . for I have less knowledge of them than of other Indians.

The writer continues by noting that the trader is to go to the Choctaws and eventually return to Coosa (in Creek territory) (Anonymous n.d.).

3. The writer hopes to secure the Choctaw—with whom the British have had little previous contact—in the British interest to advance Britain's contest with France over trade and territory. He obviously considers knowledge about their culture to be crucial to this endeavor, although there is no indication of the ways in which he plans to use the information he hopes to attain. (See Todorov 1984:99–127, for the example he makes of Cortés as a seeker of "information," not "gold".) The motivations for inquiries are important, of course, particularly in helping us understand the impact that the search for knowledge may, or may not, have had on cross-cultural interaction.) Motivation will be discussed at more length later in this chapter.

4. Although I have searched extensively, I have not been able to find the answers to these questions.

5. Margaret Hodgen suggests that the often-cited Jesuit Joseph François Lafitau; the eighteenth-century Frenchman Pierre François-Xavier Charlevoix; and Cadwallader Colden, an English administrator in colonial New York, may have directly influenced Adam Ferguson who is considered by some to be the " 'father' of modern sociology" (1971[1964]:507–508). In her study of early anthropology, Hodgen covers thoroughly the place of several proto-ethnologists within the intellectual environments of Great Britain and Europe.

6. Motivations for learning differed and will be discussed later in this chapter.

7. I am grateful to William C. Sturtevant for bringing Stagl's work to my attention.

8. Note how Petty's questions presuppose a certain (i.e., monarchical) leadership structure.

9. For a discussion of a movement in ethnology from the armchair to the field, see George W. Stocking Jr.'s "The Ethnographer's Magic: Fieldwork in British Anthropology from Tylor to Malinowski" (1983:71–73).

10. A series of questions about the Seneca posed by Lewis Cass, Governor of Michigan Territory (1813–31), sometime between 1821 and 1825, was answered in the field by a Seneca, Jacob Jemison (Fenton 1969b, 1970; for information on Lewis Cass, see Prucha 1988:628). See Nancy P. Hickerson's "How Cabeza de Vaca Lived With, Worked Among, and Finally Left the Indians of Texas" (1998:199–218) for an analysis of the link between a written record and on the ground interaction within cultural contexts.

11. See Philip Carl Salzman's "On Reflexivity" (2002) for a critique of "reflexivity." His analysis is somewhat limited, however. "Reflexivity" is much more than "self-positioning" and "self-reporting." His and others' focus on reflexivity simply in terms of anthropologists' intellectual product undermines the reflexive quality that is essential to the interactive nature of cultural contact. Reflexivity is a two-way street. It becomes useful and "real" only in the context of interfaces, interstices between individuals. George E. Marcus's "On Ideologies of Reflexivity" provides a much wider perspective on the subject (Marcus 1998b).

12. The extent to which proto-ethnologists systematized differed. Lafitau, other Roman Catholic missionaries, and Adair, for example, did so extensively, while William Johnson and Samuel Kirkland did so rarely.

13. The spelling and punctuation are true to the published version of this journal as cited.

14. *Athonni* is discussed at length by Lafitau elsewhere (1974–77, 1:339, 2:99).

15. Note that James Clifford writes, in *Routes: Travel and Translation in the Late Twentieth Century*, that the measure of fieldwork is in "its depth of social interaction" (1997:62). This may be. I suggest that it is also, however, in the depth and openness of the written text, the ethnographic writing that results from it.

16. See also Marcus (1998a) and Marcus and Fischer (1986) for information about anthropology's struggle with the nature of ethnography and its place within anthropology.

17. See *Cultural Encounters: Representing 'Otherness,'* edited by Elizabeth Hallam and Brian V. Street (2000).

18. In this they differ from many modern fieldworkers who are quite self-conscious about their impact on the field situation as well as their role in generating ethnographic texts and yet still employ frameworks that have been deemed no less allegorical than those of pre-nineteenth-century proto-ethnologists (see Clifford and Marcus 1986:101–102).

19. For different theoretical perspectives on linguistic and cultural translating, see Asad 1986; Cheyfitz 1997[1991]:xxxvii–xxvi, 175–213; Clifford 1997; Geertz 1977; Todorov 1985:219–241). See also Susan M. DiGiacomo's "Translation and/as Ethnographic Prac-

tice" for an interesting discussion of translation as more than a metaphor for cultural analysis. As she writes, "Translation shifts my position in Catalan society from observer or
even participant to agent of cultural production, with something at stake in the outcome"
(2002:10).

20. Tzvetan Todorov does more justice to the analysis of cross-cultural interaction, in
my opinion, by presenting a picture that is multifaceted. He looks in great detail at several
early Europeans and sees many differences in their own experiences, understanding, and
interpretations of Native people and their culture (1984, esp. 176–177, 185, 194–196, 237,
239–241).

21. The wording here is true to the printed text.

22. The available record of this is a deposition by Ensign Edward Ward. The information
is coming to the historian, ethnohistorian, or ethno-ethno-historian, therefore, through an
interlying layer of interpretation, of which one must be aware.

23. *Native American Testimony: A Chronicle of Indian-White Relations from Prophecy
to the Present, 1492–1992,* edited by Peter Nabokov, presents a collection of observations by
American Indians on their encounters with Europeans and Euro-Americans (1991). See also
Napier 1987; Greene 1994. More work needs to be done to incorporate American Indian
views of the Other into Indian histories. It would constitute a vital key to understanding
the cross-cultural interaction involved in those histories. The position of American Indians
as travelers who observe the people they come into contact with is another dimension that
can add to analyses of Indian histories as well as to cross-cultural interaction in general
(Hammel 1987:189).

References
Published Sources

Adair, James
  1966 [1775] The History of the American Indians, Particularly Those Nations Adjoin-
    ing the Mississippi, East and West Florida, George, South and North Carolina, and
    Virginia. London: Printed for Edward and Charles Dilly. Reprinted, Johnson City TN:
    Watanga Press, 1930; New York: Argonaut Press, 1966.
Asad, Talal
  1986 The Concept of Cultural Translation in British Social Anthropology. *In* Writing Cul-
    ture: The Poetics and Politics of Ethnography. James Clifford and George E. Marcus,
    eds. Pp. 141–164. Berkeley: University of California Press.
Axtell, James
  1981 The European and the Indian: Essays in the Ethnohistory of Colonial North Amer-
    ica. Oxford: Oxford University Press.
Bartram, William
  1995 William Bartram on the Southeastern Indians. Gregory A. Waselkov and Kathryn
    E. Holland Braund, eds. Lincoln: University of Nebraska Press.
Blu, Karen I.
  1980 The Lumbee Problem: The Making of an American Indian People. Cambridge:
    Cambridge University Press.
Berkhofer, Robert F., Jr.
  1978 The White Man's Indian. New York: Random House.
  1988 White Conceptions of Indians. *In* Vol. 4: History of Indian and White Relations.

Wilcomb Washburn, ed. Pp. 522–547. Handbook of North American Indians. William C. Sturtevant, gen. ed. Washington DC: Smithsonian Institution.

Cheyfitz, Eric
  1997[1991] The Poetics of Imperialism: Translation and Colonization from *The Tempest* to *Tarzan*. New York: Oxford University Press. Expanded edition, Philadelphia: University of Pennsylvania Press.

Clifford, James
  1997 Routes: Travel and Translation in the Late Twentieth Century. Cambridge MA: Harvard University Press.

Clifford, James, and George E. Marcus, eds.
  1986 Writing Culture: The Poetics and Politics of Ethnography. Berkeley: University of California Press.

DiGiacomo, Susan M.
  2002 Translation and/as Ethnographic Practice. Anthropology News 43(5)(May 2002): 10.

Fenton, William N.
  1969a Joseph-François Lafitau (1681–1748): Precursor of Scientific Anthropology. Southwestern Journal of Anthropology 25(2):173–187.
  1988 Lafitau, Joseph-François 1681–1746. *In* Vol. 4: History of Indian-White Relations. Wilcomb E. Washburn, ed. P. 658. Handbook of North American Indians. William C. Sturtevant, gen. ed. Washington DC: Smithsonian Institution.

Fenton, William N., ed.
  1969b Answers to Governor Cass's Questions by Jacob Jameson, A Seneca [ca. 1821–1825]. Ethnohistory 16(2):113–139.
  1970 A Further Note on Jacob Jameson's Answers to the Lewis Cass Questionnaire. Ethnohistory 17(1–2):91–92.

Fogelson, Raymond D.
  1974 On the Varieties of Indian History: Sequoyah and Traveller Bird. Journal of Ethnic Studies 2:105–112.
  1979 Major John Norton as Ethno-ethnologist. Journal of Cherokee Studies 3(4):250–255.
  1987 North American Religions: History of Study. *In* The Encyclopedia of Religion, vol. 10. Pp. 545–550. Mircea Eliade, ed. New York: Macmillan Publishers.

Fowler, Don D.
  1975 Notes on Inquiries in Anthropology: A Bibliographic Essay. *In* Toward a Science of Man: Essays in the History of Anthropology. Timothy H. H. Thoresen, ed. Pp. 15–32. The Hague: Mouton Publishers.

Fowler, Loretta
  1994 The Civilization Strategy: Gros Ventres, Northern and Southern Arapahos Compared. *In* North American Indian Anthropology: Essays on Society and Culture. Raymond J. Demallie and Alfonso Ortiz, eds. Pp. 220–257. Norman: University of Oklahoma Press.

Geertz, Clifford
  1973 The Interpretations of Cultures. New York: Basic Books.
  1977 From a Native's Point of View: On the Nature of Anthropological Understanding. *In* Meaning in Anthropology. Keith Basso and Henry A. Selby, eds. Pp. 221–237. Albuquerque: University of New Mexico Press.

Gleach, Frederick W.

2002 Anthropological Professionalization and the Virginia Indians at the Turn of the Century. American Anthropologist 104(2)(June 2002):499–507.

Griffiths, Nicholas, and Fernando Cervantes, ed.

1999 Spiritual Encounters: Interactions between Christianity and Native Religions in Colonial America. Lincoln: University of Nebraska Press. (First published Birmingham UK: University of Birmingham Press.)

Guzzardo, John C.

1976 The Superintendent and the Minister: The Battle for Oneida Allegiances, 1761–75. New York History 57:255–285.

Hallam, Elizabeth, and Brian V. Street, eds.

2000 Cultural Encounters: Representing 'Otherness.' London: Routledge.

Hallowell, A. Irving

1976 The Beginnings of Anthropology in America. In Contributions to Anthropology: Selected Papers of A. Irving Hallowell. Raymond D. Fogelson, ed. Pp. 36–125. Chicago: University of Chicago Press. First published in Selected Papers from the American Anthropologist. Fredrica de Laguna, ed. Washington DC: American Anthropological Association, 1960.

Hammel, George R.

1987 Mohawks Abroad: The 1764 Amsterdam Etching of Sychnecta. In Indians and Europe: An Interdisciplinary Collection of Essays. Christian Feest, ed. Pp. 175–193. Aachen, West Germany: Edition Herodot.

Hanzeli, Victor E.

1969 Missionary Linguistics in New France. The Hague: Mouton.

Heckewelder, John G. E.

1819 An Account of the History, Manners, and Customs of the Indian Nations, Who Once Inhabited Pennsylvania and the Neighbouring State. Transactions of the Committee of History, Moral Science and General Literature of the American Philosophical Society, vol. 1. Philadelphia: American Philosophical Society.

1820 A Narrative of the Mission of the United Brethren Among the Delaware and Mohegan Indians from Its Commencement in the Year 1740 to the Close of the Year 1808. Philadelphia: M'Carty and Davis.

1876 History, Manners, and Customs of the Indian Nations Who Once Inhabited Pennsylvania and the Neighboring States. Rev. ed. Memoirs of the Pennsylvania Historical Society, vol. 12. Philadelphia.

Hickerson, Nancy P.

1998 How Cabeza de Vaca Lived with, Worked among, and Finally Left the Indians of Texas. Journal of Anthropological Research 54(2):199–218.

Hodgen, Margaret T.

1971[1964] Early Anthropology in the Sixteenth and Seventeenth Centuries. Philadelphia: University of Pennsylvania Press.

Hudson, Charles

1977 James Adair as Anthropologist. Ethnohistory 24(4):311–328.

Ibbotson, Joseph D.

1938 Samuel Kirkland, the Treaty of 1792, and the Indian Barrier State. New York History 19(4):374–391.

Kawashima, Yasuhide

1988 Colonial Governmental Agencies. In Vol. 4: History of Indian-White Relations.

Wilcomb E. Washburn, ed. Pp. 245–254. Handbook of North American Indians. William C. Sturtevant, gen. ed. Washington DC: Smithsonian Institution.

Klingberg, Frank J.

1939 The Noble Savage as Seen by the Missionary of the Society for the Propagation of the Gospel in Colonial New York, 1702–1750. Historical Magazine of the Protestant Episcopal Church 8 (March 1939):128–165.

Lafitau, Joseph-François.

1974–77[1724] Customs of the American Indians Compared with the Customs of Primitive Times. 2 vols. William N. Fenton and Elizabeth L. Moore, eds. and trans. Toronto: Champlain Society. Originally published as Moeurs des sauvages ameriquains, comparees aux moeurs des premier temps. 2 vols. Paris: Saugrain l'aine.

McDowell, William L., Jr., ed.

1958 Documents Relating to Indian Affairs. Columbia: South Carolina Archives.

Marcus, George E.

1998a Ethnography Through Thick and Thin. Princeton NJ: Princeton University Press.

1998b On Ideologies of Reflexivity in Contemporary Efforts to Remake the Human Sciences. In Marcus, Ethnography through Thick and Thin. Pp. 181–202. Princeton NJ: Princeton University Press.

1998c Sticking with Ethnography through Thick and Thin. In Marcus, Ethnography Through Thick and Thin. Pp. 231–253. Princeton NJ: Princeton University Press.

Marcus, George E., and Michael M. Fischer

1986 Anthropology as Cultural Critique. Chicago: University of Chicago Press.

Nabokov, Peter, ed.

1991 Native American Testimony: A Chronicle of Indian-White Relations from Prophecy to the Present, 1492–1992. New York: Penguin Books.

Napier, Rita G.

1987 Across the Big Water: American Indians' Perceptions of Europe and Europeans, 1887–1906. In Indians and Europe: An Interdisciplinary Collection of Essays. Christian Feest, ed. Pp. 383–401. Aachen, West Germany: Edition Herodot.

Ortiz, Alfonso

1988 Indian/White Relations: A View from the Other Side of the "Frontier." In Indians in American History. Frederick E. Hoxie, ed. Pp. 1–16. Arlington Heights IL: Harlan Davidson, for the Newberry Library.

Petty, William

1927 The Petty Papers: Some Unpublished Writings of Sir William Petty, Edited from the Boxwood Papers by the Marquis of Lansdowne. 2 vols. London: Constable and Company.

Pilkington, Walter, ed.

1980 The Journals of Samuel Kirkland: 18th-century Father of Hamilton College. Clinton NY: Hamilton College.

Prucha, Francis Paul

1988 Cass, Lewis 1782–1866. In Vol. 4: History of Indian-White Relations. Wilcomb E. Washburn, ed. P. 628. Handbook of North American Indians. William C. Sturtevant, gen. ed. Washington DC: Smithsonian Institution.

Richter, Daniel

1992 The Ordeal of the Longhouse: The Peoples of the Iroquois League in the Era of European Colonization. Chapel Hill: University of North Carolina Press for Institute of Early American History and Culture.

Rollings, Willard

1988 In Search of Multisided Frontiers: Recent Writings on the History of the Southern Plains. *In* New Directions in American Indian History. Colin G. Calloway, ed. Pp. 79–96. Norman: University of Oklahoma Press.

St. George, Robert Blair, ed.

2000 Possible Pasts: Becoming Colonial in Early America. Ithaca NY: Cornell University Press.

Stagl, Justin

1995 A History of Curiosity: The Theory of Travel 1550–1800. Amsterdam: Overseas Publishers Association.

Stocking, George W., Jr.

1973 From Chronology to Ethnology: James Cowles Prichard and British Anthropology 1800–1850. *In* Researches into the Physical History of Man by James Cowles Prichard. George W. Stocking, Jr. ed. Pp. ix–cx. Chicago: University of Chicago Press.

1983 The Ethnographer's Magic: Fieldwork in British Anthropology from Tylor to Malinowski. *In* Observers Observed: Essays on Ethnographic Fieldwork. George W. Stocking Jr., ed. Pp. 71–120. History of Anthropology Series, vol. 1. Madison: University of Wisconsin Press.

Sullivan, James, Alexander C. Flick, Milton W. Hamilton, and Alexander B. Corey, eds.

1921–1965 The Papers of Sir William Johnson. 14 vols. Albany: University of the State of New York.

Tax, Sol

1955 From Lafitau to Radcliffe-Brown: A Short History of the Study of Social Organization. *In* Social Anthropology of North American Tribes. Fred Eggan, ed. Enlarged Edition. Chicago: University of Chicago Press.

Teunissen, John J., and Evelyn J. Hinz, eds.

1973 A Key into the Language of America by Roger Williams. Detroit: Wayne State University Press.

Todorov, Tzvetan

1984 The Conquest of America: The Question of the Other. New York: Harper & Row.

Wallace, Anthony F. C.

1970 Culture and Personality. New York: Random House.

Wallace, Paul A. W.

1971[1958] Thirty Thousand Miles with John Heckewelder. Pittsburgh PA: University of Pennsylvania Press. Reprint, New York: Russell and Russell.

Washburn, Wilcomb

1976 The Clash of Morality in the American Forest. *In* First Images of America: The Impact of the New World on the Old. Fredi Chiappelli, ed. Vol. 1:335–350. Berkeley: University of California Press.

White, Richard

1991 The Middle Ground: Indians, Empires, and Republics in the Great Lakes Region, 1650–1815. Cambridge: Cambridge University Press.

Unpublished Sources

Anonymous
  Letter to Mr. Lellycrow [or Pellycrow], n.d. Haldimand Papers Additional Manuscripts Collection, Add. MSS 21,778. British Library. London, England.

Croghan, George
  Report by George Croghan of discussion with Cayuga. Hudson, Fort Bedford, June 10, 1763. Bouquet Papers. Additional Manuscripts Collection, Add. MSS 21,655, f. 208–209. British Library, London, England.

Heckewelder, John G. E.
  Letters of John G. E. Heckewelder to Peter Stephen DuPonceau, June 20, 1816. Pp. 7–10. Manuscripts in American Philosophical Society Library, Philadelphia PA.

Johnson, William
  Sir William Johnson Papers, New York State Library, Albany NY.

Kirkland, Samuel
  Kirkland Papers. Burke Library. Hamilton College, Clinton NY.
  Journal of the Rev. Samuel Kirkland, November 1764–June 1765. Kirkland Papers. Burke Library. Hamilton College. Clinton NY.

Ward, Edward
  Ensign Ward's Deposition before the Governor [of Virginia] & Council, May 7, 1754. CO5/1328, ff. 231–234.

12. Folklore, Personal Narratives, and Ethno-Ethnohistory

JOSEPH C. JASTRZEMBSKI

The stability of myth, legend, and folk tale categories derived from a European tradition of folklore scholarship has, as Ruth Benedict underlined long ago, "prevented the understanding of the usual morphological behavior of folk tales." "Folklore incidents," she explains, "combine and recombine with ease, attaching themselves now to one plot and now to another. In the process they are necessarily reconstructed to suit the new association that has been set up. . . . Historical analysis must thus precede the psychological study of tales" (Benedict 1930–35, 6:291). Although Benedict used the term *historical* in a diffusionist sense (Boas 1891), her writings on myth and folklore make clear that problems of historical reconstruction and trait differentiation held little interest for her. Instead, she advocated an intensive study of a single body of folklore as a way of uncovering the relations between folklore and culture in a particular group and between the individual narrator and local literary conventions. "A living folklore, such as that of Zuni," she writes, "reflects the contemporary interests and judgments of its tellers, and adapts incidents to its own cultural usages" (Benedict 1935:xiv). Folk tales, however, must be "socially accepted, a process . . . dependent upon the cumulative traits and preoccupations of [the tellers'] group" (Benedict 1930–35, 6:291).

Although Benedict would go on to extend her insights into Zuni culture, folding folklore into her depiction of a group's specific culture "personality," her observations on folklore nonetheless suggest that the historian can rightly use folk tales to peer into the past of a people. That is, folk tales reflect not only a people's culture but the particular historical experience and situation that shape their "preoccupations." Indeed, Benedict avows, "in most of the world the culture reflected [in folk tales] is roughly contemporaneous—not of a distant past" (Benedict 1930–1935, 6:291).

Too often in the study of American Indian history, however, Benedict's insight has gone under appreciated, and the contemporaneous nature of folklore—the window it opens on a people's concerns at a point in time—has been subordinated to a search for structural continuity. In this regard, probably William Simmons best exemplifies both the promise in Benedict's call for an intensive examination of Native texts and the danger she warned of concerning the paucity of our methodological tools.[1]

Simmons's compilation and study of New England Indian folklore, *Spirit of the New England Tribes: Indian History and Folklore, 1620–1984*, its author notes, "represents one of the oldest continually recorded bodies of Indian folklore" ever assembled (Simmons 1986:8). Yet because "no author, English or Indian, provided an Indian folk-classification of oral narrative genres," Simmons must rely on the conventional categories of comparative folklore scholarship to organize the subject presentation of his material. As a result, legends, memorates (personal narratives of supernatural events), folk tales, and to a lesser extent myths comprise the bulk of Simmons's material. At the same time, "Giants," "Treasures," "Ghosts and the Devil," "Shamans and Witches," "Little People," and "Dreams and Shrines" constitute six of Simmons's eight classificatory rubrics for the many texts he has organized. Within these constraints, however, Simmons not only identifies several "Indian" motifs but, more importantly to his project, charts the persistence through time of a New England Indian identity. But only with the sections "First Europeans" and "Christianity" does his project capture something of the contemporaneous nature of folklore that Benedict underlines. In effect, we note a personal, Native commentary on "events" rather than simply follow Native cultural artifacts, and hence record the persistence of Native identity through "the large historical currents that affected the region and the nation as a whole" (Simmons 1986:9).

The historical consideration of "events" must take note, as Raymond Fogelson has forcefully argued, of the differential recognition and evaluation of what is eventful (Fogelson 1989:142). Further, in his discussion of the Cherokee author Traveller Bird's "corrections" to non-Native versions of Sequoyah's life Fogelson has reminded us that Native voices will cast these events in imagery that is relevant to Native traditions of narrative. In so doing, they will often reveal or explicate Native concerns or commentary that are submerged, dismissed, or overlooked in non-Native accounts or recitations of the same happenings (Fogelson 1974:109–110). For the non-Native historian seeking to recognize, identify, and understand these concerns, then, an ethno-ethnohistorical approach (Fogelson 1974:106) to Native narratives becomes all the more necessary.

KNOW

In 1993 Raymond J. DeMallie vividly demonstrated Fogelson's contentions in a presidential address he gave to the American Society for Ethnohistory, in which, among other things, he underscored the value of written Native language documentary records as an underutilized "primary" source that is particularly applicable to the ethnohistorical project.[2] One of the examples DeMallie adduced from Lakota Sioux material to illustrate his point concerned Sitting Bull's vision of the Battle of Little Big Horn as recounted by his nephew, One Bull, and recorded in written Lakota by One Bull's daughter, Cecelia Brown. Discussing the cultural ideas embodied in Sitting Bull's vision, DeMallie singled out the phrase "these have no ears" as particularly relevant. He went on to note the "ear" motif's appearance in a number of textual locations and analyzed its symbolic associations and meanings as rooted in the ear-piercing ceremony of infancy (DeMallie 1993:515–523).

Indeed, because of its ritual associations, the "ear" motif, it can be argued, occupies a secure place in Lakota Sioux rhetorical discourse. It functions as a metonym, subsuming within itself allusions to the specific range of cultural meanings found in the ear-piercing ceremony and applying them to nonritual but nonetheless appropriate situations (for example, DeMallie 1993:521–522). Similarly, "moccasins" seem to play a metonymic role in Chiricahua Apache discourse. Moccasins' obvious associations with movement and therefore one's life path are found in a number of ritual contexts, beginning with a child's "Putting on Moccasins" ceremony and continuing into the highly circumscribed and choreographed movements of a young woman undergoing her puberty rite. Thus a popular Chiricahua story concerning a group of Apaches saved from pursuing Mexican soldiers through the intervention of the Mountain Spirits conspicuously ends by noting that the soldiers' shoes, piled up outside a cave, mark the location of their demise. Unshod, the soldiers are presumed dead (Opler 1942:3 and 3 n.).

As long as the historian works with threads fixed, in a sense, firmly in the fabric of culture—language, ritual, kinship, and the like—and with clearly identifiable Native texts, then the interpretive process proceeds apace to a "reasonable" comprehension of events from a Native perspective. In other texts, non-Native in origin, the Native perspective can yet be inferred. Britton Davis, for example, a young U.S. Army officer who conducted companies of Apache scouts into Mexico in the 1880s to track their "renegade" brothers, offers clues that seem to imply that his scouts good-naturedly regarded him as a young warrior serving an apprenticeship among the men he ostensibly led. Writing of his experiences with the scouts in Mexico, Davis affirmed that past battles with Mexicans were a favorite topic of conversation among his men. A scout named Dutchy, for one, recounted to Davis an incident from his teens. Separating themselves from their raiding party, Dutchy and two friends went off to "throw a scare" into some Mexicans. Coming across a Mexican pack train, he and his friends fired their guns (old, barely operable pieces) into the air, screamed, and hollered, playing to the worst fears of Mexican travelers ambushed by Indians. As the frightened Mexicans fled, the adult Apaches, alerted by the firing, rushed to the scene, finding the boys in charge of 60 to 70 mules loaded with bolts of cloth. Relief at the boys' safety suddenly gave way to glee, as everyone grabbed a bolt of cloth and unrolled it over the desert. Later, said Dutchy, his people held a feast to commemorate the event (Davis 1929:116–119).

To the scouts under Davis's command, this story spoke to certain shared experiences unfamiliar to the "greenhorn" Davis. Apache youths usually served an apprenticeship during four raids before other adults allowed them the freedom to join or form raiding parties on their own. Ritual proscriptions circumscribed the youths' behavior while under the care of the older men, and various camp tasks occupied their time. The adults shielded the boys from danger and gave them little opportunity to thrust themselves into a direct participatory role (Opler and Hoijer 1940:617–634). If Dutchy and his friends, no doubt chafing under these restrictions, had run into concerted Mexican opposition, or had been hurt or even killed while on their spree, their adult supervisors would have been held responsible for not exercising greater care and vigilance. Intra-kin tensions may have resulted, for example, mothers angry with their brothers who should have known better than to let adventuresome boys slip away from the raiding party. When none of this happened, when the boys instead captured a pack train, relief manifested itself in good spirits and fun and later a commemorative feast; the apprenticeship was at an end. The story later bore repeating to other scouts, who in their turn had shared the trials of apprenticeship and who could appreciate its novelty, as well as to Britton Davis, who was in a sense a student himself among men more at home with the terrain and people of northwestern Mexico. Davis himself seemed to unwittingly play this role among his scouts. At one point he described himself as a " 'shave tail' second lieutenant not quite out of his army swaddling clothes" (1929:59–60), and another time he told how his scouts offered him the freshly cooked "skinned hind legs of an especially fat and juicy rat" for dinner. Davis remarked, "The rest of the scouts were grinning broadly as they watched to see what I would do, a newcomer among them" (1929:65).

Yet, in contrast to the examples examined earlier, certain symbols, images, and motifs found in systems of Native thought can have a more transient existence. They are no less "culturally specific" than "historically specific" and arise experientially from specific circumstances and situations. They are discarded, submerged, or refashioned by some when those situations no longer hold. They are, as it were, loose threads, easily overlooked or lost in the documentary record, yet discernible if reflected through the folkloric lens. Once identified as folklore, as socially accepted constructions of the "folk," they offer invaluable insight into Native historical perspectives and concerns.

Particularly important to Fogelson's project of constructing an ethnoethnohistory, however, are those folk tales that in Benedict's time still attracted little attention from comparative folklorists—personal narratives (Stahl 1983:268–276 and Stahl 1989).[3] Though American Indian cultures are replete with sacred cycles of stories, validating myths, and trickster accounts, Keith Cunningham has noted that more informal story types, such as personal narratives, are also important "signposts indicating culture because they are the most frequently employed means of communication in small groups" (Cunningham 1992:36). And more readily than formal story types, they reflect and articulate changes in the contemporary world.[4] Indeed, stories that people tell each other about each other, concerning significant events that happened to their grandmother or uncle or brother, reveal the immediate and intimate concerns of individuals at a point in time. If these concerns resonate throughout a society, if people recognize themselves in these stories, the folkloric process, as Benedict suggests, begins.[5]

Patterned into new tale types and demonstrating new themes, elements, and motifs, these narratives—precisely because they are formulaic constructions—are discernible even in translation from oral to written form and in texts in which the Native voice is seemingly subordinated to non-Native purposes. And like other socially accepted narratives, these stories can also be identified metonymically, as their tellers no longer need to furnish formal plot structures or elaborate or corroborating details. Allusions to a specific motif or other such story element bespeak a commonly shared frame of reference, a shared sense of plausibility.[6]

With their elements of suspense, danger, and dread and their plots of murder, ambush, and captivity, personal narratives of what the folklorist Marta Weigle has called "horrors," or stories associated with interethnic conflict, represent a significant number of the personal narratives that survive in the documentary record (1983:195). Indeed, among the many types of narratives, "horrors" are probably over represented since any situation of conflict, which by its nature raises barriers between groups

and perpetuates and codifies fears, creates an environment especially con-
ducive to their social acceptance and the start of the folkloric process.
Certainly in Native American history generally the persistence and adapt-
ability of certain plots, motifs, and themes are suggested by the number of
accounts of mass poisonings of signatories of treaties (White 1991:494;
Hazen-Hammond 1995:32–35) or treaty and annuity distributions that
included blankets impregnated with small pox germs (Jaskoski 1994;
Mayor 1995).[7]

Given the "cycle of conquests" endemic to the Southwest (Spicer 1962),
"horrors" especially attended the Spanish, Mexican, and American periods of this region. The Mescalero Apache scout Big Mouth, for instance,
recalled that as a child he heard the old men tell horrible and unforgettable
stories about the white man around the fire at night. Enrapt, he heard
the story of the Chiricahua Apache leader Mangas Coloradas, who "had
been promised safety in order to get him into the White Eyes' fort . . .
and [who] was treacherously murdered." Another time, he learned of a
warrior who had gone to Fort Stanton with a safe conduct only to be taken
by the soldiers and thrown into a kettle of boiling water, like the hogs the
soldiers were butchering. He listened also to the tale of a drunken soldier
who took an Apache baby by the heels "and crushed its head against a
wagonwheel" (Ball 1980:200–201).

For Apaches of Big Mouth's generation, who were children during the
American occupation of the Southwest, white atrocities constituted a not
insignificant portion of their catalog of "horrors." For Apaches born earlier in the century, those of Geronimo's or Cochise's generation, on the
other hand, the acute violence of the Mexican period in particular defined
the genre.[8] Of all the acts of frontier violence that poisoned relations between the Chiricahua Apaches and the Mexicans, arguably scalp hunting,
or the payment of a bounty for Indian scalps, was the root cause of Apache
malice. Invariably, ethnographer Morris Opler's Chiricahua informants
saw scalping as generally a Mexican practice. "The Mexicans used to
take scalps. They started it first," emphasized one informant, "—before
the Chiricahua." Another, while acknowledging that scalps were taken for
ceremonial purposes, narrowed its incidence: "Scalping is used as a last
resort on a man who has made a great deal of trouble for the Chiricahua.
Such a man, when finally caught, would be scalped and 'danced on.' He
was scalped after he was dead. The whole scalp was taken off. In the dance
the pole is in the center with the scalp on top, and they dance around it."
Significantly, he added, "This is used mostly on Mexicans who did awful
things against the Chiricahua" (Opler 1941:349).

By the second half of the 1830s, the Mexican states of Sonora and Chihuahua, unable to absorb the expenses associated with an earlier Spanish pacification program nor the losses resulting from Indian raids, had enacted "scalp" laws, in which a bounty was set on Apache men, women, and children. These statutes, especially in the decade of the 1840s, attracted a host of Mexican and non-Mexican professional and sometime bounty hunters. To be profitable, most could not rely on piecework, and so preferred to surprise large numbers of Indians under ostensibly peaceful circumstances, such as situations of trade. Using such tactics, the notorious scalp hunter James Kirker and his men, while under contract to the state of Chihuahua and later while freelancing, may have accounted for some 497 Apaches alone (*Santa Fe Republican* 1847). Yet nearly all of the initial "successes" of the system stemmed from this early phase, when it was still possible to take Apaches unaware. By 1850, the trade had peaked, becoming more difficult and dangerous, thus driving up the bounty scale. Kirker had received 50 dollars a scalp, but by the 1850s payments, as noted by Julius Froebel, a German traveler resident in Chihuahua, had increased fourfold:

> The [Chihuahuan] government has set a high reward for every Indian either captured or killed. It gives 200 dollars for every adult Indian, alive or dead. In the last case the scalp and ears of the victim must be exhibited in proof of the fact. An Indian woman, alive, is valued at 150 dollars; a living boy at the same sum, while for the one dead 100 dollars is given. [Froebel 1859:354]

Into the 1850s, the irregular town militias of Mexico's north fitfully sustained the trade, as the taking of scalps and captives, in anticipation of the payments, became a preferred retaliatory measure following Apache raids. Like the professionals, the irregulars found it expedient to prey on unsuspecting or peaceful Apaches (Smith 1964:5–22, 1965:117–140).

The New Mexican town of Mesilla, just lately American following the Gadsden Purchase agreement of 1854, typified this later phase of scalp hunting. In Mescalero Apache country Mesilla had relied since its founding on its own *guardia civil* for defense against Indian raids. Once United States forces occupied the area, responsibility for Indian affairs became the province of the army and the new Indian agent, Dr. Michael Steck. This was a jurisdictional shift that the Mesillans pointedly ignored and that the Mescaleros felt brought little benefit. One of the Mescalero leading men, Balanquito, complained,

> Since I formed and signed the Treaty I have had my horses stolen by the Mexicans, bridles and saddles taken off my horses . . . also blan-

kets and other things—some of them before my face in disregard of my remonstrances—I have complained to you and [the] alcadies [sic] of these outrages—but you have not made these Mexicans give up my horses, bridles, or saddles—they have also with impunity, outraged by women and beat my men and children . . . [T]he U. S. government has given me or my people no redress. [Barrick and Taylor 1976:25]

Despite this reproach, Mescalero difficulties continued. A short time later Dr. Steck's Mescalero interpreter and scout was scalped and mutilated while on the trail of horse thieves. And more seriously, on February 7, 1857, members of the Mesilla guard, dressed like Apaches and fortified with drink, scalped and killed three Mescaleros. They then attacked a larger party of Indians attending a trading fair at the nearby town of Doña Ana, long suspected by the Mesillans of harboring and abetting the Apaches (Barrick and Taylor 1976:27–29). Numerous Mexican towns like Mesilla engaged in such personal, sporadic warfare with the Apaches for the remainder of the century.

Apache reprisals, however, fell less on the peripatetic, "professional" scalp hunters than on the sedentary Mesillans and other townspeople of the north. Yet before the arrival of the Americans to the Southwest, little qualitative difference existed between Apache weaponry and the arms available to the citizen militias of the Mexicans. George Ruxton, a British visitor to the north in the 1840s, visited a hacienda whose men carried bows and arrows in addition to their few firearms. Ruxton again took note of Mexican arms when he was furnished an escort from El Paso del Norte. The men were armed, Ruxton said, with "bows and arrows, lances, and old rusty escopetas [muskets], and mounted on miserable horses" (Ruxton 1847:123, 170). In the 1850s, a similar state of readiness prevailed. When the Mesilla guardia civil rode after Apache raiders, each soldier had no more than three or four cartridges, and some men, judging their muskets to be of little real use, left them behind and carried clubs (Barrick and Taylor 1976:22). Even as late as 1885 the Oputo citizen-soldiers, although possessing firearms, presented a motley array of weapons. Between them, U.S. Army Lieutenant Britton Davis marveled, "they were armed with every conceivable type of antiquated firearm, aged cap and ball horse pistols, muzzle-loading, single-barrel shotguns; these, with a few Sharps rifles that had seen better days, made up the major part of the arsenal" (Davis 1929:165–166). The Mexican national and state governments could, of course, at times field large well-armed forces. In 1853 General Trias set off with a detachment of 500 infantry, 50 to 60 cavalry, and six or eight field pieces to protect Mesilla from American encroachments (Froebel 1859:398). However, until the regularization of frontier defense ushered in by President Díaz in the 1880s, such concentrations of man- and firepower were the exception. In this state of affairs, many Mexican towns turned to private accommodations with individual Apache groups. With these "partial peace treaties" they could for a time insulate themselves from Apache raiding parties and become clearinghouses for goods taken from less fortunate settlements (Almada 1952:73–74). But as the Mesilla raid on the Apaches at Doña Ana shows, peaceful contact between Apaches and Mexicans at a town often threatened to degenerate into paroxysms of violence, often ending in Apache captivity or death.

Captivity and escape narratives, therefore, exerted a particular fascination for the Chiricahua Apaches and constitute a conspicuous tale type in the "horrors" genre (Jastrzembski 1995). Eugene Chihuahua, son of an important Chiricahua Apache leader, often told the story of his maternal grandmother, Francesca. Captured by slave raiders, she and other captives "were taken to Mexico City and bought by a man who had a small maguey farm inside the north wall of the city." Escaping after six years, Francesca walked all the way back to Arizona, braving even a mountain lion attack to get back to her people (Ball 1980:45–46). John Rope, a Western Apache scout, recovered a Chiricahua captive whose experiences left her "so poor and thin that she was like an old woman, though she must have been fairly young." After she had recovered for some days, he and the other scouts "got her to make a story and it went this way": captured and incarcerated in a windowless adobe building, the woman lived imprisoned for almost a year, reckoning the passage of time by the changes in a cottonwood tree she could just make out through the chimney hole. One day a Mexican girl who used to visit her asked if she ever thought about her land and her people. "The Chiricahua woman said yes, she couldn't help but think about it, but it was no good because she thought she would never see her land again." The Mexican girl, however, responded, "I think you will see your home again" and soon effected her escape. After many hardships, the Chiricahua woman eventually reached the Chiricahua Mountains where the scouts encountered her, almost at the end of her strength (Basso 1971:113–114).

Jason Betzinez recalled a similar story that he heard many times from his "aunt" Dilchthe, a relative of his mother. Her story, Betzinez asserted, was "inspiring to those of us who later heard [it] retold around our campfires." Escaping with a companion from a penal colony in Baja California, Dilchthe made her way over 300 miles back to Arizona. Near starvation, they sat down on the side of a mountain and gazed longingly and with despair toward the north. As the morning haze lifted they saw a heartshaped mountain in the distance. "I know of only one place," cried Dilchthe, "where there is a mountain shaped like that one—in our own home country."

After building a small smoky fire to signal for help, Dilchthe was found by her own son-in-law. Both were so overjoyed that they embraced, momentarily forgetting the Apache custom of physical avoidance between a man and his mother-in-law (Betzinez and Nye 1959: 11–14). Like Dilchthe, Betzinez's own mother, Nah-thle-tla, was captured by Mexican soldiers, enslaved in Chihuahua, and then sold to a Mexican family from Santa Fe, New Mexico. She escaped and traveled for days over

steep mountains, cliffs, canyons, and rough lava beds. . . . After eight or nine days she was able to gaze far off to the south and southwest. She recognized the distinctive shape of one of the high peaks of the Magdalena Mountains, perhaps Mt. Baldy. Then at last she began to cry, for the first time since she had been captured, months before. But it was gladness that soon she might see her mother again.

Later, seeing some Apaches from a distance, she called to them. As they approached, she recognized Loco, headman of her own group. Taken to the Indians' camp, Nah-thle-tla received a wonderful surprise as she was greeted and welcomed by her mother and other relatives (Betzinez and Nye 1959:20–24).

Although all of these stories contain unique details and touches—the wall around Mexico City, the maguey farm, the mountain lion attack, the meeting with the son-in-law—they also share a number of common elements: a long incarceration or transfer deep into the interior of Mexico; a risky escape often accomplished through stealth, cunning, opportunity, or fortuitous intervention; an arduous trek homeward; an extraordinary appearance among distraught and incredulous kin; and, notably, the call of the mountains. For if the Mexicans and Anglo-Americans regarded their towns and villages as places of safety and shelter after the travails of the open road, so the Apaches in turn fastened their identity on the embracing mountain ranges of the Southwest. In these mountains, affirmed Jason Betzinez, his people "were safe among the cool pine forests and upland meadows and . . . there was always plentiful game as well as supplies of edible nuts and berries" (Betzinez and Nye 1959:27). Outside the sierras, warriors often oriented themselves to other mountains, calling them in the specialized vernacular of the raid *dò·xâ·dô̦·š̀iné'a* or "that which I have never seen before." Passing these peaks again on their return, the warriors spoke of them as *šikéyà·šikádè·s`iné'a*, literally meaning that the mountains were looking for them, telling them that home was near (Opler and Hoijer 1940:631–633).[9] In these elevations also dwelt the *gáhé* (Mountain Spirits), mighty beings whose blessings kept sickness, disease, and enemies at bay. Mountains were thus not only homes but holy places too, to be addressed in prayer: "Protect us from enemies and do not let harm befall us while we are near you" (Opler 1941:280).

In contrast to the ensheltering-mountains motif, Mexican and Anglo-American spatial entities—towns, mining camps, trading fairs, forts, even temporary encampments—provide the setting for other Apache "horrors." Unlike captivity narratives, however, these stories chronicle a "series of defeats" and inevitably end in disaster and death for their protagonists (Jastrzembski 1995). By the late 1820s, these accounts begin to appear in increasing numbers in the documentary record and can be followed into the mid-1880s, when the remnants of the Chiricahuas were transferred out of the Southwest and taken to Florida.

Residents of Santa Rita del Cobre, New Mexico, for one, staged a number of massacres of Apaches in the late 1820s and 1830s. This prompted Juan José Compá, an Apache and Mexican intermediary, to complain to his Mexican godfather, Mariano Varela, owner of the Hacienda de Ramos, that such treachery compromised his position. In a letter of April 25, 1833, Compá explained how news of these events had already reached Apache groups farther to the north, many of them informed by escapees from earlier massacres. Compá assured Varela that he would tell the Apaches "not to believe *stories and lies* [no crean de cuentos ni mientras; emphasis added]" because any Apaches so killed probably deserved it for giving the Mexicans reason to take offense. Possibly realizing how this would sound to other Apaches, he asked Varela to also send him two sealed packets of gunpowder

> because the Apaches will not be able to look at me because I have opened up to you [and] some will take it well and others will take it badly [porque los Apaches no me an de poder ver porque les he dado abrio porque unos lo tendran á bien y unos lo tendran á mal]. [Janos Archives, Reel 25]

In a letter dated January 6, 1834, Compá again reproached Mexican military officials. Justice, he maintained, had been denied the Apaches, not only in Santa Rita, but also in many other towns where civil and military authorities alike had insulted and mistreated the Apaches. Because no security could be found ("no buscan en seguridad") among the Mexicans, it was necessary for the Apaches to go elsewhere since all men value their lives ("pues todos hombres apreacia [*sic*] su vida"). It was true, Compá continued, that the Apaches had done many bad things ("han causado muchos males"), but the Mexicans had also harmed them (Janos Archives, Reel 26; the Compá family is discussed at length in Griffen 1983). In spite of Compá's remonstrances, a small group of Apaches who appeared outside the settlement to trade in 1836 were set upon by the townspeople. Inducing the Apaches to enter the town itself, "under the safeguard of affection and confidential conversation that they showed them," the townspeople suddenly attacked, and one Apache woman and two men "were beaten, speared, and shot to death" (Griffen 1988:171–172; cf. Pattie 1930:114–115).

A recurring element in the Santa Rita accounts, as Compá made clear, is the Mexican reliance on treachery: the townspeople lull the Apaches into a false sense of security through displays of "affection," "confidential conversation," and other such pretexts before springing their trap. In other stories, another common and recurring motif is the Mexican bearing alcohol (most often the distillate mescal) and the drunken, disoriented Apache (Jastrzembski 1995:181–189). The citizens of the town of Ramos, Chihuahua, for example, replayed the Santa Rita drama in the summer of 1850. Eager to collect the government bounty on Apache scalps, the townspeople welcomed an unsuspecting party of Eastern Chiricahua, plied them with mescal, and then, "just before first light [when the Indians were lying in a drunken stupor], Mexican soldiers and villagers slipped into the Indian camp. They carried ready muskets, spears, knives, and clubs. At a sudden signal violent firing broke out. Following this first ragged volley the stabbing and hacking and the clubbing of recumbent forms commenced. . . . In a short time most of the Indians were lying in their blood, dead or dying. The Mexicans fell to work with sharp knives, wrenching off the gory trophies for which they would receive gold and silver from the authorities" (Betzinez and Nye 1959:1–9). The well-known Chiricahua leader Mangas Coloradas recounted another such story, concerning a massacre at San Buenaventura, to American officials: "Sometime ago my people were invited to a feast; aguardiente or whiskey was there; my people drank and became intoxicated and were lying asleep, when a party of Mexicans came in and beat out their brains with clubs." As recalled by Major Grier in his testimony, Mangas Coloradas, "with great emphasis and in the most impressive manner," added "How can we make peace with such people?" (U.S. Congress 1867:328).

During the final months of his life in 1874, the Chiricahua Apache leader Cochise spoke of his Mexican experiences in a similar vein. Al Williamson, a one-time clerk at the reservation trading post near Fort

Bowie, Arizona, told the historian Frank Lockwood in 1934 that a certain Señor Luna, seeking a safe passage through the reservation in order to supply the fort with beans and corn, provoked the old chief into a fury, particularly as Luna traveled with a Mexican military escort. He met with Luna and through his interpreter, Narbona, denounced the merchant:

> You come in here and ask to make a treaty with me and to cross my reservation with your wagons and goods. You forgot what the Mexicans did to my people long ago when we were at peace with the Americans, and you would get my people down into your country, get them drunk on mescal and furnish them with powder and lead and tell them to come up and get big mules from the Americans. And when they would commit a depredation and steal mules, and bring them back to your country, you people would get them drunk on mescal and cheat them out of the mules. Now you are asking for a treaty . . . anyone who wants to bring their produce and trade with them [the Fort Bowie sutlers] are entirely welcome. But I warn you that you shall never cross the American line again with an escort of soldiers. You've got twenty soldiers, and what do they amount to! I can take five of my men and wipe them off the earth and capture you. [Lockwood 1938:125–126]

Embedded in narrative form, Cochise's vehement threat confirms almost 50 years of "stories and lies" about their Mexican enemies circulating among the Chiricahua Apaches. Yet, beyond their descriptive properties, their Native commentary on the nature of Apache and Mexican relations, what contribution can the analysis of these stories make to the construction of an ethno-ethnohistory? In other words, are these stories implicated in the lived reality, the history as it were, of the Chiricahua Apaches?

Contemporary anthropological work among Northern and Southern Athapaskan speakers provides some clues. Julie Cruikshank's work among Yukon Native elders reveals that oral traditions are a part of an individual's "equipment for living." One of her collaborators, Angela Sidney, for example, constantly "explained choices she had made or advice she had given with reference to narratives learned from parents, aunts, and uncles" (Cruikshank 1998:37). Moreover, Sidney's strategic use of oral narrative, her determination of when, why, and to whom to tell a particular story to produce an intended effect, shows how "good stories from the past continue to provide legitimate insights about contemporary events" (Cruikshank 1998:43–44). Likewise, Keith Basso's work among Southern Athapaskans, namely, the Western Apaches, has revealed similar narrative strategies at work. In *ágodzaahí* or "historical tales," narrators go beyond a mere description of an event to impart instead a lesson in proper social behavior to an intended audience. Further, the appearance of a particular Western Apache place name in one of these accounts not only situates a story geographically but, perhaps more fundamentally, acts as a mnemonic device thereafter that continually reminds an individual throughout his or her life of the story's message and intent. Basso goes on to posit an almost personification of place among Apaches, in which features of the landscape are forever associated in an individual's mind with that relative who employed a story for moral and didactic purposes (Basso 1983; cf. Basso 1996).

Certainly among the Chiricahua Apaches of the nineteenth century, certain kinds of stories seemed to be part of individuals' "equipment for living." Asa Daklugie, a Chiricahua Apache who experienced the closing period of resistance in the late nineteenth century, recalled, for example, that next to religious instruction he "learned of [his] people and their brave men and deeds." Such stories, he added, were "true stories told to teach" (Ball 1980:14). From the testimony of other Chiricahuas, "true stories" included captivity and escape narratives (Ball 1980; Betzinez and Nye 1959; Kaywaykla and Ball 1970) that underscored deeply held values of self-reliance, loyalty, and perseverance. As one old warrior put it after a disastrous encounter with Mexican troops, "every struggle, whether won or lost, strengthens us for the next to come. It is not good for the people to have an easy life. . . . Some need a series of defeats before developing the strength and courage to win a victory" (Kaywaykla and Ball 1970:104).

Stories of treacherous encounters at Mexico towns also provided guidance to Chiricahua Apaches whose activities, particularly in the later portion of the nineteenth century, frequently took them into Mexico. Yet unlike Basso's Western Apache stories, which encode particular geographical settings with lessons in proper social behavior, these narratives established different relations in the minds of individuals, associations with danger, captivity, treachery, and death, and thereby more explicitly suggested modes of behavior. Chiricahua leaders of the late nineteenth century, whose authority largely stemmed from their persuasive and proven abilities, for example, often drew on their personal experience of mescal and Mexican towns to frame objections to or justifications for courses of action to their followers. Leaders such as Victorio or Juh forbade their men to drink mescal when offered by Mexican villagers, explaining their actions by recounting stories of previous treacheries (these are explored at length in Jastrzembski 1995).

The actions of U.S. Army-affiliated Apache scouts ostensibly cooperating with Mexican authorities to capture the Chiricahua leader Geronimo in the 1880s can also be gauged against this cycle of stories centering on relations with Mexicans. The "Mexico" and "Mexicans" described in Chiricahua "horrors," distilled by now into a set of commonly shared presuppositions and assumptions, played a determinative role in shaping the scouts' conduct along proscribed narrative lines. In 1885, for example, three Apache scouts attached to Britton Davis's command, after purchasing alcohol at the Mexican town of Oputo, became drunk and consequently lagged behind the main body of scouts. Later attacked by Mexicans, one of the men died. When the other scouts heard what had happened, all "hell" broke loose in camp, Davis recorded. "Thirty or forty of the scouts immediately stripped for battle and started for Oputo, about twelve miles away, determined on killing any Mexicans they could find." With difficulty, Davis discouraged them from taking this course but spent the rest of the night arguing with them. "Nine tenths of them," Davis noted, "were for returning to the United States at once, killing any Mexicans they might meet en route." San Carlos, Yuma, and Mohave scouts, on the other hand, were "in a panic of a fright, arguing that the Mexicans would kill them all if [they] did not get out of the country at once." The Chiricahua scouts, however, "were the least excited." In the meantime, other scouts had returned to camp, having come across Geronimo's trail, a fact Davis seized upon to divert the rest from their proposed revenge expedition. When camp broke, however, Davis saw some of the White Mountain scouts (these were Western Apaches, as was the slain scout) scatter through the hills, and "we heard," he said, "the sound of firing in the direction they had taken. Investigation revealed that the dead man's relatives were 'taking it out' on Mexican cattle. They must have killed a score or two, but we thought it best not to interfere" (Davis 1929:161–164).

After this incident, Davis and his scouts learned that another group of Apache scouts under Lieutenant Elliot had been attacked by a force of Mexican regulars and volunteers from El Valle de San Buenaventura (August 1885). "My scouts at once," Davis recalled, "decided to pursue the Mexicans, kill as many as possible and then start for the United States." "This I vetoed," Davis added, "explaining that the Mexicans greatly outnumbered them and probably by the time they were overtaken would be in El Valle. The greater number suggestion made no appeal to them as they held the Mexicans in contempt." Davis finally dissuaded his scouts by convincing them that the Mexicans would by this time be too far away to overtake. Later two Mexican officers met Davis and informed him that Elliot and the scouts had not been attacked at all but were only being detained in El Valle. That night in the midst of a storm Davis left his camp for the town to verify the information. Suddenly in a flash of lightning he found himself surrounded by a dozen Apaches. Fortunately these were Chato and other Chiricahua scouts who had slipped past Al Sieber (the white chief of scouts) in order to follow Davis. To the relieved Davis,

> Chato afterward explained that they were determined that I should not go alone to the Mexican town for fear that I might be killed by Mexicans on the way. If I were killed they were going to take toll of those who killed me, then make their way back to Sieber and the command. [Davis 1929:184–187]

Such near encounters between parties of Apache scouts and Mexican nationals could not continue indefinitely. On January 11, 1886, the two sides clashed in battle, precipitating an international incident. Captain Emmet Crawford's command, a company of some 80 Warm Springs (Chiricahua) Apaches operating in Sonora to apprehend Geronimo and other Chiricahuas, chanced upon 154 Mexican irregulars, themselves on the trail of Geronimo. As Crawford came forward to identify his men as "American soldiers," shots came from the Mexican line, mortally wounding him. At that the scouts returned fire, killing four Mexicans instantly. For about 45 minutes both sides kept up a steady fire, while Geronimo's group, who were preparing to parley with Crawford, looked on. Eventually, identities ascertained, the Apaches and Mexicans ceased hostilities. Yet the incident was far from over. Luring Lieutenant Marion Maus, who had taken charge of the scouts, to their camp, the Mexicans now demanded enough mules to transport their wounded. Maus furnished the mounts, only to have the Mexicans refuse the beasts as unsuitable. Continuing to hold Maus, the Mexicans now ordered the hapless lieutenant to produce papers explaining his presence on Mexican soil. Maus's Apache interpreter, a Mexican named Concepción, returned to the American line to retrieve the authorization and there informed the scouts of the lieutenant's predicament (Maus 1887:571–579).

As Maus later reported,

> Then the excitement became intense. [The scouts] said they would *rather go out in the mountains than go with these Mexicans.* They began stripping for a fight, taking position in the rocks, shouting defiantly to [the Mexicans], shaking their fists at them, and using some Mexican words which they knew. They had been closely watching the Mexicans all the time. They said they did not fire for fear that Concepción and I might be killed, and indeed, if they had done so, I could not have blamed them. [Maus 1887:579]

With the example of the Crawford incident behind them, when next American soldiers and Apache scouts came close to seizing Geronimo they virtually colluded with the Chiricahua remnants to avoid the Mexican authorities.[10] According to Jason Betzinez, Geronimo informed Mexican soldiers seeking his surrender in the spring of 1886 that he had already decided to submit to General Crook. "At this," noted Betzinez, "the Mexican officer got very angry, saying that Geronimo had broken his word." Geronimo replied,

> You can see all those goods over there? They are for me and my people. These U.S. soldiers and scouts are good to my people. From the Mexicans we have received nothing but harm. So there is no use your talking peace terms. We are going back with the U.S. soldiers and scouts. [Betzinez and Nye 1959:135]

Geronimo, however, with the remainder of his followers disappeared into the night of the twenty-ninth of March 1886. Some time later, after meeting with Mexican troops near Fronteras, Sonora, to discuss peace terms, Geronimo instead once again threw his lot in with the Americans and the scouts after learning that his relatives and friends, at federal orders, were on their way to confinement in Florida. At this, Mexican soldiers commanded by the prefect of Arispe, Sonora, rode to the Americans' camp for an explanation. Apache scouts caught sight of the troops as they approached the camp and prepared for a fight. Captain Leonard Wood observed that the scouts "would not have objected to a fight. The packers also, some of them present in the killing of Capt. Crawford, had made preparations for a row. Geronimo kindly sent me word that he was on our side in case of a row" (Thrapp 1967:360–361). American officers rode out to confront the Mexicans and to warn them that trouble might ensue with the scouts. Unimpressed, the prefect and several troops rode into the American camp to challenge Geronimo directly. "It was a meeting long to be remembered," commented Wood. "The indians [sic] had decidedly the best of it, and looked upon the Mexicans with cool indifference." When the prefect asked Geronimo why he had not surrendered at Fronteras, he replied, "Because I did not want to get murdered" (Thrapp 1967:360–361). To avoid further difficulty, the Chiricahua scout Martine suggested to Lieutenant Gatewood that "he take us scouts and Geronimo's band and slip away from the Mexicans while we left still others of the soldiers to talk with the Mexicans. This we did and we were soon away from the Mexicans and they did not trouble us further" (Ball 1980:108).

Geronimo, whose apprehension Chato, Davis, Crawford, Maus, and Martine were in Mexico to bring about, echoed Martine's fears many years later when he reached back into his past to describe his experiences at the St. Louis Exposition. "I am glad," he said,

> I went to the Fair. I saw many interesting things and learned much of the white people. They are a very kind and peaceful people. During all the time I was at the Fair no one tried to harm me in any way. Had this been among the Mexicans I am sure I should have been compelled to defend myself often. [Geronimo and Barrett 1970:176]

When read against Geronimo's last and futile efforts to evade a reservation future, his incarceration in Alabama and Florida, and his later death in Oklahoma, a permanent exile from Arizona, his assessment of the St. Louis Exposition seems extraordinarily ironic or remarkably ingenuous. Such a reading, however, obscures Geronimo's long relationship with Mexico and his participation in the development and propagation of a "living folklore." Reinstated within a tradition of Mexican "horrors," with its concomitant themes, motifs, and imagery, Geronimo speaks, even in translation, in a recognizably nineteenth-century Apache idiom. [11]

Only some years after Geronimo's death, another group and largely another generation of Apache scouts in Mexico plainly displayed their predecessors' apprehensions when they found themselves actors in a region made familiar in narrative. Attached to General John J. Pershing's punitive expedition to capture Pancho Villa in 1916, these scouts, unlike their American counterparts, made no distinction among the various political factions vying for power in revolutionary Mexico. Employing stereotypical "Indian" language, Captain James A. Shannon of the Eleventh Cavalry declared, "To their simple direct minds there was only one line of conduct—'Heap much Mexican, shoot'em all!' They had to be watched pretty carefully when out of camp to be kept from putting this principle into action" (Wharfield 1964:76). By this time, of course, most Chiricahua Apaches had never been to Mexico nor had much contact with Mexican people, yet apparently their antagonism burned just as strong. In this case, at least, the lines of transmission seem clear: two of the scouts, Big Sharley and B-25, had been with Crawford 30 years before. B-25 remembered the encounter vividly—he carried with him on his jaw an ugly scar received from a Mexican bullet (Wharfield 1964:83).

Drawing largely on the experiences of a single Southern Athapaskan-speaking group, the Chiricahua Apaches, I have tried to argue in this chapter that American Indian folklore extends beyond easily recognizable motifs, characters, and themes—owls, witches, coyote stories, and validating myths in the case of the Chiricahuas. It encompasses as well the personal stories of many individuals living in a "contemporary" world, experiencing it in all of its immediacy. Some of these stories, such as "hor-rors," that are more likely to exhibit folkloric elements can consequently be identified in the documentary record.[12] Once identified, these stories, because they speak to a shared and specifically situated historical experi-ence, provide the historian with an entree into Native perspectives and so furnish a greater understanding of how, as in this case, nineteenth-century Chiricahua Apaches construed aspects of their world. For Apache scouts operating in Mexico under a U.S. flag, for example, the familiar folkloric "Mexican," treacherous and cunning, cowardly and craven, confronted them in ways reminiscent of past actual and narrative encounters—and had to be dealt with accordingly. Though the scouts also acted in an-other historical framework, that of United States and Mexican efforts to apprehend Apaches resisting the reservation, they read and reacted to events in ways that could vary widely from the non-Native soldiers they rode with. More generally, Chiricahua Apache interethnic relations must be understood against an evolving representation of the "Mexican" that influenced Apache actions even in the face of the much greater threat ulti-mately posed by Anglo-American encroachments on their autonomy and lands. Accordingly, as we gather the materials Fogelson advised for writ-ing ethno-ethnohistories, we should reexamine our documentary sources, Native and non-Native, for the folklore possibly crystallized within. In some instances, these may reflect the realities that prevailed in the past.

Notes

1. That traditional genre divisions tend to limit research by assigning artificial categories has been pointed out by Alan Dundes (1970).

2. The historian's ability to interpret events from a Native standpoint depends, DeMallie argues, on his or her grasp of the "cultural knowledge implicit in the documentary sources," on, that is, the historian's familiarity with the "culturally specific symbols and meanings" found in Native systems of thought (DeMallie 1993:533). Integrating this analytical frame-work into narrative history, DeMallie goes on to argue, will allow a "reading [of] the record of the past in a manner that as fully and verisimilarly as possible represents events as they were perceived by the actors" (533). For a comparison of written non-Native and oral Native accounts that also underlines the importance of understanding cultural context and differential perspective in interpreting events, see Cruikshank (1991).

3. Pliny Earle Goddard (1911) is a notable exception. His Jicarilla Apache texts are not limited to stories "from the beginning" or coyote stories but include "Traditions and Personal Experiences" in the form of a number of tales related by his informant, Casa Maria. Among these are stories concerning battles with Americans, Utes, and Pueblos, as well as other stories concerning Apache and American collaboration against other groups. Kit Carson and Lucien Maxwell, of Maxwell Land Grant fame, figure in these narratives. The failure of Benedict, and for that matter other Boasians, to include personal narratives in the catalog of folklore explains why their consideration of history focused less on events

than on the total "picture of [a people's] daily life . . . incorporated in their tales" (Benedict 1930–35, 6:291). History became, then, mapping the diffusion of cultural traits. However, Boas's basic insight, echoed by Benedict and his other followers, that this picture of daily life captured in folklore, including as it does beliefs and attitudes, constitutes a kind of personal ethnography has long been incorporated into the work of folklorists, particularly those interested in questions of identity. Alan Dundes, for instance, practically quotes both Boas and Benedict when he refers to folklore as a kind of "autobiographical ethnography" (1983).

4. Part of the reality reflected in personal narratives of Cunningham's informants at Zuni is the prevalence of adult onset diabetes, which is "more common among the Zunis than it is among almost any other American group" (Cunningham 1992:48). Cunningham continues:

> One of the newest and most clearly Euro-American medicines at Zuni recognizes these facts, but it also has old clear ties to Zuni culture . . . [A medical program] of exercise therapy and preventative medicine fits the Zuni idea of wellness as a natural and desirable state reached by working with the world and body, rather than against them, and ties into an old Zuni tradition of running. . . . The Zunis accepts and believe in the benefits of exercise therapy and preventative medicine, and two Zuni citizens told us personal stories of success in dealing with health problems. [1992:48–49]

5. Obviously identifying significant stories constitutes an important problem in its own right. Historians, interested in history as social processes, have tended to look for settings in which stories seemingly play a large role or have an important function. They have measured their significance in terms of contemporary response, itself measured in a variety of ways. Partially this is why historians have focused their researches on relatively bounded literary or judicial sources. See for example, Davis (1987) and Maza (1996). My focus on socially accepted personal narratives as a kind of folklore follows a similar tack, that is, identifying and measuring significance in audience acceptance, including plausibility and demonstrated effect.

6. An emphasis on a story's plausibility and by extension its demonstrated effect owes much to the work of performance-oriented folklorists (for example, Bauman 1986) who view stories as performance events that not only reflect culture but shape it as well. Yet performance-oriented folklorists' cognizance of variations in a storyteller's technique, listener response, audience composition, setting, and other contextual and behavioral aspects of the transmission of narratives often requires a long-term engagement with a trusting and familiar collaborator. When such a collaboration is possible, the results can be extraordinary. Charles Briggs, in analyzing a story performance by New Mexican Melaquías Romero about a legendary gold mine, shows how the "performance offers a critical reading of Hispano history and draws a number of lessons from the past regarding what Hispanos can do to ensure their survival in the present and future" (Briggs and Vigil 1990). Unfortunately, the historian, precluded by time from direct, participatory fieldwork, cannot always note the nuances of oral performances recorded in imperfect documentary form. Nor is the storyteller a continuous and physical presence from whom guidance can be sought and insights tested (see, for example, Cruikshank 1998:41). That is not to say, however, that given a largely coherent and accessible body of material the historian cannot subject the sources to the type of analysis that performance-oriented folklore studies outline and from that gain some insight into the creative role people play in shaping to a degree their cultural and historical

life. For an example of a performance-oriented folklore study from the Southwest drawn from the Navajos, Southern Athapaskan language family members, see Toelken (1976).

7. During his linguistic fieldwork among the aborigines of Australia, R. M. W. Dixon heard similar stories:

> In the early days, [aborigine] numbers had fallen rapidly . . . partly from the influenza they caught when the blankets they were ceremoniously given each year on the Queen's birthday got wet. But, quite a lot were shot—hunted in cold blood, like animals—and others were poisoned. There were several stories of dead Aborigines being found along the paths from their own camp to the white man's shack, where they had been given flour mixed with strychnine. [Dixon 1984:66]

Compare soldier and ethnologist John Gregory Bourke's comments on the "Pinole Treaty" negotiated by nineteenth-century Anglo-American settlers in Arizona who invited the Apaches to a parley and then served them pinole "seasoned with the exhilarating strychnine" (1891:718).

8. This chapter is primarily concerned with the nineteenth-century Chiricahua Apaches who inhabited lands in southwestern New Mexico, southeastern Arizona, and the adjacent regions of northern Mexico. The Chiricahuas consisted of three bands (possibly four): a central band, eastern band, and southern band. All were primarily a hunting-gathering people with a well-developed raiding complex (Opler 1983). There was, however, no Chiricahua Apache tribe per se, although population losses due to disease, warfare, reservation confinement, and the like did bring about a certain amount of consolidation during the later years of the nineteenth century.

9. The strictly phonetic orthography employed follows the key published in Hoijer and Opler 1938:3–4.

10. Anglo-Americans entering the Southwest in increasing numbers in the wake of the Mexican War displayed anti-Mexican attitudes congruent with Chiricahua Apache beliefs. Lieutenant J. W. Abert, who heard the story of the San Buenaventura massacre (later retold to American officials by Mangas Coloradas) at an afternoon storytelling session, provides one of the most telling examples, as it points to a cross-fertilization of folklore themes. To it, however, he added a postscript "as it [throws] some light on the character of the New Mexicans." One Apache woman, he recorded in his journal, ran to the church at the presidio to seek sanctuary, both to protect herself and her unborn child:

> but nought avails: they seize her, they drag their victim to the grand porch and cut her to pieces, tearing out a living child; they baptize it, with fiendish mockery, and then its soul is sent to join that of its dead mother!—and now, at this moment, many of the scalps of these unfortunate beings hang dangling in front of the church, a choice offering to the saints. [Abert 1848:503; see also Limon 1983 and Noggle 1959]

Richard Bauman (1972) has argued that folklore can be a means of cross-cultural identification. Such negotiations of ethnic boundaries, however, usually occur situationally (Weigle 1983:195), as in the case of American soldiers and Apache scouts on the trail in Mexico.

11. His would-be amanuensis, S. M. Barrett, made no headway in his collaborative schemes with the old leader until Geronimo "learned that I had once been wounded by a Mexican. As soon as he was told of this, he came to see me and expressed freely his opinion of the average Mexican and his aversion to all Mexicans in general" (Geronimo and Barrett 1970:48).

12. Morris Opler, for example, heard his share of these stories while conducting his

fieldwork in the 1930s, long after major Chiricahua contact with Mexico had ended. He used one of these tales in his Chiricahua ethnography in a chapter on marital and sexual life to illustrate the strength of the marriage bond between an elderly informant and his wife. What he recorded, in fact, was a classic Mexican town story: "Once when Mexican villagers were over hospitable to a group of Chiricahua," Opler summarized,

> she [the informant's wife] suspected duplicity and accepted none of the food and drink offered. As she feared, just as soon as her people were properly befuddled, a massacre began. But she remained clear-headed and managed to get her helpless husband to a hiding place. [Opler 1941:402]

Opler's use of this story suggests that older ethnographies and field notes may usefully be reread and reinterpreted. An extensive critique of the production and presentation of ethnographies exists. A useful introduction is Clifford and Marcus (1986). See also Lederman (1990).

References

Abert, J. W.
    1848 Report of Lieut. J. W. Abert of His Examinations of New Mexico in the Years 1846, 47. *In* U.S. Congress, House Executive Doc. 41.
Almada, Francisco
    1952 Diccionario de historía, geografía, y biografía sornorenses. Chihuahua: Impresora Ruiz Sandoval.
Ball, Eve, Nora Henn, and Lynda Sanchez
    1980 Indeh: An Apache Odyssey. Provo UT: Brigham Young University.
Barrick, Nora, and Mary Taylor
    1976 The Mesilla Guard, 1851–1861. *In* Southwestern Studies (51).
Basso, Keith, ed.
    1971 Western Apache Raiding and Warfare (from the Notes of Grenville Goodwin). Tucson: University of Arizona Press.
    1983 "Stalking with Stories": Names, Places, and Moral Narratives Among the Western Apache. *In* Text, Play, and Story: The Construction and Reconstruction of Self and Society. Stuart Plattner and Edward Brunner, eds. Pp. 19–55. Proceedings of the American Ethnological Society. Washington DC: American Anthropological Association.
    1996 Wisdom Sits in Places: Landscapes and Language among the Western Apache. Albuquerque: University of New Mexico Press.
Bauman, Richard
    1972 Differential Identity and the Social Base of Folklore. *In* Towards New Perspectives in Folklore. Américo Paredes and Richard Bauman, eds. Pp. 31–41. Austin: University of Texas Press.
    1986 Story, Performance and Event: Contextual Studies of Oral Narrative. Cambridge: Cambridge University Press.
Benedict, Ruth
    1930–35 Folklore. *In* Encyclopaedia of the Social Sciences. R. A. Siligman, ed. Pp. 288–293. New York: Macmillan.
    1935 Zuni Mythology. 2 vols. Columbia University Contributions to Anthropology, vol. 21. New York: Columbia University Press.
Betzinez, Jason, and William Sturtevant Nye
    1959 I Fought with Geronimo. Harrisburg PA: Stackpole.

Boas, Franz

1891 Dissemination of Tales among the Natives of North America. Journal of American Folklore 4:13–20.

Bourke, John Gregory

1981 On the Border with Crook. New York: Charles Scribner's Sons.

Briggs, Charles L., and Julián José Vigil

1990 The Lost Gold Mine of Juan Mondragón: A Legend from New Mexico Performed by Melaquías Romero. Tucson: University of Arizona Press.

Clifford, James, and George E. Marcus, eds.

1986 Writing Culture: The Poetics and Politics of Ethnography. Berkeley: University of California Press.

Cruikshank, Julie

1991 Reading Voices: Oral and Written Interpretations of the Yukon's Past. Vancouver: Douglas & McIntyre.

1998 The Social Life of Stories: Narrative Knowledge in the Yukon Territory. Lincoln: University of Nebraska Press,.

Cunningham, Keith

1992 American Indians' Kitchen-Table Stories: Contemporary Conversations with Cherokee, Sioux, Hopi, Osage Navajo, Zuni and Members of Other Nations. Little Rock AR: August House Publishers.

Davis, Britton

1929 The Truth About Geronimo. M. M. Quaife, ed. New Haven CT: Yale University Press.

Davis, Natalie Zemon

1987 Fiction in the Archives: Pardon Tales and Their Tellers in Sixteenth-Century France. Palo Alto CA: Stanford University Press.

DeMallie, Raymond

1993 "These Have No Ears": Narrative and the Ethnohistorical Method. Ethnohistory 40:515–538.

Dixon, R. M. W.

1984 Searching for Aboriginal Languages: Memoirs of a Field Worker. Chicago: University of Chicago Press.

Dundes, Alan

1970 Folk Ideas as Units of World View. In Towards New Perspectives in Folklore. Américo Paredes and Richard Bauman, ed. Pp. 93–103. Austin: University of Texas Press.

1983 Defining Identity through Folklore. In Identity: Personal and Sociocultural. Anita Jocobson-Widding, ed. Pp. 235–261. Uppsala, Sweden: Almqvist and Wiksell International.

Fogelson, Raymond D.

1974 On the Varieties of Indian History: Sequoyah and Traveller Bird. Journal of Ethnic Studies 2:105–112.

1984 Night Thoughts on Native American Social History. Occasional Papers in Curriculum, vol. 3. Chicago: Newberry Library.

1989 The Ethnohistory of Events and Nonevents. Ethnohistory 36:133–147.

Froebel, Julius

1859 Seven Years Travel in Central American, Northern Mexico, and the Far West of the United States. London: Richard Bently.

Geronimo and S. M. Barrett

1970 Geronimo: His Own Story. S. M. Barrett and Frederick W. Turner III, eds. New York: Ballantine Books.

Goddard, Pliny Earle

1911 Jicarilla Apache Texts. Anthropological Papers, vol. 8. New York: American Museum of Natural History.

Griffen, William B.

1988 Apaches and War and Peace: The Janos Presidio, 1750–1858. Albuquerque: University of New Mexico Press.

Hazen-Hammond, Susan

1995 The Poisoned Pinole Treaty at Bloody Tanks. Arizona Highways 71:32–35.

Hoijer, Harry, and Morris E. Opler

1938 Chiricahua and Mescalero Apache Texts. Chicago: The University of Chicago Press.

Janos Archives

N.d. Historical Archives, Manuscripts, and Documents of Janos. Special Collections, University of Texas at El Paso Library.

Jaskoski, Helen

1994 Andrew Blackbird's Smallpox Story. In Native American Perspectives on Literature and History. Alan R. Velie, ed. Pp. 25–35. Norman: University of Oklahoma Press.

Jastrzembski, Joseph C.

1995 Treacherous Towns in Mexico: Chiricahua Apache Personal Narratives of Horrors. Western Folklore 54:169–196.

Kaywaykla, James, and Eve Ball

1970 In the Days of Victorio: Recollections of a Warm Springs Apache. Tucson: University of Arizona Press.

Lederman, Rena

1990 Pretexts for Ethnography: On Reading Fieldnotes. In Fieldnotes: The Making of Anthropology. Roger Sanjek, ed. Pp. 71–91. Ithaca: Cornell University Press.

Limón, José E.

1983 Folklore, Social Conflict and the United States-Mexico Border. In Handbook of American Folklore. Richard M. Dorson, ed. Pp. 216–226. Bloomington: Indiana University Press.

Lockwood, Frank C.

1938 The Apache Indians. New York: Macmillan.

Maus, Marion P.

1887 Report in General Crook to Lieutenant Gen. P. H. Sheridan, January 27, 1886. In Papers Relating to the Foreign Relations of the United States, 1886. Washington DC: Department of State.

Mayor, Adrienne

1995 The Nessus Shirt in the New World: Smallpox Blankets in History and Legend. Journal of American Folklore 108(427): 54–78.

Maza, Sarah

1996 Stories in History: Cultural Narratives in Recent Works in European History. American Historical Review 101: 1493–1515.

Noggle, Burl

1959 Anglo Observers of the Southwest Borderlands, 1825–1890. Arizona and the West 1:105–131.

Opler, Morris E.

    1941 An Apache Life-Way: The Economic, Social, and Religious Institution of the Chiricahua Indians. Chicago: University of Chicago Press.

    1942 Myths and Tales of the Chiricahua Apache Indians. Memoirs of the American Folklore Society, vol. 37. Menasha, WI: George Banta.

    1983 Chiricahua Apache. *In* Vol. 10: The Southwest. Alfonso Ortiz, ed. Pp. 401–418. Handbook of North American Indians. William C. Sturtevant, gen. ed. Washington DC: Smithsonian Institution.

Opler, Morris E., and Harry Hoijer

    1940 The Raid and Warpath Language of the Chiricahua Apache. American Anthropologist 42:617–634.

Pattie, James Ohio

    1930 The Personal Narrative of James Ohio Pattie. Timothy Flint, ed. Chicago: R. R. Donnelly and Sons.

Ruxton, George F.

    1847 Adventures in Mexico and the Rocky Mountains. London: John Murray.

Simmons, William S.

    1986 Spirit of the New England Tribes: Indian History and Folklore, 1620–1984. Hanover NH: University Press of New England.

Smith, Ralph A.

    1964 The Scalphunter in the Borderlands. Arizona and the West 6:5–22.

    1965 The Scalphunt in Chihuahua. New Mexico Historical Review 40:117–140.

Spicer, Edward

    1962 Cycles of Conquest: The Impact of Spain, Mexico and the United States on the Indians of the Southwest 1530–1960. Tucson: University of Arizona Press.

Stahl, Sandra K. D.

    1983 Personal Experience Stories. *In* Handbook of American Folklore. Richard M. Dorson, ed. Pp. 268–76. Bloomington: Indiana University Press.

    1989 Literary Folkloristics and the Personal Narrative. Bloomington: Indian University Press.

Thrapp, Dan L.

    1967 The Conquest of Apachería. Norman: University of Oklahoma Press.

Toelken, J. Barre

    1976 The Pretty Languages of Yellowman: Genre, Mode and Texture in Navaho Coyote Narratives. *In* Folklore Genres. Dan BenAmos, ed. Pp. 211–235. Austin: University of Texas Press.

U.S. Congress

    1867 Condition of the Indians. Report of the Joint Special Committee. Senate Report No. 156. 39th Cong., 2d sess.

Weigle, Marta

    1983 The Southwest: A Regional Case Study. *In* Handbook of American Folklore. Richard Dorson, ed. Pp. 194–200. Bloomington: Indiana University Press.

White, Richard

    1991 The Middle Ground: Indians, Empires, and Republics in the Great Lake Regions 1650–1815. Cambridge: Cambridge University Press.

13. Events and Nonevents on the Tlingit/Russian/American Colonial Frontier, 1802–1879

SERGEI A. KAN

Introduction

Throughout 1877–78 the "Russian" (and some of the American) inhabitants of Sitka, a small town on the coast of southeastern Alaska, were anxiously anticipating an attack by the "savage Indians" whose village was located just outside the town's palisade.[1] Finally, on February 6, 1879, their worst fears seemed to have materialized when they heard loud noises of a drunken uproar, moving from the Native village to the town. Sitka's inhabitants locked themselves up in their homes, and some of the men began to prepare for a gunfight. However, when a dozen Tlingit men of the Kiks.ádi clan (some of them intoxicated), finally approached the stockade, they were turned away by the head of the local Indian police force and his kinsmen (members of the Kaagwaantaan clan) and dispersed without violence.

Despite the peaceful resolution of this crisis, throughout the month of February a number of Sitka's residents conducted nightly vigils and kept guard duty. However, the only damage suffered by the town was the theft of a portion of its palisade by the "attackers." In the meantime, Sitka's merchants and some of the other Anglo-Americans and Russians sent a petition to the commander of the British naval base at Esquimalt near Victoria, British Columbia. As a result of this, on March 1, 1879, Her Majesty's warship *Osprey* arrived in Sitka, and one day later an American customs ship also anchored nearby. Sitka's night watchmen drank heavily to celebrate their liberation from the latest Indian threat. Embarrassed by the international publicity surrounding these events, the U.S. government, which in 1877 had removed its military garrison from Sitka, finally decided to strengthen once again its presence in Alaska by dispatching in April 1879 the U.S.S. *Jamestown* to the Alaska panhandle. Earlier, the cabinet of President Harris had met to consider this crisis and had agreed that the U.S. Navy was in a better position to meet the demands of the situation than the Treasury Department, which had previously administered the affairs of the new territory, following a ten-year period of U.S. Army rule (1867–77) (see Hinckley 1972; Williams 1982).

Although memories of the "barely averted massacre of 1879" remained central to the historical consciousness of Sitka's Russian community for about half a century, the local Tlingit oral tradition makes no references to it (Kan 1979–95).[2] American officials who investigated the affair dismissed it as a simple brawl between "half a dozen drunken members of the Kiks.ádi clan and a large force of the members of the Kaagwaantaan clan" (Beardslee 1882:45–46). Thus it appears that this entire incident was so insignificant that it could hardly qualify as a major or even a minor historical event. In fact, using Raymond Fogelson's terminology (1989) we could call it a "nonevent" for most of the Tlingit and many of the Americans who witnessed it.

This, however, was clearly not the case for the town's Russian inhabitants. For them "the Indian attack" was something that Fogelson (1989) calls an "epitomizing event," a narrative that condenses, encapsulates, and dramatizes long-term historical processes. "Such events," he writes, "are inventions but have such compelling qualities and explanatory power that they spread rapidly through the group and soon take on an ethnohistorical reality of their own" (1989:143).[3]

To explain the difference between the Russian and the Tlingit interpretations of the 1879 altercation, it is necessary to focus on three topics: the history of Russian-Tlingit relations prior to the American acquisition of Alaska in 1867, the socioeconomic hierarchy and power relations within Sitka's multiethnic community, and the "Russian" as well as the Tlingit population's historical consciousness (or Fogelson's "ethno-logic") (see Fogelson 1974, 1984, 1989).[4] It is also necessary to use the ethnohistorical method. This entails combining data from various written sources with ethnographic ones and trying to play all these sources against each other so as to arrive at a more comprehensive understanding of the historical events being interpreted here (see Krech 1991; Brown and Vibert 1996).

Tlingit-Russian Relations after the Establishment of the Russian Colonial Presence in Sitka

In 1799 the Russians established the fort of St. Michael's within an area occupied by the Tlingit of the Sitka tribe (_kwaan_).[5] This action was part of a colonial expansion into North America by Russian fur trading companies that began in the 1740s. Attracted by Sitka's excellent harbor and its large population of sea otters, the Russian American Company (RAC) planned to make St. Michael's the center of its Alaskan operations.

The Tlingit, who had already been in contact with the Russians and other whites for several decades, were quite interested in trading with the newcomers—exchanging sea otter pelts for metal tools, foodstuffs, clothing, various "luxury" items, and firearms. Though the RAC refused to sell guns to the Tlingit, other Europeans and especially the Americans conducted a profitable trade in firearms in southeastern Alaska. The more "exotic items" of this trade, just like the artifacts traditionally obtained from the various Native neighbors of the Tlingit, entered the indigenous system of feast exchanges. However, with their highly developed sense of collective and personal property ownership, the Tlingit resented any infringements on their territory. Thus the Kiks.ádi clan of the Raven moiety, which claimed to be the original owner of the coastal lands in Sitka harbor, appears to have acquiesced only to the establishment of a small temporary Russian trading post on its land rather than the substantial permanent settlement inside a fort that the Russians were planning to build. By 1802 Tlingit-Russian relations in Sitka had deteriorated so much that in June of that year the St. Michael's fort was attacked by an overwhelming force (led by a Kiks.ádi headman, Shk'awulyéil, and his sister's son, K'alyáan), which burned it down and killed most of its inhabitants.

The immediate causes of the Tlingit anger against the newcomers was the decimation of the local sea otter population by the Native Alaskan (mainly Aleut and Alutiiq) indentured workers of the RAC, their looting of Tlingit graves, and the capture of some Tlingit women. More generally, despite the instructions of RAC's general manager, the Russians and their Native Alaskan workers ("slaves," as the Tlingit perceived them) did not show much *respect* to their Tlingit "hosts" and thus overstayed their welcome.[6]

Determined to regain their foothold in Sitka, the Russians returned in the fall of 1804. This time a large party of Russian and Native Alaskan RAC workers was backed by a Russian navy gunboat. The first Russian landing attempt was repelled by the Tlingit. Particular bravery was demonstrated by K'alyáan, who wore a ferocious war helmet depicting the raven (his clan crest) and dispatched the enemies with a large iron hammer.[7] However, after several days of confrontation, the Sitkans decided to withdraw from their defensive positions and made their way across the Baranoff Island, settling within the territory of a neighboring Tlingit tribe. The Russians interpreted the Tlingit retreat as a sign of fear. The Native tradition, however, invokes other reasons, practical as well as "supernatural," for their withdrawal (see Jacobs 1990; Dauenhauer and Dauenhauer 1990; Kan 1979–95).

The Kiks.ádi withdrawal from their ancestral territory undermined the clan's stature within the Tlingit sociopolitical universe. To make matters worse, their decision to get rid of their very young and the very old kin prior to departure caused a serious rift between them and the Kaagwaantaan clan of the Eagle (Wolf) moiety. Since Tlingit moieties and clans were matrilineal and exogamous, each clan recruited its spouses from one or several clans of the opposite moiety. Hence some of the slain persons happened to be Kaagwaantaan. In a society where matrilineal group solidarity was very strong, any injury to one's clan committed by another had to be compensated with payments made of human life or at least large amounts of wealth. The Kiks.ádi inability or unwillingness to fully compensate the injured clan damaged their relations with their "in-laws," whose power and influence were on the rise.[8] Moreover, from the Tlingit point of view, the battles of 1802 and 1804 were primarily a Kik.sádi, rather than a pan-Tlingit, affair. Consequently, in the aftermath of the 1804 confrontation, the Russians maintained friendlier relations with the Kaagwaantaan than with the Kiks.ádi. In fact, the former helped negotiate peace between the RAC and the Kiks.ádi.

The reasons for this peace were quite simple: both sides had a vested interest in the continuation of trading relations. While the Tlingit had already become somewhat dependent on the Russian trade items, the Russians needed the fur and especially the fish and meat that the Tlingit could procure.[9] By the early 1820s the RAC management gave permission to the Kiks.ádi, the Kaagwaantaan, and several other smaller clans to return to Sitka (or Novoarkhangel'sk, as the newcomers called it) and establish a settlement just outside its palisade.

For the next four and a half decades the two sides coexisted in what I have called a "cold peace" (Kan 1999:172–173). In other words, their relationships were never very warm but for the most part peaceful, interrupted only occasionally by violent skirmishes. Over the years the amount of food traded by the Natives to the Russians increased steadily and so did the number of Tlingit men working for the company. Realizing how dependent they had become on the Tlingit, the RAC courted their leaders, offering them lavish annual feasts and presenting them various special gifts that the Natives were eager to obtain. Some of the aristocrats as well as their lower-ranking kin became baptized and occasionally attended church services, although their understanding of and commitment to Russian Orthodoxy remained very limited (Kan 1999; cf. Grinev 1991; Dean 1994, 1995).

Despite this rapprochement, the walls of Novoarkhangel'sk continued to be constantly guarded, and the Tlingit were allowed into the town only in small groups and during certain hours. The Natives also remained suspicious of the Russians and continued to resent their permanent presence, particularly their unauthorized use of local firewood and food resources. In retaliation for what they perceived as the Russians' theft of their clan-owned property, the Tlingit periodically helped themselves to the Russian supplies. One such attempt, occurring in 1855, resulted in the last and the most serious confrontation between the RAC and the Sitka Natives, in which a number of lives were lost by both parties.

Thus by 1867, when Russia sold its American possessions to the United States, the Tlingit (particularly in Sitka) had, on the one hand, become quite dependent on their trade with the Russians and, on the other, maintained their political and ideological independence from them. This situation changed dramatically when the Stars and Stripes replaced the Russian imperial flag above Novoarkhangel'sk.

Sitka under U.S. Army Rule (1867–77)

With the establishment of the American rule in Alaska, Tlingit relations with the whites changed drastically. Unlike the Russians, the Americans were both determined and had the military power to exercise control over the entire Tlingit territory, rather than just the town of Novoarkhangel'sk, which they renamed Sitka. While their predecessors had been concerned primarily with extracting the region's fur, the Americans were eager to explore all of its resources, including fish, minerals, and timber.

Although resentful of this multifaceted attack on their way of life as well as their cultural values, the Tlingit, by and large, did not shy away from contacts with the Americans whom they saw as a source of attractive new trade goods and other valuable resources. In fact, for the first few decades after the establishment of the new colonial rule, many Tlingit families enriched themselves by working for the newcomers or selling food, firewood, and handicrafts to them (Hinckley 1972, 1996; Kan 1999:174–192).

Following the transfer ceremonies, the head of the local U.S. Army contingent, General Jefferson Davis, a Civil War veteran with a checkered military record, assumed authority over the new district of Alaska. Soon thereafter, the local American businessmen and other seekers of fortune who rushed to Sitka in anticipation of a bonanza formed a local government.[10] In the minds of these newcomers (many of them California "forty-niners"), Sitka, like the rest of Alaska, was an empty and wild frontier, its resources ready for the taking. The first thing they did upon arriving in the old Russian capital was to stake claims to the best lands in town, including some property owned by the RAC's former employees.

What the newcomers did not anticipate was the presence of a large number of "Russians" who for various reasons had not taken advantage of a free passage back to the mother country offered to them by the RAC. Thus, according to the 1870 census of Sitka, out of the total population of 391, only 32 were American-born non-Russian whites (Cracroft 1981:93–125). Though these people spoke Russian and shared many aspects of the lower-class Russian culture, the majority were actually of Native Alaskan or more often mixed, that is, Russian and Native Alaskan, descent. The latter had been officially designated as "Creoles" by the RAC and had played a major role in the company's operations throughout Alaska (Oleksa 1990). Most of them were poor, spoke no English, and felt abandoned by the RAC, which had paternalistically taken care of their needs for decades.[11] American observers described this community as destitute and demoralized. There was a very high level of alcoholism, and many of its members survived through the help of American army rations and city charity.[12] With a large percentage of widows and single women among the "Russians" and the presence of many single Anglo-American men, prostitution in Sitka was quite high.

All of this led the Americans, and particularly Sitka's small upper crust (wealthy merchants and government officials), to hold the "Creoles" in low esteem. It should be pointed out that despite this anti-"Russian" prejudice, members of the local American society's lower stratum, particularly soldiers and various frontier riffraff, did socialize with the Creoles and even began marrying Creole women and joining the Orthodox Church, which the entire Russian community belonged to.

Another major reason for this anti-Creole prejudice was the strongly negative attitude toward "half-breeds" that was so common in post–Civil War America. Thus, for instance, the Sitka newspaper characterized the local Russian Orthodox parish as being composed of a few Russians, with the rest being Indians and half-breeds, "the latter exhibiting the vices which generally come of mingling the blood of degenerate races" (*The Alaskan*, February 7, 1891:1). Another American observer referred to the Creoles as "superstitious, filthy, drunk-addicted, lazy, stupid, immoral, and generally unfit for United States citizenship" (Lain 1976:148). Not being classified as "white" by the local establishment, the Creoles, in turn, tried to distance themselves as much as possible from the "savage Indians."[13] Thus their old anti-Tlingit sentiments were exacerbated by a strong anti-Indian prejudice exhibited by the Yankees, who disparagingly referred to the Sitka Indian village as "the Ranch(e)" and to its inhabitants as "bucks" and "squaws."[14]

To keep the "savages" out of the town, the Army maintained the old Russian palisade and demanded that the Tlingit return to the "Ranch" at night. Nevertheless, compared to the Russian era, Native access to the white settlement increased significantly. On one hand, the Americans did not feel as threatened by the Indians as the Russians once did. On the other, they needed Tlingit laborers and had a commercial interest in the things the "Siwashes" offered for sale.[15]

Attracted by the new opportunities to acquire wealth and impressed with American military might, the Tlingit never openly rebelled against the occupation of their lands. In fact by the late 1870s many of them began asking American officials to establish schools and churches in their communities, to enable them and their children to acquire the knowledge that seemed to make the "Washington Men" so powerful. The few violent confrontations that did occur between them and the Americans in the first two decades after 1867 were caused by Native attempts to use the indigenous forms of retribution against physical injuries inflicted upon them or their kin by the newcomers. Thus if a Tlingit was injured by an American, his kin might capture another American as a hostage and threaten to kill him unless a substantial amount of gifts and/or money was paid to them as restitution.[16] On several occasions the army responded by bombarding the village inhabited by the "rioters." However, quite often restitution was, in fact, offered by the Americans to the injured persons and their kin as a way of maintaining peace. Thus although rumors of the "savages" planning an attack on the white settlements continued to crop up in southeastern Alaska in the 1870s, the new frontier was relatively quiet, especially compared to the situation on the Great Plains.[17] Thus it appears that as long as the Americans did not openly insult the Tlingit or refuse to compensate these proud and sensitive people for injuries, the latter were willing to tolerate the presence of the "Washington Men" in their midst.

Given this state of affairs it is very unlikely that any Sitka Tlingit would have seriously contemplated attacking the white town in 1879 or at any other time. In fact, in 1874, General Davis stated flatly, "There is no danger whatever from the Indians" (*The Alaskan*, July 13:187).[18] Having finally realized that the army's presence in Sitka and the rest of Alaska's panhandle was not really necessary and wanting to use the soldiers to suppress the Nez Perce uprising in Idaho, the American government decided to withdraw the troops during the summer of 1877 (Hinckley 1972:101–104).

The 1879 Incident

If the Tlingit posed no real threat to Sitka, what could have produced the tremendous fear of the Indians in the Creole community of the late 1870s? To answer this question, I examine the written statements generated by that community prior to and immediately after the February 1879 altercations. Their author was the local Orthodox priest, Father Nikolai Mitropol'skii, who served as both the leader of the local "Russians" and their liaison to the American community. The major document outlining the Creole concern is a report written by Father Nikolai to the Alaska Consistory in San Francisco (*Russian Orthodox American Messenger*, 1971, vol. 67:187–191), in which he asked his superiors to appeal to the Russian ambassador to encourage the U.S. government to offer some sort of a guarantee for Sitka's Orthodox community against "Kolosh" abuses.[19]

The document states that while the army was stationed in the Sitka the rights and freedoms guaranteed to the remaining Russian inhabitants of Alaska and to the Orthodox Church by the 1867 transfer treaty were protected from Indian abuses. Since 1877, however, the lives and property of Sitka's Orthodox residents had been threatened by their "savage" neighbors' misconduct. Their misdeeds included removing large sections of the old Russian stockade, looting and damaging two empty houses owned by the church, and destroying the crosses in Orthodox cemeteries. Most appalling, from the priest's point of view, was the "Kolosh" vandalizing of St. Michael's Cathedral, including the breaking of windows and, especially, playing cards and loitering on the church's porch. Father Nikolai even claimed that the "savages" had been carving "disgusting" images on the porch's railings, although he does not specify what they represented. When the church warden asked the loiterers to leave, they either paid no attention or laughed at him.

The Russian residents' private property was also under attack. At night the Kolosh would take apart the small fences surrounding their vegetable gardens and dig up whatever was growing there, thus depriving the owners of one of their few sources of food. Sometimes they even dared to enter the Russians' houses and, if no one was watching, stole their possessions. If the owner managed to chase them off, they usually came back in "gangs" of fifteen or twenty, broke the windows, and attempted to pillage the house. Intoxicated Kolosh who had been turned away from a Russian-owned house came back to avenge the owner's "insult" by throwing stones at his property. Small children, young girls, and grown-up women were also allegedly insulted by the "savage" visitors who made "scary faces" at them.

It is difficult to establish how accurate the report of these grievances was. Like the rest of his parishioners, Father Nikolai was undoubtedly troubled by the breaking of the boundary between his and the Kolosh communities, a process that intensified with the army's departure and that undermined the Creoles' attempts to distance themselves from the Indians and claim a "non-Native status." Though he most likely exaggerated the extent of the "Indian abuses," I suspect that some of the Tlingit anger against the Russian intruders, accumulated during the years of the RAC's presence in Sitka, was now being expressed in acts of petty vandalism and theft. After all, as I pointed out earlier, the Tlingit had always perceived the use of the local resources by RAC's employees as theft. What the priest fails to mention is that some of his own impoverished parishioners were also involved in helping themselves to whatever they could plunder from RAC's former property, including the palisade itself. In addition, while the Creoles spoke of the "dangerous drunken Kolosh," many of them were engaged in making home brew for their own consumption and for sale to the Natives (Teichmann 1963[1925]:172–222).

At the same time, a single sentence in the priest's report explains why stealing from the helpless Russians had become such a common practice: a number of the town's Euro-American residents were buying this stolen property from the Tlingit, thus encouraging their misconduct. A sense of freedom, of being able once again to be the masters in their old territory must also have played a role in this behavior. As Mitropol'skii puts it, in response to the Russian reprimands the Tlingit responded that "there are no soldiers here any more and we can do whatever we wish." The Native attacks on church property is particularly significant, since it indicated that they continued to view the cathedral, the cemeteries, and other church-owned structures as simply part of the Russian communities' possessions and thus fair game, rather than as something sacred and shared by the Tlingit and non-Tlingit Orthodox people.

Mitropol'skii's petition also expressed his community's frustration with the U.S. authorities, as represented by customs officials, whom the "Russians" perceived as being totally indifferent to their plight. These men are described as spending only a few days visiting Sitka and then reporting to their superiors that all was well there. Their lack of concern about America's "citizens by purchase" is illustrated by an incident that occurred in November 1877 during the customs ship's brief visit. "At that time," wrote Father Nikolai,

> the Sitka savages organized some sort of a festivity and up to one hundred
> guests from other Indian villages came to visit them. Festivities among

these savages consist of dancing and excessive consumption of home-made vodka (*hoochinoo*). Suddenly towards the end of the festivities, when the savages' minds were totally clouded by this brew, a rumor spread that they were planning to wage an open attack on the White residents and kill several of them in honor of the festivities.

The only possible sources of this rumor were the Creoles themselves. Inspired by memories of the slave killings that had accompanied major Tlingit mortuary and memorial ceremonies several decades earlier and that the RAC tried hard to stop, they were now casting themselves in the role of the sacrificial victims.[20] The Creoles' fear was further aggravated by their discovery on the day after the appearance of this rumor that the customs ship had quietly left Sitka during the night. To their relief, none of them was sacrificed—in fact, the killing of slaves had just about stopped by that time. However, Mitropol'skii and his parishioners continued to believe that every major gathering of the "Kolosh" in Sitka could put their own lives on the line. As he puts it, "God forbid, if the rumor turned out to be true. Savages cannot be trusted."

Sitka's Russian residents' plea for help, so dramatically stated by Father Nikolai, remained unheeded. In this atmosphere of fear and suspicion, which some of Sitka's Anglo-American residents shared with the majority of its "Russian" inhabitants, wild rumors continued to circulate. Combined with several incidents involving violent confrontations between individual whites and Tlingit (often precipitated by drinking) that took place in 1877–78, they contributed to the "great Indian scare" of the winter and spring of 1879.

The events leading up to this "massacre" that never materialized can be briefly summarized as follows. In 1878 five of six Tlingit crew members recruited by the captain of the ship *San Diego* to hunt fur seals perished when their canoe capsized in the Bering Sea. All of them were Kiks.ádi, and two of the hunters were close relatives of K̲'alyáan, the head of the Atóo Wax̲íjee Hít (Strong House) lineage and a direct descendant of the famous K̲'alyáan who took part in the 1802 destruction of the first Russian fort in Sitka. The sole survivor of the expedition was finally awarded 100 dollars by the company that had hired him, but most of that money had been spent on legal fees and living expenses in San Francisco, where he fought his battle against the company. Upon his return to Sitka, this man renewed his claims, arguing that the company had promised him and his fellow hunters five dollars for each day they remained on board the *San Diego*. Unfortunately, his claim could not be substantiated because the ship's captain had drowned as well. The relatives of the deceased hunters also tried unsuccessfully to get the company to pay them for the Kiks.ádi lives lost at sea (Sherwood 1965:327–328; Ushin's diary, May 1877, in ARCA, D 434).

What made the Kiks.ádi particularly unhappy was the fact that their rivals, the Kaagwaantaan, had recently turned out to be more successful in pursuing their own claims resulting from the death of one of their members (Brady Collection, Beinecke Library, Yale University).[21] The Kaagwaantaan then proceeded to tease the Kiks.ádi about their inability to get compensation from the people responsible for the death of their relatives. Another incident, which occurred in January 1879, further strained Kiks.ádi relations with Sitka's Euro-American community. When some Tlingit murdered a lone American resident of the nearby Hot Springs, a reward for their arrest was posted, and soon thereafter two Kiks.ádi men were apprehended and locked inside the guardhouse to await transportation south to stand trial. The alleged murderers' clan was faced with what it perceived to be a double standard—while five of its members had died without compensation, the killing of a white man resulted in the immediate arrest of two of their kin. This prompted the offended clan to renew their claims for just compensation for the deaths of the seal hunters. Customs collector Ball, who after the army's withdrawal became the only government official in the territory, continued to stall, while an intoxicated K'alyáan allegedly threatened to kill five Sitka merchants if payment for his relatives' lives was not forthcoming. Finally, Ball agreed to pay the Kiks.ádi an amount equal to the wages owed to each of the drowned men at the time of their deaths, which was an amount smaller than the $200 K'alyáan had been demanding for each of the five lost lives. Unfortunately, the money finally offered to the offended clan was swallowed up in legal fees.

Kiks.ádi anger mounted, fueled by further heavy drinking. Finally, on February 6, 1879, a dozen Kiks.ádi men, some of them under the influence, approached the stockade. They were turned away, not by the town's Euro-American defenders, but by "chief" Annaxóots, appointed by Davis to serve as the head of the local Indian police in 1874, and his relatives, one of whom was injured in the skirmish. According to some sources, K'alyáan was not even among the "attackers" but had left for Chilkat just before the skirmish. The "besieged" Sitkans believed that he had gone for reinforcements (Ushin's Diary, February 8–9, 1879, ARCA, D 434), but Beardslee, the fist navy commander to be stationed in Sitka in the aftermath of this conflict, subsequently learned that the Kiks.ádi leader had actually been trying to pacify his own unruly kinsmen (1882:45–46). In fact, Beardslee (1882) seems to offer the most accurate description of what happened that day when he characterizes the "Tlingit attack" on

Sitka as a simple brawl between "half a dozen drunken Kiks.ádi . . . and a large force of Kaagwaantaan." He also claimed to have learned from some Creole families that K'alyáan had that night sent to their protection some trusty members of his own family and that he himself went to the house of a Euro-American friend to defend him if molested by inebriated Tlingit men. This led the Navy officer (Beardslee 1882) to describe the Kiks.ádi leader's conduct during this incident as "brave and intelligent."

Conclusion

In sum, all available information indicates that the Tlingit, even the deeply offended Kiks.ádi, never had serious plans to attack the non-Tlingit town. Moreover, the main confrontation appears to have occurred between two rival clans: Sitka's original settlers whose fortunes had been declining somewhat since their exit from the area in 1804 and the ascending Kaagwaantaan, whose elderly leader, Annaxóots, enjoyed much better relations with the Americans than did his much younger rival, K'alyáan. The events leading up to this incident as well as the incident itself demonstrate that although the Tlingit were nurturing some serious grievances against the Americans and the demoralized Creoles, Annaxóots' strategy of reconciliation with the whites, which K'alyáan appears to have eventually adopted as well (Hinckley 1996; Kan 1999), enjoyed much greater support in the Tlingit community than the direct confrontation that some of the younger hotheads were trying to pursue.[22]

Despite the peaceful resolution of the crisis, throughout the month of February Sitka's "white" residents and their Tlingit allies conducted nightly vigils and kept guard duty, while a few Kiks.ádi continued to pillage the remains of the palisade (Ushin's Diary, ARCA, D 434). While this was going on, Sitka's merchants and some of the other Anglo-Americans, as well as many Creoles, sent a petition to the British naval authorities in British Columbia, making the following plea:[23]

> We, the Citizens of Sitka, Alaska, are now threatened with Massacre by Indians of this place. We have made application to our Government for protection, which we hope will be extended, but the intricate forms of law through which our petition must drag its way will create delay, which may result in our entire destruction before the arrival of necessary succor. Therefore we beg and pray that you will at once send or come to our assistance. We beg that you lay aside all forms of etiquette between governments, and you will take the side of an oppressed and threatened people, that you will let sympathy and charity dictate your decisions, for before the required aid from our government can be had, we may be

past assistance. Our unprotected position is well known; our appeal to you is from man to man. We ask help from you in the name of humanity. . . . Her Majesty's Government has been known for its promptness in assisting the oppressed of any nation and we hope our appeal may not be in vain. [Sherwood 1965:338]

The outcome of their appeal was the establishment of the navy rule in Alaska, which ended in 1884 when the first territorial governor was appointed by Washington. Although the Tlingit were never again accused of plotting to invade Sitka, memories of 1802–4, 1855, and 1879 were kept alive within the Creole (and, to a lesser extent, American) community. Occasional Russian visitors to the area continued to be entertained by the Creole old-timers with stories of Native treachery and Russian bravery for several decades thereafter.[24]

In conclusion, I would like to reiterate Fogelson's argument about the need for scholars concerned with reconstructing the history of Indian-white relations and understanding its cultural meanings to focus on *epitomizing events* as well as *nonevents* (to which I would also add *rumor*). All of these phenomena, refracted through the multiple sources available, tell us a great deal about the participating actors' worldviews and historical consciousness and help explain their conduct. This discussion of the 1879 "Tlingit scare" lends support to Fogelson's insightful idea and benefits from the analytical frameworks he has provided (cf. Krech 1991:354). More specifically, unlike my predecessors (Sherwood 1965; Hinckley 1972, 1996) who only utilized English-language sources and paid little attention to the Creole or the Tlingit viewpoints on this crisis, I have tried to look at it from the latter perspectives by drawing on the documents from the Alaska Russian Church Collection as well as the ethnographic data on the Tlingit collected by my predecessors and myself. My analysis of the Russian ecclesiastical sources demonstrates that the Creole fear of a "Kolosh" attack of the 1870s cannot be properly understood without taking into consideration the pre-1867 history of the Russian-Tlingit relations and an image of the "wild and treacherous Kolosh" that had developed in the Russian-Creole historical consciousness during that era. The conduct of some of the Tlingit in February 1879 makes sense only if one examines the causes and manifestations of a longstanding tension between the two leading Sitka clans, the Kiks.ádi and the Kaagwaantaan.

Acknowledgments

I would like to thank Jennifer S. H. Brown and Pauline Turner Strong for their thoughtful comments on an earlier draft of this chapter.

Notes

1. I place the word *Russian* in quotation marks because ethnically that community was mainly composed of persons of mixed Russian and Native Alaskan (Aleut, Alutiiq, Athapaskan, Tlingit, etc.) ancestry whose official designation during the Russian colonial era was "Creole." See discussion later in this chapter.

2. By the 1930s and 1940s, because of intermarriage with Anglo-Americans and the desire to distance themselves from the Natives with whom they shared a church, very few people in Sitka continued to identify themselves as Russian (Kan 1999).

3. One could also refer to the "1879 attack" as an "exaggerated event" since it was not totally invented.

4. The only detailed study of the 1879 affair is Sherwood's 1965 article. This incident is also discussed in Hinckley's monographs (1972:129–132, 1996:129–148). While drawing on these works, I was able to add new information from Governor Brady's manuscript (Brady Collection, Beinecke Library, Yale University) as well as Orthodox Church documents (Alaska Russian Church Archives [ARCA], Manuscript Division, Library of Congress). In addition, I have tried to look at the events of 1879 from the perspectives of the Tlingit people involved in them, particularly the two rival clans—the Kiks.ádi and the Kaagwaantaan, whose descendants I interviewed in 1979–95 (Kan 1979–1995, 1999).

5. The main sources on this subject are Tikhmenev 1978(1861–63); de Laguna 1972; Jacobs 1990; Dauenhauer and Dauenhauer 1990; Grinev 1991; Kan 1999:42–72.

6. On the centrality of the concept of respect in Tlingit culture see Kan 1999:10–11.

7. Both of these objects, treated as valuable treasures, remained in his clan's possession until the twentieth century when they were turned over to the local museum (see Beck 1906; Hays 1906; Shaw 1907; Corey 1987:141, pl. 26).

8. This incident remains to this day a somewhat controversial subject for Sitka's Native community. However, I feel obligated to mention it because it is crucial for my interpretation of the 1879 events. I should also point out that several references to this old tragedy have previously appeared in print (e.g., Jacobs 1990).

9. Food deliveries from Russia were costly and took a great deal of time, while the Russian and Native Alaskan inhabitants of Sitka never managed to procure enough subsistence food themselves (Gibson 1987).

10. According to Hinckley (1972:41–43) there was no clear legal sanction for that.

11. Only a few of the Creoles took advantage of the offer of citizenship made to them by General Davis.

12. Sitka was probably one of the few places in the United States where non-Indians were receiving army rations.

13. At the same time, a few remaining "respectable" "Russian" families tried very hard to distance themselves from the Creoles, downplaying their Native Alaskan and Creole ancestry.

14. This term was most likely a derivation from the term *rancheria*, commonly used by Euro-American Californians to refer to a shantytown of destitute Native Americans. In the Sitka context it had a very definite negative connotation.

15. *Siwash* was a Chinook jargon word, derived from the French *sauvage*, which Euro-Americans used as a derogatory term to refer to Northwest Coast Indians.

16. On the indigenous forms of Tlingit justice see Oberg 1934 and de Laguna 1972:594–596.

17. In fact, some of the American observers began favorably contrasting the Indians of

southeastern Alaska, whom they described as thrifty and interested in learning the ways of the white man, with the "uncivilized" tribes of the American West.

18. To maintain morale and to keep busy, however, his troops interpreted any minor incident involving a Tlingit as a major military affair. Thus, when in February 1877 a wounded fugitive Sitka Tlingit man threatened to attack them, "the military authorities prepared their Gatlings and other light Field Guns and placed them in favorable positions for defense . . . two companies, 25 men each, of the Russian inhabitants of the town were organized and armed with Springfield muskets." An attempt to organize a company among Sitka's American population failed. In the end, no Indian attack took place (*Sitka Post*, February 5, 1877).

19. *Kolosh* was the term used by the Russians all through the pre-1867 to the refer to the Tlingit. It might have been derived from an Aleut term for the labret, common among the Tlingit women, which the Russians saw as ugly. In the post-1867 period, this term was only gradually replaced by the Russian equivalent of the English "Indians." The persistence of the old term, which had become more pejorative than it had been before 1867, further illustrates my argument that the Sitka Creoles continued to view the Tlingit through the cultural lenses inherited from the Russian colonial era (Grinev 1986).

20. On the RAC's attempts to curtail the ceremonial killing of slaves see Kan 1999:120–122. On the indigenous cultural logic behind these practices see Veniaminov 1984[1840]: 426, Emmons 1991:40–46, Kan 1989:132–134.

21. According to Brady (Brady Collection, Beinecke Library, Yale University), when a high-ranking Kaagwaantaan and a close relative of one of its headmen, Annaxóots, died, having drunk undiluted liquor purchased from an American miner, his clan quickly received $250 in gold coins from the seller.

22. Cf. Fogelson's (1971) insightful analysis of the eighteenth-century Cherokee social structure was characterized by a fundamental opposition as well as complementarity between the "red" warriors and the "white" older men who advocated peace.

23. As Hinckley (1972:86–87) points out, the American merchants were less concerned with having the Navy stationed in southeastern Alaska as a defense against the Indians than in having their "spendthrift crews" as customers. Thus previous "Indian scare alarms" usually brought a U.S. Revenue Marine or navy vessels into the area.

24. Thus Shaw (1907) reported 30 years later that, according to some local (most likely, Creole) sources, in 1879 *K'alyáan* was planning to wear his famous predecessor's Raven helmet during an attack on Sitka. According to this journalist (Shaw 1907:152–153), "the ill success which accompanied his plans was supposed to be due to the loss of the charm possessed by the raven bonnet, and accordingly he buried it in the woods." Though this story belongs most likely in the realm of Euro-American mythology, it does make sense as a reflection of the Russian-Creole experience of the events of 1879 as a frightening replay of the 1802–4 confrontation between Baranov and the "wild Kolosh" led by an earlier *K'alyáan*.

References

ARCA Alaska Russian Church Archive. Manuscript Division, Library of Congress. (Available on microfilm). Washington DC.
Beardslee, L. A.
　　1882 Report of Capt. L. A. Beardslee, U.S. Navy, Relative to Affairs in Alaska, and . . . U.S.S. Jamestown. 47th Cong., 1st sess., Ex. Doc. No. 71, January 24, 1882.

Beck, George J.

1906 Soucth-shan (the Old Hat). Pamphlet published by the Women's Board of Home Missions of the Presbyterian Church. New York.

Brown, Jennifer S. H., and Elizabeth Vibert, eds.

1996 Reading Beyond Words: Contexts for Native History. Peterborough ON: Broadview Press.

Corey, Peter, ed.

1987 Faces, Voices and Dreams: A Celebration of the Centennial of the Sheldon Jackson Museum. Sitka: Division of Alaska State Museums.

Cracroft, Sophia

1981 Lady Franklin Visits Sitka, Alaska, 1870. The Journal of Sophia Cracroft, Sir John Franklin's Niece. R. N. De Armond, ed. Anchorage: Alaska Historical Society.

Dauenhauer, Nora Marks, and Richard Dauenhauer

1990 The Battles of Sitka, 1802 and 1804. *In* Russia in North Pacific. Proceedings of the 2nd International Conference on Russian America. Richard A. Pierce, ed. Pp. 6–23. Kingston ON: Limestone Press.

Dean, Jonathan

1994 "Their Nature and Qualities Remain Unchanged": Russian Occupation and Tlingit Resistance, 1802–1867. Alaska History 9(1):1–17.

1995 "Uses of the Past" on the Northwest Coast: The Russian American Company and Tlingit Nobility, 1825–1867. Ethnohistory 4:2265–302.

Emmons, George T.

1991 The Tlingit Indians. Frederica de Laguna, ed. Seattle: University of Washington Press.

Fogelson, Raymond D.

1971 The Cherokee Ballgame Cycle: An Ethnographer's View. Ethnomusicology 15:327–338.

1974 On the Varieties of Indian History: Sequoyah and Traveller Bird. Journal of Ethnic Studies 2:105–112.

1984 Who Were the Ani-Kutani? An Excursion into Cherokee Historical Thought. Ethnohistory 31:255–263.

1989 The Ethnohistory of Events and Nonevents. Ethnohistory 36(2):133–147.

Gibson, James R.

1987 Russian Dependence upon the Natives of Alaska. *In* Russia's American Colony. S. Frederick Starr, ed. Pp. 77–104. Durham NC: Duke University Press.

Grinev, A. V.

1986 Ob etnonime 'koloshi' [On the term "Kolosh"]. Sovetskaia Etnografiia 1:104–108.

1991 Indeitsy tlinkity v period Russkoi Ameriki (1741–1867). [Tlingit Indians during the Russian America Era (1741–1867)]. Nauka: Novosibirsk.

Hays, Lydia A.

1906 Kahtlian: A Chief of the Raven Tribe. Pamphlet published by the Women's Board of Home Missions of the Presbyterian Church. New York.

Hinckley, Ted C.

1972 The Americanization of Alaska, 1867–1897. Palo Alto CA: Pacific Books, Publishers.

1996 The Canoe Rocks: Alaska's Tlingit and the Euramerican Frontier, 1800–1912. Lantham MD: University Press of America.

Jacobs, Mark

1990 Early Encounters between the Tlingit and the Russians. *In* Russia in North Pacific.

Proceedings of the 2nd International Conference on Russian America. Richard A. Pierce, ed. Pp. 1–6. Kingston ON: Limestone Press.

Kan, Sergei

1979–95 Ethnographic Notes on the Tlingit. Manuscript and audiotapes in author's possession.

1989 Symbolic Immortality: Tlingit Potlatch of the Nineteenth Century. Washington DC: Smithsonian Institution.

1991 Russian Orthodox Missionaries and the Tlingit Indians of Alaska, 1880–1890. *In* New Dimensions in Ethnohistory. Papers of the Second Laurier Conference on Ethnohistory and Ethnology. B. M. Gough and L. Christie, ed. Pp. 127–160. Mercury Series, Canadian Ethnology Service Paper No. 120. Ottawa: Canadian Museum of Civilization.

1999 Memory Eternal: Tlingit Culture and Russian Orthodox Christianity through Two Centuries. Seattle: University of Washington Press.

Krech, Shepard, III

1991 The State of Ethnohistory. Annual Review of Anthropology 20:345–375.

Lain, B. D.

1976 The Decline of Russian America's Colonial Society. Western Historical Quarterly 7:143–153.

de Laguna, Frederica

1972 Under Mountain Saint Elias: The History and Culture of the Yakutat Tlingit. Smithsonian Contributions to Anthropology, vol. 7. Washington DC: Smithsonian Institution.

Oberg, Kalervo

1934 Crime and Punishment in Tlingit Society. American Anthropologist 36:145–156.

Oleksa, Michael J.

1990 The Creoles and Their Contributions to the Development of Alaska. *In* Russian America: the Forgotten Frontier. Barbara Sweetland Smith and Redmond J. Barnett, eds. Pp. 185–195. Tacoma: Washington State Historical Society.

Shaw, W. T.

1907 The War Bonnet of Kath-le-an. Alaska-Yukon Magazine 1:152–153.

Sherwood, Morgan B.

1965 Ardent Spirits: Hooch and the Osprey Affair at Sitka. Journal of the West 4:301–344.

Teichmann, Emil

1963[1925] A Journey to Alaska in the Year 1868. New York: Argosy-Antiquarian Ltd.

Tikhmenev, P.

[1861–63] 1978 A History of the Russian-American Company. Seattle: University of Washington Press.

Veniaminov, Ivan

1984[1840] Notes on the Islands of the Unalashka District. Lydia T. Black and R. H. Geoghegan, trans. Kingston ON: Limestone Press.

Williams, Gerald O.

1982 Law and Order on the Alaska Frontier: The Period of Naval Rule (1879–1884). *In* Armed Forces on the West Coast. John Lengellier, ed. Manhattan KS: Sunflower University Press.

14. Time and the Individual in Native North America

DAVID W. DINWOODIE

Introduction

The ethnographic record exhibits a division of temporal labor.[1] Africa offers up time from the point of view of segmentary social structure, latitudinal and longitudinal (Evans-Pritchard 1940; Fortes 1949). Australia offers up myth-time, past and present (Myers 1986; Munn 1970). South America and Indonesia offer variations on the idea of antihistory (Geertz 1973; Lévi-Strauss 1966). The Middle East offers the idea of experiencing biblical and Koranic events directly in the present (Thompson 1999). Time-obsessed Europe offers up the idea of social seriation in collective memory, architecture, written records, and experiential routines (Halbwachs 1980; Herzfeld 1991; Heidegger 1982). Europe also offers up the idea of the repression of memory, in both political and psychological terms. Suburban America offers up the two ideas of recovered memory, the retrieval of events that for various reasons have been inaccessible to consciousness (Bass and Davis 1994), and false memory, the vivid recollection of experiences that are proved never to have occurred (Wassil-Grimm 1996).

If all of these phenomena are evident in every society to some degree, they seem to exhibit a special intensity in the societies with which they are most closely associated. In principle, societies could be compared in terms of which conceptions of time are present and which predominate. In practice, however, a more effective and compelling approach has been to attend to individuals' efforts to navigate the temporalities of their socioculturally and historically distinctive experiences. Exploring this approach systematically, in fact, might inject life into an anthropology of time, a science that sometimes gives one the impression—after discovering that "time" is in some sense constructed—of having gone prematurely gray.[2]

In pursuing the experience of temporality, we might ask what contribution Native American studies can make. The backdrop to the ethnography of Native North America, Edward Sapir once suggested, is the "extreme psychological distance between the aboriginal American cultures and the kind of life they are expected to live today" (Darnell 1990:303). Thus viewed, Native North America offers up the experience of temporal spectra, traditional and modern, in a way that no other ethnographic area does. After all, to generalize grossly, what distinguishes Native North America among all ethnographic areas is the contiguity and sometimes confluence of practices hypermodern, archaic, and everything in between. This approach, the exploration of temporal spectra as epitomized in the experiences of representative Native Americans, would not be entirely new. A start was made in the 1930s and 1940s, particularly in the life-history work supervised by Edward Sapir and John Dollard. It has also been developed implicitly in actor-centered anthropology (Basso 1990, 1996; Fogelson 1974, 1984, 1989; Hallowell 1955) and in Native American literature (Erdrich 1984; Momaday 1968; Silko 1977; Welch 1979).

For reasons that I do not fully understand, however, North America continues to be primarily associated in the general literature not with anything as interesting or palpable as the experience and management of temporalities but with a retrograde version of the question of whether time is relative. Stated simply, this question reads: Do the Hopi have "time" (Black 1959; Gell 1992; Malotki 1983; Munn 1992)? In order to show how an undue emphasis on this approach has impoverished not only Native American studies but also the anthropology of time, I will discuss a recent incarnation of this debate and compare the sort of material on which it is based to the evidence on temporality from one revisited life history. Rather than closing the book on Native American time, so to speak, I hope to show that we have only begun to learn about the Native American experience of temporality and that a genuine understanding of Native American temporality has the potential to reinvigorate Native American studies and the anthropology of time more generally.

The Anthropology of Time in Native North America

In *Hopi Time: A Linguistic Analysis of the Temporal Concepts in the Hopi Language* (1983) Ekkart Malotki set himself the goal of refuting Benjamin Lee Whorf's analysis of Native American temporality. Alfred Gell summarized the situation as he saw it:

The first thing to say is that quite apart from the defensibility of the "Whorf" hypothesis in general, Whorf's specific claims about Hopi, for which he never provided much evidence, are very unsound. Malotki (1983) has published a lengthy monograph showing (1) that Hopi characteristically and systematically uses spatial metaphors to indicate temporal facts, the very feature which Whorf indicated as being characteristically SAE [Standard Average European]; and (2) that Hopi has a two-tense system (unmarked non-future vs. future -ni) and a very elaborate aspect system which allows for consistent distinction within the non-future between perfective-aspect/past time and imperfective aspect/present-time interpretations. Not only is Whorf completely wrong about Hopi "timelessness," but it could as well be said that of the two languages English is the more timeless. [Gell 1992:127]

Similar judgment was rendered the year before in an earlier review of the anthropological literature on "time":

[Whorf argues that] in European languages the "subjective 'becoming later' which is the essence of time" is "covered under" homogeneously quantifying and spatializing time concepts. If Whorf then takes the contrasting Hopi language to contain no "time"-referring forms (as commentators have often stressed; see 124a), it is apparently, because of his Bergsonian dichotomy of *durée* (non-spatialized, "psychological time") and spatialized "time" (192:57f., 216). Since, in his view, Hopi expresses *durée* only, he calls it (paradoxically) "timeless" (192:216). (For linguistic evidence that Hopi does in fact "spatialize" time, see 124a.) [Munn 1992:98]

Munn too suggests that the Hopi indeed "have time," at least in the sense of what Bergson called *durée*, and she suggests that they have more when she cites evidence, "see 124a"—Malotki's book as it turns out—to the effect that the Hopi language spatializes time.

By inference then both Alfred Gell and Nancy Munn, two established and respected anthropologists, credit Malotki with disproving Whorf's thesis regarding Hopi time. More careful than Gell in her evaluation of Whorf's work, Munn still implies that Malotki debunks Whorf when she suggests, with the use of parentheses, that it would be paradoxical to call Hopi "timeless." Since their opinions are highly regarded, their conclusions are sweeping, and since the evidence remains elusive we are obligated to take a closer look at Malotki's work.

Hopi Time is a 677-page book arranged into numbered sections in the anthropological linguistic tradition. Most sections consist of entries for grammatical elements. For example, "*ep* as adverb of time" is the subtitle of section 1.2.2.1.1. The section runs between pages 27 and 29. In it Malotki lists 12 sample sentences and provides 8 sentences of commentary on the variations in meaning of *ep*.

Entries vary considerably in length. They are grouped together according to themes. For example, roughly 100 entries appear under "The device of spatio-temporal metaphor," roughly 50 under "Units of time," 30 under "Temporal particles," and so forth. Thus the book is presented in the form of an encyclopedic inventory of linguistic forms and usages bearing on the reckoning of time. The book is impressive in terms of the number of entries and in terms of its sheer bulk.

Nevertheless, the framing material raises a number of questions. First, according to the author, the central contribution of the book is in the "actual presentation of Hopi language data" (Malotki 1983:10). In his words, the monograph

> elaborates . . . on the basis of the ethnolinguistic evidence which was gathered in the field and which, for the most part, constituted hitherto unrecorded source material. Crucial here is a methodology based on the broadest possible linguistic documentation from the Hopi language. It is through such an approach that new insights into Hopi language and culture are arrived at. [Malotki 1983:629]

In another passage he states that the "foremost goal of this monograph is to provide extensive Hopi information in the form of linguistic documentation and data in an area that suffers from 'tremendous gaps on the most vital points' (Hoijer 1954:274)" (Malotki 1983:7). In yet another he says that "semantic niceties and lexicalized concepts indigenous to a foreign language are not gleaned from a superficial familiarity with the source language and culture is, of course, a truism for any ethnolinguist" (Malotki 1983:631). The repeated references to data, depth of research, and degree are clearly meant to suggest that previous research fell badly short on all these grounds. Indeed, at one point Malotki comes right out and states that "there was . . . no hard core evidence stemming from linguistic research on the Hopi language to either verify or falsify his [Whorf's] findings" (Malotki 1983:6). In addition to his better known essays on "primitive thinking" and "time," which contain considerable data, Whorf also published grammatical analyses of the language (1938:275–86, 1946:158–183) and other highly regarded descriptive-analytic writings on the language (e.g., 1956). Given that, Malotki's assertion that his is the first work on Hopi temporality based on empirical research does not ring true. Is he suggesting that Whorf did no "hard core" research? Why would someone otherwise so little known pit himself against a figure whose work was highly regarded by the likes of Franz Boas and Edward Sapir?

Second, although this is not the occasion to systematically compare the work of Malotki and Whorf, it is important to note that for someone who places such a premium on the quality of data and is so dismissive of previous work, Malotki is notably vague about when he began his research and how much time he actually spent studying Hopi. He addresses neither question directly.[3] He says that Helmut Gipper of the Westfalische Wilhelms-Universität Münster, Germany, originally "kindled [his] interest in the Hopi language" (Malotki 1983:ix). He says that the initial phase was funded by a scholarship granted in 1973 and that in 1976 his dissertation on Hopi space was accepted by the Department of Linguistics at the University of Münster.

Third, given his conviction regarding the success of his restudy of Hopi time and the obvious challenge of delineating traditional time reckoning in the 1970s (as opposed to the 1930s and 1940s), we would expect Malotki to have a highly sophisticated approach to delineating the pertinent data. He presents his approach as follows:

> The approach embarked on for a considerable portion of this work is best described in terms of "linguistic archaeology." Its results may, therefore, be characterized "salvage linguistics" to some extent, for the impact of linguistic acculturation, especially in the domain of time but also in other areas, is thorough and devastating. [Malotki 1983:7]

Instead of a carefully developed approach he offers up a metaphor. Unfortunately, all that the idea of linguistics as archaeology by itself suggests is that some artifacts are located in their original context and some are not; it does not provide a way of differentiating the two. Difficult as this can be in archaeological excavation, it can be exceedingly difficult in the analysis of speech. Malotki only addresses the question of what counts as data (and then only indirectly) in his discussion of his selection of his consultants.

Most of the linguistic input for *Hopi Time*, according to Malotki, came from Michael Lomatewama of Hotvela and Herschel Talashoma from Paaqavi (Malotki 1983:ix). Malotki says that these men's "speech habits" represented an earlier time, in the sense that their speech was at the time of the research "marked by certain phonological and morphological traits that are no longer practiced by speakers of the latest generation" (Malotki 1983:7). The fact that the speech of the consultants is archaic, we are encouraged to believe, circumvents what would otherwise pose an impediment of considerable proportions. All of their utterances presumably reflect on the past. Still, we wonder how it is that these two men above all others have stood outside of time. We wonder whether these men emphasize "phonological and morphological traits no longer practiced" in some situations more than others, and, if so, we wonder what factors contribute to the variable expression of "time" in their speech. We also wonder what languages they speak (English? Tewa?) and which varieties they control (sacred varieties?), and whether these can be readily controlled for.

Malotki addresses none of this directly, but does allow that the "dialect represented throughout this monograph is that spoken in the Third Mesa villages of Hotvela and Paaqavi *by generally bilingual Hopi in ages ranging from the late thirties to the late seventies*" (Malotki 1983:ix, emphasis added). This raises more questions. Are we to infer that Lomatewama and Talashoma are generally bilingual? Are they balanced bilinguals and experience no interference from English when speaking Hopi? Do they participate equally in traditional and modern life?

Perhaps, we surmise, Malotki, notwithstanding the complex and admittedly heteroglot repertoire of his key informants, was able to delineate his data by relying on utterances produced in the context of traditional time-reckoning activities. He might use some form of the ethnography of speaking to delineate a linguistic corpus by reference to context. The likelihood that he employed such a method is diminished by what he says about his reliance on interviews: "the gigantic project could not have been concluded" without the participation of Lomatewama and Talashoma in "hundreds of hours of linguistic interviews" (Malotki 1983:x) (on the difficulties of analyzing language produced in interview contexts see Briggs 1986 and Dinwoodie 1999). Though we cannot know for sure, this reliance raises another possibility: that Malotki's data was based, notwithstanding the possible years of fieldwork, primarily on decontextualized sentences uttered by middle-age bilinguals as a part of interviews conducted in the context of a variety of wage work, far (in social distance) from the settings of traditional Hopi life.

Putting on hold for the moment the question of whether refuting Whorf would represent a meaningful contribution to the anthropology of time, then, the questions raised by Malotki's framing of his study suggest that we are not safe to assume with the secondary literature that he has effectively refuted Whorf. Pursuing this requires that we examine Malotki's data and evaluate how he extrapolates from it. But before we look into a key section of his book, it is necessary to first review the key concepts in the anthropology of time.

The Anthropology of Time

The "rhythm of social life," according to Emile Durkheim, is at the "foundation" of the "category of time" (Durkheim 1915:32). As the rhythms of social life are shaped by the formative practices of particular societies ("rites"), those are in turn shaped by the dominant institutions, and the dominant institutions vary in type and composition from society to society, so too concepts of time vary accordingly. Considerable evidence confirms that indeed they do (see Munn 1992 and Gellner 1992 for generally excellent reviews of this extensive and ever expanding literature).

This is the whole matter in a nutshell. The anthropology of time in its essentials would be simple if not for the fact that not everyone accepts the account. First, certain Marxist anthropologists, Maurice Bloch (1976) most prominent among them, claim that Durkheim inadvertently exalted the "times" of ruling classes and mistook them for a generally applicable theory of time. A generally applicable theory of time, Bloch believes, must be grounded firstly in the facts of nature, not in the nature of social groups. An approach grounded in the nature of groups would always be one grounded in class. By discounting the natural bases of time and emphasizing the significance of the social dimension, Durkheim effectively confused knowledge with ideology (Bloch 1976:279).

If Durkheim's position is, as Bloch claims, more complicated than it seems on the face of it, the same is true of Bloch's. The difficulty in his position lies not in its claim that social time always has an ideological cast—which can very well be accommodated in a modified Durkheimian approach—but in positing the possibility of knowledge completely free of social influence. Far from sharing deep appreciation of the various rhythms that inform the natural universe for their own sake, people direct their attention to those aspects of natural rhythms that are relevant for participating effectively in their social circles.

As long as they know when to take shelter or when to duck, humankind thrives with only the crudest understanding of the environment as such. It is evidently interested in the natural world only insofar as it matters for particular human purposes. In this sense, people's awareness of natural rhythms seems to be no less informed by social considerations than are social rhythms per se, which is to say, they too are intrinsically social. The only apparent exceptions are those esoteric varieties of science that are so inordinately expensive as to depend entirely on the resources and stability of entire complex societies. These observations suggest that for our purposes as anthropologists all varieties of time are intrinsically social, hence ideological in the Marxian sense.

Curiously, those who search for time in knowledge of nature tend to see nature in the time of clocks and watches, and if we read their work closely they tend to use some version of clock time as their model for "real time." This is particularly surprising when we consider that Western time concepts as expressed on clocks and watches developed not as results of increasing sensitivity to nature as such, nor in a milieu of "neutral and inevitable technological change," but as expressions of "the most far reaching [socio-cultural] conflict" (Thompson 1967:93–94). During the Middle Ages the church bell provided the standard indicator of social rhythm. In the heart of medieval European society, work rhythms and in fact all other rhythms of life were subordinated to the cycles of aggregation to worship marked by town bells. On the one hand, the bells indicated the rhythms of activity, and on the other, they served as reminders of the predominance of the Church in the matter of religion and polity, understood as a single undifferentiated sphere of life.

With the rise in significance of markets and industry came the need for new forms of "time" better suited to measuring the value of the work of individuals. In other words, labor, a category of abstract, commodified, social activity that could be bought and sold by analogy to gold, could not be instantiated without a new form of "time." Clocks with circular dials metaphorically representing "the rhythms of social life" in terms of an infinite sequence of equal spaces, every one of equal value, made it possible for work to be measured as a summation of activity units. And with this a new form of time was born. The "problem of the duration of the working day was especially acute in the textile sector," writes Jacques LeGoff; "where cloth does not occupy a dominant position, we do not observe the appearance of the *Werkglocke*" (1980:46). LeGoff continues: "in the cloth manufacturing cities" of the fourteenth century, "the town was burdened with a new time, the time of the cloth makers. This time indicated the dominance of a social category. It was the time of the new masters" (1980:46).

The "time" of these new capitalists spread relatively quickly. Initially clocks were situated in factories, behind closed doors. They were used to demarcate periods of active labor and to place values on the contributions of workers. Only factory owners and their direct representatives had access to the clocks. Workers began to worry that the owners would slow the factory clocks in order to get more labor than they were paying for. Workers had no way of independently evaluating whether they were being treated fairly. What they needed were clocks of their own. Thus a market demand emerged for cheap portable clocks.

Up until that time watches had been expensive and unreliable. They had been curiosities of the rich. With the interests of workers in mind, however, watchmakers began to produce more accurate and affordable timepieces. As workers began to acquire these watches and exert some control over the conditions of their servitude they also began to acquire "time" in another sense: they began to accept the time of the workplace as the standard for the measure of activities more generally. By the middle of the eighteenth century the clock had penetrated to the realm of personal regime. Thompson cites Laurence Sterne's novel *Tristam Shandy* (1759–67) as evidence. Tristam's

> father—one of the most regular men in everything he did . . . that ever lived—had made it a rule for many years of his life,—on the first Sunday night of every month . . . to wind up a large houseclock, which we had standing on the back-stairs head. He had likewise gradually brought some other little family concernments to the same period, and this enabled Tristam to date his conception very exactly. [1967:57]

And so the new time penetrates, if you will pardon the expression, the domestic sphere.

Time management of the capitalistic variety was also extended into schools and even into religion. As Thompson again observes, the "very name of 'the Methodists' emphasizes this husbandry of time," (1967:88). Though the Church resisted, the "time" of capitalists began to challenge the "time" of the Church, and clocks began to replace bells in town squares. Sundays, the period of highest intensity of societal participation, began to be subsumed within "weekends," periods of ritualized leisure, that is, periods of liminal reversal within the market system.

At this point the "time" of the textile industry had succeeded in supplanting other "times" so well that we have difficulty registering the fact that fairly recently there had been other idioms of temporality. Church bells in fact once represented *the* standard measure of temporality, though they do not, obviously, represent "time" as we have come to know it.

The matter is further compounded by the widespread use of celestial and other "natural" rhythms to stand above and lend credence to our social rhythms. Obviously, many temporalities underlie the workings of the natural world, and these all underlie the workings of the social world. In this sense time is certainly inherent in celestial rhythms. Upon reflecting on the situation, however, most would agree that these natural rhythms are necessary but not sufficient conditions for interpreting the "times" used to measure social rhythms within specific social groups. When a natural rhythm happens to be used to mark an important social juncture, it does not do so naturally; it does so because people resolve to use it accordingly. And doing so requires resolving who chooses which rhythm. To understand the social workings of such a rhythm we have to consider who made the decisions and how. In our everyday lives, however, it is normal for us to simplify the matter and to literally accept the metaphors implicit in time representations. We confuse the use of natural rhythms as higher order metapragmatic symbols of social rhythms with natural rhythms as such.

In summary, the basic problematic of the anthropology of time dates back to Durkheim's *Elementary Forms of the Religious Life* (1916). What we generally refer to as *time*, the standard time of the West, goes back to the industrial age. It represents a culturally and historically specific temporal system, and it serves poorly as a model for temporalities. Thus in the anthropology of time it is conventional to distinguish between *time* as the dominant form of representation of social rhythms in the West and *temporality* as social rhythms and their representation in general. With this in mind, it would be extraordinary for a non-Western society to have "time" as we know it prior to its contact with Europeans. After all, "time as we know it," is effectively a variety of European temporality. No one familiar with the anthropology of time would misinterpret such a statement with the claim that the so-and-so have no temporal concepts.

Though he does not use the term *temporality*, Whorf consistently distinguishes between the concepts of *time* and *temporality*. In situations where the two could be confused he uses modifiers to emphasize one reading over another, as in, "what we call 'time,'" or when he avoids the term *time* and characterizes 'temporality' as "the stream of duration" (Whorf 1956:57).

Ceremonial Time: The Wuwtsim

Malotki opens *The Ceremonial Calendar* (pp. 451–480) by indicating that the ceremonial cycle is the "preeminent guide for temporal orientation" (Malotki 1983:451). The first ceremony he discusses is the Wuwtsim, "tribal initiation," which occurs in late fall and marks the onset of the ceremonial year.

The Wuwtsim itself is initiated by an announcement made by the *tsa'akmongwi* ("crier" chief) when a specialist determines that the sun has passed "a certain location along the eastern horizon" known as *tingap-pi* or "announce-place" (Malotki 1983:453). At this point, Malotki presents a "text sample" to provide insights into "the Hopi phraseology in this connection." Here I rearrange the passage slightly, according to standard conventions for working with linguistic data, moving free translations into place next to Hopi clauses so they are more easily read with reference to the Hopi phrases and the adjacent morpheme-by-morpheme glosses. I have also slightly altered the translations, breaking the lines along clause boundaries and numbering each resulting line. I have no knowledge of the Hopi language, and I am claiming no expertise in using these techniques. I am simply trying to illustrate the propositional structure of the Hopi phrases in order to evaluate how they bear on the question of Hopi time:

(1) *pu' pas tingap-pi-va taawa yama.*
then very announce-place-at DIF(FUSIVE LOC) sun go through
"Then the sun rises at the 'announcement point.'"
(2) *pam pa-ng tuvoyla-t a-ng yama-k-qw pu',*
that there-at DIF marker-ACC REF-at DIF cross-k-SUBR DS w/then
"And when it has risen at that marker there,"
(3) *pam hak i-t wuwtsimu-y tiingap-ngwu-qa,*
that someone this-ACC Wuwtsim-ACC announce-HAB-REL
"[then] the person announces Wuwtsim,"
(4) *naala navoti-y'-ta-ngwe-nii-qe,*
alone knowledge-POSS-IMPRF-HAB-HAB-NEX-CAUSAL SS
"[the one who] alone knows it [lit. 'the one whose sole knowledge it is],"
(5) *oovi tingap-qw pas pàasat pu' haki-m nanapta-ngwu*
therefore announce-SUBR DS very that time then someone-PL hear-HAB PL
"and therefore people learn of it after he has announced it." [Malotki 1983:453–454]

Though they warrant more extensive linguistic and cultural interpretation than can be give here, these phrases seem well suited to illustrating the Hopi grammatical categories that are mobilized in the representation of relations between two events, and even perhaps to showing how particular speech acts are grounded in specific Hopi institutions. For purposes of considering temporality the key passage is the segment running from line (2) to line (3), glossed as follows: (2) "When it moves into position, (3) someone announces the onset of Wuwtsim." Line (2) represents the linguistic expression of a proposition to the effect that the sun moves into position; line (3) represents the linguistic expression of a proposition to the effect that a person announces the onset of the Wuwtsim. In addition, the Hopi expression of these two clauses includes in its grammar a metalinguistic message that determines the temporal relationship between these two propositions. This metalinguistic representation of the temporal organization of events is the *structure* of Hopi temporality. The nature of the metalinguistic representation in this case, which surprisingly Malotki chooses not to analyze, requires a little explanation. Line (2) seems to be a relative temporal clause linked to the following matrix clause (line 3) with a relativizing use of the form *pu'* or "then." Due to its subordinate status, the relative clause is not conjugated for tense, aspect, or mode but is in a relatively nonfinite form. One presumes a sort of progressive-by-default reading, as in the English phrase, "when it crosses," as though this could be achieved without the adding of the *-es*. Malotki indicates that the matrix verb, which is in the second clause (line 3), is in the habitual (*-ngwu*), which Malotki presumably considers as an aspect. As a point of information, this grammatical element happens to be one of three that Whorf labels "Assertions." These, as he put it, "resemble tenses but refer to realms of validity rather than of time" (Whorf 1946:176). According to Whorf, *-ngwu* "declares a general or customary truth, e.g., *ciroht pe:yawnemyan^we* "birds fly" (Whorf 1946:176). Thus we can interpret line (3) as "a person announces" in the roughly same sense as "then the congregation takes the sacrament," when speaking of church services in general rather than the way things transpire on a particular occasion.

Temporal relations between the two clauses per se, which is a separate matter altogether in this case, are apparently signaled by the inherent lexical aspects of the roots for "cross" and "announce." Both seem to have the inherent aspectual quality of punctuality. Rather than "cross" providing the typical progressive background to the punctual act of announcing (as would *talking*, for example, in a phrase like, "they were talking when he entered the room"), in a common combination of imperfect aspect in the subordinate clause, perfect in the superordinate, it is as though in this case the significance of one punctual event is being represented by the fact of its contiguity with another punctual event. Or so it appears on the basis of what is present in Malotki's text.

To go further in our analysis of time in this temporally pregnant phrase, we would want to know who uttered these phrases and under what circumstances. Is this passage from a myth in which an original temporal determination is being made and discussed by an actor? Is it the sort of formula that is typically used by narrators to sum up myths? Does it represent the form of the announcement itself (see Black 1967; Kroskrity 1992)?[4] Or does it represent a consultant's reflections on the past such as might be offered in an ethnographic interview? Whatever the case— and there is much more to know about this case—the passage provides no evidence for the presence of European "time as we know it" in the temporal organization of relations among Hopi clauses. Malotki presents the passage as evidence and yet tells us nothing about how we should look at it. Based on our crude reanalysis of the phrase we can see that the Hopi linguistic expression of temporality is indeed rich, but we can identify nothing that makes explicit or implicit reference to "time as we know it."

Together with other materials, this passage bearing on the announcement of the Wuwtsim could be used to determine how grammatical categories are managed as a system in the representation of temporal relations. Insofar as it is grounded in normative social processes, this systematic articulation of categories would represent Hopi temporality. Identifying category types alone would not answer the question of whether "time" as we know it is present in Hopi patterns of speech. Presumably, Hopi could well make use of a tense category, as European languages do, among other categories, in the management of temporality and still not manage temporality in a European fashion. In European languages temporality is a function of not merely the use of tense but its use to activate a metapragmatic system that Whorf describes as discrete and internally homogeneous units of imagined "time," aligned like bottles in a row. What is crucial for understanding the Western ideological complex of time, as Whorf puts it, is that the system of tenses "is amalgamated with that larger scheme of objectification of the subjective experience of duration . . . [which] enables us to 'stand time units in a row'" (Whorf 1956:143). Nevertheless, an analysis of the grammatical nature of temporality (which types of categories are involved, tenses, modals, aspects?) would certainly be a necessary element of such a discussion. With respect to the example from the Wuwtsim, Malotki provides no grammatical analysis, nor does he explain any "larger scheme of objectification" in terms of which it operates. Instead he continues without comment as though he believes the significance of the passage is obvious.

Malotki continues by introducing five more phrases that he seems to feel are suited to reinforcing his point about "time." Reading them we see that they seem not to represent phrases uttered as part of the Wuwtsim at all, or as a part of the announcement, or in reference to the organization of the Wuwtsim. Rather, they reflect the use of the ceremony viewed from the outside as a reference point for "locating" independent secular events or activities that are taking place outside of the ceremony altogether—much as one might use a homecoming festival as a reference for something that happened to occur in late summer but had nothing to do with the homecoming, as in "the leaves often began to change color around the time of homecoming." Consider the following example:

> hisat wuwtsimu-y e-p sutsep nuva-'iw-ta-ngwu
> long ago Wuwtsim-ACC it-at always snow-STAT-IMPRF-HAB
> "Long ago there was always snow [on the ground] at [the time of] Wuwtsim" (Malotki 1983:454–455).

Given that "snow" seems to be the verb, we might retranslate the phrase as "Long ago at/during Wuwtsim, it was always snowing." In any case, not only does this sort of sentence not contribute any more than the first to a body of evidence bearing on the question of Hopi temporality; it raises the further question of why it appears in a section entitled *The Ceremonial Calendar*? Not only does it seem not to be the sort of sentence uttered in the figuration of ceremonial time, but it seems very much to be the sort of thing that is said in response to such questions as, "When was the Wuwtsim normally held?" or "What else was going on at that time?" The same is true for all the remaining sentences.

In sum, no evidence is presented in the section on the Wuwtsim that bears directly on the question of the presence or absence of "time" in Hopi. The best that can be said for the section is that Malotki establishes that inserting the English term *time* into the translations of four sentences of unknown provenance does not render them entirely unintelligible. To evaluate conclusively whether the Malotki book contains any evidence that bears in any way on Whorf's interpretation of Hopi temporality, based on what we can see in this section we would need to go through every example individually, evaluating each.

Evaluating the evidence is further compounded by the fact that Malotki himself fails to differentiate varieties of time reckoning. For example, when he sees fit to organize his discussion of Hopi ceremonial time by reference to "the Gregorian months, beginning with November which is commonly considered the starting period of the yearly ceremonial round" (Malotki 1983:452), Malotki apparently does not realize that he is mixing Hopi and Western systems. The inevitable divergences between the two systems and his reliance on the Gregorian system lead Malotki to make the bizarre suggestion, given his interest in shoring up the integrity of the Hopi figuration of temporality, that the Hopi system is irregular:

> The sequential listing of the various major and minor rites for each month does not necessarily imply that every one of them occurred periodically every year. Some were performed on alternate years, others at *irregular* intervals. [Malotki 1983:452; emphasis added]

Is not the apparent *irregularity* of the intervals a function of failing to identify the principles that underlie the ceremonies and instead substituting the periodicities of a Western calendar? He continues: "while some were more or less fixed, *others were variable* and depended on the initiative of an individual sponsor" (Malotki 1983: 452; emphasis added). Is not the variability here again a function of viewing Hopi rites from the point of view of a Gregorian calendar? In other passages Malotki outright mixes time frames: "a preeminent reference guide for temporal orientation is provided in the calendrically scheduled rites and rituals that compose the complex Hopi ceremonial system in the course of a year. Practically every month serves as a benchmark for one or several fixed ceremonial performances" (Malotki 1983:451). "Days," "hours," "years," and "months" on the one hand and "scheduled rites and rituals" and "fixed ceremonial performances" on the other are mixed together as though they are all parts of the same system. Does Malotki realize they are not?

In sum, a closer look shows that Malotki does not analyze key evidence and that where we would expect the argument to be strongest it remains entirely undeveloped. We have not proved conclusively that Malotki marshals no evidence, but we have shown that he marshals no evidence in a, if not the, key example. We would be gravely mistaken to assume that Malotki has refuted Whorf and/or shown that the Hopi have "time as we know it."

Time and the Individual

Altogether another approach to time is present in the autobiography of the Hopi man Don Taleyesva, as told to and as edited by Leo Simmons (Simmons 1942). At a certain point in his young adult life, Don Taleyesva explained, he was strongly encouraged to go through initiation. Though he had very little choice in the matter, he agreed. The formalities proceeded without delay:

> My ceremonial father soon came and led me toward the Mongwi kiva. . . . The officers seated me with eight other boys and told us that we were now young sparrow hawks (Keles) and should cry "Kele, Kele," like young hawks begging for food, whenever a ceremonial father came to the mouth of the kiva. [. . .] We were kept awake and members of the Wowochim society taught us the special songs. My grandfather Poleyestewa beat a drum, sang softly, and repeated until we caught the tune. His song touched my heart and became firmly fixed in my mind. Other members took turns teaching us all night long.
>
> At gray dawn an Ahl member called us out of the kiva and led us, with initiates of the other societies, to the foothills just off the southeast edge of the mesa. There we threw corn meal to the rising sun and prayed for a long, happy life. Returning to the kiva, we watched our ceremonial fathers weave our new outfits, practiced songs and dance steps, ate unsalted food, and took part in some special songs and rituals which cannot be revealed. Four days were spent in this manner and it proved to be a long, tiresome experience. We were under supervision continuously and

even when a boy had to go outside, we all went together with a guide. For four nights I had to sleep under a blanket with my ceremonial father, just as I slept with my mother as a baby, in order that he might "raise me to manhood."

Early in the morning of the fifth day our ceremonial fathers washed our heads in yucca suds. Then our clan brothers, uncles and nephews repeated the operation. [. . .] We were placed in a line outside the kiva to receive new names. Each Bear Clan member proposed a name for Louis, who was first in line, and the most appropriate name was selected for him. When my turn came, Sekahongeoma held a mother-corn ear before me and said: "Now I adopt you so that you may live long and be strong and happy. You shall be called Talayesva. I belong to the Greasewood and the Bamboo clans. The Greasewood has a tassel and so does the Bamboo. The name means Sitting Tassel, for these two plants." Everybody cheered and began calling me Talayesva immediately, seeming to forget my old name Chuka, which surprised me, for this change was very sudden. [Simmons 1942:159]

His new name marked the beginning of his participation in an eminent variety of Hopi "time" that is marked by the movement of peer groups through the Wowochim and through a system of names. The movements of people such as himself served much the same function in this variety of Hopi temporality as the movements of the hands of clocks do in the most widespread Western variety.[5] From the point of view of his elders his participation and that of his peers assured the future of this variety of Hopi time.

This passage is notable in that it provides us postmoderns, Hopi and non-Hopi alike, with a glimpse of the inside experience of a variety of non-Western time, which we tend to associate with the remote past. Even in 1942, however, the passage was remarkable not only for what it revealed about the past but for what it revealed about the Hopi experience of the multiplicity of modernity. For by the time Talayesva experienced the eminent variety of Hopi temporality exhibited in Wowochim naming, he had long since become personally involved in many other varieties. For example, he had long since been involved in church time: "Every Sunday we were taken to the chapel, where we sang, prayed, and had a lesson about Jesus Christ. On those days we were supposed to wear clean clothes and have our faces washed and our hair combed" (Simmons 1942:97). He was a dedicated follower of school time: "At first I went to school every day, not knowing that Saturday and Sunday were rest days. I often cut wood in order to get candy and to be called a 'smart boy.' I was also praised again and again for coming to school without a policeman" (Simmons 1942:90). He had mastered market time: "The superintendent put us to work picking peaches with two other boys at $1 a day. Within a few weeks I was made foreman of the peach-picking outfit and did not have to work so hard myself" (Simmons 1942:144–145).

He had also been introduced to some of the esoteric varieties of Hopi time. For example, on one occasion when very young, he decided he wanted to dance as a Katchina. A kind old man of some importance "insisted that [he] could," and he went ahead and danced "as a real Katchina" (Simmons 1942:91). Also, he had once experienced the miraculous time of the supernatural when a guardian spirit came to him in a dream (Simmons 1942:121).

Even more notable than the range of varieties of time he had been involved in prior to initiation was his awareness of time frames as objects of consciousness and his ability to move from frame to frame. For example, he and some others were once on leave from Sherman Indian School at Riverside, California, working at a place called Hazel Ranch "pitching hay for board and $2 day." One day the school superintendent arrived and told them to return to Sherman and prepare to return to Oraibi. Over the next few days they changed out of government clothes and traveled by wagon, train, and then wagon from rural California to the Los Angeles area, and then headed east and reentered Indian country. After disembarking from the train at Needles, California, Taleyesva went hunting. He returned to camp to find that "the men had a big bonfire and were dancing their Katchina dances" (Simmons 1942:131–133). From market time to school time to Katchina time, Taleyesva moves without comment.

Yet other passages show that Taleyesva was not only aware of different time frames and capable of navigating them as need be but that he has even mastered the trick of participating in more than one variety simultaneously, as when holding one frame in suspension while of necessity finishing out an allotted role in another. For example:

> In May, 1906, I went to Rockyford, Colorado, with a large group of boys to work on sugar-beet plantations. We were divided into groups of eight boys each and moved from farm to farm, thinning beets during the day and sleeping in tents at night. We worked eleven or twelve hours a day at 15 [cents] an hour.
>
> One Sunday another boy and I went for a long walk and found three or four small turtles. We sat down under a tree and butchered them, taking out the meat so that we could use the shells for rattles in the Katchina dances. *I made a speech to the turtles before killing them telling them*

that we had nothing to give them now but that when we got home we would make pahos for them. [Simmons 1942:109; emphasis added]

After the Wowochim, Taleyesva feels a definite change in himself. He has come to reconsider his earlier enthusiastic forays in the space and times of the wider world:

> I had learned a great lesson and now knew that the ceremonies handed down by our fathers mean life and security, both now and hereafter. I regretted that I had ever joined the Y.M.C.A and decided to set myself against Christianity once and for all. I could see that the old people were right when they insisted that Jesus Christ might do for modern Whites in a good climate, but that the Hopi gods had brought success to us in the desert ever since the world began. [Simmons 1942:178]

His early life and his experience of Wowochim exhibit a progression from being a subject of a whole spectrum of "times" to being himself a sign of the "times." Somewhat contrary to expectations, we observe not a linear acculturation into time as we Euro-Americans know it but rather a growing sophistication about the world of times. By the "time" that he is working with Simmons the complexity increases dramatically once again as Taleyesva laminates another order of time consciousness upon the others, reframing the events of his life in terms of the chronological time characteristic of autobiography.

Conclusion

Through his involvement in the hiring of John Dollard, Leo Simmons's mentor, at Yale Edward Sapir indirectly had a hand in *Sun Chief* (Darnell 1990:334–355, 358). He was dead before it reached publication in 1942, and he and Dollard had grown increasingly apart through the 1930s, so it is certain he would not have approved of it in many ways. Nevertheless, it represented one impulse of a broad endeavor that Sapir was very sympathetic to, namely, shifting the focus of interpretation of social scientists from societies as wholes toward "individuals," viewed as "total world[s] of form, meaning, and implication of symbolic behavior which a given individual[s] partly know, and direct, partly intuit and yield to, partly [are] ignorant of and [are] swayed by" (Sapir 1949:518). Due to the "metaphysical locus" to which it was frequently assigned, Sapir felt that the concept of culture was by itself inadequate for the interpretive challenges presented by cultural change and individual adjustment (Sapir 1949:516):

That culture is a superorganic, impersonal whole is a useful enough methodological principle to begin with but becomes a serious deterrent in the long run to the more dynamic study of the genesis and development of cultural patterns because these cannot be realistically disconnected from those organizations of ideas and feelings which constitute the individual. [Sapir 1949:512]

There is certainly no right way to do anthropology, and Sapir's views in this matter are neither unique nor privileged in any way. However, in the case of the anthropology of Native North America, an overemphasis on the question of whether the Hopi have time or whether time is in some absolute sense relative or constructed has seriously limited the contributions of Native American studies to general anthropology.[6] Taking very seriously "individuals'" experiences of time in the context, to paraphrase Sapir, of the often extreme psychological distances between the aboriginal cultures and the kinds of lives they are expected to live, has provided, and will continue to provide, an invigorating alternative.

Acknowledgments

This chapter is dedicated to Raymond D. Fogelson. I hereby register my gratitude for what he taught and how he taught it, for his encouragement and for his criticism. Though this chapter wanders not in the realms of saline allegory and though it includes only one possible pun and not a single humorous line, I hope nonetheless that it exhibits something of the spirit of his work.

Notes

1. Some would argue that the division of temporal labor evident in the ethnographic record reflects nothing more than an entrenched orientalism. Here I take no position regarding the role of orientalism in the field, but I do assume that the division of temporal labor in the ethnographic record represents something about the nature of time reckoning in the societies of the world.

2. A notable exception in this regard is Carol Greenhouse's recent thesis that the experience of time is shaped by the differential application of the law (Greenhouse 1996).

3. What we know from the published record suggests that a comparison might be interesting. If we estimate that he worked continually on this project from 1973 until *Hopi Time* was published, allowing a year for publication, Malotki apparently conducted about nine years of research. Are we to assume that he spent nine years at Hopi? And if he lived in the area for those nine years, how much time was spent participating in Hopi life? And what would that mean exactly in the context of this particular monograph? Of his own research Whorf says the following in his grammatical sketch of the Toreva dialect of Hopi:

The writer's studies have been made over several years with Mr. Ernest Naquayouma, a Hopi of Toreva long resident in New York city, with the aid of funds
supplied by the Committee on Native American Languages of the American Council of Learned Societies, checked by a field trip to Toreva and the other dialect
regions made with his own funds. [Whorf 1956:158]

We would further have to consider that Whorf was intimately familiar with Uto-Aztecan
languages prior to beginning his studies of Hopi. His profuse thanks suggest that Ernest
Naquayouma was an exceptional consultant, and his linguistic peers (Sapir, Kroeber, and
Haas, for example) all considered Whorf's work to be of the highest quality (Darnell
1990:377–378).

4. An anonymous reviewer suggested this very reasonable possibility.

5. A similar movement of people in relation to names served as the basis for Clifford
Geertz's classic account of Balinese time (Geertz 1973).

6. In this respect it is interesting to consider the two epigrams that appear on the opening
cover page (Malotki 1983:vii), Whorf's famous

*After long a careful study and analysis, the Hopi language is seen to contain
no words, grammatical forms, constructions or expressions that refer directly to
what we call 'time.'*

Benjamin Lee Whorf, "American Indian View of the Universe"

This quotation, written in approximately 1936, is counterposed to a Hopi passage, of which
I will present only the translation here: "Then indeed, the following day, quite early in the
morning at the hour when people pray to the sun, around the time then he woke up the
girl again" (Malotki 1983:vii). We are apparently to see that the second epigram provides a
direct challenge to the first. Chock full, as it seems to be, with "references" to "time," the
second passage is meant to leave the reader wondering, why, as Malotki puts it, "Whorf
erred so drastically" (Malotki 1983:631). What draws our attention, however, is that the
second passage is attributed *not to a Hopi individual* but to "Ekkhart Malotki, Hopi Field
Notes 1980."

References

Bass, Ellen, and Laura Davis
   1994 The Courage to Heal: A Guide for Women Survivors of Child Sexual Abuse. 3d ed.
      New York: Harper Perennial Library.
Basso, Keith H.
   1990 Western Apache Language and Culture: Essays in Linguistic Anthropology. Tucson:
      University of Arizona Press.
   1996 Wisdom Sits in Places: Landscape and Language among the Western Apache. Al-
      buquerque: University of New Mexico Press.
Black, Max
   1959 Linguistic Relativity: The Views of Benjamin Lee Whorf. Philosophical Review
      68:228–238.
Black, Robert A.
   1967 Hopi Grievance Chants: A Mechanism of Social Control. *In* Studies in Southwestern
      Ethnolinguistics. Dell Hymes, ed. Pp. 54–67. The Hague: Mouton.

Darnell, Regna

  1990 Edward Sapir: Linguist, Anthropologist, Humanist. Berkeley: University of California Press.

Durkheim, Emile

  1915 The Elementary Forms of the Religious Life. New York: Free Press.

Erdrich, Louise

  1984 Love Medicine. New York: Bantam.

Evans-Pritchard, E. E.

  1940 The Nuer: A Description of the Modes of Livelihood and Political Institutions of a Nilotic People. New York: Oxford University Press.

Fogelson, Raymond D.

  1989 The Ethnohistory of Events and Nonevents. Ethnohistory 36(2):133–147.

  1974 On the Varieties of Indian History: Sequoyah and Traveller Bird. Journal of Ethnic Studies 2:105–112.

  1984 Who Were the Ani-Kutani? An Excursion into Cherokee Historical Thought. Ethnohistory 31:255–261.

Fortes, Meyer

  1949 Time and Social Structure: An Ashanti Case Study. In Social Structure: Studies Presented to A. R. Radcliffe-Brown. Meyer Fortes, ed. Pp. 54–84. New York: Russell & Russell.

Geertz, Clifford

  1973 Person, Time, and Conduct in Bali. In Interpretation of Cultures. Pp. 360–411. New York: Basic Books.

Gell, Alfred

  1992 The Anthropology of Time: Cultural Constructions of Temporal Maps and Images. Oxford: Berg.

Greenhouse, Carol

  1996 A Moments Notice: Time Politics across Cultures. Ithaca NY: Cornell University Press.

Halbwachs, Maurice

  1980[1950] The Collective Memory. New York: Harper and Row.

Hallowell, A. Irving

  1955 Culture and Experience. Philadelphia: University of Pennsylvania Press.

Heidegger, Martin

  1982 The Basic Problems of Phenomenology. Translation, introduction, and lexicon by Albert Hofstadter. Bloomington: Indiana University Press.

Herzfeld, Michael

  1991 A Place in History: Social and Monumental Time in a Cretan Town. Princeton NJ: Princeton University Press.

Kroskrity, Paul V.

  1990 Arizona Tewa Public Announcements: Form, Function, and Linguistic Ideology. Anthropological Linguistics 34:104–116.

LeGoff, Jacques

  1980 Time, Work, and Culture in the Middle Ages. Arthur Goldhammer, trans. Chicago: University of Chicago Press.

Lévi-Strauss, Claude

  1966 The Savage Mind. Chicago: University of Chicago Press.

Malotki, Ekkehart

1983 Hopi Time: A Linguistic Analysis of the Temporal Concepts in the Hopi Language. Berlin: Mouton Publishers.

Momaday, N. Scott

1968 House Made of Dawn. New York: Harper and Row.

Myers, Fred R.

1986 Pintupi Country, Pintupi Self: Sentiment, Place, and Politics among Western Desert Aborigines. Washington DC: Smithsonian Institution.

Munn, Nancy D.

1992 The Cultural Anthropology of Time: A Critical Essay. Annual Review of Anthropology 21:93–123.

1970 The Transformation of Subjects into Objects in Walbiri and Pitjantjatjara Myth. *In* Australian Aboriginal Anthropology. R. Berndt, ed. Pp. 141–163. Nedlands: University of Western Australia.

Sapir, Edward

1949 Selected Writings in Language, Culture, and Personality. Berkeley: University of California Press.

Silko, Leslie Marmon

1977 Ceremony. New York: Viking Press.

Thompson, E. P.

1967 Time, Work-Discipline, and Industrial Capitalism. Past and Present 38:56–97.

Thompson, Thomas L.

1999 The Mythic Past: Biblical Archaeology and the Myth of Israel. New York: Basic Books.

Wassil-Grimm, Claudette

1995 Diagnosis of Disasters: The Devastating Truth about False Memory Syndrome and Its Impact on Accusers and Families. New York: Penguin Press.

Welch, James

1979 The Death of Jim Loney. New York: Harper and Row.

Whorf, Benjamin Lee

1938 Some Verbal Categories of Hopi. Language 14:275–286. Reprinted in Language, Thought, and Reality (1956).

1946 The Hopi Language, Toreva Dialect. *In* Linguistic Structures of Native America. Harry Hoijer, ed. Pp. 158–183. New York: Viking Fund.

1956 Language, Thought, and Reality: Selected Writings of Benjamin Lee Whorf. John B. Caroll, ed. Cambridge MA: MIT Press.

Part Four

Representations

On Selves and Others,
Hybridities and Appropriations

15. Culture and Culture Theory in Native North America

ROBERT BRIGHTMAN

Introduction

Consider a Crow elder's remarks:

> You see that tin shed. It's like my culture. You can sit back here, ask questions, and describe it. But it's not 'till you get inside, 'till you see what's inside and feel it, that you really know what the tin shed is about. You can't stand outside; you've got to go inside. [Frey 1987:xv]

This brief for participation is one exemplification among many of a rich contemporary discourse by Indians on Indian cultures. Raymond Fogelson, whom we honor in this volume, has long been attentive to what he calls "ethno-anthropology" (or perhaps "ethno-ethno-anthropology" [see Fogelson 1974]), and I attempt here a skeletal and comparative discussion of North American Indian varieties. The topic is metacultural discourses on "culture," "custom," "tradition," or "convention" that are commensurable (or not) in sense and reference with the anthropological culture concept(s). Not all discourses on culture are necessarily "[ethno-]anthropological," and the latter appellation might better be limited to forms that exhibit the explicit or implicit comparativism central to the Western discipline. Throughout I employ the word *Indian*, ambiguities of correctness notwithstanding, because it remains (politicians and academics to one side) the commonest unmarked English self-designation employed by the peoples concerned.

There exist, of course, not one but multiple and heterogeneous anthropological culture concepts. As a point of reference, here is a 1930s definition by Edward Sapir: "Any form of behavior not physiologically necessary, interpretable in terms of the totality of meanings of a specific group, and the result of strictly historical processes (imitation, instruction) is 'cultural' " (1994:37).

The Boasian culture concept here explicated was plural, relative, historical or conventional, nonbiological, totalizing ("all the manifestations"), and contextualized in distinct social collectivities. Beyond these core features, there was diversity: the superorganic versus the subject, behavioral determinism versus agency, configuration versus disorder, ecology versus history, and so on. The difficulties of comparing Western and Indian ethnoanthropologies are exacerbated by a like diversity in North America. Indian groups were and are diverse in their modes of conceiving their own and other people's cultures.

Proto-Anthropologies in the New World
Natures and Cultures

Insofar as anthropology ascribes culture only to *Homo sapiens sapiens*, the concept, in classically segmentary fashion, at once unites and differentiates the species. Although both biogenetic capacity for culture and participation in historical cultures separate humans from other organic (and inorganic) entities, the plurality and particularity of these same historical cultures bespeak internal diversity. Positioned ambiguously between natural unity and cultural diversity are substantive or abstract "cultural universals"—fire, cooking, language, division of labor, incest taboos, "some form" of family, production, economy, politics, religion, art, and the like—unparalleled among nonhuman species.

It remains to be known whether this linkage of natural unity with cultural diversity and plurality is paralleled in other peoples' ethnoanthropologies. Though ideas commensurable with social and cultural pluralism are commonly present (see discussion later in this chapter), it is unclear how widely distributed is the notion of a unitary human kind. Monogenetic or polygenetic accounts of human origins in Indian mythology will afford greater clarity on the issue than the usual linguistic speculations based on polysemous nouns meaning both (one's own) "tribe" and "human." Earlier European scholars engaged in exhaustive debates as to whether New World peoples were beings like themselves, and there are few grounds for supposing that Indians never reflected in similar terms on the humanity of their neighbors or of Europeans. Thus "own tribe" may sometimes have been the focal or even unique exemplar of a human condition from which foreigners were marginalized or excluded altogether. For example, one North Alaskan Eskimo assured Richard Nelson in the 1960s that "Eskimos are the only 'real' human beings, and all other people are 'something else, I don't know what' " (Nelson 1973:289). In such cases, inter-societal cultural differences—rather than being contrasted with a natural species unity—seem to compose distinctions among humans analogous to distinctions between humans and nonhuman kinds or between varieties of the latter. Other Indians plausibly had less restrictive and more inclusive notions of "human-ness."

It remains unclear to what degree Western and anthropological distinctions between human culture and human and nonhuman natures are paralleled in Indian anthropologies. In earlier anthropology, the Fourth World societies were distinguished—to their disadvantage—from modern societies by their inability to tell the difference between nature and culture: hence animism, totemism, and prelogical participations. Subsequently, Lévi-Strauss asserted the cultural universality of the nature/culture distinction:

> The discontinuity between the rules [of nature and of culture] is undoubtedly universally recognized, and there is no society—be it ever so humble—which does not place high value on the arts of civilization through the discovery and usage of which man differs from animals.
> (1976[1961]:320)

But today the Fourth World peoples are once again being distinguished from modern societies by their inability to tell the difference between nature and culture. Now, however, they are congratulated for the achievement. Authoritative-sounding pronouncements that the nature/culture distinction is both provincially Western and theoretically misguided have proliferated since the 1980s (MacCormack and Strathern 1981; Descola and Palsson 1996; Ingold 1996). The issue, however, remains very much to be explored. In different contexts, Lévi-Strauss's universal "culture" refers either to socially learned normative (versus instinctive) rules or to the substantive "arts of civilization" (cooking, fire, marriage rules, clothing and adornment, music, language) that distinguish humans from nonhumans. As Lévi-Strauss illustrated at some length, Indian mythologies do indeed address the question of how humans came to acquire "the arts of civilization" and how animals (often their original owners) came to lose them. At the same time, some Indian societies juxtapose the human/nonhuman and culture/nature homology with theological visions of animals—and perhaps all other entities—as retaining human characteristics, including culture.

Anthropologists link the socially learned character of culture with its *conventional* or symbolic properties, contrasting these with the *necessary*

character of the innate or biogenetic aspects of human and nonhuman animal behavior. Whether Indians similarly contrast the socially learned human behavior to innate animal behavior—and thus oppose cultural "convention" to natural "necessity"—remains also to be investigated. Though Indian people had no fully conventional or symbolic theory of culture (see the discussion of "Cosmogonic Culture" later in this chapter), both children and deviants plausibly provide a universal basis for recognizing the learned versus innate character of customary behavior, and thus also for intergenerational transmission of different cultures in different tribes. Awareness of the priority of enculturative over hereditary determinations of human behavior is exemplified in the societies of the Eastern Woodlands, by the practices of resocializing juvenile and sometimes adult captives as entitled "members" (Ackerknecht 1944; Hallowell 1976; Axtell 1981). This awareness is seldom more elegantly attested than in a Shawnee oratorical address in 1764 to the English soldiers to whom white captives, long since socialized as Shawnees, were being repatriated:

> Father—Here is your Flesh and Blood . . . they have been all tied to us by Adoption, although we now deliver them up to you. We will always look upon them as Relations, whenever the Great Spirit is pleased that we may visit them . . . Father—we have taken as much Care of these Prisoners, as if they were [our] own Flesh and Blood; *they are become unacquainted with your Customs, and manners*, and therefore, Father, we request you will use them tender, and kindly, which will be a means of inducing them to live contentedly with you. [Axtell 1981:175]

The expression "flesh and blood" may be a Shawnee calque of the English phrase. In either case, we may observe here evidence for a genealogical component to Shawnee identity ("*as if* they were our own flesh and blood"). But more noteworthy is the assertion of socialization as the determinant of cultural competence ("they are become unacquainted with your Customs"). If, as may have been the case, Shawnees conceived cultural differences between themselves and Englishmen as cosmogonically ordained, it remained within Shawnee agency to transform individual Englishmen into Shawnees. As Indians well knew, behavioral characters of nonhuman animals are not commonly convertible in this fashion. It remains to be discovered whether Indians ascribed innate behaviors to animals and thus contrasted them with humans. If they did not, it would suggest that they conceived animal and human behavior as equivalently "cultural."

The semantics of lexical forms glossed as "custom" or "tradition" in Indian languages may yet provide a privileged perspective on these aspects of indigenous culture theory, although no comparative work has been undertaken along these lines and there exist, of course, formidable issues of reconstruction. In Woods Cree, for example, the verb *isihtwaa-* means "have such-and-such a custom." The verb refers to individual proclivities, but more commonly to the socially shared customs of tribal groups. Thus it is *isihtwaa-* both that Eskimos eat raw meat and that Crees do not. The Ojibwa cognate *izhitwaa-* means "have a certain custom, practice a certain religion" (Nichols and Nyholm 1995:72). The initial elements in these verb stems derive from Proto-Algonquian **ishi-* whose meaning Bloomfield reconstructed as "thus" (Aubin 1975:35). The reflexes of **ishi-* occur in many Cree and Ojibwa verbs with the resonant meaning of "particularity": do something in a certain way, be a certain way, and so on. The semantic contrasts of Woods Cree *isihtwaa-* with *itaatisi-* or "be/do such-and-such naturally" require investigation, specifically in reference to human versus animal behavior.

Social and Cultural Pluralism

Cultural forms afford dimensions of contrast both with nonhuman animals and with other humans. Until recently, most anthropologists contextualized cultures in the societies *whose* cultures they were in and within which they were conceived to be intergenerationally reproduced. The boundary-phobic social sciences of the 1980s and thereafter have emphasized the incongruent rather than isomorphic alignments of social collectivities, cultural repertoires, polities, territories, interaction frequencies, and language. As a result, the question of how or whether to segment the entities called "societies" and "cultures" out of such continua is currently much in debate.

As is well known, there originally existed no "Indians." Indians, both past and present, seem to concur with the older anthropology in recognizing plural societies or "tribes," each characterized by distinct customs. It follows that, Western solipsism notwithstanding, reflexive cultural objectification by Fourth World societies did not originate in the European imperial-colonial embrace. The *Inuhuit* or Polar Eskimo of North Greenland (Arctic), arguably the best claimants for possession of a "pure culture," seem to have sustained no contact with other Eskimoan groups—or with anyone else—for several centuries prior to "first [European] contact" in 1818. Having long since rationally concluded that they were the only people existing in the world, they were both amazed and delighted to encounter the John Ross expedition that year (Gilberg 1984:577).

The Inuhuits' sequestered circumstances were, however, exceptional.

Most Indians had "foreign" neighbors and understood themselves as members of one tribe among others, with whom diverse relations ranging from trade and intermarriage to primordial enmity might exist. The degree to which conceptions of tribal sameness and difference were continuous or discrete requires further study, but it is worth noting that conceptions of bounded group memberships were by no means absent. Boundaries were given vivid expression, for example, in the initiatory rituals to which adoptive captives were subjected, sometimes to the point of the symbolic "death" of the prior social affiliation and then "re-birth" into the tribe (Hallowell 1976; Axtell 1981).

Also like earlier anthropologists, Indians recognized plural and bounded societies as being the sites of distinguishable repertoires of custom. Tribes delimited themselves and one another by such criteria as language, territory, perhaps "genealogy," and—preeminently—custom. Indian awareness of intertribal cultural differences is especially clear in the many contexts where non-Indians brought evaluative perspectives to bear on the subject. For example, the fur trader David Thompson remonstrated in the 1790s with Chipewyan (Subarctic) men over their treatment of women, holding out to them as exemplary models the more egalitarian gender politics of their Woods Cree neighbors. The offenders responded complacently that "the Nahathaways [Crees] were a different people from—and they were not guided by—them" (Thompson 1962:106).

Another example attests Indians' recognition of functional or systemic linkages between the customs composing tribal repertoires. In 1634, the Jesuit Paul LeJeune ridiculed the animal ceremonialism of the Montagnais (Subarctic), specifically their practice of withholding the bones of slain beavers from dogs:

> As I was laughing at them and telling them that the Beavers do not know what is done with their bones, they answered me, "Thou dost not know how to take Beavers and thou wishest to talk about it" . . . I told them that the Hiroquois [Iroquois], according to the reports of the one who was with us, threw the bones of the Beaver to the dogs, and yet they took them very often; and that our Frenchmen captured more game than they did (without comparison), and yet our dogs ate these bones.

But to the Montagnais, their ritual differences from the Iroquois were entirely reasonable—indeed, inevitable—given the different modes of production in question: " 'Thou hast no sense,' " they replied, 'dost thou not see that you and the Hiroquois cultivate the soil and gather its fruits, and not we, and that therefore it is not the same thing?' " (LeJeune 1897a:213).

Relational Culture: Custom as Identity Diacritic

Earlier Indian conceptions of culture or custom plausibly comprised not the familiar anthropological ensemble of *all* socially learned or shared elements but rather a privileged subset of forms that were salient, for whatever historical reason, as diacritics of collective tribal identities (cf. Fogelson 1998). Culture or "custom" was constitutive of such identities and of those ascribed to others. Animals, children, and deviants notwithstanding, foreigners and their exotically contrastive customs were the privileged catalysts of cultural objectification. People knew each other as co-tribals partially on the basis of cultural sameness, just as they knew foreigners as foreigners on the basis of cultural difference.

The observation that customs are diacritics of collective identities is distinct from but presupposed in the claim that both identities and their diacritics are intrinsically relational. The claim that identities and diacritic customs are relational is predicated on the idea that they do not (or do not necessarily) exist independently of structural relations of sameness and difference, real or imagined, relative to the identities and customs of contiguous societies. Thus an existing element of custom, intrinsically of no semiotic account, might acquire meaning as an identity sign through its contrastive salience with parallel customs of neighbors. Virtually any cultural form can assume such significance: language, dress, marriage rules, and, famously, diet. Thus, to take a relatively contemporary example from the mid-1980s, within the merry precincts of "Mr. Arthur's" tavern on Franklin Avenue in Minneapolis, Chippewas and Lakotas reciprocally exchanged the jocular epithets "Dog Eaters!" and "Fish Eaters!" across the imaginary line that divided the place moiety-like between them.

Saussure notwithstanding, pure difference was not the only value in question: forms that were intersocietally the "same" could also be identity signs. As Lévi-Strauss wrote of the Australians, "Each group was no doubt actuated by the only apparently contradictory incentives of being like others, as good as others, better than others and different from others" (1966:90). Neither is intersocietal relationality a question only of assigning significance to prior and independently existing similarities and differences between the customs of contiguous societies. Forms might be *agentively* reconfigured or even invented as replicas or inversions of the customs of admired or devalued neighbors. Consider Lévi-Strauss on the Mandan and Hidatsa (Plains):

> Finally, if the customs of neighboring peoples exhibit symmetrical relations, the cause for it should be sought not only in some mysterious laws of nature or mind. This geometrical perfection also sums up in the

present mode the innumerable efforts, more or less conscious, accumulated by history, all aiming in the same direction: to reach the threshold, undoubtedly the most profitable to human societies, of a just equilibrium between their unity and their diversity; and to maintain an equal balance between communication, favoring reciprocal illuminations—and absence of communication, also beneficial—since the fragile flowers of difference need half-light in order to exist. [1976[1971]:255, cf. Sahlins 1993, 1999b]

Intersocietal transfers of cultural elements necessarily entail a synthesis of sameness and difference, and what Lévi-Strauss wrote of Indian myths might be generalized to other borrowings: "They appropriate it [so as] not to appear unequal to their neighbors, and they remodel it at the same time so as to make it their own" (1973:14).

Culture as Valorized Tradition

Commonly, if not invariably, customs that figured as identity signs were locally conceived as traditions. "Tradition" refers here to cultural forms whose positive value is predicated axiologically on real or imputed antiquity, on continuity with what one's ancestors are supposed to have been continuously doing for a long time, if not from mythological time immemorial. A productive example of "tradition" in this sense is afforded by Hopi conceptions that their traditions derive from prototypes practiced by the ancestors in earlier subterranean worlds. Here, however, we encounter themes of periodic cultural decline and renaissance.

Characteristically, Hopis explain the Oraibi split with a paradigm that

> is similarly applied to other major political events in Hopi history including the demise of the villages of Awat'ovi, Pivanhonkyapi, Sikyatki, and Palatkwapi, and even of the third world, below the present one. Signs of corruption and decadence, frequently indicated by immoral or antisocial behavior, begin to be noticed by the village leaders. After admonitions to improve behavior fall on deaf ears, the leaders convene in secret and ritually formalize a plan to destroy the social system in the village—including their own leadership. [Whiteley 1987:14–15]

Here, the Hopis converge with some earlier anthropologists upon notions of the degeneration and contamination of originally "pure" or "authentic" cultures. Other societies, less preoccupied with tradition, presumably have happier conceptions of their own capacity for adequately reproducing it.

Famously disposed to assimilate historic events (like new cultural elements) to mythological templates, the Fourth World peoples in general and Indian societies in particular did not always and everywhere revere "traditions" for their own sake. Woodburn (1980:106) has suggested that in foraging societies of the "immediate return" type "people often do not, at least explicitly, seem to value their own culture and institutions very highly and may, indeed, not be accustomed to formulating what their custom is or what it ought to be." Not all customs are explicitly valued, and those that are so valued are not necessarily valued specifically as "traditions." Novel forms were valued precisely because they *lacked* identity with (if not conformability to) the familiar and traditional. Needless to say, different tribes and the individuals composing them could and did differ extravagantly in their appraisals of tradition and innovation. Given white stereotypes surrounding Indian "elders," and metaphoric-metonymic tropes linking elders with traditions, it is worth noting that old people were no more universally valued than old customs. Consider the Chipewyans in the 1960s: "It would almost appear that anything old is an object of scorn. A dog is given an extra kick with the comment that it is old; a tourist fisherman is thought of as being rather peculiar, not because he is white and oddly dressed but because he is old" (VanStone 1965:66). Though it would not be implausible to argue that Chipewyans had learned to devalue the elderly from Euro-Canadians, this seems not to have been the case: Samuel Hearne (1958[1795]) reported the same sentiments two-and-a-half centuries earlier.

Cosmogonic Culture

A commonly cited difference between "traditional" and "Western societies" is

> the former's imputed lack of historical consciousness, of modern conceptions of culture and events as products or by-products of human agency. And indeed much Native American mythology represents existing cultural forms as "[super]natural," as reiterations of cosmogonic prototypes. Consider the Woods Cree myth which explains sororal polygyny. Two sisters are quarreling over which shall marry Wiisahkiicaah, the trickster/culture-hero character. Their father says to them:
> "No, don't do that [i.e., argue]. There'll be people. There'll be a lot of people in later years. They'll be short of men a lot of times. You sitting with your sister [i.e. as co-wives], that's what's gonna' happen [in] later years anyway. If you don't do it, nobody'll do it. [But] if you sleep

with him together [now], it'll be like that later on," he said. [Brightman 1988:15]

This exemplifies a common motif in Cree literature wherein customs originate in the enactment by myth-age deities of an originary prototype absent which the custom would not exist. Alternatively, Cree customs may be represented as already practiced by the animal beings of the early mythological age, and only thereafter as appropriated by human beings. However, in neither case do the Crees' own ancestors have anything to do with it.

Such mythological accounts of culture are widely distributed in North America, although customs, with the significant exceptions of religious ceremonials, comprise a relatively small percentage of the etiological motifs present in Indian mythology. They are vastly eclipsed, for example, by animal behavior and physiology (Waterman 1914). Tribal myth etiologies most commonly address people's *own* cultural forms, although the existence of foreigners and of cultural differences may also be encompassed in cosmogony. Most commonly, as in the Cree case, deities or other myth-age beings are identified as the originators of culture. Less commonly, this function is ascribed to the ancestors of modern humans.

Differences notwithstanding, the ideas in such myths parallel abiding themes in Western social thought. On the side of the sociocentric *esprit général*, mythologically engendered cultural order precedes or is bestowed upon the human subject, seeming to effect the same neutralization of individual agency as, for example, Durkheim's social morphology or Kroeber's superorganic or Foucault's discourse. At the same time, there are in these myths salient utilitarian themes that are reminiscent of contractarian theories. The mixture bears comparison with Western fusions of naturalism and constructivism discussed by Parmentier (1994). Themes of agency and design in the origination of cultural order (cf. Glacken 1967) are prominent in Indian myths. What is usually absent is attribution of these to ancestors of modern humans. In the earlier Cree example, for example, the father urges his daughters to originate polygyny as a remedy for the asymmetric sex ratios that he anticipates in the future when "There'll be people." Transformer characters of the altruistic "culture hero" type specialize in such prescience, devising social and natural orders in advance of the humans who will thereafter participate in them and with a solicitous eye for the satisfaction of their wants and needs.

The wants and needs thus providentially anticipated by the deities may, of course, reflect culturally idiosyncratic notions as to what conditions of society are worth living in. In this respect, the Crows (Plains) provide an especially interesting account of cultural (here specifically *linguistic*) diversity as the product of design. Coyote's companion Shirape directs him to institute multilingualism so that people can achieve happiness by hating each other (and thus presumably adopt Plains warfare accordingly):

> Why there are many good things you do not know [and] one of the very best things [conceivable] is that human beings should dislike one another. Why is there only one language when these people have increased so as to be very plentiful? It is bad. If some people were different, if their speech were different, and their language diverse, it would be well. Our language is one, for that reason we cannot feel anger [against one another], for that reason we cannot feel content, we cannot dislike anyone, we cannot get furious, we cannot be happy. If you made our speech different, if we could not understand each other's speech, we could get furious, we could be angry, we could be happy. [Lowie 1935:128]

Speaking of Coyote, not all customs originate from the altruistic designs of culture-hero characters. They may also come about as fortuitous and unintended by-products of a trickster character's self-gratifying projects. Looked at comparatively, Indian mythologies most commonly assign culture-originating functions to (a) distinct culture-hero and trickster characters, (b) one unitary culture-hero/trickster character, or (c) one unitary culture-hero/trickster and one culture-hero. The culture-building activities of characters of the portmanteau type may switch between design and by-product types and between stories or within single stories. In at least one case, that of Eastern Woodland and Subarctic Algonquians, the portmanteau character both introduces and violates the same custom, albeit in different narratives. He introduces the incest taboo in his culture-hero capacity and then flouts it in his trickster capacity by marrying his daughter or, yet more imaginatively, by becoming a woman and seducing his son. Boas (1940:411–414) and many others addressed the notional moral or moral incongruity posed by characters of this type. Here I will note only agreement with Ricketts (1966) that such unitary characters are plausibly of greater antiquity than their differentiated counterparts and that the conjunction of procultural and anticultural behavior is no accident. These characters' conjuncture of culture building with anticultural behavior prompted by bodily urges for food and sex affords a valuable parameter of comparison with Western nature/culture distinctions. Also of interest is the juxtaposition of themes of rational utilitarian design— remarkably convergent with materialist theories of culture—and of absolute and utter contingency (cf. Lévi-Strauss 1966:242–243).

It is platitudinous to remark that all societies are in history. Before and after the European invasion, Indian societies experienced cultural changes born of internal improvisations, external influences, and their interaction. At issue is how or whether experience of ongoing culture change was reconciled with theories of the mythological inception of custom.

Indians and other tribal peoples have long been distinguished from modern societies by the inverse values each imputedly accords to inertia and innovation. Malinowski (1954) famously interpreted mythical accounts of custom in tribal societies as both the expressions and causes of an objectively adaptive cultural conservatism (why stasis was adaptive was not made clear). Mythically ordained customs were perforce sacred and thus resistant to innovation. Lévi-Strauss (1966:217–244) subsequently elaborated a contrast between "hot" modern societies and "cold" tribal societies, which latter "try, with a dexterity we underestimate, to make the states of their development which they consider 'prior' as permanent as possible" (Lévi-Strauss 1966:234, cf. 217–244). Like Malinowski he saw the normative conservatism attested in mythically warranted custom as objectively retarding (not eliminating) the scope and intensity of directional social change in tribal societies (Lévi-Strauss 1966:234–235). One example of this is the capacity of totemic systems to reproduce themselves through periods of demographic upheaval (Lévi-Strauss 1966:66–74). Not the least interesting aspect of his argument is peoples' cultural agency as exerted in the formation of doctrines that deny this same agency. It should be noted that mythical conceptions of culture can have *either* conservative or neutral (or even innovative) effects. People can maintain the valued iconicity between mythic origins and contemporary customs equally by restricting historical deviation from the mythic precedent or by continuously reimagining the mythic precedent so as to keep up its congruency with historically changing customs. Of course, it was also Malinowski who demonstrated ethnographically that the function of Kiriwinian myth was precisely to facilitate and legitimize innovations— albeit by the expedient of assimilating them to the originary cosmogony and thus denying their existence. It has since become conventional to recognize both greater diversity in Fourth World evaluations of cultural change (Sahlins 1985:xii) and also the coexistence in all conditions of society—in different hierarchical relations—of both mythical (or otherwise naturalized) and historical/agentive conceptions of culture (Turner 1988; Nabokov 2000).

The comparative study of coexisting mythological and historical theories of custom in Indian North America remains to be undertaken. There is plausibility in earlier functionalist or structuralist claims that positive or negative values accorded to change can objectively affect its relative intensities and that customs conceived as sacred may be proportionately resistant to modification. However, I will leave to the experts on the Southwest the requisite ethnographic evidence (or lack thereof). Conversely, tribes with mythic conceptions of custom must nonetheless have welcomed the selective cultural changes afforded by the diffusion and indigenization of foreign customs. Positive or negative values accorded to change were not uniform for all elements within tribal cultural repertoires. Not all customs—not even all explicitly valued customs—were explained in tribal mythologies. And it is useful to distinguish from among all customs explained in myths that subset whose mythic origins were specifically invoked as sacred charters for their inviolability.

In broader terms, the notional incongruity between mythical and historical conceptions of custom may prove to have greater salience for anthropologists than it had or has for Indians. There is, to be sure, abundant evidence that Indian myths were often reshaped to account for cultural innovations. For Indians in general, the exemplary case of the mythologically encompassed historical-cultural event is the horse whose advent was by the late 1800s widely retold as cosmogony (Waterman 1914). On the other hand, most Kwakiutl accounts of their acquisition of the winter ceremonial complex on the Northwest Coast (Boas 1895:425–431) are fully historical in character—and exhibit an obsession with the micro details of intertribal and intratribal diffusion that is interestingly reminiscent of Boas. Some local accounts of custom are fully anthropogenic. Thus, for example, a Nootka chief explained the ritual torture attending a ceremonial by stating that "it was an ancient custom of his nation to sacrifice a man at the close of this solemnity in honor of their God, but that his father had abolished it and substituted this in its place" (Jewitt 2000:148). In some tribes, mythic and historical accounts of custom may have existed in systemic complementation, with myth defining parameters of cultural possibility and historical accounts of custom attesting a free space for human maneuver and agency. Then again, alternative mythological and historical accounts of the origin of the *identical* custom might simultaneously and peacefully coexist, as with the Kwakiutl Dzonokwe mask and its related ceremonial (Lévi-Strauss 1982:43–45). Compare the acrimony that sometimes attends competing Western anthropological theories of culture.

Elite Culture

If the anthropological culture concept was conceived in opposition to Arnoldian elitism, some Indians seemingly disagreed. They identified their "real" culture with a subset of forms monopolized by privileged status groups. One thinks of the *pavansinom*, or "powerful-important people," the Hopi (Southwest) theocratic elite whose esoteric knowledge, not least of Hopi custom, distinguishes them from the *sukavungsinom* or "common people" (Whitely 1987). Another example is afforded by the reminiscences of the Yurok (California) Lucy Thompson (1916) who makes abundantly clear the aristocratic proprietorship of "genuine" Yurok custom:

> A Talth [Thompson's word for Yurok aristos] is very reserved and never advances to meet anyone who is a stranger that is inquiring into our traditions. Our traditions and religion are too sacred to be expounded before strangers of another race; therefore the white man has received most of his allegory from the lower classes of the Indians. . . . These stories [i.e., cultural information provided by the "lower classes"] are no more like the traditions and religion of the Indian than daylight is like night. [Thompson 1916:197]

Thus contrasting modes of custom might be calibrated with respect to their excellence and authenticity within as well as between tribes.

Metacultural Objectification

Absent books, lectures, and conferences, it is reasonable to ask in what cultural forms Indian ethno-anthropologies were embodied. Theories of culture were implicit in every quotidian context, but it is possible to identify privileged sites of metacultural discourse and practice. The most visible contexts were those in which the normative order was explicitly described and promulgated: the honors accorded exemplary men and women and the punishments meted out to their deviant opposite numbers. The formal pedagogy attending socialization is well exemplified in the lengthy and didactic lectures on right conduct to which, for example, juvenile Winnebagos (Eastern Woodlands) of both sexes were subjected (Radin 1970:118–132). Myths and rituals were also privileged ethno-anthropological sites, containing both etiologies of sacred custom and exemplary and symbolic enactments of it.

If myths and rituals objectified culture through etiology and exemplary enactment, they might also do so through the rather different medium of parodic satire and transgression. Many of the comic elements present in myth and ritual were at the expense of the customary status quo. The notional incongruity of portmanteau culture-hero/trickster characters like the Winnebago Wakdjunkaga has already been noted. The clan war bundles of the Winnebago were carried reverently on military campaigns and were among the holiest of tribal sacra. What then to make of passages like the following in which our hero, while leading a war party into enemy territory, addresses the war bundle as follows:

> "It is *I* who am going on the warpath, *I*! *I* am capable of fighting, that is why *I* am going. *I* can move about easily. But *you*, war bundle, cannot do this, *you* can do nothing of value. It is only when I carry you on my back that you can move. You cannot, of yourself, move about, nor can you move anything. How, therefore, can you go on the warpath? You are simply a nuisance; that's all." Thus he shouted. Thereupon he stamped his war bundle into the ground. A part of those still accompanying him turned back at this point. [Radin 1972:7]

The Chinookan-speaking peoples seem especially disposed to reflexive cultural critique that is both serious and satirical. This notable in the Clackamas myth where excessive attention to affinal protocol results in death (Hymes 1981) and in a Kathlamet Coyote myth that satirizes the complexity of the ritual surrounding salmon fishing (Boas 1894:92–106).

In many areas of North America, clown characters were ritual counterparts of the trickster—and, like the latter, combined procultural and anticultural attributes. For example, during the winter Kuksu Society ceremonial dances of the Northwestern Maidu, about whose sanctity there is no question, the formal oratory of the officiating priest was periodically interrupted by the parodic mimicry (delivered in the Maiduan equivalent of a high-pitched Jerry Lewis–like Mongoloid-from-Hell voice) of the *Peheipe* clown—that is, when the latter wasn't providing other distractions by noisily and ostentatiously eating at inappropriate moments (Dixon 1905:315–317, cf. Brightman).

To take another case, the formal protocol attending aristocratic status transitions on the Northwest Coast is well known ethnographically. Less well known are the peoples' own satires of them. Among the Haida, for example, potlatch guests arriving by canoe on the beach were greeted both with their hosts' formal oratory and by clown baggage porters who, earnestly simulating solicitous hospitality, assisted in the unloading of the visitors' property and wound up dumping it ceremoniously into the water (Steward 1977). To the south, among the Koskimo Kwakiutl (Northwest Coast), there was the parody of aristocratic marriage performed at the Winter Ceremonial by the MaE'myaEnk or "Respected Ones," women in their twenties who formed the first of four age grades within the women's

"Sparrow" sorority (Boas 1966:174–179). While other dancing was underway in the house, the Respected Ones remained outside, vociferously demanding to be given husbands. Upon entering, their leader approached an elderly man and demanded that he be given to her as a husband. The wizened "bridegroom" ostentatiously turned over to her a single blanket as bridewealth and the two departed. Four days later at the (parodically accelerated) "repayment of the marriage debt," the "Respected Ones" distributed property (sugar water and dogs) while the nominal bride danced in a clamshell-ornamented (versus abalone shell) blanket and announced publicly that she had thrown "her husband out of the house as my great grandmother did to her husband." The presiding chief then legitimized the whole proceeding by reciting a farcical ancestral myth. Note that this theatrical makes fun both of valued customs and of their conventional mythological legitimations: both marriage protocol and the institution of the mythic "charter."

Related to but distinguishable from such satires are ritual periods of "license" in which convention was put temporarily into abeyance for the entire population, such that people were allowed or even required to transgress quotidian norms. The Northeastern Iroquoians, for example, practiced both an annual "Feast of Fools" ("Ononharoia" or "Turning-the-Brain-Upside-Down") and the "Andacwander" ceremony. The latter provided, amidst other revelry, variety-enhancing suspensions of the rule confining married adults' sexual activity to the conjugal unit (Wallace 1958:239, 240, 243, 245). The "contrary" statuses in the Plains societies afford interesting cases in which inversionary behaviors were conjoined with the positive values accorded to military prowess.

Not surprisingly, sacred clown repertoires often compounded ridicule of the people's own customs with burlesques of foreigners. Unflattering burlesques of whites were added to those of foreign Indians in the performances of ritual clowns. One such impersonation figured in the Hopi *pawamu* ceremony of 1928 and addressed itself specifically to American women. Here, "the 'kachina girls', impersonated by men, were dressed in an incongruous attire of skirts, riding boots, sombreros, and six shooters, and they carried vanity boxes" (Steward 1977:355). Then there is the Newekwe clown of the Zunis who, in the course of one ceremony, fabricated a faux telephone and proceeded to converse with the gods in Spanish (Steward 1977:347). Whether such occasions exhibit conservative or subversive or fusionally conservative-subversive effects continues to be debated. Like foreigners, trickster myths and inversionary rituals provided occasion for reflecting that the customs in place were not the only ones imaginable. And there seem to have been—among some tribes in some periods—individuals temperamentally and intellectually disposed to an anthropological sensibility. Among the Nomlaki (California) foreign travel was officially devalued. But this didn't preclude a subculture of itinerant traders, one of whom justified his vocation as follows:

> If I stay home, I won't learn anything. By going from place to place I learn more. I learn other peoples' ways and how they act and treat each other. If I stay here, I don't see anything and can't learn anything. By traveling around I learn more of different things, of talking. [Goldschmidt 1976:155–156]

Summary

A preliminary reconnaissance suggests that Indian conceptions of culture, tradition, custom, and the like converge in certain respects with the Boas-derived culture concepts and depart from them in many others. Like the Boasian concept, Native Americans conceived customs as plural, contextualized in social collectivities, transmissible via socialization, and (probably) independent of genealogical or raciological criteria. But where the Boasian construct is global, Indian notions of culture were probably focused on forms that were symbolic of social identities, associated with venerated "traditions" or with privileged elites, and significant vis-à-vis the practices of others. Where the Boasian construct is historical and (ideally) relativistic, Indian conceptions of culture mingle cosmogony with historicity, and often exhibit strongly evaluative orientations. Resonances of relativism may perhaps be identified in inversionary ritual. The question of raciological (not necessarily "racist") components in Native American cultural theory remains an important desideratum (see Fogelson 1998; Strong and Van Winkle 1996). An interestingly Lamarckian theme appears in the Zuni doctrine that the flesh of a man who had eaten Zuni food long enough to have starved four times was "therefore of the soil of Zuni" (Cushing 1979:91).

Indian Cultural Theory and the White Invasion

Euro-American culture has had diverse effects both on Indian cultural repertoires and on Indians' ethno-anthropological appraisals of their own and other peoples' repertoires. There seems to be consensus that the aggregate effect of the European invasion has been substantial leveling but not erasure of intersocietal cultural differences both among different Indian tribes and between Indians and Euro-Americans. The effects of the invasion on Indian ethno-anthropologies are less well studied. However, they plausibly include definitions of "Indian culture" as what is "traditional" or differential, doctrines of incompatibility between white and Indian forms, ideas of the" death" and "revival" of Indian cultures, ideologies of Indians as bicultural, and, most recently, theories of cultural purity and contamination.

The "Impassable" Gulf

Themes of humanism, relativism, and even primitivism notwithstanding, the dominant idea in colonial and national images of Indians, and thus in Indian policy, was the irreducible, totalizing, and allegorical opposition of white to Indian custom and "race" as triumphant civility to vanquished savagery. This primordial vision of antithesis and difference—what Pearce (1965) referred to as "the impassable gulf"—had as its message the nonviability of social contiguity and cultural pluralism. Thus a whole series of plans and programs attuned to the diverse ways that Indians might be expected or made to "vanish": extinction, isolation, removal, or cultural assimilation as rural or urban proletarians. As Greenblatt (1991, cf. Sahlins 2000) observes, such visions of the West's fatal impact upon the rest preceded actual contact between the Old and New Worlds. The earliest European commentaries on Indian societies were thus, predictably, larded with cultural critique, and Euro-American forms were commonly proposed to Indians not as augmentations to but as replacements for Indian counterparts with which they could not logically or morally coexist.

Europeans and Their Cultures

Europeans were not the first "others" with whom the tribes interacted. New discourses on Indian-European cultural differences plausibly reproduced earlier discourses on existing differences between Indians. Europeans addressed themselves early on to the question of Indian origins, and Indians, of course, undertook the reciprocal intellectual project. Although Indian accounts of white origins remain to be systematically explored (but see Nabokov 1991:3–20; Vincent and Delage 1992), whites were readily appended *a posteriori* to existing myths of human origin that variously focused on single groups, included proximal foreigners, or addressed a pan-human creation preceding "tribal" differentiation. Their appearance seemingly everywhere prophesied in advance, whites assumed variable character in Indian narratives of "first contact." If, as some of these narratives suggest, certain Indian groups initially identified whites as spirit beings, the people rapidly disabused themselves of the notion. Western Woods Cree myths, for example, derive whites either from a defective clay prototype of themselves, contemptuously hurled into the antipodes by the creator being (Brightman 1993:48–51) or from a homicidal metamorphic owl-boy expelled from Cree society in the myth age (Petitot 1888). The latter myth is not to my knowledge reported elsewhere in North America but is attested in South America (Turner 1988).

In contrast to anthropological relativisms, Indians exhibited a more diverse set of evaluative orientations toward outsiders. Chauvinism and ethnocentrism were not absent. Foreigners were sometimes ridiculed as provincials or reviled as barbarians. If ethnocentrism dominated European views of Indian culture, the Indians, on their part, were far from lacking in what Lahontan called a "Prepossession and Bigotry with reference to their own customs and ways of living" (Jaenen 1974:273). Thus, for example, at Port Royale in the early 1600s, the Jesuit Pierre Biard noted—with genuine bewilderment—that the Micmacs "think they are better, more valiant, and more ingenious than the French, and what is difficult to believe, richer than we are" (Bailey 1969:14). Few aspects of French behavior escaped indigenous critique by the Micmacs' northern neighbors, the Montagnais: capital punishment (they opined that the custom "had no sense" and "asked whether the relatives of those who were condemned to death did not seek vengeance" [Leacock 1980:34]), handkerchiefs ("If thou likest that filth, give me thy handkerchief and I will soon fill it" [Jaenen 1974:285]), and the poverty observed in Paris (the French were "foolish" to tolerate it, "the remedies being simple" [Leacock 1980:34]). Some two centuries later and further to the west, the Dakota passed judgment on that Maussian anomaly, the restaurant: "I understand that their great men make a feast and invite many, but when the feast is over the guests are required to pay for what they have eaten before leaving the house" (Nabokov 1991:22). Neither did white speech behaviors escape notice. In, for example, the neglected classic of Menominee oral narrative "How Turtle Got Drunk," the titular hero bargains for credit from a white fur trader, and the latter responds hyperbolically: "All right, Turtle, all right, all right, all right, all right, fine and dandy, Turtle, fine and dandy! Bring the fur, Turtle, bring it, bring it, bring it; I'll give you credit" (Bloomfield 1928:274, cf. Basso 1979).

A different and coexisting Indian attitude toward Europeans was a complacent relativism, probably also continuous with earlier appraisals of cultural difference. In certain contexts, this relativism was paradoxically expressed, by way of Algonquian good manners, in ready *verbal* assent to anything—however curious—that the Jesuit missionaries happened to be saying. (One thinks here of a Saulteaux Indian's courteous reaction to an anthropologist's Freudian claim that a dream about money "really" referred to excrement [Brown 1989].) Thus a formidable obstacle to Montagnais conversion in the 1630s was

> the opinion they have that you must never contradict anyone, and that everyone must be left to his own way of thinking. They will believe all you please, or, at least will not contradict you, and they will let you too believe what you will. [Hallowell 1955:137]

The combination of Jesuitical ethnocentrism with the Montagnais doctrine that "everyone must be left to his own way of thinking" was sometimes a volatile one, and there were limits to their tolerance for Jesuitical critique. In these terms, we can interpret the insults directed at LeJeune by the Montagnais during what must have seemed to them the interminable winter season they spent with him: "Shut up, shut up, thou hast no sense," "He is proud," "He is captain of the dogs," and "He has a head like a pumpkin" (LeJeune 1897:63).

Directed Acculturation and Its Discontents

The course of empire led—from east to west, sometimes sooner, sometimes later—from contexts where Indians could freely elect to acquire Euro-American customs to contexts in which the customs were forcibly imposed. If regional conquest and intersocietal projects of directed acculturation were not absent prehistorically, Euro-Americans provided Indians—under conditions of progressively diminishing political and economic autonomy—with perhaps unprecedented opportunities to severally objectify their own practices in opposition to those of the invaders. Violence, disease, starvation, imprisonment, and the abduction of children could all confront Indians skeptical of the warm embrace of Euro-American culture—as they often confronted Indians who were selectively receptive to it. In different times and contexts, Indians exhibited diverse reactions to white acculturation projects: elective participation, pragmatic accommodation, and overt or covert resistance. These different responses assumed dominant and subdominant positions in particular places and times and for different tribes or subgroups. However, they are not usefully conceived as discrete: they could coexist in unstable contiguity within the practices of a single individual.

In trading posts and in boarding schools, in prisons and in churches, Indian people were apprised that their economies, marriage customs, hair styles, clothing, religions, and languages were at once different from and inferior to their Euro-American counterparts. In these same institutions, Indians were invited, under varying modes of duress, to exchange their customs for those of Euro-Americans. Thus were the people subjected to Foucauldian disciplinary lunacies now difficult to imagine—except through archival documentation. Consider the communications of Commissioner N. S. Jones to the superintendent of the Greenville Indian School (in Maidu country Greenville, Butte County, California) in 1902 on the relations of civility to male hair styles:

> This Office desires to call your attention to a few customs among the Indians which it is believed should be modified or discontinued. The wearing of long hair by the male population of your agency is not in keeping with the advancement they are making, or will soon be expected to make, in civilization. The wearing of short hair by the males will be a great step in advance and will certainly hasten their progress towards civilization.

Jones next addressed the custom of face painting.

> On many of the reservations the Indians of both sexes paint . . . this paint melts when the Indian perspires and runs down into the eyes. The use of this paint leads to many diseases of the eye among those Indians who paint. Persons who have given considerable thought and investigation to the subject are satisfied that this custom causes the majority of the cases of blindness among the Indians of the United States.

Neither was Jones unconcerned with Indian sexuality: "Indian dances and so-called Indian feasts should be prohibited. In many cases these dances and feasts are simply subterfuges to cover degrading acts and to disguise immoral purposes. You are directed to use your best efforts in the suppression of these evils." The commissioner concluded by suggesting a variety of punitive measures, ranging from the withholding of rations to "a short confinement in the guard-house at hard labor, with shorn locks." One can note, of course, parallels—right down to the micro-regulation of bodily dispositions—between these disciplines and those to which Indians subjected white captives—and even some volunteer anthropologists (Cushing 1979:78–81,91)—in reverse contexts of cultural assimilation. The differences, however, were substantial: Indians offered their captives unqualified incorporation and participation (Ackerknecht 1944; Axtell 1981; Hallowell 1976).

Indian Discourses on Directed Acculturation

Indians predictably reacted to Euro-American cultural critique with an initially complacent relativism. Consider the Micmacs' response in 1603 to the acculturative exhortations of Jesuit missionary Pierre Biard: " 'Aoyota chaboya' they say, 'That is the Indian way of doing it. You can have your ways and we will have ours; everyone values his own wares.' " (Jaenen 1974:262).

Faced with directed acculturation *cum* colonial violence, Indians sometimes sanctified cultural relativism, representing it as the intentional design of a creator being. In 1795, the Cherokee Corn Tassel addressed an American treaty delegation as follows:

> Indeed, much has been advanced on the want of what you term civilization among the Indians; and many proposals have been made to us to adopt your laws, your religion, your manners, and your customs. . . . You say "Why do not the Indians till the ground and live as we do?" May we not, with equal propriety, ask "Why the White people do not hunt and live as we do?" . . . The great God of Nature has placed us in different situations. It is true that he has endowed you with many superior advantages; but he has not created us to be your slaves. *We are a separate people!* He has given each their lands under distinct considerations and circumstances. [Nabokov 1991:123]

Whatever primitivistic embellishments may accrue to this account, the "relativistic design" idea is genuine, for it was repeatedly asserted elsewhere. As a Woods Cree said to the Oblate missionary Marius Rossignol around 1900, "We know that God exists and that He created all men. He made the Whites of white earth and us Crees of brown earth. He has also given a particular religion to the Whites and another quite different one to the Cree. To each his own" (Rossignol 1938:68).

Other contexts seemingly suggest a surprising degree of Gramscian consent to Euro-American cultural hegemony. Consider this Hydaburg testimonial of 1912:

> We the undersigned Alaska Natives of Hydaburg, Alaska declare that we have given up our old tribal relationships; that we recognize no chief or clan or tribal family . . . that we live in one family houses in accordance with the customs of civilization; that we observe the marriage laws of the United states; that our children belong equally to the father and mother . . . that we have discarded the totem and recognize the Stars and Stripes as our only emblem . . . and we respectfully request the Congress of the United States to pass a law granting us the full rights of citizenship. [Blackman 1981:34–35]

Similarly, as late as the 1960s, some Kutchin exhibited "a generally negative view towards all things of the past," recalled the "indigenous" condition as one in which "We lived out in the bush just like wild animals," and asserted that "all that old time stuff is a bunch of nonsense" (Nelson 1973:285).

However we interpret such testimony, it seems seldom to have been the peoples' dominant orientation. The Haidas could not, of course, have become "just like White people" if they had tried—and few Indians, in any case, seem to have been trying very hard. Resistance to American-sponsored cultural genocide did not emerge ex nihilo in the activist 1960s and 1970s—it has been continuously present from the beginning. Whatever the theoretical shortcomings of earlier students of "acculturation," they compel our agreement that "The use of force [in directed acculturation] naturally arouses resentment and an added consciousness of cultural differences with, in most cases, attachment of symbolic values to many elements of the old culture" (Linton 1940b:505). Consider this Pomo discourse from the 1930s:

> My grandfather told me that the White people were homeless and had no families. They came by themselves and settled on our property. They had no manners. They did not know how to get along with other people. They were strangers who were rough and common and did not know how to behave. But I have seen that these people of yours are even worse. They have taken everything away from the Indians, and they take everything away from one another. They do not help one another when they are in trouble, and they do not care what happens to other people. We were not like that. We would not let a person die of starvation when we had plenty of food. We would not bury our dead with no show. We would kill another person by poisoning him [sorcery] if he was an enemy, but we would not treat a stranger the way they treat their own brothers and sisters. Your people are hard to understand. My brother lived with you people for twenty years, and he said that he was used to you; but he cannot understand yet why you people act as you do. You are all the same in one way. We are all the same in another. What is wrong with you? [Aginsky 1940:44]

Anthropology: Biculturalism, Cultural Death, and Composite Cultures

Ironically, the Boasian anthropologists articulated their own visions of the "impassable gulf." Recall that for Boas and his students cultures were historical and syncretic-absorptive entities. Each, at any given time, was a *mélange* of "indigenous" and "borrowed" materials. Thus Boas's astute early definition of "acculturation" as "the mutual transformation of the old culture and the newly acquired material" (1940:435). This is how Boas and his early students theorized intertribal cultural influences but *not* how they conceived Euro-American cultural influences on Indian societies. In practice, the early Boasians distinguished "authentic" (and salvageable) elements of pre-European derivation from elements borrowed from or modified by whites. We have here, seemingly, an encrypted Boasian version of savagery/civility dualism expressed in a modernist vision of the "death" of Indian culture through "replacement" by white culture. It is this orientation that informed Boas's questionable contrast between "the proud Indian of pre-White times" and "his degenerate [i.e. "acculturated"] offspring of the present" (1938). Robert Lowie, for example, strenuously professed the syncretic composition of cultures: "The attempt to isolate one culture that is wholly indigenous in origin is decidedly simpleminded" (Lowie 1935:xviii). And yet Lowie could *also* write that Crow culture was "very much alive" in 1907 and that even by 1931 "the rise of a literate generation and the advent of the automobile had not been able to kill it utterly" (Lowie 1935:xvii). If his message was the affirmative one of cultural tenacity, Crow culture was nevertheless an entity whose eventual "death" at the hands of literacy and automobiles we might realistically anticipate. One wonders whether Lowie thought Crow culture comparably endangered by the advent of horses in the eighteenth century. It was in this climate that Redfield, Herskovits, and Linton (1935) found themselves obliged to argue that Indian cultures as modified by Euro-American influences were appropriate and legitimate anthropological subjects.

Alone among the early Boasians, Radin put Indian-Indian and white-Indian intersocietal cultural borrowing in the same theoretical context. Indians, said Radin, had been through such things before—with other Indians—and the subjection of the tribes to the American state and its cultural directives did not portend the extinction of distinct Indian societies and cultures:

> But did not similar things happen before? . . . It is unwarranted to argue that, because we can demonstrate the presence of European artifacts or influences, we are necessarily dealing with cultures that are in process of deterioration or that can no longer be regarded as aboriginal in any sense of the term. These cultures have no more lost their aboriginal character because of European influence than, for instance, the Mississauga Indians of southeastern Ontario lost their aboriginal character because they were so markedly influenced by the Iroquois. [Radin 1933:121–122]

Radin's conclusions were echoed in later writing on "acculturation."

Though it seems now to be conventional to write off the anthropology of acculturation between the 1930s and the 1960s as always and everywhere infected by teleological modernization theory, most acculturation theorists exhibited characteristically Boasian concerns with the particularities of individual cases and outcomes. Linton (1940a, 1940b), for example, while disposed to use the term *acculturation* as a synonym for assimilation, recognized multiple outcomes among the cases he studied comparatively. Thus the Puyallup's "complete absorption" seemed "only a question of time" (Linton 1940c:38), the White Knife Shoshone seemed destined for "complete Europeanization" (118), and the San Ildefonso Tewa would soon experience "rapid acculturation" (462). More ominously, Ute resistance to acculturation portended "complete collapse of both the society and the culture" (206), and the Northern Arapaho had neither acculturated nor developed "an independent culture compatible with reality" (258). On the other hand, the Fox, "encysted" within American society, showed "no prospect of . . . being absorbed either racially or culturally for several generations to come" (332), and the "final assimilation" of the Carrier was "still far off" (389).

Acculturation theorists were not, therefore, always and everywhere committed to assimilationist prophecies and teleological modernization theory. Though Linton viewed assimilation as "the logical end product" or "ultimate end" of sustained cultural borrowing, he also envisioned interim emergences of "two new cultures" (i.e., Euro-American culture and the cultures of individual tribes) in a condition of stable pluralism (Linton 1940a:492–493; Linton 1940b:519). Twenty years later, Spicer distinguished "incorporative" (i.e., "indigenizing," cf. Linton 1940b:511), assimilative (i.e., "modernizing"), fusional, and compartmentalizing aspects of Indian cultural change (1961:528), and was explicit that "not every situation leads to the production of a single society out of those juxtaposed nor to the growth of a common culture" (1961:519). All subscribed to a modified version of the "cultural death" anticipated by the early Boasians, specifically "the dissolution of a particular assemblage of cultural content, configurated in a more or less unique set of patterns belonging to a nation" (Kroeber 1948:382). Culture death, however, did not portend assimilation or loss of cultural distinctiveness. What many scholars of acculturation anticipated was both the "death" of the pre-European Indian cultures and the "birth" of new hybrid Indian cultures composed of both Indian and white elements and lacking identity with either prior Indian or white cultures. Thus, for example, they envisioned the "synthesis of two new cultures with mutual adaptations" (Linton 1940a:493), or "a single system" composed of "elements of two or more distinct cultural traditions" but "combined" by principles distinct from the antecedents

(Spicer 1961:532). Distinguishing between intersocietal transfers of single elements and of whole systems or patterns, Lévi-Strauss supposed that the latter could yield for the recipient either "collapse and destruction" or, more optimistically, "an original synthesis, but one which then consists in the emergence of a third system which cannot be reduced to the other two" (1976:357). If acculturation does not necessarily portend social assimilation and cultural homogenization it did entail a discontinuous rupture or transition between successive pre-European and acculturation-catalyzed states or systems of Indian cultures.

The degree to which these ideas were paralleled in Indian ideologies of colonial culture change remains to be investigated in detail. In the remainder of this chapter I focus on shared themes between non-Indian and Indian anthropologies: conceptions of the "death" of Indian cultures, the "bicultural" segmentation of Indian and white elements in Indian cultural repertoires, and "pure" or "authentic" Indian cultures uncontaminated by foreign influences.

Cultural Death and Biculturalism as Indian Ideology

Insofar as they converged in subscribing to theories of cultural "death" and biculturalism, Indians and some anthropologists may both have been sold a bill of goods by ideologues of the "Impassable Gulf." A plausible reconstruction of Indian theories of cultural transfer in pre-European and early colonial periods is that inflows of foreign material were consistent with de facto conceptions of customs as subject to change and augmentation. When interacting with Europeans in contexts of relative political equality, Indians practiced cultural borrowing on their own terms, subordinating new cultural elements to received ends. Though particular innovations may have prompted acrimonious debate, there are few grounds for supposing that borrowed foreign elements portended the "death" of valued customs already in place.

But this was to change when Indians indigenized the white orientalist ideologies of "Indian culture(s)" and "white culture" as oppositive entities. Recall that missionaries, teachers, and Indian agents commonly represented white cultural forms as civilized alternatives to and replacements for the savage customs in place. Recall also that certain forms were sometimes objectively incompatible with Indian counterparts, as when optative polygamy was replaced by prescriptive monogamy. More than any other factor, *forced* introductions of foreign elements into Indian cultural repertoires (and forced suppressions of existing forms) lent plausibility to reciprocal Indian convictions that the gulf was, indeed, impassable. Recall finally that whites subsequently questioned the genuineness of Indians whose customs were not distinctively pre-European.

Thus Indians learned—or concluded independently—that Indian culture was what white culture was not, and vice versa. The segmentation of their own practices into distinguishable white and Indian categories—due allowance being made for long-indigenized European forms now seen as Indian—has probably been thereafter the dominant Indian conception of their cultural status. Historical refractions of this dualism exist in diverse contexts. Among the most salient are local distinctions between "progressives" and "conservatives," often mapped spatially as particular residential choices as, for example, between "on" or "off" the Res, or between different reservation communities. The literature on magical and rational "nativism" (Linton 1943) provide a potentially rich source of information on earlier Indian ideologies of white/Indian dualism, notably insofar as both ritual practices and envisioned outcomes involved practical or symbolic renunciations of white culture. Compare the radically different cultural ideology involved in the Peyote religion or Native American Church, an explicitly hybrid element of Indian culture that derives its character precisely from its simultaneous resemblance to and difference from *both* with white and "traditional" Indian religions. In any case, by the time the Boasians arrived to salvage what was left of "authentic" Indian culture, they encountered—for good historical reasons—plenty of Indians prepared to concur with them that genuine Indian culture was "dying" or "dead" and that whatever they had was something else. Among the most famous eulogists was Benedict's Paiute consultant Ramon: "In the beginning, God gave to every people a cup of clay, and from this cup they drank their life. . . . They all dipped in the water but their cups were different. Our cup is broken now. It has passed away" (Benedict 1934:333).

The reciprocal influences Indians and anthropologists may here have exerted on each other remain an interesting desideratum. Insofar as Indians distinguish discrete white and Indian components in their ways of life, they profess a theory of biculturalism sometimes also endorsed by non-Indian academics. French's (1961) analysis of Wasco-Wishram ideologies of Indian culture and of cultural change brilliantly elucidates the effects of bicultural ideology. The Wasco-Wishram, proprietors of prehistoric and historic trade centers on the Columbia River, long exhibited a cosmopolitan cultural hybridity that was exemplified by cultural borrowing, intermarriage with foreigners, and the valorization of multilingualism. After several generations of Indian agents, missionaries, and local discrimination, the Wasco reasonably enough concluded that Indian and white cultural forms were different things. By objective criteria and their own appraisals, Wascos were "quite acculturated" (French 1961:402): "In another generation, Wasco culture, if not identity, is gone" (French 1961:401). *Wasco* culture, but not, however, *Indian* culture. Wascos were co-resident with the "less acculturated" Sahaptins. They retained Sahaptin forms of the traditional "Indian-ness" culture whose Wasco counterpart the Wascos conceived themselves to be losing. Sahaptins were conceived as "physically large and strong, untidy, gregarious, clannish, irresponsible, 'nomadic,' slow to learn, conservative, uncivilized, and, above all, 'Indian' " (French 1961:404). Wascos borrowed both white and Sahaptin cultural forms, which, as respective contrasting modes of "part-time white" and "part-time Indian" cultural behavior, they associated with distinct contextual-situational genres. As for whites, so for the Wasco-Wishram and many other Indians, "white culture(s)" and "Indian culture(s)" exist in inverse relation: the more "white" you are the less "Indian" you are, and the reverse. The overall scheme recalls "compartmentalization," a "keeping separate within a realm of meaning of elements and patterns taken over from the dominant culture" (Spicer 1961:533).

By the mid-1960s, anthropologists were expounding—seemingly to appreciative Indian audiences—the bicultural or intercultural basis of Indian social problems:

> One [summer reservation] workshop discussed the thesis that Indians were in a terrible crisis. They were, in the words of friendly anthro guides, BETWEEN TWO WORLDS. People between two worlds, the students were told, DRANK. For the anthropologists, it was a valid explanation of drinking on the reservation. For the young Indians, it was an authoritative definition of their role as Indians. [Deloria 1969:86]

People, as Deloria states here, seemingly need to *learn* both that they are intercultural and that the condition is a bad one. These interpretations are not necessary corollaries of experiences of cultural change.

A similar point is made in a discussion of Cheyenne (Plains) college students:

> My experience is that the Cheyenne students who are most successful in the university do not worry too much about the differences or contradictions between their own culture and the culture of the dominant society. They become truly bicultural, slidingly smoothly between being a traditional Cheyenne and being an [Western-] educated Indian. Teachers in public schools, universities, and Native American studies programs may

> do a great disservice to American Indian students by encouraging them to concern themselves too much about the differences—to emphasize the theme of "the person caught between two cultures." Some American Indian students do not know that they are caught between two cultures until a teacher tells them. [Moore 1998:277]

Moore here distinguishes dysfunctional interculturalism from functional biculturalism but might have added that it can also be a disservice to teach people that they are bicultural—even when the condition is normalized and purged of pathology.

Biculturalism is a more positive spin on the intercultural ("between two worlds") syndrome. Bicultural cosmopolitanism may well be valued by many Indians as a good thing. The lexical form itself suggests participation in two viable coexisting cultures, not "cultural death," loss of Indian identity through assimilation, or a dysfunctional liminality. But there are also costs to excluding forms that have European origins from Indian conceptions of Indian culture. Both interculturalism and biculturalism dispose Indians to distinguish between distinct coexisting subsets of "white" and "Indian" forms that then together additively compose their total way of life. "Indian culture" thus becomes a marked domain that Indian people pick out from the totality of their own behavioral-ideational routines. The typical differentia of the "Indian culture" subset is either or both continuousness with pre-Euro-American forms and contrastive value with Euro-American forms. Insofar as Indians retain such forms, they retain their "own" Indian cultures in juxtaposition with white culture. The "white culture" subset remains "white culture" and does not become "Indian culture," usually regardless of how many generations it has been conventional within Indian societies. Indian biculturalism thus posits subjects' versatile participation in separate cultural spheres, only one of which, however, is "ours" and the other of which is "theirs" (non-Indian).

This curious position is made precarious by the implied assumption that Indian culture and white culture exist in inverse proportion, as well as by both folk and scholarly claims that Indians are "real" only in proportion to the presence of "Indian" (pre-European or contrastive forms) in their visible comportment. Given the oppositivity in question, persons and groups can appraise themselves and be appraised by others as "more or less" Indian in proportion to the ratios of "Indian culture" to "white culture" present in their customary behavior. As Deloria (1969:82) astutely noted in the 1960s, "Indian people begin to feel that they are merely shadows of a mythical super-Indian," that is, the culturally "pure" Indian of pre-European provenance. In this degree, Indian images of authentic

Indian-ness have been forged in the shadow of white stereotypy, notably the "impassable gulf" between civility and savagery that is ancestral to ideological biculturalism. Coupled with assimilationist theories predicting the gradual disappearance of Indian culture through incremental replacement by white forms, biculturalism implies a relentlessly strange version of "cultural death" ideology. Indians and many anthropologists have converged in defining "Indian culture" as an endangered and diminishing stock of "traditional" elements that are rapidly losing ground to white influences. Indians were losing "their" Indian culture and were acquiring "our" white culture—which could not, however, be simultaneously ours *and* theirs at the same time." To assert that Indians—or any other humans—have "lost their culture" suggests some bizarre and twisted cyber-punk scenario in which those so afflicted fall back by default on the species (meager) repertoire of innate behaviors in order to classify, interpret, and act upon experience. The situation of bicultural Indians is almost as anomalous. Eventually Indians will be in the abject subject position of classifying, interpreting, and acting upon experience entirely with "someone else's" culture" rather than "their own."

Indian Anthropology in the New Millennium
Biculturalism and Essentialism

By the 1990s it had become commonplace to note that the eclipse of modernism in some First World intellectual circuits was proceeding hand in hand with an increasing appetite for modernity in the Second, Third, and Fourth Worlds (Seidman 1994:1). Similarly, through a period in which anthropologists are increasingly writing off the culture concept as theoretically misguided and politically suspect, the Fourth World peoples formerly comprising the disciplinary stock in trade have never been more certain that they possess distinctive cultures and never more assertively and self-consciously engaged in their retention and objectification (Sahlins 1993:3–4, 2000:193–201).

If Indians and earlier anthropologists have been in broad agreement that there exist Indian societies with Indian cultures, then the conclusion of a more recent anthropology has been that both were deluded. A variety of critiques with roots in postmodernism, postcolonial criticism, poststructuralism, and political economy have converged in deconstructing received disciplinary concepts of "society," "identity," "culture," and "tradition." The conclusion has been variously that there are no cultures, or that cultures, insofar as they exist, do not possess the properties ascribed to them by earlier anthropologists and by the Fourth World peoples in whose Nativist or indigenist projects culture has assumed increasing importance.

The central critique of indigenous culturalism is that Indians and others profess "essentialist" theories of what their cultures were, are, or should be. The semantics of essentialism seem nowhere clearly specified, but central connotations are those of stasis and boundedness. Essentialist culture concepts stipulate qualities that cultural forms or repertoires must have in order to "count" as *the* authentic culture of *a* particular society, that is, for example, being traditional versus modern or being indigenous versus foreign. No consensus has emerged on how best to conceptualize juxtapositions of indigenous and Western-derived elements in Fourth World (or other) cultural repertoires.

Particular critiques of Fourth World ethno-anthropologies argue that they traffic in "invented traditions" that are wrongly construed as preEuropean by Fourth World peoples and credulous anthropologists. Such "traditions" are commonly deconstructed as effects of colonial domination, appropriations or inversions of European stereotypes, or pragmatic fabrications cooked in contemporary political contexts. The status of genuine traditions—that is, forms continuous with if not identical to pre-European antecedents—is commonly left under specified. If Indians and anthropologists misrecognize some modern forms as primordial traditions, then the critics of invented tradition are equally subject to the inverse error. Though the critics commonly construe essentialized traditions as instruments or effects of domination, the fact that they figure increasingly as means and ends in the political aspirations of Fourth World peoples has prompted extended debate as to whether deconstruction or advocacy is the appropriate academic posture (Dirlik 1996).

Contemporary Indian ethno-anthropologies exhibit a complex set of alignments and nonalignments with these anthropological critiques. First, many Indians do indeed profess essentialist conceptions of their cultures. The bicultural distinction between juxtaposed but sequestered "Indian" (i.e., pre-European) and "white" (or "generic") cultural elements in Indian cultural repertoires is, for example, classically essentialist. Possessing more or less stable content (defined by indigenousness and/or contrastive value with white culture), Indian culture can be "destroyed," "lost," or, more optimistically, "revived." A deferred issue, long posed by Indian hobbyists, was catalyzed in the 1980s by new varieties of wannabes: Indian culture, like Indian identity, is a social "property" that can be stolen or otherwise misappropriated by non-Indians (see Rose 1992). Also, like the "authentic" Indian cultures of the Boasians, Indian culture is susceptible to contamination through miscegenation. A particularly salient subject of such discourses today are the uses to which those virtuosos of cultural syncretism, the New Age devotees, have put what they conceive to be Indian spiritual concepts and practices. For example, according to Osage (Plains) theologian George Tinker "When you uproot something from one culture and plant it in another culture, it is not the same thing. The danger is that these mutations of spirituality will make their way back into the Indian world." But what then to make of the Native American Church? In June 1993, the Fifth Lakota Summit, with both the New Agers and their Indian preceptors clearly in mind, passed a "Declaration of War Against Exploiters of Lakota Spirituality." The declaration inveighs against "those who would exploit the spiritual traditions of our Lakota people by imitating our ceremonial ways and by mixing such imitation rituals in an offensive and harmful pseudo-religious hodgepodge." It speaks also of the need for all Indians to "preserve the purity of our precious traditions for our future generations, so that our children and our children's children will survive and prosper in the sacred manner intended for each of our respective peoples by our Creator (Johnston 1993)."

Here we encounter again the theme of cosmogonic pluralism-relativism but now conjoined with a discourse on "purity" that is critical both of Euro-American influences and of intertribal cultural borrowing. A subdominant Indian discourse that is more convergent with anthropological antiessentialism is a subject to which I return later in this chapter.

With respect to invented traditions, Indians have been no more or less gullible or calculating than other people in imputing primordial qualities to historical forms. But anthropologists have been insufficiently attentive to the modernist critiques of invented tradition posed by Indian people themselves. To take one example, there appeared in the early 1980s on one Canadian reserve a community history (of local authorship) that included a sketch of "traditional culture." In the interest, one supposes, of legitimizing increased band sovereignty, the sketch included a representation of aboriginal political organization imagined on the model of the band bureaucracy that was emergent on the reserve in the 1970s. Thus were the ancestors endowed both with a plurality of "chiefs"—diplomatic chiefs, judicial chiefs, hunting chiefs, "child welfare chiefs"—and with a structure of hierarchically organized interlocking "councils" that was in no way inferior in complexity to a bicameral legislature. This met with wide acclamation—except from a group of elders who, expressing genuine bewilderment, asserted that they had themselves neither experienced nor ever heard of such institutions and that before the treaty, as far as they knew, there had *been* no chiefs at all. Such local critiques may extend also to "invented *non*traditions," that is, customs formerly practiced but now denied. Generations of priests and other white men, for example, have succeeded in persuading some contemporary Crees that the Dravidian marriage customs of their ancestors (and some contemporaries) are incestuous. As a result, some people deny that marriage to first cross-cousins ever occurred. In the context of one such denial, my interlocutor's elderly grandmother cheerfully interrupted, pointing out that such marriages formerly occurred "all the time," She then illustrated the point at some length with examples from her own experience and genealogy.

Essentialism and invented traditions are also interwoven in contemporary Indian anthropologies in a manner that is unimagined by the critics. Specifically, Indians are increasingly engaged in modernist critiques of invented tradition on the grounds that the latter, being invented, are antipathetic to the continuity or revival of the authentic and essentialized cultures of particular tribes. Increasingly common in Indian cultural politics are "local" critiques of pan-Indian forms as inauthentic "invented traditions," coupled with reassertions of tribal and cultural pluralism in the face of pan-Indian homogenization. For many whites, Plains culture epitomizes "Indianness," and it is therefore not surprising that many non–Plains Indians have pragmatically deployed Plains images in their dealings with whites, augmented or replaced local forms with Plains forms, and even come to conceive Plains and non-Plains cultural repertoires as identical. The predominance of Plains forms in the regional varieties of pan-Indianism partially reflects these stereotypes. The critique of pan-Indianism, however, is no new thing. In the 1940s, some entrepreneurs on the Caughnawaga Mohawk Reservation in Quebec operated tourist concessions that were tricked out with such stereotypically "Indian" images as Northwest Coast totem poles and Plains teepees:

> Some of the younger Caughnawagas have studied a little of the Indian past in school and they disapprove of the front-yard [tourist] establishments. They particularly disapprove of Chief White Eagle's establishment [Stop! Pow Wow with Me! Chief White Eagle. Indian Medicine Man]; they feel that it gives visitors a highly erroneous impression of Caughnawaga right off the bat. First of all, the old Mohawks did not live in teepees but in log-and-bark communal houses called longhouses, and they did not make totem poles. [Mitchell 1993:269]

Such critiques have since proliferated. On the Northwest Coast, similar skepticism toward generic "Indian culture" was voiced by the Stolo (Halklomelem Central Coast Salish) leader Sonny McHalsie who—asking rhetorically "Are the spirits addicted?"—rejected the appropriateness of ceremonial tobacco offerings on the grounds that, whatever their appropriateness for Indians elsewhere, they were not part of "traditional" Stolo culture:

> It seems that in our quest for Stolo cultural revival, we have blended general Native American culture with the Xwelitem's [whites'] stereotypical image of the "Indian" (pan-Indianism). . . . I don't believe that a tobacco offering is or ever was a Stolo tradition. I was never taught by Stolo elders to leave tobacco as an offering. [Steele 1995:67–68]

dichotomy; modern vs. Traditional

He then proceeded to explain the hegemonic position of Plains culture to its preeminence in white stereotypes. As Steele cogently observes, "McHalsie is privileging the construction of Indian identity in relation to a specific aboriginal cultural tradition rather than in relation to a broader pan-Indian response to common aspects of post-contact history and experience" (Steele 1995:68).

The Micmac (Subarctic) "neotraditions" described by Prins (1994) provide another exemplary case. In the 1980s and 1990s, Cree and Lakota-influenced forms of the sweat lodge and the Sun Dance were introduced in Micmac communities, where they evoked disparate reactions. Elders, for whom Catholicism had long since become Micmac "tradition," derided the Sun Dance as devil worship while younger persons valued it as the recovered form of traditional Micmac spirituality. Note here an implicit Indian cultural universalism (and thus substitutability): Lakotas and Crees have retained a generic Indian culture that the Micmac have lost but can reacquire through borrowing. Though Micmacs formerly used a sweat lodge (with, however, only distant affinities to the Plains form), they did not practice the Sun Dance, and the latter provoked a reappraisal of the value of "borrowed traditions." Said a neotraditional leader:

> Our younger people must be taught, through their culture, what is considered to be sacred in our traditions and what is not. Those Micmac traditional Indians who claim that a form of peyote was used in traditional Micmac beliefs and practices are wrong. . . . The Sun dance, piercing of the skin, use of marihuana [sic], eating dogs or the use of peyote are not the ancient ways of our Micmac people, and we can't use these rituals in our native spiritual traditions. [Prins 1994:391]

Or as another Micmac succinctly put it: "Do not follow their [Sioux, Cree] ways, they are of a very different tribe" (Prins 1994:392). New-Ageism and pan-Indianism seemingly pose commensurable threats to local cultural purisms.

Its popularity among Indians and whites notwithstanding, Indian and white biculturalism is, in fact, at right angles with most of what anthropology otherwise knows about the effects of intersocietal cultural borrowing. These effects encompass everything from ideas about the "reciprocal transformation" of indigenous and exogenous elements (Boas 1940:435) and the emergent synthetic cultures of the acculturation theorists to more recent arguments that cultural history and historical culture exist as simultaneous relations of continuous reproduction or transformation between forms that compose the successive conditions of societies (Sahlins 1985).

Distinctions between the indigenous and foreign forms composing a cultural repertoire are, of course, historically perspectival. The presently "indigenous" was plausibly "foreign" in the past, and the presently "foreign" will plausibly be "indigenous" in the future. Succinctly, biculturalism exhibits a certain obliviousness to the influences exerted upon one another by the notionally sequestered but coexisting indigenous and foreign forms that compose the bicultural segments. Foreign elements introduced into a cultural repertoire and the existing elements that compose this repertoire do not and cannot thereafter exist in a condition of compartmentalization. Indian societies are composed of human beings, and human beings are incapable of such gymnastics. Indian Christianity cannot, for example, be the "same" as non-Indian Christianity because it is influenced by Indian theologies that precede or coexist with it. Conversely, these same theologies cannot exist in the "same" condition prior and subsequent to influences exerted upon them by Christianity. Since indigenous and foreign elements influence each other—hybrids like the Native American Church being only the most salient examples—they do not compose two discrete repertoires with distinguishable competencies and contexts but rather a single repertoire. Thus in practice, if not always in theory, indigenous "Indian" forms—teepees, hand games, and Sun Dances—and "white" forms—ranch houses, golf, and Easter Sundays—cannot be sorted into two coexisting but discrete bicultural compartments in people's ideas and practices—even though people may genuinely believe that they can. Ideologies of biculturalism themselves, of course, are significant forms of Indian culture that are influential on the other forms with which they coexist. Rather than engendering bicultural tendencies, it might be argued that such ideologies actually intensify fusions and interactions between Indian-derived and Euro-American-derived forms within Indian repertoires. Indians may sometimes be most "traditional" when they are attending college and most "modern" when attending naming feasts. Some irony accrues to the fact that ideologies of discrete "white" and "Indian" cultural forms developed historically in contexts of accelerated mixture, fusion, and reciprocal transformation between "white" and "Indian" forms within Indian culture repertoires.

An alternative conception is to retain existing (though much debated) ideas of cultural pluralism and holism, that is, the Boasian vision that "Culture embraces all the manifestations of the social habits of a community" (Boas 1930:79). Such phrases as *Cheyenne culture* or *the culture of the Wasco* would then refer to the totality of meanings, dispositions, and practices that are conventional among the members of the tribes in question. Since every Indian collectivity, by necessity or inclination, has long since indigenized meanings, dispositions, and practices of Euro-American historical origin (and continues to do so), the justification for excluding these forms requires elucidation. It is questionable whether "Indian culture" is usefully defined as the "traditional" residue that is left over after all modern-derived forms are subtracted. To so expand our ideas of "Indian culture" to include forms of Indian and of Euro-American (or other) derivation as well as forms specific to Indians and shared by Indians and non-Indians is consistent both with some earlier theories of acculturation and with some more recent reformulations of the culture concept, notably Hannerz's concept of creolization (1992:265–267). Such reformulations require tolerance for degrees of intrasocietal cultural difference and of intersocietal cultural sameness that are greater than those in earlier conceptions of culture. At the same time, the expanded conception does not compromise the idea that tribes have distinct cultures, both among themselves and vis-à-vis non-Indians. The Euro-American–derived forms in Indian cultural repertoires are not the "same" as their non-Indian counterparts to the degree that the former, and not the latter, bear the impress of contiguity with both earlier and coexisting elements that are continuous with pre-European cultural horizons.

Indians themselves sometimes express similarly synthetic conceptions of their own cultures. Coexisting with dominant bicultural concepts of essentialized Indian culture are ideas that see Indian culture or custom as comprising the whole repertoire of forms present in particular Indian communities. These more inclusive and synthetic Indian ideas of Indian custom may be informal, more often implicit than explicit, and unlinked with the phrase *Indian culture*. I have encountered no explicit Indian definitions of modern Indian cultures as being distinctive repertoires composed of interacting elements of both pre-Columbian and Euro-American derivation (although such may well exist).

The contrast between bicultural and synthetic Indian ideas of Indian

386   *Robert Brightman*

culture are exemplified by two passages in the June 12, 2003, issue of *Spilway Tymoo* ("Coyote's News"), the newspaper of the Warm Springs Reservation of Oregon. In the first, staff from the Community Counseling Center discuss the positive effects of cultural revival in healing the adverse effects of historical oppression: "If we realize it or not, today we carry in our hearts the grief and traumas of our ancestors. Reviving our traditions, culture, language, prayer, and songs are ways Indian nations can heal their wounded spirits." In the second, author Selena Boise announces the events scheduled for the upcoming Pi-Ume-Sha powwow: "We can look forward to the Indian dancing, stick games, softball, basketball, boxing, the parade, 10k race, endurance race, rodeo, and golf. There will be something for everyone at this annual event." Note the privileged position here accorded Indian dances and stick games but also the presupposition that basketball and golf are conventional and appropriate (and perhaps expected) powwow events for Indian participants and observers alike. Bicultural dichotomies are pushed into the background, and a form can be "Indian" without meeting essentialist criteria of pre-European origin or uniquely Indian distribution. More than whites, Indians, like the Fourth World Pacific societies described by Jolly (1992:53), may sometimes be "more accepting of both indigenous and exogamous elements as constituting their cultures." Such concepts are most often explicit with respect to foreign customs that have local historical depth. Thus a Cree elder readily identified Catholicism as "Cree custom." "And why not?" she asked, since the French, who introduced the religion in the 1880s, had themselves in turn originally acquired it from others.

Such implicit synthetic ideas of Indian custom suggest that many Indian people some of the time and some Indian people most of the time may exhibit a sovereign obliviousness to their (imputed) bicultural or intercultural conditions. Possessing sound conceptions of cultural transfer as being normal, they may lack consciousness of their ideas and conduct as being divided between Indian and white domains. Foreign forms are not "inauthentic," do not "contaminate" tradition, and do not compromise Indian identities. Neither then would the people necessarily experience that sense of distinctness or incompatibility or incongruity between "pure-indigenous" and "foreign-inauthentic" elements that is basic to both white and Indian theories of biculturalism.

On one occasion, for example, during the early 1980s, a Potawatomi friend and I were watching evening television in his home in Forest County, Wisconsin, exploring the many options afforded by his new satellite dish. After his wife retired for the evening, he opportunistically switched to the Playboy Channel. While we were watching the Playboy

Channel, my friend assumed a thoughtful air. It was the first evening I had spent in his home, and he evidently desired to dispel any concerns I might have had about my safety there. He thus casually assured me that I need not worry about "bad medicine" (sorcery) getting to me in his house. His *mndo.g* ("dream spirits"), he said, "patroled," as it were, the perimeters of the property and intercepted all such dangers. Juxtaposed with Hugh Hefner, I found this discourse entertainingly incongruous, but not so my friend.

A. Irving Hallowell (1955) bequeathed to anthropology the memorably Conradian image of Saulteaux bands growing increasingly "traditional" as one ascended the Berens River from Lake Winnipeg into the interior. In 1992, while waiting in The Pas, Manitoba's self-proclaimed "Gateway to the North," for a southbound train *out* of the boreal forest, I got into a conversation with a Cree trapper from Cumberland House named Joe McGillivray. A proud veteran of the Korean War, he shared with me his experiences as a paratrooper with Canadian forces. His reminiscences took an unexpected turn—unexpected because Crees are usually reticent about such matters—when he disclosed that his puberty dream of a *pine.siw* or "thunderbird" had providentially prepared him for his airborne combat experiences. "I'd be lying," he told me, "if I said I wasn't scared. But all the time I was over there I knew that I had that in me." Again I found some incongruity in the deployment of Cree dream blessings on behalf of the Canadian state and in the faraway skies of Korea. But McGillivray's discourse wove together fighter jets and thunderbird visions in a synthetic whole.

Hallowell also wrote extensively on incompatibilities between Saulteaux/Ojibwe and Euro-Canadian cultures, and on the psychological wages of acculturation. If Hallowell was sometimes disposed to pathologize cultural mixture, his principal authority on the culture of the Saulteaux provided a formidable counterexample. William Berens was born into a family of nomadic hunters in the bush country of Manitoba in the 1860s (Brown 1989). Born to a Saulteaux father and *Métisse* mother (i.e., mixed Indian-white ancestry), Berens identified as Saulteaux but acquired from his mixed parentage a cultural versatility exceptional at the time: "I learned the white ways from my mother and the Indian ways from my grandparents on my father's side so I know what both are like" (Brown 1989:210). Berens lived to see steamships, airplanes, railroads, outboard motors, the inception of sedentary villages, white immigration, the treaty-signing period, and the establishment of the reservation system. None of these surprised or disoriented him since he went on to master an impressive variety of Indian and white occupations and to become chief of the Berens River treaty band. Though Berens distinguished Indian and white "ways" and might have self-identified as a "bicultural Indian," his own varied life experiences more plausibly suggest the integration of Euro-Canadian forms into a Saulteaux repertoire. Absent are themes of incongruity or incompatibility. He recalled his father telling him: "Don't think you know everything. You will see lots of new things and you will find a place in your mind for them all" (Brown 1989:210).

In these three vignettes, the individuals in question are neither disposed to nor even necessarily capable of living lives segregated into distinct "Indian" and "white" domains in ideation, disposition, and practice. The cultural competence embodied in their experiences may find expression in more inclusive Indian concepts of Indian culture. Increasingly, "Indian culture" may come to mean "whatever (some or most or all) Indian people habitually do and say around here," the fact that the people in question are Indians sufficing to make what they say or do "Indian" regardless of whether the forms in question are historically indigenous, foreign, or hybrid in origin.

Acknowledgments

Over the course of many years, I have discussed ideas or materials expressed in this papers with Tim Buckley, Regna Darnell, David Dinwoodie, Kathrine French, Robert Moore, Peter Nabokov, Marshall Sahlins, Michael Silverstein, and Rupert Stasch. The inspiration for writing it came from Raymond Fogelson.

References

Ackerknecht, Erwin
　1944 White Indians. Bulletin of the History of Medicine 15:18–35.
Aginsky, B. W.
　1940 An Indian's Soliloquy. American Journal of Sociology 46:43–44.
Aubin, George
　1975 A Proto-Algonquian Dictionary. National Museums of Man Mercury Series, Canadian Ethnology Service Paper 29.
Axtell, James
　1981 The White Indians of Colonial America. In Axtell, The European and the Indian: Essays in the Ethnohistory of Colonial North America. New York: Oxford University Press.
Bailey, Alfred G.
　1969 The Conflict of European and Eastern Algonquian Cultures, 1504–1700. Toronto: University of Toronto Press.

Basso, Keith

1989 Portraits of "The Whiteman." Cambridge: Cambridge University Press.

Benedict, Ruth

1946 [1934] Patterns of Culture. New York: Mentor.

Blackman, Margaret

1981 Window on the Past: The Photographic Ethnohistory of the Northern and Kaigani Haida. Canadian Ethnology Service Paper 74. Ottawa: National Museum of Man Mercury Series.

Bloomfield, Leonard

1928 Menomini Texts. American Ethnological Society Publications 12.

Boas, Franz

1894 Chinook Texts. Bulletin of the Bureau of American Ethnology 20.

1897 The Social Organization and the Secret Societies of the Kwakiutl Indians. Annual Report of the United States National Museum for 1895. Pp. 311–738. Washington DC: Smithsonian Institution.

1930 Anthropology. In Encyclopedia of the Social Sciences. Edwin R. A. Seligman, ed. Vol. 2, pp. 73–110. New York: Macmillan.

1938 The Mind of Primitive Man. New York: Free Press.

1940 Race, Language and Culture. New York: Free Press.

1966 Kwakiutl Ethnography. Chicago: University of Chicago Press.

Brightman, Robert

1989 Acaðohkiwina and Acimowina: Traditional Narratives of the Rock Cree Indians. Ottawa: Canadian Museum of Civilization.

1990 Primitivism in Missinippi Cree Historical Consciousness. Man 25:399–418.

1993 Grateful Prey: Rock Cree Human-Animal Relationships. Berkeley: University of California Press.

1999 Traditions of Subversion and the Subversion of Tradition: Cultural Criticism in Maidu Clown Performances. American Anthropologist 101(2):272–287.

Brown, Jennifer

1989 "A Place in Your Mind for Them All": Chief William Berens. In Being and Becoming Indian: Biographical Studies of North American Frontiers. James A. Clifton, ed. Pp. 204–225. Chicago: Dorsey Press.

Cushing, Frank Hamilton

1979 Zuñi: Selected Writings of Frank Hamilton Cushing. J. Green, ed. Lincoln: University of Nebraska Press

Deloria, Vine

1969 Custer Died for Your Sins. New York: Macmillan.

Descola, Philippe

1996 Constructing Natures: Symbolic Ecology and Social Practice. In Nature and Society: Anthropological Perspectives. Philippe Descola and Gisli Palsson, eds. Pp. 82–102. New York: Routledge.

Dirlik, Arif

1996 The Past as Legacy and Prospect: Postcolonial Criticism in the Perspective of Indigenous Historicism. American Indian Culture and Research Journal 20(2):1–31.

Dixon, Roland

1905 The Northern Maidu. Bulletin of the American Museum of Natural History 17(3): 119–346.

Fogelson, Raymond D.

1974 On the Varieties of Indian History: Sequoyah and Traveler Bird. Journal of Ethnic Studies 2(1):105–112.

1998 Perspectives on Native American Identity. *In* Studying Native America: Problems and Prospects. R. Thornton, ed. Pp. 40–59. Madison: University of Wisconsin Press.

French, David

1961 Wasco-Wishram. *In* Perspectives on American Indian Culture Change. Edward Spicer, ed. Pp. 337–430. Chicago: University of Chicago Press.

Frey, Rodney

1987 The World of the Crow Indians: As Driftwood Lodges. Norman: University of Oklahoma Press.

Gilberg, Rolf

1984 Polar Eskimo. *In* Vol. 5: Arctic. D. Damas, ed. Pp. 577–594. Handbook of North American Indians. William C. Sturtevant, gen. ed. Washington DC: Smithsonian Institution.

Goldschmidt, Walter

1976 Social Organization and Status Differentiation among the Nomlaki. *In* Native Californians: A Theoretical Retrospective. Lowell John Bean and Thomas C. Blackburn, eds. Pp. 125–174. Menlo Park CA: Ballena Press.

Greenblatt, Stephen

1991 Marvelous Possessions: The Wonder of the New World. Chicago: University of Chicago Press.

Hallowell, A. Irving

1955 Culture and Experience. New York: Schocken.

1976 American Indians, White and Black: The Phenomenon of Transculturalization. *In* Contributions to Anthropology: Selected Essays by A. Irving Hallowell. R. Fogelson, ed. Pp. 489–530. Chicago: University of Chicago Press.

Glacken, Clarence

1967 Traces on the Rhodian Shore: Nature and Culture in Western Thought from Ancient Times to the End of the Eighteenth Century. Berkeley: University of California Press.

Hannerz, Ulf

1992 Cultural Complexity. New York: Columbia University Press.

Hearne, Samuel

1958[1795] A Journey from Prince of Wales Fort in Hudson's Bay to the Northern Ocean in the Years 1769, 1770, 1771, and 1772. R. Glover, ed. Toronto: Macmillan.

Hymes, Dell

1981 The "Wife" Who "Goes Out" Like a Man: Reinterpretation of a Clackamas Chinook Myth. *In* Hymes, In Vain I Tried to Tell You. Philadelphia: University of Pennsylvania.

Ingold, Tim

1996a Hunting and Gathering as Ways of Perceiving the Environment. *In* Redefining Nature: Ecology, Nature and Domestication. R. F. Ellen and K. Fukui, eds. Pp. 117–155. Washington DC: Berg.

Jaenen, Cornelius J.

1974 Amerindian Views of French Culture in the Seventeenth Century. Canadian Historical Review 55(3):261–291.

Jewitt, John.

2000 White Slaves of Maquinna. Surrey BC: Heritage House.

Johnston, David

  1993 Spiritual Seekers Borrow Indians' Ways. New York Times, December 27, 1993:A1.

Jolly, Margaret

  1992 Spectres of Inauthenticity. Contemporary Pacific 4:49–72.

Kroeber, Alfred

  1948 Anthropology. New York: Harcourt Brace.

Leacock, Eleanor

  1980 Montagnais Women and the Jesuit Program for Colonization. *In* Women and Colonization: Anthropological Perspectives. M. Etienne and E. Leacock, eds. Pp. 25–42. New York: Praeger.

LeJeune, Paul

  1897 Relation of What Occurred in New France in the Year 1634. *In* The Jesuit Relations and Allied Documents. R. G. Thwaites, ed. Vol. 6. Pp. 1–317. Cleveland: Burrows.

Lévi-Strauss, Claude

  1966 The Savage Mind. Chicago: University of Chicago.

  1973 Structuralism and Ecology. Social Science Information 12(1):7–23.

  1976 Structural Anthropology. Vol. 2. Chicago: University of Chicago Press.

  1982 The Way of the Masks. Seattle: University of Washington Press.

Linton, Ralph

  1940a The Processes of Cultural Transfer. *In* Acculturation in Seven American Indian Tribes. R. Linton, ed. Pp. 489–513. New York: D. Appleton-Century.

  1940b The Distinctive Aspects of Acculturation. *In* Acculturation in Seven American Indian Tribes. R. Linton, ed. Pp. 514–526. New York: D. Appleton-Century.

  1940c Notes on Chapters. *In* Acculturation in Seven American Indian Tribes. R. Linton, ed. Pp. 38, 118, 206, 258, 332, 389, 462. New York: D. Appleton-Century.

Lowie, Robert

  1980[1935] The Crow Indians. New York: Irvington.

MacCormack, Carol, and Marilyn Strathern, eds.

  1980 Nature, Culture and Gender. Cambridge: Cambridge University Press.

Malinowski, Bronislaw

  1954 Magic, Science and Religion, and Other Essays. New York: Anchor.

Mitchell, Joseph

  1993[1949] The Mohawks in High Steel. *In* Mitchell, Up in the Old Hotel. Pp. 267–290. New York: Pantheon Books.

Moore, John H.

  1998 Truth and Tolerance in Native American Epistemology. *In* Studying Native America: Problems and Prospects. R. Thornton, ed. Pp. 271–305. Madison: University of Wisconsin Press

Nabokov, Peter

  2002 A Forest of Time. Cambridge: Cambridge University Press.

Nabokov, Peter, ed.

  1991 Native American Testimony. New York: Penguin.

Nelson, Richard K.

  1973 Hunters of the Northern Forest. Chicago: University of Chicago Press.

Nichols, John, and Earl Nyholm

  1995 A Concise Dictionary of Minnesota Ojibwa. Minneapolis: University of Minnesota Press.

Parmentier, Richard

    1994 Naturalization of Convention. *In* Parmentier, Signs in Society. Pp. 175–192. Bloomington: Indiana University Press.

Pearce, Roy Harvey

    1965 Savagism and Civilization: A Study of the Indian and the American Mind. Baltimore: Johns Hopkins University Press.

Petitot, Emile

    1886 Traditions Indiennes du Canada Nord-Ouest: Légendes et Traditions des Cris. Paris: Maisonheure Freres.

Prins, Harald E. L.

    1994 Neo-Traditions in Native Communities: Sweat Lodge and Sun Dance among the Micmac Today. Actes du Vingt-Cinquieme Congres des Algonquinistes. W. Cowan, ed. Pp. 383–394. Ottawa: Carleton University.

Radin, Paul

    1927 Primitive Man as Philosopher. New York: D. Appleton.

    1933 The Method and Theory of Ethnology. South Hadley MA: Bergin and Garvey.

    1970[1923] The Winnebago Tribe. Lincoln: University of Nebraska Press.

    1972 The Trickster: A Study in American Indian Mythology. New York: Schocken.

Redfield, Robert, Ralph Linton, and Melville Herskovits

    1936. A Memorandum on the Study of Acculturation. American Anthropologist 38:149–152.

Ricketts, Mac Linscott

    1966 The North American Indian Trickster. History of Religions 5(2):327–350.

Rose, Wendy

    1992 The Great Pretenders: Further Reflections on Whiteshamanism. *In* The State of Native America. M. Annette Jaimes, ed. Pp. 403–421. Boston: South End Press.

Rossignol, Marius

    1938. The Religion of the Saskatchewan and Western Manitoba Cree. Primitive Man 11(3–4):67–71.

Sahlins. Marshall

    1985 Islands of History. Chicago: University of Chicago Press.

    1993 Goodbye to Tristes Tropes: Ethnography in the Context of Modern World History. Journal of Modern History 65:1–25.

    1999a What Is Anthropological Enlightenment? Some Lessons of the Twentieth Century. Annual Review of Anthropology 28:i–xxiii.

    1999b Two or Three Things That I Know about Culture. Journal of the Royal Anthropological Institute 5:399–421.

    2000 "Sentimental Pessimism" and Ethnographic Experience, or, "Why Culture Is Not a Disappearing Object." *In* Biographies of Scientific Objects. L. Daston, ed. Pp. 158–202. Chicago: University of Chicago Press.

Sapir, Edward

    1994 The Psychology of Culture: A Course of Lectures. Judith Irvine, ed. Berlin: Mouton de Gruyter.

Seidman, Steven

    1994 Introduction. *In* The Postmodern Turn: New Perspectives on Social Theory. Steven Seidman, ed. Pp. 1–26. Cambridge: Cambridge University Press.

Spicer, Edward

    1961 Types of Contact and Processes of Change. *In* Perspectives on American Indian

Culture Change. Edward Spicer, ed. Pp. 517–544. Chicago: University of Chicago Press.

Steele, Mila T.
1995 When Nationalists Become Anthropologists. BA thesis, Department of Anthropology. Reed College, Portland OR.

Steward, Julian
1977 The Ceremonial Buffoon of the American Indian. *In* Steward, Evolution and Ecology: Essays on Social Transformation. Pp. 347–365. Urbana: University of Illinois Press.

Strong, Pauline, and Barrik Van Winkle
1996 "Indian Blood": Reflections on the Reckoning and Refiguring of Native North American Identity. Cultural Anthropology 11(4):547–576.

Thompson, David
1962 David Thompson's Narrative. R. Glover, ed. Toronto: Champlain Society.

Thompson, Lucy
1991[1916] To the American Indian: Reminiscences of a Yurok Woman. Berkeley CA: Heyday Books.

Turner, Terence
1988 Ethno-Ethnohistory: Myth and History in Native South Americans' Representations of Contact with Western Society. *In* Rethinking History and Myth: Indigenous South American Perspectives on the Past. Jonathan D. Hill, ed. Pp. 235–281. Urbana: University of Illinois Press.

VanStone, James
1965 The Changing Culture of the Snowdrift Chipewyan. National Museum of Canada Bulletin 209. Pp. 1–133.

Vincent, Sylvie, and Denys Delage
1992 Traditions et récits sur l'arrivée des europeens en Amérique. Recherches amérindiennes au québec 21(2–3). Pp. 1–278.

Wallace, Anthony F. C.
1956 Revitalization Movements. American Anthropologist 58:264–281.
1958 Dreams and Wishes of the Soul: A Type of Psychoanalytic Theory among the Seventeenth Century Iroquois American Anthropologist 60:230–248.

Waterman, T. T.
1914 The Explanatory Element in the Folktales of the North American Indian. Journal of American Folklore 27:1–54.

White, Raymond C.
1957 The Luiseno Theory of Knowledge. American Anthropologist 59:119.

Whiteley, Peter
1987 The Interpretation of Politics: A Hopi Conundrum. Man 22(4):696–714.

Woodburn, James
1980 Hunters and Gatherers Today and Reconstruction of the Past. *In* Soviet and Western Anthropology. Ernest Gellner, ed. Pp. 95–117. London: Duckworth.

16. Cannibals in the Mountains

Washoe Teratology and the Donner Party

BARRIK VAN WINKLE

> The Washo watched. . . . The Washo watched through the trees as they
> ate themselves. . . . The body sprawled on the snow, split open, one of
> them standing over it with a hatchet hanging limp in his hand, the thick-
> ness of blood dripping slowly from the blade to the snow, each drop
> silently splashing red into the coldness.
>
> Thomas Sanchez, *Rabbit Boss*

The scream came at midnight, just as I had turned off my lantern. I was in
the Sierra Nevada foothills south of Lake Tahoe, at least five miles from
any other human being. In a flash I was out of my tent and into my car,
with the windows rolled up and the doors locked. The scream was real,
not some dream. It sounded like nothing I had ever heard before. I had not
woken myself up from a nightmare in which my advisor, Ray Fogelson,
was handing me yet another stack of books, another endless reading list,
another set of xeroxed articles. I heard the scream three more times that
night, once more from the west—uphill but closer—and then twice more
to the east of my camp, going away and downhill.

The next morning I was up early and quickly drove down to the Washoe
Senior Citizens Center in the Dresslerville Colony (see map).[1] It was a
crisp fall day in 1983. There I asked a group of Washoe and white elders what could have made the noise. I described it as a combination of a
woman's high-pitched screaming, dogs howling, cats screeching, and pan-
icked chickens. After animated discussion, one man, an Indian cowboy
with 40 years' experience in the Sierras said: "Oh, that was a mountain
lion." Then, leaning across the table and widening his eyes, he added,
"You're lucky it didn't eat you."

I scoffed at this notion and was told, in a confusion of voices, a well-

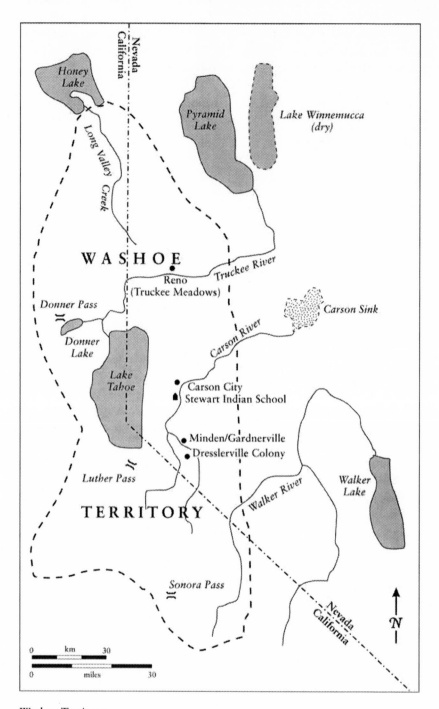

Washoe Territory

known story of two Paiute boys eaten by mountain lions in the 1920s or 1930s. I reproduce the gist of the narrative here, since my notes of this unrecorded conversation do not always make plain exactly who said what:

> It was when we were all at Stewart [Indian School]. There were these two Paiute boys from Walker River, brothers, or maybe cousin-brothers, who didn't like school. They escaped and were going over the mountains, the Pine Nut Mountains, our mountains, heading back to Walker River. The school people tracked them with those dogs, the ones they used for prisoners. After a couple of days the dogs were nervous and worried and when they found the boys, they were half-eaten, dead from a mountain lion.[2]

Over time, as more people heard *my* mountain lion story, I was rewarded with a deluge of stories about man-eating mountain lions, other anthropophagous animals, and cannibal monsters. Again and again, on that and subsequent occasions, I heard tales from Washoes of all ages about the consumption of human flesh by mountain lions, or by the now long-gone grizzly bears (as well as directions about how, in turn, to hunt them). Stories were also told about "cannibalism" by Wolf (also gone from the mountains), and there were dark allusions to the deeds of his younger brother, *géwe*, or Coyote.[3]

And there were other stories of man-eating monsters: tales of a variously formed giant, *hana'wïywïy*, who preyed on young people neglecting their duty and who was finally subdued by the cleverness of *nentúšu*, the "old woman" creator (Dangberg 1968:39–43; Inter-Tribal Council of Nevada 1976:33).[4] Then there was "Big Foot," who lured curious people to his cave by offering soup—made from human blood. Diners who complained, noticed, or inquired about the soup's ingredients themselves became the next meal (ITC 1976:35).[5] There was also Uncle Pus, the evil, man-eating uncle of the culture-hero weasel brothers, *pewétseli* and *damálali*, who was killed by the words of the older brother after he had tricked Pus and his family into lying down to hear a story (see Dangberg 1968:81–84). And the story of the *ʔáy*, a monstrous cannibal bird whose nest was in the middle of Lake Tahoe, to which the *ʔáy* would carry live captives to devour at its leisure. The *ʔáy* was also destroyed by human cleverness, although this time by a young man (see Downs 1966:61; ITC 1976:35–36). All these monsters were *ťánu ťémʔluʔ*, the Washoe phrase for a cannibal or man-eater, which literally means "having people as food."

But the most frightening revelations of cannibalism were about myself, or at least people like me. One day, as we sat in her house in the Carson

Valley in the south of Washoe territory an older woman made it plain: "Oh yes," she said, "we have those stories, but the worst cannibals were men." Tapping my knee with a finger to focus my attention, she added, "men like you, *dabóʔo*." [6]

White men? Me? I have eaten strange things—polish sausage, scrapple, head cheese, snails, hot dogs, dogs, possum, snakes, bugs, frog legs, horses—but never to my knowledge have I eaten human flesh. "Did they kill and eat Washoes, these men?" I asked. "No, no," was her answer, "each other." And she told me how, long ago, as she put it, before whites lived in Washoe territory, a "bunch" of white people traveling to California (up north of here, she said), got trapped in the mountains by snow. Her words implied that they were kin, some sort of extended family, as "bunch" is the term Washoes use to refer to their own kindreds. They ate all their food and animals, and then started eating each other.

"Oh," I said, in a masterly example of bad interviewing technique, "you mean the Donner Party!" "No, I don't think so," she severely replied, sensing perhaps that I was too dismissive of her underlying lesson. But subsequent tales and allusions to white cannibalism in the mountains reinforced my first impression. Younger people (those under 50), definitely identified the Donner Party as the "bunch," and Donner Lake and Donner Pass as the site of the story. However, much of this lore remained vague as to who was involved, where the cannibalism occurred, and why it was done. The grizzly details also varied. Here are three excerpts from other, longer conversations about cannibalism and human consumption:

> It was long ago, when Whites first came here to our country, my uncle told me, he heard it from the old people then. It was up at Donner Pass, you know, on Interstate 80, where the inspection station is. [7] There was a wagon train of White people going to California, they tried to go over the mountains when it was snowing. They got trapped and had to eat each other. Guess they didn't know how to hunt, but most White people don't know how to hunt, right, they're like you. Anyway, they starved, a lot of them, and they ate each other.
>
> I heard they drew straws and then chased the losers down and killed them and ate them. There were Washoes watching, curious about these people, and they saw that, that cannibalism. But they didn't eat the heads, just the bodies, legs and stuff you know.
>
> The old Washoes were scared of Whites—they did horrible things, you know, like eat each other up in the mountains in the winter. They must have been stupid, we didn't camp up there when it was going to be a bad winter, but we know the mountains. I heard our ancestors tried to

help them, left deer and *tágim* [pine-nuts] and porcupines.[8] But all that help wasn't enough, they still ate each other.

Other tales just mentioned the bald fact of human cannibalism. Some described chases with hatchets, the butchering of corpses, and the frenzied eating of still warm raw flesh. But if details of place and time and actions varied, the way contemporary Washoes discuss Washoe interactions with the Donner Party almost all shared several features (aside from what seemed to me to be the obligatory cautions about whites and an underlying dig at the interviewer). First, some Washoes were said to have actually witnessed cannibal acts by the Donner Party, and, second, the uniform responses were of horror, fear, and avoidance. A third feature is also often noted—compassion. Washoe ancestors were said to have left food on the outskirts of the Donner Party camps, including whole deer and haunches of venison, as well as porcupines and baskets of pine nuts.

Washoe history and lore is quite certain that Washoes witnessed this tragedy and aided the victims in some ways. However, the Euro-American history and ethnohistory of the Donner Party does not include a Washoe presence in its narrative. To Whites the Washoes were nonparticipants in this quickly epitomized event (see Fogelson 1989 for a discussion of epitomizing events). Nevertheless, however much white chroniclers may have made the Donner Party's cannibalism a historical nonevent for the Washoe of the time, the event has assumed an epitomized status for their descendants.

The Donner Party: An American Tragedy

The Donner Party and its quasi-epic experience has spawned a minor literary industry. More than a hundred works have been published about the tragedy, the earliest in 1847 (McKistry 1917), only a few months after the party's rescue and arrival in the central valley of California.[9] There are also hundreds, if not thousands, of journalistic articles over the last century and a half, repeating the same facts and suppositions and responses.[10]

The Donner Party continues to be an intriguing topic of cultural and historical reflection in western American society. It has it all: tragedy, sex, heroism, determination, murder, stupidity, and horror in a mix that continues to fascinate Americans. (Well, not really much sex, only naked corpses, but it would not be an American tragedy if there was not some or if I did not use the word.) Ric Burns produced a 90-minute segment of the Public Broadcasting System's *American Experience* about the party in 1992 (Burns 1992), a sure sign that these events are part of middle-brow American historical consciousness. More recently, as I began to write this article, the October 1996 issue of *Sunset: The Magazine of Western Living*, contained a four-page spread on the Donner Party called "Tracing a Terrible Trail." It is subtitled "The tragedy of the Donner Party is familiar to all Westerners. But familiarity can be deceptive—as new discoveries confirm." The 150th anniversary of the Donner Party's ordeal was in 1996, and the article celebrates the occasion, while cursorily reporting the findings of historians, archaeologists, and others. The "new" discoveries are not particularly revealing: tales of 20-foot-high snowdrifts are probably true, the winter was "probably not much worse than average in the Sierra Nevada," and lore about extensive cannibalism with "bodies, terribly mutilated, legs, arms, and skulls scattered" is "not supported or disproved by available evidence" (Finnegan 1996).[11]

For nonwesterners I should explain that the Donner-Reed Party, as it is more formally called, was one of the earliest migrant wagon trains to travel to California over what is now called Donner Pass, and among the first five or six to move through Washoe territory.[12] The wagon train left Independence, Missouri, in mid-May 1846. (A little late, as those familiar with the children's computer game *Oregon Trail* know.) In Wyoming, in mid-July, 19 wagons left the main pioneer trail to try the untested Hastings Cutoff, a supposed shortcut leading south of the Great Salt Lake. This move, apparently, went against the advice of the women in the group—perhaps because they wished to do the sensible thing and stop and ask for directions—but they were overruled by the men of the party.

The detour was disastrous (a typical male shortcut, as my wife has remarked more than once). Several people died, others left the group, and James F. Reed, one of the leaders, was banished from the group for killing another member of the party. Reed went on ahead by horseback, leaving his family, wagons, and stock with the main party. Most significantly, the Hastings Cutoff route required extra time and caused the remaining members of the party to reach the Truckee Meadows (the valley in which present-day Reno and Sparks are located) in mid-October of 1846.

In early September two members of the group had been sent ahead to secure supplies from California. One of these men, Charles Stanton, returned as the party began their ascent of the eastern slope of the Sierras. Stanton brought food and news, including that John Reed had arrived safely in California. Stanton was accompanied by two Catholic Miwoks, Luis and Salvador, vaqueros (or peons) from Karl Sutter's California empire. But by October 30, when the main body of 60 people reached Truckee (now Donner) Lake (elevation 5933 feet), some 1100 feet below the summit of Donner Pass, it had begun to snow. At this time most of the party camped at the east end of the lake, although the two Donner family groups camped further down the pass, along Alder Creek in Dog Valley.

It began to snow! And it kept on snowing until the drifts and snow pack were high as 20 feet. Three times the emigrants attempted to crest the pass, and three times they failed. Provisions ran out, their draft animals (oxen) were slaughtered for food (and some either escaped or were run off by the Washoe). Even the dogs were eaten, and finally hides, shoes, and belts became staples. The party was trapped at their campgrounds. Game was nonexistent under the extreme winter conditions; and eventually some members of the party resorted to eating the corpses of their dead companions.

A "forlorn hope" of five women and twelve men, including the two Indian guides, left on December 15 on snowshoes for the western slope of the Sierra. Two men, who lacked snowshoes, returned to camp the next day. The remaining members resorted to cannibalism after twelve days on the trail. The first meal was made off the arms and legs of a dead companion. By January 8, when only the five women and two white men were still alive, the two Indians left the party and struck out on their own. Two days later, tracked by their bloody footsteps in the snow, a man named William Foster cold-bloodedly shot them in the head as they lay weak from exhaustion. They were butchered immediately and eaten raw. The two Indians were, apparently, the only people deliberately killed for food. All of the other cannibalism was practiced off the bodies of the already deceased. Eventually, all five women and two men reached Johnson's Ranch, forty miles east of Sacramento in early February. From there, rescue efforts eventually relieved the last of the survivors by mid-April.

Forty-two of the 90 people who went into the Sierras survived. How many were cannibalized has never been known for sure, nor how many participated in such meals. Today the Donner Party is memorialized by a state park on the eastern end of Donner Lake, which features an imposing statute of a pioneer family that faces Donner Pass and Donner Mountain. They are also memorialized by toponyms that have supplanted and suppressed Washoe names for these geographic features. The heroic and romantic literature inspired by this party is also an enduring memorial.

The Washoes and the Donner Party

The Washoes probably numbered fewer than 5,000 people when the Donner-Reed Party spent the winter in their territory. Washoe lands were centered around the Lake Tahoe basin, some 30 miles south of Donner

Lake. Major year-round habitation sites, however, were on valley floors to its east, north, and south. The Tahoe basin was the major destination of subsistence movements from spring through fall, and even today is regarded by Washoes as "their" lake and homeland. Although almost no tribal members currently live there, its English name, an Anglicization of *dáʔaw* ("Lake") continues to testify to Washoe occupancy. Washoes also irregularly maintained year-round settlements in small valleys at higher elevations, including the upper reaches of the Truckee River near Donner Lake (d'Azevedo, 1986:467). Donner Lake itself, called *dačáhiš dáʔaw* ("? Lake") was a major fishing site for suckers, chubs, minnows, and whitefish in the spring through fall.

Washoes had had some contact with Spanish and Mexican settlements to the west and south in California since the late eighteenth century. By 1846 they had seen or heard of horses, cattle, and European clothing, and a few are said to have been conscripted as laborers in Spanish mines (d'Azevedo 1986:493). Significant penetration of Washoe lands had only begun in the 1840s, with the passage of the Bartleson-Bidwell emigrant train over Sonora Pass in 1841 (Bidwell 1928:51–60) and Fremont's expedition over Carson Pass in 1844 (Fremont 1845). Permanent settlements, however, were not founded until the next decade.

There is no documentary evidence that Washoes were camping at Donner Lake during the winter of 1846–47, nor that they witnessed the Donner Party's cannibalism or provided relief, compassionate aid, or food. The journals and diaries of party members, journalistic accounts, later reminiscences, histories, and the like *never* mention Indian camps or aid to the party from October throughout their stay at Donner Lake.

But like the Cherokee Traveller Bird, like other Indians, like other peoples—even like whites—the Washoe create their own history (or ethno-ethnohistory) to suit their own needs (Fogelson 1974). My interrogation of the Euro-American evidence regarding the lack of a Washoe presence in the Donner Party narrative does not seek to disprove the Washoes' own "ethno-ethnohistory." Rather, it seeks to show how this absence, the nonevent of Washoes aiding the Donner Party, is opposed to the vitally alive "epitomizing" status of this event for contemporary Washoes and their history.

There are two mentions of local Indians in early accounts of the Donner Party. The first is in the history of J. Quinn Thornton, who had traveled for two months with the Donner-Reed Party on their way across the plains and subsequently interviewed survivors in San Francisco in the fall of 1847 (Logan 1996:2). Thornton wrote that

On the evening of October 22d, they crossed the Truckee river, the forty-ninth and last time, in eighty miles. They encamped on the top of a hill. Here nineteen oxen were shot by an Indian, who put one arrow in each ox. The cattle did not die. Mr. Eddy caught him in the act, and fired upon him as he fled. The ball struck him between the shoulders, and came out at the breast. At the crack of the rifle he sprung up about three feet, and with a terrible yell fell down a bank into a bunch of willows. [Logan 1996:43]

The Truckee River starts at Lake Tahoe, from whence it flows north and then east, finally emptying into Pyramid Lake. (Donner Lake also drains into the Truckee, via the Little Truckee River.) Throughout much of its course it is in Washoe territory, although for the last 60 or so miles it flows through areas utilized jointly with Northern Paiutes from Pyramid Lake and other areas. The tribal identity of this bow-wielding Indian is difficult to determine, as he could have been affiliated with a variety of Washoe and Northern Paiute local groups, but it is more than likely that his fate was known to his fellow Indians.

A second mention of Indians is found in the journal of Patrick Breen, a member of the party, whose entry for February 28, 1847—long after the travelers had been trapped in the mountains and before major rescue operations had reached them—stated that "one solitary Indian passed by yesterday, coming from the lake. He had a heavy pack on his back, and gave me five or six roots resembling onions in shape, have tough fibers, and tasting something like a sweet potato" (Logan 1996:96–98).

Thornton, in his after-the-fact account, gives a somewhat more extended picture of this encounter:

Mr. Breen Says: "About this time an incident occurred which greatly surprised us all. One evening, as I was gazing around, I saw an Indian coming from the mountain. He came to the house and said something which we could not understand. He had a small pack on his back, consisting of a fur blanket, and about two dozen of what is called California soaproot, which by some means, could be made good to eat.[13] He appeared very friendly, gave us two or three of the roots, and went on his way. Where he was going I could never imagine. He walked upon snowshoes, the strings of which were made of bark. He went east; and as the snow was very deep for many miles on all sides, I do not know how he passed the nights." [Logan 1996:154]

This Indian was most likely a Washoe, although there is too little evidence to definitely assign any tribal identity. In fact, most sources about and histories of the Donner Party's ordeal in the Sierras pay short shrift to any Indian presence or potential encounters. Many, in fact, do not even mention that the Donner Lake region was Washoe territory, treating the region as empty or unused.

Whether or not these Indians were Washoes, it is possible that, unbeknown to the Donner Party, the Washoes knew of its plight. By the spring of 1847 they were certainly aware of some of the grisly details of the winter of 1846–47. As a Northern Washoe told William H. Jacobsen Jr. in 1955, people from Long Valley (the next major valley north of the Truckee Meadows) came to Donner Lake the next spring. There they found abandoned guns, money, buildings, and "dead people's heads, their hair, that were cut off at their throats, were lying around" (Jacobsen, n.d.). People I spoke to had heard similar tales from their parents and grandparents who had heard them from other relatives before them.

Besides these stories, there are other reminders of the Donner Party littered about the contemporary Washoe landscape. After all, there is a Donner Memorial Park on the site of the fatal camp with its plaques and signs and a pioneer statute and museum. The earliest published account that attests to Washoes witnessing the Donner Party dates to 1934, but it was collected around 1915 by a local doctor, S. L. Lee. Discussing an old man he called "Poker Charlie," Lee reports the following dialogue:

> He is very old, and now almost blind. I once asked him how old he was. Of course he did not know, but asked me, "You savve white man, heap starve long time ago at Truckee?"
>
> I answered, "Yes," knowing that he was alluding to the Donner party. He said, "My brother, Jimmie, see him."
>
> I asked, "Why did not Jimmie take them some ewah?" [14]
>
> He said, "Him heap praid (afraid). He never see white man before."
>
> I than asked him how old he was when those people died there and he said, 'O, I'm big boy. I'm hunt deer.' So he must have been at least 16. Assuming that such was the case, he must be at least 85 years old."
> [Lee 1953:37–38] [15]

Similar stories were current during the 1950s and 1960s, when James Downs conducted research among the Washoe. He reports in his popular monograph *The Two Worlds of the Washo* (1966) that

> During the travail of the Donner party in 1846, the Washo kept the emigrants under surveillance and from time to time left food for the marooned travelers to find. There is a story in the trans-Sierran country

that the cannibalism practiced by the Donner party was the reason the Indians were afraid of the whites. [1966:73]

In 1976 the Washoe Nation produced its own history, *Wa She Shu* (Inter-Tribal Council of Nevada 1976). Based on archival and interview research, this volume is an excellent ethno-ethnohistory of the Washoe, telling their history as they wish it to be told (cf. Fogelson 1974). The work makes it clear that, for Washoe history, the Donner Party was an epitomizing event, one that had significant consequences for the Washoe. Their description reads in part:

> Although the intruders did not always see the Washo, the Indians watched the whites pass through their land. What they saw, particularly when the Donner party reached their land in 1846, made them mistrust these strangers. . . . At first, the *Wel mel ti* wondered whether the wagon train was a monster snake.[16] If the strange wagons were a shock, what the Washo saw later stunned them. Some members of the Donner Party, desperate from suffering and starvation, resorted to cannibalism. Washo who witnessed the grim ordeal told stories which have been preserved for generations. Some tales were grisly, while others revealed sympathy for the stranded whites. The Washo offered food to the party, but became frightened when they saw the whites eating their fellows. Early tales of the Spanish missions had discouraged the Washo from contacting the whites; reports of the cannibalism at Donner Lake convinced the Washo that whites were inhuman. [ITC 1976:44]

Another story about the gruesome details the Washoes remember or construct about the Donner Party is found in a major emblematic account of Washoe history and culture—enshrined in the public spaces of numerous Washoe homes: Thomas Sanchez's novel *Rabbit Boss*. It opens with the passages reproduced at the beginning of this chapter and is almost certainly based on oral histories told to Sanchez by Northern Washoes.[17]

Washoe stories about the Donner Party highlight the differences between Washoe and white constructions of the past and present. Like Western Apache "portraits" of the white men (Basso 1979), like Native American myths and lore more generally, these Washoe stories about the Donner Party help construct a moral universe of character and behavior. They are part of the ongoing construction of Washoe identity and white alterity. After all, I was told these stories in the context of fieldwork and conversations aimed at understanding contemporary Washoes' sense of sociocultural identity, history, and language use. These were, and are, narratives that Washoes told me in order for me to understand them—and myself—better.

Unlike the Western Apache "portraits," and unlike many bodies of Indian myth, these stories about human cannibals in the mountains are not part of linguistically marked verbal genres. (Except, perhaps, as "the stories told to that obnoxious White guy who keeps asking about cannibalism.") But they do exist within the conjunction of several series of tales about relationships, equivalencies, and consequences. In one series, whites are assimilated into a collection of personages that includes mountain lions, grizzly bears, wolves, and coyotes—natural predators who are also persons and thus cannibals when they eat people. This set also contains monstrous personages—*hanáwiywiy*, Big Foot, Uncle Pus, the *ʔáy*. These are cannibal signifiers par excellence: the *tánu témʔluʔ*, those who have people as food, eaters of human flesh and blood. White men are the most extreme, frightening, ferocious members in this group—not animals, not monsters—but humans who act like animals and monsters toward their own kind and kin.

The Donner Party also stands at the extreme end of another set of stories—characterological narratives about whites and their violence and appropriation. These stories often are used to explain and justify historical and contemporary dimensions of Washoe-white interactions. Washoe stories about early contact highlight their practice of abandoning camps at warnings of approaching strangers and of constructing settlements in natural settings that hid them from view (d'Azevedo 1986:493). Historical tales about white cruelty and insensitivity range from the everyday practices of spatial exclusions, epithets, verbal abuse, and subtle harassment up through beatings, lynchings, coerced prostitution, rape, cavalry raids, and finally to the extreme of cannibalism. These stories serve as exemplars of the triumphs and tragedies possible for the Washoe in their interactions with whites. They function perhaps as verbal "weapons of the weak" in efforts to resist the cultural fashioning of modern American ideological hegemonies (Scott 1985).

Anthropologists do not escape these condemnations. There are tales of archaeologists stealing essential caches of pine-nutting equipment and of anthropologists getting informants drunk to make them talkative.[18] I was frequently told this latter story by Washoes who were going to introduce me to other Washoes. Names were not mentioned, nor much else in the way of distinguishing characteristics, but the behavior was obviously frowned upon, and the stories were meant, I believe, as a warning and admonition as to how I should conduct myself.

Whites, as the Washoe will tell you, despise and degrade people of other races. As another older woman once told me: "We've never been treated well by whites, after all, the first settlers here were Germans, and you know what they do to people of other races." In both series of stories whites are dangerous, to be avoided, tricked perhaps by cleverness if possible but never to be confronted or—unlike the monsters of the past—defeated or killed. They still surround the Washoe, making the mountains dangerous and unsafe places to venture into.[19] These stories of the Donner Party conjoin two separates series about predation and violence. And as the most extreme examples of both sets, tales of the Donner Party offer an "epitomizing event" for Washoe's construal of whites. The Donner Party is simultaneously the most ferocious example of predatory cannibalism and the most ferocious example of white violence. In both contexts the victims, the subjects of killing and consumption, are not some Others but kin, family—their own people. Whites, through the example of the Donner Party, are potentially (and actually) merciless predators, who are morally depraved and who are to be avoided and pitied for their fallings. In the 1990s Washoes reminded me of Jeffrey Dahmer (the Milwaukee cannibal) and Hannibal Lector (the fictional cannibalistic psychiatrist in *Silence of the Lambs*) as further proof of the vicious cannibalistic nature of whites.

But if whites are dangerous and terrible in these and related stories, they are also incompetent. Unlike the Washoe, and in a fashion similar to the two Paiute boys escaping from Stewart Indian School, the Donner Party and other whites do not know the mountains and the country. Whites do stupid and idiotic things (such as getting trapped in the mountains during the winter or being frightened by mountain lions) because of imperfect knowledge and understanding. Like anthropologists who do not know how to hunt, who are lucky they have not been eaten by mountain lions, or who do not like horses outside of a stew pot, such people deserve pity and compassion from more competent and knowledgeable human beings.[20]

Finally, we can understand these stories as being part of the dialogue that Washoes have been having with and about whites since they first heard of the Spanish missions from their western neighbors. These stories are powerful indicators of Washoe attitudes toward whites. Mostly they tell them to each other (if not in some "traditional" way—in the dead of winter, with the audience lying down on the floor warm and comfortable) to continually create their history and culture. Sometimes, occasionally, they tell them to those others they want to shock, impress, frighten, or tease.

Conclusion

Every few nights that fall of 1983 the mountain lion would come walking back through my campground. I presume it was hunting the deer moving down to winter in browsing grounds. But now the screams did not frighten me (as much). They were no longer a threat but just a warning, and perhaps also a salute. After all, I am a *dabóʔo* myself, a *mušégew*, a wild scary animal, a potentially predatory cannibal, even if my stalking and capture and consumption only involves the tales, practices, and words of the Washoe—and not land, natural resources, or human flesh.

I no longer bolted into my car if the screams startled or woke me. Although I was a predator myself in some Washoe perspective, I was also an inept and pitiful white man who was lucky he had not been eaten by a mountain lion. And thus I was deserving of compassion and pity from my Washoe friends, even as I stalked them and their stories. Haunches of venison I did not get, nor porcupines or baskets of pinenuts, but other gifts were offered and accepted.

So when the mountain lion screamed I just stoked up my new, more powerful lantern (a loan from the old lady who called me a cannibal), poured a tot of brandy, got out my notebooks and tapes (their words and stories being the greatest gift my Washoe friends gave me), or went back to reading one more of those endless references Ray Fogelson had given me. But I also tightly gripped the butt of a Colt .45, loaned to me by my friend, the Washoe cowboy who first told me about cannibals in the mountains.

Acknowledgments

An earlier version of this chapter was presented in the session "Representations and Self-Representations of Indigenous Peoples: Papers in the Anthropology of Power, Knowledge, and Identity in Honor of Raymond D. Fogelson," at the ninety-fifth annual meeting of the American Anthropological Association, San Francisco, California, November 20–25, 1996. I thank William H. Jacobsen Jr. for gifting me with a copy of the text I cite in this chapter. I also thank Pauline Turner Strong and Sergei Kan for their perceptive and helpful comments on the various drafts and Ray Fogelson for his support, encouragement, and example over all the years he has put up with me. Funding for my fieldwork among the Washoe was provided by the Knudtsen Award for Great Basin Research and the American Philosophical Society. I also apologize to the audience at the AAA session for my scream and to all the people who have suffered over the years from my tellings of *my* mountain lion story.

Notes

1. *Washo* is the spelling usually found in social science literature. I use *Washoe* in deference to the community, who officially call themselves the Washoe Nation of Nevada and California. My research among the Washoe was conducted in the summer of 1976; over the academic year 1976–77; and in 1982, 1983, and 1991.

2. Stewart is the former Indian boarding school, located about ten miles southeast of the State Capitol Building in Carson City, Nevada. This is where Washoe children were incarcerated from the 1890s until the early 1950s, when they were enrolled in local public schools. The Walker River Reservation is about 70 miles southeast of Carson City. Cousin-brothers, like cousin-sisters, are the children of the siblings of ego's parents. The terms for older and younger sibling in Washoe kinship terminology refer also to both parallel and cross-cousins. These terms (shown in their unpossessed root forms) are = *ʔátu* ("older brother or cousin"); = *béyu* ("younger brother or cousin"); = *ʔí·sa* ("older sister or cousin"); and = *wíčug* ("younger sister or cousin"). This equivalence of lineals and collaterals has been carried over into English with the hybrid terms *cousin-brother* and *cousin-sister*. Washoe words are transcribed here using the orthography developed by William H. Jacobsen Jr. (1964).

3. People tend not to talk about Coyote's actual deeds, but only hint of his depravity.

4. The *hanáwiywiy* is variously described as a one-eyed, one-legged giant (Downs 1966:61), a centauroid monster (ITC 1976:33), and a simple giant (Dangberg 1968:39–43). The *nentúšu* (literally, "old woman/women") is one of two or three different creators of human beings in various Washoe myths.

5. This Big Foot is not a Sierra Nevada Sasquatch, although its existence is sometimes construed that way by modern Washoe. According to Downs, the Washoe believed that "the mountains were inhabited by another race, possibly human but possessed of much more power than ordinary people" (1966:61). Ishi, the last Yana, says Downs, was thought to be one of these "wild men of their myths" by Washoes in the 1950s and 1960s (1966:62).

6. The term *dabóʔo* (archaically, *dabibóʔo*) or "white man, men" is a borrowing from a Northern Paiute form, *táiboʔo*, literally, "white-face." Whites were also called *mušégew* or "bear, scary person or monster."

7. The storyteller is referring to a California Agricultural Inspection station, just west of the California—Nevada border and north of Truckee and Donner Lake.

8. I omit a long disquisition by this storyteller on why porcupines were offered. Apparently they are good winter hunting because they stand out in the snow, talk constantly when moving, and cannot move fast in drifts. The point of this information was, I believe, to demonstrate the natural incompetence of the Donner Party (and my own) and their lack of knowledge of the mountains and its inhabitants.

9. These works include histories (Croy 1883; Farnham 1856; Fisher 1943; Houghton 1911; King 1992; Laurgaard 1981; Lavender 1996; McGlashan 1879, 1929; McHugh 1959; Pigney 1961; Read 1935; Stewart 1936, 1960, 1986; Stookey 1950; Thornton 1945, 1978), novels (Bells 1997; Burney 1891; Galloway 1983; Graham 1850; Headen 1956; Lofts 1955; Maino 1987; Rhodes 1973; Sutton 1957), collections of primary documents (Breen 1910; Harlan 1888; Lathrop 1927; Logan 1996; Murphy 1996), narrative poems (Atrocchi 1893, Keithley 1972, Whitman 1977), dramas (Polsky 1980, Summers 1972), and original works in other languages.

10. I recall reading several articles in local newspapers about the descendants of survivors when I was living in northern California and Nevada in the mid-1970s. The basic question

asked by reporters always was some variation of "So what do you think about having ancestors who were cannibals?"

11. Other new discoveries include mortality and/or survival statistics. Women, for example, had lower mortality than men; those women who did die lived longer under starvation conditions than did men. The highest survival rate was among those aged six years to fourteen years (only two out of twenty-one died). Those under five years and over thirty-five years had the highest mortality.

12. This is a necessarily abbreviated account of the Donner Party. Readers wanting more detail or a fuller narrative exposition should consult the sources listed in the bibliography. The most recent work is an attractive and well-illustrated account by Frank Mullen Jr. (Mullen 1997).

13. *Chlorogalum pomeridianum*, a member of the lily family. According to Storer and Usinger, "the delicate flowers open only in the afternoon. Scales of the bulb form a lather with water. Indians roasted the bulbs for food and used its fibers for brushes" (1963:73).

14. I presume this is some white-created pidgin word for "food," used indiscriminately with local Indians whatever their tribal affiliation. This form *ewah* does not closely resemble any Washoe form referring to food or drink (most notably, *démlu* ["food"] and *díme?* ["water"]).

15. This age calculation makes it probable that Lee had this conversation within a few years of 1915.

16. This is the curious use of separated syllables to represent *welmélti?*, "northerners."

17. The entire opening section of the novel takes up four pages and includes graphic descriptions of removing a still beating human heart and its immediate consumption, the beheading of the corpse, the subsequent murder of the heart-eater by another man, and the butchering of the heartless, headless corpse by children.

18. Given an evidentiary and documentary backing by Busby (1974) and Fenenga (1975).

19. Most Washoes (especially the more rurally located tribal members) generally avoid Lake Tahoe and Reno in part because of the crowded conditions, high prices, and general urban sprawl of both locations.

20. I do not enjoy riding horses, which struck a lot of Washoes as funny (local whites were less amused and usually contemptuous). Many Washoes told me it was because I was afraid of horses and that I didn't like them. I always replied that I like horses a lot, especially in stews.

References

Altrocchi, Julia Cooley
    1893 Snow Covered Wagons: A Pioneer Epic, the Donner Party Expedition, 1846–1847. New York: Macmillan.
Basso, Keith H.
    1977 Portraits of the "Whiteman." Cambridge: Cambridge University Press.
Betts, Doris
    1997 The Sharp Teeth of Love. New York: Alfred A. Knopf.
Birney, Hoffman
    1891 Grim Journey; the Story of the Adventures of the Emigrating Company Known as the Donner Party, Which, in the Year 1846, Crossed the Plains from Independence, Missouri, to California. New York: Minton, Balch.

Breen, Patrick

1910 Diary of Patrick Breen, One of the Donner Party. Frederick J. Teggart, ed. Publications of the Academy of Pacific Coast History, vol. 1, no. 6. Berkeley: University of California.

Burns, Ric

1992 The Donner Party [videorecording]. Lisa Ades and Ric Burns, producers; Bruce Shaw, ed.; David McCullough, narrator. Steeplechase Films Production. Presented by WGBH/Boston, WNET/New York, and KCET/Los Angeles. Alexandria VA: PBS Video.

Busby, Colin I.

1974 Pinyon Nut Gathering Equipment from the Vicinity of Gardnerville, Douglas County, Nevada. University of California Berkeley, Archaeological Research Facility Contributions 21:51–65.

Croy, Homer

1883 Wheels West: The Story of the Donner Party. New York: Hastings House.

Dangberg, Grace

1968 Washo Tales Translated with an Introduction. Carson City: Nevada State Museum Occasional Papers 3.

d'Azevedo, Warren L.

1986 Washoe. In Vol. 11: Great Basin. Warren L. d'Azevedo, ed. Handbook of North American Indians. Pp. 466–498. William C. Sturtevant, gen. ed. Washington DC: Smithsonian Institution.

Downs, James F.

1966 The Two Worlds of the Washo: An Indian Tribe of California and Nevada. New York: Holt, Rinehart & Winston.

Farnham, Eliza Woodson (Burhans)

1856 California, In-Doors and Out; or, How We Farm, Mine, and Live Generally in the Golden State. New York: Dix, Edwards.

Fenenga, Franklin

1975 A Washo Pine Nut Camp in Douglas County, Nevada. Journal of California Anthropology 2(2):205–213.

Finnegan, Lora J.

1996 Tracing a Terrible Trail. Sunset, October 1996:22–26.

Fisher, Vardis

1943 The Mothers: An American Saga of Courage. New York: Vanguard Press.

Fogelson, Raymond D.

1974 On the Varieties of Indian History: Sequoyah and Traveller Bird. Journal of Ethnic Studies 2(1):105–112.

1989 The Ethnohistory of Events and Nonevents. Ethnohistory 36(2):133–147.

Fremont, John C.

1845 Report of the Exploring Expedition to the Rocky Mountains in the Year 1842, and to Oregon and North California in the Years 1843-'44. Washington DC: Gales and Seaton.

Galloway, David D.

1983 Tamsen. San Diego: Harcourt Brace Jovanovich.

Graham, Rev. Walter

1850 Amelia Sherwood, or, Bloody Scenes at the California Gold Mines: with a Narrative of the Tragic Incidents on a Voyage to San Francisco. Richmond VA: Barclay, 1850.

Harlan, Jacob Wright
   1888 California '46 to '88. San Francisco: Bancroft Company.
Headen, William
   1956 Beyond the Pass. New York: Vantage Press.
Houghton, Eliza P. (Donner)
   1911 The Expedition of the Donner Party and Its Tragic Fate. Chicago: A. C. McClurg.
Inter-Tribal Council of Nevada
   1976 Wa She Shu: A Washo Tribal History. Reno: Inter-Tribal Council of Nevada.
Jacobsen, William H., Jr.
   n.d. The Donner Expedition. Transcript of audiotape recorded by Hank Pete, August 10,
      1955. Roy James, trans. Manuscript in Jacobsen's possession.
   1964 A Grammar of the Washo Language. Unpublished PhD dissertation, Department
      of Linguistics. University of California, Berkeley.
Keithley, George
   1972 The Donner Party: A Narrative Poem. New York: Braziller.
King, Joseph A.
   1992 Winter of Entrapment: A New Look at the Donner Party. Toronto: P. D. Meany
      Publishers.
Lathrop, George
   1927 Some Pioneer Recollections / Being the Autobiography of George Lathrop, One of
      the First to Help in the Opening of the West; and a Statement Made by John Sinclair
      Relative to the Rescue of the Donner Party; also an Extract from a Letter Written by
      Geo. McKinstry with Reference to the Rescue of the Donner Party. Philadelphia: G.
      W. Jacobs.
Laurgaard, Rachel Kelley
   1981 Patty Reed's Doll: The Story of the Donner Party. Provo UT: McCurdy Historical
      Doll Museum.
Lavender, David Sievert
   1996 Snowbound: The Tragic Story of the Donner Party. New York: Holiday House.
Lee, S. L.
   1953[1934] Ethnographic Notes on Washoe Culture. University of California Archaeo-
      logical Survey Reports 21:37–40.
Lockhart, T. C.
   1972 Zum Ende des Regenbogens. Stuttgart: Cotta.
Lofts, Norah
   1955 Winter Harvest. Introduction by Stewart H. Holbrook. Garden City NY: Doubleday.
Logan, Kristin Johnson, ed.
   1996 Unfortunate Emigrants: Narratives of the Donner Party. Provo: Utah State Univer-
      sity Press.
Maino, Jeannette Gould
   1987 Left Hand Turn: A Story of the Donner Party Women. Modesto CA: Dry Creek
      Books.
McGlashan, Charles F.
   1879 History of the Donner Party. Truckee CA: Privately printed.
   1929 History of the Donner Party: A Tragedy of the Sierra. 15th ed. San Francisco: A.
      Carlisle & Co.
McHugh, Thomas P.
   1959 Hazeldell Charivari: Christmas at Zayante, 1856, Being the Story of the Wedding

of Patty Reed to Frank Lewis, and a Recount of the Donner Party Tragedy, 1846. Santa Cruz CA: Frontier Gazette.

McKinstry, George

[1917] Thrilling and Tragic Account of a Perilous Journey Overland to California, in the Years of 1846–1847. West Hoboken NJ: Privately published by A. A. Bieber, C. Reining, printer. Originally printed in *St. Louis Reveille*, 1847.

Mullen, Frank, Jr.

1997 The Donner Party Chronicles: A Day-by-Day Account of a Doomed Wagon Train, 1846–1847. Reno: Nevada Humanities Committee.

Murphy, Virginia Reed

1996 Across the Plains in the Donner Party. North Haven CT: Linnet Books.

Pigney, Joseph

1961 For Fear We Shall Perish: The Story of the Donner Party Disaster. New York, Dutton.

Polsky, Ab

1980 Devour the Snow: A Play in Two Acts. New York: Dramatists Play Service.

Reed, Virginia Elizabeth B.

1935 A Happy Issue; the Hitherto Unpublished Letter of a Child, Virginia Elizabeth B. Reed, Survivor of the Donner-Reed Party. Foreword by Lucia Shepardson De Wolf. Palo Alto CA: Stanford University. Private printing.

Rhodes, Richard

1973 The Ungodly: A Novel of the Donner Party. New York: Charterhouse.

Sanchez, Thomas

1973 Rabbit Boss. New York: Alfred Knopf.

Scott, James C.

1985 Weapons of the Weak: Everyday Forms of Peasant Resistance. New Haven CT: Yale University Press.

Stewart, George Rippey

1936 Ordeal by Hunger: The Story of the Donner Party. New York: H. Holt.

1960 Donner Pass and Those Who Crossed It; the Story of the Country Made Notable by the Stevens Party, the Donner Party, the Gold-hunters, and the Railroad Builders. San Francisco: California Historical Society.

1986 Ordeal by Hunger: The Story of the Donner Party. Rev. ed., with supplement and three survivor accounts. Lincoln: University of Nebraska Press.

Stookey, Walter M.

1950 Fatal Decision: The Tragic Story of the Donner Party. Salt Lake City: Desert Book Company.

Summers, Robert

1972 The Seeds in the Passes. New York: The Smith.

Thornton, Jessy Quinn

1978 Camp of Death: The Donner Party Mountain Camp, 1846–47. Olympic Valley CA: Outbooks.

Thornton, Jessy Quinn

1945 The California Tragedy. Foreword by Joseph A. Sullivan. Oakland: Biobooks.

Whitman, Ruth

1977 Tamsen Donner: A Woman's Journey. Cambridge MA: Alice James Books.

17. "Vanishing" Indians in Nineteenth-Century New England

Local Historians' Erasure of Still-Present Indian Peoples

JEAN M. O'BRIEN

Histories

> It has been the lot of the unfortunate aborigines of this country, to be doubly wronged by the white men—first, driven from their native soil by the sword of the invader, and then darkly slandered by the pen of the historian. The former has treated them like beasts of the forest; the latter has written volumes to justify him in his outrages.[1]

In this passage from the first published American Indian autobiography (1826), Pequot William Apess leveled the double charge that Euro-Americans had violently seized Native homelands, then deliberately justified their outrageous conquest through their creation of historical memory. An enormous body of scholarship has more than substantiated Apess's charges, which he made through an intriguing borrowing from the writings of Washington Irving that he inserted into the "Appendix" of his autobiography.[2] Importantly, New England antiquarians had begun producing local histories in at least the decade before Apess published his autobiography. These histories, which would become a nineteenth-century cottage industry in New England that moved well beyond justifying Euro-American conquest, pressed another insidious claim: that New England Indians were on the verge of extinction, if they had not already passed from the scene.

It is somewhat puzzling that an army of antiquarians could so uniformly conclude that disappearance was the inevitable fate for New England Indians. If this scenario had played out, then why did Massachusetts and other New England states need bureaucracies for Indian affairs, and why did Massachusetts extend official recognition to the still surviving groups in the commonwealth until ending the of Indians' "wardship" status in 1869? As Commissioner of Indian Affairs in Massachusetts in the middle of the nineteenth century, John Milton Earle compiled a census that identified well over one thousand Indians in the commonwealth, a figure that is certainly too low.[3] And as scholars of nineteenth-century New England Indian history have made clear, New England Indians lived rich and traceable lives at exactly the moment historians were writing their eulogies.[4]

How could the narrative of Indian extinction coexist with the actual survival of Indian peoples in New England? As a preliminary effort toward unraveling this problem, I examine the ways in which nineteenth-century non-Indian local historians narrated their Indian past, and especially the ways in which they asserted the claim of Indian extinction. Reflecting back on the colonial past and the struggle for independence from Britain, a cadre of antiquarians asserted claims about the "glorious" achievements of residents of their communities. They did so as part of a larger effort to assert the primacy of New England in the forging of the new nation.[5] Within this broad historical narrative constructed by local historians and other published commentators on the New England past, stories about Indians often appeared. These stories usually served to justify colonialism, to confer glory upon Euro-American ancestors, and, importantly, to insist that New England Indians had vanished from the region.

I would like to suggest that these historical narratives included stories about interactions with Indians in order to establish a claim of "uniqueness" for their particular places as well as to assert an American identity. In order to stake these claims, historical narrators needed to include Indians because Indians were central to the uniqueness and Americanness of their local colonial experience and because the "glorious triumph" of colonialism was the central narrative in nineteenth-century New England. But at the same time, in these stories New Englanders told (and to some extent still tell themselves), they needed to have Indians disappear in order to justify colonialism, absolve themselves of wrongdoing and guilt, and place Indians firmly and safely in the past. Local narrators made Indians "vanish" by denying the "Indianness" of the persisting Indian peoples. They accomplished this by using the concepts of "racial purity" and unchanging Indian cultures as the criteria of Indianness—even while they sometimes wavered in their conclusions about Indian history and alleged Indian disappearance. Despite variations on the themes of Indian history and Indian fates, as possessors of cultural power what these historians accomplished was to persuade non-Indian New Englanders that Indians had disappeared from the region.[6] Needless to say, narratives about Indian "extinction" have had important consequences that continue to affect the still very present Indian people in New England.

In making this argument, I do not mean to suggest that similar cultural projects did not occur elsewhere, nor do I insist that narratives of disappearance suddenly emerged in the nineteenth century without precedent. On the contrary, the myth of Indian extinction is a long-recognized trope in the history of the United States and elsewhere, and it is not difficult to locate assertions of Indian disappearance from the earliest colonial moments. What I am trying to do in this project is ground these ideas very specifically in time and space rather than to engage in a more generalized discussion of imagery and stereotype. In addition, my narrative does not rest upon an exhaustive survey of local histories produced in New England: rather, it focuses upon 17 historical accounts from the nineteenth century, most of them from Massachusetts. I have selected these 17 because they are particularly extreme versions of extinction claims, and thus they provide material for staking out some guideposts to the problem.

Stories

Local narrators did not build the myth of Indian extinction with stark clarity and consistency. Instead, they constructed accounts that were replete with ambiguity regarding both the tension between Indian persistence and extinction and the problem of whether Indians and Euro-Americans acted honorably or dishonorably in their relations with one another, reconciling such problems within the prevailing intellectual framework of the time. No matter what accounted for the mental maneuvers that explain these contradictions, the net effect of the efforts of local narrators was a collective, multifaceted erasure of Indian perspectives on the colonial encounter, of Indian definitions of Indianness, and, ultimately, of the very existence of Indians in the non-Indian collective consciousness of New England—at least for that moment.

An 1860 account of Mashpee's history will illustrate my point. Even Cape Cod people could narrate the history of Mashpee, which has always had an undeniable Indian presence (in spite of the 1977 federal court decision that denied that "Indianness") within the trope of extinction: "Alas! the day is passed when . . . 'the conversion of the poor heathen Indians'— can be reached. They are almost extinct. . . . If *any* drop of their blood still lingers in the veins of any, let them be kindly dealt with, at least." According to this historian, "the last of the race, of purely Indian blood, was ISAAC SIMON . . . The Indian language, and the pure Indian blood, extinct, a promiscuous race of colored people, in diminishing numbers, now constitute the population of Mashpee."[7]

It is difficult to reconcile this narrator's assertion that no "drop of their blood" is carried forth by any living person with his own identification of a persisting population. In fact, he even provided numbers: in 1792, rather than the "promiscuous race of colored people, in diminishing numbers" there remained in Mashpee "not more than forty or fifty Indians of pure blood." Their miraculous recovery to 202 in 1850 and 403 in 1859 owed itself not to a population explosion but rather to shifting criteria employed by governmental officials such as John Milton Earle, who did not fully reject the idea of blood purity but did grasp more substantially than did this historian that Indianness owed something to kinship and community.[8] (His census enumerated Indian relatives by households and group affiliation, no matter where they were located.) The historian who commented on the people of Mashpee saw no contradiction in his extinction story because "purity of blood," coupled with what he saw as unambiguously "Indian" cultural practices such as language, was the criterion he used. This variety of observation depended on an ultimate (yet still somewhat unsure) denial of Indian definitions of their Indianness. These definitions involved kinship and community rather than notions of racial categories based both on the myth of blood purity and on the implicit insistence that Indian cultural change constituted a diminishment of Indianness rather than the dynamic processes of change over time.

An 1855 history of Medford offers a further illustration of how the idea of "purity of blood" governed New English interpretations of Indian prospects for the future: "The last Indian here was 'Hannah Shiner,' a full blood, who lived with 'Old Toney,' a noble-souled mulatto man. . . . Hannah was kind-hearted, a faithful friend, a sharp enemy, a judge of herbs, a weaver of baskets, and a lover of rum."[9] Hannah's assumed "blood quantum" qualified her for Indianness (as did her pharmacological knowledge and basket-making skills and, perhaps, her purported fondness of rum, which also fit within stereotypical ideas about Indians). But even though she had a mate, and may even have had children, those children could not be counted as "Indian" because their blood would have been diluted by the mixed ancestry of their father. One wonders why it was that Hannah Shiner, who died in 1822 an "Indian pauper" in Woburn, was singled out for inclusion in this history 33 years after she died in a neighboring town, and why in the revised version of this history published 31 years after that her story was not edited out.[10] In other words, what made Hannah Shiner so significant to the non-Indians of Medford? I would like to suggest that Hannah Shiner provided Medford with the opportunity to assert its "Americanness," which was most persuasively argued with reference to its Indian past.

Henry David Thoreau's journals help make my point about the unremarked-upon confusion surrounding extinction stories even more forcefully. In 1854, he noted the passing of the last Indian "not of pure blood" (whom he did not name), yet two years later he visited Martha Simons, the "last full blooded Indian" of New Bedford, and made this observation: "To judge from her physiognomy, she might have been King Philip's own daughter. Yet she could not speak a word of Indian, and knew nothing of her race." [11] Thoreau's derogatory description of Martha Simons reported that in contrast to her general "listlessness . . . the question that she answered with most interest" involved a Native plant, which might be read as Thoreau's underscoring of Martha Simon's Indianness displayed through her herbal knowledge as well as her "physiognomy." [12] Yet even her physical and (partial) cultural conformity to his own ideas about race, Martha Simons was depicted as a diminished Indian who did not speak her language (at least to Thoreau) and whom he claimed resided outside of her own history. Martha Simons became one of the most famous "last" Indians of New England not just through Thoreau's attentions but also as the subject of an 1857 Albert Bierstadt portrait, entitled "Martha Simons, The Last of the Narragansetts." This portrait reveals another confusion. Was she Narragansett, Wampanoag, or Nemasket, as she was variously identified? More importantly, was she really the last? [13]

Thoreau, Bierstadt, and the historian Daniel Ricketson (who published his narrative in 1858) would certainly have us think so. This is Ricketson: "during the middle and even to the latter part of the last century, a few of the lingering remnants of the once noble possessors of this soil remained, retaining to the last their ancient form of habitation, the wigwam, or a hut." In his view, only Martha Simons remained, residing in Dartmouth, "one solitary specimen of a full-blooded native . . . she is the last of her race." Yet Ricketson appears to have filed his lament about Indian vanishment prematurely. A year after he published his history, John Milton Earle identified 111 Indians of Dartmouth, "whose descent is not precisely known, but, of whose identity as Indians, there is no doubt." [14] And 73 years later, a historian updated Dartmouth's "last" story, though not his assumptions about the performance of Indianness:

> Charlotte Mitchell, the last descendant of Massasoit . . . rehearses Indian
> tradition and Indian lore to her visitors, and appears at historic and other
> functions in Middleboro to show adults and children how Indian women

appeared when her ancestors roamed the forests, paddled their canoes on Assawampsett pond and owned the town.[15]

What I call the "Last of the _____" genre, perhaps a deliberate empirical application of James Fenimore Cooper's literary production of 1826, circulated widely and found expression in various literary forms. John Greenleaf Whittier commemorated "The Last Norridgewock" in an 1831 poem, for example. Even local historians were liable to break into verse when narrating their Indian story, as Daniel Ricketson did in preserving for posterity his "Last of the Wampanoags" in his history, in which he did not name Martha Simons but rather memorialized defeated warriors, scattered peoples, and doomed Indians without hunting grounds for whom death "kindly to his woes has made an end."[16]

Perusal of other local histories reveals a New England thickly populated by "last" Indians throughout the nineteenth century, and occasionally (as in the case of Dartmouth) into the twentieth. These histories tell us that among the "last full blooded Indians" of New England were not just Isaac Simons, Hannah Shiner, and Martha Simons but also a married couple, Alexander Quabish and Sarah David (of Dedham), who (in keeping with the genre) it is implicitly asserted left no progeny.[17]

The Jaha family, like the foregoing "last" Indians and all persisting Indian peoples in New England, lived an Indianness that historians denied and erased. Memorialized as the last Nipmuck of Oxford, who had passed on by 1894, Julia Jaha was asserted to have been an active and devout convert to Christianity who could read and who "recalled the family [in which she was put to service] with great respect." Most of this memorial elaborated on this basic theme. In so doing, it thus trivialized and domesticated both her life and a powerful critique—acknowledging that Indians might have legitimate complaints to file—that surprisingly closed the brief sketch (and that remained uncommented on by its recorder): "Julia ever testified that her tribe were conscious of great injustice done to them in all their transactions with the English, and then added with much feeling of grief, 'They would destroy the graves of our dead as of no account and make a field of grain of our Indian sepulchre.' " Julia Jaha Dayley (then resident in Oxford) was among the 94 Dudley Indians that Earle listed just 35 years before, along with 5 more relatives in her generation plus 9 more in the next, whose immediate kinship network connected Oxford to Webster, Spencer, Worcester, and Uxbridge.[18]

On one level, it is the extreme localism of nineteenth-century histories that fueled the "last of the _____" genre that served as the most extreme statement of the extinction story. Unlike John Milton Earle, Leicester's historian failed (or refused) to understand the complex regional kinship networks that remained at the core of Indian identity in New England, despite the nearly complete Indian dispossession that English colonists accomplished.[19] It was easier for these historians to argue for extinction since they only looked locally, and even then saw Indian lives (and Indian history) only incompletely.

Their myopia exacerbated the more powerful formula that enabled their erasure of Indians. This formula centrally involved, first, ideas about race and the notion that it was dilutable: "The degenerate relics of a few of these tribes, here and there, still retain something of [the] color . . . of their ancestors from whom they trace a questionable descent."[20] And, second, it involved particular ideas about Indian cultures and their diminishment, which were related to their assumptions about Indians and history. Thoreau summarized this view nicely: "The fact is, the history of the white man is a history of improvement, and that of the red man a history of fixed habits of stagnation."[21] Putting the formula together, the New England calculation dictated that Indians are only Indians when they possess "pure" Indian blood. Even then Indianness diminishes in proportion to the failure of Indians to display certain characteristics, notably: possessing unbroken homelands, defending those homelands through diplomacy and warfare, speaking their own language, living in wigwams, engaging in hunting and fishing (and sometimes agriculture), displaying mastery of Native pharmacology, and producing Native material culture through craftwork such as basket weaving. Euro-American insistence that Indians exist within this basic and unchanging cultural repertoire both argues that Indians are only Indians when they dwell in a static and immutable past and provided Euro-Americans with an ideological framework for denying Indian persistence. The best Indians could do to measure up to this formula was to be a people numerically diminished within a falsely restrictive category ("pure-blooded Indians") who pursue a diminished form of Indianness that at the core only continued to express itself in herbalism, craft manufacture, and "wandering." Taken together, this formula produced a regionally specific stereotype of the New England Indian: the solitary, itinerant maker and seller of baskets and brooms or purveyor of Native medicine, who is often depicted as a woman.[22] As solitary survivors disproportionately cast as females, the prospects for maintaining any "purity of blood" were scripted as bleak indeed. Stereotypes about Indian men are far less prevalent in the literature I have examined, but the Indian whaler or mariner who does crop up, with his implicit lengthy absences, also feeds into ideas about disappearance. The final calculation of the formula could only add up to the final and inevitable extinction of New England Indians and their Indianness.

In some nineteenth-century accounts, the narrators followed up on their erasure of Indians by literally burying them, their culture, and their history. No trace of their former presence remained, but artifacts that from time to time were revealed. With the passing of Polly Johns, in Leicester "the only memorials of the perished race are an arrowhead, a pipe, or a stone hatchet, occasionally turned up by the plough on the spots where they built their wigwams or planted their cornfields."[23] In Medford, they remained hopeful that the true glories of an Indian past would eventually be revealed: a plough occasionally uncovered arrowheads and Indian tools, but even though "no Indian necropolis has yet been discovered . . . one probably exists on the borders of our pond."[24] Such a discovery would confer uniqueness and glory on Medford—a special place with a rich and distinctive Indian past, which is what would make it especially "American."

The juxtaposition of two narratives about Pittsfield offer a revealing glimpse at the simultaneous distancing and embrace of Indians that these narratives displayed. In an 1869 history, Indians performed their disappearing act in a typical way, yet still Indian history was etched into the landscape: "the names the red men called them by still cling to mountain, lake, and stream, forbidding us to forget the race."[25] In an 1845 celebration of the Berkshire jubilee, an orator paused to consider the history of the "River Indians," who uniquely did *not* disappear. Why? Because they moved to the Oneida nation and formed New Stockbridge, then they moved on again. These New England Indians were allowed to persist because they persisted in Wisconsin, "where with the faithfulness under God's blessing, they maintain their praiseworthy habits and character"—imparted to them by New England missionaries, John Sergeant and Jonathan Edwards, which testified to the glorious contributions of New Englanders to Indians, even in Wisconsin.[26]

The proliferation of "last" stories is perhaps the most striking characteristic of the treatment of Indian history in nineteenth-century local accounts. Yet there are other features in these accounts that substantiated William Apess's charges about ideological justification in his autobiography and his other writings, most powerfully in his "Eulogy on King Philip," which New Englanders (and others) could have turned to for an Indian interpretation of that conflict and others.[27] Especially common are stories about the military and ideological "conquest" of the "savage." Not surprisingly, King Philip's War is almost always remembered. The Pequot War, on the other hand, is often ignored, for complex reasons

I believe, which include its unthinkable brutality. Stories about conflicts with Indians almost always serve to absolve the English of culpability rather than substantiate Apess's point of view. These themes stressed the "glory" and "justice" of colonialism in the face of "savagery" along two very different trajectories: the claims that brave local residents defended their communities and the New England project by fending off brutal Indian assaults and that localities did all they could to bring the particular blessings of English Calvinism to pagans lost in the wilderness.[28]

As I have been suggesting, local stories found places in varying proportions for a cast of Indian sachems, warriors, diplomats, converts, and lone survivors. But I would argue that the central obsession of local narration focused on the issue of "just possession" of the land.[29] In narrative after narrative, historians went to great lengths in recounting the stories of how English people "legally" transferred Indian ownership of the land to themselves. Occasionally, like Dedham's historian, they even reproduced the deeds upon which they rested this claim. In my selective sample of 17, not one history failed to recount the story of how English people "legally" transferred Indian ownership of the land to themselves. I want to juxtapose the issue of "just possession" with the extinction story in some detail and then follow through with the problem of confusion about Indians displayed in nineteenth-century narratives.

In doing so, I would like to turn now to a slightly different genre, that of the published programs of historical commemorations. I'd like to ask us to listen in as the Bridgewater, Massachusetts, people commemorate the bicentennial of the "legal" incorporation of their place. If we are to believe this published program, the Bridgewater people sat through historical addresses, recited poetry, and sang hymns on this theme on June 3, 1856, an event so thorough and rich that the program itself filled 140 pages when published.[30]

In the principal historical address we are told that the Bridgewater people engaged in two legal land transactions with Indian possessors of the soil: one from the sachem Ousamequin and a second (conducted by that gentle friend of the Indians Miles Standish) from Massasoit. (The narrator failed to point out that Ousamequin and Massasoit were one and the same person. Perhaps he did not know.) These events are connected to a particular place:

> Tradition points out the spot where this act of purchase was completed, which once bore the name of "Sachem's Rock." [A revisionist footnote informs us that the rock still bears that name.] But it is sad to think, that, of all that race who then peopled this region, nothing but tradition now

remains. It is sad to recall in how short a time not a drop of the blood of the Sachem of Pokanoket, whose hand of friendship welcomed our fathers to these shores, was to be found in the veins of any living being.

In this passage, a physical landmark is invoked in order to evoke a virtuous Bridgewater history of just property transactions, to replace one set of traditions with another, and to collapse a complex history of interaction and conflict into a "short" time that culminated in a lamentable and unexplained story of Indian disappearance. Mark this carefully because I will return to the problem of Pokanoket "extinction" in a moment. For now, just note that Bridgewater people are told that their ancestors bought the land from the friendly Indians who, sadly, have exited stage left. "Not a drop of [their] blood" remained in any survivor.[31]

If we are to believe the published program for the day, after hearing the lengthy historical address, the Bridgewater people endured 111 four-line stanzas of a poem by James Reed of Boston who, appropriately, is not remembered in the annals of great poetry. Let me edit out 109 of these stanzas, and note only 2:

> So scenes will often pass from mind
> Which never should have been forgot
> Thus, not so long ago, we find
> The town of Bridgewater was not.
>
> The town of Bridgewater was not:
> How comes it that the town has been?
> 'Twas purchased in a single lot
> Of famous old Ousamequin.

The poet's admonishment to the people to remember that once "Bridge-water was not!" underscored his larger point: the virtues of Bridgewater people were displayed in the town's very foundational act; Bridgewater came to "be" only through legal purchase from a famous Indian. (Apparently Mr. Read had nodded off earlier when the historian told us there were *two* purchases.) Little else about Indians made the final draft of Mr. Read's epic poem. Three brief mentions underscored that Indians lived in the woods, were "more fearful than bears," and were "bloody-red bowmen."[32]

A commentator who followed (after the singing of a four-verse hymn that also stressed the legal purchase from the Indians), informed the audience of the exact terms of the Massasoit purchase (and laid out the going rate for Indian land): seven coats, nine hatchets, eight hoes, twenty knives, four moose-skins, and ten and a half yards of cotton cloth worth about $25 (thus establishing that Bridgewater was worth a dollar more than Manhattan). In his words:

> Such was the town valued at by the possessors, after a long period of occupation by savage tribes, and . . . was not destined to be increased in value by their mode of life, had they possessed it until the present time. Peopled by a civilized, Christian people, in the short space of two hundred years, the value of this same territory is more than five millions current money.

Thus have the Bridgewater people put Indian land to higher uses (the almighty market). They've even far outstripped neighboring Duxbury (which, we are told, has superior advantages), thus rendering "the superiority of Bridgewater the more to her credit."[33] John Locke would have been proud.

Returning more directly to my theme, let me report that for the final speech of the day the Bridgewater people were in for what could only have been the rarest of treats. For the final speaker was none other than "A representative of the Pokanoket tribe [who] made the following response":

> BROTHERS,—I have come a long way to meet you. [Indeed: all the way from extinction to Bridgewater, Massachusetts.] I am glad that our good old father Massasoit still lives in your memory. The fields were once the hunting-grounds of the red men; but they were sold to the white men of Bridgewater. The red men have been driven towards the great water at the West, and have disappeared like the dew; while the white men have become like the leaves on the trees, and the sands on the sea-shore.
>
> Brothers, our hunting-grounds grow narrow; the chase grows short; the sun grows low; and, before another Centennial Celebration of the Incorporation of Bridgewater, our bones will be mingled with the dust.

Where to begin? Well, first off, are we really to believe this could possibly actually have happened? I refer here, of course, not to the actual existence of a Pokanoket person but to his appearance in person to celebrate the people of Bridgewater and R.S.V.P. in advance for the next centennial. (It is possible, of course, that our speaker was a Bridgewater person performing in red face.) Second, let me point out that this is a perfect reversal of the trope I have been exploring so far, in which the "last of the ____" is a deliberately invoked genre in which the Euro-American narrator provides the *name* of the *last* Indian in order to precisely mark the passing of a people. Here, the Bridgewater people are feted by an anonymous Pokanoket person (who had apparently hired a speechwriter from the Plains) who proclaims that his ancestors' homelands were legally purchased by Bridge-water people. Astonishingly, our speaker goes on to predict his own peoples' extinction. Apparently, Bridgewater people had an immense capacity for reconciling contradiction. Neither the irony of the extincts' sudden appearance nor the confusion over whether it was Ousamequin or Massasoit who sold the land seemed to trouble them at all. Finally, what are we to make of the fact that the Pokanoket speech came last? That the Bridgewater people have been absolved *by a Pokanoket person* of the messier details of English conquest? That the inevitable culmination of the collision between "savagery" and "civilization" *is* Indian extinction? (Actually, the real reason this event came last was because three short hymns that were to close the celebration were "omitted for lack of time.")[34]

What to Make of It All?

Nineteenth-century narratives of New England history displayed an intriguing confusion about Indians. Taken together, they tell a story of Indian disappearance in the wake of what they insist, on balance, was a virtuous and moral colonialism. Yet some narrators, such as the historian who wrote about Mashpee, were not quite sure about the Indianness of people he did, and did not, recognize as such. This confusion is starkly displayed in the coexistence of a collective historical narrative that tells stories about Indian disappearance and a commonwealth bureaucracy that extended an official recognition to still-present Indian peoples. An emergent grasp of the inadequacy of existing categories for understanding New England Indianness found expression most visibly in work of Commissioner of Indian affairs, John Milton Earle. His census listed tribal members based on the centrality of kinship and community even while he continued to use racial labels such as "colored," "mixed," "negro," and "white" alongside Hassanamisco, Dudley, Narragansett, Punkapoag, and other tribal labels. Earle did his research, and he listened to Indian voices even if he could not completely transcend the intellectual framework of his time.

Indians, and Indian history, did continue to permeate the consciousness of nineteenth-century New England antiquarians, and there is evidence that some of them also listened to Indian voices even if they did not follow Earle's lead in struggling to come to terms with the dynamics of Indian persistence. Consider the following passage from Ebenezer Clapp's 1859 history of Dorchester:

> This year [1671] Jeremy, son of Josias Chickatabut, confirmed his Uncle Squamaug's sale to the town. The Town paid all necessary expenses to

satisfy the Indians [in their sale of lands], who were better treated then, than in later times, *'when they have been driven from their native soil by the sword of the invader, and then darkly slandered by the pen of the historian.'* The original natives of our soil have been grossly abused, *not* always *because they were guilty, but because they were ignorant* and weak. [35]

Could it be that Clapp was secretly borrowing and rewriting William Apess's stinging indictment of Euro-Americans (which had originally come from the pen of Washington Irving in the form of a twelve-page indictment of Euro-Americans, that singled out New Englanders for particular rebuke?) (Apess reproduced the piece practically intact in his 1829 autobiography.) Maybe or maybe not. But it is intriguing in any event that both Apess and Clapp saw fit to borrow from the same pointed Irving passage, which vigorously argued a Native perspective on invasion, conquest, and the power of historians to slander. It is instructive to consider the uses each of them made of his words.

Clapp's revisionism of the words he did lift from Irving (or Apess or some unknown source) began with his erasure of Irving's charge of the white man's double wrong. Although he retained Irving's wording in noting that Indians had been "driven from their native soil by the sword of the invader," in his version this occurred later and elsewhere. In Dorchester, he insists, Indians had been amply compensated for their forfeiture of their homelands, which he had earlier claimed Indians "parted with . . . without reluctance." [36] In his rewriting, this happened not just because Indians were "ignorant," as Irving had had it, but also because they were "weak." His other direct revision opens a door that Irving had slammed shut. By inserting "always" into the last sentence, Clapp suggests that sometimes Indians *were* culpable for some of the gross abuse they had suffered. All in all, Clapp engaged in exactly the sort of slander that Irving charged historians with perpetrating in the many "written volumes [that had been written] to justify him in his outrages." Audaciously, he did so by using (some but not all of) Irving's own words, wherever he got them. [37] Even if he saw only the words he used, he made his own history narrate the opposite of Irving's clear intent.

In Clapp's version of the history of Indian relations, New Englanders did not exterminate or dispossess Indians. They made every effort to "civilize" them (which language fit Irving's critique that Indians had been slandered by both invaders and historians as "savage" and "pagan"). If Clapp got the passage from Irving or Apess, he had no choice but to trip over the much fuller critique that framed the general claim. Even if he saw only what he reproduced, he edited out anything that would have bolstered the critique and argued against his story of Dorchester's honorable Indian history. Despite the laudable deeds he attributed to his New England ancestors, "civilization does not seem to agree with [the Indians'] nature, as they die out where that flourishes, or become vagrants in towns and villages, where their forefathers roamed and hunted." Instead of noting deadly hostilities, Clapp domesticated Irving's critique, justified the violence of the colonial encounter, and reiterated the disappearance story. Through Clapp's semantic maneuver even the unnamed wrongs perpetrated against Indians later and elsewhere (but never in Dorchester) would be eliminated, as Native peoples succumbed to an inevitable extinction that was their natural fate in spite of the best efforts of the well-intentioned invaders.

That Clapp used Irving (or Irving through Apess or through somebody else) without attribution fell well within the authorial conventions of the day, which did not legally prohibit plagiarism. Yet his failure to cite anybody is still puzzling, given that he provided detailed citations for other work he borrowed throughout his history. What is more puzzling is his decision to plagiarize from a passage whose purpose was to indict Euro-Americans and their historians. Even if Clapp only had access to the words that he used, he wrote to insist that Dorchester people could never have been indicted under its charge of invasion, dispossession, and slander. Clapp did his research, which included reading an Indian perspective on New England Indian history that he chose to reject. Another stark contrast differentiated Apess's and Clapp's use of Irving. While Clapp made his narrative argue for extinction and the morality of New England's Indian history, everything about William Apess's publications and life were an assertion of New England Indian persistence and change in spite of the legacy of English conquest.

The conclusions offered by Mashpee's historian about Indian relations with his ancestors echo Clapp and others in revealing a tension between justifying the past and understanding that Indian critiques contained truth. Ultimately, the persistence of Mashpee people (about which the author was so ambiguous)

> shows at least that there has been a disposition of the part of their white neighbors to extend to them a larger degree of the indulgence of humanity, than has been meted out to most tribes; for the course taken by the white man has generally, in other parts of our country, been summary and exterminating.[38]

Like Ebenezer Clapp and many others, this historian could use the language of extermination by removing it from his own immediate past and place and applying it to the rest of Indian America, and thus argue more forcefully for the unique gloriousness of New Englanders' historical legacy in connection to Indians. Leicester's historian engaged in a different sort of distancing that also permeates Clapp's account and many others: "The spread of civilization operated like an act of extermination upon the once hostile tribes, so that the early settlers were, in a few years, beyond the immediate danger of attack."[39] Time took care of everything, and an impersonal "civilization" exterminated Indians, not people.

Despite New Englanders' contradictory bent, ultimately what prevailed in the popular mind was a weighty, convenient, and erroneous ideology of extinction that took a powerful hold over the imaginations of New Englanders, and eventually became enshrined in the national historical canon. Even Dakota physician, author, and activist Dr. Charles A. Eastman recited the New England Indian extinction myth, which, presumably, he learned during his stints at Kimball Union Academy, Dartmouth College, and Boston University, where he "absorbed much knowledge of the New Englander":[40]

> The country around [Dartmouth] is rugged and wild; and thinking of the time when red men lived here in plenty and freedom, it seemed as if I had been destined to come view their graves and bones. No, I said to myself, I have come to continue that which in their last struggle they proposed to take up, in order to save themselves from extinction; but alas! it was too late.[41]

This passage stands as a testimony to the power and success of the "vanishing" story that local historians collectively told. By "vanishing" Indians from the possibility of a future in their narratives, local historians participated in the production of a powerful mythology.

In reality, New England Indians persisted, and they did so in ways that actively were constructed as "disappearance." Nineteenth-century antiquarians claimed the voice of authority about history and participated in the erasure of Indians by literally refusing to recognize New England Indians *as "authentic" Indians.*[42] They did this especially by mustering particular formulations of race and deep-seated assumptions about Indian cultures as static and fixed in the past. In this formulation, race and culture became rigid and artificial categories that could not contain the histories or identities of real New England Indians, and could not narrate a story of persistence and change.

If Indian "extinction" was their inevitable lot, if the story line had already been so conclusively plotted, why did nineteenth- century antiquarians insist that this too was part of their story in an era of stark scientific racism that posited strict separation of the "pure races"? Why did local narrators pursue this story line with such persistence and determination? The story of "disappearance" meant (and for some still means) something important to New Englanders. It allowed them (a racially and morally "pure people") to claim Indian landscapes, to justify their "benign "possession" of Indian homelands, to assert the "justice" and "glory" of their military and ideological encounters with Indians, and unambiguously to establish themselves and their social order as exclusive and dominant. Moreover, this whole process, in its selective and biased rendering of an Indian history— which erased Indian voices and critiques as well as the Indian present and future—served to emphasize the particular traits of particular places as categorically and "gloriously" pure "New English." It also asserted more broadly the Americanness of their identity. Their convenient story of Indian disappearance, which offered a kind of historical blueprint for a non-Indian people who needed a particular Indian history, contained compelling explanatory power even though it only really existed on the mythological level. This story served to naturalize colonialism and the asserted replacement of Indian by Euro-American peoples as the "triumph" of a mythological "civilization" over an equally mythological "savagery."

Notes

1. William Apess, "A Son of the Forest," Appendix, "Traits of Indian Character." In *On Our Own Ground: The Complete Writings of William Apess, A Pequot*, edited and with an introduction by Barry O'Connell (Amherst: University of Massachusetts Press, 1992), 61.

2. I would like to thank Barry O'Connell for making the Washington Irving connection for me, for other extremely useful suggestions on an earlier draft of this chapter, and for ongoing conversations about this project. For research assistance, I thank Anne Enke and Margaret Rodgers. For additional helpful input on various versions of this piece, I am grateful to William Sturtevant, Peter Nabokov, Nancy Shoemaker, Thomas Doughton, David Noble, Lisa Bower, Lisa Disch, Jennifer Pierce, Jim Merrell, David Roediger, William S. Simmons, Pauline Turner Strong, Sergei Kan, members of the Early American History Workshop at the University of Minnesota, and participants in National Endowment of the Humanities seminars at the American Antiquarian Society and the Newberry Library.

3. John Milton Earle, *Report to the Governor and Council Concerning the Indians of the Commonwealth, Under the Act of April 6, 1859: Senate Report No. 96* (Boston: William White, Printer to the State, 1861). This document was compiled in the context of the debate over the problem of Indian "wardship" in the wake of abolition. Given the prominent role of Massachusetts leaders in the abolition movement, the commonwealth found itself vulnerable to criticism about the disenfranchisement of Indians. Even the ending of "wardship" status did not mean that Indian peoples in New England ceased to exist, only that official

recognition of separate tribal status had been terminated. See Ann Marie Plane and Gregory Button, "The Massachusetts Indian Enfranchisement Act: Ethnic Contest in Historical Context, 1849–1869," *Ethnohistory* 40 (1993):587–618.

4. Thomas L. Doughton, "Unseen Neighbors: Native Americans of Central Massachusetts, A People Who Had 'Vanished,' " paper delivered at the American Historical Association, New York, 1997; Russell G. Handsman, "Native American Presence and the Politics of Representation: Indians in Nineteenth-Century Central Massachusetts," paper delivered at the American Historical Association, New York, 1997; Handsman, "Illuminating History's Silences in the 'Pioneer Valley,' " *Artifacts* 9 (1991); Barry O'Connell, "Introduction," Apess, *On Our Own Ground*; O'Connell, " 'Wandering' Indians at Home in 19th-Century New England: The Life of John Johnson," paper delivered at the American Historical Association, New York, 1997; Colin G. Calloway, ed., *After King Philip's War: Presence and Persistence in Indian New England* (Hanover NH: University Press of New England, 1996); William S. Simmons, *Spirit of the New England Tribes: Indian History and Folklore, 1620–1984* (Hanover NH: University Press of New England, 1986); Jack Campisi, *The Mashpee Indians: Tribe on Trial* (Syracuse: Syracuse University Press, 1991); Campisi, "The Trade and Intercourse Acts: Land Claims on the Eastern Seaboard," in *Irredeemable America: The Indians' Estate and Land Claims*, ed. Imre Sutton (Albuquerque: University of New Mexico Press, 1985); Ann McMullen, "What's Wrong with This Picture? Context, Conversion, Survival, and the Development of Regional Cultures and Pan-Indianism in Southeastern New England," in *Enduring Traditions: The Native Peoples of New England*, ed. Laurie Weinstein (Westport CT: Bergin & Garvey, 1994), 123–150; Ann McMullen and Russell Handsman, eds., *A Key into the Language of Woodsplint Baskets* (Washington CT: American Indian Archaeological Institute, 1987); Plane and Button, "Massachusetts Indian Enfranchisement"; Donna Keith Baron, J. Edward Hood, and Holly V. Izard, "They Were Here All Along: The Native American Presence in Lower-Central New England in the Eighteenth and Nineteenth Centuries," *William and Mary Quarterly* 53 (1996):561–586; and Frank Speck, "Territorial Subdivisions and Boundaries of the Wampanoag, Massachuset, and Nauset Indians," *Indian Notes and Monographs*, ed. F. W. Hodge, no. 44 (New York: Heye Foundation, 1928); "Reflections upon the Past and Present of the Massachusetts Indians," *Bulletin of the Massachusetts Archaeological Society* 4 (1943):33–38; and "A Note on the Hassanamisco Band of Nipmuc," *Bulletin of the Massachusetts Archaeological Society* 4 (1943):49–56. See also James Clifford, "Identity in Mashpee," in *The Predicament of Culture: Twentieth-Century Ethnography, Literature, and Art* (Cambridge MA: Harvard University Press, 1988), 277–346; *Strategies for Survival: American Indians in the Eastern United States*, ed. Frank W. Porter III (Westport CT: Greenwood Press, 1986); Laurence M. Hauptman and James D. Wherry, eds., *The Pequots in Southern New England: The Fall and Rise of an American Indian Nation* (Norman: University of Oklahoma Press, 1990); William C. Sturtevant and Samuel Stanley, "Indian Communities in the Eastern States, *The Indian Historian* 1 (1968):15–19; Ethel Boissevan, "Narragansett Survival: A Study of Group Persistence through Adopted Traits," *Ethnohistory* 6 (1959):347–62; Peter Benes, ed., *Algonkians of New England: Past and Present*, The Dublin Seminar for New England Folklife Annual Proceedings (Boston: Boston University, 1993); Colin G. Calloway, *The Western Abenakis of Vermont, 1600–1800: War, Migration, and the Survival of a People* (Norman: University of Oklahoma Press, 1990); and Paul R. Campbell and Glenn W. La Fantasie, "Scattered to the Winds of Heaven—Narragansett Indians, 1676–1880," *Rhode Island History* 27 (1978):67–83.

5. On the forging of New England regional identity, see for example Joseph A. Conforti,

Imagining New England: Explorations of Regional Identity from the Pilgrims to the Mid-Twentieth Century (Chapel Hill: University of North Carolina Press, 2001), and John D. Seelye, *Memory's Nation: The Place of Plymouth Rock* (Chapel Hill: University of North Carolina, 1998).

6. On "disappearance" stories in New England, see David Ghere, "The 'Disappearance' of the Abenaki in Western Maine: Political Organization and Ethnocentric Assumptions," *American Indian Quarterly* 17 (1993):193–207, and Simmons, *Spirit of the New England Tribes*, 3–4. On imagery and stereotypes see Robert F. Berkhofer Jr., *The White Man's Indian: Images of the American Indian from Columbus to the Present* (New York: Vintage Books, 1979).

7. Frederick Freeman, *The History of Cape Cod: The Annals of Barnstable County, Including the District of Mashpee* (Boston: Printed for the Author, 1860), vol. 1, 719 ("extinct" [emphasis added]) and 700 ("Isaac Simons"). On the Mashpee decision, see Campisi, *Tribe on Trial*; Campisi, "Trade and Intercourse Acts"; and Clifford, "Identity in Mashpee." On "last" stories, see Simmons, *Spirit of the New England Tribes*, 3–4; and Jane Van Norman Turano, "Taken from Life: Early Photographic Portraits of New England Angonkians, ca. 1844–1865," in *Algonkians of New England: Past and Present*, 121–143. Turano seems to accept the "last" stories that accompanied most of these depictions uncritically, until the last paragraph when she expresses curiosity about the phenomenon given the reality of still-present Indian peoples of New England.

8. Freeman, *Cape Cod*, 695–696; and Earle, *Report to the Governor*, 46.

9. Charles Brooks, *History of the Town of Medford, Middlesex County, Massachusetts, From Its First Settlement, in 1630, to the Present Time, 1855* (Boston: James M. Usher, 1855), 80–81.

10. Woburn, Mass., *Woburn Records of Births, Deaths, Marriages, and Marriage Intentions, from 1640 to 1900* (Woburn MA: Andrews, Cutler, and Co., 1890–1919); and Charles Brooks, *History of the Town of Medford, Middlesex County, Massachusetts, From Its First Settlement, in 1630 to 1855, Revised, Enlarged, and Brought Down to 1885, by James M. Usher* (Boston: Rand, Avery, & Co., 1886), 98–99.

11. Turano, "Taken from Life," 133.

12. *The Writings of Henry David Thoreau: Journal*, ed. Bradford Torrey (Boston: Houghton Mifflin, 1968), Journal 7, vol. 13, 96 (December 28, 1854), and Journal 8, vol. 15, 390–391 (June 26, 1856).

13. Turano, "Taken from Life," 121–143.

14. Earle, *Report to the Governor*, 9.

15. *Old Dartmouth Historical Sketches*, No. 51 (1921):33.

16. John Greenleaf Whittier, *Legends of New England* (Gainesville FL: Scholars' Facsimilies & Reprints, 1965), 137–142; and Daniel Ricketson, *The History of New Bedford, Bristol County, Massachusetts* (New Bedford: Published by the Author, 1858), 96.

17. Samuel F. Haven, *An Historical Address, Delivered before the Citizens of the Town of Dedham* (Dedham MA: Printed by Herman Mann, 1837), 63.

18. Mary de Witt Freeland, *The Records of Oxford, Massachusetts* (Albany NY: Joel Munsell's Sons, 1894), 31–32; and "Number of Persons Belonging to the Dudley Tribe of Indians, January 1, 1859," John Milton Earle Papers, American Antiquarian Society, Worcester MA, Box 2, Folder 5.

19. Jean M. O'Brien, *Dispossession by Degrees: Indian Land and Identity in Natick, Massachusetts, 1650–1790* (New York: Cambridge University Press, 1997), and O'Brien " 'They Are So Frequently Shifting Their Place of Residence': Land and the Construction of

Social Place of Indians in Colonial Massachusetts," in *Empire and Others: British Encounters with Indigenous Peoples, 1600–1850*, eds. Rick Halpern and M. J. Daunton (London: University College of London Press, 1999), 204–216.

20. Emory Washburn, *Historical Sketches of the Town of Leicester, Massachusetts, During the First Century From Its Settlement* (Boston: John Wilson and Son, 1860), 48.

21. Thoreau, *Journal*, 1858, 251–252.

22. Jean M. O'Brien, "Divorced from the Land: Accommodation Strategies of Indian Women in 18th Century New England," in *After King Philip's War.*

23. Washburn, *Town of Leicester*, 48.

24. Brooks, *Town of Medford*, 80.

25. J. E. A. Smith, *The History of Pittsfield, Berkshire County, Massachusetts* (Boston: Lee and Shepard, 1869), 45–46.

26. *Berkshire Jubilee, Celebrated at Pittsfield, Mass.* (Albany: Weare C. Little. E. P. Little, Pittsfield, 1845), 113–114.

27. In O'Connell, ed., *On Our Own Ground.*

28. On memory and King Philip's War, see Jill Lepore, *The Name of War: King Philip's War and the Origin of American Identity* (New York: Knopf, 1998). On the Pequot War see Alfred A. Cave, *The Pequot War* (Amherst: University of Massachusetts Press, 1996).

29. Consult any of the nineteenth-century works cited in this paper or the nineteenth-century history of a New England town of your choice.

30. Bridgewater, Massachusetts, *Celebration of the Two-Hundredth Anniversary of the Incorporation of Bridgewater, Massachusetts, At West Bridgewater, June 3, 1856; Including the Address by Hon. Emory Washburn, of Worcester; Poem by James Reed, A.B., of Boston; And the Other Exercises of the Occasion* (Boston: John Wilson and Son, 1856).

31. *Celebration of . . . Bridgewater*, 46.

32. *Celebration of . . . Bridgewater*, 83–97. Quotation is from p. 85. Other quotations, pp. 88–89.

33. *Celebration of . . . Bridgewater*, 136.

34. *Celebration of . . . Bridgewater*, 139–140.

35. Ebenezer Clapp Jr., *History of the Town of Dorchester, Massachusetts, By a Committee of the Dorchester Antiquarian and Historical Society* (Boston: Ebenezer Clapp Jr., 1859), 222–223; emphasis added.

36. Clapp, *Town of Dorchester*, 12–13.

37. Apess, "Son of the Forest," in *On Our Own Ground*, 61.

38. Apess, "Son of the Forest," 713–714.

39. Washburn, *Town of Leicester*, 130.

40. Charles A. Eastman (Ohiyesa), *From the Deep Woods to Civilization: Chapters in the Autobiography of an Indian* (Lincoln: University of Nebraska Press, 1977), 66. I would like to thank Jennifer Spear for directing me to this passage.

41. Eastman (Ohiyesa), *From the Deep Woods to Civilization*, 65.

42. See footnote 4 for much excellent work that has begun this task.

18. Pocahontas: An Exercise in Mythmaking and Marketing

FREDERIC W. GLEACH

> She's fearless, she's a fox . . . she's Pocahontas! Stronger than Schwarzen-
> egger and curvier than Jessica Rabbit, Disney's new animated heroine
> springs to action in this gorgeous and stirring musical loosely inspired
> by the life of the Indian princess who brokered peace between her tribe
> and Jamestown settlers. (" 'Pocahontas' Bounds into Stores," *Syracuse
> Herald-American*, 1996)

So ran one announcement of the 1996 release on video of Disney's *Pocahontas*. Never mind that this Pocahontas more closely resembles Asian-
American actress and sex symbol Tia Carrera than an early-adolescent
eastern Algonquian girl or that the story line bears little relation to the
documented events of the early seventeenth century beyond the names of
the principal characters. Distortion has long characterized the myth that
Pocahontas has become, a myth that has been constructed and marketed
in a variety of ways over the past couple of centuries.[1] Even the marketing
of tie-ins and promotional products—so overwhelming in the case of the
Disney production—is not entirely unprecedented in the history of this
American legend.

Even though I had been working with Virginia Native history for a number of years, until recently I never considered these issues of mythologizing
and marketing very interesting. I was more concerned with the actual history of the Powhatans (e.g., Gleach 1995, 1996, 1997a). This history may
be as much a cultural construction as the myths, and the "facts" it is based
on may be equally constructed and in need of interpretation. Still, one
cannot evaluate the later appropriations and recontextualizations without first dealing with the recorded evidence in its own original context.
I also believe that however difficult and problematic it may be to define

a boundary between history and myth, there is a significant difference between attempts to understand what happened in the past—subjective as they may be—and texts constructed for other purposes. My interests fell first to the former.

The story of the original Pocahontas—the favorite daughter of the paramount chief Powhatan—is known principally through the accounts of Capt. John Smith, an English commoner who rose from the ranks as a soldier.[2] Before going to Virginia, he had fought in Brittany and Transylvania; been captured, sold into slavery, and escaped; traveled extensively through eastern Europe; and sailed with pirates along the African coast.[3] In good Elizabethan fashion, he wrote accounts of his adventures. Although his first book was crudely produced by an unknown editor from a lengthy letter he wrote back to England from Virginia, he later published more carefully produced volumes over which he had more control. *The Generall Historie of Virginia, New-England, and the Summer Isles* (Smith 1986[1624]) is his most extensive work on the New World. Although much of it is drawn from his earlier works, the first account of his rescue by Pocahontas is given there.

The outline of this story is well known. Smith was captured while exploring, taken on a veritable tour of the Powhatan territory, and subjected to a series of apparent threats and several rituals during the weeks he was held captive. After finally meeting Powhatan he was suddenly seized and forced to his knees with his head on a large stone. Clubs were raised to smash his skull, when suddenly "Pocahontas, the king's dearest daughter, when no entreaty could prevail, got his head in her arms, and laid her own upon his to save him from death. Whereat the emperor was contented he should live to make him hatchets, and her bells, beads, and copper" (Smith 1986[1624]:150–151). After a final ritual the next day, Smith was returned to Jamestown.

I have written elsewhere (Gleach 1996, 1997a:10–22, 2003a:47–65) on the meanings of the events of Smith's captivity and the early history of the Virginia colony. I have demonstrated that the rescue was part of a protracted ritual complex that took up most, if not all, of the captivity, that it was Powhatan's intention to have the English settle in a particular part of his territory to supply him with the ritual/status objects he desired, and that later attacks on the colony were intended to enforce that relationship, although the English never understood the arrangement they had been brought into. After Smith left the colony in 1609 relations deteriorated, until Pocahontas again served as a cultural mediator (Kidwell 1992) by converting to Christianity and marrying John Rolfe in 1616—a move that also gave the colony hope that conversion of its Natives might succeed. Unfortunately she died in 1617 while visiting England; she had one son, but from this small start have sprung thousands of descendants.[4] Virginians proudly claimed descent from Pocahontas even at the height of anti-Indian racist sentiment. When the Virginia Racial Integrity Law was passed in 1924, defining anyone with even a trace of non-Caucasian "blood" as "colored," a formal exception was made for those whose only non-Caucasian ancestry was one-sixteenth or less American Indian, to accommodate those prominent whites descended from Pocahontas (Rountree 1990:221; Sherman 1988).

This history both shaped and reflects the development of the American nation in many ways, but so have the myths that sprung from it, even if they did not take hold immediately.[5] Through the later seventeenth and eighteenth centuries the story of Pocahontas seems to have attracted only limited attention. There was no separate publication of the *Generall Historie* in English from 1632 until the nineteenth century, and there were few printings of any of Smith's works—and those principally in empire-exalting collections of works on British world travels.[6] By the time Smith died in 1631, the Virginia colony had ceased to be the center of popular attention in England that it had been for much of the first quarter of the century. Interest seems to have remained low there until at least the late nineteenth century.

In America, however, the first history of Virginia after Smith's was published at the beginning of the eighteenth century (Beverley 1947[1705])—reflecting a native pride that is still quite evident in the Old Dominion. Another was published in 1747 (Stith 1865[1747]) and another in 1804 (Burk 1804–5).[7] The Pocahontas legend was then popularized in the works of English-expatriate John Davis (e.g., Davis 1805; cf. Tilton 1994:35–48). Following the War of 1812, as independence and the American antebellum culture stabilized, the country's historical foundation became a major focus of study. In 1819 the *Generall Historie* was republished in Richmond, Virginia—its first American publication—and from the 1830s through the 1870s many early works on colonial America were reprinted in the nascent historical journals and in reprint series, particularly those produced by Peter Force and Joseph Sabin.

This period also saw the end of the Indian Wars of the east, as the eastern tribes were largely and variously marginalized, removed, and exterminated. Easterners no longer having to fear imminent attack were free to become nostalgic for their Indians, even as the wars continued in the west. In the field of literature, the romanticized eastern Indian began to displace the narratives of Indian captivities that had been so popular at the turn of the century. The best-known example, of course, is James

Fenimore Cooper's *The Last of the Mohicans,* but the Powhatans were not spared this romanticization. Several plays based on the Pocahontas rescue were published (e.g., Custis 1803; Owen 1837; Brougham [1855]; cf. Friar and Friar 1972:22–24; Tilton 1994:72–76), and three epic poems treating the story were published in 1841 alone (Sigourney 1841; S. Smith 1841; Waldron 1841).[8] I have as yet been unable to find the proximate cause of this outpouring of poesy, but the attitude of these works is evident from Waldron's introduction:

> Pocahontas is one of those characters, rarely appearing on the theatre of life, which no age can claim, no country appropriate. She is the property of mankind, serving as a beacon to light us on our way, instruct us in our duty, and show us what the human mind is capable of performing when abandoned to its own operations.
>
> In Pocahontas we view the simple child of nature, prompted by her own native virtues alone, discharging the most generous acts of self-devotion, without seeking any reward, other than that arising from a consciousness of acquitting sacred duties. [Waldron 1841:9]

Here Pocahontas is appropriated for all humanity as a "primitive" or "natural" model to instruct us in the ideals of duty and self-sacrifice—ideals that were Christian and feminine in the context of white America in the mid-nineteenth century, and thus justifiably coming from an Indian woman who converted to Christianity. The meanings of her actions in their original context were irrelevant to this formulation, and they disappeared.

While nineteenth-century easterners were busily creating romanticized fictional Indians and as the south was moving toward secession, Bostoner Charles Deane in 1859 initiated a series of accusations that Smith had, himself, created a fictional romantic account, particularly concerning the Pocahontas rescue (Barbour 1986:lxii–lxiv; Uhry 1999:245–252). By that time sectionalists on both sides had been appropriating the legend for their own purposes for several decades (Tilton 1994:4–5, 145–175). Southerners saw in Pocahontas and the Jamestown settlement an American origin in the South (one rejected by Northerners, who emphasized Plymouth and, by mid-century, the so-called First Thanksgiving).[9] Northerners saw in Pocahontas's "mixed marriage" an innate contradiction for the slave-holding Southerners who took her as figurative mother. Although Smith was defended by such scholars as William Wirt Henry (1882) of Virginia and Edward Arber, the English editor of the great nineteenth-century edition of Smith's works, the attack on Smith's veracity largely held sway in the United States through the end of the century. It is still sometimes raised today, despite considerable evidence supporting Smith's accounts.[10] It may be tempting to dismiss a colonial Euro-American hero as a braggart and liar, but in this case to do so deprives us of much we can know about the seventeenth-century Powhatans (Gleach 1996, 2003a).

Throughout this time, and continuing through the present, the Powhatan tribes survived. They had been thoroughly marginalized in Virginia society in the eighteenth and nineteenth centuries. On two small reservations and in several nonreservation communities, however, descendants of the people who met the English colony farmed, hunted, worked, and lived, for the most part ignored by outsiders—and certainly by those who were creating new meanings for their history.[11] By the late nineteenth century they had begun giving public performances of historical plays, including the rescue of Capt. John Smith by Pocahontas, and making public appearances wearing recognizably "Indian" regalia such as buckskins and feather headdresses, an early use of pan-Indian symbols (Feest 1990). They even sent a representative, William Terrill Bradby, to the World's Columbian Exposition in Chicago in 1893 (Rountree 1990:207–210). They were, as Rountree (1990:187–211) describes, a "people who refused to vanish" (see also Waugaman and Moretti-Langholtz 2000). The adoption of pan-Indian symbols and introduction of ceremonial public presentations can be seen as a response to their marginalization, an attempt to regain, if not some of the power they had held in colonial relations, then at least some recognition from outside (Feest 1990; Gleach 1997b, 1997c). This attempt was at least partly successful: anthropologists and others began writing about their visits to the Powhatan communities in the late nineteenth century (e.g., Mooney 1907; Speck 1925, 1928; see Rountree 1990:203–208; Gleach 1997b, 1997c).

The turn of the century brought the approach of the tricentennial of the English landing at Jamestown, and in 1900 several members of the Association for the Preservation of Virginia Antiquities met and began planning for a vast historical exposition to commemorate the event (Reynolds 1909:118). The plan received the support of President Grover Cleveland in 1903, and Theodore Roosevelt, his successor, added his support in 1904 (Reynolds 1909:128–129). If anyone asked the opinion of the Powhatans I have been unable to find record of it. Held near Norfolk, facing Hampton Roads, it opened April 26, 1907, and closed November 30 with a gala ball the final evening before the closing ceremonies (Reynolds 1909:164, 182–185).[12] Almost three million admissions were recorded (of which half were free); average daily admissions were just over 13,000 (Reynolds 1909:180–181).

A number of states sent exhibitions of historical artifacts to the Jamestown Exposition, but the fair had been broadened by Congress and President Roosevelt to be "an international naval, marine, and military celebration" demonstrating American military progress (*Commemorating* n.d.:4–5). One of the more frequently reproduced images from the fair is a scene of the naval fleet in quarter-line formation in Hampton Roads (e.g., *Illustrated Souvenir* 1907). This emphasis is perhaps not surprising, coming less than a decade after the "Spanish-American War."[13] As a result of that conflict the U.S. Navy had been expanded and modernized, and this was prominently featured at the Jamestown Exposition. Several battleships seem to have been on hand throughout the fair, and there was a

> Filipino Village, typifying Uncle Sam's new ward, [which] proved entertaining to those who like to behold strange peoples, to stand and watch them busied naturally in their native habitations . . . sewing, cooking, manufacturing, or at their games and in their grotesque dances. [Reynolds 1909:177]

The Powhatans also performed their dramatization of the rescue of Capt. John Smith by Pocahontas. This was part of the process of strengthening and publicizing their political organization that had begun a decade or two earlier. The impressions made on visitors by these events were occasionally quite strong; my maternal grandfather, born that year in central Virginia, was given the middle name Powhatan by his suitably impressed parents. I suspect most viewers saw it as just another "grotesque" and "strange" entertainment, however. A rather flippant contemporary description supports this view:

> A band of these Pamaunkees on the Warpath—the modern, peaceful Warpath—nightly re-enact the historic and legendary deeds of their ancestors. As they have not had the advantage of college training, their war whoops are deficient in animation and abandon, but they have brought with them from their reservation the genuine original stone on which Captain Smith did or did not lay his head when he was or was not rescued by Pocahontas. It is at least as authentic as the Blarney Stone that was kissed by thousands of would-be flatterers at the Chicago Exposition. [Slosson 1907:124–125]

"The War Path" was the name for the midway at the Jamestown Exposition. It featured a cyclorama of the Civil War engagement of the *Monitor* and the *Virginia* and a miniature of the destruction of San Francisco, in addition to the then-typical "streets of Cairo," animal shows, and other such amusements (Reynolds 1909:178; *Illustrated Souvenir* 1907).[14]

Figure 1. Some of the souvenirs from the 1907 Jamestown Exposition. *Top row:* a desktop blotter, cup, and card tray. *Bottom left:* watch fobs and pins. *Bottom center:* watch fob: "MEET ME ON THE WAR PATH JAMESTOWN EXPOSITION." *Bottom right:* handkerchief with portrait of Capt. John Smith. *From the author's personal collection.*

Although the merchandising of this fair pales by comparison to that of the World's Columbian Exposition held in Chicago 15 years earlier, a variety of souvenirs were produced (Figure 1). Interestingly, and unlike the Columbian Exposition of 1892–93 and the Lewis and Clark Exposition of 1904–5, the federal government issued no commemorative coins for the Jamestown Exposition. The secretary of the treasury, when asked, wrote an emphatic reply against using commemorative coins as fund raisers (a practice used often both before and since), calling it "absolutely wrong in principle" (Reynolds 1909:153). Anti-Jamestown prejudice? The souvenirs sold were more mementos of the fair than of the Pocahontas legend, but the legend was also clearly represented.[15] Today the most commonly seen souvenirs of the fair are postcards (Figure 2), including historical scenes (from Jamestown through the Civil War, and even the explosion of the *Maine*) and naval ships as seen at the fair. There were 185 official postcards—only 10 percent of which deal with the events of early Jamestown. Many other postcards were produced, including advertising

Figure 2. Advertising postcard from the 1907 Jamestown Exposition. *From the author's personal collection.*

cards for insurance, chocolates, and shoes. Stereoscopic views were also produced of the Powhatan historical performance, but those seem to have been distributed after the fair rather than sold as souvenirs on site (Figure 3).

While the American military was strutting its stuff at the exposition, the Powhatans were continuing to work for their survival and for recognition from the dominant culture. This was an enterprise that has through the years seen them working as trappers, hunters, fishermen, and guides; acting in historical pageants; making public presentations to Virginia's governors; collaborating with anthropologists; and producing and marketing craft products. Beginning in the 1930s a series of art teachers worked with them to produce a pottery that would be of more interest to the incipient tourist trade than their traditional unglazed earthenwares (Stern 1951:59–66). They also developed a "picture-writing" system still used to decorate pots with the story of Pocahontas and Capt. John Smith (see also Waugaman and Moretti-Langholtz 2000:55–61) (Figure 4). Despite these efforts, the mainstream of American culture has seldom exhibited much positive interest in the Powhatans—or most other Native Americans—beyond their status as relics of the historical myths of this country's founding.

Figure 3. Pocahontas saving Capt. John Smith, performed by Pamunkey Indians at the exposition. From an original stereoview (14196), copyright 1907 by Keystone View Company, Meadville PA. *From the author's personal collection.*

After the Jamestown Exposition, the historical myth of Pocahontas took on a life of its own, generating more books and other products than could possibly be listed here.[16] One of the most fascinating publications is another epic poem (Ward 1928), an anachronistic extravaganza in which Pocahontas became a sort of flapper–Calamity Jane composite heroine—a blonde, blue-eyed girl who carried an automatic pistol and rode horses and immediately fell in love with Smith (Figure 5). Ward's poem represents an extremely unrealistic version of the Pocahontas legend, but it has at least one saving grace: it pretends to be nothing but an amusement, a satirical comedy of manners (and errors) poking fun at history and poetry, and especially at those who take things too seriously. The description of

Figure 4. Pamunkey Indian pottery of the 1980s. *From the author's personal collection.*

Powhatan's village, for example, begins with the following adaptation of one of the most recognizable poems in the English language:

> At Wocomoke did Powhatan
> A stately pleasure dome decree,
> Where wild Pamunkey's torrent ran,
> Through channels all unknown to man,
> Down to a silent sea.
> (Pamunkey's but a muddy creek
> That empties into Chesapeake.
> That pleasure dome was nothing but
> A very ordinary hut,
> Composed of wattled sticks and twigs,
> Where Powhatan, his dogs and pigs,
> His children, chickens, goats and wives
> Led rather complicated lives.
> Bare facts like these are not supposed
> In poetry to be exposed.
> In poetry, you must admit,
> One has to doll them up a bit.
> So, if you please, I shall again
> Resume the high heroic strain.) [Ward 1928:72]

Figure 5. Pocahontas as cowgirl. *Artist unknown; reproduced from Ward 1928.*

No reader, however naïve, could take this work as representing real events in seventeenth-century Virginia. It is, in a sense, an upscale *Mad* magazine version for its time, replete with art deco illustrations.

The Pocahontas myth was further spurred on by the 350th anniversary celebrations in 1957, which focused more directly than the 1907 fair on the Jamestown settlement itself. Part of this celebration was the establishment of Jamestown Festival Park, which features recreations of the Jamestown fort and ships, the colonial glassworks, and a Powhatan village (Jamestown-Williamsburg-Yorktown Celebration Commission 1958:61–84; hereafter cited as JWYCC). Over one million people attended the park during the festival, of whom over 780,000 were paid admissions (JWYCC:186)—just a bit over one-third of the total attendance of the 1907 Exposition. Marketing and product placements were more formally developed in 1957 than in 1907, and the Jamestown festival "was brought home to millions," through " 'tie-ins' with product advertising and merchandising, and similar commercial promotions, sometimes unsolicited by the commissions and occasionally on a national scale" (JWYCC:157–158). These included advertisements by Sinclair Oil and promotions by the American Dairy Association. Many department stores, from Norfolk to New York, used the Jamestown theme in window displays, following the development of a "Jamestown fashion"—colors and designs for apparel, furniture, and household wares (JWYCC:158–160):

> Ultimately "Jamestown color" or "Jamestown design" was evident in a variorum of products—fabrics, wallpaper, paints, leather, candles, costume jewelry, stationery and desk accessories, china and other tableware, and women's dresses and hats. Furniture was marketed in "Jamestown parchment tones," though the furniture itself was not represented as being reproductions of 17th-century pieces, none of which survive from the scene of old Jamestown, so far as is known. (JWYCC:159–160)

Chosen as "Jamestown colors" were "River Aqua, Indian Corn, Virginia Sky, Golden Tobacco, Glass Green, and Jamestown Clay" (JWYCC:159). Though there were numerous tie-ins of this sort—most not even recognizable today as having anything to do with Jamestown—there seem to have been even fewer products than in 1907 that included any content pertaining to the Powhatans.

Accessible, sound scholarly works were also produced in association with the 350th Anniversary festival (e.g., Swem 1957). Several books were produced for a more general audience, including works for children (JWYCC:155–156). Only a few years later, John Barth's *The Sot-Weed Factor* (1960) presented another comedic romanticized version, giving Smith a secret amatory device to enhance his sexual attraction for the Native women. More recently, Susan Donnell, whose essentialized status as a descendant of Pocahontas is proclaimed on cover of her book, published a romance novel, *Pocahontas* (1991), in which the young girl competes with her older sisters and other Powhatan women for Smith's affections. The story of Pocahontas and Capt. John Smith has also been a standard in primary school history texts for at least 150 years, and is taught even in our modern colonies, as my Puerto Rican wife can attest.

Interestingly, many people—especially outside of Virginia—seem to have internalized a version of the myth in which Pocahontas marries John Smith rather than John Rolfe. This may be simply a natural extension of the romance typically seen as the motivation for her saving Smith's life— a romantic fantasy that Rayna Green (1975) dubbed "the Pocahontas Perplex" in her study of appropriations of Indian Otherness—but it also further mythologizes the historical Pocahontas.[17] In addition to texts, there have been dozens, if not hundreds, of children's books written on Pocahontas, again beginning in the nineteenth century, but with a great efflorescence since the 1950s (e.g., Ellis [c. 1910]; Graham 1953; Seymour 1961; Wilkie 1969; Accorsi 1992). Some of these evade the issue of whom she married by stopping before that point in her life, but most do go on to present her marriage to Rolfe, allowing the morality tale of her conversion to Christianity to be presented.

The potential for romantic or sexual relations between Pocahontas and Capt. John Smith has long fascinated many. Love (at first sight) as motivation for the rescue has been traced as early as a 1755 text (Tilton 1994:41). The idea of sexual relations between the two seems to be a more recent fixation, and most recently there have occasionally been charges raised that Smith raped Pocahontas. There is no evidence to support these ideas, and it is virtually impossible that there could have been any kind of sexual relations between the two. Smith was a commoner—risen through the ranks to the status of captain but still a commoner (cf. Gleach 1997a:82). Since he perceived Pocahontas as royalty—as the daughter of an emperor—he could no more have married or had sexual relations with Pocahontas than he could have with European royalty.[18] It is worth noting that even ten years later when John Rolfe, a gentleman, wanted to marry Pocahontas, he was sufficiently worried about the perceived difference in status to write a letter begging the colonial governor's support (in Hamor 1615:61–68).

Throughout most of the twentieth century the Powhatans continued to make their annual presents to the governor. They gained further exposure in the 1990s by contesting the construction of a dam near their reservations (Latané 1996a, 1996b) and by beginning the process to obtain federal recognition (Latané 1995). These legal proceedings are still underway in early 2005. There was relatively little marketing of the legend beyond the festivals, however, aside from publications, postcards, and the occasional Pocahontas doll (which had appeared at least by the early 1960s).

That situation changed dramatically in the spring of 1995, when Disney's *Pocahontas* was scheduled to open.[19] Advertising began in May, and the film premiered in Central Park in New York on June 10 for 100,000 ticket holders chosen in a nationwide lottery that drew 500,000 entries (Daly 1995; Allan, Furse, and Schwartzman 1995).[20] A selection of newspaper headlines from reviews is indicative of the critical response: "A fairy tale history, glorious color, anthropomorphic critters and all" (Maslin 1995); "Disney animators fiddle with history in the name of romance" (Vadeboncouer 1995); "Flick all right, politics all left" (Bernard 1995:4).

Russell Means, the voice of the film's Powhatan, proclaimed it "the best and most responsible film that has ever been made about American Indians" (Means 1995), although, as Maslin observed (1995), "Hollywood's track record on this subject sure isn't hard to beat." The film began as an idea for a western romance, but Pocahontas—the mythic Pocahontas—was the story that came to mind for Mike Gabriel, the co-director and originator of the project (MacDonald 1995:28). As in some of the book versions, the desire for a pure romance probably prompted the editing out of the rest of her life. By excising the complication of her later marriage to another man Disney was also able to avoid a depiction of her religious conversion, which would be certain to draw fire from critics however it might be slanted.[21]

The film was a success at the box office but is not among the most successful Disney films. Comments I heard from children were uniformly underwhelming in their faint praise, and aside from its astounding lack of historical substance I found it quite boring, relying as it did on variations of "stupid pet tricks" to revive the audience's flagging interest at a number of points. The Native audience in general seems to have found in the film little to like and much to despise. Some, however, were also hopeful that some good might come from the film, from its positive portrayal of Native families, its use of a Native girl as heroine, and its opposition to violence as a solution (e.g., Caldwell 1995; Pewewardy 1995; Means 1995; Vincent 1995; cf. Strong 1996). Disney may have undercut those hopes, however, by presenting a saccharine-sweet romance with Pocahontas-as-babe and John Smith-as-clean-cut-blue-eyed-blonde-adventurer along with the usual overly cute anthropomorphized animals. *Pocahontas* exemplifies a body of work that Disney's many critics describe as "rife with sexism, racism, and a dumbed-down, cheered-up vision of American history and folklore" (Associated Press 1995:2A).

The merchandising of the film certainly maintains that standard, and has been criticized (gently) even in the popular press (e.g., McNichol 1995). The 1996 Academy Awards ceremony even featured a jab, in Nathan Lane's joke about a "Pocahontas home-pregnancy-test." Television commercials produced under license by Burger King—and aired even before the film opened—showed adventurous (and mostly white) boys emulating Smith by climbing on rocks and trees, and girls (again mostly white) playing quietly with their dolls. A veritable flood of products featuring Pocahontas was unleashed, from girls' makeup kits to paper plates and napkins to imprinted bandages and toothbrushes. Promotional candy packages were also licensed for Sweet-Tarts and Nestlé's chocolate, featuring images that are redolent of unequivocal trust and good will.

These products emanate not from a love of Native culture, or of material culture, or even of such general principles as Truth, Knowledge, or Goodness. The objects exist to sell the film, and the film exists to sell the objects. These are virtually pure commodities, with little embedded social meaning. What meaning is there is carefully calculated to be inoffensive (to those who share a particular set of values and beliefs): boisterous good nature, in a male, is good; seriousness is undesirable; fat people are evil, or at least insensitive; Native women are acceptable, if they're beautiful, but Native men are generally dangerous; history is a simple battle of obvious good and equally obvious evil; and so on. By extension into the realm of product marketing, candy, fast food, and breakfast cereal, makeup (for girls), and hygiene are all positively valued. Even more highly valued is artwork, the unique product of skilled (Disney) hands. An auction of 289 animation cells from the film brought over $750,000 from people who can now hang a piece of Pocahontas on their walls (Sotheby's 1996a, 1996b). Disney did at least donate the proceeds from this sale to a good cause, however: the National Museum of the American Indian and the Southwest Museum (*Elmira Star-Gazette* 1996)—an example from Disney CEO Michael Eisner of how corporate wealth is willing to help the less fortunate, perhaps. In this Disney-Pocahontas value system some products are unquestionably evil, however. A political cartoon by Pulitzer Prize winner Joel Pett (*Lexington Herald-Leader*, July 28, 1995) showed a tobacco executive exclaiming over a campaign for "Smokahontas": "I love it, but Disney will never sell the rights. . . ." The irony is that tobacco is a product that Pocahontas would actually have had some familiarity with—although its Native use was so different from ours as to render it essentially a different product.

I don't want to argue that *Pocahontas* and the other Disney products force us to see things in these ways. No propaganda is that effective. But I think there can be no question that this is the kind of worldview Disney is presenting, and the success of Disney products indicates the level of acceptance of these ideas. Just as earlier mythic Pocahontases were used to present selected values of their times, so too does Disney's. She has been adapted as a possibility for race relations to civilize the Indian, as a totem of Southern culture, as an emblem of a romanticized dying Indian culture, as an icon of Otherness, and now as a multicultural ambassador of rampant consumerism.

While each of these various adaptations can be criticized from other perspectives, the real problem with all of these mythic Pocahontases is that they obscure the original. Pocahontas was a real person, who acted in significant ways within a particular cultural context. Unlike, for example, the myth of George Washington and the cherry tree, the Pocahontas myth has been created by and for people who have absolutely no understanding of her culture. It has little relation to its historical model. And despite the accompanying historical myth of their disappearance, Native Americans and their cultures still survive today, their lives partly shaped by the myth-based perceptions of Euro-Americans. Eastern tribes now seeking recognition, including the Powhatans, can testify to the extent that we refuse to recognize them as living peoples. The myths we have made and are making of their past are a central component of our denial of their present, and future.

Notes

When I began working with Ray Fogelson as a graduate student in 1986, I gradually became more sensitive to the intricate interrelationships of Powhatan history, American founding myth, and marketing. One of the first things I noticed in his office was a wonderful poster questioning the use of Native images by sports teams, and I began thinking about these appropriations. Having grown up in central Virginia, visited the Powhatan reservations there many times as a child, and seen newspaper photographs each Thanksgiving of Powhatans presenting a deer and a turkey to the governor, I was aware of some of their public representations. Ray's classic study of Indians and their representations at the Chicago World's Fair (Fogelson 1991) was a shaping factor for part of this work. But far more important were the sorts of influences not regularly cited in scholarly literature: casual conversations over lunches and dinners; discussion of news and current events; comments and suggestions on books, old and new, while sitting amidst his library. Few people today have Ray's breadth and depth of knowledge concerning ethnohistory and Native North Americans, and it was insights drawn from those informal interactions, more than any formal teaching or scholarly product, that really shaped and guided my work—and continue to do so. A direct outgrowth of these interactions, this chapter deals with the various ways people have employed and reconstructed recorded histories.

Versions of this chapter were presented at the Northeastern Anthropological Association meeting in 1996 and the Thirtieth Algonquian Conference in 1998, and I thank those in attendance at those meetings for their comments. I have tried to add important references published since this was written—given the delay in publication, there are several—but may not have caught everything. I apologize for those I may have missed.

1. I use the word *myth* ambivalently in this paper. Scholars recognize myths as fundamental components of culture, basic truths that shape the ways people think. The veracity of these truths is not generally a matter for questioning. In popular usage, however, myth denotes something untrue. Here I argue that the developed Pocahontas story is mythic in both senses: untrue to the original history but nevertheless fundamentally related to certain aspects of American worldview.

2. I use the name Pocahontas here because that is how she was commonly called at the time, and that is the name caught up in the myth. The naming system of the Powhatans allowed for multiple names; her other recorded names were Matoaka and Amonute. Upon her conversion to Christianity she was renamed Rebecca.

3. Barbour provides both an extensive biography drawn principally from Smith's accounts (1964) and a brief summary of his life (Barbour 1986, 1:lv–lxi).

4. By the certain genealogy, her son, Thomas Rolfe, had a daughter, Jane Rolfe, who had a son, John Bolling. Bolling had a son and five daughters. The next generation saw 53 children born, the next 174, and so forth (Robertson 1887). The 1985 listing (Brown, Myers, and Chappel 1985) includes over 300 pages of certain descendants, plus another branch of probable relations. The total number of relatives indexed was over 18,000, and an additional 1000 or more were added in the next supplement (Brown, Myers, and Chappel 1987).

5. Since this was written, Ann Uhry Abrams has published *The Pilgrims and Pocahontas: Rival Myths of American Origin* (1999). This important book compares the histories of these American origin stories in great detail, and I refer interested readers there.

6. Barbour (1986, 1:lxxi–lxxii; 1986, 2:487–88) gives the publication history of the *Generall Historie*.

7. The first volume was published in 1804, the second and third in 1805. A fourth volume, finished by two other authors, was produced by a different printer in 1816.

8. Friar and Friar (1972:22–24) note a consequence of this outpouring: "As with any story too often repeated, Pocahontas was finally reduced to burlesque and satire with John Broughman's *Po-Ka-Hon-Tas; or, The Gentle Savage* (c. 1855), which contained such characters as O-Po-Dil-Doo and Col-O-Gog."

9. As all Virginians know, the first "thanksgiving" by English colonists in the New World was in Virginia, years before there was a colony at Plymouth. Of course, thanksgiving was a regular feature of Native American traditions, so it can hardly be seen as a Euro-American innovation.

10. See Lemay 1992 for the most recent presentation of this evidence. Rountree (1990:38–39) has argued against accepting Smith's account, but I question the argument (Gleach 1997a:118–119).

11. The origins of these reservations, Pamunkey and Mattaponi, can be traced to a 1646 treaty, making them at least among the earliest in North America. Neither they nor any Powhatan tribe has yet been recognized by the federal government. However, Pamunkey and Mattaponi have been recognized by the state of Virginia all along, and other nonreservation communities have recently gained state recognition. Pursuit of federal recognition has been considered at several times in the past century, and it may yet come to pass.

12. Hampton Roads, the broad area at the mouth of the James River, had been the scene of the historic naval battle between the *Monitor* and the *Virginia* in the Civil War (*Merrimac* was the original name of the ship on whose hull was constructed the Confederate ironclad; the ironclad was commissioned as the *Virginia*). The land where the exposition was held is now part of the Norfolk Naval Base Complex.

13. Actually an intervention in ongoing struggles for independence from Spain at a moment when some of those struggles were on the verge of success, the war was urged by William Randolph Hearst and others with economic and political interests in colonial expansion. It resulted in the United States controlling Cuba, Puerto Rico, the Philippines, and, less directly, Hawaii. The many interesting relationships between U.S. Indian policy (and practice) and this Caribbean expansion will be developed in a future work.

14. Gleach 2003b offers a more detailed analysis that focuses solely on the 1907 exposition and the ways in which the Powhatans, the state of Virginia, and the United States sought to represent themselves.

15. The cup shown in Figure 1, with a portrait of Pocahontas, has a general view of

the fair on its reverse. Paired portrait vignettes of Pocahontas and Capt. John Smith were featured on many items, and some showed the "rescue" itself. There were several songs composed for the fair, including "Dearest Pocahontas, Her Wooing by John Rolfe" (words by Jack Roberts, music by E. K. Heyser; shown in Friar and Friar 1972:18).

16. An extensive but still incomplete chronological list of Pocahontas-related materials compiled by Edward J. Gallagher is available on the Internet at http://www.lehigh.edu/ ejg1/ pocahontas/poca-cal.html.

17. Not only Indians can be Others, of course. While Native writers and many scholars have focused on that construction, others have seen in Pocahontas an exemplar of male domination of women and appropriation of their power (e.g., Robertson 1996).

18. These suggestions of sexual relations and accusations of rape may tell us a good deal about the cultural scene in the United States in the late twentieth century, but any knowledge of the culture of the time would dispel such notions. It is not that there was less sexual activity or better "family values" in the past. Smith, or any other colonist, could possibly have had sexual relations or conceivably even raped some Powhatan women—but not Pocahontas or others they perceived as royalty. The point cannot be made too firmly: at the beginning of the seventeenth century, the fact that a woman was only 12 or 13 years old, that she might not consent, or that she was ethnically different might be no impediment to such relations, but the class difference between commoner and royalty would effectively render them unthinkable. For evidence that the English colonists were, in fact, interested in sexual relations with Powhatan women, see Gleach (1995:121).

19. There had been earlier films of the Pocahontas story. Hilger (1995) lists two silent films: Edison's *Pocahontas, A Child of the Forest* (1908) and Thanhouser's *Pocahontas* (1910). Gallagher (2001) adds the later *Pocahontas and John Smith* (1924), in the Universal Studios "Hysterical History Comedies" series, and United Artists' *Captain John Smith and Pocahontas: A Legend* (1953), as well as a 1923 Yale University Press Film, *Chronicles of America: Jamestown*. It is notable that many of the early silent films about Indians revolved around the love of an Indian woman for a white man.

20. In another significant first for Disney, the Pocahontas premiere was the first event ever held on the Great Lawn of Central Park to require tickets. Previous events, some with twice the audience, were open to the public on a first-come, first-served basis (Lee 1995:46).

21. Even *Pocahontas II: Journey to a New World*, released straight to video in 1998, completely avoids the subject of her conversion. Although never released in theaters, the animation quality of the sequel is on a par with the original, and most of the original voice artists returned. The story, however, has even less relationship to the documented history than its predecessor, and there is an even greater reliance on animated-animal silliness and the same reductionist caricatures in place of characters. However, the video does include, in small print near the end of the closing credits, a note suggesting that viewers interested in the story of the real Pocahontas consult the American Library Association Web site or their local library—and in that note specifically mentions her religious conversion.

References

Abrams, Ann Uhry
  1999 The Pilgrims and Pocahontas: Rival Myths of American Origin. Boulder CO: Westview Press.
Accorsi, William
  1992 My Name Is Pocahontas. New York: Holiday House.

Allen, Michael, Jane Furse, and Paul Schwartzman

    1995 Multitudes Turn Out for the Big Powwow. New York Daily News, June 11:4–5.

Associated Press

    1995 Disney Depiction of Life Has Critics Up in Arms. Elmira Star-Gazette, August 6: 2A.

Barbour, Philip L.

    1964 The Three Worlds of Captain John Smith. Boston: Houghton Mifflin.

Barbour, Philip L., ed.

    1986 The Complete Works of Captain John Smith (1580–1631). Chapel Hill: University of North Carolina Press.

Barth, John

    1960 The Sot-weed Factor. Garden City NY: Doubleday.

Bernard, Jami

    1995 Flick All Right, Politics All Left. New York Daily News, June 11:4.

Beverley, Robert

    1947[1705] The History and Present State of Virginia. Louis B. Wright, ed. Chapel Hill: University of North Carolina Press.

Brougham, John

    [c. 1855] Po-ca-hon-tas, or The Gentle Savage: In Two Acts. New York: S. French.

Brown, Stuart E., Jr., Lorraine F. Myers, and Eileen M. Chappel

    1985 Pocahontas' Descendants: A Revision, Enlargement, and Extension of the List as Set Out by Wyndham Robertson in His Book Pocahontas and Her Descendants (1887). Berryville VA: Pocahontas Foundation.

    1987 Pocahontas' Descendants: Supplement. Berryville VA: Pocahontas Foundation.

Burk, John

    1804–5 The History of Virginia, from Its First Settlement to the Present Day. 3 volumes. Petersburg VA: Dickson and Pescud.

Caldwell, E. K.

    1995 Indian Summer Comes Early at the Movies. News from Indian Country 9(15):24–25.

Commemorating the Event of the First Permanent English Settlement in America, 1607. Jamestown Exposition, May 1st to Nov. 1st 1907.

    n.d. [c. 1905] . Norfolk VA: W. T. Barron & Co.

Custis, George Washington Parke

    1803 Pocahontas, or the Settlers of Virginia, a National Drama, in Three Acts. Philadelphia: C. Alexander.

Daly, Michael

    1995 For Her, Disney Magic. New York Daily News, June 11:5.

Davis, John

    1805 Captain Smith and Princess Pocahontas. Philadelphia: T. C. Plowman.

Donnell, Susan

    1991 Pocahontas. New York: Berkley Books.

Ellis, Edward S.

    [c. 1910] Pocahontas: A Princess of the Woods. New York: McLoughlin Brothers.

Elmira Star-Gazette

    1996 "Pocahontas" Auction Raises $755,320. Elmira Star-Gazette, February 25:7A.

Feest, Christian

    1990 Pride and Prejudice: The Pocahontas Myth and the Pamunkey. *In* The Invented In-

dian: Cultural Fictions and Government Policies. James A. Clifton, ed. New Brunswick
NJ: Transaction Publishers.

Friar, Ralph, and Natasha Friar

1972 The Only Good Indian . . . The Hollywood Gospel. New York: Drama Book Specialists.

Gallagher, Edward J.

2001 A Calendar of Pocahontas Materials. Online publication, available at http://www.le
high.edu/ ejg1/pocahontas/poca-cal.html.

Gleach, Frederic W.

1995 Mimesis, Play, and Transformation in Powhatan Ritual. *In* Papers of the Twenty-
sixth Algonquian Conference. David Pentland, ed. Pp. 114–123. Winnipeg: University
of Manitoba.

1996 Controlled Speculation: Interpreting the Saga of Pocahontas and Captain John
Smith. *In* Reading Beyond Words: Contexts for Native History. Jennifer S. H. Brown
and Elizabeth Vibert, eds. Pp. 21–42. Peterborough ON: Broadview Press.

1997a Powhatan's World and Colonial Virginia: A Conflict of Cultures. Lincoln: University of Nebraska Press.

1997b Race, Culture, and Anthropology: The Powhatan Indians in Virginia. Paper presented at the Ninth Conference of North American and Cuban Philosophers and Social
Scientists, Havana, Cuba.

1997c History and Anthropology: Frank Speck in Virginia, 1914–1950. Paper presented at the Northeastern Anthropological Association annual meeting, Montebello,
Quebéc.

2003a Controlled Speculation and Constructed Myths: The Saga of Pocahontas and Captain John Smith. *In* Reading Beyond Words: Contexts for Native History. Jennifer S.
H. Brown and Elizabeth Vibert, eds. Pp. 39–74. Peterborough ON: Broadview Press.

2003b Pocahontas at the Fair: Crafting identities at the 1907 Jamestown Exposition.
Ethnohistory 50(3):419–445.

Graham, Shirley

1953 The Story of Pocahontas. New York: Grosset & Dunlap.

Green, Rayna

1975 The Pocahontas Perplex: The Image of Indian Women in American Culture. Massachusetts Review 16(4):698–714.

Hamor, Raphe [Ralph]

1615 A True Discourse of the Present Estate of Virginia, and the Successe of the Affaires
There till the 18 of June. 1614. Facsimile reprint 1860. Albany: J. Munsell.

Henry, William Wirt

1882 The Settlement at Jamestown, with Particular Reference to the Late Attacks upon
Captain John Smith, Pocahontas, and John Rolfe. Richmond: Virginia Historical Society.

Hilger, Michael

1995 From Savage to Nobleman: Images of Native Americans in Film. Metuchen NJ:
Scarecrow Press

Illustrated Souvenir: Jamestown Ter-centennial Exposition

[c. 1907] Norfolk: Seaboard Publishing Co.

Jamestown-Williamsburg-Yorktown Celebration Commission [JWYCC]

1958 The 350th Anniversary of Jamestown, 1607–1957: Final Report to the President
and Congress. Washington DC: U.S. Government Printing Office.

Kidwell, Clara Sue

    1992 Indian Women as Cultural Mediators. Ethnohistory 39(2):97–107.

Latané, Lawrence III

    1995 Indian Tribes Begin the Process of Seeking Federal Recognition: It's for Scholarships, They Say, Not Casinos. Richmond Times-Dispatch, June 1, 1995:B1, B6.

    1996a Indian Campsites Uncovered: They May Provide Clues on Life in Early Virginia. Richmond Times-Dispatch, May 27, 1996:B1, B5.

    1996b "They Will Kill This River": Reservoir Proposal Doesn't Sit Well with Native Tribes. Richmond Times-Dispatch, December 8, 1996:C1, C6.

Lee, Felicia R.

    1995 Behind Premiere: Kvetchland, Permitland, and Moneyland. New York Times, June 11:45–46.

Lemay, J. A. Leo.

    1992 Did Pocahontas Save Captain John Smith? Athens: University of Georgia Press.

MacDonald, Heidi

    1995 The Making of Pocahontas. Disney Adventures 5(10):26–33.

Maslin, Janet

    1995 A Fairy Tale History, Glorious Color, Anthropomorphic Critters and All. New York Times, June 11:46.

McNichol, Tom

    1995 Pushing Pocahontas. USA Weekend, June 9–11:1, 4–5.

Means, Russell

    1995 "Pocahontas" Is an Important and Historic Achievement. News from Indian Country 9(14):26.

Mooney, James

    1907 The Powhatan Confederacy, Past and Present. American Anthropologist n.s. 9(1): 129–152.

Owen, Robert Dale

    1837 Pocahontas: A Historical Drama. New York: George Dearborn.

Pewewardy, Cornel

    1995 "Pocahontas": The White Man's Indian. News from Indian Country 9(14):31.

Reynolds, Cuyler

    1909 New York at the Jamestown Exposition: Norfolk, Virginia, April 16 to December 1, 1907. Albany: J. B. Lyon Co.

Robertson, Karen

    1996 Pocahontas at the Masque. Signs 21(3):551–583.

Robertson, Wyndham

    1887 Pocahontas, Alias Matoaka, and Her Descendants through Her Marriage at Jamestown, Virginia, in April, 1614, with John Rolfe, Gentleman. Richmond VA: J. W. Randolph & English.

Rountree, Helen C.

    1990 Pocahontas's People: The Powhatan Indians of Virginia through Four Centuries. Norman: University of Oklahoma Press.

Seymour, Flora Warren

    1961 Pocahontas: Brave Girl. Indianapolis: Bobbs-Merrill Co.

Sherman, Richard B.

    1988 "The Last Stand": The Fight for Racial Integrity in Virginia in the 1920s. Journal of Southern History 54:69–92.

Sigourney, Lydia H.

1841 Pocahontas, and Other Poems. New York: Harper & Brothers.

Slosson, Edwin E.

1907 Round about Jamestown. The Independent 63(3059):123–129.

Smith, Captain John

1986 [1624] The Generall Historie of Virginia, New-England, and the Summer Isles. The Complete Works of Captain John Smith (1580–1631). Vol. 2. Philip L. Barbour, ed. Chapel Hill: University of North Carolina Press.

Smith, Seba

1841 Powhatan; a Metrical Romance, in Seven Cantos. New York: Harper & Brothers.

Sotheby's

1996a The Art of Disney's Pocahontas; Sale 6811 [auction catalog]. New York: Sotheby's.

1996b Pocahontas Triumphantly Returns to New York City. Press release.

Speck, Frank G.

1925 The Rappahannock Indians of Virginia. Indian Notes and Monographs 5(3). New York: Museum of the American Indian, Heye Foundation.

1928 Chapters on the Ethnology of the Powhatan Tribes of Virginia. Indian Notes and Monographs 1(5). New York: Museum of the American Indian, Heye Foundation.

Stern, Theodore

1951 Pamunkey Pottery Making. Southern Indian Studies 3. Chapel Hill: Archaeological Society of North Carolina.

Stith, William

1865[1747] The History of the First Discovery and Settlement of Virginia. New York: Joseph Sabin.

Strong, Pauline Turner

1996 Animated Indians: Critique and Contradiction in Commodified Children's Culture. Cultural Anthropology 11(3):405–424.

Swem, Earl Gregg, ed.

1957 The Jamestown 350th Anniversary Historical Booklets. 23 volumes. Williamsburg: Virginia 350th Anniversary Celebration Corp.

Syracuse Herald-American

1996 "Pocahontas" Bounds into Stores. STARS [Sunday supplement], Syracuse Herald-American, March 3:13.

Tilton, Robert S.

1994 Pocahontas: The Evolution of an American Narrative. Cambridge: Cambridge University Press.

Vadeboncouer, Joan

1995 Pocahontas: Disney Animators Fiddle with History in the Name of Romance. STARS, Syracuse Herald American, June 18:17, 21.

Vincent, Mal

1995 Preview: "Pocahontas." Online publication, available at http://www.pilotonline.com/movies/mv0620poc.html.

Waldron, William Watson

1841 Pocahontas, Princess of Virginia, and Other Poems. New York: Dean & Trevett.

Ward, Christopher

1928 The Saga of Cap'n John Smith [. . .]. New York: Harper & Brothers.

Waugaman, Sandra F., and Danielle Moretti-Langholtz
  2000 We're Still Here: Contemporary Virginia Indians Tell Their Stories. Richmond VA:
    Palari Publishing.
Wilkie, Katherine E.
  1969 Pocahontas: Indian Princess. Middletown CT: American Education Publications.

19. "I'm an Old Cowhand on the Banks of the Seine"

Representations of Indians and *Le Far West* in Parisian
Commercial Culture

MICHAEL E. HARKIN

What is it about Indians and the American West that has made them such
an enduring source of European iconography? Christian Feest, addressing
this "strange fact" clearly locates it in the realm of cultural imagination
(Feest 1987a:1, 1987b:609). Excluding colonization by Euro-Americans,
face-to-face relations between Europeans and Indians have always been
extremely rare. Although the individual examples of Indians in Europe
(Pocahontas in London; the Bella Coola in Germany; the Lakota, Arapahoe, and other Indian members of Buffalo Bill's Wild West Show in
Europe) are intriguing, in the end they do not amount to much. Indians in
Europe are, even today, so rare that they often acquire a sort of celebrity
status (Deloria 1981; Feest 1987b; Haberland 1987). The roots of their
importance in the European imagination cannot be the product of any
pragmatic linkage. Rather, it is in the realm of cultural production that
we must locate the phenomenon.

Long an element in popular and literary imagination, from the time of
the DeBry's *Grand Voyages* (in the sixteenth and seventeenth centuries) to
Voltaire's *Candide* (in the eighteenth) to Chateaubriand's *Les Natchez* (in
the nineteenth), "la grande nature sauvage" of the uncolonized parts of
North America has been attractive to literate French women and men. As
the eastern parts of North America have been settled by Euro-Americans
since the eighteenth century (much to the dismay of Chateaubriand, who
met a French dancing master in the woods of upstate New York), and have
become familiar to most French people, the lands west of the Mississippi,
excluding the coast, remain a vast negative space, called "le Far West."
This space is only loosely speaking a geographical territory. Far more,
it is a mental construct with great resonance not only for the French
but for many Europeans and Americans (including some who live in the

West itself). This great negativity, in which culture is replaced by nature, European races by Amerindian ones, is a structure of French culture of *la longue durée*. The question I will look at is not the origins but the recent history of this idea. Why has it been so thoroughly deployed in the past ten years in certain areas of Paris, such as, notably, Saint Germain des Prés? What does this signify about the historical moment in which the French find themselves?

Saint Germain des Prés

Saint Germain des Prés is one of the oldest quarters in Paris. It is the heart of the Left Bank *sixième arrondissement*, which includes the Sorbonne and many other educational and training facilities. Just to the south, within the *sixième*, is Luxembourg Gardens, which is home to the Sénat. But above all, Saint Germain des Prés is associated with France's major cultural industries: literature, art, and film. Much more than any comparable place in the United States, Paris represents a centralization of all the functions of state and civilization. According to the logic of the specialization, this area of Paris is the center of matters educational and cultural (see Rabinow 1995:244–250). In the 1920s the bohemian artistic crowd, which included expatriates such as Ernest Hemingway, James Joyce, Sylvia Beach, and Gertrude Stein, began to migrate north from Montparnasse to frequent cafes such as Les Deux Magots and Café de Flore. By the 1950s important literary and intellectual circles, such as the one centered around Simone de Beauvoir and Jean-Paul Sartre, regularly met at these cafes. Numerous ateliers produce painting, sculpture, and decorative arts. Recently, the opening of the Musée d'Orsay has fortified Saint Germain des Prés's centrality in the visual arts. In addition, the film industry is located there. The famous Brasserie Lipp is home to actors and producers and serves as a venue for making film deals (Jay 1992). The inhabitants of Saint Germain des Prés are nothing if not cosmopolitan (Hannerz 1990).

Although not the wealthiest area of Paris, Saint Germain des Prés is wealthy enough. It boasts numerous chic boutiques, especially along the Boulevard Saint Germain and in the medieval market around the Rue de Buci. With all these attractions, it is an obvious tourist destination. The presence of tourists increases the wealth, and supports far more commercial establishments than could otherwise survive. Moreover, the tourist presence shapes the presentation of commodities in Saint Germain des Prés, as the area strives self-consciously to become what is expected of it. Tourists are practicing Platonists, who seek the ideal essence of a place (Harkin 1995).

All this has caused Saint Germain des Prés to become a sort of simulacrum of itself, as it strives for more "authenticity" through representational practices. A case in point is the famous restaurant Le Procope, which is advertised as the oldest continuously operating restaurant in Paris. Founded in 1686 as an Italian coffeehouse, and boasting Voltaire and Napoleon Bonaparte among its clientele, it was renovated in 1989 in "18th-century style" (with upgrades to the anachronistic plumbing and kitchen equipment included in the "restoration" project). Tourists need multiple signs of authenticity to be convinced they are in the "right place" to experience "eighteenth centuryness," or whatever quality they seek. This semiotic redundancy takes priority over other measures of authenticity, such as material continuity (Bruner 1994).[1]

Le Far West Comes to Saint Germain des Prés

This process, by which commercial sites are restored or reconstructed to become more like themselves, or what they "should" be, is the normal state of affairs. The semiotic and commercial reasons for such representational practices are quite clear and well known. However, the appearance of "le Far West" motif disturbs this simple relation between representation and tradition. There are, as far as I know, no authentic cowboys living in Saint Germain des Prés, nor is there much historical connection between France and the southern part of the American West most associated with such themes. And yet, during the spring of 1995, I counted 11 businesses with a permanent Far Western theme, and another 14 with temporary displays (e.g., window dressings, sidewalk displays) reflecting this theme.

This does not count the most famous such Parisian establishment, the Crazy Horse Saloon, which is located on the Right Bank near the Champs Elysées. Obviously, an "authentic" cowboy bar or Tex-Mex restaurant is an impossibility in Paris. Rather, the proliferation of such establishments played off three themes associated in the French mind with *le Far West*: nature as opposed to culture, American Indians as opposed to Europeans, and egalitarianism as opposed to hierarchy.

The first thing to keep in mind is that *le Far West* is not really a geographic territory but an imaginary geography. Many French are serenely unconcerned with the actualities of North American geography. Nor is this limited to commercial culture. In the North American hall of the old Musée de l'Homme a map was provided to locate tribal territories. No state boundaries were indicated (playing off fantasies of a largely uncolonized continent), but certain major cities were mentioned. On this map Chicago is located at the headwaters of the Arkansas River (i.e., in western Colorado).[2] Similarly, Chateaubriand placed a character viewing the Appalachians from the banks of the Mississippi in his essay "Natchez." It is hardly surprising, then, that "western" bars called "Le Tennessee" (playing primarily on the sonority of the Cherokee name and perhaps secondarily on the association with country and western music) and "Indiana Café" are to be found in Saint Germain des Prés. Such American placenames constitute a redundant semiotic system that refers uniformly to this Rousseauian idea of America as land of nature and natural man.[3] As Tzvetan Todorov describes it, with reference to Chateaubriand,

> The West (America) is nature; the East is culture. There are human beings in America, of course, but they are savages who live in a state of nature scarcely distinguishable from the global natural cycle, whereas on the other side of the ocean we encounter a fundamentally human world. [Todorov 1993:284]

In the modern version, this mythic place is one in which nature is always waiting to be "tamed" by nineteenth-century technology. The cowboy is integral to this image. One boutique, near the Odéon, specializes in the material culture of the working cowboy. Lariats, boots, spurs, saddles, rifles—all antique or heavily used—are material signs of this struggle against a harsh natural environment. Another boutique, on the Boulevard Saint Michel, has a sidewalk display of "dusters," the long-skirted raincoats worn by working ranchers, made both of traditional oilskin and very expensive leather (imagine mending fences wearing that!). Sadly, I never saw anyone wearing such a coat, which would have been quite a sight in the small confined spaces of a Left Bank cafe.

Numerous stores sold cowboy hats, boots and, of course, denim jeans. The latter were advertised not as the universal uniform of the student but as the apparel of the working cowboy. In certain boutiques one can purchase Levi Strauss blue jeans that have allegedly been worn by cowboys. An outlet near my Wyoming home indeed purchases used Levi's, although they have been worn more by students than working cowboys. However, they are shipped off to New York and Europe with the imprimatur of Wyoming, the "Cowboy State."[4] Boutiques with names like "Western House," "Spirit of the West," "Marlboro Collection" (evoking the well-known cigarette advertising campaign), "La Guardia Boots" (the name of the departure point for many Frenchmen and women into the western United States), and "Santa Fe" (the name of a trail, a city, and a railroad that embody the Old Southwest) all specialize in the rugged clothing and accessories required perhaps by working cowboys but certainly not by Parisians.

All of these items—dusters, cowboy hats and boots, and denim trousers
—are obviously designed to insulate the working rancher from the harsh
elements. They, like the cowboy himself, are the margin between nature
and culture. It is an image widely accepted in the West itself and ludically
represented in the sport of rodeo (Lawrence 1982). The most famous image of all, and the one that encapsulates this ethos, is the "bucking bronc"
with rider hanging on for dear life. A central rodeo event, the bucking
bronc represents the taming of wild nature or, more precisely, a space of
free play between nature and culture. Both bronc and rider are marginal
beings drawn together in a temporary and violent interface (Lawrence
1982:145–151). This event has its origins in the breaking of wild horses
that roamed the Plains before widespread European settlement, and even
remain today in isolated herds. These mustangs are plainly symbolic of
nature free and wild (Lawrence 1982:136).

In Saint Germain des Prés images of bucking broncs abound. At Le
Tennessee, a western-themed bar, a large (and quite beautiful—this being
Saint-Germain-des-Prés, an area of art schools and ateliers) mural of a
bucking bronc decorates the building front. Several *objets d'art* on that
theme are displayed in nearby shop windows. Most surprising of all to
me, who had made the long trip from Wyoming, was an old Wyoming
license plate bearing the famous image of the bucking bronc, symbol of the
state (and recently copyrighted by the state, I understand). Monumental
bronze statues of this image ornament the University of Wyoming campus
and the state capitol in Cheyenne, serving as a totem for both university
and state.

The French use of these images is in fact little different from their meaning in American culture: as myths of a mythical landscape that can never
be exactly located in space or time and that dramatize a central theme
of Western (in the broader sense) humanism. Of course, American geographical knowledge of their own country is better on average than French
people's, but even for Americans the actual location of that mythic space
("Marlboro Country") is quite vague. The transnational appropriation of
this mytheme of human control of nature is far from new, and it is a mark
of genetic kinship between French and American culture, even while it
mystifies that kinship.

An integral part of this mythic landscape is the American Indian. The
Indian is, like nature, assumed to be both noble and savage. Thus, for
Claude Lévi-Strauss, the Indian is uniquely attuned to nature and can per-
ceive that which is imperceptible to Europeans (Lévi-Strauss 1966:222;
Fabian 1983:91). In children's literature and film, Indians are invariably
tricksters. Their very closeness to physical nature allows them to out-

wit European adults. Indians are often represented as children, as in the comic book series *Les Petites Plumes* ("little feathers," that is, Indian children). Thus, they are not only united with European children in a pre-socialized developmental stage but represent the childhood of the species, as Rousseau and his many (mis)interpreters at times suggest (Berkhofer 1978:49; Deloria 1998:106–107).

Indians are not merely outside culture but at times actively oppose it. They may be a symbol of defiance and rebellion. In the early twentieth century, a group of French avant-garde composers, including Maurice Ravel and Gabriel Fauré, called themselves "Les Apaches." Though rooted in the actual historical Apache resistance, this heroic image was a generalized one. Using the symbolic vehicle of the Indian, one may stand outside of civilized society and throw rocks, much as Rousseau did with his concept of natural man. The Indian is the purest example of the "savage slot," to borrow Trouillot's coinage: positioned outside society but appropriated into, and indeed existing for the benefit of, Western utopian discourse (Deloria 1998:154–180; Trouillot 1991).

Mythic Indians can thus be threatening, like nature. However, real contemporary Indians, those on the inside who inhabit a cultural space shared by the French themselves, are seen as degraded. Like Chateaubriand in New York, the French generally look with disfavor on Indians who have been touched by European culture (which is, by now, all of them) (Todorov 1993:285). Lévi-Strauss rues the degradation that ensues when primitive and modern cultures come into contact (Lévi-Strauss 1976:360; Todorov 1993:71).[5] This cultural entropy, first described in 1855 by the nineteenth-century racialist philosopher Gobineau (Todorov 1993:137–140) creates a paradox. The closer a European culture comes to understanding a primitive culture the less worthy the latter is of being known (Lévi-Strauss 1977:33–34). As Todorov states the matter: "The best candidates for the role of exotic ideal are the people and cultures that are most remote from us and are least known to us" (Todorov 1993:265). This condition makes it impossible to positively value contemporary tribal peoples who do not live up to the ideals of their own imagined golden age. This posture denies "coevalness," as Fabian describes it, to the "savage" other (Fabian 1983).[6] In Saint Germain des Prés the Indiana Café, which trades on the connotations rather than denotation of its name, strives to be the most "authentic" of all the western bars. The decor is an elaborate essay on the theme of images of the Indian, almost museological in its scope. There we find authentic Indian artifacts, including a feathered headdress, along with portraits of Indian chiefs, finely carved wooden busts of Indians, cigar store Indians, and old Santa Fe Railroad posters depicting Indians and the Southwest. Most of the artifacts straddle the border between kitsch and cultural history—many were commercially manufactured by non-Indians or eastern groups such as the Cherokee. Nevertheless, the underlying principle of collection is clearly focused upon the image of the noble savage.[7]

These "Western bars," often called "Tex-Mex" (a term assimilated into French and referring to generic Mexican cuisine) are quite popular in Paris. Someone who frequents such establishments told me that although the food is poor the places are lively and populated especially by students. Though not all of them feature images of the American Indian so prominently, they all play on frontier nostalgia, with its idea of freedom from constraint. The beverage featured in these places is the margarita, a potent drink with famously uninhibiting qualities. It is a liquor associated with nature, symbolized by the partly dissolved worm found in bottles of "authentic" mezcal. The patrons of such establishments certainly appeared more free from normal social constraints than those at wine bars, brasseries, or traditional cafes. In part this was due to the fact that they were younger on average, but I think it clearly was related as well to the general ambience created by the decor, the drink, and the music (American pop and rock, rather than country and western, owing to the ubiquity of MTV).

The mythic American West is above all a space of freedom from constraint. Interesting in this connection is the mystification of the real relation between Indians, as aboriginal title holders to this space, and cowboys, who ultimately represented the territorial and economic interests of Euro-American society. Indeed, even before the arrival of whites to the Great Plains in significant numbers, territorial appropriations farther east made the lands west of the Mississippi contested territory among Indian tribes themselves. Thus space the right to which was (and remains to some degree) a highly contentious issue among different ethnic groups and economic interests (e.g., proletarian sheep ranchers versus aristocratic cattlemen and oligarchic railroad corporations) is transformed in myth to a space that is antithetical to the idea of bounded property itself: "Don't fence me in." By the same token, the cowhand, a subproletarian wage earner subject to the whims of cattle barons, is transformed into a symbol of freedom and empowerment.[8]

In all this the French conception does not differ in content significantly from American mythologizing. However, the position of this myth in French society is considerably different. French society is explicitly hierarchical and centralized. Everything of importance—government, education, culture, business—is centered in Paris, much of it in Saint Germain des Prés. In addition to these national structures, people feel much more strongly and permanently positioned by family, social circle, residence, and profession than do Americans, who are remarkably mobile (if they are less economically mobile than they like to think they are certainly mobile in terms of residence and occupation) (Carroll 1988:56; le Wita 1994). Although in neither society is the West an actual description of the way anyone lives, the idea of the West offers much more of a counterpoint to the French way of life than it does to the American.

Exoticism in French Thought

The hierarchical, centralized society of France contrasts with the egalitarian, diffuse ethos of the mythic American West. This is why this mythos has especially appealed to children and adolescents. They are less tied into hierarchical structures and are allowed a period of relative freedom before making permanent commitments to such structures. Games of cowboys and Indians, comic books, and other children's literature and film about the American West have long been a staple of French childhood.

The myth of the West is thus at one level a nostalgia for the freedom of youth, as well as for an imagined stage of cultural evolution. The present fascination with things western thus ties into the long tradition of French exoticism. Todorov defines exoticism as the simple inversion of cultural features of one's own society (Todorov 1993:265). Montaigne, the earliest of the French Renaissance writers to treat ethnographic evidence of primitive cultures from the Americas, sees his "cannibals" in purely negative terms:

> This is a nation, I should say to Plato, in which there is no sort of traffic, no knowledge of letters, no science of numbers, no name for a magistrate or for political superiority, no custom of servitude, no riches or poverty, no contracts, no successions, no partitions, no occupations but leisure ones, no care for any but common kinship, no clothes, no agriculture, no metal, no use of wine or wheat. [Todorov 1993:265]

This draws on an older rhetorical topos, the idea of the antipodes found in the writings of Mandeville and other medieval fantasists (see Greenblatt 1991:43–45). However, Montaigne's essay, though almost devoid of positive information about his "cannibals," is not absurd ethnographically and is based on accounts of actual groups by Lery and Thevet (see Lestrignant 1987). Moreover, while Mandeville's ridiculous tales are devoid of ethical or evaluative statements, Montaigne ultimately shows the "cannibals" in a positive light: "The very words that signify lying, treachery, dissimulation, avarice, envy, pardon—are unheard of" (Todorov 1993:265). Thus, Montaigne uses his "cannibals" rhetorically to critique his own society, painting a picture of a society nearly Edenic, surpassing all philosophers' accounts of a Golden Age (di Leonardo 1998:344; Todorov 1993:269).

This is not entirely original, for even Columbus viewed the continent of South America as Eden itself (Greenblatt 1991:78–79). Moreover, Montaigne had available to him a long tradition in Christian discourse of the noble pagan who puts the believers to shame, dating back to the gospel story of the Good Samaritan. He used the image of the cannibal to reflect back on his own society, wracked by civil war (Quint 1995). Montaigne, however, significantly extended this discourse of moral comparison by referring to cultural context. By deploying these topoi in a quasi-ethnographic rhetoric, Montaigne founded a new exoticist discourse that persists to this day (Todorov 1993:268).

The exotic Other in modern French discourse is thus a necessary companion to the domestic and familiar (see Said 1978:39–40). It allows a limited critique of one's own society. However, this critique is a peculiarly self-effacing one. This is seen especially clearly in the primitivist version of exoticism, wherein the possibility of ever adopting the practices of the Other is nonexistent. In Montaigne's formulation, the first and second parts of the quotation are connected almost syllogistically. That is to say, *if* one lived without clothing, metal, laws, and the like, *then* one could live free from envy, lying, treachery, and so forth. This has not been a possibility taken seriously by very many people (apart from periodic eruptions of political radicalism, most recently in 1968). In a sense, the image of the Other, insofar as it is an inversion of the self, reinforces the self-image. The relation between the two images is a dialectic without a synthesis.

Whatever ethical "lessons" may be learned from the Other, the most important lesson is one of identity. As Lévi-Strauss himself argues, actual contact between cultures is a "pollution" (Lévi-Strauss 1977:33). Though he had in mind the degradation of the "savage," the logical complement of that position is that we ourselves, the metropolitan Westerner, become degraded by such contact. Indeed, in Lévi-Strauss's great travelogue, *Tristes Tropiques*, all signs of Europeans in Amazonia are *a fortiori* signs of degradation (1977:157).

Not merely can exoticism coexist with nationalism, it is in many ways its natural complement. In celebrating the Other, one is always primarily concerned with defining the self. The importance of western and American Indian themes in popular German culture from the nineteenth-century through World War II is a topic for another day, but surely provides

sufficient proof that nationalism and primitivism are not mutually exclusive ideologies (Conrad 1987; Taylor 1988). In the United States, the
refinement of the notion of the primitive and the increasing sophistication
with which it was portrayed, in Buffalo Bill's Wild West Show and fairs
at Chicago and St. Louis, coincided with two other significant historical
developments of the turn of the century: the celebrated "closing" of the
frontier and the establishment of an overseas empire (Raibmon 2000).
All three of these trends intersect in the most important figure of the era,
Theodore Roosevelt.

Exoticism Today

In France of the recent past as in Germany in the 1920s, it is intriguing
that the efflorescence of the theme of American western primitivism has
coincided with the rise of far right political groups. Rather than view the
two phenomena as directly related, I believe both may be explained by
reference to many of the same conditions of French society in the 1980s
and 1990s. In a period of economic stagnation and permanently high
unemployment rates, which the French call *la crise* ("the crisis," although
it has been going on since the early 1970s), the ground is fertile for the
rise of far right groups; this much is evident (Serfaty 1993). It also has
meant a diminution of personal freedom, most obviously, economic freedom. Those without jobs have little disposable income, while those with
employment find themselves relatively powerless vis-à-vis their employer,
and have little career mobility. Students are forced to pursue studies purely
on the basis of job opportunities, and competition for spaces in those fields
has become intense (Brett 1992).

The absence of a dynamic entrepreneurial economy has meant that the
French largely missed out on the decentralizing effects of such development that Americans have enjoyed, such as small software and computer
firms, telecommuting, and the rise of self-employment in the professional
service sector. The net result for the French of two decades of *la crise*
has been to make them more dependent on the centralized, hierarchical
structures of government, large corporations, and state education. The
mythos of the American West appears more and more a perfect inversion
of French society.

At the same time, the position of France in the world has become considerably less central, which is worrying for a nation used to thinking of itself
as a sort of cultural omphalos. Most distressing is the decline of France
vis-à-vis the United States. The remarkable changes in Paris itself in recent
decades are a testament to increasing American hegemony. McDonald's

restaurants dot the landscape and are found in the most important places in the city: on the Champs d'Elysées, on the Boulevard Saint-Michel right outside the Sorbonne. Domino's Pizza delivery vehicles are omnipresent.[9] One can watch American television via cable. American pop music is the unanimous choice of the young. Indeed, they watch MTV on large-screened televisions in Indiana Cafe and other popular hangouts. Hollywood films increasingly take the place of original French films, and have pushed the French film industry itself in more commercial and American directions. And then, of course, there is Euro Disney.

The mythos of the American West satisfies a need to mystify rising American hegemony in France. If America can be imagined as a sparsely populated land of cowboys and Indians, the reality of American economic, cultural, and military domination of France since World War II can be temporarily forgotten. Moreover, as Said argues, exoticism is a means of asserting the superiority and dominance of the home culture, even when it is the exotic Other that is being "celebrated" (Said 1978:39–40). For ultimately, the home culture controls the relationship, exercising a connoisseurship that is also a type of judgment. The metropolitan elite can thus set rules for what are acceptable and unacceptable tokens of recognized types, judgments that ultimately feed back into the consciousness of the Other. I have been told that Native people traveling in Europe are better accepted if they manifest some of the features associated with the stereotype of Indianness, for example, braids and turquoise jewelry.

Not merely the United States but Europe itself threatens the centrality, and even the integrity, of French culture. Under the Mitterrand and Chirac presidencies, the French allied their destiny with that of the European Community, under the assumption that France and Germany could join together to exert dominance over that institution and thus over Europe. With monetary union (and the rise in 2002 of the Euro above the level of the U.S. dollar), Europe has perhaps begun to assert the sort of political and economic hegemony once exercised exclusively by the United States. And still, no matter how great, this is not the same as French national power.

Other problems have faced the French nation. The greatest destabilizing force has been immigration, which, especially in the wake of the fall of the Soviet Empire, has become the central political issue in France. As various walls and fences fell and borders became open for the first time since World War II, hundreds of thousands of refugees and immigrants arrived in Western Europe. Although Germany has borne the brunt of this immigration, France, especially Paris, has been affected as well. The economic cost of integrating these East Europeans into western countries has been great.

Much greater has been the psychic cost of opening the borders. "Europe" as an imagined space of modern, secular, industrialized, democratic nation-states was no more. It had been replaced by a mental geography of peasant agriculture, ethnic tribalism, and holy war. Although the French, like most Europeans, romanticize their own agricultural roots and enjoy the picturesque qualities of ancient farms, the reality of displaced peasants is different in type from the appreciation of pastoral Burgundian countryside. The latter is an aesthetic construction, a moment of viewing things as they are not (for after all, agriculture is quite mechanized in France, although still less so than in the United States). The appearance of real peasants is an unwelcome intrusion of a harsh reality. As one French man told me in the mid-1990s, it was profoundly disturbing for him to realize that just a few hours' drive from the borders of France were the horrors of former Yugoslavia. These problems add to the longstanding issue of Arab immigration, which has taken on a new urgency in the context of post-9/11 terrorism.

In such a context, the need to re-create boundaries and a sense of identity is strong. What is lacking is a clear demarcation of Europe from its Other. Exoticism is, above all, a means for establishing such a demarcation (Said 1978:39–40). Though the popularity of the American West may seem an almost trivial epiphenomenon of late capitalism, it is a potent symbolic means of establishing an opposition between a wild west and a civilized Europe, banishing the wild within. Or better, channeling that wildness into certain culturally prescribed idioms, such as the Indian and the Cowboy.

The florescence of western themes in Saint Germain des Prés is above all a type of what Rosaldo (1989:68–70) calls "imperialist nostalgia": nostalgia for a period when France was the center of Europe and America was wilderness and nostalgia for the "sauvage" cultures displaced and transformed by European colonialism. With vivid and violent images of savagery available, it is more comforting to think of the noble savage as ancestor, or collateral kinsman. As Raymond Fogelson (1991) has argued with reference to Indians and the Chicago Columbian Exposition, it is at times of rapid historical change and political and social crisis that the symbolic power of Indians is deployed. Held a mere seven years after the Haymarket Square riots, during a period of high crime and labor unrest, the Columbian Exposition presented a triumphalist vision of westward expansion, of which the presence of Indian persons and artifacts was material proof (di Leonardo 1998:4–8). Despite the success of the exposition, it was followed by a renewed period of lawlessness and labor unrest, culminating in the literal destruction of the White City by roving gangs of the unemployed (Fogelson 1991:87). The exposition was obviously unsuccessful at banishing the demons of the 1890s. The assassination of Chicago Mayor Carter Harrison at the culmination of the exposition was merely one of a long line of acts of political violence in Chicago and other cities in the 1890s. Nevertheless, it managed in its representations of American and Canadian Indian cultures to construct a powerful symbolic argument about the ascendancy of the white man on the North American continent.[10]

In most ways the French representations of Indians are superficially different from those current in the United States one hundred years ago. They are nostalgic rather than forward looking and teleological. They use highly mediated symbols of Indians and the West, not living individuals and their productions. They celebrate the fictional dominance of the Indian in a West that is imaginary, rather than the real decline of the Indian in a "real West." However, the underlying dynamic is identical. During periods of rapid change and dislocation, fears, hopes, and aspirations are projected onto an Other, who presents a convenient vehicle for thinking about Self. Popular representations of Indians and *le Far West* are thus structures of the *longue durée* that construct French identity dialectically.

The psychological dimension of the use of exotic Others should not be ignored. One might say that such a symbolic vehicle is in many ways overdetermined, especially for the French. Le Wita (1994:46) makes this very point in discussing French bourgeois identity—that it is constructed dialectically with reference to nonbourgeois Others. That is, there is no sense of self without a sense of Otherness to abet it. These mutual constructions are formed in childhood, which is viewed as a "green Elysium," an ideal time of freedom from the cares of the world, at least in retrospective imagination.

Indian and western imagery is central during this verdant dream, and viewed with great nostalgia by adults. Given these circumstances, the symbolic use of Indians and the West in adult consciousness (one a proxy for innocence, the other for nature) is almost inevitable. Such images arise out of the fog of childhood and into manifest thought at times of particular stress. This connection among the idea of the primitive, childhood, and unconscious mental states has a long pedigree in French thought. During the 1920s, surrealism appropriated ethnography as a means to access levels of consciousness suppressed by official accounts of reality. Collaborations among artists and ethnographers, such as Marcel Griaule, led to the integration of ethnological themes into Western art.

This all occurred at the height of interest in Freudian theories of the unconscious. The establishment of the Musée de l'Homme in Paris in the 1930s institutionalized such connections (Clifford 1988). Thus, the French use of the primitive as a psychological vehicle is both well established and to a certain degree theoretized. What is more, many of the more educated French are entirely aware of these connections. The locus of this phenomenon of faux cowboys and Indians, Saint Germain des Prés, is thus significant for the simple reason that a larger percentage of persons "in the street" will be aware of these structures of French thought and commercial establishments are playing on them. This very playfulness, which is characteristic of commerce in the postmodern era, is essential to its appeal (Roseberry 1996). The ironic gesture to the potential consumer—and what is more ironic than dressing as a cowboy on the Boul Mich?—brings him or her into complicity with the merchandizing strategy. At the same time, these structures of representation retain something of their original power, even while the objects of conscious thought (see di Leonardo 1998).

A final vignette brings several of these themes together. In the summer of 2002 (several years after my initial research in Paris) in the historic downtown of Laramie, Wyoming, a small Western college town with a mythic name (due largely to films and television shows such as *The Man from Laramie*), a French clothing company specializing in western apparel, Marlboro Classics, staged a two-day photo shoot, making use of historic settings such as the Buckhorn Saloon and the railroad tracks. The company, which produces exclusively for the European market, has a boutique in Saint German des Prés. Laramie was used as a setting for the French models wearing French clothing because, as one member of the crew stated, "The clothes have that Western feel and Wyoming embodies a lot of those types of characters" (*Laramie Daily Boomerang*, July 27, 2002, p. 2).

Notes

1. American tourist sites may dispense with material continuity altogether, as in the buildings in Williamsburg constructed in the 1920s. This is not something to which the French have generally resorted (see Handler and Gable 1997).

2. The American writer James Thurber commented most humorously on the French insouciance about actual American geography and history in the popular western stories of the early twentieth century (Thurber 1937).

3. As Todorov (1993:277–278) points out, these ideas associated with Rousseau were intended by him to refer to an ideal type, not an actual place or historical period, although Lévi-Strauss, among others, takes him literally.

4. Connoisseurs of secondhand jeans look for characteristic signs of wear, such as along the inner leg where the fabric rubbed against the saddle. Another telltale sign of authenticity is a circular mark on the back pocket, where tins of snuff are kept.

5. For a perspective opposed to the older entropic model of transcultural exchange, see Appadurai 1990 and 1991.

6. The term *savage* is appropriate here. "*Sauvage*" is the term still occasionally used in French to refer to tribal peoples. The connotation is broader than for the English cognate, with meanings of wild and free, but also some of the negative connotations of brutality and violence (see Sayre 1997).

7. Kitsch, a form of aesthetic bad taste and bad faith, is characteristic of ideological art. As Matei Calinescu describes it, kitsch is art that is thoroughly a product of its social context and is "entirely reducible to extrinsic causes and motives" (Calinescu 1987:240). In the case of Indian kitsch, a strong ideology about the noble but safely dead savage drives the production and consumption of such pieces (Berkhofer 1978:90). One of the most surprising pieces of such kitsch I encountered was a series of Dijon mustard jars named and styled after particular tribes (e.g., "Lakota" and "Tlingit").

8. The recent interest in African-American cowboys is quite revealing (see Love 1995). Since the greatest expansion of the West occurred in the post—Civil War era and the occupation of cowhand was among the lowest levels of wage labor, it is not surprising that recently freed slaves, especially from the Western and border states, took to cowpoking in large numbers. However, since this does not fit in with the stereotype of a biracial (or at most, triracial, including Hispanic vaqueros) frontier, the black cowboy has been seen until recently as an anomaly.

9. McDonald's and other fast-food restaurants (most of which are owned by American corporations, and the rest borrowing from an American cultural script) threaten the very existence of that archetypically French institution, the cafe. Food industry analysts estimate that the number of cafes in France in the 1990s was being reduced by 4,000 per year (8 percent of the total number in 1995) due largely to competition from fast food. On October 22, 1995, hundreds of cafe owners demonstrated against President Jacques Chirac's proposal to increase sales taxes, which unfairly disadvantage cafes (Kole 1995).

10. Of course, this view of the meaning of the White City leaves out many perspectives, especially those of the scholars, such as Franz Boas and Frederic Ward Putnam, who toiled on the ethnographic displays. I think this fairly well sums up, however, the popular and political meanings of the exposition.

References

Appadurai, Arjun
   1990 Disjuncture and Difference in the Global Cultural Economy. *In* Global Culture: Nationalism, Globalization and Modernity. Mike Featherstone, ed. Pp. 295–310. Theory, Culture and Society, vol.7. London: Sage.
   1991 Global Ethnoscapes: Notes and Queries for a Transnational Anthropology. *In* Recapturing Anthropology: Working in the Present. Richard Fox, ed. Pp. 191–210. Santa Fe: School of American Research Press.
Berkhofer, Robert F., Jr.
   1978 The White Man's Indian: Images of the American Indian from Columbus to the Present. New York: Vintage.

Brett, Patricia

    1992 Jobs, Not Politics, Preoccupy University Students in France. Chronicle of Higher Education 39(6):A33-A35.

Bruner, Edward M.

    1994 Abraham Lincoln as Authentic Reproduction: A Critique of Postmodernism. American Anthropologist 96:397–415.

Calinescu, Matei

    1987 Five Faces of Modernity: Modernism, Avant-Garde, Decadence, Kitsch, Postmodernism. Durham NC: Duke University Press.

Carroll, Raymonde

    1988 Cultural Misunderstandings: The French-American Experience. Carol Volk, trans. Chicago: University of Chicago Press.

Clifford, James

    1988 On Ethnographic Surrealism. *In* Clifford, The Predicaments of Culture: Twentieth-Century Ethnography, Literature, and Art. Pp. 117–151. Cambridge MA: Harvard University Press.

Conrad, Rudolf

    1987 Mutual Fascination: Indians in Dresden and Leipzig. *In* Indians and Europe. Christian Feest, ed. Pp. 455–473. Aachen: Edition Herodot.

Deloria, Philip

    1998 Playing Indian. New Haven CT: Yale University Press.

Deloria, Vine, Jr.

    1981 The Indians. *In* Buffalo Bill and the Wild West. George Wisseman, ed. Pp. 45–56. Pittsburgh: University of Pittsburgh Press.

Di Leonardo, Micaela

    1998 Exotics at Home: Anthropologies, Others, American Modernity. Chicago: University of Chicago Press.

Fabian, Johannes

    1983 Time and the Other: How Anthropology Makes Its Object. New York: Columbia University Press.

Feest, Christian

    1987a Indians and Europe: Editor's Postscript. *In* Indians and Europe. Christian Feest, ed. Pp. 609–628. Aachen: Edition Herodot.

    1987b Preface. *In* Indians and Europe. Christian Feest, ed. Pp. 1–3. Aachen: Edition Herodot.

Fogelson, Raymond

    1991 The Red Man in the White City. *In* Columbian Consequences, Volume 3: The Spanish Borderlands in Pan-American Perspective. David H. Thomas, ed. Pp. 73–90. Washington DC: Smithsonian Institution.

Greenblatt, Stephen

    1991 Marvelous Possessions: The Wonder of the New World. Chicago: University of Chicago Press.

Handler, Richard, and Eric Gable

    1997 The New History in an Old Museum: Creating the Past at Colonial Williamsburg. Durham NC: Duke University Press.

Hanerz, Ulf

    1990 Cosmopolitans and Locals in World Culture. *In* Global Culture: Nationalism, Globalization and Modernity. Mike Featherstone, ed. Pp. 237–251. Theory, Culture and Society, vol. 7. London: Sage.

Harkin, Michael

1995 Modernist Anthropology and Tourism of the Authentic. Annals of Tourism Research 22:650–670.

Jay, Salim

1992 Du Cote de Saint-Germain-des-Prés. Paris: Jacques Bertoin.

Kole, William J.

1995 French Cafes Hunger to Fill Empty Tables. Denver Post, October 24, 1995, p. A3.

Lawrence, Elizabeth A.

1982 Rodeo: An Anthropologist Looks at the Wild and the Tame. Chicago: University of Chicago Press.

Lestrignant, Frank

1987 The Myth of the Indian Monarchy: An Aspect of the Controversy between Thevet and Lery. In Indians and Europe. Christian Feest, ed. Pp. 37–60. Aachen: Edition Herodot.

Lévi-Strauss, Claude

1966 The Savage Mind. Chicago: University of Chicago Press.

1976 Structural Anthropology. Vol. 2. Monique Layton, trans. New York: Basic Books.

1977 Tristes Tropiques. John and Doreen Weightman, trans. New York: Washington Square Books.

Le Wita, Beatrix

1995 French Bourgeois Culture. J. A. Underwood, trans. Cambridge: Cambridge University Press.

Love, Nat

1995 The Life and Adventures of Nat Love. Lincoln: University of Nebraska Press.

Montaigne, Michel de

1958[1580–1588] The Complete Essays of Montaigne. Donald M. Frame, trans. Stanford: Stanford University Press.

Quint, David

1995 A Reconsideration of Montaigne's Des Cannibales. In American in European Consciousness, 1493–1750. Karen Ordahl Kupperman, ed. Pp. 166–91. Chapel Hill: University of North Carolina Press/ Institute of Early American History and Culture.

Rabinow, Paul

1995 French Modern: Norms and Forms of the Social Environment. Chicago: University of Chicago Press.

Raibmon, Paige

2000 Theatres of Contact: The Kwakwaka'wakw Meet Colonialism in British Columbia and the Chicago World's Fair. Canadian Historical Review 81(2):157–190.

Rosaldo, Renato

1989 Culture and Truth: The Remaking of Social Analysis. Boston: Beacon.

Roseberry, William

1996 The Rise of Yuppie Coffees and the Reimagination of Class in the United States. American Anthropologist 98(4): 762–775.

Said, Edward S.

1978 Orientalism. New York: Vintage.

Sayre, Gordon M.

    1997 Les Sauvages Americains: Representations of Native Americans in French and English Colonial Literature. Chapel Hill NC: University of North Carolina Press.

Serfaty, Simon

    1993 Europe's Main Trouble(d) Maker: An Expert on France Argues That the More Things Change, the More They Stay the Same. International Economy 7(1):22–29.

Simmel, George

    1950 The Stranger. *In* The Sociology of George Simmel. Kurt H. Wolff, ed. and trans. Pp. 402–408. New York: Free Press.

Taylor, Colin F.

    1988 The Indian Hobbyist Movement in Europe. *In* Vol. 4: Indian-White Relations. Wilcombe E. Washburn, ed. Pp. 562–572. Handbook of North American Indians. William C. Sturtevant, gen. ed. Washington DC: Smithsonian Institution.

Thurber, James

    1937 Wild Bird Hickok and His Friends. *In* Thurber, Let Your Mind Alone! and Other More or Less Inspirational Pieces. Pp. 197–202. London: Mandarin.

Todorov, Tzvetan

    1993 On Human Diversity: Nationalism, Racism, and Exoticism in French Thought. Catherine Porter, trans. Cambridge MA: Harvard University Press.

Trouillot, Michel-Rolph

    1991 Anthropology and the Savage Slot: The Politics and Poetics of Otherness. *In* Recapturing Anthropology: Working in the Present. Richard Fox, ed. Pp. 17–44. Santa Fe: School of American Research Press.

20. *"To Light the Fire of Our Desire"*

Primitivism in the Camp Fire Girls

PAULINE TURNER STRONG

I

I have a rather embarrassing confession to make. I did not first encounter the concepts of *wakonda* and the sacred fire through Ray Fogelson's anthropology classes at the University of Chicago—although these undoubtedly deepened my understanding. Rather, my first engagement with simulacra of these Native American symbols involved participating in the "council fires" of my Camp Fire Girls group. I vividly remember how I and my friends, dressed in buckskin, beads, and headbands, would circle around a campfire while beating a drum and singing the organization's stately processional, "We Come, We Come to Our Council Fire." The words, tune, and pensive mood—what Raymond Williams (1977) might call the Camp Fire Girls' "structure of feeling"—come back to me readily. All are encompassed in the concluding phrase: "To light the fire of our desire, To light the fire of Wo-He-Lo."[1]

The scene is a campfire under the stars in the Colorado Rockies. We are at Camp Wilaha or Camp Kotami. I and my sister Camp Fire Girls have each selected an "Indian name" or composed an original acronym that represents our character or our heart's desire (I'll never tell!). These personal names, like the camp names and the organization's watchword, "Wo-He-Lo," are represented by "symbolgrams" derived from Plains, Pueblo, and Woodlands iconography. Like Wo-He-Lo, which stands for "Work, Health, Love," many of the names are acronyms based on English, but others have been selected from a list of various tribal names. We have designed and beaded headbands incorporating our personal symbolgrams and fashioned ourselves fringed gowns of canvas and deerskin. The gowns are decorated with painted wooden "honor beads" strung in patterns on leather thongs. These represent our accomplishments in the areas of Home (colored orange for flame), Outdoors (brown for the earth), Creative Arts (green for nature's creativity), Frontiers (blue for the horizon), Business (yellow for the harvest), Sports and Games (red for rosy cheeks), and Citizenship (red, white, and blue).

It is the 1960s, and we are a group of varied racial, ethnic, and religious backgrounds—unified, the organization's leaders (our "Guardians") would say, by our common attachment to nature, beauty, and the values of Wo-He-Lo. Camp Fire Girls is a popular organization in Colorado, and we consider ourselves far more adventurous than the Girl Scouts. We are attracted to the outdoor activities, the romance, and the camaraderie of Camp Fire Girls, and we take the Indian-derived symbolism and pageantry quite seriously. I remember how shocked we were when my best friend's mother got an uncontrollable case of the giggles as she watched us parade in buckskin and beads at one of our "council fires."

Now, some four decades later, I laugh along with my friend's mother at our earnestness, and it is with considerable ambivalence that I admit to my participation in the venerable Anglo-American tradition of "playing Indian." But I have learned that it is fruitful to write from a position of embeddedness and ambivalence (see Strong 1996). The more I learn about the history of Camp Fire Girls the more fascinated I become with the complex and interwoven social processes that gave rise to and sustained this institutionalized appropriation of Native American symbols and rituals. Appearing in the early twentieth century in an atmosphere of modernist primitivism and cultural nationalism, and inspired by reformist movements such as first-wave feminism, progressivism, "Red Progressivism," child-centered education, the arts and crafts movement, and the back-to-nature movement, Camp Fire Girls incorporated Indian symbolism in invented traditions designed to broaden the sphere of women's activities while, at the same time, imbuing the domestic sphere of women with heightened significance and measurable value.[2] The rituals and symbolism of the Camp Fire Girls were explicitly intended to re-enchant the lives of American girls by associating modern femininity with the authentic American womanhood of Native Americans.

This is a most appropriate story to tell in honor of Ray Fogelson, both because it abounds in the kinds of irony that Ray appreciates and because it connects, either centrally or tangentially, with so many of his interests: ritual, symbolism, and what Hobsbawm and Ranger (1982) call "invented traditions"; the cultural construction of emotion and personhood; the history of anthropology, psychology, and American Indian policy; Euro-

American representations of Indians; and the process that Ray's mentor A. Irving Hallowell (1963) called "transculturation."[3] In telling this tale I am mindful of how much I have learned from Ray in all of these areas, and also of how much he will have to contribute once he has a chance to apply his famous red pencil to the book manuscript that results from my research on the appropriation of Indian symbolism in the Camp Fire Girls (research that is still ongoing).

II

Camp Fire Girls was founded in 1910 in the midst of a widespread "moral panic" over the dislocations and changing social relations associated with industrialization, urbanization, immigration, and feminism. Luther Halsey Gulick, who founded the organization with his wife, Charlotte Vetter Gulick, was a physician and "social engineer" then employed as head of the Department of Child Hygiene at the Russell Sage Foundation. Gulick favored woman's suffrage and a more public role for women but worried that the increased employment of women and girls outside the home was destroying the social, emotional, and aesthetic fabric of life. Like other antimodernists, including anthropologists Edward Sapir and Ruth Benedict, Gulick deplored the alienation and disenchantment of modern life, particularly in the realm of the workplace. Gulick sought a way, as he put it, to

> brush away from the everyday activities of the world the dull gray with which the oil and smoke of this machine age have covered them, to reveal the beauty, romance and adventure of all the common things of life; [to] waken an appreciation of the wonders going on all about us that so many of us fail to see. [Buckler 1961:39]

Pseudo-Indian rituals and symbols became central to Gulick's mission to nurture the whole person (conceived on the model of the Body, Mind, Spirit triangle he had previously formulated for the YMCA). Through these symbolic activities he hoped to offer American girls a more natural, healthy, and aesthetically satisfying way of life.[4]

While her husband was the theorist of the movement, Charlotte Gulick was responsible for inventing many of the Camp Fire Girls' practices. She coined the acronym Wo-He-Lo and developed much of the Indian-derived symbolism, originally for use at an experimental summer camp for girls that the couple operated on Lake Sebago in Maine. The Gulicks worked within a circle of social reformers that included the psychologist and social evolutionist G. Stanley Hall, an influential theorist of adolescence and advocate of child-centered education. The circle also included members of the YMCA and settlement house movements, the naturalist and amateur ethnologist Ernest Thompson Seton, and the young John Collier. At that time involved in training community leaders as the civic secretary of the People's Institute, Collier later headed the Bureau of Indian Affairs under Franklin D. Roosevelt.

Camp Fire Girls was designed as a nonsectarian organization responding to what these reformers saw as the distinctive needs of the adolescent American girl. As Collier put it, the organization sought to help the modern girl "find her own soul and then consciously to enlist that soul in group activity and world service." Following Hall's notion that the stages of life recapitulate human evolutionary history, Collier maintained that a "living contact with Indian symbolism and Indian culture" was particularly instrumental in a girl's quest for her soul because it provided "contact with universal life—with life at its fountain source of world-old, world-wide and world-foreseeing adolescent consciousness" (Buckler 1961:44, 43). In other words, Collier, the Gulicks, and their colleagues considered Indian symbolism to be particularly appropriate for adolescents because they saw Indian cultures as themselves at the adolescent stage of human development—a stage they associated with creative expression and the discovery of one's authentic nature.[5]

Fresh from helping to found the YMCA and Boy Scouts, Luther Gulick insisted that because of the inherent differences between "womanly" and "manly" virtues and pursuits it would be "fundamentally evil" for an organization for girls to model itself upon one for boys (Buckler 1961:22). The girls' organization was modeled, instead, on the Gulicks' summer camp and a small regional group already called the Camp Fire Girls. The original Camp Fire Girls was created by William Chauncy Langdon, a poet and consultant for Gulick's department at the Russell Sage Foundation, who had been charged with developing a pageant for the 150th anniversary celebration of the town of Thetford, Vermont. Invented traditions inspired by Indian rituals and symbols were central to both the Gulicks' camp, Sebago-Wohelo, and the original Camp Fire Girls. In both cases the naturalist Ernest Thompson Seton played an important role in the design of Indian-derived traditions.

Seton, the foremost proponent of the primitivist Woodcraft movement, was a friend and associate of the Dakota physician Charles Alexander Eastman (Ohiyesa), the author of numerous largely autobiographical books, including *Indian Scout Talks: A Guide for Boy Scouts and Camp Fire Girls* (1914). Along with other Indians known as "Red Progressives,"

Eastman was a cultural mediator who shared his knowledge of Dakota culture through lectures, demonstrations, and publications in an attempt to garner greater understanding and respect from the dominant society.[6] Seton was also advised by the Omaha ethnologist Francis La Flesche and other well-known ethnologists such as Alice Fletcher, Frances Densmore, George Dorsey, Frederick Hodge, James Mooney, and J. R. Walker. A crusader for Indian rights, a charismatic lecturer, and the author of numerous illustrated accounts of natural history and Indian culture, Seton formed his own "tribes" of "Woodcraft Indians," which consisted of adults as well as children. Seton was also influential in the development of the Boy Scouts. When that organization, under the influence of Lord Robert Baden-Powell, turned towards more militaristic forms of symbolism and organization, the Camp Fire Girls held fast to Seton's vision of the American Indian as a model for an authentic and spiritual life. Indian-derived symbolism likewise distinguished the Camp Fire Girls from the Girl Scout movement, which was heavily influenced by Lady Baden-Powell.[7]

The "council fires" of the Camp Fire organization built on a common association in Anglo-American culture between the circle around the campfire and the transfer of sacred or esoteric knowledge (see Hinsley 1989). More specifically, the organization drew its rituals from Seton's best-known book, *Birch Bark Roll of the Woodcraft Indians*. Similarly, the organization's pictorial symbolism and sign language were modeled on Seton's writings, including *Sign Talk* (1918), which was the product of extensive research on the syntax and vocabulary of Plains sign language.[8] The ranks through which a girl progressed—Trail Seeker, Wood Bearer, Fire Maker, and Torch Bearer—were patterned after similar ranks among Seton's Woodcraft tribes. Ceremonial gowns first appeared among Seton's Woodcraft Girls, whose activities were highly influenced by the feminist ideals of his first wife, Grace Gallatin Seton, herself a noted author, lecturer, and organizer.

At the time that Ernest Thompson Seton was assimilating Indian rituals and symbolism in an attempt to reform American character, he was also fighting the assimilation and land allotment schemes central to U.S. Indian policy. Seton shared many progressivist ideas about the preservation of tribal cultures with John Collier, who first became acquainted with Indian cultures through his association with Seton and the Gulicks. Two decades before Collier launched the "Indian New Deal" as Commissioner of Indian Affairs, he played a significant role in the formation of Camp Fire Girls, serving on its national board of directors and writing one of its central poetic texts, the "Fire Maker's Desire."

Knowing nothing of this history, my friends and I recited Collier's pledge when we progressed from the rank of Torch Bearer to that of Fire Maker:

> As fuel is brought to the fire
> So I purpose to bring
> My strength
> My ambition
> My heart's desire
> My joy
> And my sorrow
> To the fire
> Of humankind;
> For I will tend
> As my fathers have tended
> And my fathers' fathers
> Since time began
> The fire that is called
> The love of man for man
> The love of man for God.[9]

The irony of a girl's rite of passage tying her to her fathers' fathers rather than to a line of women alerts us to the way in which the fire symbolism of Camp Fire Girls reinforced patriarchal gender roles. Luther Gulick proposed fire as the organization's central symbol at a meeting held in 1910 at Horace Mann School at Columbia University. He reminded his associates that "The bearing and rearing of children has always been the first duty of most women, and that must always continue to be. This involves service, constant service, self-forgetfulness and always service." Accordingly, Gulick suggested that "the fire be taken as the symbol of the girls' movement, the domestic fire—not the wild fire—and that from the first the very meaning of the fire be explained to her, in poetry and the dance" (Buckler 1961:22).

In Collier's "Fire Maker's Desire" the Camp Fire Girl announces her eagerness to sacrifice herself, like fuel, to the fire of humankind, thus linking herself to all those who, since the beginning, have devoted themselves to tending the flames of community and spiritual love. The pledge evokes in poetic imagery what Gulick described in less mystifying terms as "service, constant service, self-forgetfulness and always service." During the ritual in which she attains the rank of Fire Maker, a Camp Fire Girl is given a silver bracelet, made somewhat in the Tshimshian style and inscribed with the watchword Wo-He-Lo.

The beauty of the bracelet and other Camp Fire honors was strategic.

In the same organizational meeting at Horace Mann School, following his suggestion that fire be the central symbol of the Camp Fire Girls, Gulick continued:

> My second point is: show how extensively it is true that beauty has been in the custody of women. Teach the old folk lore, the old folk dances, the old customs, sometimes dancing and singing by night about a fire—have that combined effect upon the senses, and you can make people over in the process and do it pretty quickly. [Buckler 1961:23]

Perhaps Gulick thought that the bourgeois self could be "made over" particularly easily, for he advocated as the next step that the adult Camp Fire Guardian teach the initiate "the possibility of leading other girls . . . the factory girls, for instance, the city girls, the mill girls, the country girls" (Buckler 1961:23). When she had successfully taught a skill to several younger or less fortunate girls, the initiate might become a Torch Bearer and, later, a Guardian herself. In this capacity she would pass on the values of Wo-He-Lo, as codified in the Law of Camp Fire:

> Seek Beauty,
> Give Service,
> Pursue Knowledge.
> Be Trustworthy.
> Hold on to Health,
> Glorify Work.
> Be Happy. [10]

III

It is disconcerting to recognize myself as someone whose subjectivity was shaped, in part, through a set of disciplinary practices that changed surprisingly little over the half century between 1910 and the 1960s—although as early as the 1940s it was recognized that the Indian symbolism, while appealing to girls, might make it difficult for others to take the organization seriously. [11] Today the Indian symbolism is downplayed and treated as the "heritage" of a group that has been expanded to include boys as well as girls. The contemporary organization, Camp Fire USA, is sensitive to charges of cultural racism and encourages members to utilize symbols and rituals drawn from their own ethnic and national heritage—a development, of course, consonant with contemporary multiculturalism and identity politics. Significantly enough, the 1996 reprint of an official publication called *Your Symbol Book*, originally compiled by Charlotte Gulick (1915), refers to the timeless nature of Camp Fire's "principles of symbolic communications and artistic design." However, it stresses that the publication reflects "the historical richness of the Camp Fire program" rather than accurate knowledge and understanding of American Indian cultures (Wallace and Kirby 1996[1951]: preface).

Reflecting on my own experiences I can attest that the spiritual and aesthetic symbolism of Camp Fire Girls touched me deeply. But I also recognize considerable slippage between the reformist goals of the 1910s and the attitude of my own Camp Fire group.[12] I am certain that we interpreted the campfire as a "wild fire" rather than a domestic fire, and suspect that the group's invented traditions may have fostered a bohemian consciousness more than a commitment to Luther Gulick's vision of woman's glorified domestic role. By the late 1960s my friends and I had dropped out of Camp Fire Girls, and I cut up the leather of my ceremonial gown to make patches for my jeans. I turned my Camp Fire Girl beads into "love beads" (and, much later, found that they were excellent teething beads for my daughters). I visited the Navajo Nation as a high school senior in an experiential education program that was descended, ultimately, from the same progressive education movement that gave rise to Camp Fire Girls. This experience and other field courses in college turned me toward anthropology, where I learned to be suspicious of invented traditions and appropriative practices—including those embedded in anthropology itself.

As George Stocking (1989) has written, there are a variety of "romantic motives" expressed in the discipline of anthropology. My Fire Maker's bracelet serves as a tangible reminder of this and links me to the ethnologist Lewis Henry Morgan, whose fraternal society, the Grand Order (or New Confederacy) of the Iroquois, centered its rituals around Iroquois fire symbolism. My "Indian name" links me not only to Charlotte Gulick, also known as Hiiteni—an Arapaho term for "life movement," made famous by anthropologist A. L. Kroeber—but also to Morgan, who adopted the name of the Oneida chief Schenandoah. My ceremonial gown ties me both to Frank Hamilton Cushing, who on occasion posed as a Zuni bow priest, and in a very different way to the Lakota scholar Ella Deloria, who served as a consultant to a local Camp Fire group while a student at Columbia Teacher's College. My design of a beaded headband incorporating Pueblo symbolism links me also to Deloria's mentor Ruth Benedict, whose *Patterns of Culture* reflects a search for authenticity not unlike that of the Camp Fire Girls—a connection signaled, perhaps, by the similarity of the book's latest cover to many Camp Fire designs. Furthermore, I suspect that my experience of what I now recognize as Camp Fire's "mimetic excess" (Taussig 1996) may have contributed to the appeal that the anthropology of "symbols and meanings" held for me when I began graduate school at the University of Chicago in the late 1970s.[13]

I point out these resonances not to equate all forms of appropriation, cultural mediation, and interpretation, but to suggest that they all bear a kind of family resemblance—or, more precisely, inhabit a common field of influences. The creators of Camp Fire Girls turned the ethnological research of Seton and others to reformist uses. Within this reform movement the future Commissioner of Indian Affairs, John Collier, developed a romantic vision that led to policies aimed at preserving the purity, authenticity, and timeliness of tribal cultures. Franz Boas, Ruth Benedict, and other Boasian anthropologists had their own reformist agendas, in some respects more radical than that of the Camp Fire Girls but equally dependent on the appropriation and reinscription of Indian cultural forms. Most poignantly, Charles Eastman and Ella Deloria performed their Indian identities in the service of their own reformist goals, using both the Camp Fire Girls and anthropology as contexts for working toward an enlarged understanding and appreciation of their Dakota beliefs and practices.

Tracing social and conceptual links between Camp Fire Girls, American anthropology, and American Indian policy, I have suggested in this chapter, enhances our understanding of the appropriation and transculturation characteristic of each of these disciplinary practices. In ongoing archival and ethnographic research I am exploring further the complex social and cultural processes involved in the distinctive mesh of primitivism, progressivism, nationalism, environmentalism, and feminism embodied in the Camp Fire Girls—as well as the processes involved in its transformation to Camp Fire USA. Though this project takes part of its inspiration from the feminist tradition of autoethnography (see Strong 1996), it would never have been conceived without the example and support of Ray Fogelson. I dedicate this research project to Ray with great affection and admiration.

Acknowledgments

Although I am not able to perform this piece as I did at the 1996 annual meetings of the American Anthropological Association, complete with renditions of Camp Fire songs and poetry, I have chosen to keep it in much the same form, as a brief overview of a larger project. I have also performed versions of this material at Scripps College, Swarthmore College, the University of Texas at Austin, and the 2005 annual meeting of the Society for the Anthropology of North America in Mérida, Mexico. Audiences at each of these presentations have offered helpful commentary, and I am grateful to Julie Liss, Bruce Grant, Janet Staiger, and Lee Baker for arranging these occasions. I also thank Stephanie Brown, Dan Segal, Richard Handler, and Barrik Van Winkle for references and insights. Not least, I appreciate the opportunity to serve on the board of directors of Camp Fire USA Balcones Council, which has helped me learn about contemporary developments.

Notes

1. The full text of the processional is posted on the official Lone Star Council web site (www.campfireusadallas.org/aboutus/Songs.htm). Accessed November 11, 2004.

2. Deloria (1998) explores several of these movements in his superb exploration of "playing Indian" in American culture from the Boston Tea Party through the New Age. Chapter 4 considers the Camp Fire Girls as part of a discussion of the role of noble savagery in the construction of modern American identities. In general, however, the literature on youth organizations is centered on the Boy Scouts and YMCA. Other notable sources on "playing Indian" include Green (1988), Lassiter (1988), Mechling (1982, 2001), and Whiteley (1993). Though the literature on early twentieth-century modernism, antimodernism, and feminism is vast, the following are especially relevant to the concerns of this chapter: Carr (1996), Cott (1987), Deacon (1997), Dilworth (1996), Evans (1989), Lears (1981), Smith-Rosenberg (1985), Stocking (1989), and Torgovnick (1990).

3. See, among others, Fogelson 1982, 1985, 1987, 1991. These interests are discussed further in the introduction to this volume.

4. Cohen (1972) and Brown (2000) discuss the "moral panic" over adolescence. For Gulick's life and philosophy, see Buckler, Fiedler, and Allen (1961), Dorgan (1934), Gulick (1920), Putney (2001), and Wallach (1989). For Sapir's concept of "genuine culture" and his critique of the alienated labor of the "telephone girl or mill hand," see Sapir (1949[1924]), Dilworth (1996), Handler (1983, 1986), and Stocking (1989).

5. For Hall's recapitulationism, see Baker (1998), Brown (2000), Gould (1977), Grinder and Strickland (1963), Putney (2001), and Stocking (1968). Clifford (1988), Dilworth (1996), and Orvell (1989), among others, critique the modernist pursuit of authenticity. For the modernist emphasis on self-realization and self-expression, particularly as exemplified by Ruth Benedict, see Handler (1990).

6. For Seton, Eastman, and other Indian progressives, see Deloria (1998) and Hoxie (1984, 1992, 1998).

7. Baker (1998), Hinsley (1981), Stocking (1968), and Whiteley (2004) offer instructive accounts of early American ethnology. For Seton, Baden-Powell, and the Scouts, see Deloria (1998), MacLeod (1983), and McDonald (1993).

8. Seton's *Birch Bark Roll* appeared under several titles and multiple editions. See Farnell (1995) for a contemporary account of Plains sign language.

9. For an illustrated version, see *Camp Fire Girls* (1914). The original text and a more recent version are posted in "Ma-ha-we's Memory Book" (http://members.aol.com/alicebeard/campfire/ index.html). Accessed November 11, 2004.

10. See Camp Fire Girls (1914:5) for the original version of the pledge, or "Ma-ha-we's Memory Book" (http://members.aol.com/alicebeard/campfire/index.html). "Worship God" was added to the Camp Fire Law in 1942. Previous spiritual references in Camp Fire Girls were primarily to "Wakonda" or the "Great Spirit." See DeMallie (1977) for a discussion

of the ethnological literature on the Omaha concept of *wakonda* that was influential in the development of Camp Fire tradition.

11. My understanding of Camp Fire Girls as a set of disciplinary practices is influenced by Foucault (1977, 1978) and by anthropologists who have offered Foucauldian analyses of colonial and capitalist practices (Lomawaima 1993; Kondo 1990; Comaroff and Comaroff 1992; Harkin 1994).

12. This slippage is illustrative of the role of power in the transmission of culture that Greg Urban discusses in his contribution to this volume.

13. The front cover of the 1989 edition of Benedict's text, designed by Michaela Sullivan, is based on Pueblo pottery patterns. For Morgan, see Deloria (1998) and Tooker (2001). Anderson (2001:101) discusses Kroeber's treatment of *hiiteeni*; see also this volume, p. 140. For Ella Deloria, see Deloria (1998) and the ancillary material in Deloria's novel *Waterlily* (1988). For Benedict, see Handler (1986, 1990).

Works Cited

Anderson, H. Allen
  1986 The Chief: Ernest Thompson Seton and the Changing West. College Station: Texas A&M Press.
Anderson, Jeffrey D.
  2001 The Four Hills of Life: Northern Arapaho Knowledge and Life Movement. Lincoln: University of Nebraska Press.
Baker, Lee D.
  1998 From Savage to Negro: Anthropology and the Construction of Race, 1896–1954. Berkeley: University of California Press.
Benedict, Ruth
  1989[1934] Patterns of Culture. New York: Houghton Mifflin.
Bieder, Robert F.
  1980 The Grand Order of the Iroquois: Influences on Lewis Henry Morgan's Ethnology. Ethnohistory 27:349–361.
  1986 Science Encounters the Indian, 1820–1880: The Early Years of American Ethnology. Norman: University of Oklahoma Press.
Brown, Stephanie
  2000 Learning Adolescence: Producing the Family and the Self in an Expert Culture. PhD dissertation, Department of Anthropology, University of Texas at Austin.
Buckler, Helen, Mary F. Fiedler, and Martha F. Allen
  1961 Wo-He-Lo: The Story of the Camp Fire Girls, 1910–1960. New York: Holt, Rinehart and Winston.
Camp Fire Girls
  1914 The Book of the Camp Fire Girls. 5th ed., revised. New York: National Headquarters.
Carr, Helen
  1996 Inventing the American Primitive: Politics, Gender, and the Representation of American Literary Tradition, 1789–1936. New York: New York University Press.
Clifford, James
  1988 The Predicament of Culture: Twentieth Century Ethnography, Literature, and Art. Cambridge MA: Harvard University Press.

Cohen, Stanley

    1972 Folk Devils and Moral Panics: The Creation of the Mods and Rockers. London: MacGibbon and Kee.

Comaroff, John, and Jean Comaroff

    1992 Bodily Reform as Historical Practice. *In* Ethnography and the Historical Imagination. Pp. 69–91. Boulder CO: Westview Press.

Cott, Nancy

    1987 The Grounding of Modern Feminism. New Haven CT: Yale University Press.

Deacon, Desley

    1997 Elsie Clews Parsons: Inventing Modern Life. Chicago: University of Chicago Press.

Deloria, Philip J.

    1998 Playing Indian. New Haven: Yale University Press.

Deloria, Ella

    1988 Waterlily. Biographical sketch of the author by Agnes Picotte. Afterword by Raymond J. DeMallie. Lincoln: University of Nebraska Press.

DeMallie, Raymond J., Jr., and Robert H. Lavenda

    1977 *Wakan*: Plains Siouan Concepts of Power. *In* The Anthropology of Power. Raymond D. Fogelson and Richard N. Adams, eds. Pp. 153–165. New York: Academic Press.

Dilworth, Leah

    1996 Imagining Indians in the Southwest: Persistent Visions of a Primitive Past. Washington DC: Smithsonian Institution.

Dorgan, Ethel

    1934 Luther Halsey Gulick, 1865–1918. New York: Columbia Teacher's College.

Eastman, Charles A. (Ohiyesa)

    1935 Indian Scout Talks: A Guide for Boy Scouts and Camp Fire Girls. Boston: Little, Brown.

Evans, Sara M.

    1989 Born for Liberty: A History of Women in America. New York: Free Press.

Farnell, Brenda

    1995 Do You See What I Mean: Plains Indian Sign Talk and the Embodiment of Action. Austin: University of Texas Press.

Fogelson, Raymond D.

    1982 Person, Self, Identity: Some Anthropological Retrospects, Circumspects, and Prospects. *In* Psychological Theories of the Self. Benjamin Lee, ed. Pp. 67–109. New York: Plenum Press.

    1985 Interpretation of the American Indian Psyche: Some Historical Notes. *In* Social Contexts of American Ethnology, 1840–1984. June Helm, ed. Pp. 4–27. Proceedings of the American Ethnological Society. Washington DC: American Anthropological Association.

    1987 History of the Study of North American Indian Religions. *In* Encyclopedia of Religion, Vol. 10. Mircea Eliade, ed. Pp. 545–550. New York: Macmillan/Free Press.

    1991 The Red Man in the White City. *In* Columbian Consequences. Vol. 3. D. H. Thomas, ed. Pp. 73–90. Washington DC: Smithsonian Institution.

Foucault, Michel

    1978 History of Sexuality, vol. 1: An Introduction. Robert Hurley, trans. New York: Random House.

    1979 Discipline and Punish. Alan Sheridan, trans. New York: Random House.

Gould, Stephen J.

1977 Ontogeny and Philogeny. Cambridge MA: Harvard University Press.

Green, Jesse

1990 Cushing at Zuni: Beginnings of American Anthropology. *In* Cushing at Zuni: The Correspondence and Journals of Frank Hamilton Cushing, 1879–1884. Jesse Green, ed. Pp. 2–27. Albuquerque: University of New Mexico Press.

Green, Rayna

1988 The Tribe Called Wannabee: Playing Indian in America and Europe. Journal of American Folklore 99:30–55.

Grinder, Robert E., and Charles E. Strickland

1963 G. Stanley Hall and the Social Significance of Adolescence. *In* Socialization: Adolescence and Society. Robert E. Grinder, ed. New York: Macmillan.

Gulick, Charlotte V. (Hiiteni)

1915 A Book of Symbols for Camp Fire Girls. New York: Camp Fire Outfitting Co.

Gulick, Luther H.

1920 A Philosophy of Play. New York: Association Press.

Hall, G. Stanley

1904 Adolescence and Its Psychology and Its Relations to Physiology, Anthropology, Sociology, Sex, Crime, Religion, and Education. 2 vols. New York: Appleton-Century-Crofts.

Hallowell, A. Irving

1963 American Indians, White and Black: The Phenomenon of Transculturation. Current Anthropology 4:519–531.

Handler, Richard

1983 The Dainty and the Hungry Man: Literature and Anthropology in the Work of Edward Sapir. *In* Observers Observed: Essays on Ethnographic Fieldwork, vol. 1: History of Anthropology. George W. Stocking Jr., ed. Pp. 208–232. Madison: University of Wisconsin Press.

1986 Vigorous Male and Aspiring Female: Poetry, Personality, and Culture in Edward Sapir and Ruth Benedict. *In* Malinowski, Rivers, Benedict and Others: Essays on Culture and Personality, vol. 4: History of Anthropology. George W. Stocking Jr., ed. Pp. 127–155. Madison: University of Wisconsin Press.

1990 Ruth Benedict and the Modernist Sensibility. *In* Modernist Anthropology: From Fieldwork to Text. Marc Manganaro, ed. Pp. 163–180. Princeton NJ: Princeton University Press.

Harkin, Michael

1994 Contested Bodies: Affliction and Power in Heiltsuk Culture and History. American Ethnologist 21(1994):586–605.

Hinsley, Curtis M.

1981 Savages and Scientists: The Smithsonian Institution and the Development of American Anthropology, 1846–1910. Washington DC: Smithsonian Institution.

1989 Zunis and Brahmins: Cultural Ambivalence in the Gilded Age. *In* Romantic Motives: Essays on Anthropological Sensibility, vol. 6: History of Anthropology. George W. Stocking Jr., ed. Pp. 169–207. Madison: University of Wisconsin Press.

Hobsbawm, Eric, and Terence Ranger

1983 The Invention of Tradition. Cambridge: Cambridge University Press.

Hoxie, Fred

    1984 A Final Promise: The Campaign to Assimilate the Indian, 1880–1920. Lincoln: University of Nebraska Press.

    1992 Native American Journeys of Discovery. Journal of American History 79:969–995.

    1998 The Curious Story of Reformers and American Indians. *In* Indians in American History. 2d ed. Frederick Hoxie and Peter Iverson, eds. Pp. 205–230. Wheeling IL: Harlan Davidson.

Kelly, Lawrence C.

    1983 John Collier and the Origins of Indian Policy Reform. Albuquerque NM.

Kondo, Dorinne

    1990 Crafting Selves: Power, Gender, and Discourses of Identity in a Japanese Workplace. Chicago: University of Chicago Press.

Lassiter, Luke E.

    1988 The Power of Kiowa Song. Tucson: University of Arizona Press.

Lears, T. J. Jackson

    1981 No Place of Grace: Antimodernism and the Transformation of American Culture, 1880–1920. New York: Pantheon Books.

Lomawaima, K. Tsianina

    1993 Domesticity in the Federal Indian Schools: The Power of Authority Over Mind and Body. American Ethnologist 20:227–240.

MacLeod, David

    1983 Building Character in the American Boy: The Boy Scouts, YMCA, and Their Forerunners, 1870–1920. Madison: University of Wisconsin Press.

McDonald, Robert H.

    1993 Sons of the Empire: The Frontier and the Boy Scout Movement. Toronto: University of Toronto Press.

Mechling, Jay

    2001 On My Honor: Boy Scouts and the Making of American Youth. Chicago: University of Chicago Press.

    1982 "Playing Indian" and the Search for Authenticity in Modern White America. Prospects 5:17–33.

Orvell, Miles

    1989 The Real Thing: Imitation and Authenticity in American Culture, 1880–1940. Chapel Hill: University of North Carolina Press.

Putney, Clifford.

    2001 Muscular Women. *In* Putney, Muscular Christianity: Manhood and Sports in Protestant America, 1880–1920. Pp. 144–161. Cambridge MA: Harvard University Press.

Rogers, Ethel

    1915 Sebago-Wohelo Camp Fire Girls. Introduction by Mrs. Luther Halsey Gulick. Battle Creek MI: Good Health Publishing.

Sapir, Edward S.

    1924 Culture, Genuine and Spurious. *In* Selected Writings of Edward Sapir in Language, Culture, and Personality. David G. Mandelbaum, ed. Pp. 308–331. Berkeley: University of California Press.

Seton, Ernest Thompson

    1915 Manual of the Woodcraft Indians; the Fourteenth Birch Bark Roll. Garden City NJ.

    1918 Sign Talk. Garden City: Doubleday, Page.

Smith-Rosenberg, Carroll

    1985 Disorderly Conduct: Visions of Gender in Victorian America. New York: Oxford University Press.

Stocking, George W., Jr.

    1968 Race, Culture, and Evolution: Essays in the History of Anthropology. New York: Free Press.

    1989 The Ethnographic Sensibility of the 1920s and the Dualism of the Anthropological Tradition. *In* Romantic Motives: Essays on Anthropological Sensibility, vol. 6: History of Anthropology. George W. Stocking Jr., ed. Pp. 208–276. Madison: University of Wisconsin Press.

Strong, Pauline Turner

    1996 Animated Indians: Critique and Contradiction in Commodified Children's Culture. Cultural Anthropology 11:405–424.

Taussig, Michael

    1993 Mimesis and Alterity: A Particular History of the Senses. New York: Routledge.

Tilton, R. S.

    1994 Pocahontas: The Evolution of an American Narrative. Cambridge: Cambridge University Press.

Tooker, Elizabeth

    2001 Lewis Henry Morgan and the Seneca. *In* Strangers to Relations: The Adoption and Naming of Anthropologists in Native North America. Sergei Kan, ed. Pp. 29–56. Lincoln: University of Nebraska Press.

Torgovnick, Marianna

    1990 Gone Primitive: Savage Intellects, Modern Lives. Chicago: University of Chicago Press.

Wallace, Frances Loomis, and Earlleen Kirby

    1996[1951] Your Symbol Book. Kansas City MO: Camp Fire Boys and Girls.

Wallach, Stephanie. Luther Halsey Gulick and the Salvation of the American Adolescent. PhD dissertation, Department of History, Columbia University.

Whiteley, Peter

    1998 The End of Anthropology (at Hopi)? *In* Rethinking Hopi Ethnography. Pp. 163–187. Washington DC: Smithsonian Institution.

    2004 Ethnography. *In* A Companion to the Anthropology of North American Indians. Thomas Biolsi, ed. Pp. 435–477. Malden MA: Blackwell Publishers.

Williams, Raymond

    1977 Marxism and Literature. Oxford: Oxford University Press.

Afterword

PETER NABOKOV

Looming with his customary impatience in the shadows behind the range of essays in this volume is a loyal, cantankerous, vulnerable, goading but supportive embodiment of the proposition that the eccentric proves the rule, the committed anthropologist and certifiable personality named Raymond D. Fogelson.

It was a tremendous honor for me to contribute to the celebrations in San Francisco that led to this collection of essays dedicated to and often inspired by Ray Fogelson.[1] For over 30 years he has been my unofficial mentor, dear friend, oftimes host, fieldwork guide, incessant nudge, and genius at exploring the hall of mirrors that has always been and will always be the discourse of Indian and white relations. And all the while he has also served as dignifier of Native metaphysics and fierce defender of Indian rights. He has put his scholarly reputation and painstaking research on the line in courtrooms adjudicating tribal recognition and treaty rights, and each July he also walks the talk during "Green Corn" at the Creek's Agena-Hachee-Dulgee stomp ground at Cedar Creek, Oklahoma.

It was an extra special pleasure to be invited into that circle by Uncle Ray's more legitimate intellectual comrades and offspring—I was always just a hanger-on, one of those structural spongers to which Rob Brightman refers in his remarks on Maidu Indian clowns. For I sort of got "adopted" by his graduate crew at Chicago through the incorporative process of fictive kinship that Ray inspired Sergei Kan to explore via the symposium that led to his *Strangers to Relatives* (2001) volume of essays. But Sergei's tack in that collection took a typical Fogelsonian twist as, under the influence of his prescient mentor, he one-upped the postmodern reflexivists by asking how anthropologists—mostly Ray's students and peers—had experienced their own reverse acculturation.

My initiation into Ray's Kula Ring began back in the 1970s after Tim Buckley told me over the phone about this unusual professor I just had to meet. And, yes, Ray proved to be, in the jazz argot of a slightly outmoded era that strangely suited him, quite the cat—as well as a hip prof who Lord Buckley might have riffed. Ray thereafter graciously served as my adoptive paternal clan uncle, one of those guides who among the Crow Indians function as quasi-guardian figures with special rights to cast their shadows over your inner life, to impose their benevolence over you on key occasions—namings, feast days (dissertation defenses), special turns in life's road—but always in such an intrusive yet mysterious manner that you never forgot that these oversize familiars were imbued with what the Crows called Maxpe—"power."

What was disconcerting, however, was that this analyst of power never waited only for those special occasions. Any wee hour would do, whether at the drag end of those intense all-night Sedgewick Street shindigs or, as Greg Urban remembers, just when you were recognizing the onslaught of a massive hangover only a few hours before your Triple-A paper was to be delivered.

During the daytime things generally went OK. I know: one of my glorious stretches under Ray's peerless hospitality was over my predoctoral McNickle fellowship in Chicago, when John Aubrey and Helen Tanner joked that we were Newberry Library's odd couple (my Lemmon to his Matthau?). Before the sun went down Ray could be so charming—pawing through his apartment's archaeological site of newspapers and magazines like the third Collier brother, emerging with a review of some exhibit he absolutely commanded that I see or book that I must memorize by morning, meditatively watering and feeding bugs to the utterly hateful jungle that steamed up his sitting room, or staring up at me with an expression bordering on adoration when he discovered that I knew how to steam broccoli.

But come the nightfall, dishes piling to the ceiling, things changed, and one fell under his assault. Now, I don't think of the scholars at that AAA gathering in San Francisco as shrinking violets, and perhaps some of them also shared my genetic allergy to advice. Yet we still refrained from committing prof-icide when, in the deep dark a.m., we felt as though we had been set upon by some monstrous amalgam of John Belushi, Franz Boas, and the Ayatollah Khomeni.

Here was both Greg Urban's "power as authority" and Rob Brightman's "anti-power as subversion" thundering at you like—dare I say it—a force of nature, telling you before you hit the books or the field to look for, listen for, stay attuned to all those multiple souls, covert categories, epitomizing events, architectural cosmograms, indigenous critiques, structural "persons," binary oppositions, and the rest of those undersize, oversize, left-handed, handcrafted, and inverted beings that could be found in those glancing moments and under-appreciated representations that just might become clues to the stories behind the stories we read about in this volume from Ray's victims. And as E. O. Wilson has said, we do love our monsters, we are transfixed by them, and I remain under my beloved uncle's spell to this day.

Ray's many long journeys into night had the same gradual effect on him as the four bounces-in-place he takes prior to his class lectures—popping him into that shamanic zone where all ambi-valences and foreign forms of self-consciousness are rendered accessible, readable, inhabitable, communicable, cross-reference-able. It was his inspired art of play.

And in this volume we encounter some of those attempts at the deeper stories inspired by Ray's teachings and writings, contributions that I briefly rearrayed in San Francisco to my liking. Prefacing my remarks to the session's papers by Tim Buckley and Barrik Van Winkle on narrative expressions of a self-and-other consciousness, I proposed that Ray's much pillaged neologism—"ethno-ethnohistory"—basically asked that we overlook the missteps of Levi-Bruhl for the moment and give "*mentalité*" another shot, or, as activist-comedian Dick Gregory used to say, let's just stop the insults—to anybody's intelligence. That posture of granting our informants and their societies an intellectual and self-reflective life on and through their own terms could open up all sorts of real work, as these scholars exemplified. Not long ago Ray was my guide through an essay I was writing on Indian concepts of history, so I can fully appreciate the interpretive twists and turns as Van Winkle and Buckley unveiled the ethno-agendas that underlay both spoken and written accounts of the past. I even wound up dedicating a book on that topic to my Chicago uncle.

Van Winkle's marvelous case of the Washo Indians aghast at the sight of starving pioneers eating each other at Donner Pass seemed to validate Ray's long fascination with diversities of the monstrous, and put the "Big" on the other "Foot" so to speak. Van Winkle's account seemed the very reverse of folklorist Jarold Ramsay's view of Indian prophecy as retroactive composition. It became a delicious example of life anticipating art and replicating cosmology, since in terms of the dark history of Washo-white relations that ensued, after this moment in time it would only be more monsters all the way.

From Tim Buckley—following on the themes of his superbly crafted entry in George Stocking's eighth volume of the *History of Anthropology* series—came another installment in his fine series of essays on California's Indians and ethnologists. For Tim's cautionary thoughts on any infinite regression of Ray's provocative prefix, *ethno-*, he turned to a database dear to both Ray's and my hearts: the rich and still largely untapped history of American Indian letters.

"Silence" was Tim's central conceit, and the hide-and-seek category of "secrecy" its twin. For as he scrolled through five Native American authors from the Klamath River region, we saw these writers caught not in the "hall of mirrors" as I characterized Indian-white relations earlier, but in a more spiraling by-play between their Native and non-Native readerly worlds.

We might imagine that those surface "ways" or traditions that the Yurok Indian author Lucy Thompson co-opts written English in order to perpetuate, and the Christianity through which she chose to communicate, were secretly contextualized by her own literate community in their oral commentary but were still silenced for outsiders. After tracking how subsequent Indian writers filled in such historical gaps—while opening new wounds and creating new secrets and silences in the process—we longed to hear more of Buckley's final Native example, the Karok scribe Julian Lang, who apparently has turned from covenants never made, or betrayed, to an altogether original and utterly unpredictable representation of his culture's ultimate secret force: "love"! What could he ever mean by this marvelous word, and who would ever have expected it?

From the conference papers of Sharon Stephens and James Brow we glimpsed the complex issues buried in self-representations that break into the public arenas of world media, international policy, and community activism. I was intrigued by Brow's concerns about the limits of what one might call "auto-essentialism" among the Sri Lankan villagers of Kukulewa. For in our reflections on the historical transformations of small-scale societies, do we not ourselves essentialize when we make ethnic persistence a one-dimensional, all-or-nothing proposition based on kinship or language or subsistence? And when we worry over self-imagings based upon yearnings for idealized pasts, might we not be ignoring those fusions of the imagined, invented and supernaturally revealed, which studies of revitalization movements have continuously pinpointed as exposing culture at its most creative? Or might not, indeed, a new revitalized day be written on paper, not just spoken or trumpeted, in some sort of indigenous, absurdist, magical novel from a Kukulewan Chino Achebe or a completely himself Julian Lang?

To some degree, Brow and Stephens have joined with the conference papers of Jamie Saris and Jean O'Brien in pointing us to the motivations and mechanics behind creations of ethnic identity. The challenge facing the circumpolar Sami that Sharon Stephens studied was less to communicate that sense of identity to themselves than to persuasively project it to others—to the policymakers and radiation scientists who hold their survival in their hands. Obviously for Fourth World peoples this is a multifaceted challenge, with the proliferation of native media being one way we are witnessing Indians rising to it.

But for these outnumbered peoples of northern Scandinavia Sharon described a much more isolated, silenced crisis since 1986—a grim story of defenseless peoples trapped in modernity's worst nightmare. It is a story that also illustrates the unexpected turns that can occur in one's research, when those who first took you in now desperately need you to venture out and advocate on their behalf. I saluted her work, which exemplified the activism implicit in Ray Fogelson's sense of ethnographic responsibility.

Finally, my remarks in San Francisco returned to Native California with Ira Jacknis and Rob Brightman. Having received great word of mouth about Ira's re-Indianizing the public persona and exhibit emphases of UC-Berkeley's Phoebe Hearst Museum, I took personal delight in learning that he had homed in on another subject close to Fogelson, Buckley, and myself: the split-plank family and sweat houses of northwestern California. Upon a rich ethnographic database, well sieved in Tim Buckley's contribution to Ray's landmark 1976 graduate seminar at the University of Chicago on symbolic encodings of American Indian architecture (which was so influential on my own coauthored *Native American Architecture*), Jacknis pioneered the next analytical step—assessing the present-day roles of these self-consciously revived built forms. His was exactly the sort of study that I pray will be repeated with Miccosukee chickees, Mexican Kickapoo wickiups, peyote tipis, and, in my own case, reservation-era roundhouses.

Lastly, I was grateful that Rob Brightman turned his trickster's sense of timing and ethnographic dexterity from the topic he was supposed to address, to one situated in the California Sierra foothills that seemed far more appropriate to our honoree and to San Francisco. For the Maidu Indian clown's exhortation at 4 a.m. from the roof of the *kum*, the ceremonial roundhouse, sounded so reminiscent of our experience on Sedgewick Street: "He kept talking all the time, telling the people what they should do—get a load of wood, go out and hunt."

On the one hand, like Pueblo *koshares* (ritual clowns)—who, as the people of Acoma Pueblo say, are men "who know something about themselves"—these central California funsters simulated the violation of morality in order to promulgate it. On the other hand, it was the mischievous wrinkle in Rob's brain that provoked us to consider, among additional interpretations, that the Maidu clown's subversiveness provided a stellar example of what Fogelson evokes by the word *ethno-anthropology*. For Rob the very presence of such a role created an antidote to all cultural rigidities, a space for multiple self-reflections and metacritiques, from which no one—street bums, session discussants, and even perspiring honorees—was exempt.

So here we have some shoots from Fogelson's tree—which has, indeed become a World Tree, flowering from North America to Sri Lanka to Scandinavia. What Ray's fascination for representations always taught me, well before the days of Marcus/Fischer and Clifford/Said, with that loving tyranny only he could get away with, was that espousing essentialisms and authenticities was always beside the point; and excavating pastiches and reconstructions was often much more revealing. It was Ray who inculcated in us a hexaphonic perspective: not only to look at and listen to any dialectical relationships between etic and emic, but also to sidestep to the left and right of one's ethnographic focus, and then to look from before and from after. For only structural ambivalences, embedded alternatives, ethno-ethnohistory, and ethno-futurology—those theories buried in prophetic discourse—could begin to fairly represent any Native perspective.

And, finally, there was his cautionary subtext that you are never exempt from the human implications of such pursuits. It was not Ray who taught me that the root of the word *lore* is *laere* and that it means "wisdom"— Ray's shoulder is too much like a boxer's to wear his vulnerable heart on it. But I have often sensed his unspoken sympathy with the James Mooneys, Paul Radins, Frank Specks, and Dorothy Lees who believe that we just may be trafficking in serious stuff here.

And it has been those deeper shadows of his scholarly journey and ethical commitments that I've always trusted from the moment Tim Buckley finally first introduced us. And that very evening I watched him take some young Yale historian to task for handling Pawnee Indian history as if no specific human individuals ever thought about, bled for, or howled with fury at the loss of their Lost Universe. Moreover, it was Ray who made the guy swear then and there that he would read the latest edition of Gene Weltfish's classic of experimental ethnography in whose epilogue she suggests the Pawnee earth lodge as a model for a modern Midwestern elderly home.

Ray has often said that masks are "social persons," and among the "persons" that join the throng of Booger Dancers during the Eastern Cherokee performance Ray has written about are a cast of multicultural lampoons. But when I think of Ray I not only think of Rob's clowns. I remember the one serious-faced booger mask with a coiled snake on his brow: the defender and dignifier of Cherokee ways, the Warrior Booger. That was the same mask, purchased during my pilgrimage to the old sacred townhouse sites along the Little Tennessee River that Ray had told me about, that I presented to Ray during my comments at the AAA in San Francisco. It was carved from buckeye wood by Davy Arch from North Carolina—not far from Big Cove where Uncle Ray researched stickball games 40 years before.

I gave it to him in honor of his role as a scholar-warrior, for his profligate scattering of generative ideas; his profound yet often subterranean impact on American Indian scholarship; his contributions to the humanizing of Indian-white relations; his splendid humor and terrible puns; his boundless friendship; his support of that circle of friends and scholars, Native and non-Native, who have been inspired by his humanism, hospitality, and scholarship; and his championing of oddballs like himself and the rest of us, no matter the cultures we hailed from.

Ray, *aho*!

Notes

1. Editors' Note: This is an edited version of remarks presented at the close of the final session honoring Fogelson at the 1996 annual meetings of the American Anthropological Association. See the editors' introduction to this volume, notes 3, 10, and 14, for references to many of the works mentioned in these remarks.

Contributors

Jeffrey D. Anderson is an associate professor of anthropology at Colby College. He is the author of *The Four Hills of Life: Northern Arapaho Knowledge and Life Movement, One Hundred Years of Old Man Sage: An Arapaho Life Story,* and various articles on Arapaho language, culture, and history. His research interests include creativity, space-time, language shift, Christianization, revitalization, ethnopoetics, epistemological imperialism, age grade systems, human rights, and comparative human development. He earned his PhD at the University of Chicago.

Mary Druke Becker is Research Associate of the Iroquois Indian Museum in Howes Cave, New York. Her research interests center on colonial encounters in North America, Native American leadership, and Iroquois perceptions of self and others. She is organizer of the annual Conference on Iroquois Research, associate editor of *The History and Culture of Iroquois Diplomacy: An Interdisciplinary Guide to the Treaties of the Six Nations and Their League,* and author of the forthcoming *Native Americans and Their Land: The Schoharie River Valley.* She received her PhD in anthropology from the University of Chicago.

Margaret Bender received her PhD from the University of Chicago in 1996 and is currently an associate professor of anthropology at Wake Forest University. Her research has focused on the relationship between language and culture in a variety of contexts—from Cherokee medicinal practice to family literacy education in Chicago. *Signs of Cherokee Culture: Sequoyah's Syllabary in Eastern Cherokee Life,* published in 2002, explores contemporary literacy practices among the Eastern Band of Cherokee Indians.

Robert Brightman is Greenberg Professor of Native American Studies in the Department of Anthropology at Reed College. Among his many publications is *Grateful Prey: Rock Cree Human-Animal Relations.* He is currently conducting research on hunter-gatherer castes in South Asia and on a variety of topics in the urban anthropology of North America. He earned his PhD in anthropology at the University of Chicago.

Jennifer S. H. Brown is Professor of History at the University of Winnipeg and author and editor of over 80 publications on the cultural and social history of northern First Nations and Métis peoples from early fur trade times to the present. Director of the Centre for Rupert's Land Studies since 1996, past president of the American Society for Ethnohistory, and British Academy Visiting Professor, Oxford University (spring 2002), she holds the Canada Research Chair in Aboriginal Peoples in an Urban and Regional Context at the University of Winnipeg. She received her PhD from the University of Chicago.

Thomas Buckley received his PhD in anthropology from the University of Chicago in 1982. Starting in 1976, he undertook long-term fieldwork with Yurok Indians that continued for the next 25 years. His most recent book, *Standing Ground: Yurok Indian Spirituality, 1850–1990*, brings into focus much of what he learned during those years as well as his study of the history of Boasian ethnology before World War I. He is presently an independent scholar and writer living in Maine.

Raymond A. Bucko S.J. is an associate professor of anthropology in the department of sociology and anthropology at Creighton University. He is the author of *The Lakota Ritual of the Sweat Lodge*, among other publications. Professor Bucko is currently completing an online version of Father Buechel's ethnographic collection held at the Buechel Memorial Lakota Museum. He continues to work on issues of identity and contemporary ritual on the Northern Plains as well as issues in computer-assisted education. The AIDS and Anthropology Research Group and the Wyandot Nation of Kansas have recognized Professor Bucko for his work in Web site development. His PhD in anthropology was awarded by the University of Chicago in 1992.

Regna Darnell received her PhD from the University of Pennsylvania in 1969. She is Professor of Anthropology and Director of First Nations Studies at the University of Western Ontario. Her fieldwork has been primarily with the Plains Cree of northern Alberta and the Algonquian and Iroquoian peoples of southwestern Ontario. Her research interests include language and culture, cross-cultural miscommunication, and the history of anthropology. In addition to several edited volumes Professor Darnell has published biographies of Daniel Garrison Brinton and Edward Sapir; *And Along Came Boas: Continuity and Revolution in Americanist Anthropology*; and *Invisible Genealogies: A History of Americanist Anthropology*. She is a fellow of the Royal Society of Canada, recipient of the Isaac Hellmuth Prize for Research Achievement, and coeditor of *Critical Studies in the History of Anthropology* (University of Nebraska Press).

Raymond J. DeMallie is Chancellor's Professor of Anthropology and Director of the American Indian Studies Research Institute at Indiana University, Bloomington. He received his PhD from the University of Chicago in 1971. He is particularly interested in Plains Indian peoples and has worked extensively with the Sioux and Assiniboines in North and South Dakota and Montana. His primary theoretical concern is the development of cultural approaches to understanding the American Indian past. Among his books and edited volumes are *The Sixth Grandfather: Black Elk's Teachings Given to John G. Neihardt*; two volumes of the papers of

James R. Walker, *Lakota Belief and Ritual* (with Elaine A. Jahner) and *Lakota Society*; *Sioux Indian Religion: Tradition and Innovation* (with Douglas R. Parks); *North American Indian Anthropology: Essays in Society and Culture* (with Alfonso Ortiz); and the *Plains* volume of the Smithsonian Institution's *Handbook of North American Indians*.

David Dinwoodie is an associate professor of anthropology at the University of New Mexico. He has conducted field research in the Chilcotin region of British Columbia. *Reserve Memories: The Power of the Past in a Chilcotin Community*, published in 2002, focuses on the roles of speech, memory, and history in contemporary First Nations life. He earned his PhD at the University of Chicago.

Frederic W. Gleach received his PhD in anthropology from the University of Chicago in 1992. He is currently Senior Lecturer and Curator of the Anthropology Collections at Cornell University. In addition to numerous shorter works he is the author of *Powhatan's World and Colonial Virginia: A Conflict of Cultures* and coeditor of *Southern Indians and Anthropologists: Culture, Politics, and Identity*, *Celebrating a Century of the American Anthropological Association: Presidential Portraits* (with Regna Darnell), and (also with Darnell) a special centennial issue of the *American Anthropologist*. He received the American Anthropological Association's President's Award in 2002 for his work on the AAA centennial. In addition to Native North America, his current research interests include Puerto Rico, tourism, postcards and other visual representations, and the history of anthropology.

Michael E. Harkin is a professor of anthropology at the University of Wyoming. His publications include *The Heiltsuks: Dialogues of History and Culture on the Northwest Coast* and *Reassessing Revitalization Movements: Cases from North America and the Pacific Island*. He has received various awards and fellowships, including two from the National Endowment for the Humanities. He earned his PhD at the University of Chicago.

Joseph C. Jastrzembski received his PhD in history from the University of Chicago. He is an associate professor of history at Minot State University in Minot, North Dakota, and codirector of the Mandan Language and Oral Traditions Preservation Project, supported by the National Park Service. He coproduced the videos *Coyote and Sun* and *Mandan Storytelling Tradition* and is currently at work on a documentary entitled *The Language of the Lodges*. Dr. Jastrzembski has published articles in *Journal of American Indian Education* and *Western Folklore*, and his work in progress includes a monograph entitled *Hosts, Friends, Subjects, and Informants: Mandan People and Ethnography on the Plains*.

Sergei Kan received his PhD from the University of Chicago in 1982. He is Professor of Anthropology and Native American Studies at Dartmouth College. Since 1979 he has conducted ethnographic and archival research on the culture and history of the Tlingit Indians, the history of the Russian Orthodox mission in

Siberia and Alaska, and the history of anthropology. He received the 1987 Heizer Prize from the American Society for Ethnohistory for his article "The Nineteenth-century Tlingit Potlatch: A New Perspective," while *Symbolic Immortality: The Tlingit Potlatch of the Nineteenth Century* was given the 1990 American Book Award by the Before Columbus Foundation. Other publications include *Memory Eternal: Tlingit Culture and Russian Orthodox Christianity through Two Centuries* and an edited volume, *Strangers to Relatives: The Adoption and Naming of Anthropologists in Native North America.* His current project is a biography of Russian anthropologist Lev Shternberg.

Robert E. Moore received the PhD in anthropology and linguistics from the University of Chicago in 2000. Since the early 1980s he has conducted linguistic and ethnographic field research in a Wasco-Wishram speech community in the Columbia River region. Out of this work has come a series of articles exploring the local dynamics of linguistic change on the Warm Springs Indian Reservation, the transformation of traditional narrative genres, and the contemporary reservation scene, where he continues to be actively involved in community efforts to document and maintain Kiksht (a Wasco-Wishram dialect of Upper Chinookan). Recent publications have also explored design, "branding," and other matters in the corporate world. Currently (2005–06) Visiting Assistant Professor of Linguistics at the University of Illinois (Urbana-Champaign), he has taught in the anthropology departments of Reed College, New York University, and the University of Chicago, and at the Institute of Design (Illinois Institute of Technology).

Peter Nabokov is a professor in the Department of World Arts and Cultures and American Indian Studies at the University of California–Los Angeles. He received his PhD from the University of California-Berkeley and is the author of *A Forest of Time: American Indian Ways of History,* and coauthor of *Restoring a Presence: American Indians and Yellowstone National Park,* among other books. He is currently completing *Where the Lightning Strikes: The Lives of American Indian Sacred Places.* Professor Nabokov's ongoing research includes an investigation of riverine culture in Tamil Nadu, South India, and a multigenerational history of a Keresan Indian family from western New Mexico.

Larry Nesper earned his PhD in 1994 at the University of Chicago. He is currently an assistant professor in the Department of Anthropology and the American Indian Studies Program at the University of Wisconsin–Madison. His research interests are in the area of Native American society, culture, and law. Professor Nesper's book, *The Walleye War: The Struggle for Ojibwe Spearfishing and Treaty Rights,* was awarded a Wisconsin Historical Society Book Award in 2003.

Jean O'Brien (White Earth Ojibwe) is an associate professor in the Department of History at the University of Minnesota, where she is also affiliated with the Departments of American Indian Studies and American Studies. Her research focuses on northeastern Woodlands Indians, social and cultural history, and English colonialism. Among her publications is *Dispossession by Degrees: Indian Land*

and Identity in Natick, Massachusetts, 1650–1790. In 1996 Professor O'Brien received the Recognition Award for Emerging Scholars from the American Association of University Women. She received her PhD in history from the University of Chicago, where Ray Fogelson served on her dissertation committee.

Pauline Turner Strong is an associate professor in the Department of Anthropology and the Center for Women's and Gender Studies at the University of Texas at Austin. Her research centers on historical and contemporary representations of Native Americans, the politics of identity and alterity, and the history of anthropology. Among her publications is *Captive Selves, Captivating Others: The Politics and Poetics of Colonial American Captivity Narratives*, which received an honorable mention for the 2000 Chicago Folklore Prize. She has served on the boards of the American Society for Ethnohistory and the Society for Cultural Anthropology, which she served as president. She earned her PhD in anthropology at the University of Chicago.

Greg Urban is Arthur Hobson Quinn Professor of Anthropology at the University of Pennsylvania. He has conducted research on the cultures and languages of native peoples in North and South America, and is author of *A Discourse-Centered Approach to Culture: Native South American Myths, Metaphysical Community: The Interplay of the Senses and the Intellect*, and *Metaculture: How Culture Moves through the World*. He received his PhD from the University of Chicago.

Barrik Van Winkle is an independent scholar who studied with Ray Fogelson as both an undergraduate and graduate student at the University of Chicago. He also completed an MA in anthropology at the University of Nevada–Reno. A linguistic and legal anthropologist, he has done research with the Washoe Nation of California and Nevada, with gang members in St. Louis, and on various criminal justice issues in Chicago. He is coauthor of *Life in the Gang: Family, Friends, and Violence*, which won the 1998 Outstanding Book Award of the Academy of Criminal Justice Sciences, and articles in *Cultural Anthropology*, *Social Analysis*, and *Chicago Anthropology Exchange*. He has taught cultural anthropology, linguistic anthropology, and criminology at several institutions.

Index

Chippewas, xiv–xv, 98

Chirac, Jacques, 470n9

Chiricahua Apaches, 305n8; captivity narrative of, xvii–xviii; characteristics of folklore of, 302–303; "horrors," 290, 293, 299; moccasins, 287; and pursuit of Geronimo, 300–302; raids and massacres, 290–299, 306n12; use of narrative by, 296–299

Chlorogalum pomeridianum, 410n13

Choctaws, 277n2, 277n3

Chosa, Mike, 101–102

Chouart, Médard, 242

Christianity, 56–59, 174, 230, 269, 434–436, 445, 450n21. *See also* Catholicism; Orthodox Church

Churchill, Ward, 221, 234n8

Clackamas, 365. *See also* Chinookans

Clapp, Ebenezer, 425–428

Clark, C. B., xxxi

Cleveland, Grover, 437

Clifford, James, 20, 278n15

Clinton, George, 273

Cochise, 296

Cohn, Bernard, xvi

Colden, Cadwallader, 278n5

Collier, John, xxi, 217, 477–479, 482

colonialism, 415, 422, 425, 429

Colville Reservation (Washington State), 202

Comaroff, Jean, xvi

Comaroff, John, xvi

commemorations, 422–425

communitas, 170

Compá, Juan José, 295–296

conjuror, 252

Conrad, Joseph, 18

Coon, Carleton, xxiii, 11

Cooper, James Fenimore, 419, 435–436

corn myth. *See* "Kana'ti and Selu: The Origin of Game and Corn"

Costo, Rupert, 225, 234n10

cowboys, 470n8

Coyote, 397, 409n3

Crawford, Emmet, 300

Crazy Lodge, 130, 150

Creeks (Muskogees), xxxi

Crees: and acculturation, 372; cultural synthesis and hybridity of, 387, 388; culture of, xix; customs of, 355; and Feast of the Dead, 245; myths of, 368–369; polygyny myth of, 359–360; traditions of, 383, 384

Creoles, Russian, xviii, 315, 317–322, 323n1

Croghan, George, 265–267

Crook, Gen. George, 301

crow belt, 251

Crow Dance, 142

Crows, 360–361, 374, 490

Cruikshank, Julie, 297

cultural production, 456

"cultural resources," 186

culture: and cosmogony, 359–361, 367, 382; death of, 373–380; dissemination of, 71, 85–87, 90–92; elite, 364, 367; and essentialism, 380–384; and folklore, 305n10; historical, 362–363; and identity, 200–204; insights on, by proto-ethnologists, 268–270, 274–276; and pluralism, 355–356, 368, 375, 382, 386; synthesis and hybridity of, 385–389; term, xiv; time, 344–345; as "tradition," 358–359

Culture and Personality (Wallace), 11, 12

Cunningham, Keith, 289, 304n4

Curtis, Natalie, 123, 133

Cushing, Frank Hamilton, xxi, 481

Custer Died for Your Sins (Deloria), 229

Dahmer, Jeffrey, 407

Daklugie, Asa, 298

Dakotas, xvii, 176, 241, 369, 478, 482. *See also* Sioux Indians

D'Arcy McNickle Center for the History of the American Indian, xxxi

Darnell, Regna, xi, xii, 21–22

Dartmouth (MA), 418–419

David, Sarah, 419

Davis, Britton, 287–289, 292, 299–300

Davis, Jefferson, 314, 316

Davis, John, 435

Davis, Lee, 235n12

Dawes Act, 216

Dayley, Julia Jaha, 419

Deane, Charles, 436

Découvertes et Établissements des Français (Margry), 243

DeFoe, Celia, 113

Delanglez, Jean, 243

Delisle, Claude and Guillaume, 243, 244

Deloria, Ella, xxi, 178, 481, 482, 483n2

Deloria, Vine, xvi, 164, 181n6, 211, 229, 378, 379

DeMallie, Raymond, xvii, 131, 287, 303n2

Densmore, Frances, 99, 148, 168, 478

Description of Louisiana (Hennepin), 243

Díaz, Porfirio, 293

Dickson Mound, xxxii

Dilchthe, 293–294

Dinwoodie, David W., xviii–xix

Disney, 447, 450n20. *See also* *Pocahontas* (film)

Naraya songs (Round Dance/Ghost Dance), 158n3

Narrative of His Exploration in Western America, 1784–1812 (Thompson), 99

narratives: captivity, xvii–xviii, 293–295, 298, 435–436; historical, 425; "horrors," 289–290, 293; importance of oral, 297; New England Indians, 415

Nash, Manning, xxviii, xxx

Natasha Goes to the Brush Dance (Norton), 233n7

Natchez, Les (Chateaubriand), 456, 459

Native American Church, 377, 382, 385. *See also* Peyote religion

Native American Graves Protection and Repatriation Act (NAGPRA), xxxii, 192

Native Americans: and architecture, 493; Camp Fire Girls and, 474–475, 477–478; evolution of study of, 185–186, 203–204; French representations of, 460–461, 468; and historical consciousness, xviii; and ideology, 376–380, 386; and land, 422–426; and purity of blood, 416–417, 420; self-study of, 211–214, 232, 261, 279n23; and temporality, 328. *See also* New England Indians; *specific tribes*

Native Americans of California and Nevada (Forbes), 235n11

Native American Testimony: A Chronicle of Indian-White Relations from Prophecy to the Present, 1942–1992 (Nabokov), 279n23

Native Healer (Lake), 228

Naturegraph Press, 235n11

Nawakwagijig, 103–106. *See also* Lac du Flambeau Ojibwe

Neihardt, John G., 178

Neill, Edward D., 243

Nelson, Byron, Jr., 219, 222–224, 226, 234n10

Nelson, Richard, 352–353

Nesper, Larry, xiv–xv

Nettl, Bruno, 149

New Confederacy of Iroquois, 481

New Discovery of a Vast Country in America, A (Hennepin), 243

New England Indians: and extinction, 414–415, 419, 428–429; and identity, xx, 286

News from Native California (Margolin), 235n11

New Stockbridge, 421

Nicolet National Forest, 111

Nicollet, Jean, 242

Nomlaki, 367

nonevent: Donner Party, 402; as event, 167; event as, 168, 169, 176, 179; Fogelson's

study of, xviii; Ghost Dance, 126–127; humor, 163, 178; importance of study of, 44–46; Sitka incident as, 311, 322

Norris, Ella, 215

Northwestern Maidu dances, 365

Norton, Jack, 219–226, 230, 233n7, 233n8, 234n10

Norton, Jana, 233n7

Norton, John, 44, 264

Notes and Queries in Anthropology for the Use of Travellers and Residents in Uncivilized Land, 266

Novoarkhangel'sk. *See* Sitka

Nute, Grace Lee, 243

Obeyesekere, Gananath, xxviii

O'Brien, Jean M., xx, 492–493

Offerings-Lodge, 133, 154

Oglala Religion (Powers), 169

Ojibwa of Berens River, Manitoba: Ethnography into History, The (Hallowell), 18

Ojibwe: crafts, 115–116; customs, 355; dreams, xiii, 21–23; geographic remoteness, 17–18; and Hallowell's study, 13; history, 17–19, 37; hunting and fishing rights, 100–101; language, 39n2; metamorphosis, 151; worldview, 29, 35. *See also* Lac du Flambeau Ojibwe

Olmstead, Frederick Law, 111

One Bull, 287

Oneida nation, 421

Opler, Morris, 290, 305n12

Oraibi, 358

orenda, 95n2

Orthodox Church (Russian), 317, 318

Osages, 382

Osprey, 310

Otherness, 444–445, 450n17, 464, 466–468

Otoes, 244

Ottenberg, Simon, xxvii, xxviii

Our Home Forever: A Hupa Tribal History (Nelson), 219, 222–224, 234n10

Ousamequin, 422–425

Owen, Charlie George, 31, 36, 37

Owen, Jacob, 31–32, 36, 37

Oxford (MA), 419

Paiutes, 191–192, 403

Pa-Ka-Hon-Tas; or, The Gentle Savage, 449n8

Pamunkey Indians: dramatization, 438, 441; pottery, 442; reservation, 449n11

pan-Indianism, 383, 384, 437. *See also* biculturalism; culture

Printed in the United States
153732LV00003B/8/A